NATIONAL URBAN POLICIES IN THE EUROPEAN UNION

This book is one of a series to be published by Ashgate under the auspices of EURICUR, the European Institute for Comparative Urban Research, Erasmus University, Rotterdam. Titles in the series are:

Leo. H. Klaassen, Leo van den Ber and Jan van der Meer (eds),
The City: Engine behind Economic Recovery

Leo van den Berg, H. Arjen Klink and Jan van der Meer,
Governing Metropolitan Regions

Leo van den Berg, Jan van der Borg and Jan van der Meer,
Urban Tourism

Leo van den Berg, Erik Braun and Jan van der Meer
Metropolitan Organising Capacity

National Urban Policies in the European Union

Responses to urban issues in the fifteen member states

Edited by
LEO VAN DEN BERG
ERIK BRAUN
JAN VAN DER MEER

European Institute for Comparative Urban Research
Erasmus University Rotterdam
The Netherlands

e·uricur

Ashgate

Aldershot • Brookfield USA • Singapore • Sydney

Published by
Ashgate Publishing Ltd
Gower House
Croft Road
Aldershot
Hants GU11 3HR
England

Ashgate Publishing Company
Old Post Road
Brookfield
Vermont 05036
USA

British Library Cataloguing in Publication Data
National urban policies in the European Union : responses to
    urban issues in the fifteen member states. - (EURICUR series)
    1. Urban policy - European Union countries
    I. Berg, Leo van den, 1948- II. Braun, Erik III. Meer, Jan van
    der, 1947- IV. EURICUR
    307.1'216'094

Library of Congress Catalog Card Number: 98-72626

ISBN 1 84014 360 6

Printed in Great Britain by The Ipswich Book Company, Suffolk

Contents

List of Charts, Figures and Maps

List of Tables

Preface

On the occasion of a meeting of Ministers of Spatial Planning and Urban Affairs (held in Noordwijk, the Netherlands, June 1997), the Dutch European Union Presidency (in this case the Dutch Ministry of the Interior) took the initiative to investigate *the state of the art* concerning urban policies conducted by national authorities in each of the 15 member states. The main consideration for this initiative was the observation that urban development is a decisive factor for the economical, social and cultural times to come in the member states and the European Union as a whole.

The European Institute for Comparative Urban Research (EURICUR) of Erasmus University of Rotterdam was invited by the Ministry to undertake this investigation, the results of which served as a source of information for the European Ministers. Without EURICUR's international network of universities and cities it would not have been possible to fulfil this request in the relatively short period available for completing this work. We would like to thank those persons all over Europe who contributed by writing a national chapter. These chapters, together with the introduction of the framework for the comparative investigation and the synthesis of the findings, form the contents of this volume.

We appreciate the valuable contributions of Herbert Purschke (Austria), Guido De Brabander (Belgium), Christian Wichmann Matthiessen (Denmark), Eero Holstila (Finland), Alain Sallez (France), Klaus R. Kunzmann (Germany), Koustautinos Efthimiou and Theodossios Psihogios (Greece), Michael J. Bannon and Mary Grier (Ireland), Ilaria Bramezza (Italy), Nuno Portes, Alvaro Domingues and Alberto Laplaine Guimarais (Portugal), Oriol Nel.lo (Spain), Jan-Evert Nilsson (Sweden) and Michael Parkinson (United Kingdom). The national chapters for Luxembourg and the Netherlands are written by the editors, as are the introductory and concluding chapters.

The investigation was carried out under the supervision of a committee composed of Mrs M.E. Bierman, Ministry of the Interior, chairman, Mr F.N.V. Hilterman (Association of Netherlands Municipalities), Mr H. Verdonk (European Unit of the City of Rotterdam), Mr G.W.M. van Vugt (City of Tilburg), Mr F. van Kuik (Ministry of the Interior) and Mr W. J. Bringmann

(Ministry of the Interior), secretary. The editors thank the supervisors and advisors for their valuable remarks and pleasant co-operation. Naturally, only the editors are responsible for the contents of this volume.

Finally, we would like to thank Ms Pat FitzGerald for her editing of the 'European' English and adapting the texts into the right format, and our secretary Arianne van Bijnen for her unequalled and pleasant dedication to seeing to it that the deadlines were met.

Leo van den Berg
Erik Braun
Jan van der Meer
Rotterdam
January 1998

Contributors

Michael J. Bannon, Professor, Head Department of Regional and Urban Planning, University College Dublin, Ireland.

Leo van den Berg, Professor, Director European Institute for Comparative Urban Research (EURICUR), Department of Regional, Port and Transport Economics, Erasmus University Rotterdam, Netherlands.

Guido De Brabander, Professor, Department of Transport and Regional Economics, University of Antwerp (UFSIA), Belgium.

Ilaria Bramezza, Senior Researcher, Centre for Regional Economics, Transport and Tourism (CERTeT), Bocconi University, Milan, and Chief Advisory Group to the Minister of Public Works and Urban Areas, Ministry of Public Works, Rome, Italy.

Erik Braun, Assistent Professor, Staff Member European Institute for Comparative Urban Research (EURICUR), Departments of Regional, Port and Transport Economics and Business Marketing, Erasmus University Rotterdam, Netherlands.

Álvaro Domingues, Professor, Department of Urban Geography, University of Porto, Portugal.

Koustautinos Efthimiou, Architect, Organisation of Athens for Planning and Environmental Protection, Athens, Greece.

Mary Grier, Planning Assistent, Wexford County Council, Wexford, Ireland.

Alberto Laplaine Guimarãis, Associate Professor, University Moderna-Lisbon, and Member of the Cabinet of the President, Presidency of the Republic of Portugal, Lisbon, Portugal.

Eero Holstila, Managing Director City of Helsinki Urban Facts, Helsinki, Finland.

Klaus R. Kunzmann, Jean Monnet Professor, Department European Spatial Planning, University of Dortmund, Germany.

Christian Wichmann Matthiessen, Professor, Director Geographic Institute, University of Copenhagen, Denmark.

Jan van der Meer, Associate Professor, Associate Director European Institute for Comparative Urban Research (EURICUR), Department of Regional, Port and Transport Economics, Erasmus University Rotterdam, Netherlands.

Oriol Nel.lo, Director Institute of Metropolitan Studies (IEMB), Professor, Department of Geography, Autonomous University of Barcelona, Spain.

Jan-Evert Nilsson, Research Director Centre for Spatial Development Planning, University of Karlskrona/Ronneby, and Professor, University of Tromso, Sweden.

Michael Parkinson, Professor, Director European Institute for Urban Affairs, Liverpool John Moores University, Liverpool, United Kingdom.

Nuno Portas, Professor, Department of Town Planning, University of Porto, Portugal.

Theodossios Psihogios, Town Planner, Organisation of Athens for Planning and Environmental Protection, Athens, Greece.

Herbert Purschke, Director Austrian Institute for Spatial Planning, Vienna, Austria.

Alain Sallez, Professor, Director Institute of Cities, Land and Real Estate (l'IVTI), ESSEC, Cergy-Pontoise, France.

1   Research Framework

Introduction

Fundamental changes in the economy, technology, demography and politics are reshaping the environment of the towns and cities in Europe. The environment of towns and cities becomes increasingly competitive and complex and they need to anticipate and respond quickly to opportunities and threats that influence their position structurally. The cities themselves develop policy measures to meet the challenges, but at the same time higher layers of government pursue policies that influence the position of the cities. From the results of a study of the urbanization and the functions of cities, undertaken for the European Commission, it appears that national policies in all member states play a critical role in shaping the social, economic and political conditions of cities throughout the European Union (Parkinson et al., 1992). The national governments serve as intermediaries between the cities and the European level of government, and create the conditions for the cities to cope with the challenges that they face. The national government draws up the financial and policy framework in which the cities design their own policies, and also formulates its own policies that affect the position of cities. The latter may be explicit – targeted to cities – or 'implicit', affecting cities either purposely or inadvertently, directly or indirectly.

Each of the national governments in the European Union tailors its policy initiatives to the specific circumstances in its country. It is of course very interesting to compare the national policy responses in the member states. What can they learn from one another's experiences? The objective of this comparative study is to present the 'state of the art' concerning the explicit national urban policy[1] in the member states of the European Union. However, the scope will not be limited to explicit national urban policy. The investigation will also stretch to national policy as far as it makes a substantial impact on the development of the cities. For each member state the investigation is guided by four central questions. First, what is the urban development pattern in the member state? Second, what are the administrative and financial relations between the national authorities and the cities? Third, what do the national authorities consider to be main issues for, and challenges to their cities? Fourth, how does the national policy of the member states respond to these issues and challenges? The research results obtained in the member states serve as input for a comparative analysis of the experiences in the member states. What are the differences, similarities, common challenges and trends in the national urban policies in the European Union?

First, the following section discusses the main features of urban dynamics in Europe. After that, we discuss urban policy in more detail. What is urban policy? What is understood by national urban policy? What factors could possibly explain the differences in national urban policies in Europe? The final section summarizes the main features of the research approach. The following national chapters present an overview of the present national urban policy in the 15 member states of the Union. The final chapter analyses the results across all member states. What can the countries learn from each others experiences?

Urban Dynamics in Europe

The European Union is one of the most urbanized areas in the world. The Union counts approximately 170 cities with more than 200,000 inhabitants and 32 cities with more than a million inhabitants (European Commission, 1995). London and Paris are the two metropolises that, with New York and Tokyo, rank among the world's largest cities. The cities with more than half a million inhabitants are distributed equally across the Union's territory. The majority of the European Union's citizens live and work in urban areas. Clearly the cities – or more accurately functional urban regions[2] – are the vital cultural, economic and innovative centres of Europe. They function as the motors of the regional and the national economy. The same can be said of the cities from a European point of view. At the same time many of these motors are confronted with serious problems such as high unemployment rates, social and spatial segregation, insecurity, and increasing pressure on the environment. Hence, cities are facing numerous challenges that will (re)shape their future. In the literature we can find a multitude of trends and developments that influence urban development structurally. In effect, these trends point to five major, closely interwoven consequences for cities: the increased competition among cities and regions; the advance of numerous urban networks at the local, national and international levels, the accumulation of such problems as unemployment, poverty and social exclusion in the larger cities; the increasing attention for sustainable urban development; the need for organizing capacity.

Increased Competition: the Shift to Urban Competitiveness

In the end, the inhabitants, businesses, investors and visitors determine whether a city is attractive or not. These (potential) customers of cities put high demands on the quality of the business and living environment. Businesses consider factors like the quality of the (potential) labour force, the economic structure, the local knowledge base, the fiscal climate, telecommunications, (international) accessibility, accessibility of markets, availability of financial resources, and local taxes rates highly relevant to their locational behaviour. In addition, the quality of the living environment has become a necessary condition for economic development as well. Attributes such as urban services, housing conditions, the availability of green areas, the social climate, the quality of public space, urban safety and leisure facilities have also become critical location factors. The weight that is attributed to these location factors has changed considerably under the influence of processes of globalization, economic restructuring, European integration and informationalization.

For years now the increase in world trade has exceeded the growth in world production. Increasingly, (economic) activities and processes adopt an international scale. Economic development in particular does not stop at national borders and spells the end of well-defined national economies. Economic activities have not just a national or international but also a *global scope*, with major consequences for cities and regions. Firms are reorganizing their production chains to create the most cost-efficient functional and geographical global route. As a consequence of that strategic reorientation, these firms have reconsidered their location(s) on a global scale as well: they have become more footloose. It goes without saying that such developments intensify competition among cities. The trend is confirmed by another observation. In the course of the 1980s the balance of power in many markets shifted from supply to demand. Buyers have adopted a critical attitude towards the delivery of goods and services from any 'supplier'. Moreover, the preferences of customers change very fast, which shortens the life cycles of products. These changes are not only relevant to consumer and business-to-business markets but apply increasingly to the services provided by different levels of government.

Internationalization is reinforced by the phased implementation of the Maastricht Treaty, which is to clear the way for a European market. The European unification pulls down economic, physical, technological and fiscal barriers within the Union, facilitating access to cities and regions and their services, labour markets, and input and export markets, and again increases the mobility of European citizens – yet another inducement to competition among cities.

The development of information technology and the combination of information and telecommunications technology open the way for what some call the *informational city* (Castells, 1991). Increasingly, innovative activities rely on information, and they need to be accessible for, and have access to, information at both ends of their production process. Information technology changes the way people and organizations communicate, learn, and do business. Increasingly, cities become parts of a network of information exchanges which in turn makes high demands on the telecommunication facilities and the education and skills of the work force in cities. Hall (1995) points to the availability of information as the new logic of location.

The interaction in Europe has also been reinforced by the changes in Eastern European countries in the last decade. These countries are offering interesting investment opportunities for international businesses that seek to benefit from the relatively low production costs, the well-educated work force and the expanding market. Cities like Prague and Budapest especially attract investment from Western Europe and rapidly expand the connections with the major cities in Western Europe. The opening-up of Eastern Europe invites new competitors to the cities of the Union. At the same time the difference in the standards of living between the West and the East has induced a lot of people from Eastern Europe to come to the West in search of a better standard of living. The majority of them have settled in the larger cities.

Along with globalization, the economic structure of cities in the European Union has changed considerably in the past decades. Industrial activities no longer dominate the urban economy; a whole array of other activities (such as trade, financial services, commercial services, cultural activities, etc.) have taken their place. Initially, these new activities are not tied to a specific geographical location. Nevertheless, technologically advanced industries like electronics, biotechnology and medical technology are thriving on the intense networks of small and medium-sized firms found in the so-called industrial districts. A similar remark applies to sectors like the fashion and the media business. Indeed, competitiveness in these (sub)sectors is still to some extent dependent on a city or region, but the initial advantages might have been developed just as well at other locations. Moreover, such highly dynamic markets are subject to rapid changes. The initial chances of cities have become somewhat more equal and it is up to them to capitalize on these opportunities. The increased attention on higher education, tourism, entertainment and arts, due to the rising wealth and income of the citizens of the European Union, also opens new prospects to many cities. These elements of culture are found mostly in urban areas. Rising wealth and income and higher aspiration levels encourage people to give attention to 'personal development and personal care'. There is, for instance, a growing demand for health care 'tailored to the needs of the customer'. Activities that once were considered special or luxurious are now aspired to by a growing segment of society. The desire to 'stay in good shape' that leads to more demand for high-quality sports and fitness facilities is another example of changed aspirations.

The Advancement of Urban Networks

Competition among cities has been promoted by processes of globalization, European integration, informationalization and the opening-up of Eastern Europe. Competition implies that cities will concentrate more on their 'core competencies', which will induce a process of further spatial specialization in Europe. Cities are also becoming more interdependent. In effect, one can expect competition to induce the 'competitive city' but at the same time to give rise to the 'complementary city'. Growing interdependency among cities implies the advancement of urban networks. The global and European segmentation of production leads to growing transport flows and consequently also intensifies interdependency among cities. The investment of the European Union in the so-called *Trans-European Networks (TENs)* makes economic activities, people and resources more mobile, thus reinforcing the need for strategic alliances among cities in Europe. With the opening-up of Eastern Europe, West European cities might also find new allies there.

There are networks at the local, national or European levels based on (telecommunication) infrastructure, functional economic relations or other strategic (political) interests. On the local level there is a widespread interest in public-private partnerships that can widen the scope of local governance. The expectation is that the scope and importance of functional urban networks linking, for instance, logistic nodes or urban financial centres, will increase further. Besides, cities get together to apply for European funding or for exchange of experiences and 'best practices' in specific areas such as the networks for Sustainable Cities, Car Free Cities, Telecities, Digital Cities.

Accumulation of Unemployment, Poverty and Deprivation in the Larger Cities

Social problems such as unemployment, poverty, crime, youth delinquency, lack of education and social deprivation accumulate in (parts of) urban areas. In many of the larger European towns a separation is defining itself between a dynamic segment of the population that shares in the new economic and social progress, and another that cannot share and as a result falls into economic and social exclusion. Such a concentration of distressed groups is especially manifest in cities that have been hit by industrial decline, but also in cities that have managed to reverse the downward economic trend. The heterogeneous group of stragglers such as the long-term unemployed, the unfit for work, single ageing persons and teenage mothers, tends to locate in specific areas within the major cities, near the city centre as is the case of the Netherlands, or in the suburbs as is usual in France. The accumulation of different but connected problems in the larger cities poses a clear threat to a balanced urban development and hampers the cities in their function as motors of the national economy.

Increasing Attention for Sustainable Development

Closely bound up with the rise of welfare and the changing aspiration levels of European citizens is the rising importance that is attributed to the environment. Concern for the environment is no longer the private territory of radical groups at the edges of society. The rising environmental awareness has promoted the idea of sustainable urban development. Sustainable development has been described as development that provides for the needs of the present generation without jeopardizing the possibilities for future generations (World Commission on Environment and Development, 1987). Very often sustainability is associated only with environmental protection, but there is much more to it, especially with respect to cities (European Commission, 1994). Sustainable development is a much broader notion and incorporates the environment, quality of life, economics and social aspects. Moreover, the majority of European citizens live in urban areas so that sustainable development in the urban areas in Europe implies for the most part sustainable development in the European Union.

The Need for Organizing Capacity

Cities find themselves challenged. They have to adapt themselves to the new logic of competition (Bramezza, 1996) and at the same time find their place in various urban networks. They compete on a widening international scale in search of mobile investment and trade but at the same time are threatened by the cumulation of societal and environmental problems. Cities have to organize themselves to deal with the complex of potential opportunities and problems. The ability of the cities to anticipate, respond to and cope with internal and external changes is getting increasing attention. The city government cannot cope by itself: challenges demand a joint effort of different layers of government as well as other public institutions and private actors. A recent investigation (Van den Berg, Braun and Van der Meer, 1997) in eight European cities has revealed that organizing capacity is an indispensable condition for balanced, sustainable urban development. Organizing capacity is closely bound up with strategic networks (both public, private and mixed networks), leadership, spatial-economic conditions, vision and strategy, and political and societal support.

Urban Policy

It is clear that the challenges presented above make high demands on urban policy. But what exactly is meant by 'urban policy'? The term 'urban policy' could be interpreted as 'policy directed to cities', to draw a distinction between non-urban or rural, regional or national policy. The term indicates only the spatial range of the policy and says nothing about the content nor about the authority that is responsible for such policies. In general terms, urban policy can be described as the whole set of government measures at different administrative levels – European, national, regional or local – which are directed to cities.

Explicit Urban Policies

In theory, all layers of government could pursue urban policy. However, the higher layers of government also formulate policy that is not specifically designed for cities but that may still have a major impact on them. This policy is not directed to cities, but is to some extent 'urban' in its impact on cities. Therefore, it is very important to make a distinction between this 'implicit' policy and explicit urban policy as defined above. Hence, what is described as urban policy above is in fact policy *explicitly* directed to cities. Consequently, the policy of local government is by definition urban policy. For higher levels of government there are two possibilities. For one thing, the government could implement policy explicitly targeted to cities. For another, the national government formulates general policies, such as housing policy, transport and infrastructure policy, economic policy, spatial planning policy, environmental policy. In most cases these policies do not make a distinction between the smallest community and the largest capital city. However, such policies that are not spatially targeted can still be highly relevant for urban development. The latter are still common practice in most European countries, but explicit urban policy might deal more effectively with the complex problems of the cities. Besides, cities are differently affected by the emerging trends of globalization and informationalization. That the risk of decline and decay is not spread equally among the cities and within cities is yet another argument for explicit spatially targeted policies. Explicit urban policy, however, requires selection and classification: which cities should get specific attention and which not.

Partial and Integral Policy

Another distinction between urban policy and other policy with an urban impact, is that between partial – or sector-specific – and integral policy. Public administration is divided into specialized departments or agencies responsible for specific policy areas, such as housing, transportation, spatial planning, etc. To some extent fragmentation reduces the complexity for policy makers. This practice is understandable in view of the complexity of the problems to be solved and in view of the political responsibilities involved, but it does carry the risk of overlooking the degree of interdependence between sectors. Independent departments are apt to consider, and deal with, their sectors alone, developing partial policies instead of integral ones, without taking heed of their possible effects on other policy sectors. Integral planning might lead to synergy effects. Otherwise, the measures may be counterproductive. Many examples suggest themselves in which sector-specific policy is quite acceptable and appreciated from the specific sector's point of view. Nevertheless, this policy might evoke negative effects on other sectors, which in the end could lead to negative effects for society as a whole.

Figure 1.1 recapitulates the types of policies that have a major impact on cities.

A Framework for National Policy Responses to Urban Issues

Naturally, there is no Europe-wide blueprint for the 'urban' policy of the national government and the relation between the cities and the national

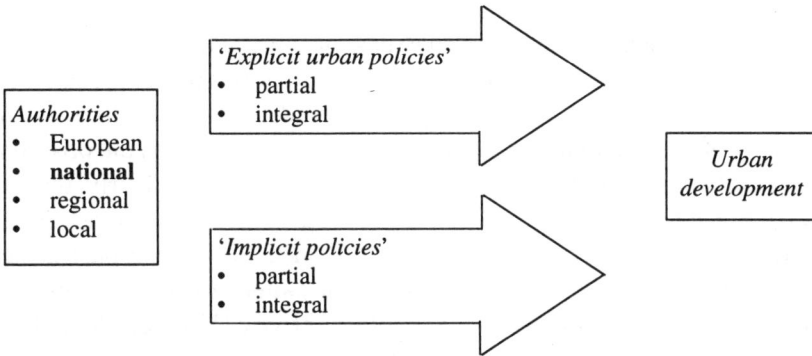

Figure 1.1   Policies that have a major impact on cities

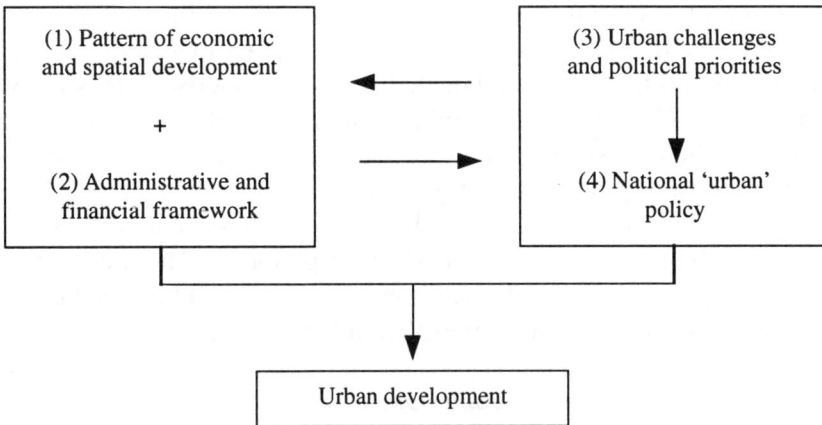

Figure 1.2   A framework for national 'urban' policy

government. Specific circumstances in each member state have led to different policy approaches in the European Union. What factors can explain the differences and similarities between the national urban policies in the European Union? This investigation defines three broad categories that could explain the characteristics of national urban policy in the European Union. National 'urban' policy ((4) in Figure 1.2) is closely tied up with the national pattern of spatial development (1), the administrative and financial framework in which the cities operate (2) and both the national perception of urban issues and challenges and the political priority that is attributed to these issues and challenges (3) (see Figure 1.2).

National Spatial and Economic Development Pattern

Different national approaches to urban issues can emerge from different spatial-development patterns in the member states. The majority of European citizens live in urban areas, but there are still major differences in the use and availability of space and in the degree of urbanization. What is the position of the larger cities within the pattern of spatial development? Clearly, the cities in Europe find themselves at different stages of urban development. International comparative research has confirmed that in the past decades cities have developed according to a cyclical pattern of urban growth and decline in terms of inhabitants and economic activity (Van den Berg, 1987). The literature identifies four stages of urban development: urbanization, suburbanization, disurbanization and, possibly, reurbanization. The process of urbanization has been induced by the concentration of economic activities. In the stage of suburbanization the larger cities lose inhabitants to the municipalities in the suburbs. The transition from urbanization to suburbanization is in this line of thought triggered by the rise of prosperity of the population. Disurbanization implies that not only the core but also the first ring of suburbs lose inhabitants to places farther away. Disurbanization is usually related to processes of degeneration in core cities. In the stage of reurbanization the city regains its attractiveness but the economic recovery is accompanied by a growing number of social problems. The urban system gets increasingly complex with each stage of development and induces the national government to implement explicit urban policy.

Administrative and Financial Framework

The challenges present themselves in the cities, which makes the local government level the appropriate one on which to deal with the city challenges. The administrative and financial framework within which the cities pursue their own policy is therefore another important factor. It makes a difference whether a federal or unitary state is concerned. The same can be said about the level of decentralization – or in other words the local autonomy. If the law provides for a high degree of autonomy of local government, a different approach can be expected from those with a lesser degree of autonomy. The degree of local autonomy is based on both administrative competencies of cities and their financial means. What makes up the urban income? What are the shares of central government sources and of local taxes in the revenues of cities? What is the role of EU contributions?

Apart from the financial aspect, the relation between the national authorities and the (larger) cities in the administrative framework is significant. What ministries are directly or indirectly involved in urban affairs and how far do they cooperate effectively? What is the role of the intermediate level of government? The spatial scope of the public administration at the urban level is another point to be considered. In the second and higher stages of urban development, larger cities and towns become the centres of functional urban regions. Almost everywhere in Europe these functional urban regions cross administrative borders, which in turn raises the matter of competent metropolitan authorities. The creation of metropolitan authorities certainly has an impact on the role of the national government in urban planning.

Urban Issues and Challenges from the National Perspective

The national spatial development pattern and administrative framework are important but equally so is the national authorities' opinion on the development and the role of larger cities within the national framework. In some cases the national government might fear that the cities would become too dominant in the national urban system; in other cases they stress the potential of cities as motors of the national economy. Furthermore most societal developments – good or bad – manifest themselves earlier and more profoundly in urban areas, which might be another incentive for giving priority to urban problems and challenges. Does the national government attribute priority to urban issues and what exactly are the main urban issues in the national perspective?

National Policy Responses to Urban Issues, Challenges and Development

Finally, the investigation concentrates on explicit urban policy in the member states of the European Union. Where have experiences been made with explicit urban policy and what is the long-term vision behind such policy? In some countries the urban issues and challenges might have been translated into direct, explicit urban policy but there are quite a few countries where indirect, implicit policy is common practice in urban affairs. To some extent the investigation pays attention to this policy, as far as it is perceived to have a major impact on cities. The previous section distinguished also partial, sector-specific policy and integral policy. Another interesting topic is the incorporation of EU policies/subsidies within the national policy framework.

For an overview of national 'urban' policy, all aspects are important. The national policy should be examined in its unique context. In the national chapters the context and background for this policy is described. They influence the 'state of the art' concerning the challenges and priorities and the national policy responses.

In Sum, the Main Features of the Research Approach

This first chapter has discussed some main features of urban dynamics in Europe: the increased urban competition, the advancement of urban networks, the cumulation of societal problems in parts of the larger cities, the emphasis on sustainability and the need for organizing capacity. These trends are general challenges for the whole of Europe but they need not necessarily have the same effects in all member states. What is their impact in the several member states and how do the national governments respond to them?

Concerning these national policy responses, an important distinction to make is between policy that is explicitly directed to cities and policy that is not, but is 'urban' in the sense that it makes a major impact on cities, such as housing policy, transportation policy, spatial planning policy, etc. Another, equally important distinction is that between partial (sector-specific) and integral (sector-exceeding) policy. Such urban problems as accessibility, quality of living and economic revitalization are so strongly connected that a more integrate approach can be far more effective. The nature of the policy responses in the member states – whether or not explicitly addressed to cities, partial or integral – is supposed to be bound up with the national pattern of spatial development, the administrative and financial framework, and the political priority a member state gives to the perceived urban problems and challenges. A systematic investigation of all these aspects in the member states permits an up-to-date and accurate presentation of the 'state of the art' of explicit national urban policy in the member states of the European Union.

Notes

1   The term 'national urban policy' refers to policies that affect the cities knowingly and directly.
2   The core city and its smaller suburban municipalities make up one functional urban region because of strong economic and social ties among them.

References

Berg, L. van den (1987), *Urban Systems in a Dynamic Society*, Aldershot, UK: Avebury.
Berg L. van den, Braun, E. and Meer, J. van der (1997), *Metropolitan Organising Capacity*, Aldershot, UK: Ashgate.
Bramezza, I. (1996), *The competitiveness of the European city and the role of urban management in improving the city's performance*, Tinbergen Institute Research Series No. 109, Rotterdam: Erasmus University.
Castells, M. (1991), *The Informational City: Information Technology, Economic Restructuring and the Urban-Regional Process*, Oxford: Basil Blackwell.
European Commission (1994), *Een duurzame stedelijke Ontwikkeling in Europa*, Eerste rapport, Brussel: Europese campagne voor duurzame steden en gemeenten.
European Commission (1995), *Europa 2000+: Samenwerking voor de ruimtelijke ordening van Europa*, Luxembourg: Bureau voor officiële publikaties der Europese gemeenschappen.
Hall, P. (1995), *Towards a General Urban Theory*, in Brotchie, J., Batty, M., Blakely, E., Hall, P. and Newton, P. (eds), *Cities in Competition*, Australia: Longman.
Parkinson, M., Bianchini, F., Dawson, J., Evens, R. and Harding, A. (1992), *Urbanisation and the Functions of Cities in the European Community*, Liverpool: European Institute of Urban Affairs, John Moores University.
World Commission on Environment and Development (1987), *Our Common Future*, Oxford: Oxford University Press.

2   Austria

HERBERT PURSCHKE

National Spatial Development Patterns

Austria consists of nine states (Länder). The capitals of eight states are centres of metropolitan regions. The most significant is the city of Vienna which is both one of the states and the federal capital and as an urban area has a population roughly equal to that of the seven other (Länder) capitals and their catchment areas. While Vienna may also be considered a large city in international comparison, the others are only medium-sized cities. This strong imbalance between Vienna and the other cities of the urban network in Austria has historical roots – Vienna was capital of the Danube monarchy up to 1918.

   In addition to the premier city of Vienna, we have to differentiate between the following city size classes:

* four large state capitals are city regions[1] with one core city: Linz, Graz, Salzburg and Innsbruck;
* two smaller state capitals, Klagenfurt and Bregenz, which are structured as polycentric city regions (the city regions of Klagenfurt-Villach and the Rhine Valley-Lake Constance area with the cities of Bregenz, Dornbirn, Feldkirch);
* the special case of S. Pölten, which was selected as state capital of the state of Lower Austria at the end of the 1980s and is a relatively small city region.

Urbanization, Suburbanization/Desurbanization, Reurbanization

In general, cities and city regions in Austria, as in most European countries, are where population and jobs concentrate. A dominant feature of spatial development in these regions, as well as in smaller cities, has been the process of suburbanization which set in at the beginning of the 1970s. Important factors for this process are:

14

- a marked rise in the number of households as compared to population trends;
- a very low density of built-up space in urban catchment areas;
- an increase of the percentage of land utilized per workplace combined with a strong dynamic of settlement of manufacturing and distributing enterprises in catchment areas.

In the 1970s the population declined in the three largest core cities in the southern and eastern parts of Austria (Vienna, Linz and Graz) the largest drop being recorded in Vienna. The core cities in western Austria grew, especially Salzburg as well as Bregenz and Dornbirn. The catchment districts had already started growing at the time. The most dynamic developments took place in the catchment area of the cities of Innsbruck and Salzburg.

In the 1980s only Graz and St Pölten lost inhabitants; the other core cities recorded increases. At the same time, the dynamic of suburbanization accelerated. The rise in population stemmed in most city regions from in-migration to the agglomerations (especially in Graz and Klagenfurt-Villach), a process accompanied by out-migration to the peripheral regions of Austria. High birth rates were recorded only in the city regions of western Austria.

Up to a certain extent a process of reurbanization set in during the 1980s. This trend is above all a qualitative trend given the fact that incentives for the restoration of old building structures were created. A substantial measure was the upgrading of city centres through the creation of pedestrian zones – this process is now under way, promoted by new ways of organizing parking space in city centres. The restoration of old buildings and historic city cores should also been seen in the light of the significance of tourism for Austria.

Important Economic or Social Indicators

Since the beginning of the 1970s labour market trends in city regions have been more dynamic than population trends. The strongest social impact has been observed in western Austria (rising gainful employment, especially women entering the labour market).

The structure of labour markets and their trends vary from one city region to another. A higher level of employment in manufacturing is to be found in the city regions of the Rhine Valley-Lake Constance areas (about 40 per cent of employed persons (ÖSTAT, 1994)), Linz-Wels (32 per cent) as well as St Pölten (30 per cent). Personal services are represented at above average levels in the regions of Innsbruck (44 per cent), Salzburg and surroundings (43 per

Table 2.1   Important figures on Austria's agglomerations

		Vienna and hinterland	Linz-Wels	Graz	Salzburg hinterland	Klagenfurt-Villach	Innsbruck	Rheintal-Bodensee-area	St Pölten	Austria
Zoning and resident population										
Inhabitants in agglomeration	1991	2,062,969	517,043	355,858	312,511	259,525	259,446	249,361	137,508	7,795,786
thereof inhabitants core city*	1991	1,539,848	255,638	237,810	143,987	144,055	118,112	67,832	50,026	
thereof inhabitants hinterland	1991	523,121	261,405	118,048	168,524	115,470	141,334	181,529	87,482	
Cadastral area in km²		4,610	1,744	1,288	1,738	2,029	2,095	724	1,230	83,859
Inhabitants/km² usable land	1991	608	379	613	443	390	828	728	171	240
Commuters										
Commuters to core city	1991	663,570	80,448	65,858	42,638	26,757	34,436	8,947	16,551	
Commuters out of core city	1991	523,705	14,587	11,579	12,054	5,309	9,182	5,279	4,864	
Economic performance index										
Gross regional product per inhabitant	1992	**136	129	110	125	96	109	101	87	100
Gross regional product per employed person	1992	**117	103	91	104	90	99	102	88	100
Labour market shares 1991										
Self-employed and employed persons according to Census										
Manufacturing w/o construction	1991	22.3%	32.2%	24.9%	23.0%	22.2%	20.6%	39.7%	29.8%	27.1%
Private services sector	1991	44.5%	35.9%	37.3%	42.9%	40.8%	43.8%	32.9%	32.0%	37.1%
Public services sector	1991	22.6%	20.7%	26.3%	22.1%	25.9%	25.0%	17.6%	20.7%	20.9%
Labour market trend										
Self-employed and employed persons according to Census										
Manufacturing w/o construction	1981–1991	-21.2%	-13.5%	-10.9%	0.3%	-7.8%	-5.3%	-5.9%	-5.7%	-12.1%
Private services sector	1981–1991	15.3%	27.6%	15.6%	25.7%	15.9%	19.9%	30.3%	24.1%	18.7%
Public services sector	1981–1991	22.4%	29.3%	17.7%	35.0%	34.1%	30.2%	133.9%	32.0%	26.3%
Employed persons total	1981–1991	5.2%	8.0%	6.2%	17.1%	10.5%	13.9%	10.5%	8.2%	4.5%
Unemployment rate										
(% of employed persons)	1995	6.9%	4.7%	6.0%	3.2%	7.3%	3.9%	4.7%	4.9%	6.4%

Austrian agglomerations

*   In the case of Linz-Wels, the sum of the municipalities of Linz and Wels, Klagenfurt-Villach; municipalities Klagenfurt und Villach, Rheintal-Bodenseegebiet: municipalities Bregenz und Dornbirn.

**   Preliminary estimate.

cent) as well as Klagenfurt-Villach (41 per cent). The public sector is very important in Graz (27 per cent), Klagenfurt-Villach (26 per cent) and Innsbruck (25 per cent) compared to Austria on the whole.

The labour market trends moved upward in the larger state capital regions from 1971 to 1981. The creation and securing of jobs was a paramount political issue in that period – city regions functioned as the driving force for economic growth. From a regional point of view, the winners regarding growth were above all Salzburg (+29 per cent) and the Rhine Valley-Lake Constance region (+27 per cent). A relatively weak dynamic of growth was observed in the region of Vienna. During this period, regions outside of the large agglomerations also grew, because regional policy concentrated primarily on industrial sites in peripheral and old industrial regions.

The period between 1981 and 1991 was characterized by a marked decline in employment levels. It has not been possible to maintain the political goal of achieving full employment in the light of the strong decline in the basic materials industries. The highest growth rates were achieved in this decade by agglomerations in western Austria. All city regions, with the exception of Salzburg, recorded job losses in the manufacturing industries (especially in Linz-Wels and Graz owing to the significance of the raw materials industries), which were more than compensated by growth in the private and public services sector.

The past years have seen labour market trends in all parts of the country successively taking on similar levels, i.e., the role of city regions as motors of economic growth and subsequently for employment has weakened. Areas which in the past served to compensate unemployment in manufacturing, no longer fulfil this task. In the medium term, the public sector cannot be expected to supply more jobs and segments of the growth sector of the producer services sector are currently stagnating. Since the beginning of the 1990s Austria has been increasingly confronted with rising unemployment rates, the situation in most city regions being more favourable than in the remaining ones, with the exception of Graz and Klagenfurt-Villach. These two regions have always been at a disadvantage because of their inadequate access to transport routes linking them to western Europe.

Development Patterns

As in all European cities, the spatial expansion of cities occurs along the main transportation axes. Vienna has grown mainly southward since the beginning of the 1970s. Vienna as potential transportation hub for eastern and western

Europe is increasingly being confronted with traffic problems. The main commuter routes and international transport routes are at their capacity limits.

In the area covering Linz-Wels and Salzburg, a coherent region with urban quality is emerging regarding the accessibility of workplaces. The metropolitan area of Salzburg is growing in the direction of southern Germany, which is also documented in the comprehensive plans for the state territories of Bavaria and Salzburg. This means that in the future, the issue of crossborder spatial planning will become crucial – the groundwork for this is being laid by EUREGIO, which was created in 1995 for 'Salzburg – Berchtesgadener Land – Traunstein'. The city regions of Innsbruck and the Rhine Valley-Lake Constance area are also increasingly orienting themselves on the metropolitan area of Munich.

Innsbruck and the Rhine Valley-Lake Constance areas are those regions in which the expansion of the agglomerations is greatly limited by the topography of the region. The density of inhabitants in relation to the amount of usable land is already the highest there. A weakening of the suburbanization process cannot be expected in light of the most recent population forecasts. The possibilities of influencing settlement trends within the regions are currently very limited owing to the political and administrative system (cf. 'Administrative and Financial Framework', q.v.).

Urban Networks

The issue of urban networks is hardly being discussed currently in Austria. In spite of the partially polycentric structure of agglomerations, no example of a functional network in Austria exists (cooperation or division of labour regarding complementary functions). Certain examples of mutual commitments for specific purposes could be considered a sort of strategic network. In this manner Linz cooperates with cities in southern Germany within the scope of the project 'The Economic Area of the Danube Cities' (*Wirtschaftsregion Donaustädte*) in the fields of location marketing, information exchange and cooperation on issues related to Danube ports. Graz is a member of the strategic network of 'Euro-cities' and cooperates with other cities in EU countries within the scope of environmental projects.

Administrative and Financial Framework

Administrative Framework

National authorities' influence on cities, direct and indirect involvement of ministries In Austria, political representation and policy-making take place on three levels: Bund (federal government), Land (state) and Gemeinde (municipality).

The division of responsibility among these three levels follows the principle of subsidiarity. Spatial development planning is the responsibility of municipalities, states take over the task of coordinating the work and defining the overall framework. Since the federal government is not explicitly made responsible for spatial planning, a proper coordination office was set up for dealing with national planning tasks that affect more than one state, the Austrian Conference on Regional Planning (*Österreichische Raumordnungskonferenz*, ÖROK). The federal government, states and municipalities are represented in ÖROK. ÖROK, however, cannot pass binding resolutions, but is only empowered to issue recommendations.

Therefore, as the Austrian constitution does not mention national urban policy as field of activity and competence of the federal government, no federal law on spatial planning or urban politics exists. There is no ministry for *Raumordnung* (spatial planning), which would include the matters of urban politics, on a federal level.

On the other hand, the federal government has oversight over important sectoral measures and planning activities with territorial reference, for example:

- the *Bundesministerium für wirtschaftliche Angelegenheiten* (Ministry for Economic Affairs) is responsible for spatial planning tasks related to the federal road network (federal roads, expressways and motorways);
- the responsibilities of the *Bundesministerium für Wissenschaft, Verkehr und Kultur* (Ministry for Science, Transport and Culture) with urban reference are the fields of transport policy, with the exception of federal roads (for example supraregional transport infrastructure, construction of public railway lines), as well as the affairs related to the public sector economy (especially regional economic policy). This ministry is also responsible for universities, institutions of higher education, specialized institutions of higher education, comprehensive and vocational colleges.

Thus technology policy as well as transport policy are not only divided among the individual territorial authorities, but on the federal level, also among several ministries. Coordination of sectoral policies for which several ministries are responsible is the task of the Federal Chancellery. The federal government determines the locations and acquires the land within the scope of its own public business administration. The municipalities do not have the formal right to be heard. However, such measures are of great importance for the municipality with regard to both its function for the region and the municipality itself.

The states as regional authorities with influence on cities The states have influence over urban development, especially regarding their competence for comprehensive spatial planning, because they have passed spatial planning laws. Based on these laws, the state governments implement *Landesraumordnungsprogramme* (state development plans) and *Landesfachplanungen* (sectoral state plans) as well as *Regionale Raumordnungsprogramme* (regional development schemes) and *Regionale Fachplanungen* (sectoral regional plans) in varying numbers and of differing natures.[2] These plans contain objectives and the determination of locations for the corresponding state or parts of it, and function as the supralocal framework for the local spatial planning of the municipalities. The spatial planning laws also lay down the planning instruments of the municipalities. In addition, states also have the duty to supervise municipal planning and to assist municipalities in their work.

Local authorities, metropolitan authorities Municipalities exercise administrative functions transferred to them by the state and the federal government. But primarily they are autonomous territorial authorities with the right of self-government with executive, but not legislative, powers.[3] These rights are independent of size and equal for all. The body that passes resolutions is the *Gemeinderat* (municipal council) and the executive body is the *Gemeindevorstand* (municipal directorate); in cities it is the *Stadtsenat* (city senate). In some states the mayors are elected by citizens, in others by the municipal council. For all tasks accomplished within the scope of self-governance in its own fields of action, the mayor is the first instance and the appeals authority is the municipal council.

One of the most important independent tasks of the municipality is local spatial planning, which includes responsibility for the building regulation plan. It gives the municipality a key role in the overall planning system. It controls permissible land use through the instrument of the *Flächenwidmungsplan* (zoning plan). In some states a *Räumliches Entwicklungskonzept* (local development scheme) must be produced before a zoning plan is drawn up, which contains guidelines for the future development of the municipality territory. In Vienna, the Urban Development Plan assumes the function of a spatial development scheme, but without legal force. The municipalities also have the *Bebauungsplan* (building regulation plan), which determines the use of building land. The state is only a supervisory authority and approves spatial planning on municipal level according to the criterion of conformity with the spatial planning laws as well as with the spatial planning on supralocal level of the state (i.e., state or regional development plans)

Municipalities are also responsible in self-governance for further significant tasks related to spatial planning, among others the issuance of *Baubewilligung* (building permits) and *Bauplatzerklärung* (building site assessments), the administration of transport routes of the municipalities and the local traffic police.[4]

Degree of administrative independency of local authorities Based on the constitutional right to self-governance of municipalities, these enjoy a relatively high degree of independence in administrative matters from the states and the federal government. Especially in the light of the autonomy of the municipalities in the area of local spatial planning and their competence for the issuance of building permits, we are able to say that decisions on the development of settlements in Austria are reached mainly on the lower tiers of the planning system.

Since the city regions in Austria cover several municipalities, the situation might occur in which municipalities independently, and sometimes even competing with one another, pursue their own spatial development goals. A city region in Austria usually does not act as a uniform planning instance that pursues a common planning goal.

Attempts to coordinate action for common goals exist in the area of Vienna through the *Planungsgemeinschaft-Ost* (planning partnership East), formed jointly by the states of Vienna, Lower Austria and Burgenland, which coordinates spatial planning activities that affect the entire region. However, it could not really successfully tackle the problem of competition among municipalities. For the city region of Salzburg, the state resolved a supralocal sectoral plan on regional level which coordinates settlement development and the location of enterprises between the core city of Salzburg and its hinterlands (Office of the Salzburg State Government, 1995).

Financial Framework, Public Business Administration

Beyond the scope of legislative competence all territorial authorities have the power to implement measures in the sphere of public business administration for which there are no competence limits and which cover economic activities within the scope of private law (e.g., land purchases, investment incentives). Every state has an economic promotion agency which, for example, sets up enterprises in business parks.

Municipalities, just as the state and the federal government, may own, acquire and dispose of assets of all types as business entities. They may operate business enterprises, administer their own budgets and write off expenses (Walter and Mayer, 1988, s. 290 ff). Thus they may apply completely independent measures from the sphere of private business administration in order to achieve their spatial planning and urban development goals.

The amounts available from the funds, which are important for the political distribution of power, illustrate the situation: of total public expenditures roughly 70 per cent comes from the federal government, 15 per cent from the states and 15 per cent from the municipalities. The share of municipalities (including Vienna) in expenditure for activities with strong spatial reference[5] is much higher though (federal 50 per cent, state 20 per cent, municipality 30 per cent). This reflects the significant role played by municipalities as important factors of influence for spatial impact trends.

Urban income sources (shares in general and/or targeted central government sources, local taxes, EU contributions, other sources) These expenditures are financed through revenue from taxes and duties. The taxation system responsible for the income funds consists basically of federal taxes (roughly 25 per cent), so-called mutual federal taxes (roughly 70 per cent) and municipal taxes (roughly 5 per cent of total tax revenue).

Of the so-called **mutual federal taxes**, municipalities receive roughly 15 per cent. Allocation to the municipalities is done by number of inhabitants, but according to a progressive population scale. According to the currently valid Revenue Equalization Law there are four levels in the progressive population scale grouped by multiples of the population of municipalities:

with not more than 10,000 inhabitants at 1 1/3;
with 10,001 to 20,000 inhabitants at 1 2/3;
with 20,001 to 50,000 inhabitants at 2; and
with over 50,000 inhabitants at 3 1/3.[6]

The allocation of mutual federal taxes therefore takes into account that larger cities need to fulfil central place functions for their hinterlands and must therefore provide higher infrastructural services. Thus the Revenue Equalization Law forms one of the most important federal regulations which takes the special position of big cities into consideration.

The most important **municipal taxes** are communal tax of three per cent on payrolls of employed persons and the beverage tax. These two municipal taxes basically determine the financial power of a municipality, and for this reason those municipalities with more plants and tourism are financially better off. Revenue equalization between municipalities does not exist in Austria.

If one compares the total tax revenues of core municipalities and their hinterland municipalities, we see that the tax per capita ratio in the centres fluctuates between 138 per cent (Bregenz and Dornbirn) and 270 per cent (Vienna) of the corresponding hinterland region. Some hinterland municipalities exceed these peak values of their core cities (e.g., Vösendorf in the Vienna area with 329 per cent, Seefeld/Innsbruck with 232 per cent, Raaba in the Grazer area with 209 per cent as well as Anif/Salzburg with 205 per cent).

Table 2.2   Tax revenue per inhabitant

City region	Tax revenue in ATS per inhabitant		
	Core city	Hinterland	Core city in % of hinterland
Vienna	29,031	10,746	270
Linz-Wels	17,786	10,944	163
Graz	14,742	8,104	181
Salzburg	18,853	11,247	167
Innsbruck	16,514	10,137	163
Klagenfurt-Villach	15,400	10,662	144
Rheintal-Bodensee	16,528	11,676	141
S. Pölten	15,481	8,148	190
Agglomerations in total	24,062	10,539	228

Source: ÖSTAT, census 1991, municipal financial statement 1994.

Fees for the use of municipal services (canalization, water supply, waste disposal, etc.) also contribute considerably to the municipalities' income: however, these funds are allocated to specific uses and for operating the corresponding infrastructure.

Moreover, municipalities are supported in the financing of infrastructure investments in several ways. The most important is the Water Management Fund followed by state funds and by a separate fund for municipalities, which is administrated by the state (granted according to need).

EU subsidies to cities are granted primarily within the scope of Community Initiatives. Since these are used to fund projects, they do not really play a substantial role for financing. The cities of Vienna and Graz receive funds from URBAN. Linz receives funds from RESIDER II, which, among other things, serves to support a location marketing initiative for selling space in the manufacturing industry. Graz is participating in several EU projects on the subject of environment and is endeavouring to establish an image as sustainable city. The Rhine Valley-Lake Constance area participates in the RETEX II initiative.[7] The initiatives EMPLOYMENT, ADAPT and KMU are relevant for practically all large cities. Vienna, Innsbruck, Klagenfurt-Villach and the Rhine Valley-Lake Constance area participate in programmes within the scope of INTERREG II.

Degree of financial independence of local authorities Regarding the contents of the overall development policy pursued, the municipalities have a relatively strong position, especially if their finances are also strong because of high tax revenues. Municipalities may apply completely independent measures from the sphere of private business administration (investments, investment incentives) in order to achieve their spatial planning goals.

Specific National Preconditions/Circumstances that Favour or Hamper Integrated Socioeconomic Policies at the Local Level

In summary, the basis for urban policy may be characterized as follows: as no formal competence for comprehensive urban planning exists, the federal government has power over important areas of urban policies, while the states and the municipalities themselves have no choice but to cooperate with one another. Moreover, the sectoral tasks carried out by the federal government are distributed among individual ministries. Therefore, no comprehensive urban policy exists on federal level in Austria.

The municipalities are in a relatively strong position because of their activities within the scope of their self-governance and their far-reaching financial autonomy. Since intercommunal cooperation between the core municipalities and their hinterland municipalities is lacking, competition between the municipalities of a city region for the location of enterprises, jobs, inhabitants, etc., exists. The more jobs, the higher the revenue from the communal tax, and more inhabitants also mean a higher share of the funds from the common state taxes. The reason for this is to be found in tax legislation and revenue equalization between the territorial authorities, which makes the municipalities highly dependent on their own income.

This competitive situation is aggravated by the fact that state administrative bodies often see themselves as representatives of the interests of the hinterland municipalities, which are weaker in terms of inhabitants and financially, as opposed to the economically more dominant core cities. The problem is especially acute in the region of Vienna, because Vienna is at the same time state and municipality, while the hinterland municipalities belong to another state (Lower Austria). This rivalry makes a development policy of integration for metropolitan areas much more difficult.

Urban Issues and Challenges from the National Perspective

Major Urban Issues, National Priorities with Regard to Urban Issues

There is no programme or concept in Austria that explicitly illustrates the national perspective of urban issues and challenges from the standpoint of the federal government.

The most important spatial problems for Austria from a national perspective for selected sectors (settlement trends, open space, regional economy, social infrastructure and technical infrastructure) are described and analyzed in the *Österreichisches Raumordnungskonzept* 1991 (ÖRK '91; Austrian Spatial Planning Concept 1991) (ÖROK, 1992), which was based on a political agreement between the federal government, the state governors and the representatives of the Union of Cities and Municipalities within the scope of the *Österreichische Raumordnungskonferenz* (Austrian Conference on Spatial Planning). ÖRK '91 should be viewed as a spatial planning framework on national level, which serves as guidance for detailed planning work, programmes and concepts of the federal government, states and municipalities. Urban policy is not treated as a separate issue here, but as part of overall spatial development in Austria in each of the sectoral areas. Since the focus is on a comprehensive illustration of Austria's spatial problems, it does not include fixing priorities or going beyond the description of measures.

A summary of the problems and development outlook for cities is contained in the national report of the Habitat II Conference of the United Nations on

Human Settlement (1995), which has also been produced jointly by the federal government, states and municipalities.

The following subjects are considered major urban issues.

Suburbanization and land consumption Metropolitan regions in Austria are confronted with growing land consumption and declining availability of reserved areas. In big cities 55 per cent of the usable land has already been built up; the percentage for the hinterlands is below 15 per cent. Austrians' favourite type of housing, the freestanding single family home, is largely responsible for this trend, because it uses up large areas at a low degree of utilization of already built up areas. Forecasts of future residential construction trends indicate that the extensive settlement area enlargements will continue at an even faster pace unless we succeed in promoting space-saving forms of construction, especially in the city hinterland municipalities.

Inefficient utilization of the infrastructure In-migration from core cities and from the peripheral parts of the catchment areas concentrates on the hinterlands near big cities with good transport infrastructure. Large investments in transport infrastructure (freeways, rapid urban transportation) are enabling an increasing number of people to realize their dream of 'working in the city – living in the country'. The expansion of infrastructure in the hinterland municipalities requires large amounts of public money, while the infrastructure in the core cities is not used to full capacity.

Environmental problems from individual short distance traffic Since settlement trends in hinterland municipalities seldom are oriented on public transport infrastructure, inhabitants are forced to depend on their own private vehicles. In addition, an increasing number of enterprises, shopping centres and large recreational facilities are being located 'in the fields', i.e., in the urban hinterlands, and are accessible only by motorized individual transport. This increases the amount of individual traffic and the pollution it causes.

Declining significance of city centres Inner city business districts of metropolitan agglomerations in Austria are threatened by out-migration of business and a declining significance, while at the same time land-consuming shopping centres are flourishing in the hinterlands.

Social segregation caused by speculative restoration of buildings In the attractive and favourably located city cores, a trend toward gentrification is emerging. For example old apartments in turn of the century buildings are being converted into offices or luxury apartments. This is driving out the longtime residents, who are socially usually not that well off, to run down districts with turn of the century buildings threatened by cumulative deterioration. Rental laws, which protect renters from having their rental contracts terminated and sets ceilings on rents for apartments of inferior quality, help to check this trend.

Integration of migrants The opening up of the border to the neighbouring countries of the east has led to an enormous inflow of immigrants to Austria over the past years, especially to cities. Although new legislation has reduced the number of immigrants, their integration remains a challenge for urban policy.

Specific Threats to Cities and Opportunities

At national level, the following factors are perceived as specific threats to cities and opportunities (= external influence on urban development).

Internationalization Although metropolitan regions have the highest level of economic activity in Austria, there are developmental problems caused by worsening location conditions, scarcity of space, increased unemployment, decline in industrial employment and a lack of innovation. The region of Vienna particularly has marked structural deficits, considering its old industrial structure directed at domestic markets and the high percentage of sectors that had been protected up to now and are hardly prepared to compete in an international environment. The city of Linz is confronted with the predominance of the large enterprises in the basic materials sector. Graz and Klagenfurt have only been able to provide weak stimuli for development to their hinterlands. Industrial and services enterprises in metropolitan agglomerations are being confronted with having to operate with fiercer competition and internationalization on domestic markets that up to now have been comfortably protected.

Opening of eastern borders Metropolitan areas in the eastern parts of Austria have been hoping for development stimuli from the opening up of the borders to the neighbouring countries of the east (Czech Republic, Slovakia, Hungary, Slovenia) due to their advantageous location as bridgehead between Western industrialized countries and the east. In particular, the cities of Vienna, Graz and Klagenfurt are hoping for development stimuli. At the same time, Austria's metropolitan areas are encountering new competition based in part on the enormous growth potential of these countries, which is where, above all, manufacturing enterprises are relocating. As reaction to the short-term and medium-term problems caused by the surplus of cheap labour and the resulting pressure on wages in Austria, immigration laws have been made more stringent.

Role and Function of Large Cities with Regard to National Development Issues

ÖRK '91 and the Habitat Report on Austria do not make any statements on the significance of large cities in Austria for national trends. The governmental statement made on 29 January 1997 did not mention this subject either.

National Policy Responses to Urban Issues, Challenges and Development

In addition to the analysis and the description of spatial problems in Austria, ÖRK '91 serves as guideline for all planning work. It is not legally binding, but rather a resolution unanimously adopted by all planning bodies and has the character of a politically self-imposed obligation (comparable to a charter). It contains goals for action in the medium term and a catalogue of measures. In addition to its function as guideline for public planning bodies, ÖRK '91 also fulfils an important informative function at national level. ÖRK '91 lists the following goals and measures for metropolitan areas.

Cooperation of municipalities of one metropolitan area It is above all in agglomerations that the establishment of a Union of Municipalities with the aim of coordinating spatial planning is necessary, in order to avoid competition among hinterlands and against city centres. The spreading out of urban functions into the countryside (residential areas, industrial areas, shopping centres, etc.) motivated solely by cheap land prices, which generates even more individual traffic, should be stopped by this measure. This requires comprehensive planning supported by all municipalities of a metropolitan area. Within a Union of Municipalities agreements under private law may also be concluded with the aim of equalizing the different levels of tax revenue in the individual municipalities (= regional revenue equalization). In addition, a Union of Municipalities will be able to negotiate as partner in a much stronger position with the state or federal government regarding subsidies for infrastructure facilities (investment in rapid urban transportation, Water Management Fund, etc.). In practice, the states have to take steps in order to be able to set up this type of partnership and to motivate municipalities to cooperate. The basic problem is that this type of cooperation will only bear fruit in the long term.

Upgrading of the periphery of core cities The peripheral areas in the immediate vicinity of core cities should be upgraded into full urban settlement areas in order to avoid the accelerated fraying of the settlement borders of core cities into the hinterlands caused by extensive land use (e.g., settlements with freestanding single family homes). To this end, available reserved space in these areas should be built up and existing low-density built up settlement areas, especially those near stations of rapid urban transport systems, should be made more dense. At the same time, however, ecologically valuable green areas should be preserved. Existing urban secondary centres should be upgraded to multi-functional centre (e.g., through traffic reduction measures) and should also be able to fulfil comprehensive urban functions.

Regional secondary centres as relief for core cities; the concept of decentralized concentration In order to relieve city centres of excessive settlement pressure while land is scarce, and to distribute traffic flows evenly according to the principle of decentralized concentration, the central places at the outskirts of metropolitan areas will have to be promoted. It is feasible to decentralize workplaces, especially in the areas of industrial manufacturing as well as in segments of central place services. The secondary centres should be linked to the core cities and to each other by a high speed public transportation network, the building of which is the competence of the federal authorities. In addition, what is needed is to ensure good prospects for the built up areas and a functioning cooperation between the core cities and their hinterlands. The objective should be to limit despoliation of the landscape in the hinterlands and to reduce the number of commuters. These principles prevail in, for example, the 'Settlement Scheme for the Eastern Region' (*Siedlungskonzept für die Ostregion*) of the PGO, the Vienna Urban Development Plan (*Stadtentwicklungsplan*) and state development plan (*Landesentwicklungsprogramm*) of the state of Salzburg.

Maintenance or creation of mixed functions in city quarters; 'the city of short distances' The inner city districts should keep their multiple functions of central place, central residential area and as location for low-emission enterprises. For this reason it is necessary to plan structural improvement measures for residential districts: among these are the socially compatible restoration of old apartment buildings, creation of more living space by adapting attics, the relocation of enterprises that cause disturbance, the clearing of interior courtyards and the improvement of the residential environment by reducing traffic and landscaping green areas. At the same time, the variety of small and medium-sized businesses in the individual city districts should be maintained (especially the local services, commerce and businesses). The aim is to keep distances short within cities where home, workplace and the most important suppliers of services are located so close together in each city district so as to reach these quickly and on foot.

Saving space Settlement trends for residential areas and for business areas in the hinterland municipalities should be concentrated in already existing settlement areas and local centres as well as in the catchment areas of stations of public transportation systems. Existing, currently widely spaced built up settlement areas, should be made more dense, and space-saving building methods should be promoted in order to minimize land consumption and land sealing. The availability of settlement land for each function (living, working, recreational, etc.) should be kept at certain proportions to reserved areas and unused building land between core city and hinterland.[8]

Promoting international competitiveness In metropolitan regions, enterprises with high capacity, intensive application of technology and which are open to world markets should be secured and/or established, especially high grade standard functions such as producer services (research and development institutions, engineering offices, planning staff and group headquarters, financial services, more cooperation between municipalities and business on the one hand, and universities on the other).[9]

Maintenance and improvement of the quality of housing and recreational facilities Prerequisites for the location and further development of principle industrial and services enterprises are high quality urban housing and recreational facilities in both core cities and in the hinterlands. Areas with countryside character in the vicinity of large cities and green and undeveloped areas should be kept or converted for recreational use. This requires ensuring ecologically sustainable agriculture and forestry.

Integration of immigrants The problem of immigration should be coped with by measures that do not violate values such as solidarity and cultural openness, but at the same time are not detrimental to the interests of the native working population.

Long Term National Vision, Sectoral Policies/Instruments Affecting Cities

Based on the multiple competences described in the field of urban policy, Austria does not have long term national visions on cities or urbanization that go beyond the scope of ÖRK '91. Some cities, however, have worked out autonomous concepts, which position them as pioneers, both in Austria and internationally (Urban Development Plan of Vienna, *Stadtentwicklungsplan Wien*, and business schemes of the cities of Linz, Graz, Salzburg and Innsbruck).

Sectoral measures of the federal government are usually carried out in cooperation with the states and municipalities. Thus the municipality of Vienna has agreed to a series of investment measures for which the federal government (Ministry for Public Economy and Transport) commits itself to supply funds for expanding transportation infrastructure.

National Opinion about the Impact of EU Policies/Subsidies on Cities

In Austria an officially published national opinion on the impact of EU policies and subsidies on cities (URBAN, TEN, Structural Funding, designation of Objective Regions) does not exist, nor on the development of European urban policy. This is probably due to the lack of competence for urban policy at federal level mentioned above, as well as with Austria's relatively short period of membership in the EU.

Experts in the field do not assess the expansion of the TEN on the north-south route via the Brenner, which has been given high priority by the EU, as being that important for internal development in Austria, because the expansion of an already existing route will not really have any influence on spatial structure. For the development of Austria and its metropolitan regions, the west-east link and the axis through the Danube Valley is much more important. In contrast, the expansion of the TEN to link Berlin – Prague – Vienna – Adria would be more significant for the cities of Vienna, Graz and Linz.

Due to the small size of Austria's territory and its federalist structure, Austria's target regions within the EU's regional policy are very small. In part, Objective 5b regions exist already in suburbanized zones at the outskirts of large cities. Based on the subsidy incentives for objective regions, the danger exists that the process of suburbanization will continue.

Conclusions

Vienna is the only metropolitan city comparably by international standards (roughly 1,500,000 inhabitants): the seven larger state capitals are only medium-sized cities in this context (roughly between 50,000 and 250,000 inhabitants). Competence for urban policies is divided up between the federal government, states and municipalities. The federal government only has sectoral competence for fields with supralocal impact such as transport routes, which is distributed among several ministries. Because the federal government has no competence for comprehensive spatial planning on national level, neither a regional development plan that covers the entire territory of Austria nor a national urban policy exist. Regional policy and spatial planning are not standardized at federal level, but rather are largely the responsibility of the states. Since every state, however, only has one to two larger city regions, the states hardly pursue an explicitly urban policy.

Metropolitan regions usually consist of a relatively large central city and several relatively small hinterland municipalities. The municipalities enjoy a relatively high degree of independence regarding self-governance tasks such as local spatial planning, and as private business administration entities they are entitled to act autonomously as private businesses. Because communal financial power depends on communal taxes, which are higher the more workplaces exist, the municipalities of a city region compete with each other for attracting enterprises and inhabitants, thus creating a situation which prevents the coordination the development of a whole region.

The Austrian Spatial Planning Concept 1991, which was based on a political agreement between the federal government, the state governors and the representatives of the Union of Cities and Municipalities, lists the following problems of urban development:

- existing competition between core cities and hinterland municipalities;
- inefficient utilization of infrastructure (expansion in hinterland regions while in agglomerations these are not being used to capacity);
- increasing environmental and traffic problems caused by the rise in motorized individual traffic;

- large areas of space consumed in the hinterland areas and, at the same time extensive land utilization;
- declining significance of city centres;
- segregation trends caused by 'gentrification';
- integration of immigrants.

Two important international trends influence the development of Austrian cities:

- the internationalization triggered by Austria's accession to the EU and increasing globalization will create more pressure especially in areas that were hardly affected by international competition up to now;
- the opening up of the border to the east has created the opportunity for agglomerations in eastern Austria to assume the role of bridgehead between east and west. At the same time, eastern European cities are becoming new competitors.

The measures proposed in the Austrian Spatial Planning Concept 1991 are only recommendations and serve only as guidance. These place special emphasis on the following:

- to increase cooperation among municipalities of a metropolitan area in order to achieve coordinated urban planning and to reduce inefficient competition for enterprises and inhabitants;
- to strengthen secondary centres of agglomerations with the aim of achieving decentralized concentration, while at the same time improving the capacity of the public transportation system in order to relieve the core city and to prevent despoliation of the landscape;
- to upgrade the fringes of core cities in order to stop the fraying of the settlement borders of core cities into the hinterlands;
- to minimize land consumption by more density in building up areas;
- to maintain the functional mix in city districts with the goal of creating 'cities of short distances';
- to strengthen international competitiveness by promoting industries producing for world markets and high quality producer services;
- integration of immigrants while safeguarding the interests of the native working population.

Notes

1   The use of the word 'city' hereinafter refers to the municipality level (cf. section on 'Administrative and Financial Framework'), in the case of urban areas it refers to NUTS III level. The NUTS III regions cover the functional urban areas quite well for Austria – it is only in the region of Linz-Wels that the suburbanized areas south of Linz are not fully accounted for.
2   Regarding metropolitan areas, regional development plans (*regionale Raumordnungsprogramme*) define green zones that are to be kept free of buildings in order to secure recreational zones in agglomerations.
3   An exception is Vienna, which is both state and municipality and therefore as in all other countries has the power to pass laws – within the scope of constitutional provisions.
4   § 118, paragraph 3, Federal Constitutional Law 1929, BGBl 1930/1 as valid in BGBl 1994/1013.
5   Expenditures with strong spatial reference are those spent by the public sector that can clearly be traced spatially (all municipal expenditures, measures of regional economic policy) or that take spatially relevant aspects into account (transportation policy, agricultural policy) or that have the effect of generating varying spatial distribution patterns (educational, housing or health policy) (ÖIR, 1992, s. 30 ff).
6   § 8, paragraph 4, Revenue Equalisation Law 1993, BGBl 1993/30 as revised in BGBl 1996/201.
7   The city of Dornbirn in this region is an Objective 2 region due to the massive decline in jobs in the textile industry.
8   A possible instrument for controlling land use would be financial incentives coordinated between all states for promoting space-saving residences over freestanding single family homes by means of housing construction subsidies, which is the competence of the states.
9   The significance of strengthening the international competitiveness of large cities is also illustrated by the fact that the city of Vienna has a proper City Councilperson for External Affairs.

References

Austrian Central Statistical Office (*Österreichisches Statistisches Zentralamt*, ÖSTAT) (1985), *Census 1981, Hauptergebnisse II, Österreich*, Vienna: Beiträge zur Österreichischen Statistik, Issue 630/21.
Austrian Central Statistical Office (*Österreichisches Statistisches Zentralamt*, ÖSTAT) (1994), *Census 1991, Hauptergebnisse II, Österreich*, Vienna: Beiträge zur Österreichischen Statistik, Issue 1.030/20.
Austrian Conference on Regional Planning (Österreichische Raumordnungskonferenz, ÖROK) (1992), *Austrian Regional Planning Concept (Österreichisches Raumordnungskonzept) 1991*, Vienna.
Austrian Institute for Regional Studies and Spatial Planning (Österreichisches Institut für Raumplanung, ÖIR) (1992), *Regionale Verteilungswirkungen öffentlicher Haushalte*, Vienna: Österreichische Raumordnungskonferenz (Hrsg.): Schriftenreihe Nr. 97.

Austrian Institute for Regional Studies and Spatial Planning (Österreichisches Institut für Raumplanung, ÖIR) (1996a), *Wirtschaftliche Entwicklungsperspektiven für die österreichischen Ballungsräume*, Vienna.

Austrian Institute for Regional Studies and Spatial Planning (Österreichisches Institut für Raumplanung, ÖIR) (1996b), *Spatial Planning in Austria*, Vienna.

National Committee Habitat II (1995), Habitat II – United Nations Conference on Human Settlement, Austrian National Report, Vienna.

Office of the Salzburg State Government (1995), *Sachprogramm Siedlungsentwicklung und Betriebsstandorte im Salzburger Zentralraum*, Salzburg.

Walter, Robert and Mayer, Heinz (1988), *Grundriß des Österreichischen Bundesverfassungsrechtes*, Vienna.

3 Belgium

GUIDO DE BRABANDER

Being part of the most densely populated and economically most productive region of the basic European urban axis, the so-called 'banana' from London to Milan, one may regard Belgium as a country in which only differences in urbanization play a dominant part. Notwithstanding important changes during the first industrial revolution, the network of urban nuclei finds its origin for the most part in the middle ages. The rise of income, combined with a very substantial growth of mobility, resulted in a massive suburbanization and urban sprawl in the period since the second world war.

For historic, cultural, economic, linguistic and political reasons, the differentiation in the urban picture has remained important. This is the more so since in the federal state of Belgium, most policy measures affecting the cities belong to the competencies of the regions Flanders, Brussels and Wallonia. It is for this reason that this chapter will deal with many of policy measures on the regional level, and only occasionally will talk about national policies. The initiatives of the individual towns, however important they may be, do not belong to the subject of this paper. Like the other contributions, we focus on the current situation and policies, and pay only marginal attention to the historic development. And of course, we look especially for developments at the top of the urban hierarchy.

National Spatial Development Pattern

The Belgian urban hierarchy is clearly dominated by the Brussels agglomeration. This is caused by the numerous national and international public functions (European Union, NATO, etc.), the attraction of headquarters of national and international companies, the concentration of employment and purchasing power and the induced commercial and service activities.

As a municipality, Brussels has a relatively small population. This is for administrative reasons. Brussels, like the other 18 municipalities of the Brussels Region, did not participate in the restructuring of the municipal boundaries in the '70s, aiming at an enlargement of the municipalities and at a drastic reduction of their number.

Social, cultural and especially linguistic reasons urged the politicians to delimit the Brussels Region as the 19 municipalities with a bilingual status. This does not reflect the geographical agglomeration, which is in fact somewhat larger. Indeed, the urban sprawl and suburbanization around Brussels goes far beyond the borders of the 19 municipalities.

The suburbanization of housing is a tradition in Belgium, as it was stimulated by a poor application of physical planning and spatial policy. The pressure of population towards suburbanization was even stronger because of the demand for space in and around the centre of Brussels by national and international public authorities, by headquarters of international businesses and by the growing service sector in general. Moreover, international civil servants as well as foreign managers dispose of a high purchasing power, such that a rise in demand for relatively large scale suburban locations was observed. The structure of public transport, as well as motorways, both oriented to Brussels, made this suburbanization process even easier. The rise in demand for good locations in the agglomeration also exercised pressure on small and medium sized industries. A lot of them were attracted to industrial estates in the neighbourhood of the agglomeration, close to a motorway where possible. Because of the proximity of the airport, Zaventem was very successful in attracting new plants. The general impact of this process clearly is that living as well as working is spread over a larger area than the 19 municipalities of the Brussels Region. In fact, the concentration of specialized jobs made it necessary to recruit in a very wide region, which of course enlarged the Brussels' functional region as well (De Brabander and Dickele, 1993; De Brabander and Verhetsel, 1995).

The second large town is Antwerp. Because of the port, chemical and diamond industries, logistic links and service activities involved, the economic profile again is quite international. Because of the merger with some of the suburbs, the population of the municipality is much larger than that of Brussels.

The spatial extension of the modern port results in a relative spread of activities. However, the most recent enlargement of the port infrastructure was westbound and took place on the left bank of the river Scheldt. As a consequence, a large part of the newest port infrastructure is on the territory of the municipality Beveren, which gave rise to some problems in the unity of management. This could only be solved by a difficult process of inter-municipal cooperation.

Just like the other larger towns, Antwerp is characterized by a selective emigration process. This results in a fall in the population figure. Moreover, the selectivity implies the growth of the share of the poorer groups. The general structure of the urban region therefore consists in a relatively poorer centre and relative rich suburbs and residential areas at the outskirts of the FUR. The suburbanization, however, was not limited to the population. Like elsewhere, industrial estates around the centre attracted new and expanding existing companies. Moreover the distribution of population, as well as the rise in mobility, resulted in an extra impulse to the spatial distribution of commercial activities, not least through the creation of new shopping centres (De Brabander, Vervoort and Witlox, 1996).

Just as Antwerp is the leading city in the Flemish region, Liège has a dominant position in the urban hierarchy of Wallonia. However, the volume of population and employment is significantly inferior to the Antwerp figures (see Table 3.1). Although the characteristics of suburbanization are more or less the same as in the Brussels and Antwerp regions, the physical position along the river Meuse has had a specific impact. From an economic point of view, the restructuring following the decline of traditional industries such as coal mining and the production of steel is certainly not at an end. In fact, the employment situation is relatively bad and the signs for amelioration are relatively weak.

Table 3.1   Some characteristics of the larger cities and their urban region

City	Population		Population density	Unemployment *	
	Municipality (1995)	Urban region (1995)	Urban region (per km^2, 1991)	Municipality 1996	
				absolute	%
Brussels	133,138	2,589,063	578	14,272	10.7
Antwerp	455,852	1,160,519	759	33,670	7.4
Liège	190,525	728,966	410	22,923	12.0
Ghent	225,464	561,171	493	15,624	6.9
Charlerloi	205,581	486,323	381	23,134	11.3

* Grouping of different categories of unemployed according to social security statistics; the percentage is calculated as a share of total population.

Sources: Bevolkingsstatistieken, 1996, nr. 1A, Brussels, NIS; Haegen, H. Van der et al., 1996; *Geografische spreiding van de werkloosheid*, toestand 31.12.96, Brussels, RVA.

The same holds for Charleroi, the second city in Wallonia's urban hierarchy. Here too the decline of traditional industries resulted in an urban decline which affected the region. The proximity of Brussels gave rise to some opportunities for commuters, although the structure of the labour force made these opportunities rather limited. The problem of industrial restructuring is not typical for the largest Walloon cities. It is a problem for the whole traditional industrial axis from Mons in the west to Verviers in the east, as well as for a number of Flemish towns in which traditional industries, such as textiles and clothing, were concentrated. What is remarkable, however, is that Wallonia's renewal occurs mainly along a new axis, starting in Brussels, passing by Wavre and Namur and going in the direction of Luxemburg. A motorway is the backbone of this future oriented economic axis.

On the Flemish side, Ghent takes second place in the urban hierarchy. Ghent was a typical textile town during the industrial revolution. It developed as a medium sized port town with some important industries such as car manufacturing and steel mills. More recently, small scale innovative industries, like bioengineering and modern services added a lot to the economic profile of the city. Although the problems of suburbanization and population structure are similar to Antwerp's, the impact on the municipality is more limited. This is caused by the administrative delimitation of the city. More specifically, the merger of the municipalities during the '70s involved a larger share of the residential suburbs than in Antwerp. Because of less local employment, Ghent's functional urban region is much smaller than Antwerp's.

The importance of the functional urban regions is quite clear if regarded in respect to the total population (see Table 3.1). In fact the Brussels' FUR contains about 26 per cent of the national population. Antwerp's FUR contains another 12 per cent, Liège's more than seven per cent, Ghent and Charleroi both about five per cent. Taken together, this means that a dependency relationship towards the five largest cities for employment and other functions exists for about 55 per cent of the national population.

Administrative and Financial Framework

The administrative situation of the municipalities has changed somewhat during the last decades because of the federalization process of the country. This means that competencies were redistributed, with a diminution for the national, that is federal, level and an enlargement for the regional level. Because the regional level contains the specific territorial competencies, most of the municipal control and the urban policies are linked to this level. This is also the reason why 'national' urban policies are not very strongly developed and why we need to concentrate on this regional level to have a picture on macro-policies towards the largest cities.

Of course, the provinces are also an intermediate level between the national and the local authorities. However, their function towards the largest cities is rather limited. They control a number of activities of the municipalities and may report deficiencies to the governor and the (regional) minister. Their impact quite often is limited to giving a helping hand and to the controlling functions mentioned above. During previous years the role of the provinces was discussed quite stringently. A few years ago, the idea existed that this intermediate level was no longer needed. In the end, however, the existence of the provinces was confirmed, although a new delimitation of their competencies was needed. Until now, only the Flemish government has succeeded in the formulation of these new functions (CBO, 1997).

The Brussels region clearly has a status other than the Flemish and Walloon regions. Indeed, for the so-called cultural competencies Brussels has no authority, while the Dutch and French speaking group do have this power. On the other hand, the Brussels regional government has the competency over an urban entity, while both other regions have different types of towns and conurbations in their territory. From this point of view, the Brussels regional government theoretically is in a better position to define and realize an urban policy. In practice, however, the specific complexities of Brussels' situation make it quite difficult to implement such a policy.

The financial situation of the municipalities is more or less in equilibrium, although the largest cities especially have some serious difficulties. This results from debts from earlier times and the payback of the loans from these periods. The debt crisis was so heavy that the higher authorities interfered. Especially in Wallonia, a large part of the debts were changed from the municipal to the higher authorities. In Flanders, this movement was much more limited, which means that Antwerp still has to pay back about seven billion francs a year until quite far in the 21st century. The Flemish Commission for the Organisation of Domestic Administration (CBO, 1997) regards this as one of the main problems for the development and implementation of the right policies by local government, at least if no significant help is given by the higher level.

Stressing the debt problem should not give the idea that municipal public finance has a very large share in the public sector. Indeed, the share of public expenditure in gross domestic product is less than five per cent (see Table 3.2). In comparison to the federal state, with more than 23 per cent, and social

Table 3.2   Expenditures of different government levels in % of GDP (1994)

Federal government	23.2 %
Regions and Communities	12.0 %
Social Security	20.0 %
Local Governments	6.5 %
of which municipalities	4.4 %

Source: Kredietbank, 1996, p. 1.

security, with 20 per cent of gross domestic product, the municipalities clearly have a rather marginal position.

The structure of income is quite specific for the Belgian municipalities. In fact, it is dominated by the 'municipal fund' and by specific local taxes. Generally speaking, the municipal fund takes about a fifth of municipal income for its account. This fund is transferred from the regional to the municipal authorities according to specific criteria in which the solidarity between municipalities and the cost of the central place functions of the cities towards their regions are taken into account. This is quite clear in the Flemish distribution system, in which Antwerp and Ghent get 42.9 per cent of the yearly fund. Another 15.55 per cent is shared by ten towns with a population between 50,000 and 150,000 inhabitants. The rest is distributed over the smaller municipalities according to their population, surface, employment, fiscal capacity of the inhabitants, population density and school-going children.

The distribution system of the municipal fund has been discussed quite frequently during the last couple of years. The specific situation of the cities most frequently was the central item in these debates. One of the fundamental questions is about the compensation for activities for non-inhabitants. According to a recent study of W. Knaepen and P. Cabus (1996) this compensation seems to be more or less complete for Antwerp, and especially Ghent, but rather incomplete for most of the smaller towns. Of course, this argument does not take into account other characteristics and needs which result from differences in the social and economic structure of the cities.

The philosophy of the Walloon distribution system of the municipal fund resembles the Flemish one, to a large extent. The two largest cities, Charleroi and Liège, get 32.5 per cent of the fund; the rest goes to the other municipalities, 22 of which have a specific protected position. The latter may be regarded as central places. Their dimension, however, is much smaller than the Flemish average. The distribution criteria make use of the volume and density of population, the fiscal situation and other elements such as the length of the roads, the service of the fire brigade, etc.

Since the municipal fund was reduced in real terms during the '80s – reduction which was not compensated for in the '90s – the municipalities had to raise the local taxes. Although a very wide diversity in types of taxes exists, two of them are quite dominant. They are the additional tax on income tax and the additional tax on the income of real estate. The first is levied by the municipality where the tax payer lives, the second by the municipality where the real estate is located. Because of the relatively high percentage of home ownership, there is a strong relationship between the location of houses and the spatial distribution of the tax paying owners. Of course, this does not hold for offices and other business related real estate.

The additional tax on income tax poses many problems, especially for the larger cities. Because of the suburbanization process, their number of inhabitants decreases and consequently the total volume of taxable income falls. Moreover, since emigration is situated most in the middle and high income classes, it is the lower income groups who take the largest share in the urban population. This twofold evolution makes it necessary to have a higher tax rate in the municipalities with a large share of lower income groups to maintain the same tax revenue. Moreover, because of the over-representation of poorer groups, the pressure for social expenditure is much higher there.

Since the value of real estate is normally higher in the larger cities, there is some compensation for the problem with the additional tax on income tax through the tax on real estate income. Here however, the suburbanization of some business activities presents an unfortunate evolution as well.

Other types of revenues are the income from municipal activities, from special funds and specific subsidies and, finally, from loans (see Table 3.3).

Table 3.3 Structure of municipal income in 1995 (in %)

Income	Flanders	Wallonia	Brussels
Taxes	44.7	47.3	42.2
Funds	20.5	14.3	19.3
Subsidies	18.1	22.7	26.3
Loans	10.3	3.0	7.7
Activities	6.5	7.7	4.7

Source: Erauw et al., 1996, pp. 77, 81 and 86.

The rise of the share of local taxes in urban income may suggest that the municipalities gained financial independence in respect of the higher authorities. However, the tax instrument has political and electoral consequences which make it a difficult one to use. Moreover, the difficult situation of local finance, especially in the larger towns, makes these municipalities more dependent on the specific funding by the regions.

As to the administrative independency, this is to be regarded as quite relative. This is not only because of the systematic control by the provincial and regional authorities, but also because of the fact that regional authorities especially have the power to prescribe new tasks to the municipalities. Local administrators often complain that it is difficult to have an efficient organization when these new tasks are introduced without a serious deliberation between the parties involved. Moreover, they complain about the fact that these tasks are added without any financial compensation for the job.

Integrated socioeconomic policies at a local level are almost nonexistent. The scale of the municipalities is normally too small to implement such a policy. Collaboration between the municipalities is organized on a free base and until now oriented to practical collaboration in specific cooperative companies called 'intercommunales'. Recently, however, some actions were taken to ameliorate the situation. A kind of socioeconomic platform has been organized to discuss social and economic problems at a sub-regional level and to elaborate appropriate policies. Moreover, the Flemish government is developing a proposal to adapt the local organization to the modern needs, in which the social and economic challenges are met.

Urban Issues and Challenges

Growing Awareness of Urban Problems

The mere awareness of urban problems by the central government came quite late. Until 1962 no general law on spatial planning existed and it was only a decade later that plans on a larger than municipal level were finalized. In the meanwhile, suburbanization went on. The dominant way of changing the face of the cities consisted in the demolition of slums (or what were regarded as slums) and quite often the replacement by rather monotonous high rise apartment blocks with parking facilities. Renovation was still to be invented.

The first initiatives for urban renewal, besides local initiatives in a few cities, consisted in the start of five pilot projects in 1973. These urban renewal projects were distributed over the country in a typical Belgian fashion: the Marollen-quarter in Brussels, Bruges and Mechelen in Flanders and Namur and Jumet in Wallonia. No specific regulation for the subsidies was elaborated and each of the five towns could decide which projects they preferred.

From 1974 onwards, urban renewal was a competency of the three regions. However, the first initiatives with an impact in the field did not come immediately. Only in 1976 was an impetus given to the renovation of monuments. The policy of renovation on a larger scale started no earlier than 1978; at least a number of Royal Decrees were published then. Their impact was limited. So, in the '80s, a new campaign for a 'social' urban renewal started. The quality of housing, especially for the lower income groups, became a priority, although the financial means remained restricted.

The most successful initiative in this period was the decree on the renewal of urban and rural neighbourhoods published in June 1982 and revised in March 1983. The response of the municipalities was overwhelming (see Akkermans, 1985 and Van den Broeck et al., 1992). No fewer than 151 neighbourhoods, distributed over 90 of the 308 Flemish municipalities, were officially accepted as renewal zones.

Typical for this policy is that:

- the housing function was regarded as the essential one for the quality of the neighbourhood; the transport function was seen as important, but problematic; other functions got less priority;
- renovation was essential, demolition was only to be accepted when no other solution existed;
- the historic structure was to be respected;
- the policy was not oriented to specific problems or opportunities in the larger cities, but to all municipalities;
- the projects accepted by the government had a price which was a multiple of the budget available; a lot of projects could not be realized or were hindered by serious delay, which resulted in a sore disillusionment not only for the local governments, but also for the population involved.

From the end of the '80s onwards, it became clear that the focus had to be broader. The situation of the underprivileged was not only a question of poor housing in bad neighbourhoods, but also of unemployment, poor education, changes in the labour market, etc. In this framework, new initiatives were taken in which priority was given to the chances of the weakest groups on the labour market. More generally, the economic function received more attention.

Nevertheless, if the hard priorities are reflected in the budgets involved, it is quite manifest that social housing was and remained dominant. Recent initiatives by the Flemish Government, such as the Domus Flandria programme, illustrate the continuity in the priority for the housing question (Peeters and De Decker, 1997).

Recent Developments

Because matters like urban renewal belonged to the competencies of the regions since the early '70s, it is no wonder that the national government paid relatively little attention to urban policy in a narrow sense. New instruments were used in the battle against drugs, safety policy received growing attention, but although these themes often are regarded as more or less specific to the larger cities, no specific integrated policy was deployed. In this respect, urban policy was no real priority for the national government, at least until recently.

In its declaration of 28 June 1995, the national government for the first time pointed at urban renewal as one of the selected priorities. In this framework, urban renewal is a fundamental part of a better society, which pays explicit attention to the strengthening of the social fabric, better quality of life, the protection of the consumer, a harmonious family policy and a strong battle against social exclusion and segregation.

This priority is explicated as:

- the fight against poverty;
- continuation of the action for the improvement of safety;
- a rigorous policy on immigration and integration;
- a more efficient policy against drugs;
- reduction of the number of traffic victims through an active safety policy;
- specific measures for the realization of safety outside the traditional police.

The integration of these measures can be realized by specific contracts or covenants between the government and the municipalities. It is in this kind of covenant that specific local actions towards the realization of a better quality of urban life are discussed and determined. Of course, the federal government stresses other priorities, such as employment and a creative economy, as well. Although the link with urban problems and opportunities is clear, this is not explicitly present in the document of the government. The reason for this is not, in my opinion, that the federal government does not make the link, but that the competencies for concrete measures in relationship to urban problems in these fields are with the regional government.

It is of course impossible to treat in detail the reactions to the urban problems of each of the three regions in a short article such as this. So, let us limit the discussion to the Flemish region, which has anyhow developed the most initiatives in this domain until now. The so-called September declaration of the Flemish government presents five priorities, one of them being the quality of life in cities and villages. This priority relies heavily on four instruments. They are: the enlargement of SIF (Social Impulse Fund); the renovation of housing, especially by the amelioration of social housing; the improvement of public transport and cooperation between the Flemish government and the municipalities by means of so-called 'mobility conventions'; and finally, improvement of the attraction of the commercial centres in inner-cities. These four instruments all get a specific budget, in which the SIF (6.5 billion francs in 1997) and social housing (9 billion francs coming from the social housing companies) are the most dominant.

Since the SIF is the cornerstone of the urban policy, we shall briefly take a closer look at it. The general goal of this fund consists in helping local governments in ameliorating the quality of urban life, and especially in redressing the environmental quality in underprivileged neighbourhoods and assisting them in the fight against deprivation and the realization of wellbeing.

The system is based on an integrated plan, presented by the municipal government, in which the different projects are presented. This plan now covers at least the period 1996–99. Its realization is financed by the use of drawing rights given by the regional to the local government. The selection of the municipalities is based on a set of measurable criteria, such as the number of houses without essential comforts, the number of social flats in the rent sector, the number of children in one parent families, the number of migrants, the number of underprivileged, etc.

The payment of the drawing rights, except for the initial one, depends on an evaluation of the results. The covenant about SIF contains a number of results to be realized. In this way, procedures or the way in which the projects are organized do not have a function in the evaluation process. The results are to be measured by the use of a number of indicators This is quite new in Flanders, although the Flemish government uses the same method in strategic plans. The method is inspired by European programmes and especially by the way the Dutch government develops its policy for larger cities.

The attention of the Flemish government to urban problems is also made clear by the appointment of a minister, whose competence explicitly mentions urban matters. The Brussels' and the Walloon government have not appointed a minister with these specific competencies, thus having the urban policies distributed over a number of partners. In Flanders, urban competencies are combined with housing and interior organization, which gives the opportunity to act directly in a number of matters which are extremely relevant to the urban question. Nevertheless, the existing division of competencies brings about an interference with a number of other ministers, e.g., where spatial planning or infrastructure policy are involved, also in Flanders.

Exactly in these fields, the priorities of the Flemish government interfere in a positive way with the urban priorities. The 'spatial structure plan for Flanders', which was adopted by the Flemish parliament by the end of 1997, shows a clear option to minimize the suburbanization process and to strengthen the urban concentration. The fundamental structure of the plan is based on the so-called Flemish quadrangle Antwerp–Ghent–Brussels–Louvain.

The central principles in this plan are coordinated differentiation and deconcentrated clustering. These imply a reduction of the dispersion of population and activities in favour of existing urban concentrations and nodal points. Although the largest urban entities are stressed in their multifunctional role, on the whole 147 municipalities out of 308 are selected to be a cluster of employment. The tendency to concentration clearly is relatively limited. The same holds for the planning options for housing, in which deconcentrated clustering acts as the highest priority.

As regards infrastructure, the orientation is to reinforce the economic infrastructure with the priority for the seaports and the major transport routes. In this framework, not only the amelioration of the motorways but also the shift to inland water transport are ranked high on the priority list. This, of course, is because of the growing problems with traffic congestion and the high appreciation of the logistic future of Flanders. In this network, the larger cities play a major role because of their function as ports and their concentration of industries.

Networks obviously are to be regarded from a national but also from an international point of view. In this respect, much attention has been given to the integration of a network of motorways. In the most recent period, however, links by other means of transport have been stressed more and more. Highest priority seems to go to the network of fast trains, at least if regarded from the financial point of view. Anyhow, the Train à Grande Vitesse already offers links with London and Paris and within a couple of years will do the same to Amsterdam and Köln. After some discussion, only Antwerp and Liège were chosen as stops (besides Brussels, of course). This choice is to be regarded as an integration of the top of the urban hierarchy in Belgium in an important

European network. It is striking that in the Flemish Structure Plan also, much attention is given to Brussels, although it is situated outside the region. This is especially because of the international functions of Brussels. It implies that Brussels needs specific urban facilities to attract and develop sophisticated service activities. Moreover, specialized industrial estates are to be developed to attract high class secondary activities. Finally, housing policy in the Flemish fringe around the Brussels region needs special care.

Other issues are of special importance for the development of Antwerp as a logistic centre. Recently a lot of attention has been given to the so-called Iron Rhine. This rail connection between Antwerp and the Ruhr area could become very important in the transport of goods between two economic heavyweights in Western Europe. Although discussions have already lasted for some time, no final decision has yet been taken.

More progress has been made in the negotiations between Belgium and the Netherlands about the deepening of the river Scheldt. This is needed to improve the accessibility of the Antwerp port for the largest category of ships. For this project, final decisions have been made and their realization will be started soon. This too is of some importance in the development of Antwerp's economic function.

All this suggests a recognition of the fundamental part of the largest cities in the economic development of the country. Nevertheless, the idea of cities as the engines of national economic growth is not widespread. In fact, most often these cities are regarded as the centres of social and even economic problems. From the point of view of the intensity of social problems, this seems right. A recent report of C. Kesteloot en H. Vandenbroecke (1996) on backward neighbourhoods in Flanders and Brussels shows this quite clearly. This report concludes that 45 per cent of all inhabitants of backward neighbourhoods in Flanders lives in Antwerp and 18 per cent in Ghent. The measures taken by both regional and national government in the framework of urban policy clearly aim at the reduction of the social problems.

Unhappily, no comparable material exists for the Walloon region. The comparison with the Brussels region, however, shows an even larger concentration of the deprived than in Flanders' two largest cities.

Recently more attention has been given to the economic strength of the major cities, especially in respect of the national and international functions of Brussels and of the growth potential of the Flemish ports and the connected industries. The recent concept of the spatial structure plan for Flanders goes in the same direction. The attention given to the commercial functions of the inner-cities in the policy of the Flemish government illustrates the attention given to these opportunities. The creation of a new Fund for Commercial Centres by the Flemish Minister for Economics and his call for proposals formulated by the municipal governments, show that a new policy is coming into existence here. However, the idea of major cities as centres for growth and innovation is still not dominant in the policies of national and regional governments.

National and Regional Policy Responses

The preceding section already makes clear that national as well as regional authorities have tried to identify the urban issues and responded by formulating a number of policies introducing new instruments without formulating, until now, a general vision on the long term development of the urbanization process. In fact, most often policies are oriented to specific sectors in the field of urban problems and opportunities. This is true for safety, infrastructure, poverty, economy, etc.

Nevertheless, in a few cases an overall idea about the future of the major cities has been developed. Perhaps the best example is the regional development plan for the Brussels region (1995). This plan tries to integrate the demands of the inhabitants, residential attraction, social equilibrium, needs for employment and environmental quality, vocation as an international centre, safety in the city, commercial functions and the service sector, reduction of pollution, cultural and tourist attraction and urban transport problems in an analysis as well as in an action plan for the 19 municipalities. The different elements that are integrated show already the fields of priority and the broadness of the approach. The attention given to spatial planning and legal instruments in the action plan illustrates the way the plan can be implemented.

The central goals of this plan are formulated in terms of populations and economics. The first is defined as a total increase by 34,000 inhabitants, to be realized in 2005. Taking into account a decrease of 17,800 according to existing trends, this means a net task of gaining almost 52,000 inhabitants. For job creation, the net task is 20,300 jobs above the growth of 20,400 according to the trend. This should be realized not only by the opportunities existing in the service sector, but also by reducing drastically the decline in manufacturing. However, no explicit relations exist between these tasks and the contents of the spatial plan.

In Flanders, besides in the Structure Plan, general visions about the larger cities and their urban regions were developed in so-called strategic plans. The initiative however came from local authorities and/or the business community. These plans, moreover, present a long list of wants and needs and seldom come to a hierarchy of priorities. The regional government nowadays tries to give an impetus to these plans, offering a new framework for discussion. However, they are still far from implementation or action as a general plan. Most often, individual actions are taken out of the list of possible priorities.

As to the instruments, some lack of integration can be observed as well. This is quite clear when we take a look at the additional financial help which is given to the largest cities in the framework of different programs. In Flanders, at least 12 specific financial instruments are to be registered:

* the Social Impulse Fund;
* the increased payment of minimum incomes in municipalities with a large number of beneficiaries of minimum income;
* specific subsidies for the institutes for elderly people;
* specific subsidies for the payment of pensions in Antwerp, Ghent and Ostend;
* financial help for Antwerp in the payment of older debts;
* payment regulations in a framework of conventions on safety and social improvement for 11 municipalities;
* subsidies in the framework of the drugs prevention scheme;
* subsidies for help centres;
* subsidies for civic guards;
* financial interventions for specialized fire brigade equipment;
* project finance in deprived neighbourhoods in Ghent and Antwerp;
* specific financial help for the larger cultural institutions.

This list is incomplete, but it already shows two things. First of all, the instruments are manifold and oriented to different sectors of society without being coordinated in all respects. Second, a lot of these instruments are used not only for the larger cities but also for smaller ones. For example, the SIF is applied to 28 municipalities. This offers the opportunity to attack the problems in all municipalities where they exist, but also implies a relatively low concentration.

One of the reasons for this is the distribution of competencies over the different departments of the government. This is a result not only of the division of competencies between the national and the regional governments, but most importantly because of the influence of traditional structures in the regional governments. In the Flemish government, for instance, the minister for urban issues is new, but a number of aspects such as employment, safety, culture, infrastructure, spatial planning, etc. are dealt with by other departments. In the Walloon government there is no minister for urban issues. Urban affairs are distributed over spatial planning, environment, housing, economics, employment, transport, social affairs and local authorities. This does not make it very easy to realize an integrated policy towards the larger cities, of course.

The most general view on Wallonia's urban development is integrated in the Plan Régional d'Aménagement du Territoire Wallon (PRATW). This plan stresses the importance of the urban concentrations and their networks. In fact, cities are regarded as incomplete, in such a way that their complementarity is the base of integration in the network. The network should be organized along the traditional lines, i.e., Brussels–Charleroi–Mons and Charleroi–Liège, on the one hand, and in perspective of international relations for Charleroi–Lille, Liège close to the Netherlands and Germany, and Arlon, close to the Grand Duchy of Luxembourg, on the other. According to J. Moriau (1996) the proposed options are in conflict with a number of existing trends, such as deindustrialization and desurbanization.

A general approach, translated in a large number of specific urban neighbourhoods, consists in Wallonia's policy of 'Zones d'Initiatives Priviligiées' (ZIP). No less than 432 neighbourhoods, distributed over 82 municipalities were selected. Here too, the improvement of the housing and the economic situation is the fundamental priority.

Recently, new initiatives have been taken in the field of spatial planning. The Walloon parliament accepted a new code for spatial planning on 19 November 1997. On this occasion, the Walloon Minister for Planning announced a new structure plan to be presented in 1998. At the time of writing this contribution, nothing was known about its contents.

As to the European level, the impact of the European instruments seems to be rather limited. The regional fund is of some help for Wallonia and thus for Liège and Charleroi but, as we saw above, the economic renovation acts more strongly along the axis Brussels–Luxembourg. The URBAN-initiative was relatively scarcely applied to Belgium until now. Most important is a pilot project in Antwerp, in one of the larger deprived neighbourhoods. Perhaps the relatively good position of Belgium in the European economy limits the application and thus the impact of EU-policies and subsidies most for the larger Belgian cities.

Conclusion

Some comparative studies on the larger cities in Europe restrict the Belgian contribution to Brussels, Antwerp and Liège. In the typology of Bonavero and Conti (1996), Brussels is characterized as a 'pure city with international leadership', Antwerp as a 'city with international leadership and a traditional industrial structure', Liège as a city going through 'a negative industrial transition, but with a tertiarisation process'. In this article, we have added Ghent and Charlerloi to the list of larger cities, since this is the approach of most Belgian analyses and of the national and regional policy makers.

Because of the federal nature of Belgium and the division of competencies between national and regional authorities, much attention has to be given to the regional level. The latter is, indeed, responsible for territorial matters.

The attention on urban problems has increased clearly during the most recent period. This is proved by the declarations of national as well as regional governments. The creation of a ministry for urban affairs by the Flemish government is another illustration.

Until now, policy makers have stressed especially the problems of the larger cities. The attention given to the social problems, backward neighbourhoods, urban decay and the housing question, as well as to safety and drugs prevention, all fit in that framework. Although some re-orientation was given to infrastructure policy, to the strengthening of commercial centres and to the integration in European transport networks, opportunities for the larger cities as propulsive forces in the economic development did not get a lot of attention from the policy-makers.

Moreover, it does not seem so easy to develop an integrated policy. A lot of instruments are brought into action by different departments. Most often, specific measures are taken for specific problems, without trying to integrate them in a general package.

A large part of these measures are not oriented exclusively to the larger cities, but to a larger number of municipalities suffering more or less the same problems. Especially in the field of spatial planning, attempts towards a more integrated approach are tried. The integration of a number of existing instruments in the Flemish SIF illustrates the trend at least to try to realize a more general approach.

Nevertheless, the attention given to urban problems implies an important shift in the priorities of the Belgian governments. One may expect that this will lead to a further development of specific and coordinated policies.

References

Akkermans, P. (1985), *Herwaarderingsgebieden in Vlaanderen: sociale stads-en dorpsvernieuwing*, 3rd edn, Brussels: Ministerie van de Vlaamse Gemeenschap.
Bonavero, P. and Conti, S. (1996), 'New Technological Paradigm, Urban Identity and Metropolitan Networks in Europe' in D. Pumain and D. Saint-Julien (eds), *Urban Networks in Europe*, Montrouge/London: J. Libbey, pp. 47–65.
Brabander, G. de and Dickele, K. (1993), 'Onderneming en werkgelegenheid in de Brusselse rand' in E. Witte (ed.), *Brusselse thema's. De Brusselse rand*, Brussels: VUBPress, pp. 21–37.
Brabander, G. de and Verhetsel, A. (1995), 'Brussels' in J. Berry and S. McGreal (eds), *European Cities, Planning Systems and Property Markets*, London/New York, E.F. Spon, pp. 65–81.
Brabander, G. de, Vervoort, L. and Witlox, F. (1996), *Metropolis, over mensen, steden en centen*, 3rd edn, Leuven: Kritak.
Brande, L. van den (1996), *Septemberverklaring van de Vlaamse regering*, Brussels: Ministerie van de Vlaamse Gemeenschap.
Brusselse Hoofdstedelijke Regering (1995), *Gewestelijk Ontwikkelingsplan Brussels Hoofdstedelijk Gewest Brussels*.
Cabus P. et al. (1996), 'Plannen voor Brussel en omgeving; concurrentie of complementariteit?', *Ruimtelijke Planning*, Vol. 3, No. 4, pp.7–32.
CBO (Commissie Bestuurlijke Organisatie) (1997), *De organisatie van het Binnenlands Bestuur in Vlaanderen*, Brussels: Ministerie van de Vlaamse Gemeenschap.
Dehaene, J.-L. (1995), *Regeringsverklaring*, Brussels: Kabinet van de Eerste Minister.
Erauw, A.-L., Dessoy, A. and Gaube, P. (1996), 'De financien van de lokale overheden in 1995', *Tijdschrift van het Gemeentekrediet*, No. 197, pp. 73–88.
Haegen, H. van der, Hecke, E. van and Juchtmans, G. (1996), 'De Belgische stadsgewesten 1991', *Statistische Studien*, No. 104, pp. 5–42.
Kesteloot, C. and Vandenbroecke, H. (1996), *De achtergestelde buurten in Vlaanderen en Brussel*, Brussels: Vlaams Ministerie van Binnenlandse Aangelegenheden, Stedelijk Beleid en Huisvesting.
Kesteloot, C. et al. (1996), *Atlas van achtergestelde buurten in Vlaanderen en Brussel*, Brussels: Ministerie van de Vlaamse Gemeenschap.
Knaepen, W. and Cabus, P. (1996), 'Centrumfunctie: duur betaald ?', *Ruimtelijke Planning*, No. 1, pp. 5–38.
Kredietbank (1996), 'De gemeentefinancien', *Weekberichten*, Vol. 51, No. 13, pp. 1–8.
Moriau, J. (1996), 'Naar een duurzame ontwikkeling in de stedelijke prioritaire zones. Wijkontwikkeling in Wallonie' in P. de Decker et al., *In de ban van stad en wijk*, Antwerpen: EPO, pp. 219–27.
Peeters, L. (1995), *Voor steden en mensen – Beleidsbrief 1995*, Brussels: Ministerie van de Vlaamse Gemeenschap.
Peeters, L. (1996), *Stedelijk Beleid: voor steden en mensen – Beleidsbrief 1996*, Brussels: Ministerie van de Vlaamse Gemeenschap.
Peeters, L. and Martens, L. (1996), *Over cijfers en gemeenten: het decreet inzake het Sociaal Impulsfonds op maat van uw gemeente*, Brussels: Ministerie van de Vlaamse Gemeenschap.
Peeters, L. and Martens, L. (1996), *Het Sociaal Impulsfonds, een instrument voor het stedelijk beleid*, Brussels: Ministerie van de Vlaamse Gemeenschap.

Peeters, L. and De Decker, P. (1997), *Het woonbeleid in Vlaanderen op een tweesprong*, Antwerp: EPO.

Van Den Broeck, J., Baelus, J. et al. (1992), *Stadsvernieuwing in beweging*, Brussels: Koning Boudewijnstichting.

Van Rompuy, E. (1997), *Een vernieuwend economisch beleid voor Vlaanderen – beleidsprioriteiten 1997*, Brussels: Vlaams Ministerie voor Economie, KMO, Landbouw en Media.

4 Denmark

CHRISTIAN WICHMANN MATTHIESSEN

Danish national urban policy, with its emphasis on the specific position of the large cities, could almost encompass all policy and planning issues, as almost all decisions have an impact on the urban system. Even the militarization of Danish foreign policy in support of UN peace operations has consequences for the growth of certain garrison cities in Denmark. Accepting high quotas of refugees will inevitably lead to social problems in parts of the larger cities a few years after the migration. National tax policy discriminates between income groups, but as on average cities differ in income level, so tax policy also discriminates between cities. Even agricultural subsidies have impact on the urban system, since the prosperity of the agricultural sector creates differences between cities. A variety of other types of policy is more clearly connected with the urbanization process. This is the case, for example, for housing policy, social policy, urban renewal policy, policies for subsidizing peripheral regions, etc. It is also clear that the whole matter of infrastructural investment policy plays an important role in growth potential for the different cities in the nation, as the infrastructural layout sets the scene in which competition between cities takes place.

Danish planning policies are concerned with issues that are certainly recognized elsewhere in Europe: decreasing densities in urban areas; urban sprawl (including recreation versus landscape conservation); regional disadvantages and peripherilization of sparsely populated areas with low accessibility; concentration to the highly accessible centres, especially to Greater Copenhagen and the regional capitals; segregation processes within the larger cities; network development and increasing international accessibility; ecological problems, especially those associated with increasing use of automobiles. Sustainability is a key word and defines a society in which economic growth and development of the cultural landscape take place without threatening fundamental conditions for the coming generations. Another key aspect is the advancement of democratic processes and the balance of top down and bottom up political processes. Finally, there is a growing interest in urban and regional marketing and strategic planning. In short, the transformation of society from manufacturing via services to information, creativity and ecology. It could be said that the transformation process of Denmark is at a stage in which the fixed environmental expenditures from production are under control and the environmental expenditures from flows are not.

Control over the land and planning its use, together with network planning issues, are of major concern. The turbulent years of transformation in the 1960s resulted in a matching of the organization of the planning machine with zoning as the main instrument. The current transformation of society demands a new organization of the machine so that it can react accordingly to contemporary problems and policies.

Only two large-scale Danish physical plans have attracted international attention. They are both anchored in the metropolitan area of Copenhagen. One is the regional development plan from 1949, the so-called 'Finger Plan'. The other is the construction of a fixed link between Denmark and Sweden with regional integration as the main objective. It is interesting to note that the first one was presented long before the establishment of a planning machine, and the second one was forwarded after the planning machine was put into low gear.

Denmark is a very rich country with social and structural problems of low weight seen in an international perspective. General policies devoted to solving problems which concentrate in the large urban units have been formulated on drugs, criminality, low quality of life, social exclusion, immigrants, ghetto formation, congestion, mass public transport, urban renewal, etc. Welfare policy and programmes have been initiated nationally or locally. Many have succeeded; others have failed. Urban renewal policy is an example of the first type. In 1960 the percentage of dwellings without a bath was 50 in the municipality of Copenhagen; in 1992 only eight per cent of the dwellings lack this amenity (Engelstoft and Jørgensen, 1997). Prevention of social exclusion and ghetto formation policies seem to have a low success rate, or even failure, when it comes to Third World immigrants.

This paper focuses on spatial urban planning in general, i.e., planning for the urban system as a whole, the organizational setup and recent shifts in policy.

National Spatial Development Pattern

Denmark has one dominant metropolitan area, Greater Copenhagen (1.7 million inhabitants, 0.9 million jobs). Copenhagen is the undisputed national leader and capital, and also plays a leading role in southern Sweden. On the national scene, Copenhagen is a city of primacy. Copenhagen is in the class of large European metropolitan units and urban competition with cities like Stockholm, Hamburg and Berlin is clear. Far below the metropolitan level, the level of regional capitals is found. Four urban units represent this level together with Copenhagen, namely Århus, Odense, Aalborg and the Triangle City.[1] They dominate their regions in many respects, but also represent some division of labour on a functional level, and their hinterlands are interwoven. Below the level of regional capitals, Denmark counts 16 towns with more than 15,000 jobs.

Urban Denmark can be defined in a variety of ways. Rankings of the larger urban units according to the different types of definitions are presented in the appendix. In this paper a compromise between the different types of definition is used, and the five large cities are overviewed in Table 4.1.

Table 4.1   Denmark: large cities

	Population		Jobs, 1995	
	Region 1995	Urban area 1994	Region	Secondary/ tertiary
Greater Copenhagen[2]	1,739,458	1,346,289	912,894	13/87
Århus	277,477	209,404	154,887	14/86
Triangle City[3]	188,836	139,456	104,985	23/77
Odense	182,617	143,029	92,448	17/83
Aalborg	159,056	116,567	87,624	17/83

System of Government

The Danish government is organized as a three-level hierarchy: national, regional and local government. Outside Greater Copenhagen, the system of local and regional government was established in 1970 and consists of 225 large municipalities (towns with local hinterland) and 12 regions (regional centres with hinterland). In Greater Copenhagen the almost century-old pattern of administrative units is still in effect, with 50 municipalities and five regional units. All parts of Denmark are covered by municipal governments and all municipalities are covered by regional governments. The rights and duties of the different local governments are almost equal, and the same applies to the regional level of government. There is a high degree of decentralization of responsibility and control of land use and structural planning, combined with centralized sectoral planning for a mix of infrastructure, including railroads, main roads, airports and harbours. The Greater Copenhagen system functions in almost the same way as the rest of the nation's governmental system. What differs is the delimitation of the municipal and regional units. The system of government is financed by local, regional and national taxes. Expenditures are paid by the responsible local, regional or national unit. In addition there is a 'downward' flow of money from the national level to regional and local levels according to a set of rules and to political decisions. Furthermore the upper levels of government operate their own systems. Of the total GNP, 50 per cent is privately used, 20 per cent is used on the national level, ten per cent on the regional and 20 per cent on the municipal level. The post-1970 system is a hierarchical one with a high degree of decentralization.

Planning and Policy History: System Organization Pre-1970

During the early phases of the suburbanization process 1950–70, urban policy consisted of zoning and land use planning. The growth of suburbs around the larger urban units was guided by master plans. Also inner city redevelopments were planned as large-scale operations.

During a period of economic growth and transformation in the 1960s, there was a clear demand for the establishment of a modern planning system. This was formulated in a series of bills on planning and land policies. In parliament, the minority Liberal side was against the complex of bills, while the majority Social Democratic side was in favour. The minority demanded a referendum because of the proposed Expropriation Bill, as Expropriation Bill proposals open up this possibility. The whole complex of bills was voted on in this referendum, and the voters said 'no'. This meant an effective barrier to political actions in the direction of improved planning, but also led to the subsequent necessary large-scale reformation of the whole system of government.

Until 1970, the administrative system in Denmark was rather complicated and worked according to tradition in a three-level arrangement topped by central government. The second level was represented by three types of authority. The national capital and three regional capitals (Århus, Odense, Aalborg) had a special status with a high degree of self-governance. The boroughs (86 in Denmark), defined as the old urban units, often clearly underbounded, had another special status also with self-governance. The rest of the country was organized in counties (25 in Denmark) with a combined state-appointed and local-elected county-government, and a low degree of self-governance. The third level, municipalities (about 1,300 in Denmark), was, as far as urban units are concerned, identical with the second level. The counties were, however, subdivided into urban or rural municipalities with few tasks, but a high degree of self-governance. The pre-1970 system counted around 1,400 units with very different types of arrangements, responsibilities and financing. One set of rules was exercised for rural municipalities, another for towns. Suburban municipalities had their own type of organizational systems, and in the four largest towns again a completely different form of government was implemented. In addition, some municipalities had special arrangements. On the regional level, 25 units, which only functioned outside the towns, were ruled by a mixture of national government civil servants and regionally elected politicians. The pre-1970 system laid a rather high degree of responsibility on central government, less on the second level, and a low degree on the third one. Government interference in local policy was generally insignificant, and the way the system operated did not secure homogeneity in development. The degree of local decision-making on the quality of public services and master plans was high. The system was financed by taxes on all levels and by proportional and automatic expenditure sharing by central and lower levels of government.

Around 1970 a new policy was introduced, namely that of planning for the pattern of settlement as a whole on national, regional and local levels. This was the consequence of the ongoing, increasingly general suburbanization. It was also the result of a policy favouring regional equality or even conformity. To this is added the deconcentration process of manufacturing from Copenhagen and the weak counterurbanization process.

1970-reformation of Organization of Government and Planning: Spatial Equalization Policy 1970–92

In 1970 a dramatic administrative reform was carried out, soon followed by a massive increase in planning operations. The policy was intimately linked to the construction and implementation of the welfare state (Jensen, Jørgensen and Nielsen, 1996). Spatial allocation principles should ensure an equal spatial development of the entire country. Irrespective of geography, the aim was to guarantee equal levels of living conditions and welfare to citizens. The new system was meant to be homogenous, functional and democratic at all levels. The first level is central government. The national plans have the form of directives, proposals on different matters, sector plans, land reservations for national purposes and control operations. Since 1970 national control has been increased by a rising number of laws conducting many matters of daily life and thus continuing the policy of equalizing, also on a regional or local scale. The second level of government is defined as regions with a major city as a node and with geographically and economically defined boundaries (labour market, traffic system, hinterlands of higher education, hospitals and cultural activities). 14 regions (or 16 when also counting the two metropolitan municipalities of Copenhagen and Frederiksberg as regions) are established in Denmark. Regional policy has to do with regional functions, and planning deals with the urban system, land zoning and regional infrastructure. Control with municipalities within the region is important, and so are decisions on assignments of quotas of growth (different types of land: housing, manufacturing, etc.). The third level was constituted by the 1970-established municipalities (then 277 units, later reduced to 275). A unit is defined as a city and its daily hinterland. This was, in many cases, impossible to fulfil for reasons of tradition, policy, lack of cities at a proper distance, and so forth. The whole administrative reform was negotiated within the former system, and most of it was the results of compromises. The municipalities take care of a variety of tasks and obligations conducting daily life. On the planning level, they elaborate master plans for the local urban system, structure plans for the function of this system, and zoning plans for detailed development.

The post-1970 system places a rather high degree of responsibility on central government, less on the regional level, and a high degree on the municipality level. The way the system operates assures some homogeneity in development, but regional and local decisions define quality of services. The system is financed by taxes on all levels and by reimbursement of some law-defined expenditures from national to lower levels of government.

In the 1970s national government persuaded each municipality to identify one settlement as a growth pole for services and manufacturing. This was the reaction to the rise in public service and to the subsequent decentralization following the municipality reform. From 1979 the concept was combined with the policy of establishing a settlement hierarchy. Outside Copenhagen, four cities (Århus, Odense, Aalborg, Esbjerg) with between 100,000 and 200,000 inhabitants were given the status of regional centres. The third urban level was the district centres, with at least 20,000 residents.

The principle of 'one city one municipality' was not exercised in the Greater Copenhagen area, which was excluded from the reform, although some municipalities in the outer parts were amalgamated (based on Bruun,

1995). On the contrary, the Greater Copenhagen area was excluded from the reformation because a unified local government organizing 33 per cent of the national population would be politically unacceptable. It was also argued that it would mean a total abandonment of local democracy.

The consequence of the 1970-reform has been a major standard improvement of public services and infrastructure in the more sparsely populated parts of the nation. So the fact is that the implication of a organizational policy has played an important role as an instrument of relative decentralization away from the larger urban units, and especially away from Greater Copenhagen.

1997 Planning System and Issues

The purpose of the actual Planning Act (here cited from Ministry of Environment, 1994) is to ensure that the overall planning synthesizes the interests of society with respect to land use and contributes to protecting the country's nature and environment. Consequently, sustainable development of society with respect for people's living conditions and for the conservation of wildlife and vegetation is secured.

Denmark has one of the world's simplest and clearest spatial planning systems, with an extensively decentralized delegation of responsibility. The municipalities are responsible for comprehensive municipal and local planning. The counties are responsible for regional planning, and the Minister for the Environment can influence this planning by directives, call in procedures and veto rights, but usually exercises national interests by negotiations. The planning process is controlled politically and public participation is an important part of the procedures.

The spatial planning policies of the Danish government are mainly expressed in an obligatory national planning report submitted to parliament by the Minister for the Environment after each national election.[4] National planning includes topics and projects in spatial planning that are considered of national significance. It comprises a framework and a supplement to the regional planning carried out by the counties, and to the municipality and local planning carried out by the municipalities. Detailed management and approval of regional or local planning are not the purpose. National interest, however, sometimes requires intervention in decisions that the local authorities cannot or will not make on the location of projects vital to society. National planning can stop or change local projects that are inappropriate in an overall perspective. Specific trends can also be promoted. A committee of state civil servants assesses all regional plan proposals during the public comment period to determine the need for national interference. Local plan proposals can be vetoed by a state authority and if no agreement is reached, the Minister for the Environment has the final decision.

The national level of planning uses a variety of instruments to achieve national goals. The minister can issue directives, which is done a few times each year, thus binding the counties and municipalities. Directives can be used to locate specific activities and thereby determine part of a regional or local plan, such as the path of main electricity lines or motorways. They are also used to determine or regulate more general features like the building distance from the coastline. When it comes to approval of regional or local plans, the national level does not have general obligations. In practice, however, the ministry plays a role. It can give orders to a county or a municipal council to produce a plan with a specific content, but seldom does, as negotiated solutions are normally reached. The minister can call in a plan and decide to assume the authority granted by law to the county or municipal councils in connection with proposed regional, municipality or local plans in order to make national motivated necessary changes or negotiate changes. The ministry can also exercise a veto to regional and local plans during the public comment period.

On the regional level, 16 counties[5] cover nationwide and provide a planning framework for land use in Denmark. A regional plan must contain guidelines for land use and a report accounting for the premises on which the plan is based. The plan balances sectoral considerations and is the basis for the county's decisions and administration. Regional plans are renewed every four years and present a 12 year guideline for urban development, the countryside, nature, environmental protection and large technical facilities. The degree of detail must not be greater than required by national and regional interests. The report must account for the premises, which means describing the existing state of the region (nature, demographics, regional economy, transport and supply pipelines, etc.), analyzing evaluations and making forecasts of future trends, and presenting the objectives of the planning and explaining the choices made. A regional plan obligates the county authorities and determines the framework for municipality planning.

On the municipal level, 275 municipalities cover the whole nation. Municipal plans include a report, a structural plan and a framework plan for detailed local planning, which is also carried out by the municipalities. The report describes the premises and relations to regional and national planning.

It also discusses objectives, alternatives and choices, and relates to previous planning. The structural plan provides the objectives for land use and designs areas for type of use. It also coordinates sectoral planning and budgets. The framework lays out land uses in more detail, and also encompasses transport facilities. These plans are renewed every four years and are increasingly used as political instruments. They function as a strategic basis for efforts and actions far beyond their urban development and function purpose. They govern urban renewal, policies on attracting commercial development or on improving the environment. They link sectors, and ensure that the municipality's activities are coordinated. They are coordinated with or even coordinate the budgeting process. Opportunities and potential are in focus, and not just regulation. Land use is, however, still controlled in detail by local plans, which determine development, and they are legal documents which must be followed by everyone.

By law each municipality's municipal and local plans must be in accordance with the regional plan. The county council must ensure that the proposed municipal and local plans comply with national planning directives and the current regional plan. The council must veto proposals when contradictions occur.

National Policy Responses to Urban Issues, Challenges and Development

Danish towns are becoming increasingly dependent on international developments as international barriers for movements are breaking down.[6] Cooperation across the national borders will be expanded. The geographical mobility of companies will be enhanced. The exchange of goods and services will increase and international competition will become keener. As a consequence, it is expected that future international competition in Europe will be more between urban regions than between nations. Denmark is often considered to be one region when observed from an international standpoint, and regional differences in standards of living are certainly small. Denmark, however, consists of different labour markets or urban regions, which, in many ways, are relatively independent of each other. Internationalization will lead to increased specialization and division of labour among the urban regions. Each individual urban region will thus have its own unique role to play in the international division of labour determined by the strengths and weaknesses of the regions.

Against this background the Danish government has found it important to mobilize strategic network and urban system planning. A series of reports on these challenges was published recently. In the discussion of the development potential of towns, the following questions are considered in detail: which are the factors supporting the local companies (labour force supply, education, facilities, services)? What is the actual role within the international economy? Which are the structural advantages? What are the infrastructural position and the international links? Is the environment in jeopardy and can action to improve the environment be taken? How healthy are the cultural resources of the urban region in question? All these aspects of potential urban development are discussed in the governmental reports, and against the background of a series of studies the potential of Danish towns is evaluated. Potential here means the ability of the towns and their trade and industry to generate earnings for owners and staff, now and in the future. The report about the urban regions of Denmark aggregates the strengths and structural characteristics of each individual urban region in six broad themes under the headings network, production, creativity, international orientation, social merits and tourism. The profiles are synthesized and presented in a map. The metropolitan region of Greater Copenhagen is in a class of its own with regard to networks, and especially creativity and international orientation. The region clearly distinguishes itself from all other regions in the country. In addition to the metropolitan region, Århus, Triangle City, Odense and Aalborg make their marks in several areas. All get top marks for creativity, Århus and the Triangle City furthermore for networks and international orientation, Odense for international orientation and tourism and Aalborg for tourism and networks. An important geographical feature is that the metropolitan region overshadows all other urban units on the islands of Zealand, Lolland and Falster, where the other urban units present weak profiles. It is also clear that the regions with high marks in production almost all are located in the Jutland peninsula and that all units with significant profiles in regard of international orientation apart from Greater Copenhagen and Odense are found in the same peninsula.

The Greater Copenhagen Experience: Regional Planning and Lack of Regional Government

Comprehensive planning in Greater Copenhagen started in the 1940s, largely inspired by British town planning. The initiative was private and the 1947 regional plan for the structure of Copenhagen and the location of different land uses never attained legal status. Nevertheless, the 'Finger Plan' played a major role, because practically all decision-makers concerned with urban development agreed with it. The plan called for outward growth of the million inhabitant centre of Copenhagen along five fingers, each in the direction of other towns, with settlement structured by new commuter train lines and highways. Land uses were controlled such that jobs were centralized while housing and local services were decentralized. Strict zoning secured that the green areas between the fingers would remain green. In time the plan started to erode. Economic growth seemed inevitable, growth in business land consumption was rising, families decreased in numerical size but increased in square metres of living space required, in-migration from rural areas turned out to be higher than expected, business activities started to decentralize to the finger areas, and local politicians gave way to industrial land use in the green areas between the fingers.

By 1960 the population reached 1.5 million and the national government produced a new and revolutionary plan for Greater Copenhagen. This was a high growth plan which provided for the establishment of a new hand to the west of the existing Copenhagen hand. One million new inhabitants and large-scale urban renewal were major elements of the new plan, which had very little impact because of the 1963 referendum on planning laws. Growth continued, nonetheless, and instead of a major metropolitan change a new south finger was added and developed by national laws and by nationally appointed agencies.

The problems of making the Greater Copenhagen area function increased during the 1960s and it seemed a must to form some kind of regional government, although the national policy was clearly negative towards this issue. In 1974 the Greater Copenhagen Council was established for the 1.7 million residents of the metropolitan area, and a relatively weak type of regional government was introduced. Indirectly elected representatives from the county councils formed the council. The council never gained independent taxation rights but relied on transfers from the counties. The tasks included public transportation, regional planning and environmental control. The council was in fact primarily a transportation body. Around 97 per cent of its budget went on public transportation. A new regional plan was activated. It was a structural plan, a land use plan and a zoning plan, and entailed yet another revolution. Halfway out in the fingers a new infrastructural zone around Copenhagen was to be established with major motorways, railroads and other new networks. Growth was to be concentrated to the nodes where this zone and the fingers intersect. But Copenhagen's population stagnated: the population remains 1.7

million today. The regional plan did influence the location of some new activities, but space in the older areas was abundant and the significance of the regional plan dwindled in time.

In 1989 the Greater Copenhagen Council was discontinued. The decision to abolish the council was sudden and surprising, but in accordance with European trends (based on Bruun, 1995). Regional plans are subsequently made by five regional units sharing the metropolitan area. The current regional plan for Greater Copenhagen is an enlarged version of the 'Finger Plan', combined with a reorientation in the direction of the forthcoming bridge to Sweden (see below). Lack of regional government is evident.

During decades Greater Copenhagen has been a rich part of Denmark. The nearly fixed 34 per cent of the Danish population creates a tax base of 42 per cent. This has had the consequence that the provincial parts of Denmark have forwarded a policy of redistribution of wealth from the rich metropolitan region to the rest of the nation. Year after year, parliament and national government taxed the rich municipalities and transferred the resultant sums (1996: six billion Danish kroner) to poor municipalities. Together with discriminating hierarchical transfers and national investment policy (sums up to 14 billion Danish kroner per year in favour of the provincial areas), these flows have almost totally balanced out the differences in wealth. It has become a major policy toward growth in the Greater Copenhagen area because the flows of money across the regional border efficiently blocked the potential migration flows the other way. Thus, this policy has had a very stabilizing effect on the urban system.

Inside the Greater Copenhagen region, the same policy of transfers from rich to poor municipalities has meant flows of money from rich suburban municipalities to poor central city municipalities, thus in fact acting as a social conflict moderator within the functional urban region.

Lack of reforms in local and regional government structure and function in the metropolitan area, and the abolition of the Greater Copenhagen Council implies that no common Greater Copenhagen policy can be established to counteract the national policy of transfers of money to the provinces.

The Danish capital outgrew the territorial division 100 years ago. Series of discussions have focused on incorporation, amalgamation or superstructures in the region. It seems that everybody agrees that some kind of regional authority has been and is a necessity. It also seems that, when it comes to realizing such a body, everybody loses their decision-making power. Even the weak Greater Copenhagen Council was discussed, undermined and at last given up. A new discussion in 1995–96 formulated alternative types of metropolitan government but no such thing was decided upon in parliament because of traditional Copenhagen opposition.

Cross-National Metropolitan Development in the Öresund Region

In spite of the failure to create any type of metropolitan government in the Greater Copenhagen region, a shift from politics negative to Copenhagen into those positive to Copenhagen occurred around 1990. The shift was relatively sudden, and engendered very little argument, although it represents transformations from politics to economics, from welfare orientation to market orientation, and from spatial equalization policy to a focus on metropolitan competition (Jensen, Jørgensen and Nielsen, 1996). The recent policy change has mostly had its impact on national infrastructural investment policy in favour of Greater Copenhagen, but has also meant large investments in cultural institutions and activities (European Cultural Capital 1996). The shift was a consequence of the ongoing internationalization of economy, 1989–91, expressed first and foremost by the establishment of the European Inner Market. With this background it is clear that Danish urban policy could only identify one internationally known city with potential for international competition, Copenhagen. The ambition is to lift Copenhagen in the European urban hierarchy by integrating the Danish and Swedish urban areas in the Öresund area, the instrument being a 12 km long bridge.

The bridge in construction between Copenhagen and Malmö on the Swedish side of the Sound, combined with Swedish entrance into EU, open up for development of the first cross-national integrated large-city region outside the European centre. A fusion of Greater Copenhagen and the Malmö-Lund agglomeration gives the two hitherto non-interdependent urban economies access to more specialization and opens up the possibility for cooperation as yet unforeseen. Synergy and further new specialization will be the obvious consequences. To these changes in growth potential will be added the effects of optimism and increased world interest associated with the event itself. Large-scale engineering and construction projects are of international interest, and a fusion of two agglomerations, which cooperate very little at present, is a world-class event. In many respects, Copenhagen, together with the South Scandinavian centres, are expected to experience increased economic growth. When the fixed links between Scandinavia and the European continent are in place, regional organization can be integrated.

The construction of the 15 billion Danish kroner bridge is a mega-event in itself, but using the event as a tool in strategic planning is a challenge. Development of the large cross-boundary infrastructure is going to alter the spatial organization of the territory, which again will encourage cross-border collaboration in institutional planning processes. This will activate creative and innovative new arrangements as regards industries, institutions, procedures, management or any public action tool. Already the principal investment decisions have been followed by a series of other investment decisions, altogether adding up to 110 billion Danish kroner. Most of them are public, such as a new mini-metro, intraurban motorways, railroads, airport railroad station, new Swedish university and large scale urbanization; some are private, such as a new airport terminal and more to come. The dynamics are clear.

The Brundtland Report and its Impact on Planning Ideology

This report (Bruntland Commission, 1987) has had a clear impact on governmental behaviour in the 1990s. The messages in the report were by no means new, but they actualized and underscored the importance of environmental concern. Sustainability became a leading motive in public planning. Transport planning should not only focus on flows and network functioning, but also on sustainability to create a new balance between development and environment. The task is to develop and change the total system of transportation so that the necessary mobility can be obtained inside limits defined by consideration of consumption of resources and environmental strain, e.g., in terms of energy, climate, air pollution, traffic accidents and noise. These types of argument have been forwarded by a series of reports from ministries of environment, planning, traffic and communication. This environmental or ecological profile is penetrating into planning organization at all levels but is still far from having succeeded. One example of this is the considerable reduction of private car traffic in the city centre of Copenhagen without any decrease in urban core activities: on the contrary, there was an unforeseen rise in the number of people using the carfree public space.

Strategic Planning

Marketing (demand) orientation and strategic planning have been brought to the fore during the late 1980s and are playing a growing role. Regional issues with the main goal of increasing the international competitiveness of the region in question have been added to traditional urban marketing. The Örestadsplan of Copenhagen is the first and only example of a comprehensive development plan for an area subordinated to strategic objects. The strategic object is formulated as advancement of regional productivity in order to give Copenhagen a better platform in international competition with other metropolises. To that end, a large area of highly accessible open land in physical proximity to both the city centre and the airport is in the process of being developed. Large investments in infrastructure, including a new light rail system, are in progress, and a mixture of metropolitan functions with residential land use is planned for according to a comprehensive plan derived from an international architectural competition.

Strategic planning on the national level gives perspectives for the spatial structuring of Denmark in the future Europe, published as national reports (Ministry of Environment, 1992). It also expresses the current national policies for urban development and change in the urban system. The national plan is a reference framework for the decisions taken by Danish authorities and the business sector, which have physical and functional consequences. The perspective is Denmark's basis for participation in European cooperation on physical planning and decisions on land use, location and urban development. This is based on fundamental goals. The environment must be protected for future generations and economic growth and increased welfare must be ensured. Developments must be of a high standard and decisions must be taken as close to individuals as possible. The actual national plan presents two north-south and one east-west international traffic axes, and in addition a number of major links to neighbouring nations. The Öresund region plays a crucial role in this superior structure. Denmark's urban system of the future will consist of many centres. It will be hierarchically based on one city of European significance, Greater Copenhagen or the Öresund region. The four regional capitals, including the runner up, Triangle City, plus Esbjerg, are seen as important nodes with substantial international relations, and numerous other cities and towns will present different international specialities.

Summary

In a small country such as Denmark with only one large city and four minor regional capital type cities, national policy for the large cities is not very explicit, since Greater Copenhagen houses 34 per cent of the national population and creates 42 per cent of all taxes paid. Any massive policy in favour of this clearly identifiable unit creates a minor revolution amongst the 66 per cent of the population which lives outside Copenhagen. But many reports have been produced and many discussions undertaken. Large city policy has especially been formulated in this way on the national level, mainly expressed in the obligatory national planning report which the Minister for the Environment submits to parliament after each national election (Ministry of Environment, 1994). From time to time a more comprehensive document on national planning strategies is presented. The latest version was presented 1992 (Ministry of Environment, 1992). The main agent is the Ministry of the Environment, but other ministries and agents have been active, too. This combination of reports and many agents does not mean that no policy is exercised on this issue. On the contrary, it is clear that national policy in the 1970s and 1980s was in favour of Denmark outside Greater Copenhagen. It is also clear that a shift in policy in favour of the Danish capital and only metropolitan unit occurred in the beginning of the 1990s, and that this policy is active and dynamic 1997.

The pre-1992 policy was intimately linked to the construction and implementation of the welfare state (Jensen, Jørgensen and Nielsen, 1996). Spatial allocation principles should ensure an equal spatial development of the entire country. Irrespective of geography, the aim was to guarantee citizens living conditions and welfare of equal levels. This policy terminated abruptly between 1989–92. The shift was relatively sudden, and was the subject of very little debate, although it represents transformations from politics to economics, from welfare orientation to market orientation, and from spatial equalization policy to a focus on metropolitan competition. The recent policy change has mostly had its impact on infrastructural investment policy in favour of Greater Copenhagen, pointing out also a new metropolitan reality in the Öresund area. It also gives rise to new focusing on the four regional capitals. The shift is probably a consequence of the ongoing internationalization of economy, which between 1989–91 expressed itself first and foremost in the establishment of the European Inner Market. It was also forwarded by a series of informal meetings at the same time between Union ministers responsible for this kind of question, followed by European documents and green books advocating spatial planning with an European perspective. With this background it is clear that Danish urban policy could only identify one internationally known city with potential in the international competition, Copenhagen.

The Danish capital outgrew the still existing territorial boundary 100 years ago. Series of discussions have focused on incorporation of suburban municipalities (of which many today must be considered urban), local amalgamation or superstructures in the region. It seems that everybody agrees that some kind of regional authority has been and is a necessity. It also seems that, when it comes to realizing such a body, everybody loses their decision-making power. Even the weak Greater Copenhagen Council (1974–89) was discussed, undermined and at last given up. The decision to abolish the council was sudden and surprising, but in accordance with European trends (based on Bruun, 1995). The council was in fact primarily a transportation body. Around 97 per cent of its budget went on public transportation. A new discussion in 1995–96 formulated alternative types of metropolitan government (Indenrigsministeriet, 1995) but no such thing was decided upon in parliament. A majority of existing establishments are not interested in giving away any power to a new regional government. National politicians elected in the provinces are not in favour of changes that would strengthen Copenhagen at the national level. In fact, it is interesting to observe the contradiction between the introduction of a new metropolitan policy parallel with the absence of any regional superstructure.

Notes

1 Triangle City is not an official unit, but a name used for the concentration of urban units in the centre of Denmark. The cities Kolding, Vejle and Fredericia form a triangle with distances between urban centres of 25 km. Together with neighbours, this cluster is making its way into the ranks of regional capitals.
2 Greater Copenhagen. The urban area is defined according to the statistical definition. The region is the area of the 1990-abolished Greater Copenhagen region.
3 Triangle City is defined as the five municipalities, Børkop, Fredericia, Kolding, Middelfart and Vejle, located in the centre of Denmark. The urban area in Triangle City is defined as the urban areas of the cities of Fredericia, Kolding, Middelfart and Vejle.
4 This section is mainly based on the Ministry of Environment and Energy, Spatial Planning Department (1994).
5 14 county councils plus the municipalities of Copenhagen and Frederiksberg, which also have the status of counties.
6 This section is based on Miljøministeriet (1992).

References

Bruntland Commission (1987), *Our Common Future*, Oxford: Oxford University Press.
Bruun, F. (1995), 'Dilemma of Size: The Rise and Fall of the Greater Copenhagen Council' in L.J. Sharpe (ed.), *Government of World Cities*, Chichester: John Wiley and Sons.

Engelstoft, S. and Jørgensen, J. (1997), 'Copenhagen: a redistributive city?' in C. Jensen-Butler, A. Shachar and J. v. Weesep, *European Cities in Competition*, Aldershot: Avebury.
Jensen, O.B., Jørgensen, I. and Nielsen, J. (1996), *Interreg II C – A Loophole for Transnational Spatial Planning*, Nord REVY: Denmark.
Indenrigsministeriet (1995), *Hovedstadsområdets fremtidige struktur*, Betænkning nr. 1307.
Miljøministeriet (1992), *Danmarks byregioner*.
Ministry of the Environment (1992), *Denmark Towards the Year 2018*.
Ministry of Environment and Energy, Spatial Planning Department (1994), *Spatial Planning in Denmark*.

Appendix

The traditional concept of urban areas is delimitating what is urban strictly based on physical features. Delimitation on labour market regions where town and hinterland are seen as one unit gives the most liberal definition of urban Denmark and clearly represents an overbounding of the units. Again another listing is found when urban Denmark is defined by administrative definitions.

Statistical information describes urban areas, labour markets, municipalities and counties. None of these categories fulfils demands for a precise definition which can describe the urban system in a homogenous way. An urban area is, for example, a continuously built-up area, which means that the distance between houses does not exceed 200 metres, except owing to public parks, churchyards, athletic grounds, industrial plants, etc. Using this definition, the top ten units measured by population data are:

Population in urban areas (1994)

Greater Copenhagen	1,346,289
Århus	209,404
Odense	143,029
Aalborg	116,567
Esbjerg	73,149
Randers	55,515
Kolding	51,205
Horsens	47,365
Vejle	46,718
Helsingør	41,266

Delimitation on labour market regions, where town and hinterland are seen as one unit, gives the most liberal definition of urban Denmark and clearly represents an overbounding of the units. The top ten are:

Labour market regions	Population 1993
Greater Copenhagen	1,796,380
Århus	405,079
Odense	361,589
Aalborg	263,162
Kolding	163,413
Vejle	154,985
Esbjerg	154,810
Randers	149,735
Holbæk	124,197
Slagelse	119,453

Yet another listing is found when urban Denmark is defined by administrative definitions. The use of administrative definitions gives rise to one problem. The Greater Copenhagen area was excluded from the major administrative reformation 1970 (see below), and a comparison between the Greater Copenhagen area and the rest of the country is biased.

Municipalities	Population 1996
Greater Copenhagen (50 municipalities)	1,752,078
Århus	279,759
Odense	183,564
Aalborg	159,980
Esbjerg	82,905
Randers	62,013
Kolding	60,040
Herning	57,965
Horsens	55,747
Vejle	53,261

5   Finland

EERO HOLSTILA

Introduction

In order fully to understand Finnish urban policies it is essential to bear in mind that Finland was a very agrarian country until the late 1950s. Consequently, urbanization started quite late, but the process has been very rapid during the last 40 years. Urbanization still continues and immigration to big cities is still actively going on. Finland has only a few large cities and most of them are in many ways different from usual cities in other EU countries. Urban areas in Finland are typically relatively sparsely populated. The housing stock is quite new – mainly built during the last 35 years – and the majority of dwellings are in multistorey buildings in suburbs.

Past governments pursued active regional policy to keep the country evenly populated and control the urbanization process. The recession at the beginning of the 1990s also brought massive unemployment to big cities. At the same time, public economy cuts have brought hard challenges to the sectorally controlled social policy. So far the institutions of the welfare state have managed to keep social development stable and to prevent the emergence of social crisis. Still, the threats of social segregation and deprivation are acute in Finnish cities.

European integration, together with economic growth and industrial structure changes in Finland, will affect future regional development and urbanization in our country. This brings new challenges to urban policy, as well. In 1996, the Finnish government commissioned a report on urban policies, called 'Cities as Generators of Growth', showing a new approach to problems of regional and urban policy. On the basis of this report the government appointed a working group for the years 1997–99.

National Spatial Development Pattern

Historical Background of Finland's Late Urbanization

Finland is a sparsely populated country of 337,000 km^2. Although the country has seen rapid urbanization since the second world war, the percentage of urban inhabitants (63 per cent) is still one of the lowest in the European Union.

In 1950, only 26 per cent of Finland's inhabitants lived in urban communities, and the percentage of primary production among the gainfully occupied population was 46 per cent. Forestry had a key position in Finland's rapid industrialization in the 1950s and 1960s. Paper and pulp mills were built near raw material sources, which essentially favoured employment in inner parts of the country. Historian Laura Kolbe (1994) has written that the glorification of the countryside was one of the crucial ideas of the national romantic movement in the 19th century, and that this tradition has remained strong in Finland throughout the 20th. After the second world war, for example, many new farms were founded in sparsely inhabited rural areas in Eastern and Northern Finland with subsidies from the government. The aim of the state's regional policy has been to keep the whole country populated.

The industrial structure in Finland has changed dramatically during the last 45 years (Table 5.1). The proportion of primary production has decreased from 46 to 8 per cent. In spite of the rapid change, the share of agriculture and forestry is still much higher than the average within the European Union. The proportion of services has increased to almost two thirds, respectively.

Table 5.1   Employed persons by industry in Finland, 1950, 1970 and 1995

	1950 %	1970 %	1995 %
Primary production	46	20	8
Secondary production	28	36	28
Services	26	44	64
Total	100	100	100

Since 1950 cities have grown very rapidly, too. In a European perspective, a feature typical of Finland is that urbanization is still continuing vigorously. If urbanization in Finland is gradually approaching the average EU level, the urbanization process will be going on for decades yet. This is one of the crucial issues in Finnish urban policy.

The Urban Structure of Finland

According to the latest population statistics (1996), Finland has eight urban regions with more than 100,000 inhabitants. In total, these regions account for more than 2.3 million inhabitants, which makes 46 per cent of the country's population. 1.1 million – almost half – of these urban citizens live in the Helsinki region, which is by far the largest urban region in Finland. It consists of 12 municipalities, among which the biggest are Helsinki (525,000 inhabitants) and its immediate neighbours Espoo (191,000) and Vantaa (166,000).

Helsinki's growth is a good example of the late but rapid urbanization in Finland. In 1875, Helsinki had only 23,000 inhabitants, but by 1917, when Finland declared itself independent, the population already numbered 162,000. In 1946, Helsinki incorporated considerable adjacent land areas and communities, which raised its population figure to 341,000. The whole capital region then had around 450,000 inhabitants.

From the 1960s on, growth in the Helsinki region increasingly took place in suburban municipalities to the west and north of the city. The population in the city of Helsinki started decreasing in 1969, but returned to growth in 1980s. The population of the whole Helsinki region has increased continuously.

The Helsinki region is an urban area of 1.1 million inhabitants. It is the only metropolitan area and the economic and administrative centre of the country. Its position in Finland can be demonstrated by the following figures: the proportion of the Helsinki region is one-fifth of the population, one-quarter of the employed persons, and almost one-third of the GDP of the whole country.

As Table 5.2 shows, the major cities in Finland are growing rapidly, particularly the regions of Helsinki, Oulu and Jyväskylä. Tampere and Kuopio have grown fast, too, while Turku's growth has been modest. All these cities have universities.

The population growth figures of cities dominated by traditional industries are modest or negative. Among the large cities, Lahti and Pori belong to this category – neither having a university. Today, though, some vocational training schools in these cities have been given the status of third level institutions, thus upgrading their status.

Oulu has received international attention as a region where the effects of the university have been particularly beneficial. The city has seen the traditional

Table 5.2   Some characteristics of the biggest urban regions in Finland

Region/city	Population 1996	Growth % 85–96	Economic performance	Tertiary/ secondary
Helsinki	1,121,000	14	high	80/19
city	525,000	9		
Espoo	191,000	25		
Vantaa	166,000	17		
Tampere	283,000	10	average	66/32
city	183,000	9		
Turku	265,000	7	average	66/31
city	165,000	2		
Oulu	160,000	15	high	72/26
city	109,000	13		
Lahti	151,000	2	low	59/36
city	95,000	1		
Jyväskylä	128,000	15	average	69/28
city	74,000	14		
Pori	110,000	-2	low	62/34
city	77,000	-3		
Kuopio	106,000	10	average	75/20
city	85,000	10		

factories close – but also a compensation for this loss in the form of new information-related jobs. Since the early 1980s, the city, university and local business community have joined forces to develop modern resources in the field of information, data and telecomm technology. In the 1990s, the example of Oulu has been used for the nationwide programme for centres of expertise, which is today an important part of the national urban policy (see below).

There are also a number of provincial centres (fewer than 100,000 inhabitants) dominated by administration and education, such as Joensuu, Vaasa and Rovaniemi, which have grown fairly rapidly.

In medium-size and small provincial centres, population growth has, on average, remained about at the same level as in the whole country, i.e., growth has been slow. Today, in most small towns and rural communities population is declining.

Other Cities

Finland is divided into 452 municipalities (in 1997), of which 104 have the status of a town. According to official Finnish statistics, the country is divided into 88 labour market regions, of which 37 urban regions were studied by the Finnish Urban Policy Group, appointed by the Ministry of the Interior. The total population number of these regions was 3,920,000, i.e., 77 per cent of Finland's population.

The major city regions (over 100,000 inhabitants) were mentioned above. The list of the smaller urban regions is as follows. The proportion of rural population in Finland is among the highest in Western Europe. According to OECD's classification, communities with fewer than 150 inhabitants per km^2 are defined as rural. If this definition is used, only 21 per cent of the inhabitants of Finland live in urban communities, while 47 per cent live in rural and 32 per cent in very rural communities.

These figures also demonstrate that international classifications are not always suitable for describing Finnish cities, which in many cases are rather sparsely constructed. The average population density of Finnish cities is 500–600 inhabitants per km^2, versus 1500–1700 in Sweden and Norway. The difference is even greater when compared with Denmark, Holland or Germany.

Unemployment

In the 1980s, Finland's GDP grew clearly faster than the EU countries', but at the beginning of 1990s, Finland suffered the hardest recession in Western Europe. During the period 1991–93, Finland's GDP decreased by 12 per cent. In the 1980s, some 20 per cent of Finnish exports went to the Soviet Union on a bilateral basis. The sudden collapse of exports to the East, at the same time as exports to Western Europe declined, thanks to the poor competitiveness of Finnish firms and declining demand, led the country into the severest depression of this century.

Soon after, the Finnish economy had to adjust to the requirements of the common market. Finland became a member of the European Union on 1 January 1995. In 1994–96, Finland's GDP has grown rapidly again, and growth forecasts for the year 1997 are between four and five per cent.

As late as in 1990, unemployment was a marginal problem in the Helsinki region, which, in fact, suffered from a shortage of labour. During the years of recession, the rate of unemployment reached almost 20 per cent in the country as a whole and over 20 per cent in many larger cities. In spite of the rapid

Table 5.3   The population of smaller urban regions in 1996

Urban region		Centre town	
Kouvola	101,825	Kouvola	32,078
Kotka-Hamina	90,457	Kotka	55,903
Joensuu	90,434	Joensuu	50,431
Vaasa	87,232	Vaasa	55,502
Hämeenlinna	86,650	Hämeenlinna	44,891
Lappeenranta	75,304	Lappenranta	56,664
Lohja	74,003	Lohja	15,265
Mikkeli	71,578	Mikkeli	32,812
Ylä-Savo	70,823	Iisalmi	24,042
Porvoo	66,795	Porvoo	21,155
Kemi-Tornio	65,500	Kemi	24,696
Rauma	61,744	Rauma	38,162
Salo	60,816	Salo	22,802
Kajaani	58,109	Kajaani	36,860
Seinäjoki	57,174	Seinäjoki	29,039
Rovaniemi	57,045	Rovaniemi	35,236
Kokkola	52,988	Kokkola	35,552

economic growth during the last few years, the unemployment rate has remained high. According to statistics, Finland's figures, which are comparable with those of EUROSTAT's, the unemployment rate in autumn 1997 was 13 per cent. There is another source for employment figures, the register of unemployed persons of labour authorities. According to their statistics the unemployment rate of the country was 15.3 per cent in October. In spite of the evident overestimation, this is the only source which is available for municipality-level unemployment statistics.

The Threat of Segregation

All city regions show a common feature: unemployment is decreasing more slowly in the central municipality than in the suburban ones. Poorly educated, unskilled people and other risk groups of labour markets are concentrated in central cities. This is particularly obvious in the Helsinki region. The rapid population growth in most big urban regions also contributes to unemployment rates. Although the number of jobs increase, unemployment decreases only slowly, due to in-migration and consequent growth of labour force.

Table 5.4   Unemployment rates of the big cities in October 1997

Helsinki Region		12.6 %
of which	City of Helsinki	14.0 %
	Espoo	9.6 %
	Vantaa	11.7 %
Tampere (city)		18.3 %
Turku (city)		17.4 %
Oulu (city)		16.9 %
Lahti (city)		20.6 %
Jyväskylä (city)		20.9 %
Pori (city)		21.9 %
Kuopio (city)		17.7 %
Finland		15.3 %

Source: Labour authorities.

Long-term unemployment, in particular, has become a problem in big cities. Local concentration of this unemployment in certain residential areas is now, for the first time, posing a threat of social segregation in the Finnish society. Social differentiation has locally been very mild in Finland, so far. In Helsinki, the situation has also been worsened by the inflow of immigrants, another new phenomenon. Since 1990, the number of immigrants has increased by some 400 per cent in Helsinki, where the proportion of foreigners, however, is still not greater than 5 per cent today. Unemployment is an especially severe problem among immigrants: in Helsinki the unemployment rate among foreigners is about 50 per cent.

Economic Competitiveness of Urban Regions

Employment in the cities is picking up again after hard years. The following conclusions are based on a survey made by Mika Pikkarainen (1996) for the Ministry of the Interior.

Economic prospects for Helsinki are good on a short-term perspective, but even more on a long-term perspective. The Helsinki region is by far Finland's greatest and most versatile economic zone. The region has the best chance for growth, since it can offer the best development resources for knowledge-intensive and international enterprises. However, there is no reason to feel too confident about Helsinki's attractiveness, compared with other metropolises in the field of telecomm and knowledge infrastructure.

In terms of international contacts, knowledge-intensity and network economy, the regions of Tampere, Turku and Oulu come next after Helsinki, and their prospects are looking good, too. According to an index representing the competitiveness of industries on a short perspective, Oulu has the brightest future, while Tampere has reasonable prospects, but Turku has problems with service industries. The problems of Kuopio and Jyväskylä, as well as other cities of eastern and northern Finland, are that the expert service sector which is supported by the public sector, has weak links with the local competitive business community.

The problem of traditional industrial cities, such as Lahti and Pori, is that manufacturing, however successful and prosperous, is hardly creating any new jobs today. Growth potential could be created by internationally oriented industrial clusters and by offering new knowledge-intensive company services.

Table 5.5   Short-term prospects for Finnish urban regions from 1995 on (the greater the index figure, the greater the threat of increasing unemployment; 100 = average of city regions)

Urban region	Structural sensitivity of manufacturing	Structural sensitivity of services	Extent of the public sector
Helsinki	122	51	96
Tampere	109	124	106
Turku	155	197	108
Oulu	57	38	133
Lahti	116	140	88
Jyväskylä	108	174	138
Pori	163	46	101
Kuopio	65	128	149

Administrative and Financial Framework

Local Self-governance

The basic unit of Finnish local administration is the municipality. Local self-governance of municipalities is guaranteed by the Finnish constitution. Every four years, the local council is elected by the residents of each municipality.

The most important services provided by municipalities concern education, children's day care, social welfare, health care and maintenance of technical infrastructure. Finland's strong local self-governance derives from independent taxation rights. Municipalities finance nearly half of their costs from municipal tax revenue. In large cities, this proportion is even higher.

Finland is divided into 459 municipalities of very different sizes. In terms of population the biggest one is Helsinki, with more than half a million inhabitants. Finland's smallest municipality has 130 inhabitants.

In many fields, such as health care or education, it is usual for municipalities to cooperate to provide services, e.g., hospitals or schools. Joint municipal boards are formed to manage these services.

There are 19 counties in Finland, in addition to the autonomous province of Åland. They are governed by regional councils, which are intermunicipal joint authorities. Regional councils bear statutory responsibility for regional development and planning. There are no regional elections in Finland. Member municipalities elect representatives to the regional council for a four-year term.

The city of Helsinki, for example, belongs to the Uusimaa Regional Council, in the administrative area of which there are 1.25 million inhabitants. The Helsinki region's share of this is 90 per cent, whilst its share of the administrative area is only 45 per cent. The big municipalities of the area, Helsinki, Espoo and Vantaa have been discontent with their role in the Uusimaa Regional Council, which has an important role in the implementation of the government's regional policy. Since January 1997, the influence of the Helsinki Region has been increased in the council.

State Administration at Local and Regional Level

Finland has been divided into 12 provinces, each having a provincial government representing the government. From 1 September 1997 on, the number of provinces will be reduced to six, including the autonomous province of Åland. Provincial governments are multisectoral authorities. Their significance to large cities like Helsinki has become minor ever since their responsibilities in the field of regional policy were shifted over to regional councils a few years ago.

This year will also see the introduction of a reform aiming to assemble the state administration of local industrial and labour policy into one regional organization. The idea of this reform is to cut the number of the state's administrative units at regional level. As a result of the reform, 15 industrial and labour policy centres will be founded to house the regional administration of the Ministries of Trade and Industry, Labour, and Agriculture and Forestry.

Metropolitan Authorities

In Finland there is no statutory administration for urban areas consisting of several municipalities, with the exception of the Metropolitan Area Council operating in the Helsinki region. Its existence is based on a law on cooperation in the metropolitan area, consisting of the cities of Helsinki, Espoo, Vantaa and Kauniainen. The population of this area is some 900,000 inhabitants. The duties based on law of the Metropolitan Area Council are waste management and recycling, and public transport. In principle, the member municipalities may assign other tasks to the council, but in practice, it has mainly restricted itself to its basic duties which are defined in law.

The Metropolitan Area Council is led by the Council government, to which the member municipalities appoint their own representatives. The members also cover those expenses which are not covered by service fees.

The municipalities of the Helsinki region also cooperate directly, without the intermediary of the Metropolitan Area Council. The mayors convene regularly and start joint projects. Furthermore, separate cooperation organizations have been founded, such as Helsinki Metropolitan Development Corporation Ltd, in the framework of which, for example, some of the cooperation between the Helsinki region and the cities of Moscow and St Petersburg takes place. In 1995, the universities and cities of the region founded a joint development company, Culminatum Oy Ltd, to promote the introduction of university-generated innovation into the business community. This expertise centre has also been funded by the state and the EU. On the initiative of the City of Helsinki, a foundation was founded in 1996, the aim of which is to carry out the projects pertaining to the celebrations in the year 2000, when Helsinki has its 450th anniversary and carries the title of Cultural Capital of Europe. The University of Helsinki, the City of Espoo, the Helsinki Chamber of Commerce and the state are also members of the foundation.

Most of the other big urban regions have unofficial cooperation between the municipalities. The Oulu region, for example, has a voluntary organ for carrying out the marketing campaign for 'Oulu Technopolis'.

Direct/Indirect Government Involvement

Most of the duties of municipalities concerning service provision for inhabitants are strictly controlled by law. Otherwise, the national government does not interfere directly with the internal affairs of cities. But its indirect influence, particularly in terms of government grants, is most significant (see the following subsection). Among other important means of influence of the government there are regional policy grants, which are connected to the EU's structural foundations. It should be mentioned that none of the urban regions of Helsinki, Tampere, Turku, Oulu, Jyväskylä and Kuopio are entitled to EU's regional grants, being so-called white areas. Instead, Pori and Lahti belong to the category of regressing industrial cities.

In addition to government grants to municipalities and regions, the allocation decisions concerning transport and other infrastructure, universities and educational institutions, and other public investments, significantly affect the development of urban areas and other regions. There is a long tradition in Finland of using public investments as an instrument of regional policy. For example, the university institution, which earlier was strongly concentrated in Helsinki, was decentralized in the 1960s and 1970s.

Urban Income Sources

The expenditure of local authorities makes up two-thirds of all public expenditure in Finland. This means that the scope of municipal activities is wider than in many other EU countries.

The basic principle in the public finance in Finland is that the government receives the revenue from commodity taxes, consumption taxes and progressive income tax. Municipalities receive the revenue from proportional municipal income tax and property taxes. The revenues from corporation taxes are divided between the government and municipalities. Regional councils have no taxation rights, but receive their finance from member municipalities and the government.

The basis of municipal finance is the municipal income tax. Each city council decides independently on its income tax rate. No upper limit is set. In 1996, the average municipal income tax rate was 17.5 per cent of personal taxable income. Among the big cities, the lowest tax rate is 17 per cent and the highest 18 per cent. The extremes in Finland are 15 and 20 per cent.

Furthermore, municipalities levy property taxes for land and constructions. There are upper and lower limits for property tax rates prescribed by law. In spite of the fact that the system of property taxation was totally reformed in Finland a few years ago, the significance of the real estate tax as an income source for municipalities is minor, compared with other EU-countries.

The municipal tax revenue means that cities, the large ones in particular, are fairly independent of the government, by all-European standards. Differences in tax revenue between 'richer' and 'poorer' municipalities are balanced by the system of government grants. Municipalities receive government grants enabling them to cover the costs of services and other functions required by law. The government pays a contribution to both operating costs and investment costs. The amount of grants received by a local authority depends on factors such as the size and structure of the population, and the number of users of different services.

The Financial Position of Big Cities in the 1990s

The economic basis of big cities in Finland has traditionally been quite strong. The recession, especially in 1991 and 1992, cut revenue from municipal income tax, which was the main income source of big cities. This income cap had to be covered by expenditure cuts and by loans. But in smaller municipalities, especially in the countryside, the system of government grants compensated, to a large extent, the decrease in tax income.

Before the recession the financial standing of every big city was very good compared with the average of all municipalities. Now the situation has changed and the relative financial position of big cities has weakened. The financial standing of cities of Helsinki and Tampere are still good. Espoo, Oulu, Kuopio, Turku and Pori are now close to the average of all municipalities. But the financial positions of Jyväskylä, Lahti and Vantaa are rather poor.

The economy of Finnish municipalities is expected to tighten in coming years, because the government has cut grants to municipalities to decrease the budget deficit. Still, the financial position of big cities may improve, provided that the Finnish economy increases according to forecasts and unemployment continues decreasing.

Urban Issues and Challenges from a National Perspective

Background

Urban policy is a new phenomenon in Finland. It is only under the present government that the cities' situations and the joint effects of sectoral policies have been studied. In summer 1995, a working group on urban policy (the Finnish Urban Policy Group) was set up by the Ministry of the Interior. Last year, the group made a proposal concerning development policies needed in Finnish cities.

On 13 November 1996, the national government, in an unofficial meeting, received the working group's proposals, but no decisions were made. In December 1996, the Finnish government appointed a new working group for city policy, with the task of 'observing and evaluating the development of city regions, defining the contents of the government's urban policy and making suggestions about it in cooperation with the rural policy'. According to the decision of the government, the working group is supposed to support nationwide, regional and local urban development. It is also supposed to increase the competitiveness and other resources which urban regions will need in the future.

Problems and Challenges

The main points presented in a memorandum for an unofficial government meeting are as follows.

The starting point for the urban policy is the contention that one of Finland's strengths has been the even nationwide regional structure, which is the result of a deliberate policy pursued for several decades. Finns live in small and medium-sized cities rather than internationally oriented major cities.

European urban problems in the form of local concentration of poverty and social problems are still comparatively rare in Finland, according to the working group, which also mentions that up to the late 1980s, the government made continuous efforts to control the growth of the capital and its suburbs.

According to the report, it looks as though urbanization has started increasing again in Finland since the mid 1990s. People are moving from the countryside to the cities, and from smaller urban communities to larger ones. The degree of urbanization in Finland seems to be steadily approaching the average European 80 per cent level.

Unemployment, which earlier used to be a problem in faraway rural areas, has now taken a firm grip on cities, too. The unemployment situation in certain suburb residential areas may yet, according to the report, become even worse. In some residential areas of Helsinki, unemployment is almost up to 30 per cent, and in two housing estates in provincial centre Hämeenlinna, it is almost 40 per cent. The same trend can be seen in most larger city regions in Finland.

The 1990s have seen increasing differences in economic growth between Finnish city regions. An alarming feature from both a regional and national point of view is the fact that several city regions are among the unsuccessful urban regions.

As the report sees it, innovations are the motor that creates new enterprise and keeps existing companies going. Crucial competition factors today are the supply of well-educated professionals and good cooperation between the business community and various institutions for education and research. 'Big urban communities provide the best conditions for innovation. Favourable growth processes in cities have widespread effects in the regions' (Valtioneuvoston iltakouluun 13 Marraskuuta 1996 tehty muistio kaupunkien kehitiämisen jatkotoimista, Sisäsiainministeriö 11 Marraskuuta 1996; Memorandum concerning further measures for the development of cities, prepared for the unofficial session of the Finnish government on 13 November 1996, Ministry of the Interior, 11 November 1996).

Discussion

In Finland, the national urban policy is only today seeking a direction. Besides the appointment of the working group there has, so far, been no governmental planning or decisions that could be called a concrete urban policy.

This reflects the fact that Finland is still one of the European Union's most rural countries. The national urban policy that is now being drawn up is linked with the national rural policy in order to achieve a 'nationwide balanced regional structure'. This formulation may be interpreted as an argument in favour of continued control of escalating urbanization. The assignment given to the new working group separately points out that the urban policy has to be prepared in cooperation with the traditionally strong rural policy.

Today, the big cities in Finland have perhaps Europe's highest population growth percentages. At the same time, the population of the countryside and small towns is decreasing. The state's documents on urban policy do not make any clear point with regard to the new growth wave. But some recent statements suggest that Finland should be prepared for continued urbanization, reaching the average European level. On the other hand, attitudes have been expressed that urbanization is a threat which should be fought by supporting the countryside by special measures.

The social and environmental problems of Finnish cities have been regarded as fairly minor, but there is also an awareness that the problems may soon become much worse. The high rate of unemployment and uneven distribution of unemployment between residential areas is seen as a serious problem which may eventually lead to clustering of poverty, deprivation and to social and ethnic segregation.

The weaknesses of the industrial structure of certain cites and their uneven economic development have also been seen as a problem. One of the goals of urban policy is to strengthen the cities' potential for economic growth. This view is incorporated in a theme of the urban policy working group, which is entitled 'cities as generators of growth'.

It should perhaps be noted which issues have *not* been mentioned on the narrow list of 'challenges for the cities'. Criminality is not mentioned at all, nor are environmental problems. Both are, of course, problems in Finnish cities, too, although not on very large scale in an all-European perspective. One thing which the governments has noted, though, are the high infrastructural costs per capita in sparsely constructed urban areas. The rapid growth in the number of immigrants has not yet found its way onto the government's list of problems. In Helsinki, the number of foreign nationals has increased fivefold over the 1990s, and according to some estimates more than half of them are unemployed. This problem is, so far, mainly restricted to the Helsinki region.

In the above-mentioned urban policy outlines, the importance of competitiveness is underlined, but the international aspect is not emphasized too much. The importance of international transport links for the competitiveness of Finnish cities has also been almost forgotten.

The increasing housing need caused by recent growth in cities has also passed unnoticed. Instead, the need for repair and socioeconomic reform in postwar housing estates has rightly been noticed.

In these reports, so far, no special position has been attributed to big cities. However, their role is indirectly recognized by stressing the importance of knowledge-intensive and innovative economic activity. The background report ordered by the working group on urban policy (Pikkarainen, 1996) states, however, that urban and regional policies ought to recognize the differing roles of various city regions for Finland's economic development. 'The role of Helsinki, in particular, as Finland's only international knowledge-intensive major city area needs to be promoted for the simple reason that it competes more with major cities in other countries than with urban regions in Finland. The other regions that have most international contacts and the most developed network economies are Tampere, Turku and Oulu.'

National Policy Responses to Urban Issues, Challenges and Development

Vision

As pointed out earlier, Finland does not yet have a national urban policy ratified by the government. The working group for urban development which gave its report last year presented a vision for urban policy in the headline of its report: 'Cities as generators of growth'. The view of the group was that the future growth of Finland's national economy depends on the economic activity in cities, above all on the clustering of knowledge, know-how and innovations. For a sparsely populated country like Finland, cities have a particularly important role: prosperous cities spread prosperity and wellbeing widely into their surroundings.

The memorandum for an unofficial meeting of the government in November 1996 is to some extent contradictory with regard to the urbanization process in Finland. On one hand it states that Finland will gradually achieve the average EU degree of urbanization – around 80 per cent. At the same time it points out that Finland's strength today is its balanced regional structure. In practical terms this means a more rural structure than in the European Union on average. It remains to be seen whether the government's goal will be to maintain the present regional structure or to promote urbanization.

A Strong Tradition of Sectoral Policy

The foremost aim of Finnish postwar regional policy has been to achieve balanced regional development in the whole country. Considerable resources have been put in to maintaining the vigour of distant rural areas and keeping the whole country populated. The government has pursued a strong sectoral policy carried out by ministries. Although local self-governance is relatively strong in Finland, the government's sectoral legislation has been the dominant standard for how municipalities should implement their services concerning health care, social welfare and education. The system of government grants has levelled out the economic differences between richer and poorer municipalities. As an example, the significant reforms of public health care, education and children's day care during the 1970s were first carried out in distant parts of the country and only later in big cities in the south.

The financial crisis of the public sector in the 1990s has caused considerable cuts in government grants, and consequently, the sectoral policy of the government has been weakened, to some extent.

The effects of the so-called 'free municipality programme' carried out in Finland, according to Scandinavian models, have been somewhat similar. It gave those municipalities which took part in the experiment more independence and rights to deviate from the sectoral legislation. The programme is now over, but it had the consequence that the sectoral legislation was altered in a slightly more liberal direction.

In general terms it can be pointed out that the strong sectoral control by the government is still typical for Finnish local authority policy. This also applies to the so-called 'principle of universality', according to which all regions and municipalities of the country shall be treated according to the same principles and criteria. Under these conditions, there has been no fertile ground for the development of separate urban policy.

The Need for an Integrated Urban Policy has been Acknowledged

According to a memorandum of city policy presented to the national government on 13 November 1996, 'strong development in cities requires a determined and consistent attitude from the state. A commonly approved urban policy is needed – and the will to pursue it. We need a shift from separate sectoral policies to a more integrated policy'.

The memorandum contains a list of seven crucial measures:

1   increasing the cooperation between the government and the urban regions;
2   setting up research on cities;
3   strengthening knowledge and culture in the urban regions;
4   promoting employment in the urban regions;
5   improving and developing the urban structure within urban regions;
6   the economic basis for development initiated by the cities themselves;
7   the special position of the Helsinki Metropolitan Area.

In its unofficial meeting, the government noted the need for a new urban policy. Still, no decisions were made. Many steps and measures are only in their early stages. In the following, we shall see a few examples of new urban policy initiatives across the sectoral borders.

Cooperation

On 19 December 1996, the government appointed a working group for urban policy for the years 1997–99. As mentioned earlier, the task of the group is to increase the cooperation between the government, various ministries and cities. According to its stated assignment, the group is supposed, e.g.:

- to promote common practices, reforms, experiments and projects concerning cities; and
- to find a common view on urban policy for the preparation of documents and decisions in the field of regional and urban policy.

The aim of the Ministry of the Interior is to provide financial resources for the working group to be used for urban programmes, pilot projects and research. These funds would complement the Ministry's financing to cities and the financing of EU programmes.

By urban programmes is meant common development programmes of separate local authorities and other partners in an urban region. These programmes serve to combine the plans of various organizations for developing industry and commerce, population development, internationalization, arts and culture of the region. The idea is that the programme should consist of projects and cooperation agreements engaging all agents.

In the autumn of 1997, the working group on urban policy chose 13 urban programmes to be carried out during the next few years.

The Centres of Expertise Programme

Although the Centres of Expertise Programme has started in the name of regional policy reform, instead of urban policy, it can, nevertheless, be considered the most concrete measure of urban policy on the government's part.

The Centres of Expertise Programme was launched in 1994 by the Finnish Ministry of the Interior. Its objective is to improve the local conditions that enable the location and development of internationally competitive knowledge-intensive firms. At regional level, the most important organizations for cooperation are the universities, research institutions, private firms, regional authorities and cities. The programme aims at improving the building of networks between these parties.

The programme is an example of the change in regional policy in Finland in the 1990s. Earlier, the regional policy applied the ideology of local balance and supporting weaker areas. Conversely, the Centres of Expertise Programme aims at finding the strengths of each area and making the areas develop their assets.

In certain chosen fields of expertise, the programme assembles common projects – or 'centres of expertise' – involving universities, research institutes, centres of technology, private firms and local administration. The achievements of these centres may be, for example, innovations, new firms or the birth of new 'local economic motors'. Indirect effects would be the development of local networks, accumulation of know-how and the improvement of local practices of cooperation. The long-term aim is to give cities vitality and create new jobs.

Since 1994, 11 expertise centre programmes have been launched, involving the big cities of Helsinki (Uusimaa province), Tampere, Turku, Oulu, Jyväskylä and Kuopio. The Ministry of the Interior has granted a total of 15 million FIM per annum to these centres. The financing has been channelled through the regional councils. Thanks to this 'seed money', the centres of expertise have found additional finance from public and private sources, including the ESR-fund of EU. The total funding for the centres of expertise in 1996 was 450 million FIM.

According to a evaluation report by the Ministry of Interior concerning the Centres of Expertise Programme, the 11 centres have created their own applications of the generic model. Planning and actions have reflected regional characteristics. The programme's innovative nature has affected the outcome producing highly diverse action and results. At best, the programme can result in new, innovative practices.

Referring to the encouraging results of the Centres of Expertise Programme, the working group for urban policy proposed that additional funds should be granted to the programme.

Promoting Employment

The memorandum prepared for the above-mentioned unofficial meeting of the government on 13 November 1996 contained several suggestions for how to promote employment. These proposals can be divided into two groups, first, experiments for creating service jobs in cities, and second, improving the chances of providing employment in cities. One suggestion was that the Ministry of Labour would prepare a proposal for how to weight long-term employment in the local allocation of employment funds.

We may state that although the local accumulation of long-term unemployment in certain residential areas of big cities has been recognized as a problem, no cross-sectoral measures of urban policy have yet been defined to alleviate the problem – nor have financial resources been provided.

Improving Urban Structure

The memorandum on urban policy of 13 November 1996 points out that future construction and development in cities should use and complement existing urban structure with its municipal engineering and other infrastructure. City centres are developed, and buildings and constructions with historic or cultural value are protected and maintained. In order to safeguard consumer services and to limit the increasing problems caused by car traffic, the control of locating large super- and megamarkets will be improved.

In addition, the memorandum points out that the special problems of urban regions concerning land use planning and cooperation between municipalities are taken into account in the coming reform on planning and construction legislation. Incentives leading to a more scattered urban structure will be dismantled.

The special problems of several suburban residential areas constructed in the 1960s and 1970s in big cities have been noticed during the last years. Many of these areas suffer from high unemployment and social problems, as well as from problems concerning the condition and quality of housing, local environment and local services. There have been several projects by the Ministry of Environment and big cities in the field of improving suburban residential areas. In the future, funds of EU will be used for this kind of project also. The joint proposal of the cities of Helsinki and Vantaa, concerning the development of Myllypuro-Kontula area in Helsinki and Koivukylä-Havukoski area in Vantaa, was approved for the 'Urban program' of EU in 1996.

The Special Position of the Helsinki Region

According to the memorandum, the Helsinki region has a special position in Finland. There are special requirements, both national and international, for functional solutions within administration, planning and other cooperation. Thus the memorandum suggests that the Ministry of the Interior studies what special legislative or other administrative measures are needed for granting the functionality of the Helsinki region in the future.

Conclusions

In Finland, the urbanization process is still continuing. Growth is concentrated in the Helsinki region and the other large university cities. According to a report by the United Nations, Helsinki will be the fastest growing major city in the European Union in the late 1990s.

Local authorities enjoy considerable autonomy in Finland, and the economic significance of the municipal sector is great compared with many other EU countries. Almost two-thirds of public expenditure is municipal. The economic autonomy is based on local (= municipal) income tax, which is on average 17.5 per cent of citizens' income.

The 1990s have seen a drastic weakening of the formerly strong economy of big cities. In the recession years of 1991–93, municipal tax revenue fell decisively, and cities had to take on debt. Today, tax revenues are back at 1990 level, but in the meantime government grants have been cut. The big cities are, however, no longer in economic crisis.

The government's attitude towards the present wave of post-urbanization is prudent, but it has not started reviving the traditional Finnish policy of trying to restrict growth in big urban centres. Instead, it has started preparing a new kind of urban policy.

In a report on urban policy (1996), the Ministry of the Interior has stated that the country's regional structure is balanced and that no larger environmental problems have occurred, the worst problem being the severe unemployment. Unemployment was very marginal in big Finnish cities up to the 1990s, but then reached 20 per cent. Today, long-term unemployment, in particular, has clustered in big cities. The extent of present unemployment and the simultaneous rapid population growth gives rise to fears that social marginalization and local segregation will become a problem in big cities. Another threat clearly seen is the growing difference between cities in terms of economic development.

The most important task of urban policy is felt to be the strengthening of the economic growth potential in cities. This thought is expressed in the title of a report of a governmental working group for urban development, 'Cities as generators of growth'. According to the view expressed in the report, knowledge and innovation are the motors which generate new business enterprise and maintain the success of existing companies. 'The conditions for innovation are particularly favourable in the big cities. Favourable economic growth in these cities has widespread regional effects.'

So far, the Finnish national government has not launched an official urban policy. But on the basis of the report just mentioned, the government did have an unofficial discussion on urban policy in November 1996. In December, it appointed a working group for urban policy, with representatives of several ministries, certain cities and a number of urban researchers. The task of the group is to observe and evaluate the development of city regions, to define the contents of the state's urban policy and make suggestions about it in cooperation with the working group on rural policy. The group has also decided to support nationwide, regional and local intersectoral urban development programmes. This programme is based on the idea that measures taken by the cities themselves lead to a better result than measures directed by the government.

The most significant project of urban policy, from the big cities' point of view, is the current programme for centres of expertise, which the Ministry of the Interior launched in 1994. There are 11 expertise centre projects under way, e.g., in the regions of Helsinki, Tampere, Turku, Oulu, Jyväskylä and Kuopio. The objective of these programmes is to improve the local conditions enabling the location and development of internationally competitive knowledge-intensive business enterprise. At city level the most important cooperation organizations are universities, research institutes, private firms, regional authorities and cities. The projects have been funded by ESR.

None of Finland's big cities enjoy EU Regional Development Fund, with the exception of Lahti and Pori, which are included in the Target 2 programme of the structural funds. One city in Finland – Joensuu – has, so far, been granted community development funding from the URBAN-initiative. Finland's national government has proposed that a similar Urban-programme be launched in the cities of Helsinki and Vantaa.

Urban policy has become a matter of discussion only during the last few years in Finland. It has been noticed that local activity and a state sectorial policy are no longer powerful enough to solve the new urban problems and keep new threats at bay. New cooperation across the sectorial boundaries of the ministries and the borders of the urban regions are needed. The task of the government in this context is to create a framework for it.

References

Ahlbaek, Erik, Rose, Lawrence, Strömberg, Lars and Ståhlberg, Krister (1996), *Nordic Local Government, Developmental Trends and Reform Activities in the Postwar Period*, Helsinki: The Association of Finnish Local Authorities.

Helin, Heikki (1996), *Kaupunkinen talous 1990–1994: Lama koetteli keskuksia muita enemmän* [The finances of the cities 1990–1994], Sisämininisteriö, Kaupunkien kehittämistyöryhmän julkaisu IV [The Ministry of Interior].

Kattelus, Kaija (1996), 'Helsinki – a city of work and unemployment', *Quarterly from the City of Helsinki Information Management Centre*, Kvartti 3B.

96   *National Urban Policies in the European Union*

Kaupungit kasvun luojina (1996) *Kaupunkipolitiikan kehittämisryhmän loppuraportti* [*Cities as generators of growth. The final report of the working group on urban policy*], Sisäministeriö, Kaupunkien kehittämistyöryhmän julkaisu VI [The Ministry of Interior].

Kolbe, Laura (1994), 'Helsingin pääkaupunkiasema 1809–1990 ja kaupunki-identiteetin kehittyminen [Helsinki's position as a capital 1809–1990, and the development of an urban identity]' in *Kaupunki käännekohdassa* [City at turning point], Helsingin kaupungin tietokeskus [Helsinki City Urban Facts].

Laakso, Seppo (1996) *Helsingfors folkmängd ökar – hot eller framtidshopp* [The growth of population – chance or threat for Helsinki?], Kvartalspublikation från Helsingfors stads factacentral 4.

Lehto, Elina (1997), *Näkökohtia kaupunkipolitiikasta* [Aspects of urban policy], Helsingin kaupungin tietokeskuksen Muistioita [Helsinki City Urban Facts, Memorandum], 3.

Pikkarainen, Mika (1996), *Kaupunkiseutujen kasvu ja kilpailukyky* [*Growth and competitiveness of the city regions*], Sisäministeriö, Kaupunkien kehittämistyöryhmän julkaisu VII [The Ministry of Interior].

Söderström, Lars (1996), *Local Public Finance in Europe: The Case of Finland*, University of Gothenburg: Institute for Economic Studies.

United Nations (1995), *World Urbanization Prospects*.

Uusikallio, Irma (1997), 'National overview on distressed urban areas in Finland', *The Finnish Environment 85*, Ministry of the Environment.

Valtioneuvoston iltakouluun 13 Marraskuuta 1996 tehty muistio kaupunkien kehittämisen jatkotoimista, Sisäasiainministeriö 11 Marraskuuta 1996 [Memorandum concerning further measures for the development of cities, prepared for the unofficial session of the Finnish government on 13 November 1996, Ministry of the Interior 11 November].

6 France

ALAIN SALLEZ[1]

Introduction

In France more than 80 per cent of the population lives in cities or suburbs, a figure which is not significantly different from other northern European countries. At least 12 French cities have populations in excess of 500,000.

Although France has lagged behind other industrialized countries with regard to urbanization, strides have been made since World War II, and development has proceeded in both urban centres and peripheral areas. The rural population exceeded the urban one throughout the 19th century. A state of equilibrium was reached in 1928, when there were as many people in rural areas as in the cities. As a comparison with other European countries, rural populations outnumbered urban residents in 1850 in Great Britain, in 1875 in the Netherlands and in 1890 in Germany (Braudel, 1986).

In the following pages we will identify cities which are recognized as 'agglomerations' in the statistical sense of the word. There were 29 agglomerations (see insert) of over 200,000 inhabitants in France in 1990, as compared with 14 in 1954.

Cities and 'urban areas' (*aires urbaines*): a new statistical approach
Urban development patterns in France after the second world war made it necessary to redefine areas in order to draw up better adapted statistical measures. 'Agglomerations' were defined as communities of over 2,000 living units based on urban continuity (that is, no more than 200 metres between buildings), thus differentiating rural and urban areas.

Nevertheless, recent changes make it increasingly difficult to define town limits using the old characteristics of 'agglomerations'. That is why the state's Institute of Statistics (INSEE, Institut National des Statistiques et des Études Économiques) has recently proposed a new entity, called 'urban area'. Urban areas which receive over 5,000 people coming to work within their geographical region are considered as an 'urban pole'.

Cities sending more than 40 per cent of their work force to this urban pole compose the 'suburban ring'. The combination of the urban pole and suburban ring together comprise the 'urban area'.

This definition seems better adapted to French urban development patterns of the '80s and '90s. In fact, according to this definition, urban areas are better able to compete with their European neighbours by their size, economic power and the relationships between urban poles and their suburbs.

Despite this progress, France has not yet succeeded in fully compensating for what can be called the 'French anomaly'. Its capital is the largest core city in Europe, and Greater Paris, with its 9.3 million inhabitants, is larger than Greater London. Moreover, Lyon, the second largest French city, ranks 24th in the European classification of cities with over one million inhabitants. The differential between Paris and the other French cities is unique in Europe.

In contrast, the number of small and middle-sized cities in France exceeds the European average. This might constitute a strength which is balanced by the dearth of large cities. Nevertheless there is a significant problem, because the lack of other large cities slows balanced development, as will be further discussed below.

This major distortion has forced the French government to sustain cities since the end of World War II, in order to balance the spatial and economic development of its regions, as opposed to the Paris area (Ile de France). The administrative and financial links between the national authorities and French cities is the subject of our second section.

Two recent periods appear of major importance in urban development. On the one hand, the oil crisis of 1974 and subsequent progress in technology have brought on social, spatial and economic change, both at local and international levels. On the other hand, a decentralization process was engaged by the government in 1982–83 *(Loi de décentralisation*, 2 March 1982). As a consequence of these changes, cities face new challenges and issues, to which old solutions are no longer pertinent. The national opinion on these questions is developed in our third section.

As a consequence of new challenges, which local governments alone cannot easily take up, the French government has followed a number of old policies or adopted new ones. The last section is a description of the most important government actions in favour of French towns.

National Spatial Development Pattern

63 per cent of French people live in communities of over 10,000 inhabitants (72 per cent for Europe as a whole) (Pumain et al., 1996) and 76 per cent in urban areas, but French urban development patterns vary throughout the country. There are many cities near northern borders and in the east of the country. In the South of France, around the Mediterranean Sea and on the border of the Rhone River, the situation is similar, but the other regions suffer from a lack of sufficient urban density, a situation which implies economic

handicaps and threats to spatial development. As a rule, we can observe that French cities mostly stand along rivers and coasts.

Moreover, the last census in 1990 revealed that large French cities have shown an increase in population since 1982. This trend is comparable to that of 1975–82, except that core cities have stopped their decline (loss of population during the '70s) and that the rapid rate of growth in urbanization has slowed slightly. Each year since 1982, the urban population has risen by 0.39 per cent. In the 29 agglomerations of more than 200,000 inhabitants, this figure reaches 0.5 per cent.

However, traditional French centralization of political power, which has existed since the 13th century, and which increased with the royal absolutism of the 17th century and republican supervision after the French Revolution, explains why urban hierarchy is atypical. Paris is overdeveloped compared with other French cities. The influence of large provincial cities on political and economic life is not very significant. As a consequence, the high number of middle-sized cities really does not close the gap.

The French Urban Hierarchy

There are four types of cities in France:

- the capital;
- developing urban areas (with important differences between the first three cities and the others);
- large provincial cities with administrative functions, which are often overdeveloped compared to their economic power; as a consequence, their international influence is relatively weak;
- small and middle-sized towns, which offer services to rural areas but which depend on other large towns for major urban functions (economy, universities, research and development, health care).

Size of urban units (agglomerations) The more services a town offers, the better the level it reaches in the urban hierarchy. This is why the following classification depends on the level of services more than on the number of inhabitants.

At the top of the pyramid stands Paris, far ahead of the second agglomeration. Lyon is seven times smaller than the French capital, and Bordeaux, the fifth agglomeration in France, is 13 times smaller than Paris. This ratio is an exception in the European Union; no other European capital

Map 6.1   Main French cities

matches the power of Paris over the country's other large cities.

The Parisian region concentrates national and international political functions, and strategic ones in finance, management, marketing and so forth. Nearly 60 per cent of French executives work in the Greater Paris area. Two high-level civil servants out of five work in the capital; senior civil servants and executives from private companies are 12 times less numerous in Lyon than in Paris.

Paris has over three-quarters of the headquarters of the 500 largest companies in France (Noin, 1990), including 92 companies of the hundred most important ones.

More significant is Paris's financial power. Over 91 per cent of financial decisions (Noin, 1990) and stock exchange transactions are made in Paris, which is really an exception. Lyon only accounts for 0.65 per cent of that power.

One student out of three lives in the Greater Paris area, along with three researchers out of five, due to state subsidies to strategic research and development programmes. Nevertheless, the situation is changing thanks to government plans (Universités 2000) for the further development of universities and research and development throughout France.

Generally speaking, the share of the Paris region is still prevailing for strategic functions since they represent 20 per cent of French industrial employment, 58 per cent for research, 46 per cent for finance, 39 per cent for services and 74 per cent of alumni of ENA (École Nationale d'Administration), the elite of civil servants.

In order to cope with its future, Paris region has been reorganized according to the 1965 Regional Master Plan of Paul Delouvrier. This project was completely implemented and resulted in five new towns, which are home to half of the increase in the regional population, and the new business district of La Défense. Also as a result of the plan, Greater Paris has three major ring highways, a rapid transit system (RER) and the country's busiest airport, Roissy-Charles de Gaulle.

The second level includes eight cities with over 500,000 inhabitants but this figure has to be compared with more than 15 similar towns in Great Britain and Italy, and over 20 in Germany. These towns exert a significant influence over a wide area; this is why they are called 'regional metropolises'. They have enough amenities to prevent their inhabitants from going to Paris. They have administrative offices, an academic tradition and a cultural history.

But they are often too weak, from an international point of view, to compete successfully with other large European cities (Bonneville et al., 1992).

Nevertheless, despite their lack of demographic weight and economic power, some French cities are internationally well known for their specific vocation, as is the case of Toulouse with its aerospace industry and Clermont-Ferrand with Michelin.

In fact, these metropolises have grown because of their geographical location: they all stand on the coast, the border, or a European crossroads, and are far from Paris. Such a situation has enabled the development of exchanges and commerce over the centuries, without significant supervision from the capital. Within this group, some cities have depended on other countries for centuries (Lille, Strasbourg, Grenoble, Nice, etc.).

Among this category of cities are Lyon, Marseilles and Lille on the one hand, and Bordeaux, Toulouse, Nantes and Strasbourg on the other. Metz – Nancy, Grenoble and Nice also belong to this group, even though they are slightly less well equipped.

Lyon, Marseilles and Lille have to be differentiated within this group. Although they are the second and third cities in France, Lyon is the 24th largest city in Europe, and Marseilles the 28th. Nevertheless, they undoubtedly have an economic influence out of proportion to the size of their populations. The difference between the Parisian population and that of these three metropolises has been decreasing for the past 70 years. They offer specific services, especially to companies (banks, insurance, French Grandes Ecoles and universities, headquarters, consulting firms, etc.), which other cities lack.

In fact, this group of cities is the one benefiting from a specific policy of the '60s, called 'métropoles d'équilibre', implemented by the French government. It consisted in making them second capitals in order to offset the pre-eminence of Paris. They had already reached the rank of regional capitals in the '70s (see Map 6.1 for the eight *'métropoles d'équilibre'*).

The third level of cities is comprised of ten regional centres: Grenoble leads the group which includes Rennes, Nice, Clermont-Ferrand, Rouen, Dijon, Montpellier, Saint-Etienne, Caen and Limoges. They are less well-equipped than the previous group but offer many services for firms and households. They all have regional or departmental administrations. Rouen and Le Havre appear as an exception: even though they are large cities, they may be considered as an extension of the Greater Paris area, since they are the natural gates to the French capital, on the Seine River. Therefore they figured in the Delouvrier plan of 1965 for the Paris region ('Schéma directeur d'aménagement et d'urbanisme de la région parisienne') and in the Lower-Seine master plan of 1967.

In this group stands a multitude of small and mid-sized towns. They include

Table 6.1 Development of large metropolitan areas

	Conurbations	Population in (1990) (in thousands)	Annual growth rate 1975–82	Annual growth rate 1982–90	Unemployment rate 1990
1	Paris	9,318	0.1	0.5	8.7
2	Lyon – Saint-Etienne	1,575	-0.1	0.3	10.1
3	Bordeaux	697	0.4	0.9	12.8
4	Toulouse	650	0.5	1.6	11.4
5	Marseilles – Aix en Provence – Vitrolles	1,231	0.3	-0.2	17
6	Lille – Roubaix – Tourcoing	959	0	0.2	13.7
7	Nice – Grasse – Cannes – Antibes	853.1	1.2	1.2	12.1

Table 6.2 Development of the six largest regional 'capitals'

Agglomeration	Population in 1990 (in thousands)	Annual growth rate 1975–82	Annual growth rate 1982–90	Unemployment rate (1990)
Nantes	496.1	0.4	0.7	11.9
Toulon	437.8	1.2	0.8	16.8
Grenoble	404.8	0.2	0.3	9.9
Strasbourg	388.5	0.3	0.5	9.7
Rouen	380.2	-0.3	0	13.9
Nancy	329.4	0.1	0.1	10.5

old industrialized towns in Lorraine or in Northern France and departmental administrative centres distributed all over the French territory, in the hinterland of the regional metropolis. This group is far from being homogeneous: each town offers different kinds of services but generally suffers from the lack of others.

Despite the predominance of Paris and the number of small and mid-sized towns, we observe that city distribution does not fit with the size/rank law (Moriconi-Ebrard, 1993) or with Christaller's urban distribution. In Table 6.4 we can observe that there is a relationship between the groups that cities belong to and their populations.

Table 6.3   **Development of nine cities with populations of between 200,000 and 300,000**

Agglomeration	Population in 1990 (in thousands)	Annual growth rate 1975–82	Annual growth rate 1982–90	Unemployment rate (1990)
Montpellier	284.4	0.8	1.1	15.6
Tours	282.2	0.7	0.5	11.0
Orleans	243.1	0.8	1.2	9.4
Rennes	244.9	0.3	0.6	9.8
Dijon	230.5	0.1	0.6	10.3
Mulhouse	208.2	0.5	0.7	12.9
Angers	206.5	0.2	0.4	13.0
Metz	193.1	0.3	0.4	12.4

Table 6.4   **Ranking of cities in France according to their size**

Size	Rank	Average population (1990)
Capital	1	9,300,000
Regional metropolis	3	973,000
Regional capital	9	362,000
Departmental capital	24	177,000
Middle-sized town	54	78,000
Small town	158	25,000

Cities and Urban Development in France

National urban and regional planning ('aménagement du territoire') policies in the '50s aimed at balancing urban development by favouring the growth of cities, except that of Paris, whose growth had to be limited. Nevertheless, the Greater Paris population also grew as much as the total of the 26 next largest French agglomerations. As a consequence, the capital still produces 27 per cent of the GDP and is home to 16.5 per cent of the French population. Prospective studies revealed at the beginning of the '90s that the Parisian population would grow to approximately 13 million people by 2015.

In fact, Paris draws an abundance of young people, who come to study and then continue living in Greater Paris, because they can find better jobs more easily than in the other regions.

Between 1982 and 1990, the capital attracted twice as large a labour force as between 1975 and 1982. During the same period, emigration was halved.

Moreover, the population inside Paris's administrative limits has decreased. People settling in the area recently have preferred Paris's neighbouring cities and the suburbs.

Most larger metropolitan centres have lost population too. In contrast, Greater Lyon and Greater Lille have acquired population, which is not the case for Marseilles, caught in a downward trend. Marseilles's centre suffers from an illness similar to North America's large cities, that is, pauperization, violence, unemployment, building decay and so forth. That is why specific help has come from the government (see GPU, q.v.) in the form of a public body (Etablissement Public d'Aménagement, EPA) set up in 1995, in order to improve its centre's quality economically and socially. This EPA is called Euromediterranée.

In the case of Lille, the development of modern infrastructures, especially the TGV which joins the city to Paris, London and Brussels, and of an ambitious economic policy will foster city growth after the difficult period of the '70s and the '80s.

In fact, large cities in France have to fulfil several conditions if they intend to increase their population. European and national studies have shown that the number of engineers and executives employed by firms is of the utmost importance. Second, cities have to be located on major highways or main railroads, and preferably on infrastructure networks. Moreover, their success is correlated with an interest in scientific and financial exchanges, a high level of services, research or professional training, a good quality of life including services to households, environmental protection and policies to renovate slum districts. The cities meeting these conditions have shown rapid growth of population and employment since the beginning of the '80s. The others, such as old industrial towns or many commercial ports, have clearly declined. In fact, the economy of these cities often relies on overspecialization in declining industries. This is the case of many towns in north and northeast France like Valenciennes,[2] Lens-Liévin, Béthune or Douai, the economies of which relied mostly on coal mining. As for ports, they suffer from inadequate nautical conditions and mostly from the competition of Rotterdam and Anvers. Only those having a mix of industrial, tertiary and commercial activities like Nantes and Bordeaux have known healthy dynamics.

Consequently, the gap between dynamically developing towns such as Bordeaux, Toulouse, Montpellier, Orleans, Rennes, Tours, Angers or Reims, and the network of old industrialized cities, which suffer from a lack of services and executives, is growing, which could menace the balance of the French territory.

Table 6.5   The decline of specialized cities

Agglomeration	Population in 1990 (in thousands)	Annual growth rate 1975–82	Annual growth rate 1982–90	Unemployment rate (1990)
Valenciennes	338.5	-0.5	-0.5	20.4
Lens-Liévin	323.2	-0.2	-0.2	18.5
Saint-Etienne	313.5	-0.8	-0.2	13.8
Béthune	261.6	-0.3	0.1	15.2
Clermont-Ferrand	254.5	0.2	-0.1	11.2
Douai	199.6	-0.6	-0.2	18.9

Table 6.6   Stagnation of ports with populations between 100,000 and 350,000

Agglomeration	Population in 1990 (in thousands)	Annual growth rate 1975–82	Annual growth rate 1982–90	Unemployment rate (1990)
Le Havre	253.7	-0.5	0	15.8
Brest	201.4	-0.1	0	13.7
Dunkerque	190.9	0.7	-0.2	17.4
Saint-Nazaire	130.4	0.4	0.1	15.9
Lorient	115.5	0.1	0.5	16.5
Calais	101.8	0.1	0.1	18.1
La Rochelle	100.3	0.1	-0.2	16.6

Table 6.7   Annual growth rate of the French population according to type of community

Type of communes\period	1962–68	1968–75	1975–82	1982–90
Core cities	1.29	0.58	-0.06	0.12
Suburbs	2.66	2.09	0.93	0.86
Rural communes at city peripheries	-0.27	0.12	1.19	0.95
Traditional rural communes	-1.35	-1.64	-1.05	-0.52
Metropolitan France	1.15	0.81	0.46	0.51

Source: INSEE.

French towns in crisis have unemployment rates higher than the national average. In 1990 the level reached 13.5 per cent in cities between 100,000 and 200,000 inhabitants and from 12 to 13 per cent in smaller cities and has probably worsened by about two points on average since then. Between 1982 and 1990 nearly 92,000 inhabitants of those cities changed residence in order to live in Greater Paris.

The economic crisis has had more significant effects on the suburbs of large towns. Unemployment, drugs and Mafia organizations are not only North American symptoms; they affect French suburbs as well. The middle class has abandoned large housing complexes and expensive city centres in favour of residential suburbs. Indeed, many wealthy people prefer individual homes to city dwellings. The lower tax level outside cities also attracts companies. Thus the outskirts of large cities enjoy the fastest growth.

Administrative and Financial Framework

The excessive number of French communities, added to their relatively limited size, is due to the historical organization of the civil service. The French situation is exceptional: with 36,664 'communes' (the smallest territorial divisions), France has as many local councils as the rest of the European Union countries put together, before the last enlargement. This dispersion of power appears as a handicap in the perspective of border opening. However, despite the French attachment to small communities, cooperation between local councils has existed since the end of the 19th century.

French State centralization is less significant than before. Nevertheless, the law of 2 March 1982 did not abolish all administrative and financial frameworks for local communities; at the commune level, financial dependence still exists.

Local Administrative Hierarchy in France

There are four administrative levels in France. At the top of the pyramid, the French state still stands very powerful. The more powerful a local community, the older it is. 'Communes' correspond to the parishes of the old regime, before 1789. They may have anywhere from ten people to several million inhabitants. There are over 2.2 million Parisians. There are 25,000 communes with fewer than 700 inhabitants, while half of the French population lives in communities with more than 10,000 inhabitants.

Table 6.8   Distribution of population in French communities

Size (inhabitants)	Number of communes	Proportion	Population	Proportion
< 700	25,249	69.00%	6,897,540	12%
700–2,000	6,908	19.00%	7,933,928	14%
2,000–5,000	2,655	7.00%	8,062,265	14%
5,000–10,000	898	2.46%	6,168,826	11%
10,000–20,000	445	1.22%	6,231,927	11%
20,000–50,000	293	0.80%	9,087,761	16%
50,000–100,000	67	0.18%	4,443,077	8%
100,000–300,000	31	0.08%	4,742,423	8%
>300 000	5	0.01%	4,116,977	7%
<10,000	35,710	97.70%	29,062,559	50.38%
>10,000	841	2.30%	28,622,165	49.62%

Source: DGCL.

Created in 1789 along the lines of an idea of the geographer R. de Hesseln, departments were substituted for former royal provinces. The main idea of the department was that inhabitants could go back and forth to the main administrative city (*chef-lieu*) of the department within a day on horseback. Notwithstanding technical progress, the number of departments has not changed and has remained steady to date, except for the Paris region, which was subdivided into eight departments in 1964. Each department raises a portion of its own financial resources.

Regions are the most recent local entities. They were first created in 1972, as a new administrative level between the state and the departments, but without financial power. Since 1982 the regions have been referred to as *collectivités territoriales*. They are administered by an elected president and an assembly, whose role continues to expand as regards economic development. Regions are made up of several departments and nearly correspond to the former royal provinces.

There are 22 regions, 95 departments and 36,664 communes in France. Nevertheless, each local community received new responsibilities after passage of the law of 2 March 1982. Regions were given financial responsibility and draw up their own budgets. Our study will deal with communes' responsibilities only.

Communes are managed by a council led by a mayor. Councils are elected by local populations every six years and are composed of between nine and 69 councillors, depending on the commune's size. Election modes change between communes with less than 6,500 inhabitants and the larger ones. Councils are in charge of the local administration (registry office especially), police and municipal budget management. They vote on all deliberations concerning the commune's responsibilities and powers (bylaws, city planning, etc.). They can hire or dismiss municipal employees. The most significant power is the financial one, that is, to vote the yearly budget and supervise its management.

The local council elects the mayor among council members. The mayor is concurrently the commune's representative and the state's at the lowest administrative level. S/he is subject to a higher authority, the prefect.

As the state's representatives, mayors are in charge of the publication and application of laws, the organization of elections, the carrying out of the census and other administrative acts, the implementation of general safety measures. They have to see to registries (marriages, births, deaths, etc.). They are judiciary police officers, that is, they are allowed to note penal infractions and draw up charges.

As the commune's representatives, they are the chiefs of staff. They have specific powers in town planning and are the local police authority.

Since the law of 2 March 1982, communes have received new responsibilities, as prescribed in the 7 January 1983 and 22 January 1983 laws. They are described in Chart 6.1.

Inter-communcal Cooperation

Faced the over abundance of communes, the French legislator has regularly passed various laws to encourage inter-communal cooperation.

By 1997, nearly 19,000 inter-communal public cooperation bodies (Etablissement Public de Cooperation Intercommunale, EPCI) had already been created. Each commune belongs to at least one of these institutions, and to five on average (*Inter-Régions*, August–September 1996, No. 201, p. 24). Such institutions are not a fourth level of local administration but only a way of making the management of some services (water, waste management, etc.) more coherent, and if possible, a way of creating some financial solidarity between communes.

These institutions (EPCI) receive powers delegated by communes, which decide on the financial resources (fiscal contributions or subscriptions) to be

Chart 6.1   The responsibilities and powers of communes

Area	Responsibilities and powers
Town planning (since 1983–84)	Local councils vote legal measures concerning the way municipal territory can be occupied (building size, architectural styles, reserved or protected areas, etc.). Such documents may concern several communities, in which case a common document is drawn up. Mayors allow people to occupy the territory according to these documents (licences to build, etc.).
Social action and health (since 1984)	A local social department draws up records about aid requests and analyses the social needs of the population. Because of specific financial contributions, communes may take on certain department responsibilities.
Professional training (since 1983)	Communes establish training plans.
Education (since 1986)	They create, build, equip and maintain nurseries and primary schools.
Economic development (since 1983)	Communes draw up charters for economic development and planning with other communities.
Regional planning and environment (since 1983–84)	They can optionally adopt programmes to develop rural areas. They propose or accept the creation of architectural and urban heritage protection areas. They agree to the creation of nature reserves.
Lakes and harbours (since 1984)	Communes are in charge of the creation and operation of leisure harbours.
Lodging (since 1983–84)	Communes define local housing programmes.
Transportation (since 1984)	They are in charge of financing and planning urban and school transportation.
Cultural activities (since 1986)	Creation and management of local libraries and museums. Local archive conservation.
Inter-community cooperation (since 1992)	Communes can cooperate with foreign communities within the limitations of their powers.

allocated. Together they spend nearly 80 billion francs, (compared with an additional 320 billion francs spent by the 36,664 communes) (*Les Cahiers du CNFPT*, No. 42, Patrick Labia, p 111). Investments represent 60 per cent of this spending.

There are three types of EPCI:

- specialized syndicates;
- institutions with self-financing systems, including all types of communes;
- institutions with self-financing systems for urban communes.

One commune out of four belongs to an EPCI with a self-financing system: more than 22 million inhabitants are concerned by these bodies.

Specialized syndicates are the oldest type of EPCI, amalgamating communes in order to manage one (Syndicat à Vocation Unique, SIVU) or several (Syndicats à Vocations Multiples, SIVOM) services of common interest (water management and recycling, waste collection, etc.). They were created by the 22 March 1890 law for the first type and in 1959 for the second. Syndicates are financed by contributions from communes.

Two types of EPCI have self-financing systems and concern urban communes as well as rural ones: they are called 'districts' (*district*) and 'communes' communities' (*communauté de communes*).

The first ones were created by the regulation of 5 January 1959 for urban communes and extended to all communes in 1970. Housing and fire brigades must be managed. These EPCI automatically replace older specialized syndicates and have had self-financing systems since 1990.

The second ones were created by the 6 February 1992 law concerning territorial administration (Loi pour l'Administration Territoriale de la République, ATR) aimed at drawing up a common project for a set of communes. Moreover, EPCI administrators have to choose at least one responsibility among the following: environmental protection, housing, quality of life, administration of public thoroughfares, cultural and sports equipment. They are allowed to receive the local companies' taxes (*taxe professionnelle*)[3] if two representatives out of three vote in favour of a fiscal transfer.

The last type of EPCI with a self-financing system concerns 'urban communities' (*communautés urbaines*), 'communities of cities' (*communautés de villes*) and 'new town syndicates' (*syndicats d'agglomerations nouvelles*): only urban communes can join such organizations.

Communities of cities are quite similar to the communes' communities. They have the same powers and responsibilities but they receive the companies' taxes de jure, their only fiscal resource.

Urban communities were set up in 1966 to make the development of large cities more coherent. They concern agglomerations with over 20,000 inhabitants (50,000 until the 6 February 1992 law). Such communities enjoy extended responsibilities for spatial planning, economic development, public facilities, public services management. They have a self-financing system based on four direct local taxes: the council of the community votes tax rates, land taxes on buildings and free properties ('taxes sur le foncier bâti et non bâti'), inhabited house duty (*taxe d'habitation*) and companies' tax (*taxe professionnelle*).

New towns were created by the 10 July 1970 law better to balance urban growth in metropolitan areas, especially the Paris region. New town syndicates and development corporations (*etablissement public d'aménagement*) were in charge of town planning, investments, housing, transportation, various networks and economic development. They benefit from specific subsidies allocated by the state.

Chart 6.2 gives figures for each type of EPCI.

Chart 6.2   Types and evolution of the EPCI

Type of EPCI (with date of creation)	1972	1980	1988	1993	1995	1996
SIVU -(1890)	9,289	11,664	12,907	14,584	14,551	14,551
SIVOM (1959)	1,243	1,980	2,287	2,362	2,106	2,106
Districts (1959)	95	147	165	289	322	318
Communauté urbaine (1996)	8	9	9	9	9	10
Syndicat d'agglomération nouvelle			9	9	9	9
Communautés de communes (1992)				554	756	894
Communautés de villes (1992)				4	4	4

Source: Perben's Report, 1996.

Financial Framework: State Aids to Communes

Each commune in France receives endowments from the state. There are four types of endowments: one for current expenses ('dotation globale de fonctionnement', DGF), another for investments (*dotation globale d'équipement*, DGE), another resulting from state decentralization ('dotation globale de décentralisation', DGD), the lastly for urban solidarity ('dotation de solidarité urbaine', DSU).

DGF was created in 1979, and was modified by the laws of 29 November 1985 and 1 December 1993. Every commune receives the DGF, which aims to help cover current expenses (wages, building maintenance, debt interests, office supplies). DGF is indexed to the value added tax, and its level depends on various criteria: the size of the commune, levels of local taxes and specific data such as the number of pupils and subsidized lodgings. Communes may receive more if they are small and poor, if they are a tourist centre, if they are under population pressure or if they receive less in tax resources than the average commune of the same size. According to the 1996 budget, the state distributed 100 billion francs under DGF provisions.

DGE was created in 1982 and modified in 1995 in favour of communes with over 2,000 inhabitants since the 20 December 1985 law. It is financed by the state, the region and the department. In communes under 5,000 inhabitants, subsidies from the department are the major source of funding. State contributions prevail for communes with over 10,000 people.

The DGE amount depends on the size of the population, the size of the road system, the number of pupils, housing construction, and on the 'fiscal potential'[4] of communities with over 2,000 inhabitants. The DGE is increased by ten per cent if it concerns an EPCI or if the community is poor. DGE is based on physical and financial criteria only.

The state has distributed 47 billion francs under the DGE.

DGD was considered a counterpart to the 2 March 1982 law, delegating state powers and responsibilities to the local communities. It allows communes to finance expenses in accordance to their new responsibilities: town planning, communal libraries, primary school maintenance and school buses. The communes received 19 billion francs from the state in 1996 under DGD.

DSU is a way for the state better to balance the resources of each commune: the state acts as intermediary and collects money from rich communes in order to help poorer ones. The conditions to be met in order to receive this aid are either that the ratio 'number of subsidized lodgings/population' has to exceed 10 per cent for a population over 10,000 or there must be 1,100 subsidized lodgings on communal territory. Communes receiving more taxes than the average for their size finance the DSU in favour of communities less well off. The DSU represented two billion francs in 1996.

Urban Issues and Challenges from the National Perspective

The Economic Development of Large Cities in Light of European Competition

The economic, financial and political position of Paris is clearly predominant, as has been shown in the first section. As we have said, Paris concentrates over 90 per cent of the financial power, compared to less than one per cent of strategic financial decisions made in Lyon, the second city in France. In fact, large French cities still have not reached strategic positions, since the range of services they offer is incomplete (certain service sector companies, international headquarters, etc.). As a consequence, large towns are not as competitive as other major neighbouring cities in Europe.

The French government has been aware of this situation for a long time.

In 1963, for instance, the Department for Planning and Regional Action (Délégation à l'Aménagement du Territoire, DATAR), newly created by de Gaulle, decided to promote eight urban areas as second capitals. All these towns were situated at the periphery of France; some of them included two or three satellite towns, i.e. Lille – Roubaix – Tourcoing, Nancy – Metz, Strasbourg, Lyon – Saint-Etienne – Grenoble, Marseille – Aix – Berre, Toulouse, Nantes – Saint-Nazaire.

These towns benefited from special policies in the fields of rapid transportation (highways, TGV, etc.), regional planning (Organisme Régional d'Études d'Aires Métropolitaines, OREAM) and grants ('primes à l'aménagement du territoire') for the implementation of services. The Paris region itself was reorganized with a rapid transit system and powerful new towns as a consequence of the Regional Master Plan for the Paris region (1965). The city centre of Paris, completed by the company headquarters district of La Défense, was favoured by urban policies in order to confirm Paris as the first or second business, financial and cultural centre in Europe.

The 'second capitals' (*métropoles d'équilibre*) policy had been implemented by OREAM, which was in charge of developing regional master plans. As part of these master plans, the new towns were developed by development corporations (*etablissements publics d'aménagement*), financed by the state at the outset, and headed by boards of directors composed of civil servants and elected representatives. The directors were generally civil servants from the 'Ponts et Chaussées' corps and the president was a locally elected representative.

In order to reinforce the industrial structure of these towns, the DATAR negotiated the settlement of great consortia in the provinces. Consequently, some regions have specialized since the end of the '60s: iron and steel industry in Fos near Marseilles, shipbuilding in Nantes – Saint-Nazaire, telecommunications in Brittany. Lyon was promoted for international business, Marseilles as the Mediterranean's largest port, Toulouse as a major worldwide centre for aerospace and aeronautics.

Recent studies conducted by DATAR have shown that a town is better able to profit from economic development if it belongs to a region with a dynamic metropolis. For instance, the unemployment rate in the latter and that for cities far from any dynamic metropolis varies from seven per cent to 20 per cent per cent (DATAR, 1996, p. 53). That is why the development of large French cities is crucial throughout France and stands as a government priority. It cannot rely only on the results of the policy of the '60s in favour of large towns.

Urban Development and Social Issues

Position of European cities Lack of housing after World War II forced the French government to undertake massive building projects in order to develop subsidized apartments, especially in the suburbs of large cities. In such an emergency, little attention was paid to what the so-called *grands ensembles* would become. These tower blocks and low-income housing flats received lots of inhabitants, who were attracted to a new level of comfort (bathrooms, WC, etc.). People often commuted to companies located on the outskirts of cities.

But wealthier populations left these housing developments as soon as they were able to do so and moved to better districts. Consequently, such suburbs mostly house poor people nowadays: the unemployed, immigrants and the elderly.

The economic situation of these districts worsened after the crisis of 1974. Many youths felt excluded, causing the following problems: school failures, insecurity, drug use, violence, desertion of economic activities. Moreover, these areas are often located far from core cities, preventing urban mixing and reinforcing the feeling of exclusion. They suffer from lack of public services, small shops, cultural and sports facilities, parks and meeting places such as pubs, all of which impoverish social life.

The quality of life is also threatened because of housing decay, pollution (especially noise, since such districts are often located along main roads) and the lack of public transportation. According to a study from the National School for Administration (Ecole Nationale d'Administration, ENA), the unemployment rate in slum districts is as high as 20–40 per cent, the number of homeless people has increased, the availability of housing has worsened, as have health problems (e.g., AIDS, tuberculosis, scabies) (in *Territoires*, R. Dupiret, April 1995, p. 25).

In fact, there are 690 slum districts listed in France (in Tabard, 1993), many even poorer than the town near which they stand, when that town is also poor and small. These districts include over a million people. They can be indexed according to several criteria (in Castellan et al., 1992). About 60 per cent of these districts belong to agglomerations of over 10,000 inhabitants, and 25 per cent are located in cities of over 50,000 inhabitants. Only ten slum districts belong to urban units under 10,000 inhabitants. In making comparisons, Paris slums house more population than the others, but the Nord – Pas-de-Calais region takes first place for the proportion of people living in such areas.

Table 6.9   Slum districts and unemployment

Criteria/area	Slum districts	Agglomerations	France
Unemployment rate	19.7%	11.5%	10.8%
Unemployment rate of young men/women (20–24)	24%/34%	NA	14.8%/25.3%
Families of more than six persons	7.5%	3.1%	3.3
Foreign population	18.3%	9.0%	6.3%
– of which foreign population from outside the EU	81%	67%	63%
Young people under 20	33%	26%	26%

Source: Castellan et al., 1992.

There are 96 slum districts in the Paris region (Ile de France), including three in the core of Paris. In the other regions, 37 per cent of these districts stand in remote suburbs, 49 per cent in neighbouring suburbs, 14 per cent in core cities. They are located along main roads and railways, which separate them from core cities, and four slum districts out of ten have a railroad station.

Slum districts often exist in blocks and towers of the '60s (*grands ensembles*). But, except in the Paris area, 58 per cent of these districts are mixed areas, composed of tower blocks or low-income housing and individual houses. Former workers' housing estates have also become slum areas.

In 1990, the slum districts could be compared to the whole of the country and the agglomerations to which they belong.

Two types of slum districts have to be differentiated: 23 per cent of them belong to poor regions or cities, accurately reflecting the weakness of their environment. But 30 per cent appear as excluded areas, with high unemployment rates, far from rich core cities. Nevertheless, whatever the type of slum district, families are often numerous.

As stated above, violence has been increasing in these areas. Chart 6.3 concerns the whole of France, but the geographic enquiry shows that there are two types of areas concerned: suburbs of large towns and holidays areas.

Crimes and offences in France Before addressing these issues, the French government needed to define the limits of slum districts in order to make its policies more efficient. In fact, on the one hand, it seems that there is no correlation between the geographic location of a district or its urban form and the fact that its inhabitants feel excluded. Exclusion seems rather to reflect

Chart 6.3   Crimes and misdemeanours in France

	1977	1980	1992
Crimes and misdemeanours	2,097,919	2,627,508	3,830,996
Delinquency on public highways	NA	1,100,812	2,146,447
Other crimes and offences	NA	1,526,696	1,684,549

Source: Chaire d'Economomie Urbaine de l'ESSEC, 1994, p. 16.

the lack of social representation than a physical organization. On the other hand, it is very hard to establish a hierarchy between slum districts and to define priorities among them.

Today, the challenge is to help these districts achieve a social identity, according to economic, cultural and religious criteria. The creativity of inhabitants must be recognized.

A number of preconceived ideas must be abandoned. In fact, 75 per cent of unemployed people live outside ghetto districts (from 'Les annales de la recherche urbaine', D. Behar, No. 68–69, p. 10). Private residences house twice as many of the unemployed as subsidized lodgings, which are the major type of housing in slum districts (ibid.).

At the same time, the former links between rich and poor districts must be rediscovered: elites and research activities of core cities communicate through networks, involving new core development, while poor peripheral districts lose their cohesion and are increasingly excluded. For precisely that reason the city has to be treated as a whole.

Therefore urban policies must try to improve the accessibility of all parts of the city. Every district has to find its specific character, which can be reached through a balanced distribution of housing, the labour market and urban functions (training, culture, leisure).

Urban Development and Environmental Issues

Most people have to commute to work. So city development has depended on the development of the car, and has resulted in an increase in distance among the different functions: housing, work, leisure, and consequently the development of numerous harmful effects on the environment, which are not always endured by those responsible for them.

Moreover, spatial occupation has developed anarchically in certain areas. In 1990, 35,000 km^2 were occupied by housing, infrastructures and activity areas, representing 4,000 additional km^2 of urbanized areas within the space of eight years, the majority for housing (DATAR, p. 212). This urbanization was allowed without any consideration for peripheral rural areas and forests. In the past 15 years, the average distance between home and the work place has grown from seven to 14 km, and has involved the use of transportation and, consequently, the increase of pollution (local and total pollution, contributing especially to the greenhouse effect) and energy consumption. At present, individual vehicles are responsible for 76 per cent of urban pollution, compared with 56 per cent only ten years ago (ibid.).

Another problem in France is the access to cities, especially large cities. The outskirts have large commercial zones, which compete with small shops from city centres. Such areas are badly defined, lacking in housing and social life, and they increase the exclusion of certain populations in the town periphery.

Waste treatment is a third problem, added to water pollution and unwanted noise. 70 per cent of waste comes from agricultural activities and agribusiness, 25 per cent from other industries and 5 per cent from urban waste (*Territoires*, A.S. June 1996, p. 29). In France, households produce 30 million tons of waste per year, that is, 1.5 kg per inhabitant per day. In the cities, 70 per cent of garbage comes from home waste products and the rest from park waste, mud and sewage waste. It is treated by incineration, sorting and compacting (tri-compostage), recycling, or placed in refuse dumps, the latter set to disappear in 2002, according to the law.

Participation in environmental issues is a responsibility of concerned citizens. But in France, habits, customs and proceedings concerning the environment are sometimes slow to change: environmental defenders and planners, builders and inhabitants act too often as enemies instead of finding solutions together. The challenge is to get the various actors together upstream of the decision process, to change mentalities by developing a sense of participation and overcoming inertia.

National Policies, Responses to Urban Issues, Challenges and Development

Financial relations between regions and the French state are defined by special Planning Contracts (Contrats de Plan). They are voted by concerned parties, every five years. Contracts can also concern cities or departments in certain cases.

All national policy guidelines involving urban issues, challenges and development appear in such planning contracts. We can distinguish two types of policies: the first aim to reinforce the economic structures of cities under the supervision of DATAR; the second at preventing social problems and threats from becoming even worse, under the supervision of the DIV (inter-ministerial department for cities).

City Networks and Large City Charters

As seen above, the French urban hierarchy is skewed because of the lack of large cities. Small and mid-sized cities cannot expect to attain competitiveness at a European level if the status quo is maintained. Consequently, French cities could suffer from economic handicaps, which would increase in future in relative terms, due to European expansion.

Large city charters To foster growth, the French government drew up a policy for large city development in 1963 (policy of *métropoles d'équilibre*): the eight largest cities in France were promoted as regional capitals, in order to offset Paris's power. This policy was extended through the 'large city charters' (*chartes d'objectifs*) in 1990.

Large city charters now include 11 agglomerations in France: Bordeaux, Brest, Clermont-Ferrand, Lille, Lyon, Marseilles, Metz – Nancy, Nantes – Saint-Nazaire, Rennes, Strasbourg and Toulouse. Brest was selected for political reasons, Clermont-Ferrand because of its central location. Except for Clermont-Ferrand, all these cities stand on French borders or a European crossroads. This is not fortuitous but a way of developing cities in the perspective of an enlarged Europe.

Charters define several specific vocations for each agglomeration (i.e., maritime activities in Brest, aerospace in Toulouse, European institutions in Strasbourg, mail order in Lille). On the basis of these vocations, it is hoped that they may be able to develop and become European towns, assuming more regional functions. Each agglomeration has to propose specific objectives likely to make them benefit from their local forces and missions.

Specific vocations are chosen within the following fields: university, research, technological transfers, training and economic sectors. The national government acknowledges the agglomeration's choices through charters, signed by the representative of the government (the prefect), by the chairpersons of the regional and departmental councils, by the president of the urban community and by the mayor of the town concerned. The proposals of the large city charters have to be agreed by the ministers in charge of the related fields. They ascertain that other policies in planning contracts (*contrats de plan*) contribute to these objectives. Each agglomeration receives seven million francs from the state to help implement charter objectives. Other local communities together contribute matching funds.

Official texts clearly declare that large cities will be accompanied in their development. In fact, cities find it difficult to implement their strategies because they concern long term policies (20–25 years), while short term policies are more successful vis-à-vis local voters. Cities have enjoyed more and more independence since 1982 (see section 'Administrative and Financial Framework' above), and they do not want national authorities to remove their power. The charter policy may appear to some representatives as an indirect way for the state to control their economic development.

In fact, things are not so simple. In order to develop this policy, prefects are in charge of creating working groups, composed of representatives of each local community involved. These working groups, if created, have not proposed any action to date.

Consequently, although the mayors of large cities are aware of the necessity of reaching a competitive size to improve their European status, the allocations for large city charters had not yet been spent in April 1997. The charter policy still has not produced any effects. The charters for the cities of Lyon and Marseilles have been abandoned. Clermont-Ferrand's has not been written yet, although the city wants it to be signed. Finally, it seems that the large towns have not fully understood the advantages of such a charter.

The other ones are signed or about to be signed, but they seem to be only pious wishes at this point.

Chart 6.4 sums up the objectives for each charter signed.

Small and medium-sized cities Small and medium-sized cities in France are facing other challenges: their vitality is linked to their capacity to maintain private and public services and to operate as employment centres. Their development depends on their ability to unite efforts at the local level, which does not really fit with the French traditional attachment to local communities.

City networks (*réseaux de villes*) were created by the same official text as that which created large city charters. Any city may enter into a network, but there is no obligation. This policy aims at reinforcing economic city development in ways adapted to their specific identities, at balancing the spatial development at national and European levels. City networks aim to promote high quality services throughout France, and to further solidarity between towns and depressed areas.

Chart 6.4   Charters and their objectives

Agglomeration	Specific vocations	Objects
Brest (8.3.95)	Maritime activities Tourism and culture Metropolitan position	Development of activities linked to the sea
Nantes Saint-Nazaire (28.3.1994)	Six economic sectors Harbour functions Metropolitan position	International development Economic development of wood, agribusiness, harbour functions, ecotechnology, mechanics
Rennes (4.8.1995)	Three economic sectors Metropolitan position	Development of biotechnology, nutrition, environment, mechanics Development of services and culture
Strasbourg (20.9.1994)	Institutional functions Universities and scientific functions	Development of institutional and diplomatic functions Development of transportation, R & D (chemicals and pharmaceuticals)
Toulouse (29.2.1996)	Five economic sectors	Development of aerospace industry, aeronautic industry, electronic industry, services, health care.
Bordeaux	Five economic sectors Cultural heritage	Maintenance of the architectural and cultural heritage
Clermont-Ferrand	Four economic sectors Metropolitan position	Economic development around the tyre industry, agribusiness, health care and polymers Reinforcement its metropolitan position thanks to city networks, services, training, R & D, cultural heritage
Lille	International development Six economic sectors Training, R & D	Cultural and institutional development Development of agribusiness, mail order, insurance, textile industry
Lyon	Five economic sectors	
Marseilles	No project	
Metz-Nancy	Main roads Urban quality University and research Culture Economic development	Development of infrastructures and services Valorization of historical areas and cultural alliances Development of university cooperation, of R & D (mechanics, wood, water, software, health care)

Source: DATAR, *Chartes d'Objectifs: bilan et propositions*, October 1996.

Within city networks, cities compare their experiences, means and methods. They also realize economies of scale and develop complementary actions in the following fields: industry, higher education, transports, medical care, cultural and tourist facilities, training, town planning, promotion and advertising.

Over 60 cities have decided to join a network. They are middle-sized and small towns, department capitals or cities wanting to reinforce their independence vis-à-vis a neighbouring metropolis. Working groups define the network's programme; they are composed of representatives from the different cities, socioeconomic organizations, and are led by the regional prefect. Some networks employ a standing representative, in charge of developing the programs and promoting the network.

A club (Club des Réseaux de Villes) was created in 1992, organizing meetings to compare experiences. The Department for Regional Planning (Délégation à l'Aménagement du Territoire et à l'Action Régionale, DATAR) acts as a councillor, attending meetings and exchanging information with network representatives. One person in this department is entrusted with the charters.

Each region receives five million francs from the state, whatever the number of networks created.

This policy has been more successful than the large city charters policy, but there is a high disparity between the different networks. Seven years after the beginning of city networks, the policy can be assessed. The credits spent depend on the regions.

Money has been spent where cities freely join the network, where actors are really motivated, where there is a solidarity between cities, where there are meetings to plan concrete actions, where there is real cooperation among the cities concerned, where elected representatives communicate with socio-professional citizens, where cities develop common promotion actions, where projects are voted by all representatives, where economic, social and institutional actors are implicated in effective action, where there is a specific stimulating person, representing the network.

In contrast, experience has proved that networks fail when cities join the network without any real willingness, when there are no regular working meetings, when cities only fight to defend their self interest, when this interest overrules the network's interest, when a city is the only leader of the network, when the projects are short term actions.

In fact, cities have learned to work together, a fact that was not so obvious before. Thanks to their common promotion and marketing efforts, cities attract companies, effectively offering them more varied and complementary services. In the past, companies often refused to move in when competition was too keen between cities of the same region.

In fact, city networks were hard to establish. Nevertheless, an increasing number of cities chose to adopt this method. Representatives of the cities concerned have understood the benefits of cooperation. This process is even more significant than state subsidies in helping to develop efficient measures. City networks were reinforced from the national point of view, by the preamble of the 4 February 1995 law for spatial development and planning (*loi pasqua*), which insisted on the necessity of cities' networking to enhance spatial development in France. Thus was found a way of filling the gap between French small and middle-sized cities and their European neighbours.

But in fact, 89.5 million francs were earmarked for city networks; only six million were spent (Gondry, 1996, annexes).

*Concerted Programme for Urban Development (*PACT urbains*) and Town Contracts (*Contrats de Villes*).*

The National Assembly devoted a special two-day session to the urban policies in April 1993. It drew up a list of urban problems and suggested new orientations for town policy. Following this debate, new planning contracts have been introduced to favour urban development. Urban contracts (*contrats de villes*) and planning programmes ('programmes d'aménagement concerté du territoire', *PACT urbains*) are destined to meet social and environmental challenges. Such policies are decided by inter-ministerial committees. Only certain cities can benefit from state financial aid through urban contracts or planning programs: those facing social difficulties, especially old industrialized cities or former fishing ports. The list of towns benefiting from special aids is specified in each planning contract.

An urban contract (*contrat de ville*) is a commitment by which the state, the region, communes and departments, if necessary, decide together upon a programme which will be valid for several years (*contrat pluri-annuel*). This programme encourages economic, social and urban development in order to fight against exclusion, improve slum districts and better integrate them into the city or its agglomeration. This policy aims to encourage inhabitants at reinforcing citizen participation.

Urban programmes may concern cities, agglomerations or districts only. They often deal with housing policy, prevention of delinquency and violence and drug addiction. Their goals are economic and social insertion (with attention to youth employment and insertion), environmental improvement, education and training, public service improvement, cultural development. At the district level, inhabitants, associations and organizations take part in decisions concerning collective projects, local town planning, health care and so on.

Credits may vary from one region to another. For instance, national ministries gave 116 francs per inhabitant and the region 16 francs per inhabitant in Lorraine, 62 francs and 18 respectively in Pays de Loire. In some cases, credits can be delivered without any reference to a planning contract. In fact, the state may aid whichever city needs it.

Urban contracts are often associated to the 'Programmes d'Aménagement Concerté du Territoire' or *PACT urbains*. They concern areas suffering from declining industrial sectors or serious social handicaps. 26 territories in 12 regions benefit from this policy, the list of which was drawn up by the 12 July 1993 inter-ministerial committee for spatial planning and by the 29 July 1993 inter-ministerial committee for cities. The following regions, which suffered heavily because of the 1974 crisis, are particularly concerned: Nord – Pas-de-Calais, Picardie, Lorraine and Rhone – Alps.

Projects are drawn up within a partnership among locally elected people and more important representatives of economic and social life. National authorities act as advisers. These programmes also aim to:

- improve facilities and public services;
- encourage small shops and craft industries;
- improve special areas such as industrial waste treatment, office and industrial parks, housing programmes and environmental quality, in order to attract new companies;
- take part in continuing education, in upgrading professional skills and in training jobless people.

The PACTs are funded by the state: 425 million francs have been allocated to this policy for the current four-year contract period. All the areas concerned by planning programmes may receive FEDER credits; government and local community aid may also be complemented by European funds.

At the national level, two inter-ministerial departments are in charge of the follow-up of PACT policies: one is devoted to planning and regional action (Délégation à l'Aménagement du Territoire et à l'Action Régionale, DATAR) and one specializes in dealing with city social and exclusion districts (Délégation Interministérielle à la Ville, DIV).

Other City Policies

Urban projects (Grands Projets Urbains, GPU) GPUs are agreement protocols by which the state and some communes fix long and middle term urban policy objectives. The state explains how it will financially and technically support the communities.

GPUs concern communities with serious social problems, needing more help than that which is proposed in the other contracts (large city charters, networks, PACTs, city contracts). There are 11 GPUs in France, including eight in the Paris region, designated by the inter-ministerial Committee for Cities on 2 February 1994.

Cities covered by a GPU:
Paris region: Argenteuil; Aulnay-sous-Bois; Le Mantois (Mantes-la-Vile, Mantes-la-Jolie, Buchelery); Clichy-sous-Bois, Montfermeil; Saint-Denis, Aubervilliers, La Courneuve; Genevilliers; Grigny; Vénissieux.
Rest of the country: Marseilles; Roubais, Tourcoing (near Lille); Vaux-en-Velin (near Lyon).

Financing: between 500 and 700 million francs allocated and distributed through each agglomeration.

The financing of GPUs is shared by the state and local communities. The budget is fixed in the planning contracts. A working group is created, made up of representatives of the state, local communities and the concerned associations (from the districts). This group leads political decision-making and acts as a board of directors. Another structure acts as a contracting authority: it can be a public body for planning (*etablissement public d'aménagement*, EPA), a mixed private and public company (*société d'économie mixte*, SEM) or a public interest company (*groupement d'intérêt public*, GIP). Activities concern urban rehabilitation, local economic development, employment policy and social rehabilitation. Urban integration requires easier exchanges between slums and the city centre. This can be done with road networks, balanced distribution of housing and town planning actions.

Economic development is planned through the employment of young people in environmental upkeep or in services to households. To make social rehabilitation successful, public services will be further developed (schools as well as police offices). The associations of slum districts are subsidized and the inhabitants are involved in decision-making.

In fact, this policy is running into certain difficulties: local communities do not have enough funds to lead the GPUs, thus showing the handicap of financial multipartnerships.

From HVS (Habitat et vie sociale – 1977) to tax free areas (zones franches – 1996) The French government has been implementing social policies specific to cities for 20 years.

The first aimed at improving housing. But the lack of financial and administrative means, owing to the innovative quality of such a policy, forced the government to reduce its ambitions. Moreover, efficiency depended on backing from the middle class, which leads the associative life. Its departure from certain districts involved the decline of many associations. Nevertheless, social policy was efficient from a rehabilitation point of view: life in the tower blocks of the '60s improved thanks to the actions programmed under HVS policy.

In 1981, the new socialist government ordered several studies (two of them were led by mayors, Dubedout in Grenoble and Bonnemaison) in order to define its urban social policy:

- the 'Dubedout' report in 1982 dealt with the global treatment of slum districts and initiated DSQ policy (*développement social des quartiers*);
- the 'Bonnemaison' report in 1982, on delinquency prevention, founded the National Council for Delinquency Prevention (Conseil National pour la Prévention de la Délinquance, CNPD);
- the 'Schwartz' report evaluated youth insertion, especially in professional life.

'Banlieues 89' was a programme proposed by Roland Castro and Michel Cantal-Dupart, aimed at improving life in the district; school failure was treated through the ZEP process (*zones d'enseignement prioritaires*).

At the end of the '80s, the French administration attended to these policies by creating special departments in charge of urban policy, i.e. the Department for Cities and the Inter-ministerial Committee for Cities. These organizations concentrate all the missions started in the early '80s (Banlieues 89, DSQ and CNPD). The Inter-ministerial Committee for Cities operates under the administrative supervision of the prime minister, but does not benefit from political representation.

In 1991, as a consequence of riots in Vaux-en-Velin (near Lyon), the French government decided to give a political dimension to urban policy. The Ministry for the City was created, and it included a Department for Cities (DIV). An economic dimension was proposed with a suggestion for a consortium from the building sector to benefit from contracts, if they employed young people from slum areas. The DIV refused this principle, on the grounds that it was against free market functioning.

Town contracts developed the territorial dimension of urban policy (see above). They treated the districts not as specific areas but as parts of the whole city.

In 1993, the Ministry for the City became the Ministry for the City and Social Affairs. Simone Veil developed social policies in favour of slum districts, doubling the budget for urban policy, with new credits destined for the associations.

The most recent policy proposed by the state was decided by the 28 March 1996 law, in the 'pacte de relance pour la ville', voted by the National Assembly on 31 October 1996. It delineated 44 tax free areas (*zones franches*), 700 distressed urban areas (*zones sensibles urbaines*) and 350 areas for urban renewal ('zones de redynamisation urbaine'), all intended to attract companies and retail trade by fiscal exemptions. The state compensates the loss resulting from the exemption of the companies' tax.

Tax free areas apply to cities with over 10,000 inhabitants, whose labour force exceeds 25 per cent of population and whose youth exceed 36 per cent of the total. The number of over 15 year-olds without any diploma has to be higher than the national average of 29 per cent. The fiscal potential (see above) must be less than 3,800 francs per inhabitant.

In fact, the cities concerned have more than 600,000 inhabitants, an unemployment rate twice as high as the national average, a young population reaching 46 per cent of the whole population, including 44 per cent without any diploma.

Firms established in these areas or belonging to it enjoy tax exemptions if they work in the following fields: construction, car sales, small shops, restaurants, taxis, health care and social actions, waste collection, culture and sports, services to households. They have to choose over 20 per cent of their employees from the tax free area.

At the same time, the government finances 53 per cent of the jobs for young people directly working in associations, services to households or the local environment. To fight against delinquency, 2,000 extra police officers were assigned to these areas, along with associations and organizations to improve contacts between the population and the justice system, education, housing. DSU (see above) is increased in such districts.

The budget for urban policy came to 11 billion francs in 1996, and it should remain at that level in 1997.

Environmental Policy

The first French law aimed at 'protecting nature' was voted in 1976. Since then, laws have become increasingly specific concerning environmental issues.

There are three ways citizens can participate in such issues, in order to ensure that legislation is respected. The 6 February 1992 law (Administration

Table 6.10   List of tax free areas.

Tax free areas:
Paris region: Bondy (northern districts); Champigny-sur-Marne/Chennevières-sur-Marne (Le Bois l'Abbé); Clichy-sous-Bois/Montfermeil (district of the GPU); Garges-lès-Gonesse/ Sarcelles (Dame Blanche, La Muette, Lochères); Grigny (GPU); Les Mureaux; Mantes-la-Jolie (Le Val Fourré); Meaux (Beauval, La pierre Collinet); Montereau-Fault-Yonne (Surville).
Rest of the country: Amiens (northern districts); Belfort (Les Résidences); Bourges (northern districts); Calais (Beau Marais); Bordeaux – Cenon – Floirac – Lormont (Hauts de Garonne – Bastides); Charleville-Mezières (Ronde Couture); Chenôve (Le Mail); Creil (Plateau Rouher); Dreux (eastern districts); La Seyne-sur-Mer (Berthe); Le Havre (Mont Gaillard, Bois de Bléville; Mare rouge); Le Mans (Les sablons); Lille (south of Lille, faubourg de Béthune); Marseilles (Plan d'Aou, La Bricarde, La Castellane); Metz (Borny); Montpellier (La Paillade); Mulhouse (Les Coteaux); Nice (L'Ariane); Nîmes (Pissevin, Valdegour); Octeville-Cherbourg (Les Provinces); Perpignan (Le Vernet); Reims (Croix rouge); Roubais-Tourcoing (GPU); Saint-Dizier (Le Vert Bois); Saint-Etienne (Montreynaud); Saint-Quentin (Le Vermandois); Strasbourg (Neuhof); Valence (Fontbarlette, le Plan; Vaux-en-Velin) (GPU).

Territoriale de la République, ATR) specified the use of referenda for decisions concerning environmental issues, but the referendum's results do not bind the communal council. The 10 July 1976 law established 'impact surveys' (*étude d'impact*), showing the consequences of a project on the environment. In 1983, a law (*loi Bouchardeau*) set up public utility inquiries (*enquête d'utilité publique*), comparing points of view during meetings, but results have been relatively disappointing to date.

Conclusions

The urban policies followed by the French government after World War II were first oriented towards reconstruction and the building of large blocks of flats, then towards establishing equilibrium throughout France. The latter aspect has resulted in a policy of national urban and regional planning (*aménagement du territoire*) developing eight regional metropolises and producing a master plan for the Greater Paris area. The '70s witnessed efforts to develop medium-sized cities and particularly to restructure city centres.

For the most part, these policies have been conducted by central government through the Ministry of Construction, later called the Ministry of Equipment and Transportation, and the inter-ministerial DATAR.

Starting in 1981, the politico-administrative environment, the internationalization of commerce in a liberal context and rising social problems changed priorities for urban policies.

Decentralization of power and responsibilities, particularly in urban and economic development, and instituted by laws in 1982 and 1983 in favour of local communities, has progressively reoriented urban policies and development, until then directed by central government, towards economic contracts signed by the state, the region and the urban community. Territorial development policies, while continuing to favour distressed areas, also sought to promote international competitiveness of cities in a context marked by the developing European regional policy.

Rising unemployment and social problems in neighbourhoods of social exclusion led the state to propose specific policies in favour of these neighbourhoods, under the heading 'city policy'. First aimed at material renovation, the policies have evolved towards social solutions and fiscal incentives with the setting up of companies in these neighbourhoods. The inter-ministerial delegation for cities is in charge of implementing these policies.

In France, current objectives with regard to urban policies were laid out in the 1994 law orienting territorial development. They were further specified by a pact for re-launching cities in 1996, then by a pre-project for a master plan for territorial development ('schéma national d'aménagement et de développement du territoire') and an inter-ministerial committee on 10 April 1997. Some may regret that there is not a single large ministry for cities or a single inter-ministerial delegation to coordinate the economic, social and development policies concerning urban and territorial development. Others feel that these policies are not decentralized enough at the regional level.

Notes

1 With the assistance of Raphaëlle Gondry.
2 This city has recently benefited from the decision of Toyota to build a plant employing 2,000 employees.
3 This tax amounts to half on average of the four local taxes for communes.
4 Fiscal potential is the ratio found by comparing the taxes paid by each inhabitant of a commune with the national level.

References

Bailly A., Baumont, C., Huriot J.M. and Sallez A. (1995), 'Représenter la ville', Paris, *Economica*.

Bailly A., Sallez A. et al. (1995), 'L'Aménagement du Territoire et la Science Régionales' in *Stratégies Spatiales, Comprendre et Maîtriser l'Espace*, Monpellier: GIP Reclus.

Bonnemaison G. (1987), *La sécurité en liberté*, ed. Syros, IRERD: Grenoble.

Bonneville M., Buisson, M.A., Commercon N. and Roussier N. (1991), *Les villes européennes et internationalisation – LET*, Programme Rhône Alpes 1992.

Braudel F. (1986), 'Les villes d'abord in l'*Identité de la France*' in *Les Hommes et les Choses*, tome 2, Paris: Arthaud Flammarion,.

Buisson M.A. et al. (1994), *Prospective des villes en 2010, LET de Lyon*, DATAR, octobre.

Castellan M., Marpsat M. and Goldberger M.F. (1992), *Les quartiers prioritaires de la politique de la ville*, Paris: INSEE-première, No. 234.

Catan N., Pumain, D. et al. (1994), *Le système des villes européennes*, Paris: Anthropos-Economica.

Chaire d'Economie Urbaine de l'ESSEC (1994), *Politique de la Ville: Bilan et Prospective*, Juin.

Cheshire P.C. (1990), 'Explaining the recent performance of the European Community's Major Urban Regions', *Urban Studies*, 27, 3.

CNRS (1994), *La ville*, Paris: Le Courrier du CNRS, no. 81.

CNRS (1996), *Cities, Ciudades-Villes*, Paris: Le Courrier du CNR, no. 82.

Commissariat Général du Plan (1993), *Séminaire– Les nouveaux enjeux de la Péri-Urbanisation*, Novembre, Paris: Direction de l'Architecture et de l'Urbanisme (DAU).

Commission Européenne (1994), *Europe 2000 +, coopération pour l'aménagement du territoire européen*, Bruxelles.

Damette F. (1993), *Métropoles en France, dynamique des fonctions 1985–1990*, DATAR, Université Paris 1.

Damette F. (1994), *La France en villes*, DATAR, Paris: La Documentation Française.

DATAR (1996), *Schéma National et d'Aménagement et de Développement du Territoire: propositions des commissions thématiques*, Paris: La Documentation Française.

Délégation Interministérielle à la ville (1996), 'Commentaire de la loi relative à la mise en oeuvre du Pacte de Relance pour la ville', Paris: Les Cahiers, 7.

Drewe P., Rosenboom H. (1993), 'Indicators of the Urban Quality of Life, with Special Reference to France,, paper prepared for the colloquium *Réseau des villes européennes, état des recherches comparatives*, ENS, Delft University of Technology, Saint Cloud, 21–22 October.

Dubedout, H. (1983), *Ensemble refaire la ville*, Paris: La Documentation Française.

Gondry, R. (1996), *Les chartes d'objectifs, bilan et propositions*, DATAR/IVTI, novembre.

Guichard, O. (1987), *Propositions pour l'Aménagement du Territoire*, Paris: La Documentation Française.

Guigou, J.L. (1995), *Une ambition pour le territoire, aménager l'espace et le temps*, éd. de l'Aube, Paris: DATAR.

Julien P. and Pumain, D. (1996), 'Fonctions stratégiques et image des villes', Paris: *Economie et Statistique*,.

L'Atlas Région (1996), 'La dynamique des villes', *Les Echos*, 21 octobre.

Laborie, J.P., Langumier, J.F. and de Roo, P. (1985), *La Politique Française d'Aménagement du Territoire*, Paris: La Documentation Française.

Le Jeannic, T. (1996), 'La délimitation des nouvelles aires urbaines' in *Données Urbaines*, Coll. Villes, Anthropos, Economica, no. 19.

Loi d'Orientation pour l'Aménagement et le Développement du Territoire (1995), Paris: Supplément à la lettre de Matignon, No. 472 et J.O. du 5 février.

Monod, J., de Castelbajac, P. (1993), 'L'aménagement du territoire, Que sais-je?', Paris: *PUF*, 7ème édition, février.

Moriconi-Ebrard F. (1993), *L'urbanisation du Monde depuis 1950*, Paris: Anthropos-Economica.

Noin, D. (1996), *L'Espace Français*, 9ème édo, Paris: Armand Colin.

Pumain, D. (1993), *Les villes, lieux d'Europe*, Paris: Editions de l'Aube.

Pumain, D. , Rozenblat, C. and Moriconi-Ebrard, F. (1996), 'La trame des villes en France et en Europe', *Données urbaines*, Paris: Anthropos-Economica.

Pumain D. and Saint Julien, Th. (1995), *L'espace des villes*, Atlas de France, GIP Réclus, Montpellier: La Documentation Française.

Sallez, A. (1993), *Les villes, lieux d'Europe*, éd. de l'Aube, Paris: DATAR.

Sallez, A. (1995), 'Dynamique urbaine, une analyse qualitative et économétrique pour la France', *Revue d'Economie Régionale et Urbaine*, No. 5.

Sallez, A. and Verot, P. (1991), 'Strategies for Cities to Face Competition in the Framework of European Integration', *Ekistics*, Vol. 58, December.

Schwartz, B. (1983), *L'insertion professionnelle et sociale des jeunes*, Rapport au Ministre, Paris: La Documentation Française.

Soldatos, P. (1991), *Les nouvelles villes internationales, profil et planification stratégique*, Aix-en-Provence: SERDECO.

Tabard N. (1993), *Quartiers pauvres, quartiers riches, position dans la hiérarchie socio-spatiale*, Paris: INSEE.

Terrier, Ch. (1996), 'L'emploi se concentre en ville' in *Données Urbaines, Collection Villes*, Paris: Anthropos-Economica.

7 Germany

KLAUS R. KUNZMANN

Urban Germany: an Introduction

With its mere size as well as its well known and often envied polycentric urban structure, the Federal Republic of Germany is a special case in a Europe-wide assessment of national urban policies. Given the politico-administrative structure of the country, urban policies are being formulated and implemented both at the federal (national) level, and at the level of the 16 *Länder* (states and city states). Embedded in a culture of consensus, there is neither a clear top-down command structure, nor an effort to harmonize urban policies at the *Länder* level. Each *Land* or city state may pursue its own urban policy, as long as it does not contradict legally bound federal regulations. And all *Länder* do it with more or less enthusiasm. Hence, these urban policies vary from *Land* to *Land* according to the respective regional tradition and culture of decision-making. Their aims and objectives vary with the mainstream ideology: some countries (such as Bavaria, Saxony or Turingia) are strongholds of the conservative party, while others (Northrhine-Westphalia and Saar, Hamburg and Bremen) have been dominated for decades by socio-democratic governments. Understanding present urban challenges in Germany and the respective policy responses, means: i) being aware of the long urban history of the country, and of the fact that urban development after World War II had to cope with tremendous efforts of reconstructing widely destroyed cities; ii) understanding the established decentralized federalist system which gives considerable power to established regions (*Länder*); and, iii) knowledge of the practical repercussions of the recent reunification of Germany in 1989. These dimensions can be described as follows.

First, Germany has an urban history of more than 2,000 years. The Romans founded a dense network of colonial cities in the then province 'Germania', with cities such as Augsburg, Regensburg, Trier, Xanten or Cologne. The Middle Ages saw the emergence of independent cities (*Freie Reichstädte*, such as Nürnberg, Ulm or Fankfurt) and the powerful networks of Hanseatic cities (Bremen, Hamburg, Lübeck Rostock and many others). In feudal times, new cities were established by feudal sovereigns to demonstrate their power and their dedication to the arts and higher education (for example, Mannheim, Karlsruhe, Würzburg, Düsseldorf, Dresden or Potsdam). The 'age of industrialization' then saw the evolution of industrial cities such as Bochum, Essen, Wuppertal Gelsenkirchen or Oberhausen in the Ruhr, or Offenbach, Ludwigshafen and Chemnitz. The foundation of industrial new towns during the period of the Third Reich (Salzgitter, Wolfsburg) was then the last effort to complement the already dense network of the urban system in Germany. Postwar urban development policies in the country did not quite succeed in promoting the idea of new towns launched by architect planners, and the few projects initiated (Sennestadt, Wulfen, or Chorweiler) became in the end just suburbs or dormitory towns. There is another historical fact which has to be taken into account: during World War II all larger German cities were heavily bombed and demolished. Hence their present physical stock of buildings stems mainly from intensive reconstruction during the '50s and '60s, with a few gentrified islands of 19th century urban quarters. Where bombs did not succeed, architects and developers contributed heavily to the functional internationalization of once traditional medieval townscapes.

Secondly, Germany benefits from its decentralized federal system. This system was established by the allied forces in West Germany after the second world war, built on a long history of scattered regionalism in Germany, labelled *Kleinstaaterei*, in the 18th and early 19th century. It has also been an explicit policy to avoid the revival of a strong imperial Germany. The result were eight so-called *Länder* (such as the old kingdom of Bavaria or the newly created Nordrhein-Westfalen), two city states (Bremen and Hamburg), and West Berlin as a particular urban enclave within East Germany. These *Länder* were equipped with a set of powerful tools, ranging from independent parliaments, a *Länder* senate (*Bundesrat*) controlling the national government and parliament from local and regional perspectives, and a policy monopoly in education and culture, to the power to formulate and to implement their own urban development policies and strategies. Their state capitals (*Landeshauptstädte*, such as Hannover, Munich, Duesseldorf, Stuttgart or Mainz) became regional centres of politico-administrative power, pursuing their own policy interests.

Thirdly, while, prior to 1989, the urban systems in East and West Germany developed quite differently for more than 40 years, the reunification allowed their full integration into the established West German system, to immediate effect. The required transformation process in the re-established five new *Länder*, and in their cities, has been financed by a considerable transfer of funds from West to East Germany (around 200 billion DM/year). This was necessary as the endogenous economic base eroded within a short period and left a deindustrialized country extremely vulnerable and quite unprepared to handle the mechanisms of the Western market economy.

There is a one more aspect which has to be added to the above three dimensions. Urban policies in a country are formulated in a certain country-specific socio-cultural and politico-administrative context which favours or eventually hinders certain policy decisions. This country-specific context of decision-making has a strong historical dimension and, additionally, is loaded by mainstream paradigms of spatial planning and development, more visible to the general public in the form of physical urban development. The experience of past policy failures, and the influence of mainstream paradigms, preached by institutional and academic policy advisors and transported by the media, have an enormous influence on the directions and general acceptance of urban policies in a country. Germany is no exception.

The National Spatial Development Pattern

Germany has a population of around 81 million (1993), which results in a population density of 228 inhabitants per km^2. Around 63 million (77.8 per cent) live in West Germany and 18 million (22.2 per cent) in East Germany, including Berlin. In 1993, according to official definitions, 53.3 per cent of the German population lived in 'urban agglomerations', 29.8 per cent in 'urbanized areas', and the remaining 16.9 per cent in 'rural areas' (Figure 7.1 and Tables 7.1, 7.2a and 7.2b).

Compared with many other countries in Europe, the urban system in Germany is well-balanced. Given the politico-administrative system in Germany, large urban cities are scattered throughout the country, resulting in a dense functional network of rural, medium and large cities. According to international statistical definitions, large cities (*Großstädte*) in Germany are cities with a population with more than 100,000. In 1997 there were 84 such large cities in Germany, with reunited Berlin being the largest one. In 1995 three cities had a population of more than one million (Berlin, Hamburg and Munich), nine cities one of more than 500,000 (Cologne, Frankfurt/Main, Essen, Dortmund, Stuttgart, Düsseldorf, Bremen, Duisburg and Hannover) and 18 one of in between 250,000–500,000 (Figure 7.1 and Table 7.1)

As a rule, and throughout Germany as a whole, the population in larger cities has been stagnating or declining over the last decade, while the many small and medium-sized cities in the nearer and wider hinterland of the central core cities are steadily growing. Suburbanization and hyper-urbanization processes are prevailing, favoured by aggressive promotional policies of local governments on the urban fringe, and only partially blocked by regional physical plans and strong land use regulations. Hence, as elsewhere in Europe, urban administrative boundaries in Germany do not reflect the full urban reality in the country. Most large cities in Germany have a wide urbanized or suburbanized hinterland, reaching increasingly out into the rural hinterland, incorporating small and medium-sized urban cities into the larger conurbation. Polycentric 'city regions' or larger 'urban fields' have evolved, which extend far into the agricultural belts around the cities. Pertinent examples are the Rhein/Main conurbation with Frankfurt, Wiesbaden, Mainz, Offenbach and Darmstadt, or the Region Mittlerer Neckar with among others Stuttgart, Reutlingen and Tübingen (Tables 7.3 and 7.4). Thereby, the RheinRuhr region is a particular case. This large polycentric urban region in the heart of Northrhine-Westfalia has a population of more than 10 million. This region, however, does not appear as one entity in official statistics or comparative city studies.

The most recent effort of the Federal Government to develop a strategic framework for spatial development in the whole country (*Städtebaulicher Orientierungsrahmen*), has identified a system of ten larger urban agglomerations in Germany ('Agglomerationen mit internationaler bzw. großräumiger Ausstrahlung') (BMBau, 1994). These agglomerations are RheinRuhr as the largest one, followed by Berlin, RheinMain, Stuttgart and Munich and a group of smaller agglomerations, comprising Bremen, Hannover, Leipzig, Dresden and Nürnberg) (Figure 7.1). These ten urban agglomerations have clear individual profiles. The urban system of larger urban agglomerations in Germany, however, would not be so vital were it not complemented by a dense network of hundreds of economically viable small and medium-sized cities with central place functions.

It is essential to also know that the larger agglomerations in Germany are perfectly interlinked by high speed trains (IC, EC and ICE) which operate at one or two hours intervals. Hence the average travel times between the larger agglomerations are comparatively brief (Table 7.5a). This, however, is less true of the linkages to larger agglomerations in neighbouring countries (Amsterdam, Brussels, Zurich, Prague or Warsaw). Some of these targets can be easily reached by train, although at much less frequent intervals (Table 7.5b). Being aware of the growing importance of these intercity linkages, the German Bahn AG is continuously optimizing and accelerating intercity

Table 7.1   Large cities in Germany (with a population of more than 100,000) 1997

Stadt	Fläche in km²	Einwohner F'95	je km²	Stadt	Fläche in km²	Einwohner F'95	je km²
Städte über 1 Mio.Ew.				Kassel	106.77	201,789	1,890
Berlin (Hptst.)	889.12	3,471,418	3,904	Freiburg i.Br.	153.06	198,496	1,297
				Saarbrücken	167.06	189,012	1,131
Hamburg	755.33	1,707,901	2,261	Mainz	97.75	184,627	1,889
München	310.47	1,244,676	4,009	Hamm	226.38	184,020	813
Städte mit 500,000 bis under 1 Mio. Ew.				Herne	51.41	180,028	3,502
Köln	405.14	963,817	2,379	Mülheim a.d.Ruhr	91.26	176,513	1,934
Frankfurt a.M.	248.36	652,412	2,627	Osnabrück	119.79	168,050	1,403
Essen	210.35	617,955	2,938	Ludwigshafen	77.67	167,883	2,161
Dortmund	280.24	600,918	2,144	Solingen	89.46	165,973	1,855
Stuttgart	207.33	588,482	2,838	Leverkusen	78.86	161,832	2,052
Düsseldorf	216.99	572,638	2,639	Oldenburg	102.95	149,591	1,454
Bremen	326.72	549,182	1,681	Neuss	99.48	148,870	1,496
Duisburg	232.82	536,106	2,303	Darmstadt	122.24	139,063	1,138
Hannover	204.07	525,763	2,576	Heidelberg	108.83	138,964	1,277
Städte mit 250,000 bis under 500,000 Ew.				Potsdam	109.37	138,268	1,264
Nürnberg	185.81	495,845	2,669	Paderborn	179.36	131,513	733
Leipzig	150.12	481,121	3,205	Bremerhaven	77.51	130,847	1,688
Dresden	225.75	474,443	2,102	Würzburg	87.66	127,946	1,460
Bochum	145.42	401,129	2,758	Göttingen	116.89	127,519	1,091
Wuppertal	168.37	383,776	2,279	Recklinghausen	66.41	127,139	1,914
Bielefeld	257.66	324,067	1,258	Wolfsburg	203.96	126,965	622
Mannheim	144.95	316,223	2,182	Gera	151.94	126,035	830
Gelsenkirchen	104.84	293,542	2,800	Cottbus	150.33	125,643	836
Bonn (Reg.-Sitz)	141.23	293,072	2,075	Regensburg	80.81	125,608	1,554
Halle/Saale	133.69	290,051	2,170	Remscheid	74.60	123,069	1,650
Karlsruhe	173.44	277,011	1,597	Heilbron	99.86	112,253	1,224
Chemnitz	141.48	274,162	1,938	Bottrop	100.60	119,669	1,190
Wiesbaden	203.93	266,081	1,305	Schwerin	130.04	118,291	910
Mönchengladbach	170.43	266,073	1,561	Pforzheim	97.84	117,960	1,206
Magdeburg	192.94	265,379	1,374	Salzgitter	223.91	117,842	526
Münster	302.62	264,887	875	Offenbach a.M.	44.84	116,482	2,598
Augsburg	147.16	262,110	1,781	Ulm	118.68	115,123	970
Braunschweig	192.06	254,130	1,323	Siegen	114.67	111,541	973
Städte mit 100,000 bis under 250,000 Ew.				Ingolstadt	133.37	110,910	832
Krefeld	137.55	249,662	1,815	Koblenz	105.08	109,550	1,043
Aachen	160.82	247,113	1,537	Fürth	63.34	107,799	1,702
Kiel	116.74	246,586	2,112	Reutlingen	87.04	107,782	1,238
				Moers	67.68	107,011	1,581
Rostock	180.66	232,634	1,288	Hildesheim	92.96	106,095	1,141
Oberhausen	77.04	225,443	2,926	Witten	72.37	105,423	1,457
Lübeck	214.16	216,854	1,013	Bergisch Gladbach	83.12	105,122	1,265
Hagen	160.36	213,747	1,333	Zwickau	59.86	104,921	1,753
Erfurt	269.07	213,472	793	Jena	114.22	102,204	895
				Kaiserslautern	139.71	101,910	729
				Erlangen	76.97	101,450	1,318

Source: Baratta, 1996.

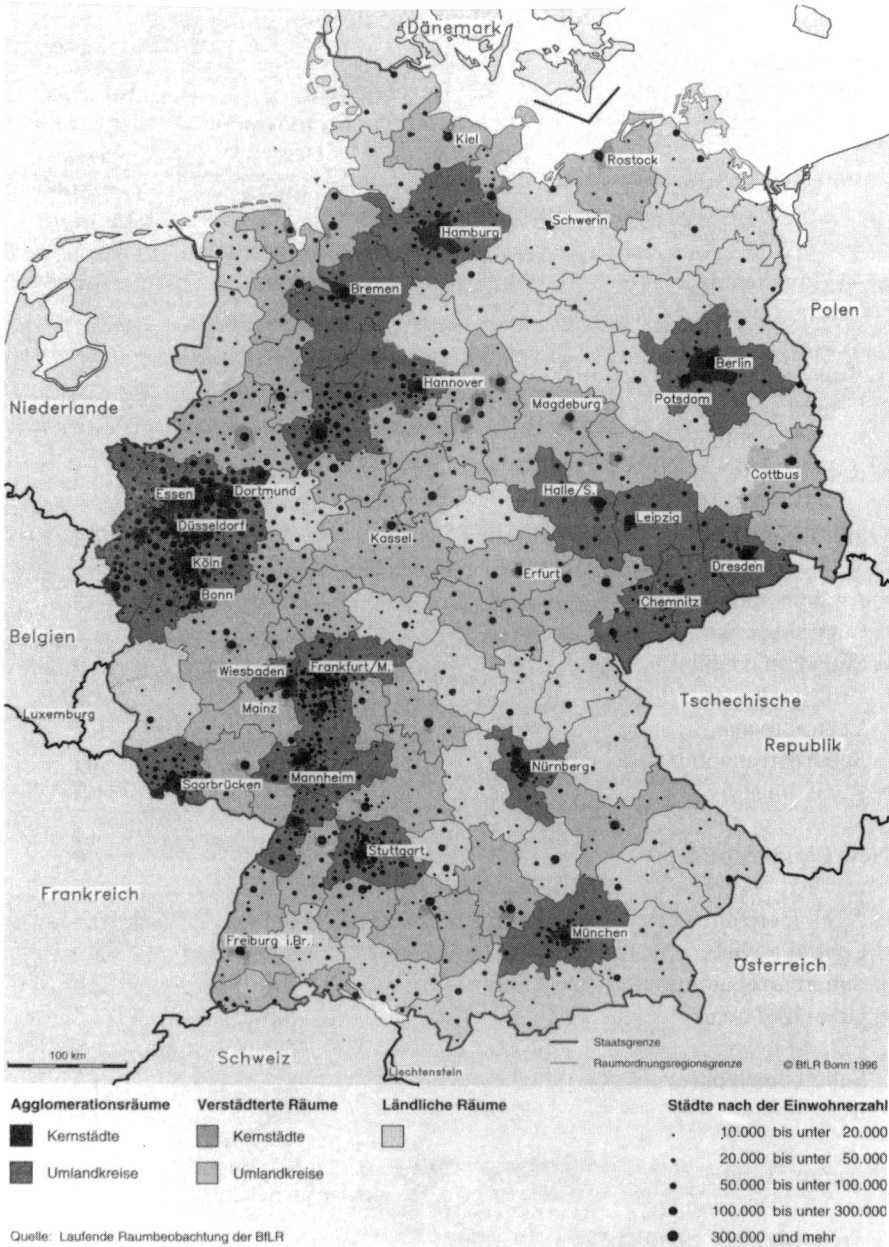

Figure 7.1   The urban settlement system in Germany 1997

Source: BMBau, 1996b, p. 18.

Table 7.2a   Population and employment development

Settlement structural area types	Development		Internal migration balance 1991/92 per 1,000 inhabitants
	Population 1989–93 in %	Employment 1989–93 in %	
• Agglomeration areas	4.2	5.5	1.8
Central towns	2.7	3.5	-1.6
Suburban counties	5.4	8.3	4.5
• Urbanized areas	6.0	8.0	1.7
Central towns	3.8	4.8	1.3
Suburban counties	6.5	9.2	1.8
• Rural areas	5.7	8.4	4.4
Old Länder total	**5.0**	**6.6**	**2.2**
• Agglomeration areas	-2.8	-22.7	-4.3
Central towns	-1.2	-24.6	-3.0
Suburban counties	-5.0	-20.3	-5.9
• Urbanized areas	-6.1	-30.9	-8.9
Central towns	-6.5	-62.5	-9.4
Suburban counties	-6.0	-20.9	-8.7
• Rural areas	-5.2	-29.7	-11.5
New Länder total	**-4.3**	**-26.6**	**-7.0**
• Agglomeration areas	2.6	-2.3	0.4
Central towns	1.7	-4.1	-2.0
Suburban counties	3.5	0.1	2.6
• Urbanized areas	3.1	-5.2	-0.7
Central towns	1.0	-15.7	-1.5
Suburban counties	3.6	-1.4	-0.5
• Rural areas	2.9	-5.4	0.4
Germany total	**2.8**	**-3.6**	**0.0**

Source: BMBau, 1996b, p. 21.

Table 7.2b   Population settlement structure

Settlement structural area types	Inhabitants in 1,000	Share of inhabitants in %	Inhabitants per km^2	Share of s&t[1] in the total area in %
• Agglomeration areas	34,146	53.7	509	18.6
Central towns	15,108	23.8	2,085	50.4
Suburban counties	19,039	30.0	318	14.8
• Urbanized areas	18,979	29.9	197	11.8
Central towns	3,445	5.4	1,194	35.9
Suburban counties	15,534	24.4	166	11.0
• Rural areas	10,437	16.4	123	8.8
Old Länder total*	**63,563**	**100.0**	**256**	**12.6**
• Agglomeration areas	9,229	51.9	352	12.3
Central towns	5,336	30.0	3,064	55.2
Suburban counties	3,893	21.9	159	9.3
• Urbanized areas	5,255	29.6	150	8.0
Central towns	1,147	6.5	1,489	32.6
Suburban counties	4,108	23.1	120	7.5
• Rural areas	3,291	18.5	69	6.0
New Länder total*	**17,775**	**100.00**	**163**	**8.2**
• Agglomeration areas	43,375	53.3	465	16.9
Central towns	20,444	25.1	2,275	51.4
Suburban counties	22,932	28.2	272	13.2
• Urbanized areas	24,234	29.8	185	10.8
Central towns	4,592	5.6	1,256	35.2
Suburban counties	19,642	24.1	154	10.1
• Rural areas	13,729	16.9	104	7.8
Germany total	**81,338**	**100.0**	**228**	**11.3**

1 S&T = settlement and traffic areas
* Berlin is regarded as belonging to the new Länder

Source: BMBau, 1996b, 1996b, p. 19.

Table 7.3   Population in the ten largest agglomerations of Germany (1987)

Agglomeration	Population in agglomeration core	Population in agglomeration fringe	Total population
RheinRuhr Bochum, Bonn, Cologne, Dortmund, Düsseldorf, Duisburg, Essen,	8,978,503	1,776,051	10,754,554
Berlin Potsdam	3,750,845	209,196	3,960,041
Hamburg	2,077,770	203,422	2,281,192
RheinMain Darmstadt, Frankfurt, Mainz, Offenbach, Wiesbaden,	1,185,271	753,325	2,038,596
Munich	1,370,554	241,266	1,611,820
Stuttgart Esslingen, Reutlingen, Sindelfingen	1,079,397	422,515	1,501,912
Bremen Delmenhorst	786,669	292,818	1,079,487
Hannover	687,760	343,785	1,031,545
Nürnberg Fürth	707,261	211,554	918,815
Dresden	687,337	105,964	793,301

Source: NUREC, 1997.

Table 7.4 Characteristics of the 10 largest urban agglomerations in Germany

RheinRuhr Bochum, Bonn, Cologne, Dortmund, Düsseldorf, Duisburg, Essen	Largest conurbation in Germany with Düsseldorf: capital of NRW, banking and German fashion centre/Cologne: the culture- and media centre/international fairs/Bonn: the former federal capital of West Germany/a considerable number of other large and medium sized cities/no joint policy body and much internal competition/growing internal disparities; partially high unemployment/and/industrial cities of the Ruhr
Berlin Potsdam	Former and new capital city of Germany, one of Germany's centre of culture, higher education and research/East Berlin: considerable urban problems in
Hamburg	Free and Hanseatic City/City State/Germany's most important sea port/industrial centre (logistics, chemical industry, ship building)/trade (German import-export-centre)/publishing and services (banking, insurances, media, higher education)/ cultural industries
RheinMain Darmstadt, Frankfurt, Mainz, Offenbach, Wiesbaden	German banking centre/Frankfurt fair/industrial cities of Offenbach and Hanau/chemical and motorcar industries/ Hightech centre Darmstadt/capital of Hessen, Wiesbaden/ capital of Rheinland-Pfalz, Mainz/media and publishing
Munich	Capital of Bavaria, modern Hightech and traditional cultural centre of Southern Germany/automobile and defence industries/banking and insurances/universities and research centres/media and publishing
Stuttgart Esslingen, Reutlingen, Sindelfingen	Capital of Baden Württemberg/industrial centre/automobiles/ regional centre of higher education and research
Bremen Delmenhorst	Free and Hanseatic City/City State/Trade (import-export)/ defence and aerospace industries
Hannover	Capital of Lower Saxony/Germany's international fair centre/ EXPO 2000
Nürnberg, Fürth	Second industrial centre in Bavaria/electronics/distributive trade/German gateway to the Czech Republic
Dresden	Capital of Saxony/hightech centre of East Germany/symbol of war demolitions and socialist urban reconstruction

Table 7.5a   Exemplary travel times by train between urban agglomerations in Germany, 1997

from/to	to/from	average travel time/ hours
RheinRuhr (Duesseldorf)	RheinMain (Frankfurt)	3.0
RheinRuhr	Hamburg	3.5
RheinRuhr	Berlin	5.5
RheinRuhr	Hannover	2.0
Munich	Stuttgart	2.0
Munich	RheinMain (Frankfurt)	3.0
Munich	Nürnberg	1.0
RheinMain (Frankfurt)	Berlin	3.0
RheinMain	Hannover	2.0
RheinMain	Stuttgart	1.5

Source: DB railway schedules.

Table 7.5b   Exemplary travel times by train between urban agglomerations in Germany and larger agglomerations in neighbouring countries, 1997

from/to	to/from	average travel time/ hours
RheinRuhr (Duesseldorf)	Amsterdam	2.5
RheinRuhr	Brussels	2.5
RheinRuhr	Paris	6.0
RheinMain (Frankfurt)	Zürich	3.0
RheinMain	Paris	4.0
RheinMain	Vienna	6.5
Berlin	Prague	3.0
Berlin	Warsaw	2.5
Hamburg	Kopenhagen	3.5

Source: DB railway schedules.

connections within the country and has developed a policy to modernize the central railway stations and to turn them into huge inner-city shopping and 'infotainment' complexes.

The Politico-administrative and Financial Framework of Urban Policies in Germany

As elsewhere in Europe, urban policies in Germany are embedded in, and influenced by a rather complex politico-administrative and financial system of decision-making and control. This system is increasingly linked to a wider European system of sectoral policies.

The Politico-administrative Framework

Being well-anchored in the federal *Grundgesetz* (basic constitution), the local authorities in Germany have considerable power to regulate their own urban affairs in the context of the established legal framework. The bigger and the more powerful they are, and the better their local economies perform, the less they depend upon federal or *Länder* urban policies.

The formulation of national urban policies in Germany is conducted at two tiers, at the federal level and at the level of the 16 *Länder*. At the federal level, the Bundesministerium für Raumordnung, Bauwesen und Städtebau (Federal Ministry for Regional Planning, Building and Urban Development) is the key actor in formulating policies for national spatial, urban and housing policies, with the Ministries of Transport and Environment being quite influential in urban transport or urban environmental matters. At the *Länder* level, the formulation of spatial (regional) and of urban policies is not necessary done by one ministry. Moreover, policy responsibilities in the *Länder* may change from time to time, depending on the outcome of elections and the resulting strategic coalition arrangements. This, however, varies in the *Länder* according to institutional arrangements, as well as to intensity and power.

Under the wide and open umbrella of federal policy frameworks, spatial (regional, settlement) policies are formulated by the respective ministries usually in accordance with the respective *Staatskanzlei* (the policy coordinating office of the prime minister in the *Land*); in NRW, for example, the Ministerium für Umwelt, Raumordnung and Landwirtschaft; in Bavaria, the Bayerisches Staatsministerium für Landesentwicklung und Umweltfragen; in Saxony, Sächsisches Staatsministerium für Umwelt und Landesentwicklung. Urban and housing policies, in turn, are, usually, the responsibility of other ministries (in NRW, for example, the Ministerium für Stadtentwicklung, Kultur und Sport and the Ministerium für Bauen und Wohnen). The city states of Hamburg, Bremen and Berlin are special cases. There, policy formulation and substantial implementation of regional and urban policies go hand in hand.

In addition, two standing conferences of the state ministers responsible for spatial planning and housing, the Ministerkonferenz der (Länder)-Minister für Raumordnung (MKRO) and the Arbeitsgemeinschaft der (Länder)-Minister für Bauen (ARGEBAU), debate, review, harmonize and approve federal policies if required. In mutual accordance (based on the established countercurrent principle of decision-making), their unanimous vote is crucial for the acceptance or for the rejection of federal policy initiatives.

A number of established policy support institutions at the federal level provide substantial information and organizational capacity to do the necessary spatial and urban monitoring, basic and applied research, as well as information dissemination. Such institutions include, among others, the Bundesforschungs-anstalt für Landeskunde und Raumordnung (Federal Research Institute for Regional and Spatial Planning) in Bonn recently renamed Bundesamt für Bauwesen und Raumordnung, the Akademie für Raumforschung und Landesplanung (Academy for Regional Research an Spatial Planning) and the Akademie für Städtebau und Landesplanung (Academy for Urban and Regional Planning), as well as three urban research institutes in the new *Länder*.

Another powerful actor in the complex system of urban policy making is the well-established German *Städtetag* (an association of the larger cities in Germany), which is headquartered in Cologne. Supported by its own think tank, the Deutsche Institut für Urbanistik (German Research Institute for Urban Affairs) in Berlin, and as an advocate of its member cities, the Städtetag is much involved in the formulation of federal urban development policies.

Apart from the established city states, there are only few metropolitan authorities which aim to coordinate spatial development within their metropolitan boundaries. These authorities are the Kommunalverband Ruhrgebiet, the Region Hannover Association, the Kommunalverband Mittlerer Neckar or the Umlandverband Frankfurt. Their power in coordinating local authorities and harmonizing their local urban development, however, is quite limited. Intra-regional competition for taxpaying households and firms often overrides the more strategic aims to make the whole functional metropolitan region internationally competitive.

This well established multi-tier system of decision-making in spatial planning and urban policy is characterized by a strong will for mutual consultation and consensus finding, often called 'consensus culture'.

The Financial Framework

The main income of local authorities in Germany is a 15 per cent share of revenues from wage and income tax. To complement this share, the local authorities are entitled to raise their own taxes. The *Gewerbesteuer* (industrial/ trade tax) is the most important one, while the property tax is too low to contribute significantly to the local budget. The contribution of another local tax, the local entertainment and beverage tax is almost negligible. All these taxes together cover about 35 per cent of local expenditures. The level and the levying of taxes is decided by the federal or the *Land* government, leaving very limited possibilities for local authorities to raise or to lower tax levels.

The second important source of local income are grants from the respective *Land*, and to a lesser extent, from the Federal Government. In total, this amounts to another 30 per cent share of the local budget. Grants from the *Land* are either freely dispensable (revenue allocations) or marked for specific purposes only. They stem from the communal revenue equalization system, which is the well-established revenue sharing mechanism in financial relations between the *Land* and the local authorities, based on the relative taxation power of the individual communes.

The third important source of communal finances are fees and contri- butions. Benefiting from mainstream deregulation policies, this source of income has grown over recent years to cover the full cost of a certain communal service (such as water, waste disposal, plot development). It is generally accepted, however, that some communal services and activities (for example operas, museums or kindergärten, etc.) cannot be fully covered by such fees.

Moreover, the communes have the possibility to lend capital on the free market. However, the money cannot be used for recurrent expenditure. Loans are reserved solely for investment projects and have to be approved by the supervisory authority of the *Land*.

Since the early '90s, most German cities are facing huge budget deficits, particularly the urban cores of city regions and cities in old industrial regions, where the local tax base is eroding. The situation is quite serious. Many local authorities are forced to bring any new investment to a halt and to postpone the necessary renewal of public facilities and utilities. As a rule, the communal debt of the larger cities is much higher than that of the smaller ones, is higher in Northern than in Southern Germany (1995: Frankfurt DM 9,810/head, Duesseldorf DM 6,127, Cologne DM 5,194, Bonn DM 4,664, Munich DM

2,100, Augsburg DM 1,976). Since 1992, the budget of the city of Frankfurt has been frozen as the city, over the years, has accumulated a debt of more than eight billion DM to develop into a modern, culturally-minded metropolis (FR, 20 February 1997). Now it is forced to sell its money making jewellery and to cut the expenses for cultural facilities and events. On the other hand, many affluent communes on the urban fringe continue to benefit from the cultural services of the urban core without contributing to their costs.

At the *Länder* level the respective figures reflect the closer relationship between the *Land* and local authorities. The budget for urban development of the Minister for Urban Planning, Culture and Sports in Northrhine Westphalia, for example, amounts to 390 million DM for more than 250 projects with an emphasis on the modernization of the cities in the Ruhrgebiet (WAZ, 27 February 1997).

The share of the Federal Ministry of Raumordnung, Bauwesen und Städtebau in the national budget in 1996 was ten billion DM or 2.2 per cent of the national budget (450 billion DM). This is less than the shares for defence (48 billion DM), transport (51 billion DM), for research and development (16 billion DM), or for agriculture (12 billion DM). Moreover the major part of this budget goes into housing subsidies. For other activities, such as preparing and following-up, or even implementing urban policies, there is very little space for innovative manoeuvring.

Urban Issues and Challenges from a National Perspective

The main urban policy issues and challenges in Germany, as reflected by political rhetoric and media coverage, include: i) the concern about urban development in East Germany, the physical reconstruction of Berlin as the old and new capital city and the cushioning of envisaged repercussions for the old capital Bonn; ii) a fair distribution of functions to the major urban agglomerations in the country; and iii) the immensely squeezed budgets for cultural facilities and activities in cities (the local authorities bear the responsibility for cultural facilities and for most recurrent costs of the comprehensive local cultural industries apparatus!). All this is overshadowed by the concern for employment. Unemployment in Germany reached a historic peak of 4.5 million in January 1997, with 15 per cent in some sub-regions of Germany, and unprecedented high figures in some traditional industrial cities (Duisburg, 17 per cent and Dortmund, 16 per cent). However, the urban concerns obviously vary from interest group to interest group:

- Private industries, the business community and liberal professions, aided by their support institutions and clientele, complain about costly comprehensive environmental and land use control mechanisms and slow bureaucracies in granting building permission and business licences. They also deplore the ailing competitiveness of airports, motorways and infrastructure facilities, the business-damaging effects of inner city traffic calming initiatives and the tight control of new developments on virgin land.
- The more environmentally-conscious argue vociferously for a total reformulation of economic growth policies, energy reduction and ecological small-scale agriculture, reducing unnecessary instead of promoting additional mobility, reconsidering the further extension of airports and motorways, and making the further consumption of open land even more difficult.
- Others, more concerned with the growing social problems in cities, point to increasing poverty and homelessness, to crime and drug problems in certain urban quarters, to visible social segregation and to the spatial concentration of social and economic problems in urban backwater districts (*quartiers en crise*), as a consequence of increasing unemployment.
- The fine and performing arts milieu, together with the traditional bourgeois middle classes in cities, feel threatened by the relative demise of the public sector, which used to provide them with a wide range of cultural activities at comparably low costs. They consider the closure or merging and regional consolidation of local theatres, operas and philharmonic orchestras to be fatal to a lively and safe European city.
- More general academic concerns include the European-wide polarization effects of globalization trends, the resulting competition among major cities for inward investment and inter-regional or supra-national events, the shifting priorities from equity to efficiency in urban and spatial development, and the slowness with which the widely accepted sustainability aim is being enforced and implemented much to the costs of the environment. They consider the demographic development trends, particularly the aging of the society and the multi-cultural society, as key challenges to cities at the turn of the millennium.

The official view, in turn, as expressed in the National German report to the HABITAT Conference in Istanbul in 1996, sees five urban policy challenges with which federal (and *Länder*) governments are confronted (BMBau, 1996. pp. 45–8). These five challenges and aims of urban development policies are described in the document, as follows:

- *Sustainable resource utilization.* The way resources are used in the city region, and material flows are organized between the city and its hinterland, usually contradicts the principles of sustainable urban development. Consequently, efforts have to be undertaken to increase the density of cities, to alleviate the functional division of labour within the city, and to aim for a higher degree of urban polycentrality. Such policies should follow the paradigms of *Dezentrale Konzentration* (decentralized concentration), *Stadtinnenentwicklung* (internal urban development) and of the 'Stadt der kurzen Wege' (short distance city).
- *Socially compatible urban development.* The creation of socially compatible urban development is seen as critical to cushion the most negative social impacts of the free market economy, and to avoid the emergence of socially disadvantaged urban neighbourhoods and urban slums. The remedy is seen as lying in an urban policy which strengthens the self-organizing power of disadvantaged neighbourhoods, the creation of affordable social infrastructure, and in better targeting of housing policies to minority groups.
- *Affordable housing for everybody.* The awareness of growing social imbalances in the German society means that the provision of affordable housing is considered to have high political priority on the urban policy agenda. This is thought to be possible; for example, the improvement of fringe benefits of private housing investment, the provision of cheap land for private development, the promotion of owner-occupied housing at affordable costs, the modernization and partial privatization of an obsolete housing stock in the former East Germany.
- *Sustainable urban infrastructure.* The explosion in the costs of maintaining public infrastructure is increasingly exceeding the financial capacity of cities. Large, centralized utilities and facilities in particular have proved to be to costly in the terms of maintenance, and unsuitable for incorporating local or even household responsibility in their day-to-day management and operation. Decentralized service structures are favoured rather than highly centralized utilities and facilities, enabling private-public partneships and improving the involvement of local residents and households.
- *Attractive cities.* The physical attractiveness of cities and the local investment climate are seen as essential factors in attracting inward investment and retaining the existing local business community. However, given the financial constraints of local authorities, and being caught in the obvious conflict between modernization and sustainable development, ways and means are being sought to compromise between two well-justified urban development objectives.

The report draws the following final conclusions (BMBau, 1996b, p. 48):

With all the differences in the problems and experience, all the regions and towns are faced with the challenge of exercising a sustainable settlement and urban development. The following principles could serve as guidelines for this:

- Decentrality rather than centrality in the towns and regions
- Promote settlement density, protect free space
- Improve function mixing in the towns and regions
- Strengthen inner cities and centres of urban districts
- Give more consideration to the needs of disadvantaged groups
- Utilize savings potentials of land, energy and water and avoidance potentials of traffic more effectively
- Stimulate environmentally-friendly action more effectively via prices
- Protect regional potentials and place service before aftercare
- Strengthen regional cooperation of the communes
- Promote the participation of all social groups

These demanding principles are a challenge to all the settlement policy players. It is a question of maintaining and improving our developed towns, the European town, in this economic and social quality and with its natural foundations.

Summing-up the official view on urban development in Germany, one could argue that the large conurbations in Germany are clearly considered to be the economic engines of development in the country. However, there is little enthusiasm, legitimation and power at the federal level for actually intervening in metropolitan development affairs. Political priority is given to creating a favourable investment framework for the private sector, in a global competitive world. The federal and *Länder* efforts to promote urban sustainable development are well absorbed by the planning community and the more visionary local politicians, who, as in Freiburg or Heidelberg for example, are eager to turn their mainly middle-sized cities into environmentally sound and liveable places.

National Policy Responses to Urban Issues, Challenges and Development

In recent years, the Federal German government has intensified its efforts to formulate future oriented urban development principles and guidelines. This was caused by the need to incorporate the spatial and urban development of new East German *Länder* into the territory of the reunified Germany, and additionally strengthened by European (Europe 2000, Europe 2000+) and international initiatives (Rio Summit). The outcome has been a few documents aimed at both policy areas, at national *Raumordnung* (spatial planning) and at local *Stadtentwicklungsplanung* (urban development planning). In these two highly interrelated policy fields, a number of documents have been launched which pull various policy strings together. They are described below.

The 'Raumordnungspolitische Orientierungsrahmen' (principles for national spatial development, officially translated and published in English as 'Guidelines for Regional Planning') This is a concise policy document which outlines and communicates the prospects, principles and strategies for spatial and urban development in the Federal Republic of Germany. The intention of this document is given in the introduction (BMBau, 1993, p. 1):

> These Guidelines are intended
> * to promote equivalent living conditions in all parts of the Federal territory and above all in the new Länder;
> * to integrate the fundamentally changed situation in Europe (completion of the internal market/opening up of Eastern Europe) into a spatial precept;
> * to safeguard and develop the poly-central spatial and settlement structures; and to protect the environment and natural resources.
>
> The Guidelines for Regional Planning are addressed to decision-makers at Federal and Länder level as well as in the communes and local-authority associations, whose plans and measures exercise a prominent influence on spatial development. At the same time, they are intended to provide the private sector with a timely orientation for the future capital spending decisions. ...
> The general principles outlined in the Guidelines of Regional Planning are to be viewed as basic patterns and principles of orientation for the desired spatial structure. Accordingly, they are not meant as firm, detailed plans. This is particularly true of the maps, which are merely intended to illustrate the information in the text. They need to be adjusted and updated at regular intervals. The planning frameworks applicable in the individual Länder, e.g. their sub-regional structures and their systems of central places, will continue to determine the further development of spatial and settlement structures in Germany.

This document presents its principles mainly in five sections (the headings follow the published translations):

* *General Principles for Settlement Structure*. Observing growing spatial

interdependencies and tremendous spatial imbalances between the old and the new *Länder*, these principles aim at measures to: develop and strengthen the polycentric urban system; encourage urban cooperation in agglomerations ('urban networks'); avoid agglomeration diseconomies in urban regions which suffer from development pressure (Berlin, Hamburg, RheinRuhr, Rhein/Main, Greater Stuttgart and Greater Munich); stabilize the settlement system in sparsely populated rural areas and to develop their endogenous potentials; and enhance Greater Berlin's evolution into the network of European metropolises.

- *General principles for the environment and land use.* Monitoring a rising number of land use conflicts in the densely built up territory of the Federal Republic of Germany, these principles strive for the protection of resources through 'safeguarding and ameliorating the quality of environment, putting ecological quality to use, remedying damage to the environment alleviating and avoiding pressures on the environment. Special mention is given here to the conversion of former military sites, both in East and West Germany.
- *General principles for traffic planning.* Starting from the fact that urban agglomerations in Germany are heavily affected by traffic congestion, these principles aim at promoting the restructuring of inter-regional transport networks in reunited Germany, at the improvement of linkages between inter- and intra-regional traffic networks and the deconcentration of traffic flows, the reorganization of intra-regional traffic flows, the development of appropriate settlement structures to relieve traffic pressures, the extension of the high speed rail network, and the deconcentration of inter-regional traffic.
- *General principles for Europe.* Acknowledging the growing importance of the European dimension of spatial planning, and stressing the geographical situation of Germany being at the crossroads of Eastern and Western Europe, the principles in this section of the document aim at expanding interrelations and transborder cooperation in Europe, and at supporting the idea of a European spatial development concept following the principle of subsidiarity.
- *General principles for planning and development.* Committed to the overriding goal of contributing to and the achievement of equal living conditions for all citizens in the country, these more general principles are a plea for more regional endogenous development, strengthening forces and actors in cities and regions, suggest a redefinition of the allocation mechanisms of federal and *Länder* regional promotion funds, and for linking regional structural policies with spatial policies.

The widely distributed and well received document ends with some general recommendations as to the required flexibility and openness for new development.

The 'Raumordungspolitische Handlungsrahmen' (federal action plan for national spatial development) This is a follow-up document to the *Orientierungsrahmen* (BMBau, 1995) with an emphasis on implementation. The document presents the explicitly so-called 're-orientation' of its spatial development policy in the following ten action areas:

- encouraging regional development concepts and regional conferences;
- stabilizing structurally weak rural areas;
- promoting intra-regional cooperation through urban networks;
- controlling urban expansion and securing resource conservation in urban agglomerations;
- enhancing spatial cooperation in the European Union;
- strengthening German metropolitan regions within the European network of metropolitan regions;
- intensifying inter-regional cooperation across inner European borders;
- conserving natural resources;
- relieving urban agglomerations from car traffic;
- adapting German spatial planning legislation to new development.

The action area in the document which refers to the strengthening of German metropolitan regions within the European network of metropolitan regions deserves special attention. It is a new, hitherto rather neglected field of interest of the German government. The document defines six metropolitan regions in Germany as being of European importance: Greater Berlin, Greater Hamburg, Greater Munich, RheinMain, RheinRuhr and Greater Stuttgart, and suggests that particular emphasis is given to the development and promotion of these six metropolitan regions. The measures proposed to the *Lander* and the local authorities in these metropolitan regions are:

- the strengthening of international accessibility by plane and train and infostructures;
- the promotion of inter-metropolitan networks and cooperation;
- cross-border development concepts where appropriate;
- the coordination of federal, *Länder* and local authorities in infrastructure development in metropolitan regions;

- inter regional cooperation in the protection of natural resources and of *Ausgleichsräume* (compensation space);
- regional marketing abroad;
- the linking of small and medium sized urban centres to European metropolitan regions.

These recommendations, however, are quite general. In the end they remain an expression of orientation rather than one of action, as the Federal Government has very little will to implement such measures. Hence the enumerated action areas can only be used by policy makers in the *Länder* or in metropolitan regions to support their own arguments.

The 'Städtebaulicher Bericht: Nachhaltige Stadtentwicklung' (Federal Report/ Green Book on Sustainable Development) The report on sustainable urban development (BMBau, 1996) is the most recent document of the Federal Ministry of Regional Planning, Housing and Urban Development to enhance sustainable urban development in the country. It marks a new dimension of urban policies in Germany. By fostering the application of sustainable development principles to urban development policies in the country as a viable strategy, it offers a new *Leitbild*, a new doctrine, for the urban future. Based on comprehensive empirical evidence of the multifold challenges of sustainable urban development in Germany, the report first explains why the concept of sustainable development must be the overall paradigm for urban development in the decades to come. It then develops its arguments along four policy areas where urban action is required. These areas are:

> *Stadterneuerung und Stadtumbau* (urban regeneration and urban redevelopment);
> *Vitalisierung des Stadtrandes* (vitalization of the urban fringe);
> *Stadterweiterung* (urban expansion);
> *Stadtregionale Entwicklung* (development of the urban region).

The required policy measures are:

> *Haushälterische Bodenpolitik* (restrictive land consumption policies);
> *Stadtverträgliche Verkehrspolitik* (appropriate urban transport policies);
> *Städtische Umweltpolitik* (urban environmental policies).

The report concludes with describing economic and essential social dimensions of sustainable urban development in Germany.

The new official *Raumordnungsbericht*, the quadrennial report on national spatial development in Germany, is under elaboration. The last report stems from 1994. Its contents are widely incorporated into the above documents.

Only recently, the Ministry of Regional Planning, Housing and Urban Development, in light of the experience in the Netherlands, has felt the need to reach a wider public and has published a document *Raumordnung in Deutschland (Regional Planning in Germany)* better to communicate the aims and principles of spatial and urban development (BMBau, 1996a)

As an official contribution to the HABITAT Conference in Istanbul in 1996, a *National Plan of Action for Sustainable Development* has been produced. This (English language) report sums up the contents of the above reports, presents best practice projects of urban development in Germany and discusses its transferability (BMBau, 1996b)

Given the limited legitimacy the Federal Government has in urban development, one of the few available instruments are EX-WOST programmes, federal action research programmes which aim at exploring and experimenting innovative urban policy fields. The programmes which have been initiated over the last years have been the following:

Nachbesserung von Grosssiedlungen (housing estate rehabilitation);
Städtebauliche Dorferneuerung (village redevelopment);
Stadtoekologie und umweltgerechtes Bauen (urban ecology and environmentally sound housing);
Ältere Menschen und ihr Wohnquartier (senior citizens in urban neighbourhoods);
Städtebau und Wirtschaft (urban economic development);
Städtebau und Verkehr (land use and transport);
Städtebauliche Qualitäten im Wohnungsneubau (new quality in housing);
Städtebauliche Entwicklung grosser Neubaugebiete (urban expansion);
Kosten- und flächensparendes Bauen (small budget housing);
Städtebauliche Erneuerung (urban redevelopment);
Wohnsituation Alleinerziehender (housing for single parents);
Konversion (conversion);
Wohnungsversorgung Obdachloser (housing provision for homeless);
Schadstoffminderung im Städtebau (pollution reduction in urban development);
Beschleunigte Vermoegenszuordnung im Wohnungswesen (acceleration of housing finance procedures);

Neue Wege der Finanzierung (new ways of housing financing);
Städtenetze (city networks);
Nutzungsmischung (mixed land use);
Zentren (revitalization of city centres);
Raumliche Integration von Ausländern und Aussiedlern (integration of immigrants);
Städte der Zukunft (cities of the future).

Developing Berlin into the capital city has been a major political concern since the German parliament decided in 1991, with only a small majority vote, to move the capital function from Bonn to Berlin. The Minister for Regional Planning, Building and Urban Development personally has been made responsible for managing and hastening the transfer. Consequently, the urban development of the government quarter in Berlin (together with the physical reconstruction of the former imperial and socialist city centre of Berlin) has become a dominant urban policy issue in the country. The well argued politically supported efforts of merging Berlin and the *Land* Brandenburg, in order better to coordinate the future spatial expansion of the capital city with its hinterland and to make it a competitive European metropolitan region, have failed. They did not receive the majority vote of the population in a plebiscite in 1996, although spatial planning in the metropolitan region is now being coordinated. However, implementation remains in the hands of the respective governments and local authorities.

Urban Policies at the State Level: the Example of Northrhine-Westphalia

Given the particular federal conditions in Germany, it may be beneficial briefly to present the urban policy of just one of the *Länder* in the country. Northrhine-Westphalia, the biggest German *Land*, with a population of 18 million, may serve as an example for the kind of quasi-national policies a *Länder* government in Germany exerts. Obviously, given the diversity in tradition and size the urban policies vary from *Land* to *Land*. Some of the *Länder* have extremely elaborate and complex urban policies with more or less innovative strategies to cope with urban issues. Others are less willing to guide and promote urban development. The essential elements of the state's urban policy over the last 30 years can be sketched as follows.

- *Strengthening balanced urban development.* Since the '60s, and based on the theory of central places, spatial and urban policies have been targeted to a hierarchical system of central places and development corridors, which has guided the public sector contributions to urban development.
- *Urban containment.* Through a combination of incentives and disincentives, urban containment has received policy priority. Containment has been partially achieved by providing considerable funds and project support (*Grundstücksfond NRW*) for the reuse of derelict industrial land, by strong land use control through *Gebietsentwicklungspläne* (regional physical plans) and a policy concept of *Stadtinnenentwicklung* (intra-urban development).
- *Conserving the urban heritage.* Preserving the historical heritage and the character of historical town centres has been a prime concern of urban policies over the last decades to control excessive profit-oriented redevelopment and to conserve the quality of life in small towns all over the country.
- *Stabilizing disadvantaged urban quarters* Supported by financial means from EU structural funds, recent urban policies aim at stabilizing neglected urban quarters (*quartiers en crise*), which threaten to polarize cities (mainly in the RheinRuhr agglomeration).
- *Sustainable urban development.* Following the Rio Declaration and the overall concern for sustainable urban development, urban policy is increasingly targeted towards more sustainable urban development by encouraging cities to reduce their overall resource consumption through combining various local policies from *Verkehrsberuhigung* (traffic calming) to energy reduction in new pilot housing projects.
- *The Internationale Bauausstellung Emscherpark (International Building Exhibition Emscherpark, (IBA).* A particular successful urban policy has been the establishment of the International Building Exhibition *Emscherpark*, which, in contrast to its misleading label, is not an exhibition of buildings, but a comprehensive, integrated and imaginary redevelopment strategy for the most disadvantaged industrial zone in the Ruhr. For that purpose, a new agency has been developed to initiate, encourage and implement, together with individual cities, innovative urban development projects (alternative flagship or anchor projects) from housing to technology parks in former pits, from urban art events to a huge inner-urban green belt (called *Landschaftspark*) stretching from Duisburg to Hamm.
- *The Tourism Master Plan for the Ruhr.* The most recent strategic effort to support sustainable urban development (and to create employment in a

weak service sector) in the industrial region, has been the launching of a tourism master plan for the Ruhrgebiet. This was encouraged by the success of the IBA and that of a state supported development of a large entertainment park in the Ruhr and has attracted the interest of the younger generation to the region which is full of visible and (now) accessible legacies of its industrial past.

*   *Cultural development.* Acknowledging the growing importance of culture as a 'soft' location factor in urban development, and monitoring the erosion of local budgets for cultural facilities and activities, a Ministry of Urban Development and Culture has been established to combine urban and cultural policies and to create new synergies for making the cities more liveable.

However, it has to be noted that, for political and cultural reasons, there is no explicit urban or spatial policy to strengthen the international competitiveness of the RheinRuhr agglomeration. At present, and in contrast with the pro-active policies in the '60s and '70s, physical planning at the state level (*Landesplanung*) receives very low priority. Traditional sectoral policies truly dominate at the state level, with regional economic policy residing with the Minister of Economics, Technology and Transport, as the leading and most powerful force. Their overall aim is further to improve the international accessibility of the *Land* and its densely populated RheinRuhr agglomeration by plane, rail and road, by promoting international new communication infostructures, and by further strengthening the well-established activities such as the holding of international fairs in the RheinRuhr agglomeration.

Summing-up: Which Urban Future in Germany Beyond the Year 2000?

Which urban future does Germany have? There is much evidence that globalization, the single European market, the European Monetary Union, the gradual development of a more efficient trans-European transport network and mainstream deregulation paradigms, as elsewhere in Europe, will continue to favour the larger agglomerations in the country. They will further expand into the wider hinterland and gradually bring more and more smaller and medium size urban settlements under their influence and dominance. Boundaries will not change, hence the many local governments in the urban agglomeration will be forced to combine their strengths and initiatives in order to increase their competitive advantage at the European or even global level. New regional cooperative efforts will be made in these agglomerations to cope with the various implications of tight communal budgets on infrastructure maintenance, employment and cultural facilities. The social disparities within these agglomerations will further increase, dividing the urban region into pockets of poverty and walled islands of wealth, glamorous inner-city stages and urban backwater spaces.

The more attractive small and medium-sized towns on the fringe of these larger agglomerations will be the winners of such development, particularly those who, in the past, have succeeded in preserving their townscapes and architectural heritage, agreed on strict environmentally-conscious local policies standards, resisted developing large industrial parks for land-consuming industries and warehouses, and created an image of 'livability'.

It will take more time to regenerate the smaller and medium-sized towns in Eastern Germany. Given the present economic conditions, they can only wait for anticipated spill-over effects from Berlin.

However, a few more decades will pass, until Berlin, as the reinstated capital city of Germany, regains some of its former importance. This will mainly depend on the overall economic and political development in the various states of Eastern Europe. The earlier the standards of living in the cities of Eastern Europe reach present Western European levels, the more Berlin will strengthen its geopolitical and cultural position.

As a whole, Germany's existing polycentric urban system will be sustained, with only a few peripheral, non-urbanized regions in Eastern and Northern Germany.

Note

In this report the following translations have been used:

Landesentwicklungsplanung: land development planning;
Nachhaltige Stadtentwicklung: sustainable urban development;
Raumordnung: spatial planning;
Regionalplanung: regional planning;
Siedlungspolitik: settlement policy;
Städtebau: urban design;
Stadtentwicklung: urban development;
Stadtentwicklungspolitik: urban policy;
Umweltplanung: environmental planning;
Wohnungsbau: housing.

References

Baratta, M. von (Hg.) (1996), *Der Fischer Weltalmanach 1997*, Frankfurt: Fischer Taschenbuchverlag.

BfLR (Bundesforschungsanstalt für Landeskunde und Raumordnung) (1993), *Materialien zur Raumentwicklung, Heft 57, Raumentwicklung*, Bonn: Politik für den Standort Deutschland.

BfLR (1995a), *Trendszenarien der Raumentwicklung in Deutschland und Europa*, Bonn.

BfLR (1995b), *Informationen zur Raumentwicklung, Heft 2/3, 1995*, Hauptstadtregionen in Europa, Bonn.

BfLR (1996), *Nachhaltige Stadtentwicklung*, Bonn.

BMBau (Bundesministerium für Raumordnung, Bauwesen und Städtebau) (1993), *Guidelines for Regional Planning*, Bonn.

BMBau (1994a), *Raumordnungsbericht 1993*, Bonn.

BMBau (1994b), *Sanierung und Entwicklung der Städte und Dörfer – Ein Weg in die Zukunft*, Bonn.

BMBau (1995), *Raumordnungspolitscher Handlungsrahmen*, Bonn.

BMBau (1996a), *Raumordnung in Deutschland*, Bonn.

BMBau (1996b), *HABITAT II, Human Settlements Development and Policy*, Bonn.

BMBau (1996c), *HABITAT II, National Plan of Action for Sustainable Settlement Development*, Bonn.

BMBau (1996d), *HABITAT II, Verstädterungsprozeß und Nachhaltigkeit, Heraus forderung für Politik und Gesellschaft in Deutschland*, Wissenschaflter beziehen Stellung, Bonn.

BMBau (1996e), *HABITAT II, Gobale Best Practices-Initiative zur Verbesserung der Lebensumwelt*, Bonn.

BMWI (Bundesministerium für Wirtschaft), *Standort Deutschland – Die Herausforderung annehmen*, Bonn.

EUROSTAT (1993), *Portrait of the Regions, Volume 1: Germany, Benelux, Denmark, Brüssels*.

IBA (Internationale Bauausstellung Emscher Park) (1996), *The Emscher Park International Exhibition – An Institution of North-Rhine Westphalia*, Gelsenkirchen.

ILS (1996), *Jahresbericht 1994/95*, Dortmund.

Krautzberger, M and Selke, W. (1996), *Perspektiven der bundesstaatlichen Raumplanungspolitik in der Europäischen Union*, Wien.

Kunzmann, K. (1996), 'Das Ruhrgebiet: deie Lasten und neue Chancen' in *Agglomerations räume in Deutschland – Ansichten, Einsichten*, Aussichten, Hannover: ARL

Kunzmann, K. and Wegener, M. (1991), *The Pattern of Urbanisation in Western Europe 1960– 1990*, Institut für Raumplanung, Universität Dortmund.

Landesregierung NRW (1996), *Landesentwicklungsbericht Nordrhein-Westfalen*, Düsseldorf.

NUREC (Network on Urban Research in the European Union) (1994), *Atlas of Agglomerations in the European Union*, Duisburg, Amt für Stadtentwicklung.

NUREC (1996), *Report on Integrated Large City Projects*, Duisburg, Amt für Stadtentwicklung.

8 Greece

KOUSTAUTINOS EFTHIMIOU AND THEODOSSIOS PSIHOGIOS

Introduction

The objective of this paper is a comprehensive review of the Greek national urban policies, especially with regard to the role of the large cities.

Large urban centres and metropolitan areas in particular are acquiring increasing importance in the European spatial and economic system; they are the derivatives of the extensive urbanization which occurred during the transition phase from manufacturing to service industries. This phenomenon is a consequence of the revolution in communications and technology and the consequent radical changes in the international spatial distribution of the chain of production, with the maximization of the globalization of capital, the creation of a wider international economic space and of new phenomena of regional integration, the deregulation of markets and the intensification of economic competition.

The European area is becoming the focus of major changes leading towards a wide and deep Europe, with rich and developing regions, trends towards the expansion of the European centre, efforts for economic and social cohesion in the second- and third-speed regions of the European perimeter, as well as visible trends for further expansion of the European Union towards Central and Eastern Europe.

The growth of cities however, with the increase in economic activities and their territorial concentration and high density of uses and traffic, often creates conditions which encourage them to malfunction, creating a crisis of the urban environment and an increase in social inequalities leading to the creation of areas of social exclusion. Efforts towards the development of actions to ease problems through new forms of planning are universal.

National Spatial Development Patterns

Urbanization in Greece took place much later than in the cities of the European north, and at much a faster rate.

The special character of the urbanization process in Greece has contributed not only to the economic growth but also to social and political integration. The provision of housing was based almost exclusively on the system of individual production and owner occupation, on extensive small landownership and on lack of capital.

The dominant mechanism was massive acquisition and subdivision of agricultural land at the urban fringe and construction by the individual owner. This was an illegal operation, but tolerated by the authorities, although in its original form, when it was first applied to house the waves of refugees in the '20s it was realized through more formal channels, such as building cooperatives and private suburban development companies. In the '50s a new form of housing production mechanism was established which was applied for the massive reconstruction and expansion of the urban centre through a system of 'in kind' exchange between property owner and builder for the construction of condominium-type apartment buildings (*antiparochi* system). What was left from the exchange was then sold on the open market. Thus no initial capital was required and the whole operation was usually financed entirely by the prospective buyers. Both processes resulted in massive housing production, widespread and extensive owner occupation (the highest in EU after Spain) for both popular and middle-classes, and social diffusion of control over urban land.

The production of housing favoured informality and flexible organization of small-scale units. In fact, these are elements that characterize a large part of the urban economy of Athens and, indeed, of national economy. Productive activity and services are diffused over a large number of very small firms. More than half of total employment (57 per cent) is in firms of fewer than ten employees; these constitute 97 per cent of all firms, while the average size of firm is 3.1 (census year 1991). The share of waged labour in total employment is very small by European standards.

In relation to the other European countries, Greece is characterized by various indices of economic development and urbanization. This is because of the delay in the emergence of industrialization, the special structure of the Greek economy and the particular geographic characteristics.

Following the first world war and mainly after the second, Greece faced a wave of urbanization (see Table 8.1). The urban population (cities of more than 10,000 inhabitants) represents 58.8 per cent of the total population.

The period from the '50s to 1973 was marked in Greece by high rates of economic development and both external and internal migration. Strong measures were also taken to ensure financial stability. The influx of rural

Table 8.1   Urban, semi-urban and rural population

Census year	Population urban	semi-urban	rural	total	Population distribution in % urban	semi-urban	rural
1920	1,148,341	760,500	3,108,048	5,016,889	22.9%	15.2%	62.0%
1938	1,931,937	899,466	3,373,281	6,204,684	31.1%	14.5%	54.4%
1940	2,411,647	1,086,019	3,847,134	7,344,800	32.8%	14.8%	52.4%
1951	2,891,994	1,130,188	3,622,619	7,572,801	37.2%	14.9%	47.8%
1961	3,628,105	1,085,856	3,674,592	8,388,553	43.3%	12.9%	43.8%
1971	4,667,484	1,014,421	3,081,731	8,763,636	53.3%	11.6%	35.2%
1981	5,664,191	1,125,547	2,955,729	9,745,467	58.1%	11.5%	30.3%
1991	6,036,660	1,312,774	2,910,466	10,259,900	58.8%	12.8%	28.4%

migrants provided the necessary low-cost labour. Industrial production was oriented primarily to consumer goods for this market: food, clothes, footwear, textiles, etc.

The construction sector played a very important role in the economy. In the '60s, infrastructure projects of national and supranational significance were constructed. Protectionism was strengthened and industrial investments diversified into branches of intermediate and capital goods. Growth rates achieved record levels (Table 8.2). The construction sector became pivotal to the development process in which its share in total employment almost tripled in a decade. The economic development had the result of preserving unemployment at very low levels.

Table 8.2   Rates of growth 1960–87 (Greece, EC, OECD)

	1960/73	1973/87	1973/79	1979/81	1982	1987
Greece	7.7	2.9	5.6	0.6	-0.2	-0.7
EC				0.6	2.2	
OECD	5.0	2.4	2.8	1.2	-0.6	2.5

Source: OECD 1987 (Economou, 1990).

The population which was displaced chiefly from the agricultural regions to the central regions of the country up to 1971 was principally oriented towards the metropolitan areas of Athens and Thessaloniki.

Actually, Athens – taking advantage of her favourable geographic position, the mechanisms for concentration of capital and labour force and the expansion and enlargement of the state mechanism – 'won over' the larger part of the internal migration in the context of the urbanization procedure. In parallel, the non-urban areas have been subjected to an economic shrinkage, following mass emigration, and this is evident primarily in small and medium-sized cities.

The urban network thus shaped (see Table 8.3 and Table 8.4) is characterized by the primacy of Athens, with 30.1 per cent of the total population in 1991 and 51.3 per cent of the urban population and Thessaloniki with 7.21 per cent of the total population and 12.25 per cent of the urban population. In total, the two metropolitan centres house 37.38 per cent of the population and 63.55 per cent of the urban population.

Table 8.3   Population and the number of housing settlements according to size category

Size category	Number of housing settlements	1981 Population	% as against the total population	Number of housing settlements	1991 Population	% as against total population
1,000,000 Athens	1	3,027,331	31.08	1	3,096,775	30.17
250,000–1,000,000	1	706,180	7.25	1	739,998	7.21
Thessaloniki						
10,000–100,000	55	1,450,630	14.89	63	1,675,923	16.33
0–10,000	5,729	4,080,889	41.90	5,721	4,231,529	41.23
Total	5,790	9,740,417	100.00	5,790	10,264,156	100.00

On the other hand, there are only four cities with population over 100,000 which form the 'S-shaped' development in the Greek map and concentrate 5.07 per cent of the total population and about 8.6 per cent of the urban population. This is probably due to the morphology of the country as well as the transport links. The main land-link connecting Greece to the rest of Europe is the Athens–Thessaloniki national road.

As can be seen also from the table, during the recent decade one witnesses a deceleration of 'hydrocephalization', which is due in large part to the degradation of the environment and the 'anti-economies of concentration', which are present in Athens and render the city a non-preferred place of residence, and a demographic development of the medium-sized cities of which some seem very dynamic owing to infrastructure or location on a transport axis.

Table 8.4   Population and number of cities according to size

Cities		1920	1928	1940	1951	1961	1971	1981	1991
I Metropolis	Number	2	2	2	2	2	2	2	2
	Population	627,432	1,046,680	1,402,564	1,675,750	2,233,357	3,097,601	3,733,511	3,836,773
Ia Metropolitan centre of Athens	Population	453,042	802,000	1,124,109	1,378,586	1,852,709	2,540,241	3,027,331	3,096,775
Ib Metropolitan centre of Thessaloniki	Population	174,390	251,254	278,145	297,164	380,648	557,360	706,180	739,998
II From 50,000 up to 200,000	Number	1	1	2	3	5	5	6	9
	Population	52,174	61,278	138,202	216,412	361,531	419,214	593,360	812,469
IIa From 100,000 up to 200,000 inhabitants	Number	0	0	0	0	1	1	4	4
	Population	0	0	0	0	103,985	120,847	475,009	529,521
IIb From 50,000 up to 100,000 inhabitants	Number	1	1	2	3	4	4	2	5
	Population	52,174	61,278	138,202	216,412	257,546	298,367	118,351	282,948
III From 10,000 up to 50,000	Number	26	35	39	43	48	49	53	58
	Population	451,886	731,680	814,995	920,056	990,345	1,105,106	1,282,317	1,356,992
IIIa From 20,000 up to 50,000 inhabitants	Number	10	15	16	20	21	25	29	
	Population	234,226	467,415	482,848	590,826	610,223	753,135	941,553	
IIIb From 10,000 up to 20,000 inhabitants	Number	16	20	23	23	27	24	24	
	Population	21,766	264,265	332,147	329,230	380,122	351,971	340,764	

On the other hand, the stabilization of the population and the growth of the Athens area are clarified in the law 1515/85 concerning the Master Plan of Athens (*Rythmistiko Schedio* of Athens, known as RSA 1985).

Demographic rates show that the wave of urbanization has been checked, in part because of the measures of systematic regional development policy. The composition of employment is marked by the overwhelming prevalence of the tertiary sector, something which reflects the modern changes in the structure of production following in part, and somewhat distorted by, the models of the metropolises in the developed world.

Today, the Greater Athens area is undergoing a phase of de-urbanization towards the non-urban areas of the Attica Basin, with trends of demographic growth in the network of hinterland settlements, as well as a marked wave of secondary residences along the coastal fronts. There is growing evidence from studies of local plans of various Athens neighbourhoods that people (and especially families) tend to move away from the congested city centre toward the suburbs (especially in the northern and southern areas of the county) (i.e., suburbanization). On the other hand, where renewal plans were implemented in central neighbourhoods (e.g., Plaka) people (especially from higher income groups) return to these central areas (i.e., reurbanization).

To elucidate the Greek reality as far as the urban structure is concerned, Table 8.5 shows the population of the main cities within the relative regions, for all of the Prefectures of Greece (except Athens and Thessaloniki).

Administrative and Financial Framework

In Greece until very recently, central government was responsible for planning and regulations at all levels. Local government has very limited planning power. A locally elected tier of prefectures governing the areas of a *nomos* – province (54 for the whole country) was introduced in January 1995 (Law 2234/94). The prefecture is the lowest tier to which planning powers are decentralized (according to recent law) although in exceptional cases some powers have been delegated to municipalities. The recent changes to the government structure mean that the locally elected prefecture is likely to take responsibility for planning. However, until now local authorities have had no significant responsibilities in spatial planning.

The approval of the plans – even the local ones – is in responsibility of the central government (although Law 1337/83 mainly introduced the public participation process).

Table 8.5 **Prefectures (excluding Athens and Thessaloniki) and their main cities**

Prefectures (excluding Athens and Thessaloniki	Main city	Prefecture's population	Main city's population	Greater area's population
Etalia and Akarnania	Messologi	228,180	12,103	46,990
Argolida	Argos	97,636	22,289	45,342
Arta	Arta	78,719	21,2861	78,719
Arkadia	Tripoli	105,309	22,463	46,363
Achaia	Patra	300,078	153,500	231,058
Beotia	Livadia	134,108	19,295	61,575
Grevena	Grevena	36,797	9,619	36,797
Drama	Drama	96,554	38,546	96,554
Dodekannesa	Rhodes	163,476	43,558	101,348
Evros	Alexandoupolis	143,752	38,220	52,556
Evia	Chalkida	208,408	51,646	134,845
Evritania	Karpenisi	24,307	6,178	24,307
Zakynthos	Zakynthos	32,557	10,237	32,557
Ilia	Pyrgos	178,429	28,660	142,446
Imathia	Veria	139,934	38,713	104,766
Iraklio	Iraklio	264,906	117,000	137,111
Thesprotia	Igoumenitsa	44,188	7,022	15,655
Ioannina	Ioannina	158,193	57,000	136,670
Kavala	Kavala	135,937	58,025	71,905
Karditsa	Karditsa	126,854	20,289	126,854
Kastoria	Kastoria	52,685	15,710	52,685
Corfu	Corfu	107,592	36,293	105,356
Kefallonia	Argostoli	32,474	7,401	17,134
Kilkis	Kilkis	81,710	13,128	61,387
Kozani	Kozani	150,386	32,010	79,652
Korinthia	Korinthos	141,823	37,412	141,823
Cyclades	Ermoupolis	94,005	13,030	26,049
Lakonia	Sparti	95,696	14,084	47,768
Larisa	Larisa	270,612	113,000	151,223
Lasithi	Agios Nikolaos	71,279	8,574	23,258
Lesvos	Mytilini	105,082	25,000	56,980
Lefkada	Lefkada	21,111	6,721	21,111
Magnisia	Volos	198,434	111,696	163,380
Messinia	Kalamata	166,964	44,052	68,510
Xanthi	Xanthi	91,063	37,463	91,063
Pella	Giannitsa	138,761	25,392	65,988
Peiria	Katerini	116,763	45,281	116,763
Preveza	Preveza	58,628	15,119	58,628
Rethymno	Rethymno	70,095	24,064	36,801
Rodhopi	Komotini	103,190	39,927	81,250
Samos	Karlovasi	41,965	5,357	33,039
Serres	Serres	198,828	50,390	101,491
Trikala	Trikala	138,946	48,962	110,481
Fthiotida	Lamia	171,274	44,084	105,115
Florina	Florina	53,147	12,622	53,147
Fokida	Amfissa	44,183	7,189	28,926
Chalkidiki	Polygyros	72,576	5,684	72,576
Chania	Chania	133,774	50,077	93,394

The process for the creation of framework and regulatory instruments in spatial planning in Greece was initiated between 1971–80, following the restoration of parliamentary regime in the country (1975). This period is more generally characterized by the effort to establish a centralized planning system able to cope with the economic crisis, in combination with the goals of regional development and economic restriction.

Following the constitutional provision of 1975, Law 360/76 was laid down, which constitutes the first comprehensive act concerning the establishment of a spatial planning system in Greece. Law 360/76 reflected the values and administrative practices as well as scientific doctrines of the time, namely doctrines and practices of a centrally controlled, 'holistic' planning concept. It introduced two kinds of plans and programmes: the 'spatial' plans and programmes; and those for the protection of the environment.

The Law recognized three kinds of spatial plans or programmes:

- the national plan and programme for spatial development, referring to the entire country;
- regional plans and programmes;
- special plans/programmes, referring to a particular sector, function, activity or infrastructure network.

The relationship of the plans is hierarchical, in the sense that the lower (geographical) level or special plan has to conform with the higher level or general plan respectively.

The responsible body for the formulation of spatial planning policy, as well as for the elaboration and approval of spatial plans (national and regional) was the Council for Spatial Planning and the Environment, a body at ministerial level including the major sectoral ministries under the coordinating capacity of the then Ministry of Coordination and Planning (now Ministry of National Economy). No other competence in regional planning was described in the Law, either at a regional or local level, confirming the absolutely centralized character of the planning system being established.

Needless to say no particular provisions existed for public participation. Even the participation of local authorities themselves in the decision-making was not envisaged in the Law, and it was only at the discretion of the central authorities that local representatives could be called to attend the meetings of the Council, without the right to vote.

In the early '80s, after a lengthy maturing of the need for planning which would go beyond the local level not only for the Greater Athens area, but also for the remaining urban network of the country, a single planning framework was established for all cities in Greece with the new development law and the Urban Restructuring Agency, and the lengthy efforts were completed, as a full institutional multi-level framework. Thus Law 1337 of 1983 created the legislative urban planning framework. In the same period, efforts were made in the area of spatial planning with the elaboration of the five-year plan of economic and social development 1983–88.

Law 1337/83 initiated the General Urban Plans (Geniko Poleodomiko Schedio, GPS) for the urban areas, and the Urban Development Control Zone (Zoni Ikistikou Eleghou, ZOE) which are the tools for applicable spatial planning.

The General Urban Plans constitute a planning framework for a municipality's spatial management as well as development activities and potential on the basis of environmental, historic, cultural and socioeconomic criteria. General Urban Plan requirements such as transportation and traffic management, urban renewal and neighbourhood upgrading activities etc. are further elaborated through special town plans (*Poleodomiki Meleti*) and finalized by means of project-specific Implementation Acts (*Praxi Efarmogis*) (the only stage that is not approved by the Minister of Environment but by the prefect).

The Urban Development Control Zones apply to the surrounding areas of Greek urban centres and can be compared to the local development plans existing in some European countries. The Urban Development Control Zones Act requires land use, allocations, building regulations, infrastructure requirements, environmental management mechanisms, etc., and comes into force through a Presidential Decree following the proposal of the Minister of Environment.

During the same decade, the master plans (*Rythmistiko Schedio*) of the two major metropolitan areas of Greece – Athens and Thessaloniki – were approved by law (1515/85 for Athens and 1561/85 for Thessaloniki) institutionalizing the guidelines with policy goals, orientations, measures and building interventions for the development of the two metropolises, and strenghtening the environmental dimension.

The two Organizations for Planning and Environmental Protection of the Metropolis were established. These Organizations constitute autonomous public authorities under the auspices of the Minister of Environment. They operate in total administrative and financial independence as public service authorities and are responsible for urban planning, environmental management and the promotion of major interventions of regional significance within the

Greater Athens/Thessaloniki areas respectively.

The principal activities of the Organizations are related to:

- coordination, monitoring and follow-up actions towards the implementation of the Athens/Thessaloniki structure plan;
- promotion of proposals of sound equitable and sustainable development, as well as preservation of the historical, cultural and natural resources;
- coordination of programmes, projects and measures proposed by other agencies such as ministries and local authorities within the Greater Athens/ Thessaloniki areas and development of the five year action programme (annually reviewed).

The importance of the Urban Planning Law of 1983 (Law 1337) was underscored by the introduction, during the same period, of a number of other laws pertaining to decentralization and the structure of local authority system:

- Law 125/1982, among other things, renewed the composition of the Prefecture Council through the participation of local authorities, the business community, professional associations, agricultural cooperatives, etc. Added to that, it delegated the responsibility to these councils to decide about the distribution of national funds in their prefecture (Public Investment Programme).
- Law 1622/86 is envisaged:

  the redefinition of regions and the creation of regional councils where the government and the local authorities (first and second grade) are represented;
  provision for the creation of second grade local authorities (prefecture level);
  the reshuffle – on a voluntary basis – of the geographical areas of communes/municipalities with the purpose of becoming larger units;
  the delineation of the process of (economic) planning at national, regional, prefecture and local levels, through the presentation and approval of short-term (one year) and medium-term development plans/ programmes, with the participation of the local authorities at commune and prefecture levels, the regional councils and the central ministries.

However, the institutional innovations remained incomplete, as far as spatial planning was concerned. More specifically, the separation of responsibilities for economic and spatial planning in two ministries (of National Economy and of the Environment respectively) required that the Law 1622/ 86 would provide a mechanism by which the two aspects of planning – spatial and economic – would be coordinated and made compatible to each other. But such institutional provisions did not exist in 1622/86 or any other law.

Thus, the historical moment of the mid-'80s – when a concerted effort was made to give governmental policy in different areas more coherence and synergy – was lost for spatial planning, since the spatial structural plans, although formulated in accordance with the guidelines of the five year development plan of the country and the development plans at prefecture level (expressed in the form of public investment programmes), never found a proper form of institutionalization. This does not mean that they lacked validity, since they performed for many years their role as the main guidance document to assist (and educate) the Prefectural Councils in their new decision-making competencies on the spatial distribution of mainly public investments.

In view of all the above, the Ministry of the Environment has been involved (the last 2–3 years) in the preparation of the new outline law for spatial planning. The draft law consists of three main parts, the first referring to the general goals and principles, the second to the structure of the responsible bodies and decision-making processes and, finally, the third part referring to instruments and mechanisms of spatial planning.

Urban Issues and Challenges from the National Perspective

During the 1980s , the increase in urban population started diminishing (+6.8 per cent against +21.3 per cent for the previous decade), a trend that was detected chiefly in the smaller urban centres (+1.5 per cent for the Athens metropolitan area, +6.1 per cent for the Thessaloniki metropolitan area, but +13.1 per cent for the other urban centres of Greece). An increase was also registered in semi-urban population, whereas the rural population continued to diminish, but at a slower rate than in the past. Despite this, the network of urban centres continues to be characterized by a concentration structure, which is dominated population-wise and economically by the capital. Another important fact of this decade from the standpoint of population movements is the appearance of a net repatriation, a tendency which began to emerge in the late 1970s. In fact, the larger percentage of repatriated Greeks moved to the urban centres.

The decrease of the relative attractiveness of the urban centres is due, in part to the decrease in the inequality of the standard of living between agricultural and urban regions and in part to the deterioration of the quality of life in the large urban centres.

Traditionally, we note in Athens and in Greece in general the creation of a mixed land use system, which, except in the case of some incompatible functions, has important advantages of social cohesion in relation to the strict systems of land allocation present in other European countries. These systems were imposed after the war and have now being questioned, because they increase commuting between residential areas and work, consumption and entertainment areas, and consequently increase the imported pollution because of high traffic of vehicles, as well as reducing the sociability of residential areas. The mixing of uses in the capital is directly linked to the way it grew and in particular to the housing production system which prevailed after the war, as well as to the parcelling of land which was carried out from the beginning of the century and led to a regime of multiple ownership, and large percentages of ownership-occupancy.

While other countries in postwar Europe were strengthening their efforts for reconstruction through mass programmes of organized construction with a strong intervention of public authorities, in Athens, and in Greece in general, the role of the public sector was limited to institutional measures for the incorporation of areas in the approved city plan. The public sector was responsible for the limited-range construction of settlement programmes of social character for low income families, refugees, etc.

The main problems facing the Greek metropolis and the other urban centres are the need for social infrastructure, especially in the 'popular' peripheral neighbourhoods, for technical infrastructure, especially transport as well as for parks and the projects that will improve the quality of public space. These problems are further aggravated by high land prices, fiscal constraints and a highly centralized public administration system (at least up to recent years).

Today, the Greater Athens area struggles under the load of pressing problems related to environmental quality, social disparities, transportation and infrastructure inadequacies and last but not least spatial disorder. The current aggregation of these problems may, to a large extent, be attributed to rapid growth without the benefit of comprehensive planning. Unemployment has risen to record levels since the '50s and shows signs of further increase. The highest rate is exhibited in Athens, which has reached 10.57 per cent in 1991 compared to a national figure of 8.12 per cent (Table 8.6)

Table 8.6   Unemployment in active programme – 1991

Urban areas	10.08%
Athens	10.57%
Thessaloniki	9.09%
Other urban	9.64%
Semi urban	6.64%
Rural	4.14%
National average	**8.12%**

Source: NSSG provisional census.

Recent estimates of the Institute of Labour of the General Confederation of Labour raise national unemployment rates to ten per cent. Although this is lower than rates in other Mediterranean regions, in Athens there is no evidence of a restructuring adaptation taking place. Added to these figures, one must consider the effect of extensive underemployment which is not accounted by national statistics. Further, institutional structures are not prepared to deal with this situation. The absence of adequate mechanisms in the form of welfare provisions, training and reintegration further aggravates the situation. Indications of high rates of youth and long-term unemployment are also very critical. Low rates of public and private investment, deindustrialization and the closure of manufacturing plants, the further reduction of the public sector as a result of attempts to reduce inelastic expenditures in implementing an austere convergence programme, are all factors that will contribute to a further increase of unemployment rates in metropolitan areas, and particularly in Athens. The two sectors that will be worst hit are those in which Athens has the highest share in employment: manufacturing and the public sector.

Although Greece has moved to the last position in terms of per capita income among its European partners, evidence (Tsakloglou, 1991; Karantinos and Cavounidis 1992; Eurostat 1990) shows that the percentage of households living in relative poverty, by European standards, was much less in Greece than in Spain or Portugal, although it is twice that of EU average. Further, income and most other economic inequalities have diminished since 1974 while the percentage of households in relative poverty also diminished. According to the above studies both absolute and relative poverty have diminished spectacularly since 1974, at least until the mid-'80s, when relevant data exist.

Poverty, until the '70s, was predominantly a rural phenomenon. Although, according to the evidence, until the '80s it remained so, it is at the same time increasingly associated with urban conditions. As urban unemployment rises, it is safe to assume that poverty also rises among the unemployed, especially the heads of households (since individuals are still supported through family and kinship transfers, see Tsakloglou, 1991). Further, as a result of deindustrialization, many areas in Greece which specialized and had high concentrations of employment in specific industrial sectors which have since declined are facing widespread poverty problems as plants close down. Indeed, in the region of Attica, the city of Lavrion, with 10,000 inhabitants, is perhaps the most severe case in Greece of an area hit hard by plant closures. The rate of unemployment is over 65 per cent, and almost half of the population lives in conditions of absolute poverty.

Minorities as well as foreign immigrants face various problems ranging from overall social rejection to difficulties in integrating themselves and settling down, and exclusion and desperation of the magnitude experienced in other cities of the European north. They have developed defences and survival practices that are compatible with their resilience and contribute to polyvalence but also to the informality of the metropolitan structure and to the further development of gray and black market areas. In that sense, they contribute to the development of conditions that resist change and modernization in the economy, as well as in the physical structure of the city.

All aspects of the social exclusion examined above suggest that we are in a transition phase: family ties and kinship, the structure of the labour market, the persistence and indeed growth of informal activities, the structure of urban property and of the housing market have acted as barriers against increasing dangers of exclusion in the absence of services, programmes and policies, or their ineffectiveness and poor quality. As problems grow in number and in importance it is increasingly becoming apparent that such traditional structures and practices – themselves undergoing major transformations – cannot provide adequate solutions. It seems likely that problems of social exclusion will increase in intensity.

In Greece there are no such phenomena yet as those exhibited in the 'historic' suburbs of a western metropolis. Public housing complexes are very few and 'suburbs' are of a middle class character. The 'popular' suburbs of metropolitan regions are extensive areas which have developed spontaneously mostly through illegal practices of new migrants, as described above.

There has been a considerable lag in infrastructure spending, both technical and social, in the Athens area, where high rates of urbanization and of private investments, combine with low presence and laxity of planning and regulatory mechanisms. This lag has not only contributed to conditions leading to congestion and environmental degradation in the high growth formative years but has also prevented corrective action in the more recent years of decline.

Policies in favour of regional development were, in more recent years, complemented by policies to contain the growth of the capital. Several significant attempts have been made in recent years to plan the future of the capital. Starting from the early '70s, the major preoccupation of all the master plans that were drafted for the capital was containment of its growth. Problems of congestion and environmental degradation were to be confronted primarily through restoring regional balance. With respect to policies for Athens, this was to be achieved by controlling further urbanization, and job creation.

Planning controls were proposed that aimed at restraining further expansion of the city and of its productive activities, especially in the industrial sector. These proposals lead to the enforcement of restrictions prohibiting the establishment of new industrial plants in the Athens area, except for few high technology non-polluting sectors, and the expansion or modernization of old ones. Further, strict land use controls with respect to location and relocation of industries were applied which, combined with prevailing defensive attitudes among the Athenian population towards any industrial installation, have probably contributed to the decline of the sector and have certainly resulted in an increase of informal activities.

Thus, in spite of the persistent economic crisis and the need to redirect limited resources to support more competitive sectors and regions, there has been no major shift in national and regional policy plans against the capital.

Today's approach in confronting the problems of the large cities in general is to first emphasize programmes and actions directed at immediate improvement of the area's proper functioning, followed by longer-term planning activities and legislative actions designed to ensure the future sustainable development of the region. Policies seeking to direct or attract development to particular regions or areas experiencing high unemployment and the growth of 'location marketing' to encourage inward investment as well as indigenous growth are common aspects of economic development policy. Other objectives which economic development policies seek to address are the improvement of infrastructure and other physical conditions to encourage investment and economic growth, the encouragement and support of small and medium-sized firms, the promotion of sustainable economic development and the need to maintain a productive manufacturing sector, whilst accommodating growth in service sector employment.

Specially for the prefecture of Attica, because of the environmental problems, a comprehensive programme known as 'ATTICA SOS' has been elaborated in the last two years, giving the axes and priorities to urban issues. The programmes objectives are: protection of suburban open space with the approval of Urban Development Control Zones Act; renewal of industrial districts; unification of archeological and open green spaces in the centre of the cities; support for the public transport system; protection and management of the coastal areas, etc.

National Policy Responses to Urban Issues Challenges and Development

Planning a large city, and especially a metropolis, can only be multiform and must incorporate the principles of sustainable development in all its dimensions – economic, environmental, social. The major features of a metropolitan planning meeting the needs of our times pertain to the need to combine:

• a positive provisional planning with economic and institutional public initiative for the execution of the necessary projects of technical and environmental infrastructure and energy and the institutionalization of the protection of the natural environment, as well as of the cultural heritage, in urban, suburban and non-urban areas;
• flexible urban development planning which will incorporate economic, social and environmental dimensions and which will be based on strategic programmes which will strengthen the international position and the role of the metropolis in the wider network of urban centres and which will allow the enhancing of its comparative advantages. It will also promote a programme of selective interventions/restructuring of urban development importance which will create together with the restoration of the urban fabric, the frameworks for the distribution of private productive investments.

During the 1990s the interventions which affect the development and organization of our urban system and the metropolis are:

• the new Development Law 2234/94 in the context of which Community funds are used for the strengthening of the secondary and tertiary sector;

- legislation and the beginning of the implementation of the second level of local government with Laws 2218/94 and 2240/94 with the establishment of the regional councils as well, for the organization of the housing network and strengthening the role of the main settlements of each territorial unit so as to become regional centres;
- the creation of operating units through cooperation of the first degree local authorities which will help in increasing the local revenues;
- the creation of housing units which, with their rational operation, will ensure the same standards of living and quality of services to all the country's residents.

The regional councils which are set up in regions include local authorities with common geomorphological/economic/political/operational (infrastructure networks and services) characteristics. Their aim is 'planning and programming the development of their region, the execution of works and the realization of supplies, the provision of services for the mutual accommodation of local authorities, their members and the inhabitants of their regions';

- promotion of the new legislative framework for spatial planning and of the new housing law;
- the promotion of a strategic plan on a country level;
- the elaboration of research studies at a country level for sectors which concern spatial planning (housing network, vacation home, rural areas, land use policy);
- the promotion of strategic plans at district level;
- the elaboration of specific spatial plans in areas with severe problems;
- the construction of works for upgrading the environment and the standard of living of the urban centres and the other settlements;
- projects of national significance under the European Community Support Framework (CFS) 1994–99 which intensify the role of the two metropolises;
- a new parameter in the evolvement and organization of the urban network in our country after 1985 constitutes the formulated policy of the EU for regional development with programmes and initiatives, by means of which significant objectives are promoted which were set in Vancouver (Habitat, 1976);
- the CFS with infrastructure works for the upgrading of the standard of living in urban centres shapes the policy for upgrading urban areas and the development of medium-sized cities;
- initiatives such as URBAN and RECITE and city networks indicate the

intention for expanding and possibly formulating an urban policy in the EU;

• the programme RECITE with the development of city networks promotes the self-organized operation of urban centres.

The Ministry of Environment, Spatial Planning and Public Works, through the actions of the Community Support Frame as well as the Community Programs (EGES, URBAN) promotes integrated interventions in the urban centres of our country. These interventions are connected to specific regenerations in order that the standard of living be improved and that economic activities be simultaneously promoted to set the specific urban centres on a trajectory of development.

The interventions are oriented solely towards one aim: to have urban centres acquire a social and productive cohesion, and an environmental and cultural one, as well as lasting development compatible with their particularities and their comparative advantages.

The Ministry of Environment, Spatial Planning and Public Works implements interventions by way of the Community Initiative URBAN in the large urban centres of the country, where deindustrialization, unemployment, the devaluation of the standard of living and the deterioration of the environment preside. The basic aim is the improvement of technical and social infrastructures, the upgrading of the environment, and the creation of social infrastructure networks in order that economic activities be attracted which will change the image of these urban regions, remedy a significant part of unemployment, and set the foundations of development for the greater area.

The integrated programme of urban interventions, aims at the 'enterprise city', the 'social city of employment/welfare/health/security', the 'operative – with sufficient infrastructures city', the 'ecological city', the 'cultural city', the 'participative and informed city', the 'regionally integrated international city'. All these 'cities' within the body of the 'city' ought to be 'visible' to all citizens.

Recent national and regional economic development programmes are beginning to recognize not only the problems of congestion, environmental degradation and economic stagnation but also the need to develop appropriate policies to exploit the resources and the potential of the city as an engine of economic growth (KEPE, 1993). Thus the national priorities for the strategic regional development, as far as the large cities and mainly the two metropolises are concerned, according to the SPA 1994–99 are:

- improvement of the operational conditions of the cities providing the necessary infrastructure which will reduce the production cost of economic activities and will improve the environmental conditions and the citizens' quality of life;
- the modernization and increase of the productive potential for the creation of new jobs and countering unemployment.

To that end a number of large scale projects have been planned in recent years for the city of Athens, with a view to improve the living conditions and the image of the capital (e.g., the Athens Archeological Park and the Acropolis Museum) to provide supranational transport infrastructure (i.e., the new city airport conceived as a strategic project to turn Athens into a hub for international transport) and to relieve traffic congestion (i.e., the Athens Metro and the surface rail in the historic centre).

Because of its geographical isolation from the rest of the Community, Greece is currently promoting cross border transport networks as part of her economic objectives. Thus, the national strategic development on transportation concerns (SPA, 1994–99):

- the country's international connections (infrastructure to facilitate the connection of the country with the EC through Italy and Yugoslavia;
- inter-regional connections;
- inter-local connections;
- the transportation infrastructure of the large cities (deviation of the central areas and priorities according to the regional development programmes).

Conclusions

The need for flexible and effective approaches to the planning of space which will comply with uniform principles, dictates the main strategic goals for the city's sustainable development and ensures clear priorities in the implementation of its strategic development plan.

Current trends in the metropolitan areas in Europe affect the achievement of a provisional 'positive planning' with a view to providing the city with modern systems of transportation, communications energy infrastructure and environmental protection and planning which will 'react' positively and attract private sector investment to modern sectors of the economy by creating appropriate and organized receivers for development activities.

Strategic planning must be implemented through a strategic action plan and its permanent management and updating by pursuing the best coordination between lower administrative levels and planning organizations of central and local government with a view to applying an ongoing development and environmental planning in harmonious cooperation between the public and private sector.

Summary

Current trends in Greece show that population growth is moving towards medium-sized cities (rather later than in northern European countries). This is due to policies promoting regional development which were initiated during the last few decades and aimed not so much at controlling the growth of the capital, but rather at providing the necessary financial incentives for the factor of production to move to the periphery.

Several significant attempts have been made in recent years to open up new economic opportunities – other than agriculture – in many medium-sized cities.

Until very recently, the spatial planning process in Greece was central government's responsibility. A locally elected tier of prefects governing the area of provinces *nomoi* was introduced in January 1995, but until recently local authorities have had no significant responsibilities for spatial planning in addition to having limited financial independence from the central government.

The new outline law for spatial planning that is in its final stages, gives the potential for coordinated spatial planning in the country and attempts to improve Greece's situation among the other member states of the European Union.

Current strategic policies in spatial planning concern: effective inter-urban transportation and transport links with major urban centres; improvement and development of competitive productive activities; improvement of technical infrastructure for upgrading the standards of living in urban centres; urban integrated interventions in order to improve the image and the economic activities of the cities; elaboration of specific spatial plans in areas with severe problems; environmental, economic, social and cultural re-emergence of the main urban areas.

References

Arvanitaki-Fischer, A. (1995), 'Spatial Planning in Greece after 1974 and Public Participation; practices, experiences and prospects', *European Regional Planning*, No. 58.

Economou, D. (1990), 'Recent trends in the Organisation of Greek Industry' [in Greek], *The Greek Review of Social Research*, No 76.

European Commission — EUROPE 2000+ (1995), *Cooperation for Spatial Planning in Europe*, G.C. Eleftheroudakis SA (ed.).

European Commission — EUROPE 2000 (1992), *Development Perspectives of the Community's Region*. ed. G.C. Eleftheroudakis SA.

Gerardi, K. (1996) 'Strategic Planning for the Greater Metropolitan area of Athens for Sustainable Development', proceedings of the international conference on *Athens–Attica: Strategic Planning towards Sustainable Development*, Athens, May (unpublished).

Gerardi, K. and Gialyri, T. (1996), *Planning of the spatial development as a necessary instrument of strategies for sustainable development* [in Greek].

Karantinos, D. and Cavounidis, J. (1992), Consolidated report on Greece E.C. Observatory on National Politics to Combat Social Exclusions, National Centre for Social Research, Athens, [in English].

Katochianou, D. (1989), *The Greek System of Urban Centers* [in Greek], Athens: KEPE (Center for Planning and Economic Research).

KEPE (Center for Planning and Economic Research) (1993), *The Regional Development Plan for Greece 1994–1999* [in Greek], KEPE, Athens.

Manola, K. (1996), 'The Role of the Two Greek Metropolises in Relation to the Other Urban Centers', proceedings of the international conference on *Athens–Attica: Strategic Planning towards Sustainable Development*, Athens, May.

Ministry of National Economy (1994), *National Overview on Distressed Urban Areas*.

Pyrgiotis, Y. and Demathas, Z. (1994), 'Athens', report submitted for *Document Europe 2000+* to the European Institute for Urban Affairs, John Moores University, Liverpool.

Tsakloglou, P. (1991), *Poverty in Greece, Methodological Issues, Overview of Studies, Trends and Perspectives* (unpublished).

9 Ireland

MICHAEL J. BANNON AND MARY GRIER

Introduction

The population of Ireland, according to the 1996 *Census of Population*, was 3,621,025. Of that figure, almost 61 per cent is considered as an 'aggregate urban population' (i.e., those in urban clusters of 1,500 or over). The rate of urbanization has increased particularly since the 1960s. This growth is largely attributed to various economic, social and cultural changes which the country has experienced. Several policies have been considered at national level and many have been implemented, all of which have had a profound impact on the spatial development pattern of the country.

Following a brief introduction to the national spatial development pattern which has evolved, the most pertinent policies will be discussed in subsequent sections. Particular emphasis will be placed on issues which have emerged as being relevant to the urban areas, and the most recent policy responses which have been adopted in an attempt to deal with them. Table 9.1 provides an overview of the size and the economic performance of Ireland's five major urban areas as of 1996.

Table 9.1   Characteristics of the urban areas 1996

Name	Population		Year	Economic performance	Industry tertiary/ secondary[2]
	City area	City region[1]			
Dublin	480,996	1,056,666	1996	very high	69/31
Cork	127,092	420,346	1996	high	61/39
Limerick	165,017	316,875	1996	high	55/45
Galway	57,095	188,598	1996	high	65/35
Waterford	42,516	94,597	1996	medium	58/42

Source: *Census of Population, Preliminary Report*, 1996 and *Labour Force Survey*, 1996.

181

National Spatial Development Pattern

Accelerated Urbanization

Ireland had for centuries existed as a predominantly agriculture based economy. However, since the 1960s there has been a perceived need to diversify, with successive governments attempting to introduce measures facilitating the development of a more modern urban industrial society (Hourihan, 1991, p. 141). Problems such as long term unemployment, increasing emigration rates and regional disparities led to a consensus in the early 1960s that the development of a spatial plan for the country could assist in accelerating economic growth. The strategies pursued over the remainder of that decade have collectively been referred to as the Growth Pole Policy (see Figure 9. 1). The government commissioned a number of advisory plans which influenced the future development pattern of urban areas.[3] These plans followed the 1965 statement on regional policy where the government expressed support for the

---

1961 – Government appointed Committee on Industrial Organization. Main recommendation was that aid to underdeveloped areas should be withdrawn and that future investments should be directed towards a small, carefully selected number of growth centres.

1964 – The government defined nine regions for physical planning and administration purposes.

1965 – Government statement on regional policy.

1966 – The government appointed Buchanan to carry out the regional etudies report.

    – The government issued a white paper on regional policy.

    – Report of the Committee on Development Centres and Industrial Estates. The committee supported the idea of development centres, claiming that they would act as a stimulus for regional growth and were also desirable from a social viewpoint.

1967 – Publication of the Myles Wright and Nathaniel Lichfield reports for Dublin and Limerick respectively.

1969 – Publication of the *Buchanan Report on Regional Policies in Ireland* and the establishment of the nine advisory Regional Development Organizations.

1972 – Publication of the government *Statement on Regional Policy* and the unveiling of the 'Regional Industrial Plans, 1973–77' by the Industrial Development Authority.

Figure 9.1 Measures constituting the 'Growth Pole Policy'

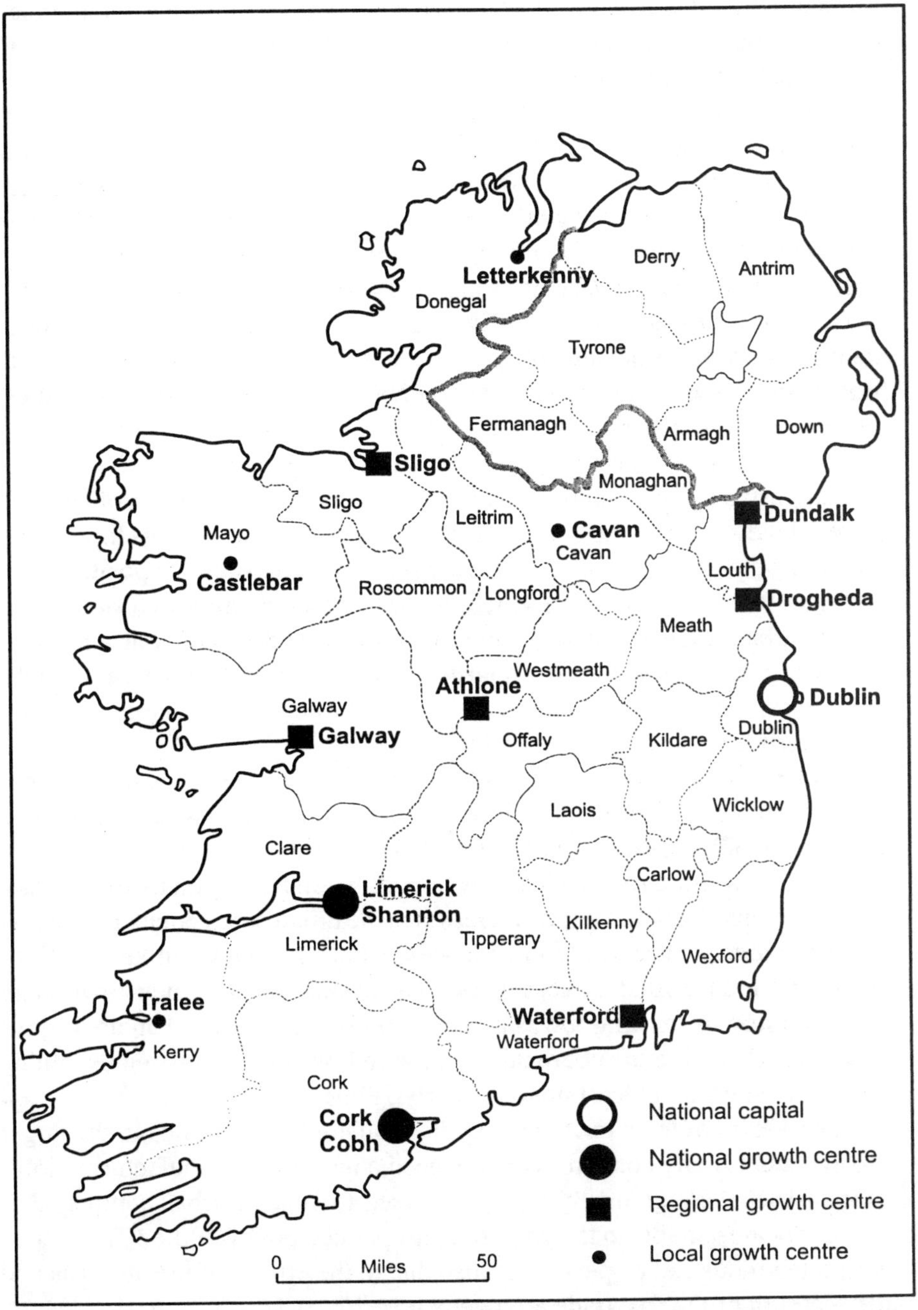

Map 9.1   Recommended policy for growth centres

development of urban centres as they were likely to 'become the commercial, financial, educational, health, social and administrative centres of each region' (Brunt, 1988, p. 149).

Regional Studies in Ireland, otherwise referred to as the Buchanan report, was a national strategy which proposed guiding strategic centres towards accelerated urban expansion. The strategy sought to support government aspirations of achieving development through a balanced concentration and dispersal policy. Dublin was envisaged as the primary centre in the hierarchy, with Cork and Limerick serving as national growth centres in order to combat against primacy (see Map 9.1). Six potential regional growth centres were identified – Waterford, Dundalk, Drogheda, Galway, Sligo and Athlone, with four other towns being selected as suitable local growth centres (Tralee, Letterkenny, Castlebar and Cavan).

A 1972 government statement proposed a higher degree of dispersal than that suggested by Buchanan. In addition to the planned expansion of first and second level centres, the government was also anxious to develop county towns or other local urban centres occupying suitable strategic positions.

The 1972 statement represented the last official attempt to formulate an explicit urban settlement policy. Since then, various other economic and social policies, particularly policies relating to the development of the service industry, have facilitated the growth of a number of the larger centres, particularly Dublin.

The composition of the population, the changing economy and the demands of society have had considerable influence on the manner in which the internal structure of the urban areas has developed. A significant proportion of migration in the 1970s was internal, with a flow of population from rural to urban areas, principally into Dublin. Despite increases in the urban based population, many inner city areas continued to experience decline, as new suburban locations were favoured for residential purposes. The development of 'new towns' and the expansion of existing towns adjacent to the traditional urban areas gave rise to a high degree of suburbanization, with low density housing becoming the accepted norm, at least up to the early 1990s.

The 1980s were characterized by high unemployment rates in the larger urban areas.[4] Many core areas experienced a net loss in manufacturing jobs, as industries were gradually being dispersed to smaller urban centres. This was partly attributable to the government-operated policy of the 1970s which advocated industrial dispersal and also due to the effects of the oil crisis and the securing of the free trade arrangement.

Industrial policy was gradually reformed as government intervention in industrial development and job creation became necessary. Attention turned towards the development of high technology industries and the service sector, to which the larger urban areas were particularly suited. Dublin's dominance increased as the necessary infrastructure was already in place to enable the service industry to compete on an international basis (Hourihan, 1991, p. 148).

The Primacy of Dublin and the Trend Towards Urbanization

Although Ireland has lagged behind its European neighbours in terms of urbanization, the country is now experiencing a consistent urbanization (see Figure 9.2). The most significant urban growth has tended to be confined to the five largest cities, particularly Dublin, with the city being described as 'an extraordinarily isolated giant'.

In the course of development, the major urban areas followed a pattern whereby the core areas accommodated a large volume of commercial and office developments, while on the residential front, the inner cities continued to go into decline as low density housing in suburban locations was favoured. The suburban growth of Dublin has been both consistent and very extensive. The rate of population increase was slower in Cork and Limerick, thereby

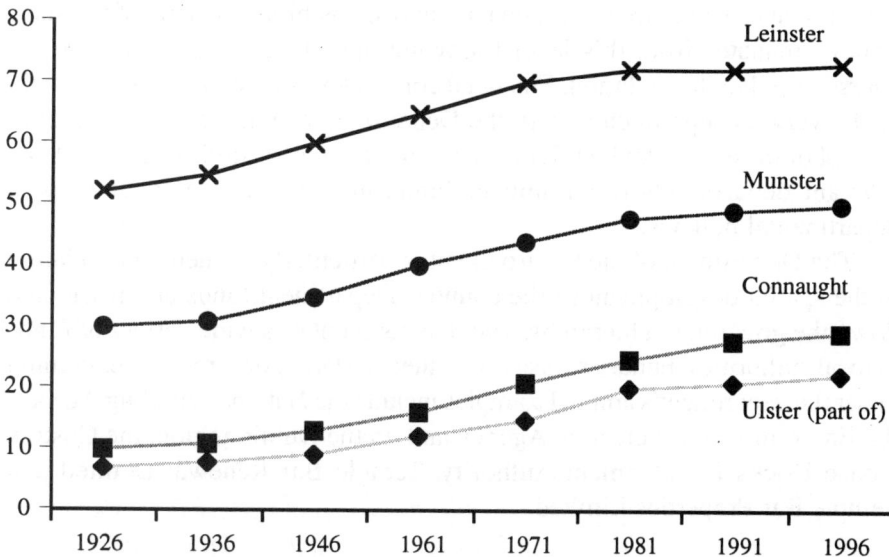

Figure 9.2   **Urban population as a percentage of total provincial population, 1926–96**

avoiding the excesses of urban sprawl which the capital city was experiencing. Galway benefited significantly from the development of the service sector and from the national policies of decentralization, and is today still regarded as one of the fastest growing small cities in Europe.

Through the introduction of measures such as the Urban Renewal and the supporting Finance Acts, the urban cores have gradually been restored and a residential population attracted back. Concurrent with this, suburbanization is continuing, with a trend towards ex-urban, 'edge city' type developments, particularly in the case of Dublin. The peripheries of urban areas now accommodate out-of-town regional shopping centres, retail parks, leisure complexes and other business and industrial parks. Due to the volume of patrons of the new facilities, it has been necessary to improve the transport infrastructure.

Administrative and Financial Framework

Three tiers exist within the national administrative framework in Ireland – the national government, the regional authorities and the local authorities.

National Government At the national level, there are 15 government departments (see Figure 9.3), each having responsibility for particular issues. Policy emanates from this level following appropriate negotiations in the course of policy formulation. Financial control tends to remain in the domain of the various departments, with the Department of Finance having overall control of the annual budget. It then becomes the responsibility of each of the relevant departments to administer funds in accordance with their own departmental policies.

The Department of the Environment is particularly influential in relation to the spatial development of the country. Department funds are distributed down the government hierarchy, with the payment of a wide variety of funds to local authorities. Funds are also distributed to state sponsored bodies coming under the department's ambit. Examples include the National Building Agency, the Environmental Protection Agency and, in the Dublin region, the Custom House Docks Development Authority, Temple Bar Renewal Limited and Temple Bar Properties Limited.

Regional authorities Eight statutory regional authorities came into effect on 1 January 1994.[5] One of the main functions of the authorities is to promote coordination, consistency and compatibility with the programmes, plans,

People

EC Law

Constitution

Government

Departments

Taoiseach — NESC — CSO

ADM — Urban initiatives

Partnership companies

Civic Trusts

Transport, Energy and Communications

Equality and Law Reform — Bord na Mona

Tanaiste — CIE

NESF

Marine Institute Central Fisheries Board

Regional Fisheries Board — Habour authorities

Irish Georgian Society

Education

Marine — NRA

An Bord Pleanala

Health Boards

VECS

Health

Local authorities

Professional organizations

Environment

Justice — CHHDA — NBA — EPA — Regional Authorities

Dublin Transport Initiative

Defence — Temple Bar

Finance — Shannon Development

Intereg

IBEC

OPW

ACCRA

Trade and Tourism — Bord Failte

Regional Tourism Organizations

Forbairt Forfas IDA Ireland

County Enterprise Boards

CIF

Enterprise and Employment — FAS

Social Welfare

Arts, Culture and the Gaeltacht — National Heritage Council

Arts Council

Udaras na Gaeltachta

An Taisce

Foreign Affairs

Agriculture, Food and Foresty — Coillte — Teagasc

LEADER

Semi-state bodies:

Regional:

Other initiatives:

Local:

Other groups:

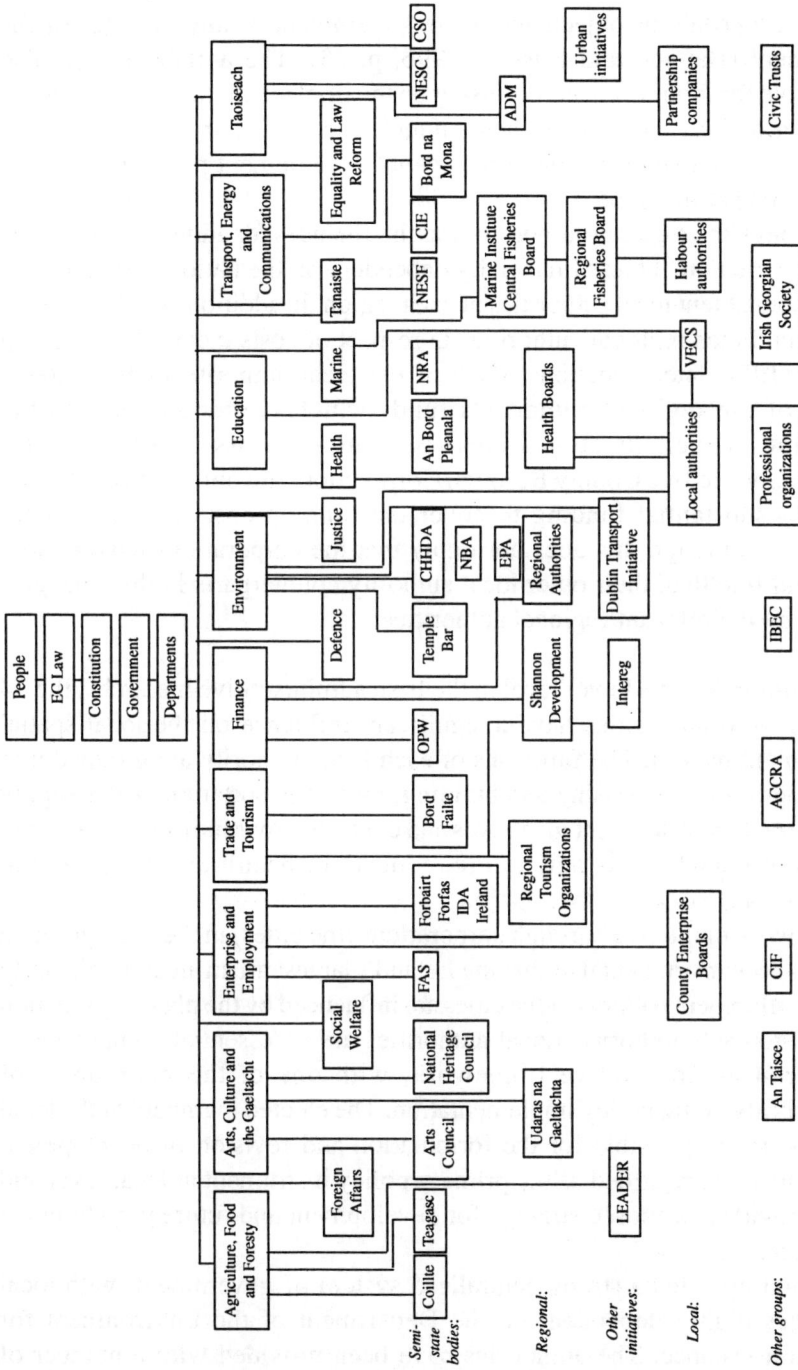

Figure 9.3 Overview of principal spatial policy-making institutions in the Republic of Ireland, 1996

policies, proposals or objectives of the government or any minister of the government (Bannon and Russell, 1996, p. 35). The authorities are also responsible for monitoring and advising on the implementation of EU funding in the regions As they are in their infancy, a commentary on the level of influence of the authorities on urban spatial development patterns would be inappropriate at this time.

Although the regional authorities require finances for administrative costs only, they are nonetheless financially dependent on the national government and the constituent local authorities of each region. In addition the Department of Finance funds regional authorities in respect of costs incurred in carrying out their EU-related functions. Each of the local authorities contributes a portion of the regional authority's funds which is proportionate to the population of their functional area (Bannon and Russell, 1996, p. 36). Accordingly, the five County Borough Corporations are obliged to contribute relatively substantial funding to cover the running costs of the regional authorities, although this does not imply that the corporations have a more influential role than their other local authority counterparts in the strategies pursued by the relevant regional authorities.

Local authorities At a lower level in the Irish administrative hierarchy, the 34 principal local authorities have a significant influence on the local spatial development pattern. The functions of each local authority are grouped into eight programmes – housing and building, road transportation, water supply and sewerage, development incentives and controls, environmental protection, recreation and amenity, agriculture, education, health and welfare, and miscellaneous.

The work of the five borough corporations (the cities) in these programme areas has been instrumental in shaping Ireland's largest urban areas, particularly as the development patterns of the cities are influenced by the planning function assigned to each authority. Local authorities are an essential component of the overall administrative framework, with one of the main areas of responsibility being policy implementation. The elected members of the local authority are responsible for the formulation and revision of development plans, which are regarded as the primary policy instrument at local level and which provide a proposed strategy for development and future growth in the area concerned.

Ireland operates a strong centralized system of government, with local authorities highly dependent on the Department of the Environment for financial assistance. The authorities have been provided with a number of grants, principally the 'Rate Support Grant', with service charges also providing an important source of income. The latter included the imposition of an annual fee on householders and others utilizing local authority services, in most areas, such as refuse collection and the provision of a water supply. However, there are plans to abolish all such charges. The government now believes that a charge for domestic water and sewerage facilities is 'more in the nature of a tax' and should therefore be consolidated into general taxation. Plans are also afoot to replace the Rate Support Grant.

In December 1996, the government published major reform proposals for *Better Local Government*. The aim of the programme is to modernize the Irish local government system and bring it more into line with European norms. Four core principles underlie the programme:

- enhancing local democracy and widening participation;
- serving the local authority customer better;
- developing efficiency;
- providing proper resources to fund local government (Department of the Environment, 1996a).

Both rural and urban areas of Ireland have gained significantly from European Union contributions, particularly as the Republic of Ireland is classified as an Objective One region for the purpose of receiving European funding.[6] Following the submission of the *National Development Plan 1994–1999* to the EU in an attempt to secure funding, the *Community Support Framework 1994–1999* emerged. This framework document contains a variety of operational programmes. Although financial assistance benefiting urban areas has been forthcoming under initiatives such as the Operational Programmes for Tourism, Transport and Industry, it is the *Operational Programme for Local Urban and Rural Development 1994–1999* which has had the greatest impact on the development, and in some cases the redevelopment, of the larger urban centres.

As Ireland lacked a single administrative structure with responsibility for integrated local development, the operational programme provided an opportunity to expand and integrate the various approaches that had been made to local development. The programme recognized the 'particular importance of locally-based measures for socio-economic development especially in communities characterized by long term unemployment and severe disadvantage' (Government of Ireland, 1994a). Many communities of this socio-economic profile are located in Ireland's urban areas.

Local Authority Independence

The system of local government in Ireland was intended to be a form of local self-government, providing the smallest community units possible with the opportunity to participate in the democratic process. In comparison to this ideal, the current role of local government may be considered subordinate, where local authorities have little influence of their own, as their functions and powers are derived from the Oireachtas.[7] The restrictive nature of the range of functions performed by local authorities has been recognized by the government. Local authorities are not 'in a position to offer a comprehensive response to problems confronting local communities ... causing communities to look to central Government to solve their problems, or to propose new arrangements locally' (Department of the Environment, 1996a, p. 7). Instead, they have been regarded as fulfilling a limited role as 'providers of environmental services and protectors of the environment'. However, the Local Government Acts of 1991 and 1994 have enhanced the powers of local authorities, offering hope for their future enhancement.

Fortunately, the level of independence of the local authorities is set to increase. A Devolution Commission was established in 1995. Its mandate included developing recommendations for a phased programme of devolution and a widening of the role of local government. A further report is being prepared by the Devolution Commission regarding the range of 'functions suitable for devolution to local government' (Department of the Environment, 1996a, p. 27). The recommendations are intended to provide the greatest possible level of independency to local authorities. In addition, the government report on *Better Local Government* proposes the strengthening of and greater independence for the local government tier as a result of the folowing:

- role of local elected members to be strengthened with a stronger focus on policy development through Strategic Policy Committees comprising two thirds representation from the local elected members and one third from sectoral and other interests;
- greater emphasis on serving customer needs; quality initiatives will be implemented to improve particular services;
- performance indicators will be used to measure and compare local authority activities; a major programme wil be put in place to ensure maximum efficiency and effectiveness; and
- the introduction of new arrangements for local government funding.

In addition, it is to be hoped that the recent publication *Sustainable Development – a Strategy for Ireland*, together with the policy of drawing up planning guidelines on land use policy issues, will provide a comprehensive policy framework for land use planning in Ireland (Department of the Environment, 1997).

National Conditions and Integrated Socio-economic Policies at the Local Level

Many of the national conditions which have an impact on the formulation and implementation of socio-economic policies at the local level have the dual effect of contributing both positively and negatively to these policies.

The structure of state sponsored bodies At the national level, a plethora of state sponsored bodies exists. Approximately 100 bodies have been established under the care of a number of government departments. They are established 'by or under statute and financed wholly or partly by means of grants or loans made by the Minister of State or the issue of shares taken up by the Minister'.

State sponsored bodies have contributed positively to the development of the country, but the absence of horizontal integrating mechanisms tends to weaken their impact in terms of integrated socio-economic policies. One of their main advantages is that they combine the experience of individuals involved in the public and private sector in order to guide and enhance the performance and management of state enterprises.

As each of the national bodies has a single purpose remit, there is some difficulty in securing comprehensive agreement on socioe-conomic policies, often due to the limited approach taken by the bodies and their sponsor departments to horizontal coordination. Additionally, many organizations are at a disadvantage due to differing levels of autonomy, which depend on the nature of the function performed by the relevant body, the financial position of the body and its source of funds.

The limited role of the regional authorities The regional authorities currently have a limited role. Operating under severe financial and policy restraints at present, it is hoped that the authorities may eventually play a more instrumental role in local socio-economic development.

One of the current problems being addressed is the need to increase the level of commitment from the majority of public bodies, to the work of the regional authorities. The Department of the Environment has called upon local authorities to give increased commitment to the regional concept (Department of the Environment, 1996a, p. 67). In a recent publication, *Better Local Government – A Programme for Change*, it is stated that although functions such as the provision of public services will remain with the primary local authorities, the 'regional authorities will become the focus for strategic planning for these services' (Department of the Environment, 1996a, p. 67). Additionally, other public bodies involved on the operational committees of the regional authorities will be required to 'make a modest financial contribution ..., to improve their sense of "ownership" of the regional authorities' policies and work ...' (Department of the Environment, 1996a, p. 68).

The overall role of the regional authorities is becoming more defined, with authorities having responsibility for the preparation of regional development reports which take account of the strengths and opportunities of each region and include appropriate objectives. In a bid to achieve maximum efficiency within the regional system, there are also proposals to review a number of existing regional boundaries.

The restricted role of local authorities The authorities have frequently been criticized for their perceived role as 'administrative organs allocated functions by the central authority as convenience dictates (Chubb, 1992, p. 264). Their subordinate role is emphasized by their financial dependence on the national government and the fact that their main function has been to provide environmental services and to serve as protectors of the environment, thereby giving them little opportunity to actively participate in the development of integrated socio-economic policies. Ireland's local authorities do not have as broad a range of responsibilities as most of their European counterparts,[8] a fact which was recently highlighted as a negative aspect of local government by the newly appointed manager of Dublin Corporation (*The Irish Times*, 10 July 1996).

However, efforts have been made in recent years to improve the role of local authorities. Reforms introduced since 1990 include:

- 'the introduction of broad powers of general competence for local authorities to act in the interests of the local community – relaxing substantially the archaic "ultra vires" rule';
- 'the provision of broad powers for the making of bye-laws to regulate a variety of local matters'; and
- 'the removal of a large range of statutory and administrative controls in

areas such as local authority personnel, land disposals, traffic management, etc. ...' (Department of the Environment, 1996a, p. 8).

The government policy for *Better Local Government* published in December 1996, is designed to continue and to accelerate the process of strengthening local government and includes a proposal that Ireland sign the European Charter of Local Self Government.

Administrative boundaries The nature of boundary divisions, particularly those of the urban areas, presents extreme difficulty in local level policy coordination. In many instances administrative boundaries do not reflect the urban realities of today. Most of the five major urban areas have greatly exceeded their administrative boundaries. This is particularly evident in the case of Dublin, where development pressures have led to the residential population spreading to areas beyond the former county boundary. In planning for the needs of the current population of the Dublin 'region', policies are required to deal with a much larger area. This is typified by the development of the Dublin Transportation Initiative (DTI) whose study area encompassed the commuting areas of counties surrounding Dublin. Although more realistic, the DTI area is not recognized as an administrative boundary. Similar situations exist in Waterford and Limerick, where in both cases development has spread beyond the corporation boundaries. As some of the suburban areas officially come under the functional area of neighbouring local authorities, coordination of policies between authorities is often difficult to achieve. *Better Local Government – A Programme for Change* addresses such issues and it is therefore hoped that reasonable solutions may be forthcoming.

Favourable National Conditions

The National Development Plan and the EU Community Support Framework are committed to local level development in urban and rural areas. One of the principal aims of the documents is to 'turn investment into employment – in industry, services, natural resources, tourism and construction' (Environmental Protection Agency, 1996, p. 239). In order to translate this national level aspiration into local areas, the operational programmes, which are derived from the Community Support Framework, place a high level of emphasis on the issue of local development. The *Operational Programme for Local Urban and Rural Development 1994–1999* is having the most direct impact. Through the assistance derived from the various sub-programmes relating to city and county Enterprise Boards, partnership companies and the local authorities, the social, economic and physical impacts are clearly visible, particularly within the urban areas (see Figure 9.4 for a list of local level developments that have taken place in the urban areas aimed at ameliorating area-based disadvantage).

Urban areas assisted under sub-programme two of the *Operational Programme for Local Urban and Rural Development 1994-1999*

Dublin

Ballymun	Dublin Inner City
Tallaght	Finglas/Cabra
Clondalkin	Blanchardstown
Ballyfermot	Coolock/Darndale/Kilbarrack
Crumlin/Kimmage/Walkinstown	

Other Urban Areas

Cork city	Tralee	Pockets of disadvantage
Limerick city	Bray	in South County Dublin
Galway city	Drogheda	and Dun Laoghaire
Waterford city	Dundalk	
	Wexford	

Figure 9.4   Local level developments in urban areas

County strategy groups were established in 1995 to serve as coordinating bodies for a variety of local development initiatives such as the partnership companies and county Enterprise Boards. A strategy group was established in each local authority area, with its members drawn from a wide range of disciplines, such as elected representatives of the local authorities, the social partners, voluntary groups, partnership companies and a wide range of other professional services. However, the county strategy groups may soon be replaced by 'community and enterprise groups' (CEG) in an effort better to integrate local government and local development systems. It is intended to bring about increased collaboration on projects, thereby creating a firm base for socio-economic development at the local level.

Urban Issues and Challenges from the National Perspective

Major National Urban Issues

'The creation of employment and the consequent reduction of unemployment and involuntary emigration is the primary objective of the Government' (Government of Ireland, 1991, p. 43). The problem of unemployment is exacerbated in the urban areas, due to greater concentrations of unemployed, particularly the long term unemployed. Partnership 2000 acknowledges that unemployment is the 'single biggest contributor to social exclusion and poverty' (Government of Ireland, 1996, p. 19).

As the urban areas continue to expand, it is important to note that unemployment figures within both the Dublin region and the Greater Cork area quadrupled between the 1970s and 1994 compared to the 199 per cent increase experienced over the rest of the country (Dublin Regional Authority, 1966, p. 25). Similar, although less aggravated, trends have also been identified in the other urban areas.

Urban Development Problems

The growth of population in urban areas has brought with it a number of unexpected issues. There has been extensive pressure for land resources, resulting initially in the spread of the urban areas outward, thereby contributing to the phenomenon of suburbanization. Concurrent with the trend of suburbanization, many Irish cities have experienced a regeneration of the core areas – a recent trend which is partially attributable to the introduction of the Urban Renewal Act of 1986 and subsequent Finance Acts.

Suburbanization has led to the obliteration of traditional roles and the street patterns and the identity of many villages and small towns. As the suburbs accommodate the increasing population, demand for further services is stimulated and, in many cases, the services have not been forthcoming. Extensive suburbanization of residence, coupled with city centre working locations, has given rise to serious commuting problems, with associated pollution problems. Additionally, where the core unemployment area was once the inner city, the problem has now partially shifted to 'new towns' on the peripheries.

Since the late 1980s, the regeneration of core urban areas has led to a change in the demographic structure and the social mix of the areas. Encouraged by recent trends of private sector apartment construction in the inner city, a new inner city population is now slowly emerging, with young, single professionals settling among the established local communities. Generally, there is little evidence of social mixing between this new population and the older traditional communities.

Limited Land Resources

Ireland has experienced a residential property boom in recent years, which has resulted in soaring property prices. Research conducted by estate agents indicates that Dublin house prices have risen by approximately 20 per cent during 1996, with further increases of up to ten per cent likely in 1997 (Hamilton Osborne King, 1996, p. 12). Contrary to the government policy of encouraging a social mix and combating segregation, the increases in house prices and land values have in fact contributed to further social segregation as certain areas of the cities become more elitist.

There is evidence that the scarcity of land has caused an intensification of use in most areas. Demand for development space in the inner suburbs is particularly high, where the market is favouring the construction of apartments. With a growth in the number of one and two person housing units and the resulting demand, a change in building types is becoming evident. Developers are now catering for the maximum number of residential property purchasers possible within the constraints of the particular site. Recent studies of the property market have concluded that the average size of residential units in urban and suburban locations may decrease even further over the coming years, in line with decreases in household size.

The Loss of Open Space and Amenity Areas

The pressure for development on the limited land resources of the major urban areas may result in the loss of valuable amenity areas and other open space. Under the Local Government (Planning and Development) Act of 1963, the relevant local authorities are charged with the responsibility of ensuring that their development plans contain adequate zoning for open space and amenity purposes.

As the largest urban area, Dublin has come under the greatest development pressure. In order to safeguard existing amenity areas two Special Amenity Area Orders were confirmed by the Minister for the Environment in 1990 and 1995,[9] following the submission of the orders from the relevant local authorities. The two areas to benefit from the protection are the Liffey Valley to the west of the city and Bull Island, a coastal nature reserve on Dublin Bay. It is likely that the Dublin region will benefit from a third SAAO in the near future, with the local authority currently preparing an order for a part of Howth Peninsula.

Environmental Concerns

In an age of growing concern for the protection and enhancement of the environment, the condition of urban areas has become increasingly important. Because of poor air quality levels for some areas, particularly caused by smoke and sulphur dioxide concentrations, regular monitoring procedures have now been put in place.

Water quality and the provision of an adequate water supply pose a threat to a number of major urban areas. Given that the five major cities of Ireland all occupy coastal locations, their degree of urbanization and the large proportion of the population which they are home to represent a threat to the environmental quality of the areas. Much of the coast near the urban areas is of a high scenic quality and is therefore intensively used for recreation purposes. However, studies of beaches in areas close to the urban centres have revealed a disappointing aesthetic quality. Additionally, much of the urban coastline is still used for effluent disposal and, in some cases, for port related activities, which have a significant potential to cause increased environmental pollution. There is a general recognition that there is a need for improved environmental management of the urban coastline.

Traffic Congestion

Traffic congestion is a phenomenon frequently associated with the structure of the city and increases in vehicle ownership rates among urban dwellers. The physical spread of the development of the cities has created complex journey patterns. Travel between the suburbs and the core areas had become the established norm and efforts were being made to cater for this through the improvement of public transport systems and stricter traffic regulations. However, owing to recent commercial and industrial development on the periphery of urban areas, travel patterns are changing, with increased journeys between suburbs and also a higher level of traffic flow from the core to the periphery.

The majority of public transport systems currently in place lack the efficiency to cope with increased demand on alternative routes. This issue is now being addressed in the capital city in the form of the Dublin Transportation Initiative (DTI).[10] Earlier attempts were also made to improve public transport systems, with the commissioning of the Cork Land Use/Transportation Study (LUTS) 1976 and reviewed in 1990.[11]

As public transport is not regarded by many as a viable alternative method of travel, traffic congestion has gradually worsened. The increase of vehicles on the streets has led to near gridlock situations in a number of cities. Many of the road systems are inadequate to cope with the level of traffic and it is an issue which is under constant review by the National Roads Authority,[12] whose task it is to 'secure the provision of a safe and efficient network'. The present economic boom has led to a major growth in traffic volumes, particularly in goods vehicles.

In addition to contributing to air and noise pollution and representing serious road safety implications, traffic congestion also has the potential to impact negatively on the economy of the urban areas, primarily through discouraging potential clients from using the facilities and services of the cities.

Crime and Health Concerns

Common to all urban areas is a rise in the incidence of crime and vandalism. Crime statistics released for 1995 show that 70 per cent of all criminal offences committed in Ireland were in city areas, with 80 per cent of indictable offences also occurring in the urban centres (Dublin Regional Authority, 1996, p. 58).

One of the greatest concerns in Irish cities in recent times has been the rise in drug abuse and associated crime. There are serious concerns for the safety of children and youngsters who are being introduced to the illegal substances in certain urban localities. The problems are compounded in those parts of urban areas, both inner city and suburban, which are characterized by multiple deprivation. In turn, drug abuse gives rise to a wide range of criminal activity, leading in turn to the establishment of vigilante groups as a reaction to the threat to the communities, especially to children.

National Priorities regarding Urban Issues

The central priority of the Irish government is a decrease in the nation's unemployment level, particularly in the urban areas, which are most severely affected. Initiatives aimed at reducing the level of unemployment are intended to have a cumulative effect, whereby the creation of employment opportunities

Strengths	Weaknesses
Heritage of the built environment Inner city renewal Generous fiscal policies encouraging urban renewal Strong historic identity Close proximity to the coast Nearby ports and airports Increasingly educated society	Weak hierarchical urban structure Inadequate infrastructure Lack of integrated policies for urban areas Peripherality of Ireland Unplanned urban overspill Some inner city dereliction Creation of inner city and suburban ghettos

THE FIVE MAJOR
URBAN AREAS

Opportunities	Threats
Improved services and facilities Creation of a balanced social mix Better educated population Development of local areas from the bottom-up Growth in services and high-tech industries Flows of inward investment Increased tourism potential	Environmental pollution Transport problems +costs Pressure for development Land speculation with negative effects Over-reliance on traditional manufacturing industries Long term unemployed Rise in crime/drug abuse Increased competition between European cities

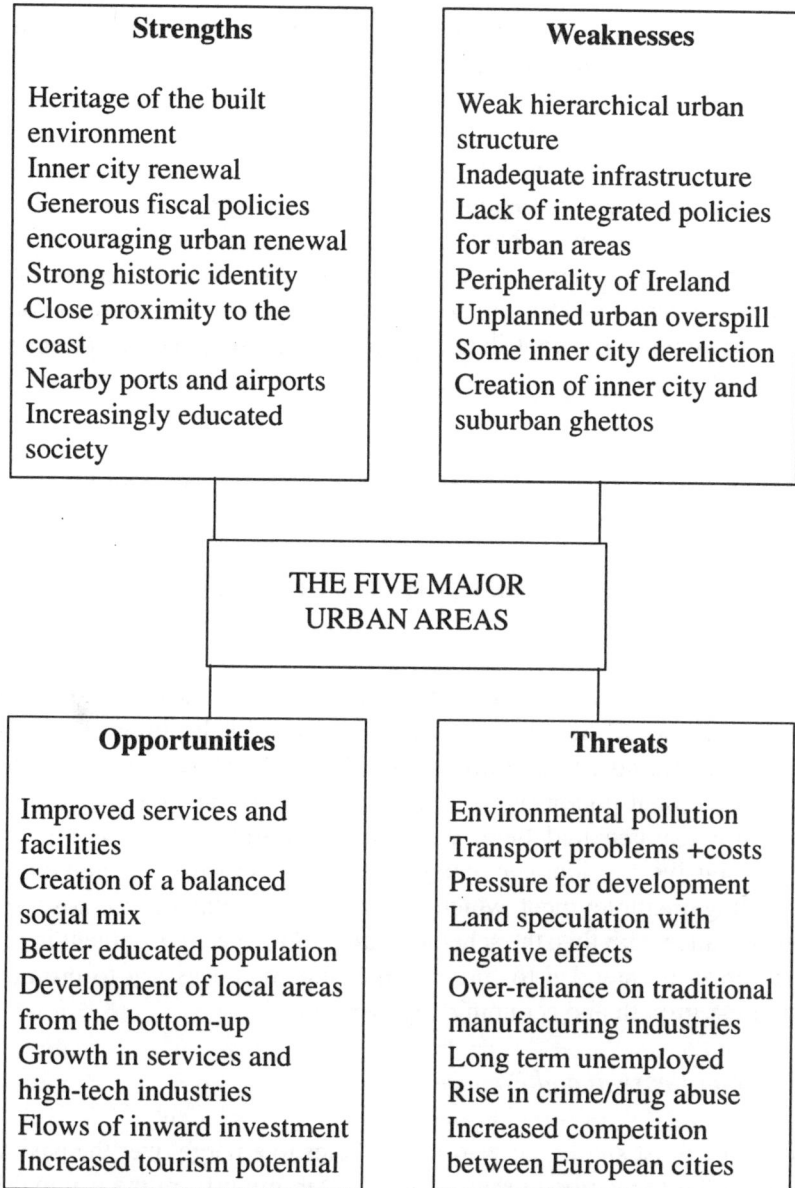

Figure 9.5 SWOT analysis of Ireland's urban areas

may lead to an improvement in the social and economic circumstances of greater numbers of the population.

The urban development pattern of recent years has proven that the creation of further jobs can achieve a diversity in the physical development of Irish cities. As previous sections of this chapter have demonstrated, new trends in city centre apartment, townhouse and mews living have emerged. One of the primary drivers of such changes has been the availability of increased job opportunities in the service sector, generally located at the core of the five major urban areas.[13] The policy of attracting people to the urban cores as a place of residence has contributed towards the reduction of the doughnut city idea.

National Policy Responses to Urban Issues, Challenges and Development

National Policy and the National Vision for Cities and the Urbanization Process

Considerable efforts have been made over the last decade to introduce policies which will assist the process of urbanization in the long term. The EU *Community Support Framework 1994–1999* is the closest representation of a realistic national policy, as its objectives were formulated after the level of available finance had been decided. Although it does not provide a comprehensive development policy, it nonetheless focuses on vital issues such as tackling unemployment, which is perceived as Ireland's foremost problem. In accordance with this, the scheme of upgrading the environment in selected urban areas is intended to 'provide the impetus necessary to promote self sustaining growth and economic regeneration'.

The Urban Renewal and Finance Acts

One of the most significant national policies to emerge over the past decade has been the focus upon urban renewal. Stemming from the original Urban Renewal Acts of 1986 and 1987, the overall approach is intended to provide for comprehensive redevelopment of urban areas. The urban renewal programme encourages the refurbishment of existing buildings and the improvement of the streetscape through landscaping and other material works, and it is also intended to provide increased educational opportunities, and facilitate the development of social and community services in urban areas.[14]

As Ireland's inner cities were characterized by high development costs and serious problems of site assembly, public intervention in the form of urban renewal incentives was considered necessary. The incentives regulated the market forces which would otherwise have led to new private commercial and residential developments being located outside the urban cores.

As Table 9.2 demonstrates, the success of the urban renewal policies has been particularly noticeable in Dublin where inner city wards experienced a constant decline in population between 1951 and 1991. The decline of Dublin's inner city areas was as a combined result of the private sector preference for suburban living, the local authority decision to provide housing in 'new towns', and the gradual loss of manufacturing industries in the core areas.

Table 9.2   Dublin inner city population 1995 –96

DED	1951	1961	1966	1971	1979	1981	1986	1991	1996
Arran Quay	24,987	20,242	19,091	17,434	13,954	13,654	11,944	10,120	11,424
North Dock	17,192	13,977	13,548	12,035	9,107	8,510	8,063	7,049	7,265
Ballybough	12,847	9,533	9,965	8,525	7,578	7,429	6,164	6,047	6,125
Inns Quay	20,298	13,649	13,078	11,996	9,435	8,781	7,947	7,335	7,649
Mountjoy	17,512	13,123	11,402	10,344	6,939	5,792	4,863	4,640	5,103
North City	7,454	4,195	2,966	2,311	1,588	927	1,206	819	2,391
Rotunda	13,602	8,241	6,757	6,064	4,681	3,870	3,028	2,733	3,522
Mansion House	14,405	9,859	8,827	6,328	4,389	4,403	3,803	3,613	3,849
Merchants' Quay	25,476	19,394	19,225	16,898	14,530	13,763	11,142	10,534	11,687
Royal Exchange	10,599	6,165	5,293	4,577	3,455	3,175	2,477	2,323	3,872
St. Kevin's	9,614	6,512	5,900	4,918	3,595	3,497	3,067	3,047	3,549
South Dock	10,714	6,914	5,818	5,122	3,370	3,123	2,968	2,589	3,294
Ushers Quay	23,938	18,765	19,316	17,711	14,820	13,898	11,023	10,298	10,476
Wood Quay	11,103	8,908	8,723	7,968	6,397	6,436	5,509	5,411	6,166
Total	219,741	159,477	149,909	132,231	103,838	97,258	83,204	76,558	86,372

Source: *Census of Population, Volume 1, 1951, 1956, 1961, 1966, 1971, 1979, 1981, 1986, 1991 and 1996*, Central Statistics Office, Dublin.

However, the introduction of the urban renewal incentives has rejuvenated the inner city, with all 14 wards in Dublin's inner city recording population increases for the period between 1991 and 1996. Similar evidence is now available also for the other cities.

The Establishment of Independent Authorities for Urban Renewal

A number of independent authorities have been established for the purpose of overseeing urban renewal activities in Dublin city centre. The Custom House

Docks Development Authority (CHDDA) was established under the Urban Renewal Act of 1986, with its general duty being to 'secure the re-development of the Custom House Dock area'.[15] The functions assigned to the CHDDA included acquiring, holding and managing land for redevelopment, the provision of infrastructure and the preparation of a planning scheme for the development, redevelopment and renewal of the area. The development of the Custom House Docks area is ongoing and progress has been made, with notable developments including the Irish Financial Services Centre, extensive residential schemes and the provision of a hotel.

Following the success of the CHDDA, Temple Bar Properties Limited and Temple Bar Renewal Limited were established in 1991. Through the use of compulsory purchase powers, the area has benefited from comprehensive redevelopment. The functions of the authority include the renewal of the area, the regeneration of the residential population; 'the marketing of Temple Bar with the aim of attracting an increased amount of business, activity and people to the area; and the improvement of the Temple Bar environment in co-operation with the appropriate authorities' (Temple Bar Properties, 1992, p. 7). The combined work of the two bodies has resulted in the regeneration of an inner city area, which has been internationally commended and is now regarded as Dublin's cultural quarter.

Legislation was enacted in 1996 to establish the Dublin Docklands Authority to oversee the redevelopment of an extensive area to the east of Dublin's city centre. The Dockland's Authority is in the process of finalizing a master plan for the development of this area.

Impacts of Urban Renewal

The original 1986 Urban Renewal Act, has been criticized for its initial negative impact on the urban areas. Together with the Finance Act, the incentive package offered had been heavily biased in favour of commercial, rather than residential, developments. This resulted in an oversupply of offices in many of the urban areas, particularly in locations not traditionally associated with tertiary development. Dublin's inner city was most severely affected, with a vacancy rate of 45 per cent in new office buildings in the designated areas in the early 1990s.

However, this situation was reversed as developers turned their attention to residential developments. In addition, during the past three years the 'expansion in key areas of financial services, telemarketing, data processing and software development' (Lisney, 1996, p. 4) has created a strong office market. A record take up of 112,000 m^2 of office space was recorded in 1995 in the Dublin area, with the first nine months of 1996 accounting for a 100,000 m^2 take up (Hamilton Osborne King, 1996, p. 3). There is currently a shortage of new prime office space as speculative development has been slow following the mistakes of the 1980s. In comparison to office vacancy figures for the late '80s, it is now expected that the vacancy rate in 1997 will dip below 4 per cent (Hamilton Osborne King, 1996, p. 3).

The original urban renewal initiative was also a source of disappointment as it encouraged a change in the urban fabric of the inner cities. Demolition and new construction was widespread, rather than the retention and refurbishment of existing buildings. It is estimated that in the decade since the introduction of the urban renewal programme, the refurbishment of the existing stock has accounted for just 11 per cent of the total work. *A Study on the Urban Renewal Schemes* is critical of the manner in which development work was undertaken, claiming that it was piecemeal, with 'little prioritization of urban design objectives'. The report, prepared for the government, recommends that future urban renewal tax incentives should be linked to area based plans which take account of commercial development, employment, design and urban conservation (Department of the Environment, 1996b).

A third criticism of the urban renewal incentives has been that they failed adequately to take into consideration the existing population of the inner cities. Numerous inner city communities are classed as socially deprived and therefore do not possess the initial capital required to facilitate their participation in tax incentive led development. With escalating land prices in the designated areas and the entry of the economically privileged social classes into the inner cities, the traditional communities can ultimately experience further social exclusion.

Changes in the Urban Renewal Programme

Although the initial urban renewal programme covered a limited number of areas in the five largest cities, the programme was gradually extended to cover over 100 designated areas in 35 urban centres. Drawing on the experiences of the early years of the renewal programme, a government decision was taken in 1994 to introduce a revised urban renewal programme, with an increased emphasis on the development of residential properties in the urban core, particularly favouring the refurbishment of existing buildings.

Two of the most innovative incentives introduced in 1994 were the 'Living over the Business Scheme' and the creation of new enterprise zones. The latter measure aims to attract clean industries into inner city locations. The scheme has had the dual purpose of creating jobs and assisting the regeneration process. Enterprise zones have been successfully developed in Dublin, Cork and Galway.

Other incentives include:

- 50 per cent capital allowances for commercial development;
- double rent allowances for ten years for business occupiers;
- rates relief on a sliding scale for ten years;
- 100 per cent relief for owner occupiers of refurbished houses and flats.

Further improvements were added to the urban renewal programme in 1995 as the Minister issued a comprehensive set of guidelines for the development of apartments (Department of the Environment, 1995a). The guidelines recommended minimum floor areas for one, two and three bedroom apartments, in addition to minimum floor areas for individual rooms in each unit. In the interests of achieving an improved demographic structure (i.e., encouraging couples and families to live in the urban cores) the guidelines stipulate that no more than half the units in residential developments in tax designated areas may be one bedroomed. It is also required that a proportion of large three bedroom apartments must be included in developments comprising 50 or more units.

Housing Policy

Over the past number of years successive governments have broadly followed similar housing policies, with the main objective being to enable 'every household to have available an affordable dwelling of good quality, suited to its needs, in a good environment, and, as far as possible, at the tenure of its choice' (Department of the Environment, 1995b, p. 4). Ireland has one of the highest rates of home ownership in Europe, with an estimated 80 per cent of dwellings being owner occupied. National policies have encouraged this trend through the provision of a number of fiscal incentives. The primary incentives offered are tax relief on mortgage interest, which has been curtailed in recent years, and the first time buyer's grant.[16]

However, the government accepts that home ownership may not be within the financial capabilities of all households. Therefore, a housing policy exists which aims to provide either local authority housing or housing provided by voluntary groups. In 1995 the government introduced a policy document entitled *Social Housing: The Way Ahead*. It is aimed at changing the role of local authorities from providers of housing to a more enabling role, where local authorities will assist tenants in acquiring their properties. This is achievable through measures such as shared ownership schemes,[17] mortgage allowances for tenants and the provision of serviced sites. The primary aim of the document is to counteract housing segregation and to encourage an improved social mix – two problems which are most often encountered in Ireland's five major cities. There is also a growing emphasis on housing management issues.

Other Policies Affecting the Built Environment

The Building Control Act of 1990 provides a modern basis for regulating the products of the building industry. The Act provided the Minister for the Environment with the power to introduce regulations regarding the design and construction of buildings, material alterations or extensions, the provision of services, fittings and equipment, and to material changes of use. Regulations introduced to date have been instrumental in raising the standards of numerous developments throughout urban areas.

In 1996, the Department of Arts, Culture and the Gaeltacht issued a document which is intended to be the forerunner of Ireland's first government policy on architecture. *Developing a Government Policy on Architecture* marks an appreciation of the cultural and social significance of Ireland's architecture, particularly the fine examples of notable architectural periods which exist in some of the major urban areas. The proposed policy is aimed at improving the quality of the built environment, particularly through the promotion of the concept of sustainability and also through the development of a clear 'framework within which the building profession and other organisations can focus their efforts more effectively' with the assistance of the state (Department of Arts, Culture and the Gaeltacht, 1996, p. 69).

Environmental Policies

Although Ireland benefits from a relatively high quality natural environment, it has occasionally been necessary to implement programmes on national environmental action. Many of the activities were particularly necessary in the urban areas where greater concentrations of population and traffic tended to contribute to a decrease in air quality. The *National Development Plan 1994–1999* clearly states the value of a quality environment in developing the overall economy of the country – '[i]t is the primary objective of this Plan to enhance economic performance through sustainable growth and development. Ireland's reputation as a clean and green country offers an important opportunity for competitive advantage in development ...' (Government of Ireland, 1993a, p. 141).

Over the past decade, the Air Pollution Act which came into effect on 1 September 1987 has had a positive effect on the quality of the urban environment. The Act gave legal expression to a previously issued EC Directive (80/779). It was the first comprehensive air pollution act in Irish statute and has since been used effectively to prohibit certain emissions and has allowed for the designation of 'special control areas' (Sweeney, 1991, p. 233). It is of general benefit in all major urban areas, although it was originally enacted to cope with the problems of increasing smog in the Dublin region. Following a 1988 Dublin City Council order designating a small area of a south city suburb as a special control area, the government prohibited the sale of all bituminous coal throughout the Greater Dublin area in 1990 and similarly in the Greater Cork area in 1995.

Ireland's urban areas have also suffered from air pollution caused by increases in vehicle numbers. The concentration of vehicles results in smoke emission from internal combustion engines and in some cases visible exhaust products. Despite causing a deterioration in air quality, there has not been any direct policy on vehicle emissions in Ireland since SI No. 190 of 1963, Road Traffic (Construction, Equipment and Use of Vehicles) (Timoney, 1992, p. 240). Instead, EC legislation is relied upon, particularly the 1991 Directive which consolidated all former complex legislation into one (91/441/EEC). In 1991, the Department of the Environment published a discussion paper on the directive. Entitled *Implementation of Vehicle Emission Standards in Ireland*, it summarized Irish requirements in this area and stated that the minister proposed to meet the latest EC requirements (Scannell, 1995). The most recent EU legislation which the national government has been obliged to take into account dates from 1994 and concerns emission standards for all vehicles (94/12/EC – Mechanically Controlled Vehicle Emission Control Regulations).

Since the 1970s, various legislation has been enacted requiring the issuing of licences and permits for certain activities, such as air emissions or waste disposal from industrial developments. The relevant local authorities were responsible for the issuing of the licences. Since 1994, a more efficient system has been in operation, with licences and permits now combined as an Integrated Pollution Control Licence, which the newly established Environmental Protection Agency has responsibility for issuing.

The Environmental Protection Agency (EPA) was established in 1993, with the primary purpose of controlling and regulating scheduled activities which are likely to pose a major threat to the quality of the environment. Two of the EPA's functions which have a positive effect on the environmental quality of the urban environment are the agency's monitoring of the environmental quality and the licensing, regulation and control of scheduled activities for the purpose of environmental protection. A comprehensive report on the current state of the environment has recently been completed by the Environmental Protection Agency.

In 1990 *An Environmental Action Programme* was launched by the government and it provided a framework for environmental protection founded on the principles of sustainable development, integration and precautionary action (Bannon and Russell, 1996). The programme indicated an environmental investment directive of up to Ir. £1 billion over the decade of the 1990s. Ireland's urban areas have been improved through a variety of measures suggested in the programme. These include increased efforts to attract environmentally-friendly industries through offering higher rates of industrial grants, the promotion of waste recycling which many local authorities have become involved in, and a general increase in the awareness of environmental issues affecting the urban and rural areas. The latter policy of increasing national awareness has been assisted through the establishment of an environmental information centre in Dublin city centre.

Economic Policy

The primary objective of the country's economic policy is to 'secure and strengthen the economy's potential for sustainable employment and economic growth' (Government of Ireland, 1994d, p. 51). Successive documents have outlined policies aimed at achieving this,[18] the majority of which support the development of a programme of structural measures covering industrial policy, manpower policy, tax and social welfare reform and changes in health and education policies (Bannon and Russell, 1996, Part II, p. 54).

Industrial policy has undergone a transformation in recent decades. The formulation and evaluation of policy has taken a much broader approach, with the acceptance that 'national development involves all sectors of the economy, and that the industrial sector alone cannot provide enough jobs to meet our national requirements' (McMenamin, 1975, p. 196). Industrial policy in the 1990s takes into account issues such as 'the level and structure of taxation, the cost and quality of infrastructure, the relevance and effectiveness of education and training' (Industrial Policy Review Group, 1994, p. 9). There has been a shift in emphasis from traditional manufacturing industries to a favouring of the service sector of the economy. Prior to the introduction of service sector policies, the decline in secondary employment served as the catalyst for the decline of the inner urban areas. The positive role of the services sector has been highlighted in the Culliton and Moriarity reports,[19] which were commissioned with a view to industrial policy reform. It is now realized that the tertiary sector is a valuable source of job creation, with the potential to encourage the regeneration of Ireland's urban areas. *Shaping Our Future – A Strategy for Enterprise in Ireland in the 21st Century* recently projected that over 300,000 jobs can be created in the services sector over the next 15 years, provided that the right policy framework is in place (Forfas, 1996, p. 25).

In an effort to accelerate industrial development in specific locations, the recently signed national agreement, *Partnership 2000* refers to accelerated planning procedures to facilitate certain major projects.

The formulation of a manpower policy is also becoming increasingly important. It is aimed at improving the skills of those currently in employment and developing the skills of the unemployed through the establishment of training and education schemes. Beneficial action has been taken as a result of funding received under the Community Support Framework. Government policy supports the development of area-based programmes for the unemployed, the development of which has often been facilitated by the *Operational Programme for Local Urban and Rural Development* and the *Operational Programme for Human Resources*. The programmes illustrate that national policy now supports the bottom-up approach to economic development. The area-based programme, which was originally developed under the PESP,[20] has proved highly successful in a number of disadvantaged urban locations characterized by high levels of unemployment.

Commercial and Retail Policies

Ireland lacks a direct policy concerning commercial development. Above average amounts of commercial development have generally been accounted for by a growth in the services sector. The greatest concentration of commercial activity has taken place in the Dublin region, with the other large urban areas also benefiting, largely through the introduction of the Urban Renewal Act in 1986. As the original incentives offered in the 1986–94 period favoured commercial rather than residential development, by January 1994, £263 million had been spent on commercial developments, with 342,000 m^2 of office space constructed in the designated core areas of the cities.

The benefits of the incentives were also apparent in the south west Dublin suburb of Tallaght. This area developed as a 'new town' from the 1960s, and although it had a population in excess of 61,000 in its catchment area by 1986, the 'town' remained devoid of a centre providing basic service and facilities. Upon designation in 1988, the concept of the Tallaght Town Centre was created. The area is now host to The Square – Ireland's second largest regional shopping centre, the Tallaght Retail Park, a large number of industrial warehouses, a substantial number of office developments, a hotel and a variety of recreation facilities.

Similarly to commercial policy, Ireland is also deficient in terms of a national retail policy. Development pressure in recent years has led to the creation of large regional shopping centres and other retail forms, such as warehousing. The most relevant document addressing retail issues dates from 1982 – a ministerial directive on *Planning Policy on Large Scale Retail Shopping Developments*.[21] However, with the changing development trends and particularly the shopping patterns in urban areas, the issues covered in the Directive need to be reassessed. Recent years have seen the opening of a number of large shopping complexes in the Dublin region and a variety of smaller shopping centres in the other urban areas. There are also advanced plans for further major shopping developments, particularly in Dublin.

One of the most recent trends to emerge in Ireland is retail warehousing. Planners were initially reluctant to allow the development of retail parks in locations other than industrial estates. However, successful retail park developments in Tallaght and Galway have led to a change in opinion. Due to the lack of pertinent legislation, it is the responsibility of the relevant local authorities to safeguard against undesirable retail developments. Each authority may adopt its own policy on retailing and include it in its statutory development plan. However, this can lead to difficulties, as policies may run contrary to those of neighbouring local authorities.

Transport Policy in Urban Areas

At the national level, the general thrust of transport policy for the coming years is reflected in the EU funded *Operational Programme for Transport 1994–1999*. The overall aim of national transport policy is to meet the identified needs of all transport users, with a view to improving transport services for industrial and tourism purposes, as a method of assisting regional development and encouraging the urban renewal process.

Positive action regarding transport policy is of vital importance to the future development of Ireland's urban areas and indeed the development of the entire country. It had been argued that Ireland's economic performance is hampered by its peripheral position, principally the fact that it is now the only remaining EU Member State without a direct land link to the continent. In a bid to counter this disadvantage, national policy is geared towards improving air and sea transport. Consequently, a number of the major urban areas have benefited from such actions due to the close proximity of the three largest international airports and some of the principal seaports.

Although it is necessary to secure adequate cost effective air and sea transport, the national transport policy also highlights the importance of developing adequate transport infrastructures within Ireland, linking regions and urban areas. Significant investment in the internal transport system is planned over the coming years, as the government recognizes the possible 'contribution that a high quality transport infrastructure can make to economic development' (Bannon and Russell, 1996, Part II, p. 48). This investment will focus principally upon new national roads and upon the implementation of the Dublin Transportation Initiative.

Education Policy

Education is regarded as being of major social and economic importance. A large amount of public expenditure is committed to education. There has been a tremendous growth in educational participation, particularly in third level colleges. However, the negative reality is that the formulation of medium to long term policies is constrained by reliance on the annual budgetary system (National Economic and Social Council, 1990, p. 309). The education policies which have been pursued to date have not been explicitly related to the urban areas, rather they have had indirect impacts in the areas. However, urban areas do have specific concentrations of educational need.

The majority of third level institutions in Ireland are situated in major urban areas and it may be assumed that this would have a positive impact on the areas, given the research and development opportunities, and the increased contribution to the local economy which is derived from the user populations.

However, there are negative effects, most of which centre around the issue of equality. Policy instruments exist which aim at improving the equality of opportunity in education. However, attendance at third level institutions in the late 1980s was associated with rising costs as the government favoured the idea of the student bearing increasing costs. The *Programme for Action in*

Education 1984–1987 suggested that 'students should be required to meet a greater share of the costs and that fees should bear an increasing proportion of the cost' (Department of Education, 1984). This effectively discouraged participation among individuals from deprived and disadvantaged areas. Fortunately the past decade has seen a change in policy regarding third level education. In 1995, the Minister for Education announced the abolition of all fees at undergraduate level. This was partially implemented for the academic year 1995/96 and became fully operational at the start of the academic year of 1996. It is expected that the abolition of fees will encourage greater numbers of lower socioeconomic classes to seek entry to higher level education.

The Department of Education and the individual institutions are aware that inequalities in the system still exist, with research showing that a low proportion of students attending the urban based institutions actually come from the localities. To counteract this, a collaborative scheme was recently announced between the Department of Education and Dublin City University. DCU is located in a northern suburb of Dublin, with neighbouring suburbs including some of the most socially and economically disadvantaged areas of Dublin. Many of the areas are characterized by a pattern of early school leaving, followed by long term unemployment. The recent announcement concerned the decision to make available 50 special places at DCU for students from the disadvantaged local area, under a scheme known as the North Dublin Access Initiative.[22] Rather than going through the CAO system,[23] interested students will submit their application to the college, where it will be directly assessed.

Efforts are also being made at secondary level to combat the effects of disadvantage. The *Programme for Economic and Social Progress*, which was launched by the government in 1991 states that efforts will be made to 'increase retention rates in education among disadvantaged groups' (Government of Ireland, 1991, p. 31). This is to be achieved through early identification of children suffering educational or social disadvantage, followed by positive action in the form of remedial teaching, guidance and counselling and the development of home and schools links.

Justice Policy

With the incidence of crime on the increase, particularly in the larger urban areas, there has been a need for the Department of Justice to introduce new initiatives to deal with the problem. The Garda Schools Programme which has been in existence for some time is intended to change children's 'attitudes towards vandalism, substance abuse and general authority'. In 1991, it was considered necessary to extend the programme to new areas of Dublin, Cork, Limerick and Waterford, where crime statistics were becoming of public concern.

It is also the aim of the Department of Justice to ensure that Ireland's urban areas become safer places in which to live and work. In order to achieve this, the number of annual recruits to the national Garda Training School has been increased and large numbers of those qualified are being deployed to the major urban centres. Additionally, a limited number of closed circuit television systems were installed on some major urban thoroughfares. Research has shown that the CCTV system has been instrumental in reducing the number of crimes in the area and has also assisted Gardai (police) with their enquiries. As a result there are plans to extend the system to other parts of some urban areas.

The Impact of EU Policies

At the current time, the European Union is considered to have little impact on urban areas, due to the lack of a comprehensive urban policy at European level. Many regional and local authorities operating in Ireland's urban areas echo the sentiments expressed by the Committee of the Regions and draw attention to a recent document which called for an urban policy. The document stated that

> urban areas have not been one of the focal points of EU policy development. In fact, EU policies and funding programmes have developed almost on an ad hoc basis. As a result, the European Union cannot claim any coherence in its policies on urban development (Dublin Regional Authority, 1996, (excerpt from C.o.R. 235/95) p. 75).

In an effort to assess the impact of various EU funding programmes, a midterm review and evaluation of the operational programmes is required under the Community Support Framework 1994–1999. It is expected that a review of the *Operational Programme for Local Urban and Rural Development* and the *Operational Programme for Human Resources* will be completed by mid-1997.

Although it is widely accepted that the European Union has a limited legitimacy on urban policy, it is conceded that the potential for increasing influence does exist due to levels of funding being provided by the Union. As previous sections of this chapter have outlined, Ireland is designated as an

Objective 1 region, for the purpose of administering structural funds. The assistance has been welcomed and has facilitated large scale change in urban and rural areas.

Objective 1 regions are defined as those territorial units whose per capita GDP is less than 75 per cent of the Community average. Funding provided to Objective 1 regions is intended to 'promote the development and structural adjustment of regions whose development is lagging behind in EU terms' (Dublin Regional Authority, 1996, p. 69). Funding for Ireland as a region is derived from all four of the Structural Funds – the European Regional Development Fund, the European Social Fund, the European Agricultural Guidance and Guarantee Fund and the Financial Instrument for Fisheries Guidance, although the latter two sources of funding are of relatively little benefit to urban areas.

While Ireland's GDP, as a percentage of the EU average, was below the 75 per cent threshold in 1993–94, this has increased above the 75 per cent threshold of eligibility for funding. There is concern at national level that Ireland may lose its Objective 1 status in subsequent rounds of the structural funding. In order to safeguard against this, there have been suggestions that Dublin, which has the best economic performance, should be classified as a separate region, thereby losing its Objective 1 classification, but allowing the remainder of the country to retain its status where GDP rates may still fall below the 75 per cent threshold.[24] The Regional Authority for Dublin is opposed to this, claiming that the 'use of GDP criteria is unsuitable as the sole indicator of eligibility for EU Structural Funds' (Dublin Regional Authority, 1996, p. 69).

Positive Impacts

Following from the Community Support Framework, a series of action programmes were implemented. The majority of the operational programmes have been of some benefit to the development of urban areas. However, the *Operational Programme for Local Urban and Rural Development* has proved to have had the greatest impact.

The Local Enterprise Sub-Programme involved the establishment of City and County Enterprise Boards. The boards fill a gap which had existed in the 'range of support services available for local enterprise initiatives' (Government of Ireland, 1994a). Although they have only come into existence in the relatively recent past, the boards have already made a valuable contribution towards stimulating economic activity in areas. The more disadvantaged urban areas have particularly benefited, as many of the long term unemployed utilized the assistance offered by the Enterprise Boards as a means of breaking the cycle of unemployment, poverty and low self-esteem. In addition to providing financial assistance to individuals wishing to start or expand their businesses, the Enterprise Boards also offer practical assistance through the provision of information services and the promotion of an enterprise culture. The benefits of the work have been seen by many local communities, particularly through the improvement of economic circumstances.

Sub-Programme two of the *Operational Programme for the Integrated Development of Designated Disadvantaged and Other Areas* operates in a similar manner, with the most disadvantaged areas being targeted (see Figure 9.4 above). The partnership companies have been established in the areas with the assistance of ADM,[25] through the administration of the Global Grant. The partnerships have provided enormous support to communities and have greatly assisted in planning for local area development. Local communities have been enabled to help themselves through their involvement in capacity building exercises. The problems of social exclusion and marginalization are being tackled, and individuals are gaining new skills and increased confidence through participation in partnership programmes, therefore bringing social and economic benefit to the disadvantaged areas.

The Urban and Village Renewal sub programme has had the greatest effect on the physical environment (Department of the Environment, 1995a). Many inner city areas have experienced a social and economic rejuvenation through the projects which have been undertaken under measure one of the sub-programme (see Figure 9.6 for a list and details of the five major initiatives). Financial assistance was allocated to the five major urban areas, with each of the relevant local authorities choosing a flagship project to lead the way in the regeneration of a core area of the urban centre. It is thought that the redevelopment of such core areas may have a cumulative effect in that the improved physical environment will attract new investments, further developments and a subsequent increase in the population of the urban cores, leading to a change in the demographic pattern of Ireland's inner cities. However, there may be some necessity to curtail projects of a complex nature, as the local authorities are obliged to provide matching funds for any financial assistance received from the European Union. The sub-programme also has the added advantage of dovetailing into already on going development under the Urban Renewal Acts.

1   **Dublin**
    The initiative became known as HARP – the Historic Area Rejuvenation Programme. It consists of the partial regeneration of a large area immediately north of the river Liffey, with its other boundaries formed by O'Connell Street, Collins Barracks and Henrietta Street to the east, west and north respectively.
2   **Cork**
    The Cork initiative is part of the local authority's 'Historic Centre Action Plan'. The initiative primarily concentrates on the medieval core of the city, taking in North and South Main Streets and Shannon Street and Barrack Street.
3   **Limerick**
    The funding received by Limerick Corporation was deployed to the King's Island Area of the city, to assist in achieving the aims of an overall integrated action plan.
4   **Galway**
    The eastern bank of the river Corrib, as it passes through the core area of Galway city is the area benefiting under Measure 1 of the subprogramme. A regeneration of the core area, linked to Eyre Square (the main square) is in progress.
5   **Waterford**
    Waterford Corporation have chosen an initiative which has a significant emphasis on the river. The South Quays and the Stony Steps area are benefiting from the restoration of a number of historic buildings, with additional plans to develop the area as an 'arts and crafts quarter'.

Source: Department of the Environment, 1995, p. 10.

Figure 9.6   The five Major Urban Reneral Initiatives funder under the EU Operational Programme

The URBAN Community Initiative

Another EU programme which is considered to have a positive impact on the urban areas of Ireland is the URBAN Community Initiative. The initiative has been implemented in three areas – two in Dublin and one in Cork – and it is especially useful as it complements the measures of the Community Support Framework, in particular those projects being implemented through the *Operational Programme for Local Urban and Rural Development 1994 – 1999*. URBAN takes a broad approach to urban development, and is considered to 'act as a catalyst by undertaking key schemes to help deprived urban areas achieve a lasting improvement in living standards for their inhabitants' (Goodbody Economic Consultants/Service Industries Research Centre, 1996, p. 1).

The implementation of the URBAN Initiative in Dublin and Cork follows the guidelines of the Commission of the European Communities, as it addresses in an 'integrated way a range of problems associated with socio-economic exclusion within deprived sections of inner cities and peripheral urban areas throughout the European Union' (Government of Ireland, 1966, p. 6). The government of Ireland accepts that addressing the problems in all urban deprivation areas is impossible, owing to the scale of the task involved. However, it is thought that indirect benefits may be derived from the URBAN initiative for all urban areas, as the actions undertaken within the selected areas are intended to serve as a demonstration of techniques that may be applied in other urban areas. From this point, it then becomes possible to build on the structures already in place.

Trans European Networks: Urban and Settlement Implications

The introduction of the Trans European Network initiative has also had an impact on the urban areas of Ireland. 'It is clear that Ireland's location at the western extremity of Europe is a handicap which needs to be overcome'.[26] It is imperative that trans-European links are developed in order to allow integral aspects of the Irish economy, such as trade and tourism, to develop to their full potential. A number of road, rail and sea routes have been identified for investment in the *Operational Programme for Transport* which form integral parts of the Trans European Network. The introduction of the TEN's initiative has encouraged increased cooperation between governments in various member states. For example, the Irish Department of Transport, Energy and Communications, the Department of the Marine and the United Kingdom Department of Transport have jointly commissioned a feasibility study on the commercial viability of combined transport links between Ireland and Great Britain (Government of Ireland, 1994c).

Transport improvements instigated as a result of the Trans European Network initiative include the extensive redevelopment of Dublin Port and Dun Laoghaire Harbour as well as Rosslare Harbour in the south east of the country.[27] It is intended that the actions will strengthen the 'land bridge' route between Ireland and Europe. Upgrading of roads leading from the north Wales port of Holyhead are on going, resulting in improved access from Ireland to the motorway network of the UK, and particularly to the ports of the east and south coasts and the Channel Tunnel.

Attention has also been given to the rail system in Ireland recently. Journey times are set to improve between urban areas as a result of the upgrading work which has been undertaken. Passenger train speeds are being increased on the Dublin–Cork and Dublin–Belfast rail lines as part of the Trans European

Network of High Speed Rail. Speed and safety systems are also set to improve on rail routes from Dublin to Limerick, Sligo, Galway, Waterford and Rosslare.[28]

Conclusions

An attempt has been made in the preceding sections to outline the pattern of urban spatial development which Ireland has experienced. In doing so, the policies which initially affected that development were discussed, particularly those which were introduced from the 1960s onwards. The range of strategic, industrial and other economic and social policies to emerge from central government in the years following the 1969 *Buchanan Report* have been responsible for the most radical changes in the spatial development pattern of the urban areas since the formation of the state in 1921.

A hierarchical urban structure has emerged, with Dublin as the premier city, having a strong dominance over the remainder of Ireland in terms of its proportion of the population, its large service sector and the presence of other industries and the capital city's strong administrative role. Cork and Limerick follow in the hierarchy, having established themselves as regional centres. Despite this, both cities have failed to develop to their expected potential in social and economic terms. Galway and Waterford follow in the urban structure. Although they too have emerged as regional centres, they have a low population density and are small in physical size in comparison to the other regional centres and indeed to other cities in Europe. All of the five cities have experienced large scale suburbanization which has been on going since the early to mid-20th century. However, recent government attempts to regenerate the inner cities, both physically and economically, have been successful, with the results visibly evident, particularly in Dublin's inner city. Question marks still arise over the social success of urban renewal initiatives, particularly those involving tax led investments.

The physical development of each of the urban areas is overseen by the relevant local authorities, primarily through their role as protectors of the environment. Through the powers bestowed on them under legislation such as the Local Government (Planning and Development) Act of 1963 and subsequent planning legislation, each of the local authorities has an influential role to play in the development of urban spatial patterns. However, there is a level of discontent regarding the lack of autonomy experienced, particularly by the local authorities. Local authorities are ultimately dependent on central government for most of their funding. While the 1996 report on *Better Local Government: A Programme for Change*, signals a new approach to the role and funding of local government, it will take time to realize the benefits of new policies. In addition to this, further dependency is derived from the fact that much of the work undertaken by the local authorities is as a result of financial assistance provided by the European Union.

Given that Ireland's major urban areas have increased dramatically in population, a number of issues have come to the fore which are of national concern. The current unemployment levels are regarded by central government as the issue which needs to be addressed and rectified most urgently. The urban areas are among the worst affected with many experiencing large concentrations of unemployment which are significantly above the national average. This in turn has resulted in an intolerable chain of events, with the unemployed, especially the large volumes of long term unemployed, often experiencing poverty and social isolation. In some extreme cases, turning to crime is considered a method of alleviating their problems. There has been a sharp rise in the crime rate of the urban areas, with drug related crimes and violent incidence rising dramatically. This has led to increased concern for the safety of the general public in some parts of the urban areas.

The state of the environment in the urban areas has also given rise to some national concern. The use of bituminous substances in many urban homes in the years preceding the 1987 Air Pollution Control Act and the continuing worsening traffic congestion have been cited as the instigators of high levels of pollution recorded in many urban locations. Action has been taken to rectify the matter as seen through the aforementioned 1987 act, and the traffic problems are also being addressed. Current transport policy displays an increased government understanding of the need to improve the overall infrastructure of Ireland in an attempt to lessen the negative impacts of its peripherality. In addition to this, considerable efforts are being made to develop a comprehensive integrated transport system in the Dublin region, and this may serve as an exemplary model for future transport improvements in the other urban areas.

Undoubtedly, one of the most beneficial policies to emerge from central government in recent times has concerned urban renewal. Prior to the introduction of the Urban Renewal Act in 1986, the major urban areas had been characterized as decaying inner cities where commercial and residential properties had been vacated in favour of suburban locations. With the introduction of generous fiscal policies, the core areas of the cities have benefited from new commercial and retail ventures, which have created much needed employment opportunities. The built environment has improved in most cases, despite a level of concern over the early tendency for new construction rather than refurbishment of existing structures. An improved balance is now being achieved and as a result many urban areas are now benefiting from their restored heritage. The principal achievement of the urban renewal incentives has been the attraction of an increased residential population to the city cores, stimulating the revitalization of areas that were once in danger of becoming little more than 'doughnut' cities. However, the social integration of these new populations with the traditional communities remains a task for the future.

Notes

1   The population figures for the Dublin city region comprises the population totals for Dublin County Borough and the counties of Dun Laoghaire–Rathdown, Fingal and South Dublin, which make up the overall Dublin region. Accurate figures are unavailable for the remainder of the city regions.
  The Cork city region includes the Cork County Borough and the remainder of the County area. Limerick city region corresponds to that of the Mid West region. The Galway region includes the population of the Galway County Borough and Galway County.
  Waterford City region refers to the population of Waterford County Borough and County.
2   The tertiary/secondary employment ratio is derived from the *1996 Labour Force Survey*. In the case of Cork, Galway and Waterford, the only figures available were those relating to the regional authority areas in which the cities are located (southwest, west and southeast respectively). Therefore, figures for the three areas may be considered approximate.
3   The plans were the Myles Wright Plan for Dublin (1967), the Limerick Plan by Nathaniel Litchfield and Associates (1967) and a national plan prepared in 1969 by Buchanan and Partners.
4   Population growth in the cities was the result of a number of factors, including high levels of natural increase, the immigration of people from rural areas of Ireland and in some cases, particularly in the 1970s, the return of emigrants from abroad.
5   The former Regional Development Organizations were regional based non-statutory authorities which were disbanded in 1987.
6   Objective One regions are considered to require assistance for development and structural adjustment as their general development is lagging behind other areas of the European Union.
7   The Oireachtas is the national parliament of Ireland. It consists of the President and two Houses – the House of Representatives and a Senate. The functions of all three are derived from the constitution of Ireland, and law.
8   Ireland was one of the few countries which did not sign the European Charter of Self Government, which was adopted in 1985 and which provides that local authorities shall have general competence.

9   Special Amenity Area Orders may be made under Section 42 of the Local Government (Planning and Development) Act of 1963, as amended by Section 40 of the Local Government (Planning and Development) Act of 1976.

10 The Dublin Transportation Initiative is a comprehensive approach to transportation planning which receives 75 per cent funding from the EU and is sponsored by the government. DTI deals with all forms of surface transport and examines the way in which transport issues may be integrated with other policies, particularly those of urban renewal, economic development and the overall environment.

11 LUTS was initially commissioned with the aim of developing a strategic plan for the orderly growth and coordinated development of Cork city and its catchment area. It was intended that the plan would support and promote the economy of the area, make efficient use of available resources and provide for an acceptable level of accessibility to the area, ensuring mobility and safety for residents. Projections were made to 1991, with the plan including policy recommendations and programmes for 'investment in public transport, roads, parking and traffic management measures to best serve the needs of the area in the 1990's' (Cork Land Use/Transportation Plan, 1976, and revised 1990).

12 The National Roads Authority (NRA) is under the jurisdiction of the Department of the Environment and was established on 1 January 1994. It is a 'Prescribed Authority' specified in the Local Government (Planning and Development) Regulations of 1994, under Section 21 of the Local Government (Planning and Development) Act, 1963.

13 The valuable economic contribution of the services sector has been realized over the past decade and there has been a shift in industrial policy accordingly.

14 The aims of providing increased educational opportunities and social and community services were not adequately catered for in the Urban Renewal Acts of 1986 and 1987. However, an increasing awareness of the need for such developments in the urban area prompted the government to seek funding from the European Union under the URBAN Initiative. The Department of the Taoiseach has undertaken to manage the programme at national level. Two partnerships have been formed in Dublin city and another in Cork, all with the intention of utilizing the EU funding to assist in alleviating the economic, social and environmental problems of these deprived urban areas in the coming years.

15 Section 9 (1) (a) of the Urban Renewal Act of 1986.

16 The first time buyers grant is a cash grant of £3,000 provided to first time buyers of modestly sized new homes, by the Department of the Environment.

17 The shared ownership scheme is a cooperative arrangement between the local authority and the householder. It is designed to assist householders, who may not be able to acquire full financial assistance through conventional methods of house purchasing, to gain ownership of their home in stages.

18 Documents include the *Programme for National Recovery, the Programme for Economic and Social Progress* (PESP), the aforementioned *Programme for Competitiveness and Work 1994–1996* (PCW) and most recently *Shaping Our Future – A Strategy for Enterprise in Ireland in the 21st Century*, produced by Forfas in 1996.

19 In recent years, the principal documents on industrial policy have been *A Time For Change: Industrial Policy for the 1990s* (the 'Culliton' report); *Report of the Moriarity Task Force on the Implementation of the Culliton Report* (the 'Moriarity' report); and *Employment Through Enterprise*, which was the government's response to the Moriarity report.

20 PESP is the 'Programme for Economic and Social Development'.

21 Minister for the Environment, *Planning Policy on Large Scale Retail Shopping Developments*, SI No. 264 of 1982.

22 A pilot scheme has been in operation in DCU since 1990, with a small number of places being made available to students of Ballymun Comprehensive School. Following the extension of the programme, students from 14 local schools are eligible. Applicants must meet certain criteria such as proof of their socioeconomic disadvantage, a commitment to education and a certain level of academic achievement.

23 Students wishing to gain entry to third level colleges normally proceed through the Central Applications Office (CAO), where places on college courses are allocated on the basis of a points system, following receipt of the final second level examination results.

24 Under the current regime, the Dublin region has the lowest per capita structural fund allocation of the eight regions in Ireland.

25 Area Development Management Limited. ADM is the intermediary company designated by the European Commission to manage the Global Grant through which Sub-Programme two is funded.

26 EC Committee for Regional Affairs, Chairperson Bruce Millan, 1990.

27 Rosslare Harbour is considered Ireland's 'Europort' and benefits from integrated road, rail and sea transport systems. With direct sailings to and from Europe, the port serves as a gateway to/from Europe and is linked to the Trans European Road Network. The E101 links the port with Dublin and northwards to Belfast and the port of Larne.

28 The improvements form part of the Trans European Network of Conventional Rail.

References

Bannon, M.J., Bourne, L. and Sinclair, R. (eds.) (1991), *Urbanisation and Urban Development – Recent Trends in a Global Context*, Dublin: Service Industries Research Centre, University College Dublin.

Bannon, M.J. and Russell, P. (1996), *Compendium of the Planning Systems and Policies in the Republic of Ireland* (draft) Dublin: Service Industrial Research Centre, UCD.

Blackwell, John (1988), *A Review of Housing Policy*, No. 87, Dublin: National Economic and Social Council.

Brunt, Barry (1988), *The Republic of Ireland (Western Europe: Economic and Social Studies)*, London: Paul Chapman Publishing Ltd.

Buchanan, Colin and Partners (1969), *Regional Studies in Ireland*, Dublin: An Foras Forbartha.

Centre for Retail Studies (1993), *Dublin Shopping Centres: Statistical Digest, 1993*, Dublin: University College Dublin.

Chubb, Basil (1992), *The Government and Politics of Ireland*, 3rd edn, UK: Longman Publishing.

Department of Arts, Culture and the Gaeltacht (1996), *Developing a Government Policy on Architecture: A Proposed Framework and Discussion of Issues*, Dublin: Government Stationery Office.

Department of Education (1984), *Programme for Action in Education 1984–1987*, Dublin: Government Stationery Office.

Department of the Environment (1991), *An Environment Action Programme*, Dublin: Government Stationery Office.

Department of the Environment (1993), *The European City and Its Region* (conference papers), Dublin: Government Stationery Office.

Department of the Environment (1995a), *Urban and Village Renewal Sub-Programme –
    Implementation Guidelines*, Dublin: Government Stationery Office.
Department of the Environment (1995b), *Social Housing – The Way Ahead*, Dublin: Government
    Stationery Office.
Department of the Environment (1996a), *Better Local Government – A Programme for Change*,
    Dublin: Government Stationery Office.
Department of the Environment (1996b), *Study on the Urban Renewal Schemes*, Dublin:
    Government Stationery Office.
Department of the Environment (1996c), *Housing Management Group – First Report*, Dublin:
    Government Stationery Office.
Department of the Environment (1997), *Sustainable Development: A Strategy for Ireland*,
    Dublin: Government Stationery Office.
Department of the Taoiseach (1996), *Operational Programme for URBAN – Ireland 1996–
    1999*, Dublin: Government Stationery Office.
Devlin Group (1969), *Report of the Public Services Organisation Review Group 1966–1969*,
    Dublin.
Dublin Regional Authority (1996), *Dublin: A Regional Focus – Overview*, Dublin.
Environmental Protection Agency (1996), *State of the Environment*, Wexford.
Feehan, John (1992), *Environment and Development in Ireland*, Dublin: Environmental Institute,
    University College.
Forfas (1996), *Shaping Our Future – A Strategy for Enterprise in Ireland in the 21st Century*,
    Dublin.
Goodbody Economic Consultants/Service Industries Research Centre (1996), *Appraisal of
    Urban Initiative Plans* (draft), Dublin.
Government of Ireland (1991), *Programme for Economic and Social Progress*, Dublin:
    Government Stationery Office.
Government of Ireland (1993a), *National Development Plan 1994–1999*, Dublin: Government
    Stationery Office.
Government of Ireland (1993b), *Dublin Transportation Initiative (phase 2) Interim Report*,
    Dublin: Brunswick Press Ltd.
Government of Ireland (1994a), *Operational Programme for Local Urban and Rural
    Development 1994–1999*, Dublin: Government Stationery Office.
Government of Ireland (1994b), *Operational Programme for Human Resources 1994–1999*,
    Dublin: Government Stationery Office.
Government of Ireland (1994c), *Operational Programme for Transport 1994–1999*, Dublin:
    Government Stationery Office.
Government of Ireland (1994d), *The Programme for Competitiveness and Work 1994–1996*,
    Dublin: Government Stationery Office.
Government of Ireland (1996), *Partnership 2000 for Inclusion, Employment and
    Competitiveness*, Dublin: Government Stationery Office.
Hamilton Osborne King (1996), *Property Outlook*, Dublin, H.O.K.
Hourihan, Kevin (1991), 'Culture, Politics and the Recent Urbanisation of the Republic of
    Ireland', in Bannon, Bourne and Sinclair (eds), op. cit.
Industrial Policy Review Group (1994), *A Time for Change: Industrial Policy for the 1990s*
    (Culliton report), Dublin: Stationery Office.
Lisney (1996), *Lisney Property Review 1996/1997*, Dublin: Lisney.
MacLaren, A. and Drudy, P.J. (eds.) (1996), *Dublin – Economic and Social Trends*, Vol. 2,
    Dublin: Centre for Urban and Regional Studies, Trinity College Dublin.

McMenamin, P.S. (1975), The Industrial Development Process in the Republic of Ireland 1953–72 in J. Vaisey, *Economic Sovereignty and Regional Policy*, London: Gill and McMillan.

Meehan, B. (1995), 'Planning Decisions and Integrated Pollution Control', *Irish Planning and Environmental Law Journal*, Vol. 2, No. 1, pp. 30–5.

National Economic and Social Council (1981), *Urbanisation: Problems of Growth and Decay in Dublin*, NESC Report No. 55, Dublin.

National Economic and Social Council (1990), *A Strategy for the Nineties: Economic Stability and Structural Change*, NESC Report No. 89, Dublin.

National Economic and Social Council (1997), *European Union: Integration and Enlargement*, Report 101, Stationery Office, Dublin.

Partnership 2000, for Inclusion, Employment and Competitiveness (1996), Dublin: Stationery Office.

Scannell, Yvonne (1995), *Environmental and Planning Law in Ireland*, Dublin: Round Hall Press.

Shannon Development (1996), *Regional Policy – A Report by a Regional Policy Advisory Group to Forfas*, Shannon Development.

South West Regional Authority (1996), *Strategic Action Plan 1996–2001*, Cork.

Sweeney, John C. (1992), 'Modelling Dublin Smoke Pollution – An Epilogue?' in Feehan (ed.), op. cit.

Temple Bar Properties Ltd (1992), *Development Programme for Temple Bar*, Dublin.

Timoney, David (1992), 'Internal Combustion Engines and Exhaust Emissions' in Feehan (ed.), op. cit.

10 Italy

ILARIA BRAMEZZA[1]

Introduction

In Italy there is no urban policy that is primarily focused on the development of larger cities, although the allocation of funds is mostly directed to larger cities for the improvement of their accessibility and regeneration of degraded areas. The main goal of this urban policy is to limit further urbanization and to improve the quality of urban life by eliminating the conditions that have determined urban degradation, and overcoming the lack of infrastructure and services.

This case study starts giving an overview of the pattern of spatial development in Italy. The second section deals with the administrative and financial relations between the national government and cities. The third section illustrates the national authorities' points of view about the development of large cities, the major urban issues and challenges that cities are facing, while the fourth is focused on the direct and indirect policies that have been developed to solve urban problems and face urban challenges. Finally, some conclusions are drawn.

National Spatial Development Pattern

Strong centrality has always been the main characteristic of the urbanization process in Italy. Over time, cities have maintained the most important functions internally, affecting the following developments connected with their growth. More than 8,000 municipalities are spread over the territory. However, in 1991 only six of them are there more than 640,000 inhabitants, while the majority of the municipalities have no more than 5,000 inhabitants (about 6,000 municipalities). Demographic trends in the last two decades show a slowing down of demographic growth, because of the decreasing internal migration and birth rate. This phenomenon mainly concerns the large centres, but also affects the smallest ones over the whole territory, except for some areas in southern regions. With respect to metropolitan areas, the development pattern is characterized by stagnation, or even decreasing population in the centre and moderate growth in the ring. The causes of the development are found in the differential cost of housing and in the search for a better quality of living environment.

Urban growth mostly occurs in small urban centres characterized by relatively good accessibility to larger centres. These areas start with a residential function, but industrial activities, especially small and medium-sized activities, also take place, according to a decentralization pattern of production. In the city centres, strategic public and private functions and services remain.

Thanks to urban sprawl, the mass diffusion of the use of automobiles and decentralization of production, the urbanization pattern in Italy has gradually changed. Italy has become a country organized into main areas of complex development. Within these areas changes take place at all levels, while outside of them, development patterns in urban centres tend towards stable or even declining trends.

Italy has 103 administrative chief-towns (provinces), among which 12 can be considered as large cities. The nine largest cities recognized by the legislation as metropolitan cities are Torino, Milano, Genova, Venezia, Bologna, Firenze, Roma, Napoli and Bari. Three other cities located in the two largest islands (Sicily and Sardinia, which are regions with a special status) are also considered large cities: Palermo, Catania and Cagliari (see Map 10.1).

The Tables 10.1 and 10.2 give an overview of the characteristics of large cities in Italy, according to some social and economic indicators. Table 10.1 shows the number of inhabitants by municipality, the rest of the province and total number of inhabitants, density of population and unemployment rate.

At the end of the '80s, the largest cities and metropolitan areas found themselves at different stages of urban development, which, according to the urban life-cycle theory, can be sketched as follows (IRES, 1991): Palermo and Cagliari in the southern part of the country still fell into the stage of urbanization, while Catania had entered the suburbanization stage, together with other southern cities like Bari and Napoli. Cities moving towards desurbanization were Roma, Firenze and Bologna. Genova, Torino and Venezia were already in the desurbanization stage, while Milano was the only large Italian city moving towards reurbanization.

Table 10.2 shows the rank of the 12 largest cities with respect to indicators related to quality of life (Il Sole-24 Ore, December 1996)[2]: tenor of life (income, savings, insurance premiums, pensions, housing prices, inflation effects), business and work (number of protests, bankruptcy, new firms,

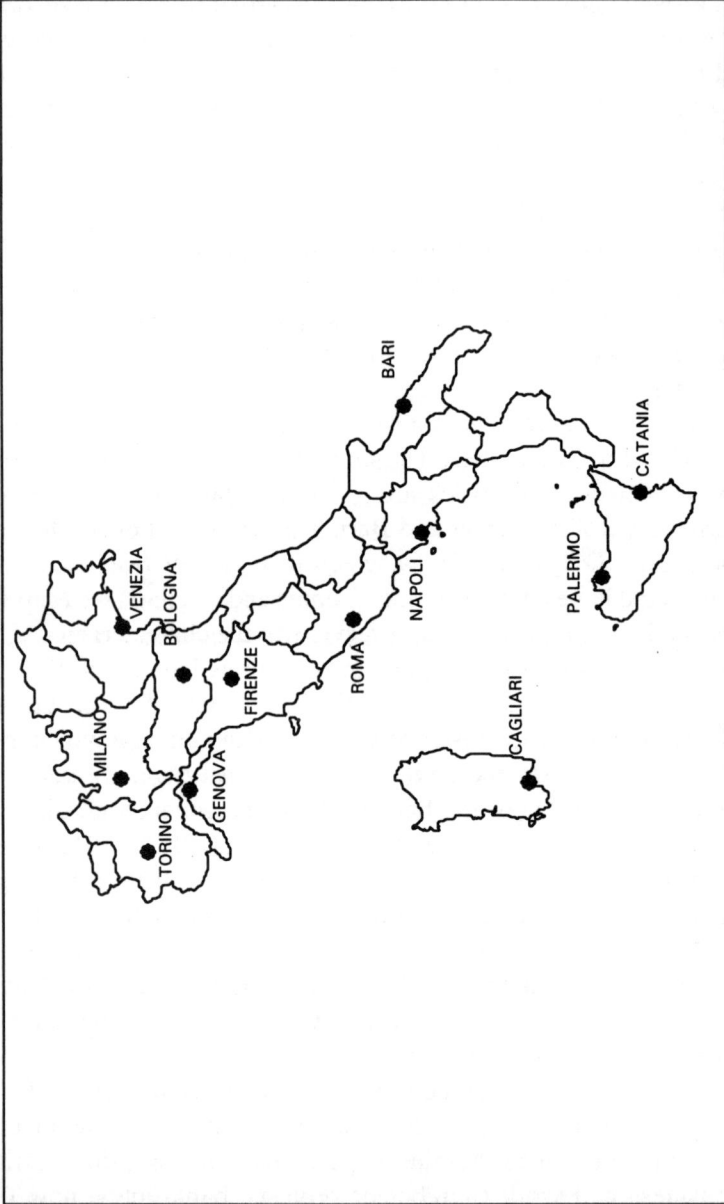

Map 10.1   12 largest cities and metropolitan areas

Table 10.1   Characteristics of the 12 largest cities and the metropolitan areas in Italy

Large cities	Inhabitants (million, 1991)			Density* (1995) (n. inh. per km²)	Unemployment* (1995) (per cent)
	City	Province	Total		
Torino	1.0	1.3	2.3	325.1	10.7
Milano	1.4	2.2	3.6	1,901.7	8.2
Genova	0.7	0.2	0.9	508.7	13.0
Venezia	0.3	0.5	0.8	332.3	8.1
Bologna	0.4	0.5	0.9	244.7	5.1
Firenze	0.4	0.6	1.0	271.1	8.1
Roma	2.7	1.0	3.7	705.4	12.8
Napoli	1.0	2.0	3.0	2,645.6	28.8
Bari	0.3	1.2	1.5	303.7	14.3
Palermo	0.7	0.5	1.2	248.4	24.7
Catania	0.3	0.7	1.0	306.4	19.8
Cagliari	0.2	0.6	0.8	111.7	25.2

*   average national density = 190.3; average national unemployment rate = 12.0

Source: Presidency of the Council of Ministries, 1996 and Il Sole 24 Ore, December 1996.

Table 10.2   Quality of life in the 12 largest cities and metropolitan areas (1= best performance)

Large cities	Life's tenor	Business and work	Services and environment	Criminality	Population	Leisure	Quality of life
Torino	5	3	6	8	7	6	5
Milano	1	7	11	12	9	5	5
Genova	4	4	8	9	12	4	3
Venezia	7	2	1	1	8	7	7
Bologna	2	1	2	5	9	2	1
Firenze	3	5	5	10	11	1	2
Roma	6	12	3	11	6	3	4
Napoli	12	8	4	4	4	11	10
Bari	10	11	7	7	2	12	11
Palermo	9	9	12	6	5	9	12
Catania	11	10	9	2	1	10	9
Cagliari	8	6	10	3	3	8	8

Source: Il Sole 24 Ore, December 1996.

insolvency, employment register offices, unemployment), public services and environment (time to cash pensions, mailing time, waiting time for a telephone connection, space for students, urban ecosystem, road traffic), criminality (murders, stolen cars, robberies in apartments, juvenile criminality, frauds, pickpockets), population (birth trend, deaths, demographic density, tumours, net rate of internal migration, legal separations) and leisure (artistic and cultural associations, sport events, expenses for theatre and music, cinemas, fitness centres, bookstores).

Tables 10.1 and 10.2 gives evidence of a clear dichotomy between north and south Italy. The northern cities perform relatively better with respect to unemployment and quality of life. Among them Bologna shows the best performance. Milan has serious problems concerning public services and criminality. It seems that the city is losing the traditional image of efficiency. Criminality also affects cities like Firenze and Roma. In the south, Palermo, Napoli and Bari are the most problematic cities, with highest unemployment rates and worst performance in quality of life. Napoli, in particular, registers almost 29 per cent of unemployment.

Comparing the figures for quality of life with the previous years, only three large cities (Torino, Bologna and Firenze) have slightly improved their position in the rank with respect to previous years. High quality of life is difficult to achieve in large cities. The biggest problems relate to the quality of services (only Roma and Bologna are in a slightly better position), criminality (Roma and Milano score rather badly) and demography (Napoli has more than 2,600 inhabitants per km^2). However, large cities score relatively well in tenor of life (Milan is the first) and leisure (Bologna and Firenze compete for the first position).

Administrative and Financial Framework

Administrative Organization, National/Regional Authorities' Influence on Cities, Metropolitan Authorities

The current four tier administrative system in Italy includes the national government, the regions, the provinces and the municipalities. The Italian administrative system is based on historical foundations rather than on modern functional relationships. However, important changes at institutional level have been recently set by the government, in line with the general European trend of decentralization of tasks and competencies.

In 1990 the Italian parliament passed law 142/90. It is an attempt to adapt the situation to the developments occurring across Europe. The law has cancelled the entire normative structure that regulated the life of local systems (dated 1915 and 1934) and it attempts to introduce innovations. This law is aimed at making the transition from centralization to decentralization. The local administrative institution should achieve a statute power and regulate itself with wide autonomy. According to the law, each local institution (municipality or province) would have its own administrative structure and organization, flexible in time and adapted to its own dimension and context.

Innovation has been introduced in several aspects of the reform. Besides the statute autonomy, other important points of innovation concerning municipalities, provinces and regions foresee:

- active participation of citizens in the local administration;
- greater transparency of actions and activities concerning citizens;
- the possibility of the fusion of more municipalities and the constitution of new municipalities;
- the institution of metropolitan areas and metropolitan cities;
- the direct election of the mayor and the president of the province; and
- financial and fiscal autonomy.

The tasks of the various administrative levels, according to the reform introduced by law 142/90, can be summarized as follows:

- *municipality*: all those functions which are related to the population and the relevant territory;
- *province*: programming, managing of administrative functions in sectors like environment, culture, transport, information systems and technical-administrative assistance for the local entities;
- *metropolitan areas* (Torino, Milano, Venezia, Genova, Bologna, Firenze, Roma, Napoli, Bari and Cagliari)[3]: they will substitute the provinces from an administrative point of view (not as territory). Their delimitation is decided by the respective regions. However, no region has yet come to any consistent result. The metropolitan cities, besides the tasks carried out by the province, will also have other functions, such as spatial planning of the metropolitan area, traffic, protection of cultural assets and of hydrogeology assets, gathering and distribution of water and energy, services for economic development and large retail, urban services generally defined of metropolitan level;

- *regions*: discipline of functions, procedure of programming, forms of association and collaboration, metropolitan areas, controls and partial distribution of financial sources;
- *central government*: it maintains its role of controller (Ministry of Internal Affairs) over the various institutions through institutional figures such as the civil governor, and manager and supporter of decisions concerning metropolitan areas (Ministry of Public Works with delegation for urban areas).

Where it is established by law, the regions have to decide the territorial extension of the metropolitan areas. Problems related to this matter have delayed the full implementation of the law. They arise because the law establishes that the metropolitan area cannot also coincide with the territory of the province, disagreeing with Article 114 of the Italian constitution which says that the republic is divided into regions, provinces and municipalities. An active debate has emerged in the last few years among those supporting the delimitation of large areas and those who are in favour of more restricted areas. The debate has not reached any resolution. In three cases – Bologna, Genova and Venezia – voluntary forms of associations among municipalities are evolving, in anticipation of or as alternative solution to the formal institution of the metropolitan areas.

Urban Policy at the Level of the Ministries

Urban policy in Italy has long been a non-priority for central government. Article 1 of Urban Law No. 1150, still valid, is dated 1942. It establishes that 'the Ministry of public works watches over urban activities also to ensure, within the process of renewing and widening of cities, the respect of traditional characteristics, to favour desurbanization and hamper the trend towards urbanization'. Despite this, urbanization did occur. All Italian urban legislation, of which the above article is the main expression and point of reference, begins and continues with constraint as the norm, since it hampers urbanization. Until the '80s, urban laws did not permit any programming of the phenomena of urbanization on national territory, a correct definition of such phenomena with respect to the economic and social aspects, and, consequently, they have not even permitted any valid control system over such phenomena (Pierotti, 1991).

An attempt to link economic programming to the territory was made in the late '60s with the elaboration of *Progetto 80*, which, however, has never been implemented. Starting from the evidence of an imbalance in the urban and economic development, it proposed a three-directional action:

- urban restoration in the urban system with metropolitan characteristics;
- strengthening of neighbouring urban systems which have potentials of readjusting territorial balances; and
- creation of urban systems which could be the alternative solution to the spontaneous trends of urbanization.

The plan failed mainly because of the lack of organizations able to manage economic policy and programming of those agglomerations.

In the '70s, the methodologies of intervention changed: instead of focusing on the large movements of population and economy, attention moved towards the best possible use of existing sources and more moderate interventions. For the first time in urban legislation, the notion of programming appears. In the '80s and '90s a new perspective emerged. Instead of looking for a balanced development by means of centralized control of localization and flows of population and economic activities, the attention focused on the endogenous components of those processes, that is, on the answers that each local system can give to global changes. The logic of regeneration replaces the old logic of re-equilibrium, and the notion of competitive advantages substitutes the one of comparative advantages.

This evolution starts from the recognition of the impact of the fundamental changes at social, technological and economic levels that are affecting urban development. Quality of the living environment and quality of life, on the one hand, and specificity of local context on the other hand, assume strategic value and become the main factors that determine competitiveness.

The above-mentioned weaknesses with respect to urban policy are reflected also at the administrative and institutional levels. Currently, in Italy, the responsibilities of the Ministry of Urban Areas have been delegated to the Ministry of Public Works. The latter may count on three departments dealing with urban matters: Di.Co.Ter. (*Dipartimento per il Coordinamento territoriale*); CER (*Comitato per l'Edlitia Residenziale*), and *Officio Rapporti con l'Unione Europea*. However, other ministries also deal indirectly with urban matters. For example, the Ministry of Internal Affairs, together with the Ministries of Public Function and Regional Affairs, and of Treasury and Budget, have been involved in Law 142/90 which deals with the administrative reorganization of some Italian regions into metropolitan areas. Also, the Ministries of Transport, Environment, Culture and Social Affairs often have a role in decision-making on matters concerning urban affairs. For instance, in 1995 the Ministry of Transport, together with the Ministries of Public Works, Treasury and Budget, and Environment, have produced a reform of urban transport (Law 549/95), setting three main goals: to transfer the financial and management powers to decentralized administrations (the regions); to overcome the current situation that sees the state as responsible for local rail services and the regions as responsible for road and urban services; to allow regional and urban governments to modify the share of financial resources assigned to local transport, i.e., to include these resources in the regional budget and let the regional government decide about the use of funds.[4]

The Ministry of Public Works with Delegation for Urban Areas (from now on called Ministry of Urban Areas), besides the tasks of coordination, outline, promotion of initiatives of monitoring, verification and control, is delegated to deal with the management of urban areas, the management of public services (also in cooperation with private actors), the operational management of interventions for *Roma Capitale* and of the problems related to the *2000 Jubilee*.

In particular, the Ministry of Urban Areas has the task of promoting, together with the other competent ministries, the following actions:

- programmes of completion and enlargement of parking and integrated systems of transport in urban areas, metropolitan areas, and in the areas between them, also with reference to the European systems (with the Ministry of Transport);
- interventions of the central administration for the decentralization of administrative and production activities, reuse of abandoned areas, limitation of noise and pollution, respecting the regional and local autonomies and by means of programme agreements (with the Ministries of Industry and Environment);
- financial assistance concerning the above two points, and definition of the criteria, by activating the already-decided financial dispositions, but also promoting public-private partnerships and agreements with financial and credit institutions (with the Ministry of Treasury and Budget);
- predisposition of all interventions, legislative and administrative, related to the definition, assessment and management of metropolitan areas (with the Ministries of Internal and Regional Affairs);
- institution of committees of research, consulting and technical support for specific matters (Jubilee and others) (with the Ministries of Tourism and Transport);

- designation of representatives by the presidency of the Council of Ministries in institutions, committees, research, technical-administrative and consulting agencies operating on the above matters in other administrations and institutions;
- promotion, in cooperation with the other competent ministries, of programmes aimed at the optimization of public services in urban areas;
- elaboration of proposals for the constitution by the prime minister of an organ of coordination of relations between the state and urban and metropolitan areas, for the promotion of economic, social and cultural activities and the introduction of innovation technologies in the same areas.

To implement the above actions, the Ministry of Urban Areas may count on the *Dipartimento per le aree urbane* (Department for Urban Areas), and the *Ufficio del programma per Roma Capitale* (Office of the Programme for *Roma Capitale*). The first organization has been created by the presidency of the Council of Ministries and depends on the Ministry of Urban Areas (currently delegated to the Ministry of Public Works). *Roma Capitale* is an organization controlled by a committee chaired by the Minister of Urban Areas, made by the Ministries of Transport, Environment, Culture, besides other local authorities (region, province and municipality of Roma). Its specific objectives are the realization of the necessary interventions concerning the city of Roma conceived as special territorial entity because of its role of capital city (for more details see Law 396, 15 December 1990).

The Urban Income Sources

Before the introduction of law 142/90, the financial situation of local administrations had undergone a disordered and uncoordinated evolution. In particular, the fiscal reform of the '70s (DPR 616/1977), in the name of the unity of public finance, had eliminated almost every form of autonomous taxation by the local administrations. The latter were dependent almost exclusively on central government. Before this reform, municipalities and provinces had a certain degree of fiscal autonomy, and local taxes were the largest part of their income. Autonomy and self-sufficiency of finance disappeared with the fiscal reform.

Currently, the situation is still marked by a centralized fiscal system, established in 1977: fiscal drawing is carried out by central government which then redistributes the resources to regions and municipalities. The redistribution of funds favours medium-sized cities and neglects the bigger cities, despite their larger need of financial resources (Presidency of the Council of Ministries, 1996).

Article 54 of Law 142/90 has only fixed some general principles that the expected reform of the government is supposed to respect when legislating about local finance. The main role is played by autonomous financing as the major source of urban income: each city is supposed to have its own duties, taxes, rights, tariffs on competent services, and its own income from its properties. Public transfers are assumed to guarantee the services of first necessity, while local income is targeted at the financing of public services considered necessary for the development of the community. In other words, local financing is expected to have a propelling role, ensuring citizens not only new services but also higher quality services of first necessity.

Yet the law specifies that public transfers from the central administration occur according to objective criteria that consider the population, the territory, the social and economic situation; the government can also distribute specific contributions in case of exceptional situations of need. A national ordinary fund contributes to local finance for the realization of public works of relevant social and economic interest, while a special national fund finances public works in areas or situations defined by law. Shares are defined by the government according to parameters that are fixed during the period of the government's budget (three years), so that local administrations have more certainty about the consistency of the funds that they will receive during that period. Regions co-finance the local administrations for the implementation of the regional plan of development and the programme of investments. Moreover, on the basis of regional programmes, the resources for investments established by the central government are distributed to municipalities and provinces.

Since 1990 several decrees have been prepared which start the process of decentralization of the fiscal system. The most relevant decrees are those that have instituted the property tax (ICI) (Decree No. 504, 1992), the municipal tax on advertisements and on occupation of public areas (TOSAP) (No. 507, 1993) and the tax for disposal of solid urban waste.

Some cities have also taken advantage of EU financial contributions. About 135 million ECU have been invested for the rehabilitation and recovery of decayed areas in 16 cities with the URBAN programme. A large share of funds have been given to Objective 1 regions (about 95 million at a first stage, plus 12 Million at a second stage), while cities located outside Objective 1 regions received about 28 million (21.7 in the first stage plus 6.4 in the second stage). Despite the limited funds, with URBAN there has been an attempt to integrate at local level different sectoral policies (Presidency of the Council of Ministries, 1996). Thus, Italy benefits also from the allocation of EU funds for eight Objective 1 regions, all in the southern part of the country. These funds also have impact on cities of those regions. However, the weak integration and coordination of policies, resources and actions at the national level results also in the lack of support at the local level concerning EU initiatives of funding urban development. This deficiency has also determined another aspect: Italy spends only 15–20 per cent of European funds for urban development (Presidency of the Council of Ministries, 1996).

Specific National Preconditions that Hamper Integrated Socioeconomic Policies at the Local Level

The high political instability of Italian governments and the national debt constraint are two specific national circumstances that have hampered the development of integral policies at the local level. Indeed, political instability has had a strong influence on the problem of competencies and the coordination of actions and interventions. The second aspect affects the amount of investments dedicated to infrastructure and resources that are necessary for the development and implementation of policies at local level. This problem also focuses the attention on ways to decrease public deficit, at the expense of effective integral socioeconomic policies.

Law 142/90, which concerns the reform of local autonomies, has not changed much the administrative culture, as today planning and programming are still quite sectoral and there is still little coordination among the various sectors and levels of government. There is, as yet, no governmental organization able to gather and organize knowledge about territorial plans and programmes. The preliminary conditions to implement effective procedures of coordination and discussion among the various sectors and levels of spatial government are still missing. Consequently, local administrations have little trust of national programmes.

The main problem concerning territorial planning is to define rules and procedures able:

- to express a system of guidelines about spatial development at the national level, consistent with the guidelines of spatial development given by the EU and by other European countries;
- to ensure coherence of territorial plans defined at different levels of local government;

- to ensure an effective coordination between the programming of the national infrastructure and spatial planning at different levels of competence.

Urban Issues and Challenges from the National Perspective

Major National Urban Issues

Until the '90s there has not been an explicit urban policy in Italy, for the reasons that we have already mentioned. With Law 142/90, the concept of metropolitan cities has been introduced for the first time. Although the national government has started a discussion about administrative reform linked to the urban context, an explicit urban policy is still missing in terms of contents. The lack of a ministry dedicated exclusively to urban areas confirms it. Thus, we can say that there is an implicit policy concerning cities.

Unemployment, poverty, traffic congestion, crime and inadequacy of infrastructure are major concerns of the (implicit) national urban policy, as the consequences of these phenomena seriously affect quality of life, especially in the largest cities (see also Table 10.2). Unemployment is a phenomenon that interests the largest cities in the south of Italy especially, where it registers rates up to 33 per cent, while northern cities show relatively better figures. This phenomenon needs to be faced by prompt interventions of economic policy. However, no measure has yet provided any solution with strong impact (for instance, the redeployment of people without jobs into socially useful activities). In that respect, the government is preparing some interventions to fight unemployment. One of the major interventions supports small and medium-sized enterprises (SMEs) in urban areas (Presidency of the Council of Ministries, 1996). SMEs are seen as a possible solution to the creation of job opportunities. The wellbeing of the largest cities that had gone through economic restructuring in the '70s and '80s largely depends on the ability of local SMEs to create wealth and employment. There is a need to adopt a coordinated policy to regulate the restructuring processes and restrain the increasing gap between the north-central areas and the southern part of Italy. Recently, attention has moved towards the development of forms of cooperation between the different levels of administration in the definition of measures in favour of SMEs and projects for interventions of this kind have been developed for slums in large cities.

Other interventions have regarded the promotion of tourism, which in Italy represents an extremely important economic and employment resource

(Presidency of the Council of Ministries, 1996). An agreement on a programme for innovative projects related to the development of tourism has been prepared jointly by the central government (the office of prime minister) and several ministries (tourism, urban areas, civil service and regional affairs). The idea is to promote projects that use cultural and environmental assets for tourism, submitted by private operators. The capacity for creating new productive jobs is among the evaluation criteria.

The increasing flow of immigrants has exacerbated the problems of crime and poverty. The problem of immigration and its impact on cities is becoming serious. There is a high percentage of illegal immigrants in Italy looking for employment. Despite the obvious difficulties they encounter in finding a job, they tend to remain in Italy anyway. Many problems related to immigration derive from the inability of the competent institutions to manage the phenomenon efficiently. The impact of immigration on cities is relevant: there are problems of integration and cohabitation with immigrants and usually the latter are relegated in degraded areas.

National Priorities with Regard to Territorial Management

In Italy, as all over Europe, the attention of public authorities is focused mainly on the definition of guidelines for projects of urban regeneration, safeguarding the environment and adequate management of territorial transformations.The Ministry of Public Works, with technical and propositional competencies for guiding and coordinating the territory, acts mainly, with respect to urban matters, along two lines: the first refers to the definition of the fundamental outlines of the national spatial assessment of the territory, assuming the role of promoter and coordinator of local initiatives; the second is based on the necessity to foster cooperation at international level among competent institutions, harmonizing the various actions according to the various interests diversified by territorial scale (supranational, national, local). In this respect, the ministry has started a range of initiatives that include the collaboration with the EU in relation to the TENs (Trans European Networks) policy, to assess outlines that are consistent with the framework of development of the European system.

The problems that territorial management in Italy currently has to face are related to four areas:

- the movement from a sectoral-hierarchical process to a more complex decision-making process that imposes complementarity and subsidiarity of competencies and the necessity for a wide harmonization of choices, especially with respect to the relationship between central administration and local autonomies and between local interventions and national and community development programmes;

- the need to overcome the logic of management of financial transfers and think in terms of management of local taxes, management of the processes of exploitation of existing assets and involvement of private actors;
- there is a growing need for investment in reorganization, infrastructure and regeneration of housing and premises, but scarcity of funds drives the search for greater effectiveness of public expenditure in social, economic and employment fields;
- the lack of infrastructure has generated the need to change also the logic of development based on the simple addition of housing into the logic of development focused on the reorganization and regeneration of housing and premises and large infrastructures.

Generally, there is the tendency to move from quantitative towards qualitative aspects of the urban development, respecting the general condition for sustainable development expressed by the European Union in the document *Europe 2000+*. This trend implies a reorganization of institutions, especially with respect to the relationship between local autonomies and central government and the quality of juridical, planning, evaluation and managerial tools. The key problems are:

- the relationship between national programming and local planning (attempted by Law 142/90);
- the effectiveness of the process of infrastructuring;
- effectiveness of territorial policies.

Specific Threats and Opportunities for Cities as Perceived at the National Level

In Italy, as all over Europe, cities are confronted with specific urban challenges. The process of globalization of the economy has been translated into growing competition at national and international levels. The effects of competition occur very rapidly. However, economic growth is not directly and automatically linked to growth of employment, improvement of quality of life, social progress and improvement of the quality of the living environment. The fact that cities are very much exposed to the effects of the global economy constitutes a stimulus to innovation and enhancement of the level of competitiveness, but also it implies that cities must be able to manage this process. Likewise, problems arise on the one hand from the scarcity of production factors – with the exception of labour which remains heavily unemployed – and, on the other hand, the availability of new information technologies which allow the composition and integration of production factors located in other regions and countries. In this respect, changes occur very rapidly: innovation processes permit rapid improvements in levels of competitiveness and the quality of life, but also create problems of continuous adjustment to innovation. Lastly, as far as the need for maintaining high levels of efficiency is concerned, the preliminary factors that are preconditions for the competitiveness and economic development of cities (infrastructure, production sites, strategic centres, and research and development centres) require large investments and a clear definition of priorities.

The need for cooperation among cities and the need to anticipate relations of cooperation at the European level, and with countries that will probably take part in the EU in the future, are considered to be challenges. Furthermore, cooperation is also necessary at the local level, especially in those areas which are made up of many local administrations.

The general reduction of public sources for intervention in infrastructures and services has favoured the development of public and private partnerships. Further development of this measure of project financing must be developed. Among the conditions that favour the creation of public and private partnerships opportuneness, transparency and certainty about the actions of the public administrations that manage the territory are very important.

Globalization and increasing competition often force policy- and decision-makers to privilege the objectives of effectiveness, rather than of equity. Policies of social and economic cohesion, solidarity, social and cultural development and, in general, the furthering of the wellbeing of citizens must be privileged as much as economic policies for sustainable development. In that respect, sustainable development requires the implementation of long term integral policies that consider, at the same time, economic development, social cohesion and environmental improvement. Policies of territorial reorganization should also be considered as part of an integral policy for sustainable urban development.

Urban areas are also concentrated zones of unemployment. To face this challenge, the conditions for the favourable development of new economic activities and the support of those already existing is needed, in addition to the exploitation of economic potential to enlarge the supply of labour compatibly with the characteristics of demand.

Last, there is the tendency to develop privileged areas within cities, where the level and quality of services and infrastructure is higher than in other parts of the cities. This tendency stresses the problem of social segregation. Projects of urban regeneration and interventions on infrastructure should start a process of redistribution of the values and qualities of the city (in the form of better services, infrastructure, conditions of mobility, architecture and quality of the living environment) that guarantees homogeneous and balanced development.

National Policy Responses to Urban Issues, Challenges and Development

National Policy Based on (Long Term) National Vision on Cities and the Urbanization Process

Urban renewal and regeneration are important matters for national authorities, on account of the urbanization effects which have provoked great demand for housing, and the need to manage urban growth. Concern has moved towards the need for urban quality and the consequent necessity to regenerate existing quarters. New tools have been recently introduced with legislative dispositions. Urban renewal plans, regeneration plans and integrated programmes aim at reorganizing the cities with innovative forms of project-financing that foster the active intervention of private actors and consider the use of inter-sector resources.

Urban renewal programmes move attention from housing to infrastructure. They focus more on infrastructure and aim at increasing and improving the accessibility and quality of the living environment of residential areas. They include initiatives of primary and secondary urbanization, urban design and completion and integration of urban programmes. These programmes stimulate the active intervention of private actors. Proposals are made by public and private actors, often together, to the municipalities. The latter evaluate the proposals according to existing and future priorities and select those which also respect the procedural form of the so-called 'programme agreement'.

Urban regeneration programmes are the complementary tools to the two just mentioned. Regeneration concerns maintenance and urban restructuring, rehabilitation of buildings and urban design, urbanization and environmental reordering. It depends on the specific context as well as revitalization and reorganization needs. These programmes also take into account the effects that they can generate over the whole urban area. They concentrate their action on specifically identified urban areas and intervene with programmes of primary and secondary urbanization, nonresidential and residential buildings. In this case also, project financing and degree of integrity are criteria used in the selection of programmes, which are presented to the competent central agency (Ministry of Public Works, Di.Co.Ter.) that performs the selection and also has task of monitoring the proceedings of the projects and controlling their implementation.

Integrated programmes (Article 16, Law 179/92 and Law 493/93) are tools for regenerating the whole urban, housing and environmental structure in consolidated cities. Indeed, they encompass a plurality of functions that affect sustainable urban redevelopment, involve different actors and make use of various financial sources. The impact of these programmes is determinant and the level of efficiency in their management is relevant too, thanks to the direct relationship between the national authority and cities that avoid the mediation of intermediate actors (regions). However, integrated programmes are a valid tool as far as the coordination of actors and financial sources is concerned. For coordination is only ex post facto: the programmes do not arise from a pre-evaluation and definition of prior objectives.

Many cities are experimenting with new ways of initiating processes of revitalization and redevelopment, using these innovative tools. They are, therefore, considered important. Innovation relies especially on the plurality of actors, functions and uses involved in the programmes, on transparency and new forms of public and private cooperation, according to the logic of integrated urban planning. However, these innovative tools are not yet fully integrated forms of intervention as they need some technical and procedural adjustments. For instance, the economic aspects concerning public and private partnerships, local government's experience in activating project financing and incompatibility with some existing regulatory systems are aspects that need to be better defined to transform these tools into ordinary forms of intervention.

Sectoral Policies for the Sustainability of Cities' Growth

The 12 largest Italian cities host some 22 million inhabitants, i.e., 38 per cent of the total population. Quality of life has been seriously affected in the last decade because of the heavy environmental and social pressure resulting from economic restructuring. Problems of lack of sustainability arose and plans for interventions have been developed. Italian cities must face various challenges because of the peculiarity of the urban system: environmental aspects, the importance of historic and cultural assets, industrial activities and tourism. The coexistence of several strategic elements which contribute to urban development makes it clear that an integrated approach that considers them all is the only answer. Land management, urban planning and environmental policies are proposed by the government integrally, equally to the international experiences. The sectors of interventions are:

- action for decreasing motor vehicle traffic and air pollution. Action is taken at different levels: expansion of the rail transportation system (high speed system, subways, tramways), coordinated development of parking lots located in strategic sites and cycling paths; regulations concerning the limits of acceptability of the warning and alarm thresholds for air pollution in cities, with monitoring systems and technical facilities for controlling emissions; incentives for reducing the emission of the various means of public transport; agreements with the oil companies to reduce the level of benzene and aromatic compounds in petrol;
- action against noise pollution. A law dated 1995 has introduced new standards concerning road infrastructure and the railways for reducing noise pollution in large cities, by means of technical solutions and the relocation of rail structures and buildings from critical areas. Air traffic has also been the objective of this law from the point of view of airport activities and over-flying aeroplanes. Measures have been adopted to reduce noise at the source and provide targeted plans relative to land surrounding airports. Severe controls by the Ministries of Environment and Culture are adopted when acting on airports and highways
- waste management. Italy has a relatively high percentage of waste compared to other European countries. Aware of this weakness, the government intends launching projects for the construction of incinerators in line with the EU legislation and campaigns for increasing the awareness of citizens and industries through programmes of environmental education. The instruments are mainly: differentiated waste collection and recycling; transformation of the tax on solid urban waste into a tariff proportionally related to the quantity of waste produced; and the introduction of the 'ecotax' to limit the use of dumps (to be paid where a dump is used for elimination of waste);
- water resources management. Water purification plants are under construction and interventions on water purification aim also at restoring the rivers

as natural resource for leisure inside the cities (for instance in the Tevere river in Rome). Water tariffs have been introduced on the same principle of the 'ecotax' for those citizens not directly served by purification plants;
*   urban green parks. Many initiatives are under way to increase the number of parks in cities, especially in the largest cities, and to increase the awareness of the need for parks protection. This issue is rather problematic, as Italian cities have little green space, for structural reasons. Owing to the architecture of cities, urban parks tend to be developed in peripheral areas adjacent to cities, but remain disused because they are not in the cities;
*   industrial risk. Many industrial areas of relevant dimension are adjacent to cities, e.g., Genova, Venezia, Napoli and Milano. The risk of accidents is high. To reduce them, the government has imposed the technological conversion or relocation of plants located near urban agglomerations;
*   areas at risk of an environmental disaster. Some areas, e.g., Napoli and Milan among the larger cities, have been classified as being at risk of an environmental disaster. The government's attention is moving towards prevention and monitoring interventions;
*   environmental education. The government has created several national reference centres and spatial laboratories for providing information, planning and diffusing environmental education, to orient the culture of citizens towards sustainability of urban growth (Presidency of the Council of Ministries, 1996).

The National Idea about the Development of a European Urban Policy

Collaboration with the EU has already been consolidated and new initiatives continue to be taken to further develop cooperation with the European countries concerning the definition of guidelines about large scale planning and the development of innovative planning and knowledge-development tools. The Ministry of Public Works has been active since 1993 on both aspects, having presented a framework for the development of the European territory (SDEC) and the necessary tools for the exchange of knowledge and the analysis of phenomena of spatial change (*Osservatorio sulle politiche territoriali*). SDEC should offer a framework at the European level to evaluate the effects on the territory of environmental, social and economic phenomena that will probably occur in the near future within the EU neighbouring countries. The aim is to build a range of operational tools that provide indications, support, tools and codes of behaviour to the national, regional and local administrations of the EU, and ensure conditions for sustainable development based on complementarity of the different structures.

More particularly, at the European level, the idea is that the EU should promote wide sensibility on the requisites of urban quality to be guaranteed to all citizens; on the most effective planning, economic and administrative instruments to start structural processes of urban regeneration; and on the type of actions that favour an equal redistribution of the economic results and benefits originating from the interventions of urban regeneration. In other words, the main role that the EU should assume is the favouring of the transition from strategies of support for marginal urban areas towards strategies that are based on a balanced economic and social development.

Conclusions

Until the '90s there has not been an explicit urban policy in Italy. With Law 142/90 the concept of metropolitan cities has been introduced for the first time. Although the national government has started a discussion about administrative reform linked to the urban context, an explicit urban policy is still missing in terms of content. The main reason behind the lack of a clear urban policy is that, in Italy, urban policy has been a non-priority for the central government for a long time. Since 1942 Italian urban legislation has been based on Article 1 of Urban Law No. 1159, which favours desurbanization, rather than managing the process of urbanization. Therefore, at least until the end of the '80s, urban laws have not permitted any programming of the phenomena of urbanization, nor even a correct definition of such phenomena with respect to the economic and social aspects.

Only recently has the national government started thinking in terms of urban planning and programming. The instruments for the development of an integrated urban policy have been set, although they require better definition. Although an explicit national urban policy still does not exist, central government is implicitly paying growing attention to cities. The scarce coordination and cooperation between the several departments and institutions at the national, regional and local levels of government is the main obstacle to the development of a clear national urban policy that favours the sustainable growth of Italian cities.

To overcome this obstacle, it seems necesary to organize the many urban policies and programmes better, entrusting one department only, at the national level, with their coordination. The Department for Urban Areas, in this case, seems the most appropriate seat.

Notes

1 The author would like to thank the Ministry of Public Works for the valuable information given, without which this contribution would not have been possible. Particular thanks go the Minister of Public Works with delegation for urban areas, Paolo Costa, Arch. G. Fontana (Di.Co.Ter.), Dott. D. Attubato (Roma Capitale and Presidency of the Council of Ministries), and Dott. S. Finocchiaro and Ing. Sammartino (Dipartimento Aree Urbane). Also, the author thanks Lanfranco Senn, professor in Urban and Regional Economics at Bocconi University, for his valuable comments.

2 The rank is based on the elaboration made by Il Sole-24 ore. One might argue about the choice of indicators and the methodology (widely described in the dossier). However, in this context, the aim is to give a general idea about the situation in the largest cities in Italy.

3 Palermo and Catania have not been included, because Sicily is a region with a special status.

4 So far, only the first issue has been faced. No actions have been undertaken to implement the other two goals.

References

Bramezza, I. (1996), *The Competitiveness of the European City*, Amsterdam: Thesis Publisher.

Cempella, F. (1996), 'Territorio, infrastrutture e ruolo dell'amministrazione centrale' in Clementi, Dematteis Palermo (eds), q.v.

Clementi A., Dematteis, G. and Palermo, P.C. (eds) (1996), *Le forme del territorio italiano. Temi e immagini del mutamento*, Vol. 1, Bari: Laterza.

Cori, B. (1991), *Città, spazio urbano e territorio in Italia*, Milan: Franco Angeli.

ENEA (1996), 'L'osservatorio delle trasformazioni territoriali' in Clementi, Dematteis and Palermo (eds), op. cit.

Fubini A. and Corsico, F. (1994), *Aree metropolitane in Italia*, Milan: Franco Angeli.

Il Sole-24 Ore (1996), *Dossier on Quality of Life*, No. 355, 30 December.

IRES (1991), *Le aree metropolitane tra specificità e complementarietà*, Turin: Dibattiti IRES.

Pierotti, P. (1991), 'La politica delle città in Italia' in Cori, op. cit.

Presidency of the Council of Ministries (1996), 'Piano nazionale di azione', report for the *World Conference on Human Settlements, Habitat II*.

Presidency of the Council of Ministries (1996), 'Rapporto sulla condizione abitativa in Italia', report for the *World Conference on Human Settlements, Habitat II*.

Presidency of the Council of Ministries, Dipartimento Aree urbane (1996), 'Il territorio del sistema urbano dell'Unione in funzione dell'art. 10 fesr, quale strumento della commissione nel quadro di una strategia di sviluppo urbano', report written by D. Attubato.

Presidency of the Council of Ministries, Dipartimento per le Aree urbane (1996), *Competenze, finalità, aspetti organizzativi ed operativi. Quadro normativo di riferimento e linee di azione*.

SEC, Social and Economic Committee (1996), *Advice on the Role of the European Union about Urban Matters*, Brussels, 25/26 September.

Sichera C. (1995), *L'ordinamento delle autonomie locali*, IV edn, Milan: Pirola.

Vandelli, L. and Mastragostino, F. (1996), 'I comuni e le province' in *Le autonomie territoriali*, 2, Bologna: Il Mulino.

11 Luxembourg

LEO VAN DEN BERG, ERIK BRAUN AND JAN VAN DER MEER[1]

National Spatial Development Pattern

Luxembourg's surface measures 2,600 km^2, which is less than 1/1000th of the total EU surface area. In this smallest among the EU member states live about 400,000 persons, one third whom are foreign residents. The spatial development pattern clearly shows an urban hierarchy: by far the most important town is the capital city of Luxembourg-Ville, where almost 25 per cent of the inhabitants live. Foreign residents make up slightly more than 50 per cent of the population of the capital city. Next to the capital city are some secondary towns, most of them located close to Luxembourg-Ville. The population of the four largest towns is presented in Table 11.1.

Table 11.1   Largest cities of Luxembourg

City	Population
Luxembourg-Ville	about 85,000 inhabitants
Esch sur Alzette	about 25,000 inhabitants
Differdange	about 16,000 inhabitants
Dudelange	about 15,000 inhabitants

Source: Ministre de l'Interieur, Luxembourg.

The three secondary cities are some 20 km away from Luxembourg-Ville and are all located in the canton Esch-sur-Alzette, south of the canton of Luxembourg. The canton of Esch-sur-Alzette is densely populated, with some 470 inhabitants per km^2, about as much as in the city of Luxembourg itself (Eurostat, 1996). This concentration of people originates from the growth of the iron and steel industry in this part of the country following the discovery of iron ore around 1850, which marked Luxembourg's economic take off. An important steel industry came into being, drawing tens of thousands of immigrant workers into the mines and steel factories. Until the middle of the

246

20th century this part remained the centre for economic activity. The decline of the steel industry has resulted in a decline in welfare. Still, Luxembourg houses Europe's fifth steel complex (the ARBED Group). Steel exports constitute one quarter of Luxembourg's export trade.

The neighbouring cantons of Luxembourg-Ville and Esch-sur-Alzette together constitute what can be indicated as the 'functional urban region' of Luxembourg-Ville. The urban area thus defined occupies about half of the Luxembourg territory and numbers 230,000 inhabitants (almost two thirds of total population). The cantons in the east and north are mainly rural and less densely populated (just over 40 inhabitants per km^2). During the decade 1980–90 the total Luxembourg population grew by 4.1 per cent, while the urban area grew by only 0.4 per cent.

The extension of the capital's role as a European and financial centre from 1970 onwards led to the development of an important new centre of economic activity. Owing to a fiscal regime, Luxembourg is an attractive location for banks (more than 200 settlements), investment funds (about 900) and holding companies (about 7,000). In addition, Luxembourg is the home base for European institutions (Court of Justice, Court of Auditors, European Investment Bank and three annual sessions of the Council of Ministers). Luxembourg has a strong economic performance. The unemployment rate is far below the EU average and the GDP per inhabitant is about 30 per cent higher than the EU average, which makes the country comparable with affluent European regions such as Piemonte and Baden-Wuerttemberg (Eurostat, 1996).

Administrative and Financial Framework

Given the limited size of Luxembourg, only one administrative layer apart from the national government exists: the municipality. There are 118 municipalities with an average population of just over 3,000. The four largest cities together accommodate more than one third of total population. For administrative purposes the country is divided into three districts ('cantons'), each of which is headed by a commissioner appointed by the central government. This official has no executive powers, his or her main function being to serve as a liaison between the central government and the municipalities (Committee of the Regions, 1996).

In general, decisions which can effectively be taken at the municipal level will be taken at this level. This holds true for urban policies as well. Local authorities are thus quite independent. The legal basis for this principle stems from a decision made as early as 1789. However, in order to avoid municipalities' taking decisions which have a national impact, the Minister of the Interior has the authority to interfere in such decisions. This possibility for interference applies also to urban plans, following a 1937 law. The national government does have nationwide policies for different kinds of subjects. These policies do include urban areas, but they are not specifically directed towards them. The policy subjects include: employment, economic affairs, housing, transport spatial planning and the natural environment. Different ministries have policies for subjects of their competence, which influence the urban development. In this sense ministries have indirect influence.

Because of the size of the country there is generally a close relationship between the central and the local level of government. This relationship is strengthened by the fact that more than half of the 60 members of the national parliament also are mayors or members of municipal councils. Different public institutions cooperate continuously. On the basis of projects, teams with participants from the ministries and municipalities involved are formed to handle a specific issue, thus creating effective partnerships. An example is a project aiming to reorganize the public transport system in the city of Luxembourg and surrounding municipalities. The management of this project is carried out jointly by the Ministry of Transport and the city of Luxembourg. Advice committee's are set up also, to handle a specific subject. These advice groups constitute a formalized way of cooperation between ministries, as they have members from different ministries and/or municipalities. Some of these advice committees have a permanent existence, such as the committee for planning matters, the committee for housing matters and the committee for sites and monuments.

The main sources of revenue for local government are general grants (31 per cent), specific grants (4 per cent), local taxes (34 per cent) and charges and fees (31 per cent). Local taxes consist of a real property tax (5 per cent of local taxes) and the far more important trade tax (95 per cent of local income), levied on the capital and income of companies. In 1991 the Law of Local Finance was reformed with the intention of rearranging the general grant system. This reform was a reaction to an increasing disparity in the municipal revenues caused by very unequal income from the trade tax. In order to equalize the differences in the municipal tax bases (which favoured the cities) the disadvantaged municipalities (mainly in the rural area) now receive a greater share from the Municipal Fund as a compensation for their weaker tax bases (The Committee of the Regions, 1996). Finally, borrowing must be approved by the Minister of the Interior.

The national government has set up some funds (under their own control) to help to overcome specific urban problems, some of them directly targeted at Luxembourg-Ville:

- the fund for affordable living facilities, which aims to facilitate the building of cheap houses, for rent and for sale;
- the fund for the urbanization and planning of the Kirchberg plateau, created in order to facilitate the planning, acquisition and building of a new district of Luxembourg-Ville, at the Kirchberg plateau;
- the fund for the renovation of the ancient city, which aims to facilitate the renovation of four islands in the inner city of Luxembourg-Ville.

Urban Issues and Challenges from the National Perspective

As indicated in the previous section, there is no general policy for urban matters at the national level. There are nationwide policies on specific subjects which matter for cities.

A supreme objective at the national level is the optimal utilization of the land. For this reason, deterioration should be avoided, as should wasting financial means. Failure to meet these two objectives can result in the national government's interfering in local planning. For this local planning, a spatial plan is obligatory.

In order to develop a more effective land use policy, national and regional industrial zones have been established. Their purpose is to help to consolidate the manufacturing structure in the south and to stem the rural exodus in the north and east.

An aid scheme for specific development areas has been introduced by law focusing on both industrial and service activities (Eurostat, 1994).

Apart from the instruments to exert indirect influence on municipal policies, the Ministry of Physical Planning has initiated a series of plans created specifically for urban development, most importantly on the issue of transport. Thus, this is direct involvement by the national government.

National Policy Responses to Urban Issues, Challenges and Development

An important national government instrument to allow interference in municipal planning and policies is the national planning vision. This is a long term vision, which strives for a coherent use of specific policies, in order to avoid unbalanced development. It aims for balanced national and regional plans. Thus, urban policies are judged in a national context.

The following subjects are considered especially relevant in this respect:

- housing: the focus should be on the renovation of ancient buildings. A substantial rise in the demand for housing in Luxembourg-Ville is expected. Measures are taken in order to accommodate this growth. These housing projects are developed in close cooperation between ministries, such as the Ministries of Physical Planning, the Environment and Transport. However, rather than focusing on housing alone, the vision is that the rise in prices due to the rise of the tertiary sector in the city centre poses a problem;
- urban planning: the policy objective is to spread economic and social functions. This relates to the problem as identified above. Policy measures are the development of regional parks for economic activity. This is because a large expansion of Luxembourg-Ville will result in high infrastructure costs, pollution and other negative effects. For this reason, Luxembourg is striving to spread economic activity;
- public services: the government is aiming to reduce the number of government offices in the city centre by relocating these offices elsewhere. This will generate space for new activities in the city centre;
- transport: the policy objective is to increase the public transport system in the urban agglomerations;
- environment: the policy objective in this respect is to ensure durable economic development.

The cities in the former industrial area have experienced problems due to the decline in the metal industry. Also, these cities accommodate many immigrants, who have to cope with low incomes. Houses are not well maintained, which has led to a decline of housing prices and consequently, in some districts, to social segregation. Policies are set up to improve this situation. The conditions for successful policies are present; for instance the availability of former industrial sites, which can be used now to locate other economic activities. New businesses are willing to locate at these sites due to excellent accessibility and communication connections with the centre of the country. In the town of Esch-sur-Alzette, such rehabilitation policies were set up in the '80s, and are now almost complete.

The municipalities of Differdange and Dudelange are developing policies, in cooperation with the Ministry of Housing, to overcome urban problems, also caused by a decline in industrial employment.

The canton Esch-sur-Alzette, where both municipalities are located, receives European support in the frame of the Structural Funds (Objective 2). Differdange and Dudelange are also involved in the URBAN-initiative. Projects are under way to improve public services. In both cities, a project was set up to renovate an old building, located in a problem district, for public services, most importantly as a day-care centre for children. For the renovation work, people from the district relying on social welfare payments are employed, in order to increase the participation of the local community. An advantage of such projects is that they generate a certain dynamism in policy making, which has resulted in the cooperation of different municipalities in South Luxembourg to create an integral plan for the region, a plan which is currently lacking.

The opinion of the national government with respect to the European urban policy is that problems – which are more or less similar in all large cities – should be studied at the European level, in order to prevent each city having to find its own solution. A common treatment of urban development and related questions allows better policy practices.

Conclusions

The Grand Duche of Luxembourg is considerably smaller than most larger European cities. Hence it is no surprise that national urban policies specifically directed to large cities have not been developed here. The national spatial pattern shows a sparsely populated rural north and east part, and a rather urbanized area in the south, comprising the capital city Luxembourg-Ville and the industrial area of the canton Esch-sur-Alzette. This industrial south once formed part of one of Europe's leading industrial regions, spreading over the north of France via Luxembourg to Saarland. This concentration of the capital city and the old industrial belt, comprising the four largest towns, has resulted in what can be indicated as the 'functional urban region' of Luxembourg-Ville, with about 230,000 inhabitants.

Despite the decline in the iron and steel industry, the Luxembourg economy ranks among the most affluent in the world, with, among other things, a very low unemployment figure and a GDP per inhabitant that is about 30 per cent above the EU average. Nowadays Luxembourg-Ville is an important commercial and administrative centre specializing in financial services, and home base for EU and other international institutions.

The national administrative structure is simple: next to the national government there are municipalities. Most decisions regarding municipal issues are taken at the municipal level; however, to avoid municipalities' taking decisions which have a national impact, the Ministry of the Interior has the authority to interfere in municipal decision-making.

The national ministries do have nationwide sectoral policies. There are no policies specifically directed to cities. There does exist continuous cooperation between different public institutions. Specific issues are dealt with by project teams or (permanent) advice committees in partnership between ministries and local authorities.

The municipalities are financially quite independent. The three major revenue categories of national grants, local taxes and local charges/fees are roughly of equal size. A trade tax levied on companies makes up about 30 per cent of local income. This especially holds for cities. Since 1992 the rural areas are compensated by the Municipal Fund in order to equalize the increasingly diverging incomes of urban and rural municipalities.

National government controls some specific funds aiming at financing some priority projects in cities, such as affordable housing, the development of a major real estate project in Luxembourg-Ville and the renovation of the ancient part of the capital.

A policy priority at the national level is the development of a more effective land use policy. To this end, a national vision on spatial planning has been formulated. Local plans have to fit into the national plan; if not, the national government can intervene. Some specific objectives of the spatial policy are the consolidation of the industrial structure in the south, stemming the rural exodus in the north, spreading new economic activities and relocating public services away from the crowded city centre, and improving public transport.

Luxembourg-Ville experiences some traffic congestion, some suburbanization, and pressure on land for commercial activities, leading to a considerable increase in land prices. The city, however, does not seriously suffer from the same diseases that are manifest in most major cities in the rest of Europe. In order to prevent high infrastructural costs, pollution and other negative effects, spatial planning policies are directed to spreading economic activities by developing business parks outside the city.

Most social problems exist in the old industrial quarters in the canton Esch-sur-Alzette. Many immigrant workers have settled in this part. Housing quality is low and some social segregation is noticeable. The EU has indicated this region for financial support in the frame of both Objective 2 as well as the URBAN initiative.

Note

1   With the assistance of P.W. de Langen

References

Committee of the Regions (1996), *Regional and Local Government in the European Union*, Brussels.Eurostat (1994), *Europe in Figures*, Vol. 1.

Eurostat (1996–1, 1996–2 and 1996–3), *Statistics in Focus*, regions.

Ministre de l'Interieur (1997), *Questionnaire relatif a la conference des grandes villes d'Europe*.

'Rapport National du Grand-Duchi de Luxembourg "Habitat II"' (1996), *Deuxième Conférence Mondiale sur les Etablissements Humains*, Istanbul.

12 The Netherlands

LEO VAN DEN BERG, ERIK BRAUN AND JAN VAN DER MEER

National Spatial Development Pattern

The Netherlands is one of the most densely populated and urbanized countries in Europe. Over four-fifths of the population lives in urbanized areas. The urban system is marked by a reasonably balanced spread of local units by size classes. There is no single dominant primarycity; there are rather a few large towns which – in general terms – are treated as equivalent by the national government. An uncommon aspect is that the national capital (Amsterdam) is not the seat of the government (The Hague).

That the Netherlands does not recognize a primary city does not mean that population and activities are distributed evenly across the national territory. The urban system has its centre of gravity in the western part of the country, where the four largest cities, together with the suburban municipalities oriented to them and some towns of medium size, form the more or less ring-shaped structure known as Randstad Holland. Physically as well as economically, Randstad Holland constitutes the core of the Netherlands. Six and a half million people live, work and move there, yet the Randstad is not formally a recognized statistical unit, nor does it have an administrative structure of its own.[1] It is primarily a planning unit in the framework of national physical planning.

The predominantly rural character of the Green Heartland is unique to the Randstad, enclosed as it is within the strongly urbanized ring-shaped structure. It is that phenomenon that distinguishes this (pseudo-)metropolis from other very large demographic concentrations in Europe, such as Paris and London, and makes it to some extent comparable with the Rhein-Rhur area. To the inhabitants, the term Randstad is a concept of relative meaning. They feel first and most attached to their own place of residence in their own region within the Randstad. Moreover, the different parts of the Randstad have kept their own character; although their centres are quite close to one another,[2] they are nevertheless a collection of separate (large and small) urban regions. Most of them have their own distinct socioeconomic identity. The tradition of intensive government commitment to physical planning has prevented the

254

development of one unbroken urbanized space. On the other hand, that kind of planning has engendered much traffic, and hence congestion. Holland has the highest number of private car kilometres by km^2 in Europe. Furthermore, urban regions are increasingly showing overlaps, as is evident very clearly from commuting statistics.

Characteristically, the principal physical structure is gradually emerging as corridor-shaped zones that link the Randstad to urban regions in Belgium and Germany. The national economic core appears to extend from the west in easterly and southerly directions along these corridors, which have evolved along the principal transport axes. The economic activities that have settled in these corridors are often concentrated around the large and medium-sized towns within the corridor. The expectation is that, by and large, this spatial pattern will continue developing in the coming years: a metropolis-like core area with a few urbanized zones fanning out towards Germany (Hamburg/Berlin and Rhein-Ruhr) and Belgium (Antwerp/Brussels). The pattern also reveals that the prospects are still poor for the northeast, traditionally the least urbanized and economically most problem-ridden part of the Netherlands.

The notion of 'major city' is a relative one that has its own special interpretation in the Netherlands. Indeed, by world standards, the Netherlands cannot boast any genuine major city at all, for none of them reaches a population of one million. However, if by 'city' is understood a functional urban region, including the central city and the surrounding places strongly oriented to it in terms of commuters and services, then the Netherlands has two urban regions of more than a million inhabitants (the Amsterdam and Rotterdam regions), and three counting between half a million and one million (the regions of The Hague, Arnhem/Nijmegen and Utrecht). In 1996, the Netherlands counted 23 municipalities of more than 100,000 citizens, and 33 of between 50,000 and 100,000. In 1990 the corresponding figures were 17 and 27. The average municipal population is about 25,000 (1996).

In the Netherlands it is quite normal to speak about 'the major four' (Amsterdam, Rotterdam, The Hague and Utrecht), but for the national physical planning as practised in the early 1990s, 13 urban nodes (urban regions) were distinguished; the present government initiated in 1994 the Major-Cities Policy, primarily for the 'major four', but soon extended to 15 municipalities of medium proportions (not coinciding with the 15 largest towns); another six will be added shortly. That is typical of the national preference for equal treatment and aversion to selectiveness.

During the postwar period (1950s and 1960s), the Netherlands went through processes of industrialization and urbanization, reflected in the growth of the major cities. Metropolitan growth continued to the mid-1960s. The increased prosperity, manifest in higher disposable incomes, greater mobility and a demand for more comfortable housing and living, determined the transition to suburbanization in the 1960s and 1970s. Disurbanization characterized developments in the 1970s: an exodus from the largest central cities, abetted by the then prevailing national policy of allocating housing contingents to a limited number of designated suburban municipalities (growth towns), a policy meant to curb unbridled dispersal of the population. The disurbanization was to a degree attended by the social and economic degeneration of, in particular, the older inner-city neighbourhoods surrounding the city centres. Large-scale town renewal efforts during the 1980s, added to such external global trends as informatization, internationalization and economic structural change (from industry to services), tended to restore the position of the major towns, or rather, of the metropolitan areas. For the most dynamic zones were found, besides some city centres, among the newly-developed sub-centres which evolved around the major cities. Re-urbanization (defined here as the restoration of the economic position of metropolitan regions) has failed to reduce the problems of major cities that are the consequence of the concentration of underprivileged groups. At the moment, national policy is focusing on improving the quality of life and safety in metropolitan areas, in addition to the efforts towards town renewal, social innovation and spatial-economic revitalization already in progress.

As do many major cities abroad, the Dutch cities combine economic functions that are reasonably- to well-developed with a cumulation of social problems. These problems are concerned with the population and with housing (caused by the fragmentation of households and a permanent inflow of migrants), with spatial segregation and social polarization, or with a spatial-economic mismatch (most jobs in the city being in the hands of people living elsewhere). The problems are most manifest in the 'major four' cities. The towns of medium dimensions are on the whole less affected, although a few of them are falling victim to typically metropolitan worries. The fact is that in the medium-sized urban regions urbanization has proceeded more evenly, so that they have not suffered such drastic absolute population losses as their larger sisters. At most, the population has remained stable or its growth somewhat slowed down.

Since the 1980s, the Dutch urban system has been reasonably stable. The great differences in growth among the towns (losses in the major cities, growth in the designated growth cores) that had marked the 1970s, have disappeared. National policy and that of the cities themselves have certainly played a role to that effect.

To round off this introduction, Table 12.1 gives a survey of the Dutch towns with more than 100,000 inhabitants and Tables 12.2 and 12.3 give a review of some characteristics of the four largest Dutch cities (urban regions).

Table 12.1   Municipalities and agglomerations of over 100,000 inhabitants in 1996

	1970		1980		1990		1996	
	core	region	core	region	core	region	core	region
Amsterdam	832	1,040	717	958	695	1,045	718	1,102
Rotterdam	699	1,1061	586	1,018	579	1,044	593	1,080
's-Gravenhage	551	719	457	675	442	685	443	695
Utrecht	279	455	237	482	230	530	234	548
Eindhoven	194	335	195	369	191	384	197	398
Groningen	169	201	161	200	168	207	170	209
Tilburg	153	203	152	217	157	229	164	239
Apeldoorn[a]	124	–	138	–	148	–	151	–
Enschede	139	230	143	244	146	251	148	254
Haarlem	172	239	158	225	149	214	148	211
Nijmegen	149	203	148	218	145	243	148	251
Arnhem	133	270	128	287	130	301	135	315
Zaanstad	116	137	130	141	130	142	134	148
Breda	121	147	117	151	123	159	130	167
's-Hertogenbosch	85	167	88	184	91	196	125	202
Maastricht	113	143	109	145	117	162	119	164
Leiden	101	163	103	173	110	187	116	196
Dordrecht	99	169	107	196	109	206	116	216
Amersfoort[a]	84	–	88	–	99	–	115	–
Almere[b]	–	–	12	–	71	–	113	–
Zoetermeer[c]	17	–	64	–	96	–	106	–
Haarlemmermeer[d]	59	–	78	–	96	–	106	–
Zwolle[a]	76	–	82	–	94	–	101	–

Notes

a   Not classified by the CBS as 'urban agglomeration'.
b   Suburban municipality in the Amsterdam region (not, however, included in the statistical region as applied here).
c   Suburban municipality in the region of The Hague.
d   Suburban municipality in the Amsterdam region.

Table 12.2   Profiles of urban regions with (inter-)national economic functions*

Profiles of urban regions with international function:

Amsterdam: good international accessibility (Schiphol airport); strong international and export orientation; (inter-)national decision centre; strong representation trade, financial services and commercial services; strong distribution function; first rank in business and leisure tourism; two universities.

Rotterdam: world's largest seaport for cargo; strong wholesale, distribution and trade; decision centre (e.g., Unilever); leading in petrochemicals; growing in insurance and commercial services; strong international and export orientation; weak industrial function; export above national average; university.

The Hague: seat national government and related international institutions, embassies, head offices (e.g., Shell), services, etc.; limited industrial function; technical university (Delft).

Profiles of urban regions with national function:

Utrecht: central location; major rail traffic junction; increasingly popular as location for growth sectors, especially services; leading trade fair function; export above average; university.

Arnhem/Nijmegen: halfway Randstad and Rhein-Rhur region; strong consumer industries; important corporate head office (AKZO Nobel); industrial orientation; increasing international orientation owing to foreign investments; strong export position; university (Nijmegen).

Eindhoven: situated on Randstad-Rhein-Rhur (south) corridor; corporate head offices (e.g., Philips, DAF, Océ); strong cluster in electronics; industrial orientation; technical university.

Groningen: situated in periphery in rural area; regional economic centre; strong position in consumer industries; export below national average; university.

*   According to qualification by spatial planning policy (VINEX).

Source: INRO/TNO, VVK and RPD, 1994.

Table 12.3 Characteristics of urban regions with (inter-)national economic functions[a]

Urban region	Population (x 1000)		GRP 1983–95[b]		Industry/ services	EU funding
	region[c]	city	region	city		
Amsterdam	1,373	724	2.7	1.5	15/84	URBAN
Rotterdam	1,304	599	2.6	1.9	23/76	URBAN
The Hague	922	445	2.5	1.2	13/87	URBAN
Utrecht	1,056	234	3.6	1.9	19/81	URBAN
Arnhem/		134		2.8		
Nijmegen	668	147	2.9	3.2	23/76	Objective 2
Eindhoven	671	196	2.8	1.1	37/62	Objective 2
Groningen	351	171	1.8	2.0	23/76	Objective 2

Notes

a   According to qualification by spatial planning policy (VINEX).
b   Annual change; national average: 3.0 per cent growth (source: Vegt and Manshanden, 1996).
c   CBS COROP-regions (usually larger than VINEX-urban region).

Administrative Framework

The Kingdom of the Netherlands started out as a federal republic, composed of parts that were to a high degree autonomous. In the 19th century the Netherlands grew to be a 'decentralized unitary state' with three administrative levels: state, provinces, and municipalities. That political structure is laid down in the constitution and still forms the framework within which the three government levels operate. The tasks, responsibilities and funding of provinces and municipalities are also laid down in law. The law considers all municipalities of equal status.

In the last century, the national government left plenty of room for municipalities to design their own policy. In the course of the present century, however, the national government has issued ever more policy measures and drawn up more and more rules – in a variety of policy areas – by which the municipalities have had to abide. Municipalities and provinces are committed to respect, and help implement, the decisions of the state. Up into the 1980s the national government influenced ever more explicitly the policy of the lower authorities in the decentralized unitary state. One important reason is that the Netherlands are so densely populated that the available space needs to be used with caution, and the national government has actively tried to control spatial developments by careful physical planning. Another reason is that the Netherlands are very keen on equality, or at any rate on keeping differences as narrow as possible. The Netherlands accommodate Roman Catholics, Protestants, socialists and liberals. None of these categories is dominant, and a succession of coalition cabinets has tried to protect the interests of them all. That tendency has its spatial reflection: the discrepancy between the Randstad and the rest of the Netherlands has figured high on the political agenda.

Administrative Innovation

At the moment, the Netherlands comprise 12 provinces and some 560 municipalities. In the 1980s new discussions were started about a reform of the administrative organization. The national government has proposed to abandon one of the foundations of the decentralized unitary state, namely, that the administrative structure of all municipalities should be the same in general terms. Under the administrative renewal policy, seven metropolitan regions were elected for an extraordinary administrative reform. Besides the four major cities Amsterdam, Rotterdam, The Hague and Utrecht, the regions of Eindhoven/Helmond, Arnhem/Nijmegen, and Enschede/Hengelo were designated as so-called 'BON[3] regions'. Each BON-region was invited to submit a plan to the Ministry of the Interior, which then proceeded to prepare a bill opening the way for the gradual introduction of 'city provinces'. However, negative outcomes of referenda held on the subject by the city corporations of Amsterdam and Rotterdam held up the process considerably. The cabinet has now launched a revised proposal featuring 'city provinces' for only two urban regions (Rotterdam and Eindhoven). The 'city provinces' are to be entrusted mainly with spatial-economic tasks. The parliament still has to decide on the issue.

Financial Revision

The funding of the municipalities is a shared responsibility of the Ministry of the Interior and the Treasury. Financially, the municipalities are largely dependent on the national government. Dutch municipalities have far less opportunity to acquire revenues of their own than most of their counterparts abroad. By far the greater part of taxes are collected nationally. In 1995, only 16 per cent of municipal expenditure was covered from the municipalities' own revenue. The greater part derives from the state in the shape of general and specific payments (see Table 12.4). The state determines the size of the general payment by a number of criteria. The municipality is responsible for the allocation of the funds. The state also determines the specific payments, and also involves itself actively in their allocation by regulations and checking procedures. The relatively large share of specific payments in municipal financing constrains the freedom of municipalities to develop their own policy. More recently, the state has taken measures to expand municipal policy freedom. For one thing, a number of specific payments have been combined into broad target payments, leaving municipalities sufficient elbow room to adjust the allocation of the financial means to the local situation, within the responsibility of the state. For another, some specific payments have been transferred to the general payment, thus increasing the policy freedom and permitting a more integral weigh-off on the local level. Since 1987, there has been a distinct change in the ratio between the various sources. The effect of the policy adopted has been to increase the municipalities' own revenues and the general payment (see Table 12.4). The expectation is that this trend will continue in the coming years, in particular as far as the ratio between general and specific payments is concerned.

Table 12.4   Municipal funding in guilders

Income sources	1987		1990		1995	
	billion	%	billion	%	billion	%
Municipal taxes	2.8	5	3.1	6	4.4	8
retributions, duties	1.6	3	2.0	4	4.2	8
general payment	12.1	23	13.9	28	17.8	32
specific payment	36.1	69	31.6	63	28.3	52
Total	52.7	100	50.5	100	54.7	100

Source: Ministry of the Interior/Ministry of Finance (1995c).

The ultimate object of the distribution of national resources has always been to give all municipalities an equal starting position. However, the system that was introduced in the early 1980s upset the financial relations among municipalities. The money for the general payment, which derives from the so-called Municipal Fund, used to be for the most part allocated by size characteristics. The disadvantage of the system was that the distribution did not really take account of the expenses of the municipalities. Municipalities with a regional function and a relatively poor social structure were at a particular disadvantage; they were often, though not always large and medium-size towns (Ministry of the Interior/Ministry of Finance, 1995). Recently, the Act regulating the financial relation between the state and municipalities was revised completely so as to put the municipalities back on an equal level of services. One reason for the revision, apart from the need for a more cost-oriented allocation of resources, was the greatly increased political and social concern with the problems of major cities. In the new system, half of the resources are dependent on the social structure (38 per cent) and the function of regional centres (13 per cent). At the same time the new structure allows for adjustment of the distribution code, thus permitting a transfer from relatively rich to relatively poorer municipalities (the large ones among them).

To end this section, here follows a short typology of the role of the ministries in the policy for large towns.

Review of the Role of Ministries with Respect to the Major Cities

The Ministry of the Interior The Ministry of the Interior is traditionally responsible for public administration, and since the 1980s has pursued an explicit metropolitan policy by means of the proposed administrative reform. Moreover, the Ministry shares with the Treasury the responsibility for the funding of municipalities through the Municipal Fund. Since 1994, the Ministry of the Interior has coordinated the Major-Cities Policy (in Dutch: *Grote-Stedenbeleid*, or GSB for short), in which 11 ministries are involved to a greater or lesser extent.

Ministry of Housing, Physical Planning and the Environment The Ministry of Housing, Physical Planning and the Environment is closely involved in the development of the major cities. An important policy instrument is the *National Report on Physical Planning*, issued once every decade since 1960. This report culminates in a so-called 'physical planning key decision', which sets the course for provincial and municipal physical plans and provides the framework for national spatial policy, in which the spatial aspects of sectorial policy (house-building, traffic and transport, economy, etc.) need to be fitted. The currently prevailing report is *VINEX (Vierde Nota Extra, Fourth Report on Physical Planning Extra)*. Another matter coming under the Ministry of Housing, Physical Planning and the Environment is town renewal. The

Ministry participates in GSB, among other things by co-investing in houses built in deprived neighbourhoods to be sold on the market (see 'National Policy Responses to Urban Issues, Challenges and Development', q.v.).

The Ministry of Economic Affairs Up to the 1980s, this ministry had hardly any explicit truck with major cities. With the greater attention on the role of major cities in national policy, regional policy (a responsibility of this ministry) has also begun to give some thought to the cities. Regional policy is mostly of the condition-creating type. Moreover, the ministry participates in the GSB by according subsidies and by creating opportunity zones (see 'National Policy Responses to Urban Issues, Challenges and Development', q.v.).

The Ministry of Social Affairs and Employment The Ministry of Social Affairs and Employment participates in the GSB, among other things, through the so-called 'Melkert-jobs' (mentioned to the responsible minister in charge) and by according additional funds for employment services in the major cities. Before the new policy was introduced, this ministry had not adopted any explicit metropolitan policy. Nevertheless, many of its policy measures have effects on cities, as is the case of the 'social reform' (taken in hand jointly with the Ministry of the Interior).

The Ministry of Transport, Public Works and Water Management This ministry is responsible for the traffic and transport policy and for investment in infrastructure, as laid down in the *Second Transport Structure Plan (1988)*. The objective of the policy is to control mobility in a consistent way, improve accessibility and raise the standard of living. It involves explicit attention to nodes and main ports, which often coincide with metropolitan regions. Many infrastructural projects, such as the high speed rail network, are directly oriented to the accessibility of the major cities. Transport, Public Works and Water Management also participates in the GSB.

Other ministries involved The Ministry of Justice is involved in the GSB through its safety policy. Other ministries involved are those of National Health, Welfare and Sports, Education, Culture and Sciences, and Agriculture.

Urban Issues and Challenges from the National Point of View

Until the 1960s, the major cities were important centres of industrial growth and their population was growing fast. So fast, in fact, that the government decided to adopt an overspill policy to prevent the cities' becoming too large and too densely populated. However, after 1970 the birthrate dropped rapidly, and a selective migration process developed which had a very negative socioeconomic influence on the largest towns. The selective migration made for a one-sided population structure. Within the urban regions the contrasts between central cities and ring zones were becoming more pronounced, with the central towns housing disproportionate numbers of single person households, low income categories, persons entitled to social benefits, unemployed persons and people of foreign descent. The performance of the housing market is often blamed for the concentration of underprivileged groups, because only in the major cities can the housing supply provide for the limited choices of the lowest income groups. The erosion of the status of the central cities spelt the loss of power and hence of function (de Boer, 1996).

Remarkably enough, for dozens of years the national policy failed to observe the negative socioeconomic developments in the towns. Through the physical planning then practised, policy was even in part responsible for the way things developed. Lacking a proper vision of the nature of cities, national policy followed the social developments rather than responding to it with anti-cyclical control.

In the course of the 1980s, thanks in part to the efforts of local governors, the problem of poor urban housing was recognized as a task for the state. An extensive policy of town renewal (developed for the largest towns, but applicable in the entire country) was taken in hand on a large scale. Originally the concern was mostly with 'bricks and mortar', and the renewal was entirely directed to the bottom of the housing market. Only the existing city was taken in hand; there was no vision of what the future city ought to look like (de Boer, 1996). Only in the course of the 1990s did the town-renewal policy evolve towards a more integral strategy. When it appeared that without a flanking social policy decay promptly set in again, the state proceeded to stimulating 'social renewal'.

When in the mid-1980s the national economy appeared to be recovering from the effects of a grave recession, and the goal of economic growth was given national priority, one result was a new perception of the major cities: not only as social problem areas but first and foremost as powerful motors of the national and regional economies. That new point of view was supported on the national level by spatial as well as regional-economic policy measures, and not without success. Thanks to (co-)financing of major urban renewal projects and an enterprising attitude on the part of the city councils, the major cities managed an economic revival. Plenty of money was invested in offices, shopping provision, tourism and commercial housing. The government invested in, among other things, infrastructure, art and culture, in public buildings and in the quality of open spaces. That form of integral spatial-economic renewal, meant to improve the urban competitive position, proceeded successfully. Some town centres (e.g., Rotterdam and The Hague) underwent a metamorphosis, and in Amsterdam a large-scale office complex of European status arose. However, the social benefits of that urban economic renewal were not evenly distributed. Underprivileged groups hardly profited from the new urban vitality. The differences between haves and have-nots widened rather than closed. Moreover, urban renewal was attended by an increase in crime and drug-related problems, breeding feelings of insecurity.

Metropolitan problems gained new national attention in the early 1990s after some influential reports about the position of the major cities had been published. But no recovery plan ensued. Propositions were indeed launched to attack the urban problems in a different administrative context, for instance by creating regional governments in the largest agglomerations. However, the implementation of these plans has come to a standstill.

The recognition that the social problems were getting worse, in particular as far as safety, living climate and lack of jobs were concerned, induced the joint governments of the four largest cities in the spring of 1994 to submit a salvage plan for the metropolitan agglomerations (*Delta Plan for the Major Cities*) to the politician charged with the formation of a new government. This plan was taken over by the new coalition cabinet. The problems of the major cities, especially with respect to the living climate and safety, were made a priority concern of national policy. One reason was that the aggravating problems threatened to put a spoke in the wheel of the motors of the economy: the major cities. The result was the announcement of an integral policy for major cities (GSB) and the appointment of a state secretary for the major cities. Because the GSB is primarily an administrative operation, the Ministry of the Interior was designated as coordinator. The core of the new approach is integrality. The departmental segregation is recognized to have obstructed an effective approach to the problems. By a coherent perception, for instance, of town renewal, social reform, safety, education and economic activity, and by addressing them locally, in close consultation with the citizens, the problems may be efficiently solved.

The challenge for the government and local governors is to take care that the city keeps its attraction as a location for companies, and once more becomes an appealing residence for all income categories; that mobility is better controlled; that the entrepreneurial climate improved to offer a chance to new entrepreneurs; and finally, that the city becomes a safer and cleaner place, where even vulnerable groups can feel at home.

To attain these ambitious objectives, the state investment level must be raised substantially. Whether and how that will happen is not clear for the moment (1997).

National Policy Responses to Urban Issues, Challenges and Development

Introduction

This section deals with the national policy for the major cities, in part sector by sector, and in part chronologically (by sector). Only since the late 1980s has explicit attention been given to the (economic) role of major cities, initially notably in spatial policy. Policy measures towards town renewal and social innovation were not explicitly focused on major cities, despite the fact that the worst problems there are precisely in those policy areas. In the coalition agreement of 1994, the problems of large towns were emphatically and integrally put forward, not least because of an urgent plea from the four greatest cities themselves. This chapter discusses the aspects of national policy that most affect the functioning of the major cities. The themes treated are, in succession: spatial policy (including housing policy); town renewal policy, regional-economic policy; traffic and transport policy; social renewal; and finally, the policy for major cities in operation since 1994.

Spatial Policy

Characteristic patterns The national spatial policy designed to control the urbanization process was primarily a policy of spatial concentration. To preserve sufficient open space in the strongly urbanized west, policy makers have, since the 1970s, persistently tried to guide building towards concentration. A limited number of so-called growth towns was designated by the state, mostly suburban municipalities of the four largest urban regions. That policy proved very effective, for in the 1980s 95 per cent of population growth in the three largest urban regions took place in the seven 'growth towns' designated there (Van der Meer, 1989). However, that growth was attended by a strong (and selective) reduction of the population in the major cities. At the end of the 1980s the focus of the concentration policy was shifted from the 'growth towns' to the major cities and their immediate environment. New housing locations now have to be found in the large towns themselves or as near as possible to them. This policy is 'compact-town policy'. This (anticyclical) strategy has helped to restore population growth in the largest towns since the mid-1980s. The objectives of the modified concentration policy are to increase urban support, limit the growth of mobility, encourage the use of bicycles and public transport, and protect rural territory serving as green buffer.

A second characteristic development (not only in spatial policy) is progressive decentralization. Increasingly, the hierarchical planning system has been reformed into a system of checks and balances, within which, on the higher policy levels, indicative plans are accompanied by directive competencies (Needham et al., 1994). Thus, at the end of the 1980s the state shed the care for all details of national housing. Under the present spatial policy, the national government just hands out criteria and proposals for the development of new business or housing estates. The regional and local governments are expected to regard these criteria and proposals in their weigh-off.

Fourth report on physical planning: breakaway from the past The foundation for the present spatial policy was laid in the 1980s, when the national economy was cautiously picking up from a serious recession. The new approach emphasized the need for economic growth and the relevant role of the market sector. The economic dimension was new to spatial policy. Until then, the focus had been on the spatial distribution of housing contingents, the expectation being that the market sector, led by the locational behaviour of business companies, would duly follow. New accents were also put on internationalization (among other things, the increasing competition between major European cities) and the negative effects of the fast rising car mobility on the environment as well as on the transport and distribution sector. The policy emphasis on economic growth, international competition, accessibility of economic centres (in particular the main port complexes of Amsterdam and Rotterdam), and the quality of the environment, very explicitly put the major cities (as motors of economic growth) in the centre of policy attention. Such a central position of the major cities in national spatial policy was a new phenomenon. The need for urban revitalization was emphasized, to be effected by outward expansion as well as by restructuring inner-city locations that had lost their functions, since the creation of high quality living and working locations was considered to contribute to the urban quality.

The policy and its instruments were based on the concept of the urban region, that is, a central city together with suburban municipalities functionally oriented to it. That implied an anticipation that policy proposals would reform the administrative structure in the largest urban regions through the introduction of regional governments.[4] The stagnation of that administrative operation necessitated inter-municipal administrative cooperation in the urban regions. Subsidies and instruments of the state were adjusted to encourage that.

One implication of a decentralized national policy is that the state will only fund projects of its own implementation. In many cases, private co-financing is required to carry through the preferred policy. Investments initiated by central government are mostly those meant to strengthen the national competitive position. That objective is translated, among other things, as: a) promotion of an internationally competitive metropolitan location environment (the state giving priority treatment to, for instance, international accessibility and the development of top locations for offices); b) strengthening the position of urban nodes (see below); and c) reinforcement of the main port functions of Schipol Amsterdam Airport and the Rotterdam seaport complex, both crucial to the national economy.

Urban-nodes policy The designation, in 1989, of 13 so-called 'urban nodal points' was distinctly in the interest of the major cities. These cities get priority in the allocation of national funds for high grade public services, especially for telecommunication and accessibility. A positive effect on the market sector is hoped for from the concentration of services. The cities have to draw up their own profiles and to indicate by what 'strategic projects' they mean to re-inforce those profiles. The central government will then conclude more detailed agreements about investment in one (or a few) 'key projects'. The first concern of this policy is to capitalize the city's spatial-economic potentialities. In the first instance, very little money is involved. The primary aim is to open up important sources of investment in transport provisions (Ministry of Transport and Public Works), housing locations and soil cleansing for the sake of business environments (both Ministry of Housing, Physical Planning and the Environment), the upgrading of industrial estates (Ministry of Economic Affairs), and so on. An interim evaluation (after seven years of urban-nodes policy) has revealed positive developments but also criticism. Positive points are the realization of some key projects, the concentration of services in town centres, and improved accessibility. There is criticism with respect to the set of financial instruments, which is mostly dependent on other departments (where sectoral priorities presumably outweigh the 'urban node' criterion), and the lack of selectiveness: 13 urban nodes seem too much of a good thing

(Ministry of Housing, Physical Planning and the Environment, 1996).

Location policy To curb intra-city car traffic, promote the quality of living in the cities and improve the mutual adjustment of living, working, services and public transport, in the early 1990s the central government introduced a location policy, addressed to business companies and services. This policy comes under the joint responsibility of the Ministries of Housing, Physical Planning and the Environment, Economic Affairs, and Transport, Public Works and Water Management. The underlying motive of the policy is to put 'the right business in the right place'. To that end, three types of location are distinguished according to their accessibility by public transport and/or motorcar. Ideally, only companies with a corresponding mobility profile should establish at each type of location. The profile is determined by such criteria as intensity of visitors and workers, and dependency on business transport or goods transport. Municipalities are thus no longer entirely free to develop new business or office estates.

Housing policy; 'VINEX-locations' The Netherlands distinguishes itself from several other member states by the government's strong influence on the housing supply. Within the national policy of physical planning, the spatial distribution of house building is the main instrument with direct influence on the spatial structure. (Financial) support from the central government to municipalities for the construction of houses depends on this distribution. In addition, the national government is closely involved in the building of both rented and owner-occupied houses for the lower income categories. Although the housing policy is not explicitly metropolitan, the greatest challenges with respect to future housing do occur in and around the largest cities. Under the new policy, decisions about the kind of dwellings to be built, and where, are as far as possible weighed off against policy decisions about work locations, services and public transport on the level of urban regions. To attain the required administrative cooperation (among municipalities in an urban region) as well as functional integration (among the departments involved), various policy instruments have been newly inserted or adjusted. Some themes involved are the possibility of joint land policy, instruments to control land prices, distribution of housing space, public transport, and mobility policy (e.g., parking policy).

Although the national government takes responsibility only for the lower income groups, here, too, the desired development cannot be realized without the participation of the market sector. The municipalities are committed explicitly to enlisting the private sector (investors and developers) in their spatial policy. The central government has invited the urban regions to propose large scale locations ('VINEX-locations'), where a minimum number of houses has to be realized within five years.[5] For the inner-city locations, a link-up is sought with the town renewal policy, which so far has not considered building lots outside the built-up area (see below).

A new element with regard to the designation of the VINEX-locations is the negotiation model. Agreements have been made about funding, housing, infrastructure, soil cleansing, etc., by covenants between the state and urban regions, for a ten-year term. National grants for land exploitation, public transport and soil cleansing have been adjusted. The covenants assume that the market sector is prepared to invest generously in the construction of houses. Although opinions differ on that point, the central government does not believe there is a serious risk, given the rate of acquisition of VINEX-land by private developers (Needham et al., 1994). The integral implementation and the financial responsibility rest mostly with the municipalities. By now, most covenants have been signed (with some delay). Between 1995 and 2005, some 460,000 houses are to be built, of which one-third is in the cities themselves and two-thirds in expansion zones. The four largest urban regions are supposed to account for half that quantity. In the four major cities, 58,000 dwellings have to be realized.

Town Renewal Policy

By the national government's direct commitment to the housing policy, it is deeply involved as well in town renewal, which in the Netherlands was taken in hand relatively early (in the 1970s), and was primarily meant to improve the poor quality of the housing conditions in large parts of, mostly, the largest towns. In those low grade town quarters there was a concentration of low incomes and unemployment. The accumulation of problems was no longer thought acceptable. The government expressed its intention to try to make good at one leap that qualitative lag by a large-scale and intensive town renewal policy. That 'catch-up' operation was to be complete around the year 2010. The Town and Village Renewal Act (1985), and its related funds, assured the municipalities of state grants and, moreover, of generous policy freedom in the spending of the funds, so that, for instance, town renewal in Amsterdam proceeded quite differently from that in Rotterdam. From the title of the Act, it is apparent that town renewal was not addressing the major cities exclusively, where the arrears were most severe.

Municipalities receive payments according to a distribution code (among other criteria: proportion of prewar houses; average per-capita income). Before 1990, the town renewal policy was primarily a policy of housing rehabilitation, with business in the old neighbourhoods quite often being sacrificed. Since the 1990s, attention has shifted from the physical to the environmental aspects. In the long run, efforts in the area of national housing appear meaningful only if attended by efforts to upgrade the environment (Ministry of Housing, Physical Planning and the Environment, 1989). Such more integrated urban renewal implies, among other things, a zone-oriented rather than a street-by-street approach. And that requires cooperation with departments primarily focused on aspects of the quality of life (social affairs, employment, national health, justice, education, economic affairs, etc.), and hence has important administrative consequences in terms of departmental integration. So far, integration has mostly been attempted through intensified consultation. Many separate financial schemes have by now been combined into larger funds, leaving more spending freedom. Largely because of political responsibilities, the combinations are mostly intra- rather than interdepartmental. In 1994, the distribution code was again adjusted; the share of the four major cities in the average annual payment from the Town-Renewal Fund (now holding over a thousand million guilders) was raised from 46 to 55 per cent (bij de Leij, 1995). Amsterdam now receives almost a quarter of the national payment.

From a first evaluation (Ministry of Housing, Physical Planning and the Environment, 1990) the conclusion was that town renewal was comfortably on schedule. Another conclusion was that the municipal town renewal policy was becoming more and more varied, with integrated urban renewal[6] and management figuring besides housing rehabilitation (Ministry of Housing, Physical Planning and the Environment, 1992). That development induced the central government to reconsider, because the idea of a 'finite catch-up operation' thus threatened to change into a broad definition of town renewal without a clear horizon. The primary purpose of the reconsideration is a better management of national expenditure on housing. Decentralization and deregulation are central to the new point of view ('less government and more market'). As the government withdraws, investment risks are progressively put on the plate of the private sector, in particular the owners of low- and moderate-rent housing (the housing corporations), and the municipalities.

Traffic and Transport Policy

Through its traffic and transport policy, the Ministry of Transport, Public Works and Water Management plays an important part in the national investment policy. The traffic and transport policy as laid down in the Second Traffic and Transport Structural Plan (1988) marches in unison with the spatial policy formulated in the VINEX. Since the 1980s, the policy is no longer trying only to remove impediments to accessibility, but also to contribute to the quality of living. Control of (car) mobility is an important element. The position of the economic centres and the two main ports Schipol Amsterdam Airport and Rotterdam seaport are central to the policy.

Areas with a great (potential) demand for transport thus form the spearheads of the policy, because there the investments in road infrastructure and public transport yield the highest social and economic returns. At the same time, the quality of living is more under pressure in the dense traffic and transport nodes than elsewhere. For that reason, the policy has chosen first and foremost to improve accessibility and raise the quality of living by cultivating public transport and substantially increasing its use (Ministry of Transport, Public Works and Water Management, 1996). That choice is reflected in the investment budgets, which for the major part are spent on public transport. The investment in high-grade regional public-transport networks, in particular, is supposed to keep the pressure on the road network within acceptable limits. Thus, for the south wing of the Randstad the introduction of a light-railway network has been under study for some time, and funds have been reserved for a new underground service in Amsterdam. The Dutch government also sets great store by the high speed railway that is to give Amsterdam and Rotterdam a better connection to the European network. The priority for easy access to economic centres and main ports has consequences for investment in road infrastructure. The hinterland connections of the main ports and the main transport axes – in particular the connections among urban regions – are thus given priority before other projects.

Regional-economic Policy and EU-support

The main objective of Dutch regional-economic policy is the classic one of reducing socioeconomic discrepancies between regions, comparable to the present regional policy of the European Union. With the exception of some (mostly medium-sized) towns in problem regions, until recently no explicit large-cities-oriented economic policy had been pursued. Because of the serious economic recession in the early 1980s, the traditional approach ('equity policy') was converted into a two-track policy, in which 'efficiency policy' was also given a place. That found expression among other things in efforts to have all regions contribute to the best of their ability to the development of national employment and prosperity, while on the other hand funds available for regional policy were considerably reduced. That reduction was only in part compensated by payments from the European Structural Funds. The drive for less regional discrepancy has now become first and foremost a matter of European policy. A portion of the 'Objective 2 funds',[7] meant for economic restructuring, will now also benefit some – medium-sized – towns (Eindhoven and Enschede among them) in the designated objective regions. The Netherlands has also received a European contribution in the framework of the Community Initiative URBAN (for each of the four major cities). The URBAN-funds have been integrated in the GSB.

Response to economic development potentialities implied the redirection of some policy attention and subsidy flows towards strengthening the competitive position of the 13 urban nodes. Since 1992, policy has tried to stimulate investment in the construction and opening-up of industrial estates. The available funds were small, however, and not earmarked for certain cities. Meanwhile, the accent has shifted to the prevention of spatial bottlenecks which threaten to thwart economic development. Space for economic activities needs to be reserved in good time, for in a small and densely populated country like the Netherlands the various – sectoral – spatial claims for physical planning (the building of houses, for instance), nature and environment, leisure, infrastructure, etc. are more and more likely to clash. The claims of economic activities are quite often in danger of losing out (Ministry of Economic Affairs, 1995).

Social Renewal

As well as the spatial-economic policy, quite a few policy measures have already been issued which were aimed directly at overcoming socioeconomic disadvantages. In the early 1990s, 'social renewal' was launched, not as an explicit policy for the major cities, although they were most in discussion, at least in the beginning. The idea had been hatched in Rotterdam and subsequently adopted on the national level. The principal objective is to fight persistent social disadvantages by an integrated and sector-crossing approach (Sociaal Cultureel Planbureau, 1993). Such social disadvantages are most obvious in the larger towns. The policy of social renewal aimed at integrating the measures to fight disadvantages by a new administrative approach. The administrative reform was to be given shape in covenants between municipal authorities and the central government, in which directions were given on how to set about social renewal.

The contents of social renewal were arranged in three circles: 1) labour, education and income; 2) quality of the daily living environment; 3) cultural and social innovations. The policy was to be given shape mostly on the municipal level, since decentralization and deregulation were key notions in social renewal. The first circle referred to the deficient labour market participation in underprivileged areas. Job pools were created in which the long term unemployed could work without losing their unemployment benefit. The second circle was concerned with the physical and social services in the town quarter. The third circle refers to the restoration of social cohesion and the social defensive capacity of the citizens in underprivileged areas.

Some state payments to municipalities have been combined in the Social-Renewal Funds. Moreover, in the distribution of funds much more account was taken of the cumulation of problems. By the disadvantage criteria by which the national means were distributed, a major portion of them landed in the larger towns. The social renewal has certainly been effective, but could not meet all its ambitions because of both the way it was set up and lack of time.

1994: Major-Cities Policy (GSB); Transition to an Integral Approach

While spatial policy outlines long term strategic developments and points the way for important national investments in housing, urban renewal, industry locations, services and infrastructure, in general terms the physical elements, the main concern of the policy for major cities is to solve the metropolitan socioeconomic problems in a wider context than had been usual before.

With the new cabinet's assuming office in 1994, a new stage in the policy for the major towns began. The cabinet made the problems of the major cities one of the principal themes of the coalition agreement. In addition, a project deputy minister for the large towns was appointed. His office comes under the Ministry of the Interior and coordinates the so-called 'Major Cities Policy' (*Grote Stedenbeleid*, GSB). This policy is not the responsibility of the Ministry of the Interior alone; it is cabinet policy involving virtually all departments. The GSB's objective is to fight the disadvantages in the large towns by relating them to promising developments. Between 1994 and 1998, an annual sum of about 3,700 million guilders is available for the GSB, found mostly by combining and/or earmarking existing funds.

The acknowledgement of the special position and problems of major cities has had a long history. From 1973 there had been periodic consultation – the so-called 'agenda-consultation' – between the national government and the 'major four' ('G-4'), Amsterdam, The Hague, Rotterdam and Utrecht. Until the early 1990s, the agenda-consultation provided a platform for discussing the problems of the 'major four'. The consultation between the national government and the four large towns is now laid down in the GSB. The initiative for this explicit policy has been inspired, among other things, by the progressive political and social attention for the major cities. The increased attention had already found some reflection in the policy pursued in the 1980s and early 1990s, as described above.

The initiative for the GSB was taken by the 'major four', who shared the wish to put the problems of the major cities even more prominently on the political agenda. They made that quite clear at the time of the cabinet formation in 1994 by presenting a collective programme for the major cities. For quite some time the 'major four' had collaborated in representing their common interests before the national government, and their new coordinated action fits in that tradition. The so-called *Delta Plan* (the *Major Cities Memorandum*) stresses job creation, increasing safety, and raising the quality of living in the major towns. In addition, the 'major four' plead more administrative flexibility and decision power for the major cities, and financial means enabling them effectively to use the policy space thus created (Major Cities, 1994).

The Dutch government has duly read the signal, and subscribed to the analysis and recommendations from the *Delta Plan*, turning it, as it were, into the starting point of the GSB. The GSB also gives evidence of a clear vision of the role of the major cities in the Netherlands: that of motors of the Dutch economy and society (Ministry of the Interior, 1994). The conclusion is, then, that flourishing major cities are important not only for the cities themselves, but also for the future of the entire country (Deputy Minister of the Interior, 1994). The four major cities are highly important social, economic and cultural centres, whose functioning is regrettably obstructed by a cumulation of social problems in certain town quarters. Much persistent unemployment, one-sided income distribution, debts, crime, insecurity, degradation of the living environment, and social nuisance keep the cities from functioning properly. The GSB emphasizes the threat of a divided town, and intends to overcome the disadvantages by relating them to promising developments. In short, the motor of economy and society must be permitted once more to run at full power, making full use of the development potential of the major cities and putting a stop to the cumulation of problems. That vision and its specification in objectives for concrete themes are laid down in the 'Major Cities Policy Covenant'.

To realize that objective, the GSB-covenant formulates three key themes:

- employment and education: priority for schemes meant to deal with the persistent unemployment in underprivileged town quarters and to improve the adjustment between education and the labour market;
- safety: the GSB has to bring about a reduction in registered crime as well as reduce inhabitants' and visitors' feelings of insecurity;
- quality of living and care: the quality of the living environment in underprivileged areas has to be improved (Ministry of the Interior, 1995).

Those are the three themes of the *Delta Plan*, with education and care also included.

A considerable part of national policy is directly or indirectly relevant to the development of the major cities: the administrative reform and the revision of the municipal fund on the part of the Ministry of the Interior; the urban node policy, the VINEX and town renewal on the part of the Ministry of Housing, Physical Planning and the Environment; social renewal on the part of the Ministry of the Interior and the Ministry of Social Affairs and Employment; the Second Traffic and Transport Programme on the part of Transport, Public Works and Water Management. From the first it has been clear that the GSB does not replace the policy initiated in the 1980s and 1990s, but builds upon it. The policies conducted by the various ministries with respect to the major cities had been observed to lack coordination. An important inspiration for the GSB was the wish to improve the coordination of both the 'old' and the 'new' policy, making both more effective. Thus, the GSB represents the conversion from implicit to explicit national urban policy. This explicit policy rests on three pillars: integrality, partnership, and result-oriented working.

Integral policy The principle underlying the GSB is that the problems of the major cities can only be dealt with by an integral approach. The problems of a major city cannot be captured within one policy area and are tightly interwoven with its potentialities. National policy was too fragmentary to deal properly with that complexity. The major cities had for quite some time been urging a better coordinated policy. The GSB is expected to break open the segregate segments of national policy, and in that way to achieve the matching and integration so sorely needed. In practice, as many as 11 state departments are more or less concerned, and directly or indirectly involved in the policy. It is the task of the Project Deputy Minister of the Interior to coordinate their efforts without relieving the departments of their responsibilities. The success of the policy depends entirely on the cooperativeness of the politicians and civil servants involved.

Administratively, implementation of the integrated GSB is no easy task. The integral approach of the GSB has to find a place alongside the political responsibility for separate policy areas of the sectorial departments. To ensure the integrality of the policy, a political direction group has been appointed under chairmanship of the prime minister. Members of this group are the ministers of Finance, the Interior, Social Affairs and Employment (SZW) and Justice, as well as the project deputy minister (Van Poelje Instituut, 1995). The ministers of Housing, Physical Planning and the Environment, Economic Affairs, Transport, Public Works and Water Management, Agriculture, and National Health take part in the consultation when there are items on the agenda that concern them. The project deputy minister maintains contact with the governors of the major cities and other interested parties, such as the Association of Dutch Municipalities (VNG). On the civil servant level as well, adequate adjustment is essential. To that end an interdepartmental project group has been created. This project group in turn has formed work groups for each policy theme, in which the local authorities are represented.

The efforts to diminish the segregation of national policy to some degree find support in the reform, on the departmental level, of the financial flows to the municipalities. The departments of Housing, Physical Planning and the Environment, and of Social Affairs and Employment have combined certain subsidies into, respectively, the Work Fund and the National Housing Fund, a step that makes for greater clarity towards the municipalities. Under the GSB, the desegregation on the national level should be attended by a corresponding move on the municipal level. In the major cities as well, the adjustment of policies can be improved.

The URBAN-programme of the European Commission has so many points of agreement with the GSB that it has been integrated.

Partnership The GSB is orchestrated by the cabinet, but the approach to and implementation of the policy is an interplay between the state and the cities. The national government is continuing the decentralization of policy begun in the 1980s, assuming a facilitating role. The national government wants to march in unison with the major cities, as partners. If the GSB is to be successful, a basis of confidence has to develop between the government and the cities. At any rate, they are agreed on the contents of the central themes. The volume of the resources to be set aside for the problems of the major cities is established on the national level, with relatively little influence from the cities.

The division of financial means, set beforehand, is the point of departure for further consultation between the state and municipalities. The national government invites each major city to draw up an integrated plan specifying the approach to the specific problems. A committee with representatives of the departments checks the entire programme. After the check, the national government concludes agreements with each separate municipality, which again will be laid down in a covenant. The agreements establish the objectives of the policy and the rights and commitments of the national government as well as the municipality. In principle, a new phase in the relations between the national government and the municipalities has been heralded: primacy will be less with the state than before; either party can appeal to the other's share in the joint responsibility.

Result-oriented working: the GSB-Monitor The GSB is continuing on the course already set out in the social reform policy. Under that policy, municipalities had already acquired more freedom than before as to the spending of the available funds. Likewise, the GSB gives the cities elbow room to tailor their policy to local problems. Cities and state are jointly responsible for the results, and evaluate jointly whether the adopted policy has the desired effect. As far as possible, the objectives of the policy are expressed in quantifiable variables. The statistics are combined every year into the *Major Cities Policy Monitor*. To that end, indicators have been devised to express the developments in matters of employment, education, safety, care and quality of living. Moreover, a so-called thermometer of the quality of living has been evolved, encompassing among other things, the ownership relations in the housing stock, the nuisance caused by drug addiction, and the appreciation of the level of services by the citizens (Verwey et al., 1995). Admittedly, all parties are aware that some objectives of the GSB are difficult to quantify meaningfully. Disappointing results appearing in the monitor are not expected to have consequences for the budgets allocated to the cities. For the cities, the crucial phase is that of the judging of the plans. It is still too early to predict whether the monitoring will in the event bring about a more effective policy. At any rate, some response has been given to the demand of the cities to bear more responsibility themselves.

The major cities in the GSB-context: G-4, G-15, and G-6 Originally, the GSB was meant for Amsterdam, Rotterdam, The Hague and Utrecht, but its jurisdiction has expanded. In the slipstream of the 'major four' ('G-4'), a number of medium-sized towns have organized themselves, arguing that they too – albeit on a lesser scale – are facing the cumulation of problems for which the GSB offers relief (Ministry of the Interior, 1995). Their arguments were heard by the national government and eventually these 15 medium-sized towns[8] – the so-called 'G-15' – were included in the GSB. Covenants were concluded with the government, stating agreements comparable to those contained in the covenant with the G-4. Nevertheless, the G-15 do not have quite the same status as the G-4. The latter enjoy an exceptional position: they get proportionally more money and need not fulfil quite such stringent conditions.

The chance of extra financial support and the inclusion of 15 medium-sized towns in the GSB incited still other municipalities to strive for the status of 'major city'. Evidently, equity is still at least as important as efficiency in the Netherlands, for ultimately the government decided to include another six ('G-6') municipalities in the policy for major cities. That decision means, on the one hand, recognition of the problems of medium-sized towns, but on the other makes the policy more difficult to carry out, and renders the coordinating role of the Ministry of the Interior very awkward indeed. It should be noted that the 25 municipalities involved in the GSB are not the 25 largest.

The GSB-themes More harmony, in terms of policy, among departments, between the government and municipalities, and within municipalities, is not an objective as such. In the end, administrative partnership is needed for an integrate approach to the problems of major cities. The national government and the four major cities have formulated objectives and measures with respect to the three principal themes: employment, safety, and quality of living, as well as with respect to education and care. The themes are closely interwoven. Investment in education and in the quality of living may incite entrepreneurs to invest in a certain area, to the benefit of employment. In turn, new jobs created to have an eye kept on public spaces are promoting safety and quality of living.

a) *Employment and education*

Employment growth in the large towns trails behind that in the rest of the country, and a large proportion of the long term unemployed and others entitled to benefits live in the underprivileged neighbourhoods of the larger towns. In those towns, labour participation is too low. The aim of the GSB is to raise employment growth to the national average and to help the long term unemployed to find jobs. A reasonable growth of small and medium-sized enterprises in the large towns would provide the necessary stimulus.

The Ministry of Social Affairs and Employment contributes most in

Table 12.5 Summary of GSB resources for the G-4 (in million guilders)

	Amsterdam	Rotterdam	The Hague	Utrecht	Total
40.000 jobs plan[a]	640.3	491.3	307.3	171.1	1,610.0
JWG/Banenpool	40.1	30.5	23.5	12.8	107.0
RBA's in G4	54.5	53.0	27.2	30.4	165.0
Purchases RBA	41.2	31.6	22.8	12.5	108.2
Stirea	37.5	28.5	22.0	12.0	100.0
quality of life/					
urban economy[b]	43.1	32.8	25.3	13.8	115.0
URBAN[c]	26.0	26.0	26.0	26.0	104.0
Public safety	34.6	26.2	20.3	11.0	92.1
Others	22.5	17.1	13.2	7.2	60.0
Total	939.8	736.9	487.7	296.9	2,461.3

Notes

a Exclusive of jobs in the care sector.
b Once-only contribution.
c Payments from the state as well as the European Union.

Table 12.6 Summary of GSB resources for the G-15 (in million guilders)

	Quality of life/ urban economy*	Purchases RBA	Youth safety	Drug safety	Total
Almelo	4.07	2.70	2.99		11.18
Arnhem	9.09	7.07	5.08	0.59	24.99
Breda	8.34	4.36	5.08	0.52	21.2
Deventer	4.27	1.96	2.92	0.45	11.08
Eindhoven	13.03	6.66	7.24	0.64	32.10
Enschede	9.09	5.45	6.06	0.56	24.31
Groningen	11.07	10.15	5.64	0.59	31.30
Helmond	4.68	2.5	3.2		12.01
Hengelo	4.28	1.91	3.34		11.01
's-Hertogenbosch	6.85	3.49	3.90	0.59	17.22
Leeuwarden	5.62	4.01	3.48	0.28	15.36
Maastricht	7.54	4.07	4.32	0.65	19.20
Nijmegen	10.19	8.15	5.36	0.51	27.76
Tilburg	10.86	5.98	6.61	0.55	27.77
Zwolle	6.03	2.54	4.38	0.42	15.47
Total	115	71.	69.6	6.4	302.0

* Capitalized.

the shape of the so-called 'Melkert-jobs'. Such jobs have to be created in the public as well as the private sector. The Melkert scheme is intended to help the long term unemployed back onto the labour market. People who have been out of employment for over a year are eligible for one of the three Melkert schemes. In the present government period, Melkert I will provide 40,000 new jobs in the public sector, of which 20,000 are in municipal services and 20,000 in the care sector. Of the 20,000 municipal jobs, some 70 per cent will be accounted for by the large and medium-sized towns. Three categories of employment have been selected: surveillance (in schools, on industrial estates, in public transport, etc.), management of public space, and work in day nurseries. Recently, education was added to the list. The subsidy for these Melkert jobs is permanent. The envisaged employment in the care sector is not restricted to the large towns, but the ministers involved have expressed the intention, though without committing themselves, to create a sizeable portion of the jobs in the cities. The introduction of the 'municipal jobs' is said to be on schedule; the development in the care sector lags behind expectations.

Melkert II aims at 20,000 new jobs in the market sector in this period of government. In contrast to Melkert I, in Melkert II, employers receive an initial subsidy towards wage costs, which is in fact paid out of the benefits saved. In time, the job will have to be financed completely from the market. Again, a substantial portion goes to the large towns. Much water will have flowed under the bridge before the 20,000 'market jobs' are a reality. Melkert III, finally, is oriented primarily to social rather than labour market participation. The scheme addresses people who are not eligible for Melkert I or II; many of them are doing, or will be placed in, voluntary work. Apart from the Melkert jobs, the Ministry of Social Affairs and Employment gives the municipalities involved more freedom to enlist the Regional Employment Services. Some money will still be available for the Guaranteed Youth Employment Schemes.[9]

The Ministry of Economic Affairs contributes to the revalidation of business parks in the inner cities, and together with the Ministry of the Interior has drawn up the action plan 'Economy and Work'. A striking element of this scheme is the designation of so-called 'opportunity zones', an attempt to put back some economic dynamism into the underprivileged neighbourhoods of the major towns by dint of deregulation, a more generous interpretation of prevailing rules, and some fiscal incentives. In sum, a integral spatially-targeted approach that combines the GSB-measures to fight crime and raise the quality of living, schooling and care, with temporary deregulation and financial relief on behalf of designated areas (Werkgroep Stadseconomie, 1996). In each of the G-4 cities and in two G-15 towns a neighbourhood has been designated as an opportunity zone.

Employment growth and education are closely related. In the underprivileged areas where the overall educational level is relatively low, young people appear to have considerably more school problems than elsewhere. Relatively more youngsters leave school without a certificate and truancy has assumed undue proportions. Money has been set aside to achieve a better match of education and work in backward areas, and to help ethnic minorities overcome their linguistic arrears. As from August 1997, the input of additional means to attack educational arrears in elementary and vocational education will be a matter for the municipalities.

b) *Safety*

Since the deputy minister's office for the major cities comprises the so-called Integral Safety Policy, it is not to be wondered at that safety is an important element of the GSB. In the large towns, the compromise of safety by crime, accidents and nuisance is between two and six times worse than in smaller municipalities. The GSB sets out to relieve most of the feelings of insecurity among citizens. Safety measures can no longer be the exclusive responsibility of police and justice, but need broad administrative support (Ministry of the Interior, 1995). Safety is eminently a matter for the local administration. For every neighbourhood in the large towns, a safety plan has been developed, in which all local parties – public and private – are involved. In financial terms, the cabinet has set clear priorities in the Integral Safety Policy. Extra money has been allocated to large towns for reducing the nuisance caused by youthful delinquents and for the fight against nuisance due to drug consumption. At the same time, the living environment and various forms of surveillance have been given a place in the safety policy. In this policy, the municipalities have to do with several ministries, such as those of Housing, Physical Planning and the Environment (living environment); Social Affairs and Employment (surveillance jobs); the Interior (public administration), and of course, Justice. To the Ministry of Justice, the Integral Safety Policy represents an important step towards policy reform. The Public Prosecutor opens subsidiary offices in the neighbourhood and appoints an account manager who takes up the local problems.

c) *Quality of living*

In the 1970s and 1980s, the Netherlands invested much in town renewal, the emphasis being on the technical rehabilitation of as many dwellings as possible. Physical rehabilitation sometimes was not enough: the living environment, unemployment and lack of safety had to be taken in hand as well. The Ministry of Housing, Physical Planning and the Environment suggested a conversion in the policy of national housing ('from building to living'). That line has been continued in the GSB. More than that, the present policy aims at putting an end to the physical segregation of those who have and those who lack chances in life, a segregation reinforced in part by the 'old-style' town renewal policy, which focused mainly on the needs of the socially weak who, unlike the more affluent citizens, were unable to move to the suburbs. The new strategy is to build houses for the affluent in problem areas, for rent or owner-occupation, and to reserve parts of the new 'better' VINEX-building locations for low-rent houses. The aim is to restore balance to the demographic structure and the quality of the housing stock. To enhance the quality of living in the backward neighbourhoods, comprehensive neighbourhood management programmes are being drawn up, intended to improve the direct living environment, the social parti-cipation of citizens, public safety and the ratio between population groups.

Under the heading of care, even the most vulnerable groups in the urban society are given a place in the GSB. The towns want to improve care for the homeless, the drug addicts, the hopelessly indebted and the mentally unstable.

Finally: Future Investment

ICES[10]-funds are the returns on natural gas, which will be partly used to restore the government investments, which have been trailing behind for some time, to a higher level. These investments concern the functions of working, living, communication, and greenery. The decisions on the volume and direction of the annual investments will be an element of the coalition agreement of the next government (which will take office in 1998). The allocation is a matter for the whole cabinet. The Ministry of Economic Affairs and the Treasury will serve as budget keepers of the Fund for Economic Structure, into which ICES-money will be paid. The present expectation is that up to 2010, 2–4 thousand million guilders will be invested. Another expectation is that notably large scale infrastructural projects will be co-financed from these ICES-resources (such as the cargo railway from the Rotterdam harbour to Germany, a high speed rail connection to Germany, the expansion of airport capacity, and the construction of Randstad Rail). These investments greatly affect the accessibility of those major cities that are profiting directly, such as Rotterdam and Amsterdam. To make them more accessible is a vital national policy objective. Better access to the economic centres can have a positive effect on such aspects as economic development, the environment, and mobility (rail instead of road and air transport). In June 1998, the ICES is expected to submit a proposal concerning the distribution.

Synthesis

Spatial Pattern and Urbanization Process

Owing to the uneven spatial distribution of population and activities, the western part of the Netherlands especially is very densely populated and urbanized. In the western part of the country, the four large urban regions (of Amsterdam, Rotterdam, The Hague and Utrecht) together with some towns of medium size, form a ring-shaped structure ('Randstad Holland') encircling a dominantly rural area ('Green Heartland'). Since the 1950s this structure has dominated physical planning. To concentrate as much as possible the growing need for space, and to keep the Green Heartland and other buffer zones as open as possible, are elements of traditional Dutch planning, with the spatial distribution of housing contingents as an important instrument. That policy has greatly influenced, and not always positively, the development of the large towns. For one thing, the suburbanization because of rising prosperity (in the 1970s) was inadvertently stimulated by the concentration of house building in some suburban municipality. That process was to the detriment of notably the three largest central cities (Amsterdam, Rotterdam, The Hague), which between 1965 and 1985 not only lost 23 per cent of their (collective) population, but also found themselves confronted with an increasingly lopsided demographic composition dominated by the less affluent and the deprived. Thanks to an intensive policy of town renewal (since the late 1970s) and a change in spatial policy in favour of building houses in or near the cities ('compact-city policy' pursued since the late 1980s), the development of the urban system is now reasonably stable. Since the middle of the 1980s there has even been some new growth (reurbanization) in Amsterdam (6 per cent between 1985 and 1995) and Rotterdam (4 per cent).

The Hague and Utrecht stayed more or less at par. At any rate, in no single town of some importance have there been signs of remarkable growth or decline in the past decade.

Administrative Framework

Until the 1980s, the central government exercised a growing and ever more emphatic influence on the policy of provinces and municipalities. That was especially manifest in the distribution of financial means, about nine-tenth of which derived from the state and which were, moreover, often earmarked for special targets. Since then, a strong decentralization of competencies has been carried through. The central government admittedly still hands out criteria and proposals, but leaves the implementation to the local authorities. The new approach has been attended by a reduction of the (co-)financing of housing, on the assumption that market parties would take over that task ('more market, less government'). Many specific payments have now been combined (by each separate ministry) into 'broad target payments', which gives municipalities more policy freedom. Early in 1997 the system of municipal financing was changed in favour of 'problem cities'. Nevertheless, the cities' own local revenues are still relatively poor at an average of 16 per cent.

Another characteristic of central policy until the end of the 1980s was that no distinction was made among municipalities: all were treated alike. Not until the late 1980s was that principle abandoned, albeit very cautiously, in the awareness that especially the state of affairs in the major cities called for a more tailored policy. In 1994, a deputy minister for the major cities (coming under the Ministry of the Interior) was appointed, whose task is to coordinate as much as possible the policies addressed at the major cities.

National Policies Directed to Cities

Perhaps the first metropolitan challenge which the national government accepted (although not explicitly with its eye on towns) was to undertake a massive town renewal. Considerable state resources were made available for that purpose; the objective was to complete the whole 'catch-up operation' by 2010. Initially, the policy was concerned only with improving the housing function for the financially weakest in the qualitatively lowest neighbourhoods. In time, that 'cement-and-stone' strategy has evolved into an integrated approach, taking account as well of the quality of living as of the preservation or restoration of economic functions. Efforts are now being made as well to bring about a more balanced demographic composition by merging the income classes. The implementation is in the hands of the local governments, which to that end enjoy a high degree of freedom.

The first explicit policy attention for the major cities dates from the end of the 1980s and was concerned with spatial policy. The economic crisis of the early 1980s gave rise to greater concern about the economic aspects of physical planning and the international competitive position of the major cities. At the same time the need to raise the quality of living in the towns was recognized. That insight resulted in a 'priority position' for 13 town regions ('urban nodes'), based on their economic potential. The Ministries of Transport, Public Works and Water Management and of Economic Affairs subscribed to that positioning. Investments aiming to improve the (international) accessibility of the four large town regions and of their public transport systems were given priority, because congestion was becoming a threat to the economic function and the quality of living. Another objective was to diminish car mobility with the help of spatial planning and mobility constraining measures. In regional economic policy, some attention was switched to stimulating the quality and availability of industrial estates at the urban nodes. To supplement the economically-oriented 'policy of urban renewal' in the early 1990s the policy of social renewal was introduced. That policy was also addressed, if not explicitly, to the major cities. Efforts were made to combat social arrears by a more integral multi-sectorial approach (effected again by combining several social grants into a broad target grant).

The recent new growth in some major cities is not all honey and roses: on the one hand international trends and other developments have strengthened the economic position of the urban regions, and the major cities are now considered by the national government to be the motors of the regional and national economies; on the other hand there is a growth of social discrepancies and typically metropolitan problems, which are not only considered socially unacceptable, but also seem to put the motor function in jeopardy. The new population growth in the central cities derives mostly from underprivileged groups. As a result, the social discrepancies within the central cities and between the central cities and their neighbouring areas, continue to widen. That situation has given rise to increasing care and attention on the part of the government for the position of the major cities, stimulated by repeated pleas from the governors of the four major cities. The authorities have more and more woken up to the fact that the major cities need a special approach.

1994: Major Cities Policy

Since 1994, the major cities have attained a priority position in the present government policy. Under the leadership of the prime minister and in cooperation with a large number of directly or indirectly involved departments, a policy explicitly addressing the large towns has been given shape: the Major Cities Policy ('GSB'). By 'major cities' were initially understood the 'major four', the cities which had hatched the idea and presented it to the new government coalition, but soon 15 other municipalities were added to the list and in 1997 another six, so that currently there are 25 participants. While spatial policy indicates the long term strategic development and the direction of state investments, the GSB focuses on an integral approach to metropolitan socioeconomic problems. An important motive underlying the GSB is the need to coordinate the old and new policies directed to towns. More explicitly than before, the 11 participating departments channel a portion of their subsidies, investments and/or policy measures towards the major cities. At the same time, the separate ministries have combined several of their financial flows into broad target payments, to enable local governments to deal with the problems integrally. Core themes of the GSB are employment and education, safety and quality of living. Its implementation rests on three pillars: integrality (desegregation on the state and municipal levels); partnership (among departments but also with local governors); and orientation to results (through monitoring). One of the most important elements is the creation of job opportunities in the public sector (mostly surveillance, management and day nurseries) for the long term unemployed. The integrated safety policy has an interesting structure. The first monitor results have inspired a cautious optimism about the new approach. The coordinating deputy minister believes that for the future development of the GSB, investment in the economic segment will be most needed.[11]

Notes

1 About two-fifths of the Dutch population lives in Randstad Holland. The population density amounts to some 1,000 persons per km^2.
2 For instance, the distance between the centres of the The Hague and Rotterdam regions is no more than about 25 km.
3 *Bestuur-op-Niveau-gebieden* (regions designated for administration at the proper level).
4 That reform has not yet been carried through, but the existing relevant legislation (Common Rule Act) offers the state sufficient possibilities of discussing the matter on the basis of urban regions.

5   At least 2,000 dwellings at expansion locations and 1,000 at inner-city locations.
6   Unlike improvement of existing, mostly social housing stock (= town renewal), by 'urban renewal' is mostly understood the addition of new elements, primarily aiming at urban economic growth, elements that help to provide the city with a renewed socioeconomic basis.
7   3,000 MECU for the 1994–96 period.
8   Eindhoven, Nijmegen, Arnhem, Hengelo, Enschede, Groningen, Bois-le-Duc, Almelo, Maastricht, Deventer, Leeuwarden, Tilburg, Breda, Zwolle and Helmond.
9   Existing national policy to create temporary employment for young people, thus enhancing their chances on the labour market.
10 ICES stands for Interdepartmental Committee for reinforced Economic Structure.
11 The authors gratefully acknowledge discussions with the following people:

> Dr E. Holstvoogd, Ministry of Social Affairs and Employment;
> Dr R. Hoogerboord, Ministry of the Interior;
> Dr M.A. de Jong, Ministry of Transport, Public Works and Water Management;
> Mr L.H. Kokhuis, Ministry of Housing, Physical Planning and the Environment;
> Dr A.T. Leeuwenstein, Ministry of the Interior;
> Dr J.P.J.P. Menger, Ministry of Housing, Physical Planning and the Environment;
> Dr H.J.Th. Nieuwenhuis, Ministry of Economic Affairs;
> Mr W.E.H. Sloots, Ministry of the Interior;
> Dr L. van Vliet, Ministry of the Interior;
> Dr K. Meersma, Ministry of the Interior.

References

Boer, M. de (1996), *Ter wille van stad en land*, Gemeente Rotterdam: Burgerzaallezing.
Deputy Minister of the Interior (1994), 'Brief van de staatssecretaris van Binnenlandse Zaken inzake het Grote Stedenbeleid', *Tweede Kamer*, vergaderjaar 1994–1995, 21 062, No. 28, 's Gravenhage: SDU.
INRO/TNO, VVK and RPD (1994), *De vitaliteit van het Nederlandse bedrijfsleven 1988–1993*.
Kolpron Consultants (1996), *Inventarisatie van VINEX-bouwlocaties*, Rotterdam.
Leij, G. bij de (1995), *Stadsvernieuwing en woningverbetering*, EIB.
Major Cities (1994), *Een deltaplan voor de grote steden, Memorandum aan de kabinetsformateur*.
Meer, J. van der (1989), *Wat beweegt de stad*, Rotterdam: Proefschrift EUR.
Ministry of Economic Affairs (1995), *Ruimte voor regio's. Het ruimtelijk-economisch beleid tot 2000*, 's Gravenhage: SDU.
Ministry of Housing, Physical Planning and the Environment (1988), *Vierde nota over de ruimtelijke ordening, Deel a: beleidsvoornemen*, 's Gravenhage: SDU.
Ministry of Housing, Physical Planning and the Environment (1989), *Nota Volkshuisvesting. Van bouwen naar wonen*, 's Gravenhage: SDU.
Ministry of Housing, Physical Planning and the Environment (1991), *Vierde nota over de ruimtelijke ordening, Extra, Deel 3: kabinetsstandpunt*, 's Gravenhage: SDU.
Ministry of Housing, Physical Planning and the Environment (1992), *Nota beleid voor*

stadsvernieuwing in de toekomst, 's Gravenhage: SDU.

Ministry of Housing, Physical Planning and the Environment (1993), *Vierde nota over de ruimtelijke ordening, Extra, Deel 4: Planologische Kern Beslissing Nationaal Ruimtelijk Beleid*, 's Gravenhage: SDU.

Ministry of Housing, Physical Planning and the Environment (1995), *Interim rapportage Grote Steden Problematiek*, 's Gravenhage: Physical Planning Agency.

Ministry of Housing, Physical Planning and the Environment (1996), *Voortgangsrapportage stedelijk knooppuntenbeleid*, 's Gravenhage: Physical Planning Agency.

Ministry of Housing, Physical Planning and the Environment (1997), *Herijking Belstato, Ministry of Housing*, 's Gravenhage: Physical Planning Agency.

Ministry of the Interior (1994), *Covenant Cabinet, Amsterdam, Den Haag, Rotterdam and Utrecht, 's Gravenhage*.

Ministry of the Interior (1995a), *Grote-stedenbeleid Kabinet – G15*, 's Gravenhage.

Ministry of the Interior (1995b), *Nota Veiligheidsbeleid 1995–1998*, 's Gravenhage.

Ministry of the Interior/Ministry of Finance (1995c), *Wetsvoorstellen Herziening Gemeentefonds*, 's Gravenhage: Haagse drukkerij/Lakerveld bv.

Ministry of Transport, Public Works and Water Management (1988), *Tweede Structuurschema Verkeer en Vervoer: deel a: beleidsvoornemen,*'s Gravenhage: SDU.

Ministry of Transport, Public Works and Water Management (1996), *Samenwerken aan Bereikbaarheid*, Koninklijke Drukkerij Broese & Peereboom.

Needham, B., Zwanikken, T., Mastop, J., Faludi, A. and Korthals Altes, W. (1994), *Evaluatie van het Vinex-verstedelijkingsbeleid*, Ministry of Housing, 's Gravenhage: Physical Planning and the Environment.

Sociaal Cultureel Planbureau (1993), *Evaluatie sociale vernieuwing: een tussenrapport*, Rijswijk.

Van Poelje Instituut (1996), *Naar een effectief grote stedenbeleid*, Faculteit Bestuurskunde Twente.

Vegt, C. van der and Manshanden, W.J.J. (1996), *Steden en stadsgewesten*, Den Haag: SDU.

Verwey, A.O., Goezinne, B. and Dijkstra, A. (1995), *Opmaat tot signalering: instrumentontwikkeling voor de monitor Grote-stedenbeleid*, Rotterdam: ISEO.

Werkgroep stadeconomie (1996), *Actieplan Economie en Werk Amsterdam, Den Haag, Rotterdam, Utrecht, '* s Gravenhage: Ministry of the Interior.

13 Portugal

NUNO PORTAS, ÁLVARO DOMINGUES
AND ALBERTO LAPLAINE GUIMARÃIS

Introduction

Portugal has been emphasizing a territorial structure characterized mainly by a notorious imbalance, through a fast urban growth concentrated along a narrow seaboard strip and the diversified forms of urban concentration, in particular the scattered urban development of the northern half of that strip, and further still by the fragility in the system of mid-sized townships which have persisted in improving their urban quality within depressed regions and yet not reliable alternatives to the predominant trends.

On the other hand, within the last 20 years Portugal has developed well-dimensioned local institutions with political autonomy, but with a range of attributes and resources still insufficient vis-à-vis the necessary requirements for urban development policies. Whilst awaiting the inception of a future regional level, the central administration holds the majority of public resources – financial, legal and technical – albeit with a persistently layered character and imposing that rationale also to the actual application of the structural funds.

The overlapping of these situations has contributed to the delays experienced in the clarification and deployment of cohesive urban policies at the level of the national urban system and its role in the regional development policies.

This assessment is all the more important, when the rise of the new urban policy concept as a cornerstone of national and regional development highlights the importance of integrating clearly and durably the necessary sectoral programmes, whether governmental or local.

It is true that Portugal has neither developed a culture of entente and implementation of inter-institutional programmes, nor has it done so in terms of partnerships or social contracts with the community. In addition, this culture does not allow for synergies to be developed or for isolated actions to be extended further. Earlier in the decade, instead of responding to the effects of urban problems, several cities started to focus on the problems themselves.

290

The local level – at present the city level, in the future the regional level – seems to be the most adequate for coordinating the different policies and programmes horizontally and in terms of time (i.e., definition of priorities).

Thus the local strategies began by being the basis for claims and negotiations with the national sectoral administrations. In the future they should become more than just that: city contracts, resulting from those negotiations and common multi-institutional contracts of a broad spectrum based upon objectives as consensual as possible.

National Spatial Development Pattern

Introduction

Portugal is the least urbanized of the member countries of the EU according to current statistics. The estimated weight of the population resident in the metropolitan areas and in localities with more than 2,000 inhabitants is approximately 50–55 per cent. Meanwhile, 23 per cent of the population resides in parts of the country where urban centres barely exceed 2,000 inhabitants. Notwithstanding this low weight, this is above all because of the strong urbanization processes in the past 15–20 years.[1]

There are major asymmetries in the pattern of the population and urbanization process. This situation is above all due to the following factors:

- continued weight of agricultural employment, which today still accounts for about 10 per cent of the working population;
- a process of emigration and rural exodus which have above all contributed to urbanization processes in the destination countries;
- the specific nature of the diffuse rural industrialization process which contributed to the urbanization and industrialization process 'between cities', above all in the northwest of the country;
- the late development of the tertiary sector;
- 74 per cent of the resident population, the two metropolitan areas (MAs) of Lisbon and Oporto (LMA and OMA) and the essential part of economic activity are to be found in the coastal strip to the north of Setubal. The population is dense (exceeding 200 inhabitants per km^2 in most of the municipalities in the northern coastal strip and in the LMA), and the diffuse urbanization and industrialization processes have increased, particularly in the northern coast area. The only two cities which have more than

100,000 inhabitants not included in the metropolitan areas are also located in this area,(Coimbra and Braga: a third, Setubal, is part of the LMA, and a fourth, Funchal, on the Atlantic island of Madeira);

- in the interior of the country, where the demographic density of municipalities is almost always less than 50 inhabitants per km^2, the urban system is very rarified and the urban agglomerations are small (Evora and Viseu are the largest cities, with about 40,000–45,000 inhabitants each);
- this asymmetry is combined with serious functional imbalances. The MAs concentrate more than 39 per cent of the population resident in the country; about 67 per cent of the urban population; 52 per cent of all employment, and levels of employment in the service sector in excess of 62 per cent, particularly in the FIRE services (about 74 per cent). The two MAs generate more than half of the total GAV (46 per cent of all industrial GAV).

This concentration of resources within the MAs coincides with a concentration of problems, above all in peripheral municipalities: lack of infrastructures, lack of urban quality, uncontrolled and illegal urban development, inherited lack of facilities and the problems associated with social exclusion.

The urban hierarchy suffers from serious discontinuities, above all at the level of the fragility of the systems of medium-sized cities. After the three cities with 100,000 inhabitants, the following level involves population levels of from 40,000–50,000, which accounts for 13 cities; almost all of the remaining urban agglomerations have less than 23,000 inhabitants (see Map 13.1 and the relevant tables).

Essentially, the following tendencies can be identified:

1   A strong polarization, namely in the two metropolitan areas, although with very different results and models, i.e., the lack of high level decision services in the case of Oporto. This polarization is evident in terms of demography, but much more so in terms of employment, investment, gross production value, added value, qualified employment, advanced service functions and infrastructures, concentration of elites and power, etc.

The models of the two metropolises are very different: the LMA corresponds more to the idea of agglomeration normally associated with metropolises, with a strongly tertiarized central nucleus; the OMA was established artificially in a more extensive regional area distinguished by diffuse urbanization and industrialization and where the urban condition is manifested in various manners, from recognizedly urban conglomerations

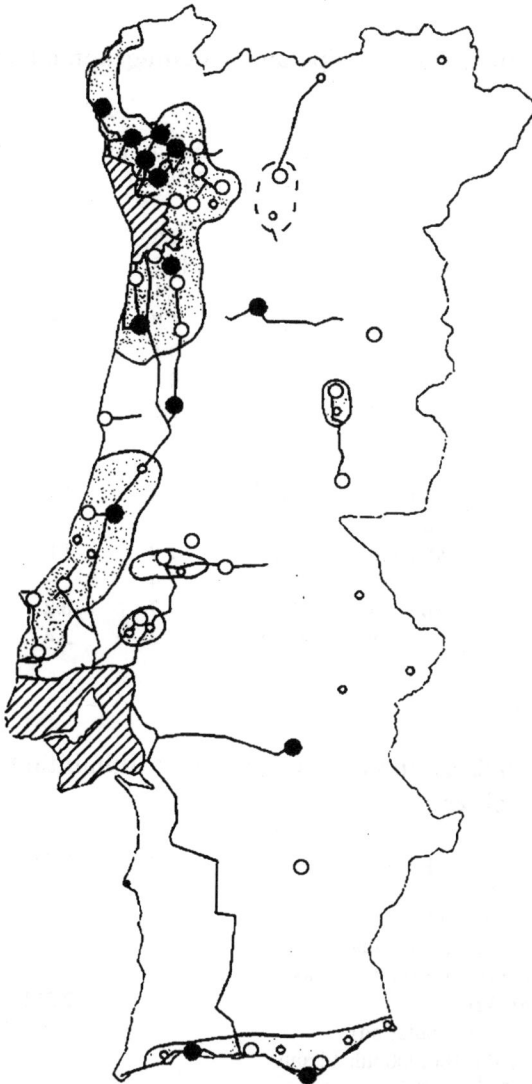

source: "Estudo de Avaliação dos Programas Regionais em Portugal", doc. int., Geoideia, 1993

Metropolitan Areas

High Density Urban Areas

Economic and Demographically Depressed Areas

—— > 5.000 Vehicles (average annual daily traffic)

Urban Centers

● > 40.000 inhabitants

○ 21.000 - 40.000

o 10.000 - 21.000

• Sines port

Map 13.1 The urban and regional archipelago

Table 13.1   The 'regional/urban archipelago' – demographic trends, 1981, 1991

	Population 1991	National mainland %	Demog. evolution 1981/91, %		
			Effective	Natural	Migratory
Lisbon Metropolitan Area	**2,551,750**	**27.2**	**2.0**	**3.2**	**-1.8**
Lisbon	659,649	7.0	-18.35	-2.5	-15.4
Other LMA municipalities	1,892,101	20.2	11	5.9	5
North Atlantic region	**3,000,604**	**32.0**	**5.8**	**7.5**	**-1.8**
Oporto Metropolitan Area	1,152,596	12.3	3.1	4.5	5.9
Oporto	297,506	3.2	-9.1	2.5	-10.1
Other OMA municipalities	855,090	9.1	9.5	7.3	2.2
Other North Atlantic regional municipalities	1,832,589	19.6	6.6	8.6	-2
West Littoral region	**410,417**	**4.4**	**4.3**	**3.4**	**1.0**
Littoral Algarve region	**324,518**	**3.5**	**6.9**	**0.8**	**6.1**
Small islands (municipalities)	**994,323**	**10.6**	**-1.9**	**1.8**	**-3.7**
Small islands (cities)	597,385	6.4	2.4	–	–
Depressed areas	**2,169,206**	**23.1**	**-7.7**	**-0.2**	**-7.6**
Total national mainland	**9,371,448**	**100.0**	**0.3**	**3.4**	**-3.1**

Source: GEOIDEIA, 1993.

Table 13.2   The 'regional/urban archipelago': MAs' inhabitants and number of cities

North Atlantic region (total pop.)	**3,000,604**
Oporto Metropolitan Area	1,152,596
No. urban centres 41,000–100,000 inhabitants	8
No. urban centres 21,000–40,000 inhabitants	9
No urban centres 10,000–20,000 inhabitants	1
Lisbon Metropolitan Area	**2,551,750**
West Littoral region (total population)	410,417
No. urban centres 41,000–100,000 inhabitants	1
No. urban centres 21,000–40,000 inhabitants	4
No urban centres 10,000–20,000 inhabitants	3
Littoral Algarve (total population)	**324,518**
No. urban centres 41,000–100,000 inhabitants	2
No. urban centres 21,000–40,000 inhabitants	2
No urban centres 10,000–20,000 inhabitants	4
Depressed areas (total population)	**3,494,576**
No. urban centres 41,000–100,000 inhabitants	3
No. urban centres 21,000–40,000 inhabitants	9
No urban centres 10,000–20,000 inhabitants	10

Source: GEOIDEIA, 1993.

to small urban groupings and strongly urbanized axes which coexist without discontinuity, in a nebulous urban-industrial mix which characterized the whole conurbation's reaching a population level near that of the LMA.

2 Coastal development, particularly between Setubal and Viana do Castelo, which includes the two MAs and, also on the southern coast of the country, the Algarve.

   As can be seen from Map 13.1 and the relevant tables, this coastal development process has given rise to urbanization standards and subsystems that are very different in terms of extent, functional cohesion urban density and demographic concentration. Taken as a whole, the Atlantic Strip has about 85 per cent of the country's urban population, some of the dominant characteristics of which are as follows:

- the development of diffuse urbanization patterns, fed by diffuse industrialization outside urban conglomerations. The result of this is that the relative weight, in demographic terms, of the cities, in terms of the surrounding areas, is reduced;
- a lack of structure in the urban system which results in: excessive demographic and above all functional bi-polarization in the two metropolitan conglomerations, and an unresolved tension between the logics of hierarchical relations which intersect with as yet unstabilized logics of functional specialization and complementarity. In the case of strongly urbanized and industrialized regions, the density and proximity of urban agglomerations has been developing towards the consolidation of urban subsystems and city axes, with a cohesive functional complementary and specialization logic of which it is now proposed that a new intervention policy should take advantage;
- the proliferation of small cities and the relative absence of medium-size agglomerations. Braga, with about 100,000 inhabitants, in the diffuse northwest conurbation, and Coimbra, which is located in a relatively empty regional area, are the only two exceptions;
- the split in the two metropolitan agglomerations, between the functional infrastructure and demographic size. Despite the stabilization of the population in the two MAs, there are strong internal reorganization processes (peripheral demographic growth) which are not accompanied by the development of infrastructures and the provision of facilities.

3   An increasing tenuousness and great fragility of the urban system in the declining regions (experiencing demographic decline) i.e., all the Alentejo and the central and northern interior of the country. All this area has been marked by processes of demographic decline and ageing and by a serious economic crisis, although this has been accompanied by the recentring of the functional role of some cities, e.g., Viseu and Evora. The following can be indicated as weaknesses of the urban system in these declining areas:

- an urban economic base that is excessively dependent on public investment, state payments (retirement and other pensions), or remittances by emigrants. As a result, the functional strengthening and the attractiveness of these cities has shown that this has not been accompanied by private investment (except in the building sector) which threatens the sustainability of the urban development process;
- the 'separation' of the cities from the surrounding regions as a result of the economic crisis in the latter and the external influences which feed the development of urban centres;
- in many cases, inadequate access and geographical isolation;
- most cities combine reduced demographic and economic size with great institutional fragility and lack of resources (in quality and quantity). The exceptions, Evora or Viseu, are the result of increased competitive advantages caused by: specific capital agglomerations (heritage, tourist attractions, the existence of higher education institutions, etc.), favourable logistic position in terms of strategic communication arteries or cross frontier relations.

The 'Archipelago-country': Territorial Dynamics and Urbanization Pattern

In a recent study (GEOIDEA, 1993), we can see a more accurate account of the situation described in the first section (see Map 13.1 and Tables 13.1–13.3). The authors use the metaphor of the 'Archipelago-country' to emphasize the effects of territorial fragmentation in continental Portugal: metropolitan areas; large 'islands', where the territory is characterized by diffuse urbanization and industrialization, and small 'islands', the small and medium-sized cities located in 'submerged' territories, i.e., where there are circumstances of considerable depopulation and urban, economic and institutional decline.

Table 13.3 Small and medium cities ('small islands' in depressed areas) scores

Cities ('islands')	Population 1991	1981/91, %	Equipment* 1990
Coimbra	102,499	1.4	10.39
Evora	45,817	10.8	4.07
Viseu	44,947	3.0	3.49
Santarém/Cartaxo	44,800	1.9	3.26
T. Novas/Entroncamento	42,815	7.3	1.94
Covilhã/Fundão	42,587	-6.3	2.64
Fig. Foz	37,207	15.3	1.53
Vila Real	28,633	3.0	2.59
Castelo Branco	27,279	12.3	2,73
Tomar	23,931	-4.3	1.35
Abrantes	23,607	-7.6	1.07
Beja	23.391	-4.1	2.28
Guarda	21,236	4.6	2.39
Chaves	19,768	-4.1	1.52
Lamego	18,925	-11.2	1.10
Bragança	18,047	12.6	2.43
Portalegre	17,979	-4.6	2.36
Elvas	13,917	2.3	0.83

* Relative scores in accordance with the attributed importance to the public social and administrative equipment.

Source: GEOIDEIA, 1993.

Tendencies:
- the demographic stabilization of the MAs (3.1 per cent OMA and 1.3 per cent LMA, 1981–91: national average, 0.3 per cent); peri-urban and suburban growth; decline of central nuclei; increased rate of vehicle ownership; spatial dilation of mobility; new central areas (shopping centres; tertiary strengthening of new and old centres); reduced average family size; increased consumption of residential space per capita; second homes;
- growth and the increased polarizing influence of some medium-sized urban centres. In the interior region, by 'suction' from the surrounding rural areas and as a result of increasing public facilities and services. On the coast by

'condensation' of the population or by the coalescence of nearby urban centres, thus tending to form small conurbations;
- growth of diffuse forms of urbanization, namely on the industrialized Atlantic coast: (NUTS Cávado, Ave, Entre Douro e Vouga, Pinhal Litoral, Algarve);
- extensive urban growth, that does not accord with the stabilization or low rate of population growth.

The Metropolitan Areas of Lisbon and Oporto – National Framework and Recent Evolution (see Tables 13.4–13.6)

With about 2.5 million inhabitants and 27.3 per cent of the national resident population in 1991, the LMA is the largest urban agglomeration in the country. There has been major population growth, particularly in the '60s and '70s. During the '80s, the demographic dynamics of the LMA stabilized (about two per cent (1981/91), to a national average of about 0.3 per cent). Nevertheless, the population of Lisbon has declined during the current decade (the city lost almost 150,000 inhabitants, with the relative weight of the LMA changing from 32.3 per cent in 1981 to 25.9 per cent in 1991). Centrifugal demographic tendencies within LMA gave rise to population variation levels, which in seven peripheral municipalities are between 15 and 30 per cent (1981/91).

The demographic stabilization of the LMA nevertheless coincides with the increasing intensity of urban land use (the variation of the number of dwellings between 1981 and 1991 was 22.5 per cent and in respect of buildings was 20.1 per cent), and with the over-enlargement of the land area encompassed by the urbanization process.

This internal reorganization of the LMA is combined with social dualization and segregation. This situation has led families in the middle income groups to leave the capital city. Those who remain are the better off section of the population which stimulates the supply of luxury housing; the poorer strata of the population (precarious accommodation and public housing); and an undifferentiated sector that pays old rents.

In the case of the OMA, the situation is considerably different. Despite the decline in population also experienced in Oporto (-9 per cent, as against -18.4 per cent in Lisbon), the existence of a rapidly growing urban crown is not so clear. The territorial model of the OMA is more or less one of demographic concentration in a regional conurbation marked by the increasing density and diffusion of its population. In the case of the OMA, the fragility of the rail and road public transport networks and systems and the absence of

Table 13.4 Lisbon and Oporto MAs' employment: national mainland share; Lisbon and Oporto cities' share (%) of LMA and OMA respectively); employment sectoral distribution (% of total MAs' employment) (1990)

Main economic sectors	% national, by sector		% Lisbon in the LMA	% Oporto in the OMA	% sector /total emp.	
	LMA	OMA			LMA	OMA
Manufacturing	21.8	19.2	27.8	21.9	29.6	48.6
Construction; public works	30.6	17.0	47.0	35.0	8.0	8.3
Total manuf. and const.					**37.6**	**56.9**
Commercial services; hotels	43.8	18.6	60.0	61.5	27.2	21.6
Transports; communications	50.0	16.4	81.1	68.7	10.6	6.5
Finance, ins., real estate; prod. serv.	56.2	17.6	84.8	82.9	10.7	6.3
Personnel and public services	50.7	16.8	65.3	64.1	11.7	7.3
Total services					**60.2**	**41.7**
Total employment	**33.3**	**17.8**	54.6	41.7	706,305	377,395
Population	**27.3**	**12.3**	25.9	25.8		

Source: Ministry of Employment, 1990; INE, 1991.

Table 13.5 Employment national mainland share (%) evolution in the LMA, OMA and Littoral North region (1983–90)

	Manufacturing			Commercial services; hotels; restaurants			Finance, insurance, real estate; producer services		
	1983	1987	1990	1983	1987	1990	1983	1987	1990
Lisbon metropolitan area	28.1	23.2	20.6	47.5	45.3	43.6	60.6	55.7	56.7
North Atlantic Oporto metropolitan area	20.0	19.3	19.1	19.3	18.8	18.0	17.2	19.9	17.6

Source: Ministry of Employment.

Table 13.6 Research and development and human resources expenses – national share (%), 1986 NUT II

	R&D investments		Human resources*	
	North region	Lisboa region	North region	Lisboa region
Universities	25.2	43.7	27.9	45.3
Public laboratories	3.4	89.4	3.5	87.2
Non-profit private institutions	20.4	76.2	21.6	75.1
Private firms	27.3	55.8	31.9	55.3
Total	17.5	65.8	18.4	65.6
Absolute values (1,000 Esc.)	3,473.6	13,054.0	1,938.7	6,928.5

*   Full time equivalence

Source: SEFOR/JNICT, Nov. 1988.

inter-modal solutions is a good indicator of this deficit in territorial cohesion at the metropolitan level. Demographic change during the '80s resulted in increases of from between 5–15 per cent both in the local municipalities that comprise the OMA, and in the conurbation, between Braga and Aveiro, of which the OMA is a central part (see Map 13.1).

Although the same characteristics are to be found here as those which influence the production, acquisition and rental of housing on a national level, the dualization processes in the NW and the OMA are more compensated by the significant role played by housing cooperatives and by the construction of residences by owner-occupiers in a territory that is still marked by fragmented land ownership and by links with small scale agriculture.

The urban fabric around the city of Oporto is therefore characterized by its fragmentary character – a result of the 'spontaneous' and diffuse growth model – which does not impede the as yet incipient growth of suburban centres.

The tendency towards the functional bi-polarization of the two MAs will undoubtedly be increased, particularly as a result of the effects of the different trends of concentration of top level decision services in the two principal metropolises and their increased internationalization capacity (see relevant tables). This bi-polarization is, nevertheless, quite uneven and biased towards the LMA, above all given the indicators regarding the agglomeration of advanced services, particularly those of businesses, spending on research and development, the concentration of foreign investment or cultural and leisure infrastructures.

There persists, however ,a clear infrastructure deficit and lack of attendance to and coordination of the public transport systems in both MAs. The implementation of investment in this type of road, track and structuring systems, will determine a very active territorial reorganization process, not only at the level of the redefinition of the geometry and content of the centres, but also at the level of the many more peripheral areas, particularly those affected by the opening up of new urbanization fronts as a result of the development of new transport axes.

The economic position The recent transformation of the economic base of the two MAs has been marked, above all, by processes involving the development of the tertiary sector and the internationalization and reorganization of the industrial base. These processes have had, nevertheless, a very uneven effect on the two metropolises which, after all, were previously very different (see relevant tables).

The LMA went through a period of serious crisis and instability that marked the '70s and the first half of the '80s. The industrial aspect of the crisis affected basic sectors of the industrial ring around the capital, particularly those sectors dominated by large companies in the ship building, steel production and basic chemical industries.

More recently, and despite the loss of employment in manufacturing industry, the tendency is towards a productive restructuring involving modernization, which is reflected in productivity gains, increased qualified employment and the emergence of new structuring and pull sectors, as in the case of the automobile 'filière'. Admittance to the EEC, the major injection of community funds (Setubal OID), the implementation of programmes to provide incentives to productive potential (PEDIP in particular), the acceleration of privatizations and the reorganization of major economic groups, the progressive liberalization of the financial system and the increased penetration of foreign capital triggered by the perspective of the Open Market in 1993, are factors that explain these processes. In the meantime, the strong macrocephalic tendency, which has always affected the country, became resurgent in the context of the EU and of the greater openness to the overall process of the internationalization of the economy.

The territorial effect of this type of tension induced increased growth of the tertiary sector and the redefinition of the central areas of Lisbon, and a major movement of manufacturing out of the city. In the light of the investment made or still envisaged in access, it is to be hoped that the model of territorial cohesion, which is still far from being stable, will become clarified. In this connection, the role of foreign capital in industry has been important (e.g., the case of large projects such as FORD/VW), and above all in the real estate, financial, hotel and restaurant and business services sectors.

In these and other sectors of the tertiary sector – e.g., the case of the major impact of shopping centres and their attraction effect – unpredictability, the size of the investments, or the new ways associated with them, introduce too much uncertainty, a factor which is incompatible with conventional forms of urban management planning. In order to respond to these impacts, demand-oriented 'negotiated planning' will have to attract and manage opportunities, coordinate public and private financial resources in order to promote the improvement of the urban space and counter the negative impact of these major interventions.

In the case of the OMA, the position was and remains completely different. The diffuse model of industrialization by which it is characterized is overwhelmingly comprised of small and medium-sized family businesses in traditional sectors (textiles, clothing and footwear above all) which are geared to the export trade, and proved to be much more flexible when faced with the industrial crisis in the '70s and the beginning of the '80s. Accordingly, none of the traumas that affected the LMA were experienced. The other side of the coin of this extensive industrial growth with full employment is also well known: industry in the north, based as it is on the low cost and the 'docility' of its labour force, and in sectors in which external competitiveness was based on a very devalued escudo, postponed investment in technological intensification (almost completely imported) and chose industry with low added value and an intensive work force specialized in medium and low quality final consumption goods. At the same time, northern economic groups with an industrial base emerged and grew during the turbulent period during which the nationalizations and subsequent privatizations occurred.

The position of the OMA also differs from that of the LMA with regard to the so-called tertiarization process. The OMA, and above all its central nucleus, are currently engaged in a tardy tertiarization process which is doubly limited; first by over-polarization of the public administration sector in the capital, and secondly, by the nature of the northern productive fabric which is particularly lacking in service intensive industries that are able to dynamize, diversify and improve the quality of the establishment in the OMA of a supply of services more congruent with the economic weight of the industrialized northwest. The high-level decision services deficit therefore inhibits a greater centripetal effect in the OMA which is rather negative, if the extent of its economic potential is considered. Despite its increasing commercial and logistic services and business-oriented hotels and restaurants, the OMA is increasingly restricted to being a regional metropolis. The recent cycle of public investment in access broke a long period of spontaneous and diffuse urban growth (since the first half of the '60s), which meant that the old image of 'Oporto and environs' moved rapidly towards greater territorial cohesion. The affirmation and strengthening of the new centres, fed by the expansion of services (here more dependent on private than public capital, and more on regional than on foreign capital), is the clearest evidence of the break with the traditional model. There are currently positive expectations with regard to the OMA's internationalization capacity. This metropolitan nucleus continues to be the international relations platform of a regional productive structure which is very export-oriented. This is especially visible in its importance in terms of transport and international trade (as can be seen from the dynamism or significance of international transport infrastructures and services, fairs and exhibitions and the development of business hotels). Another prospect is greater cohesion along the axis that links it to Galicia. The great unknown lies in the current uncertainty regarding the modernization of the manufacturing base. This has not, as a whole, shown great signs of diversification, although there are some nuclei of excellence (e.g., the recent SIEMENS project) in sectors such as electronics and automation, the automobile *filiére* industry and moulds. However, important projects such as the Science and Technology Park are experiencing considerable start-up problems; the financial sector has abandoned Oporto for Lisbon; and advanced services continue to show signs of fragility.

Administrative and Financial Framework

The Structure of Administrative Powers and Responsibilities

Portugal is currently a country with only two levels of government – central and local – although an intermediate regional level, which has been proposed in the constitution since 1976, is currently being discussed. Special mention is made of the two Atlantic archipelagos of the Azores and Madeira, which are autonomous regions. The main difference between the two autonomous regions and the (future) administrative regions lies fundamentally in the level of autonomy of the former in terms of legislative power. The powers and responsibilities of the administrative regions will certainly not be so wide, depending on the degree of decentralization of ministry departments. The indications are that they will be responsible for the elaboration of regional plans and the important task of 'horizontal' coordination development between the decentralized government departments and the local authorities' projects.

Despite its centralist tradition, reinforced by almost half a century of authoritarian regime (1926–74), the country has, since the 19th century, had a fairly balanced municipal structure of about 305 municipalities for a population of about 10 million and a continental area of less than 100,000 km². Despite their reasonable size, Portuguese municipalities have fewer powers than other EU member countries; fewer financial resources of their or supplied by the state (less than ten per cent of the state budget); less decision-making autonomy, namely in the area of urban planning, where most statutory documents require government ratification or approval before they are effective.

Only exceptionally or in a subsidiary manner are areas such as education, health, social work, security, housing and transport municipal obligations. The same is also true of activity to promote culture and tourism. Local authorities have almost no powers or responsibilities in the areas of the economy and employment.

The territorial planning system has, since the last decade, been divided between the local authorities (physical local plans) and the central state (regional physical plans and special plans), with frequent overlaps and impositions by the latter over the former. Only recently have more programmatic or strategic documents become more widespread (the physical plans are basically land use zoning regulations) which may give investors greater security and which above all seek to encourage synergies between the various administrations and private entities, if any.

The recent use of these negotiated and programme-oriented methods, and the search for greater flexibility in the regulatory function of jointly agreed plans, are the result of the need for better justifications in applications for structural funds and for similar national funds.

The coincidence of these challenges with the growing importance of measures to safeguard the environment and heritage (sustainable development) has been an obstacle to the acceptance of increased flexibility in order to take advantage of unexpected opportunities and a more frequent use of partnerships. The growth of local movements and pressure groups (environmental and heritage defence), and the recurrent suspicion that public/private contracting could favour private interests also contributed to this and made it difficult to make the necessary compromises.

Finally, regulation by plan was introduced in Portugal much later than in the rest of the EU and was not accompanied by operational urban planning measures which would enable the local authorities to intervene more effectively in the land market to assure the provision of infrastructures, in the implementation of large scale urban development operations with a mix of activities and types of promoters, which are necessary to reconstitute or link the most critical areas of major agglomerations. Projects such as EXPO 98 and Alto do Lumiar in Lisbon, or the Western Zone of Oporto, and the South Matosinhos project, which is still at the preliminary stage, have compelled new legislation or exceptional forms of management because of the lack of a generally applicable system, and are almost always constructed on publicly owned land. Indeed, the lack of publicly owned land is a critical factor affecting the viability of public housing programmes, urban regeneration or the relocation of factory units. Recourse to compulsory purchase is well known to be prohibitively expensive for local authorities and the creation of partnerships or mixed urban development companies has, as yet, not be permitted by legislation.

The Powers and Responsibilities of the Metropolitan Authorities

The two large agglomerations polarized by the cities of Lisbon and Oporto are naturally the object of government attention, not only because of their political weight but because they are also the areas with the greatest competitive potential and at the same time of greatest conflict.

The MAs' special associations of local authorities, were only created in 1991. They have an executive committee comprising the mayors and an assembly indirectly elected by the local authorities within the metropolitan area. These have not, however, been given their own resources or technical staff and have no exclusive responsibilities or powers other than the coordination of municipal investment plans and projects and the relation thereof with state investment. Accordingly, these institutions have so far been unable to play a relevant role in the definition of metropolitan strategies and even less in their implementation.

The government or autonomous state authorities continue to have the dominant responsibility and powers for the elements that structure the territory, such as road, rail and port networks or even sewage and waste disposal. One of the few exceptions is the recently formed Oporto Subway Company which is controlled by the OMA, although it is financed by central government.

Accordingly, the results reflect the two processes which continue to be used, which are either an aggregate of municipal programmes (with those local authorities with greater financial or technical capacity and/or political weight having the advantage), or, they are the result of impositions by the departments or sectoral companies of the central state, which also have little inter-coordination.

One of the few examples of cooperation between local authorities has been in connection with the selection and prioritization of the projects to be proposed for financing by the Community Support Framework or by programmes promoted by the Commission.

There are examples of major dualization between central local authorities (Lisbon and Oporto) and the surrounding territory. This dualization is the result of the obvious differences in relation to the capitation of resources (local rates, central government subventions and EU funds) and is reflected in the lack of infrastructures, the peripheral nature and degradation of environmental systems. As we shall see later, there are variations in the capitation of municipal income which can be as much as 100 per cent between Lisbon and Oporto and some densely urbanized peripheral local authorities, not to mention the distortions that are caused by central government investment in sectoral projects with a significant urban impact, whether in terms of quantity or quality (e.g., the considerable investment being made in Oporto University affects the whole of the city centre; the same is also true of EXPO 98 in Lisbon).

To summarize, therefore, the major urban changes have been the result of sectoral investments made by central government (the attraction of which is one of the most visible tasks of local government representatives), or private investment, as can be seen from 'National Policy Responses to Urban Issues, Challenges and Development', q.v.

Both the LMA and the OMA have sought to obtain studies of business and competitiveness tendencies, of access or the improvement of environmental systems (more in the OMA than in the LMA). These studies have not been consequential in terms of the elaboration of strategies for the agglomeration that involve institutions, private companies and civil society.

Metropolitan policies, such as access to housing, the environment and first rate facilities, appear to have greater priority with the current government, just as the policy for medium-sized cities was launched earlier. However, the appropriate institutional forms and sufficient financial resources for such aims have yet to be found.

The MEPAT is the ministry most directly involved in urban policy, above all at the level of investment in infrastructures, transport and housing, even though there are still coordination difficulties between its various departments on the ground. This coordination should be extended to other ministries with an involvement in urban matters, such as the Ministry of the Environment, Culture and the Economy. The Ministry of Social Solidarity and Employment have also intensified their programmes to fight poverty and social exclusion. It is to be hoped that urban rehabilitation policies and the rehousing of pockets of insecure housing will be better coordinated.

The urban coordination of sectoral policies in strategic areas to promote sustainability and competitiveness – i.e., to consolidate and upgrade the 'city-innovative environment', and modernization of the productive fabric, science and technology, employment and vocational training, tourism and external promotion – is still incipient or almost completely lacking.

This underlies the implicit nature of urban policy even though, as we have stated, some steps are being taken to define an explicit policy, more coordinated at the various levels of the state.

Urban Income Sources – Degree of Independence of Local Authorities

The data available from the urban policy finance structure, is limited to the

Table 13.7 Municipal receipts structure: Lisbon and Oporto metropolitan areas, 1994

Municipal receipts	Total national		LMA, 1994			OMA, 1994		
Current receipts	10^9 Escudos	%	10^9 Escudos	%	% National	10^9 Escudos	%	% National
Municipal taxes	326.23	40.9	97,55	60.5	41.3	33.08	54.0	14.0
Current transferences	123.09	21.3	18.08	11.2	14.7	8.02	13.1	6.5
Central administration	122.86	21.3	17.90	11.1	14.6	7.97	12.0	6.5
EU	0.23	0.0	0.16	0.1	69.7	0.04	0.1	19.2
Total	359.31	62.3	115.62	71.7	32.2	41.09	67.0	11.4
Capital receipts								
Municipal source	61.98	10.7	20.56	12.7	33.2	8.45	13.8	13.6
Current transferences	155.58	27.0	25.22	15.6	16.2	11.75	19.2	7.6
Central administration	106.44	18.5	18.20	11.3	17.1	8.13	13.3	7.6
EU	49.14	8.5	7.03	4.4	14.3	3.62	5.9	7.4
Total	217.57	37.7	45.78	28.4	21.0	20.20	33.0	9.3
Total receipts	576.88	100.0	161.40	100.0	28.0	61.29	100.0	10.6

Source: DGAA, *Direcção Geral da Administração Autárquica*, 1994.

Table 13.8 Municipal expenses structure: Lisbon and Oporto metropolitan areas, 1995

Current expenses (10^9 escudos)	AML, 1995	AMP, 1995	AML, %	AMP, %
Personnel	59,77	19,68	38.5	31.9
Durable goods	0.36	0.35	0.2	0.6
Nondurable goods	6.26	2.82	4.0	4.6
Services purchasing	21.39	8.48	13.8	13.8
Current transferences	11.06	4.94	7.1	8.0
Transf. to 'freguesias'	4.17	1.53	2.7	2.5
Others	6.89	3.41	4.4	5.5
Financial charges	3.61	1.16	2.3	1.9
Other current charges	2.17	0.69	1.4	1.1
Total current expenses	104.63	38.12	67.3	61.8
Capital expenses (10^9 escudos)				
Land acquisitions	1.74	1.71	1.1	2.8
Housing	14.14	5.04	9.1	8.2
Other buildings	8.19	4.70	5.3	7.6
Sport, edu., cult., rec., equip.	2.08	2.71	1.3	4.4
Other	5.95	1.83	3.8	3.0
Public words	21.12	9.78	13.6	15.9
Roads and streets	10.32	5.13	6.6	8.3
Sewage	2.27	0.24	1.5	0.4
Water	0.54	0.16	0.3	0.3
Rural roads	0.93	0.25	0.6	0.4
Waste disposal	0.84	0.03	0.5	0.0
Others	6.21	3.97	4.0	6.4
Transport materials	1.21	0.73	0.8	1.2
Machines and equipment	3.65	1.37	2.3	2.2
Others	0.74	0.20	0.5	0.3
Total capital expenses	50.79	23.53	32.7	38.2
Total	155.42	61.65	100.0	100.0

local authority budgets, central government and EU fund subventions, and can be identified according to whether they are current income (services) or 'capital' (investment).

The great significance of normal overheads as part of the total overheads, i.e., just over 50 per cent, is clear from the analysis of the relevant tables. It follows therefore that there is little investment capacity. An example of this is the way in which these receipts were distributed between the various areas of municipal investment, in the case of the LMA and OMA in 1995 (see Table 13.8).

The total municipal income is approximately 250 ECUs per inhabitant/ year. The LMA (18 local authorities with about 25 per cent of the national population) has 28 per cent of the income, and the OMA (nine local authorities and 12 per cent of the population) has 10.6 per cent of the income. This distribution does not appear to be very distorted, with the exception of the two major cities, Lisbon and Oporto, in which the capitation is twice that of the most populated peripheral local authorities.

Since local authorities do not have the same responsibilities as local authorities in other EU countries, i.e., for inter-municipal or regional infrastructures, public transport services, education, health (except at the most primary or local level), and new housing or housing rehabilitation programmes (to which they contribute only 50 per cent of the total investment), the urban investment and services which are the responsibility of central government should be added. Only thus is it possible to make a proper assessment of the geographical distribution of the resources that finance urban policy. No such analysis has been published and the elaboration thereof is clearly outside the scope of this report.

National Urban Issues and Challenges from the National Perspective

The main urban issues faced in Portugal today should be differentiated according to the types of cities and agglomerations identified in the first section of this paper.

It can be stated therefore that dualism does not appear to be declining in the two main agglomerations, the LMA and the OMA, despite the concentration of financial and human resources that has taken place in recent decades.

The lack of the development of a welfare state in Portugal during the period of postwar growth is a further explanation of the continued lack of facilities and infrastructures, above all in local authorities on the metropolitan periphery, which are more sensitive to intra-metropolitan access, sewage and waste disposal systems, educational, social welfare and health resources. Central government has recently concentrated national and community investment in order to correct this historic backwardness, since such investment is beyond the capacity of the local authorities, particularly those where there has been faster population growth.

The two major agglomerations these days exhibit a superimposition of paradigmatic situations in which there coexist: urban development, characteristic of underdevelopment; the stabilized administrative or bourgeois city; and, since European integration, the aspiration to high levels of economic competitiveness and cultural affirmation at an international level.

Poverty, social marginalization and unstable employment, aggravated by housing conditions; traffic congestion in road access to central areas; environmental deterioration particularly in derelict areas, aggravated by insufficient urban sewage and waste disposal systems; are problems and challenges the solution to which cannot be delayed and which mobilize substantial amounts of public sector investment, to the obvious detriment of the non-metropolitan urban network.

From a schematic point of view it can be stated that the two major agglomerations suffer from physical deficits the extent of which is a source of concern, while the smaller cities, which have relatively better environmental conditions and urban services, struggle to attract productive and cultural investment in order to retain the population and offer attractive conditions to youth and upper professional groups.

Medium-sized and small cities, and above all in those that are spontaneously organized into subsystems and regional axes, nevertheless have as yet to implement and invigorate policies based of networks of synergies and complementarities, in order to take advantage of the effects of agglomeration, polycentrism and inter-specialization of the overall system. In small cities in declining regions, the challenge goes beyond strictly urban policies. In such cases the city has to recover its role as the locomotive force in relation to rural regional areas which are subject to major changes: tourism could, for example, be one of the most promising opportunities.

For these middle-sized cities, national programmes to build inter- and intra-regional roads cannot be further delayed, although they conflict with the satisfaction of basic needs and the requirements of excellence in the metropolitan areas and particularly the LMA, because of the amount of capital required. The resolution of this conflict requires great selectivity in the interventions to be undertaken, in the context of a strategic vision which is able to reconcile the improvement of the advantages arising from the effects of agglomeration, internationalization and the externalities at play in large cities, with the consolidation and sustainability of the development of small cities.

National Policy Responses to Urban Issues, Challenges and Development

At the intra-urban level, the main policy instruments are the PMOTs (Municipal Physical Plans) As has already been mentioned, these are physical plans that regulate land use, based on land zoning but do not include policy priorities or the operational programmes envisaged. They are approved by the municipal councils and ratified by central government.

With the exception of the applications to national and community programmes already referred to, the urban policies of local authorities have centred on the completion of infrastructure networks, namely road and sewage and waste disposal systems, and the construction of facilities (sometimes by restoring old buildings) destined for cultural, sporting and leisure use and social and youth work. This type of investment is rendered possible by recourse to EU funds.

It should further be noted that there has been a proliferation of programmes to revitalize historic areas, which, in dozens of cases, have led to the creation of specialized technical services which conceive and support the various private and public initiatives demanded by this type of intervention.

At the inter-urban level (regional urban systems and subsystems), there is still a considerable lack of coordination of government policies The PROTS, regional physical plans, (introduced in 1988 and revised in 1990), are plans for which central government is responsible which have little impact on the definition of urban policy. The PROTS were meant to be a method of inter-sectoral coordination (prediction of infrastructures and public services) and also to reconcile and coordinate land use policies at the local authority level, but they are above all used to control land use from an environmental defence perspective.

So far as the regional urban framework and system is concerned, the investment made by the various ministries or departments has contributed to the creation of a hierarchy of urban centres, above all by way of decisions to site public facilities and services with regional impact and the programming of road investment.

Urban policy is a recent goal at the national level It is above all in the major planning options for 1996 and 1997 that a series of policy instruments that are more explicitly interlinked with what could be understood to be a national urban policy, started to be developed.

The formulation of this policy is far too polarized at two levels: the so-called 'medium-sized cities' and the Lisbon and Oporto metropolitan areas.

Medium-sized cities In June 1994, the MPAT created the PROSIURB programme with the explicit objective of developing urban centres which have a strategic role in the organization of the national territory (except for the Lisbon and Oporto MAs), by giving them facilities and infrastructures that support economic and social dynamics.

According to the law, the general objectives of PROSIURB are to:

* restructure and modernize the urban system, as part of a coordinated land use strategy;
* promote the economic revitalization of urban centres and promote the consolidation of the framework of strategic social and economic facilities;
* improve the effectiveness of measures on the organization of the territory and to promote cooperation between the various institutional levels in urban development actions;
* protect of urban heritage;
* support the integrated development of infrastructure facilities in, and the development of urban centres;
* increase coordination in frameworks of interrelations at the level of axes and neighbouring urban systems;
* promote collaboration and partnerships between different institutions and parties (public, private and associations); promote complementarities, coherence and synergies between measures in various ways.

PROSIURB has a very small budget and was conceived as a complementary financial programme (additional aid in the financing of large scale investments included in the Community Support Framework); functional and financial complementarity (support for measures that are not sufficiently catered for in the other programmes), and complementarity in the programming of measures (coordinated management of a group of structuring and multi-sectorial measures to be supported in each agglomeration).

Local authorities were required, as part of PROSIURB, to prepare strategic plans for each city or system of cities (a condition of candidacy under Sub-programme 1); a city office (a consultative body linked to the preparation, approval and monitoring of the plan); and a city contract (between MPAT departments, local authorities, institutions involved and other ministries that grant financial aid for the measures proposed in the strategic plan).

It was in this way that the philosophy of strategic urban planning began, after the experience of the local authorities in Lisbon and Evora (1990–93), encompassing the methodology of public-private negotiation, the explicit existence of a coherent urban policy and the definition of a strategy to direct urban policy in the medium and long terms well as collaboration within institutional frameworks and complementarity between systems and city axes that structure nearby regional areas.

It is still too early to evaluate the results of this policy. Strategic planning introduced serious cleavages in the organizational cultures of local authorities (for which there had been no preparation) and tried to establish urban policy objectives which are normally beyond the area of municipal action, above all those which involve a major non-material component: employment, economic attraction, cultural promotion, social promotion, etc.

It is proper also to state that the cities covered by PROSIURB started out from very different circumstances, both in terms of demographic size (most cities have fewer than 20,000 inhabitants; the two largest cities have approximately 100,000 inhabitants), location in relation to the main arteries and development areas, and the quantity, variety and quality of their resources and institutions.

The metropolitan areas There are some obstacles that still persist at the policy level for the metropolitan areas of Lisbon and Oporto, whose policy instruments are discussed hereinafter, which derive from two sources:

- the non-consolidation of the metropolitan councils as bodies which coordinate and establish a true metropolitan policy;
- the circumstance of strong dualization between the central local authorities of Lisbon and Oporto and the surrounding territory, which is distinguished by peripheralization, lack of infrastructures, chaotic town planning levels and a general lack of urban environment;
- the continued existence of a confused institutional architecture, with the uncoordinated measures of various institutions, offices and companies directly responsible to central government, with strategic powers and responsibilities in terms of urban policy: road and rail access, urban transport, port infrastructures, airports, housing, etc.

Since the middle/end of the '80s, the sectoral policies with greatest impact in the metropolitan areas have been in the areas of basic infrastructures, transport, housing and social policy. The investment in the construction of new arteries (internal and external ring roads, motorways and rail systems) is one of the most important portions of public investment and the most important in terms of the functional structuring of the metropolitan area.

In the area of the fight against social exclusion the following are worthy of note: the National Programme against Poverty, and the INTEGRAR Programme, and the implementation of the national minimum wage. In the area of housing PER, 1993, RECRIA, 1988, the production of controlled cost housing, and other specific programmes of the INH and the IGAPHE, in partnership with local authorities, are noteworthy. In other sectoral policies, (above all in the areas of sewage and waste disposal, the environment and natural resources, transport and communications infrastructures, cultural, leisure, sports, education, civil defence and housing), contract-programmes have been made between central government and local authorities.

The metropolitan areas have (like other cities) increased their diversity and functional quality, by increasing the extent of public facilities, by recourse to annual central government investment programmes, PIDDAC, and specific operational programmes co-financed or not with Community funds. The efforts in the area of culture (museums, cultural centres, libraries, etc.), in education (above all in higher education), health (new hospitals and the modernization of old ones), and sporting and leisure facilities are also important.

The following programmes, plans and projects within the ambit of urban renewal programmes are worthy of mention. In the LMA:

- the URBAN programme and the national urban rehabilitation programme, which aim to renew decayed areas from the physical, economic and social point of view, has enabled some localized intensive multisectoral interventions. The interventions in the LMA were in the municipalities of Lisbon (Casal Ventoso), Amadora, Oeiras and Loures;
- the policy which is being followed by the Lisbon City Council is to create specific institutions (of a technical nature, as in the case of the recuperation of historic areas; commissariats, as in the case of URBAN; municipal companies, such as that which operates car parks and on-street parking; or mixed companies, like AMBELIS which promotes the city's image and also runs special projects at the request of the city council, for example in Chelas);
- the EXPO 98 project (created in 1993, EXPO 98 is a company with

314 National Urban Policies in the European Union

exclusively public capital, subject to special legislation, to organize the International Lisbon Exhibition, including the environmental and property development aspects and infrastructures, in part oriented to the creation of a new urban centralities on the basis of new high standard facilities, required for the international exhibition). This project is a vast operation (more than 300 hectares) which, in addition to the EXPO, also involves a series of interventions in Lisbon's eastern zone. The area of the intervention is a shore of the Tagus estuary which is extremely degraded from both the environmental and functional point of view and is isolated in terms of access to the urban fabric. The EXPO 98 project also triggered a series of other investments with a strong structural impact which include the new bridge over the Tagus linked to national and metropolitan networks, an extension of the subway line, a new railway station on the Oporto line and the construction of a new centre for the treatment of urban waste for the northern local authorities of the LMA;

- in the municipalities on the periphery of the LMA there are important interventions in the areas of urban rehabilitation and housing; research and development and higher education (TAGUSPARQUE, Oeiras; Universidade Nova de Lisboa, Almada; Setubal Polytechnic, etc.); the improvement of historic areas (Sintra World Heritage); and access and transport systems (inner and outer ring roads, underground rail extensions). Almost all the investment involved in this type of project come from central government policies and resources and community aid.

In the OMA:

- the intervention plan in the historic area, coordinated by the Oporto City Council, is currently being implemented and has been enhanced by the recent classification of the city as part of World Heritage. The plan, the objective of which is to reinstate and revitalize the historic centre, places a considerable emphasis on public housing policy, the improvement of public spaces, the rehabilitation of architectural and urban heritage, and local revitalization. The action is managed by a Technical Commissariat and by a Foundation for the Development of the Historic Area of Oporto in order to take the best advantage of the national and community aid available in the social, employment, training and other areas;

- the metro project (managed by a company with mixed capital, part of which is municipal) is in the start up stage of its first phase (the link to two municipalities that adjoin Oporto) and is meant to be the fundamental element in the modernization and multimodal coordination of the metropolitan public transport system;

- the URBAN programme (Vale de Campanhã, Oporto; and S. Pedro da Cova, Gondomar) and the urban revitalization programme (Espinho and Vila do Conde), with the objectives already stated, are combined with other actions within the ambit of housing policy (INH and IGAPHE programmes which also involve participation by cooperatives and local authorities);

The URBAN programme in Vale de Campanhã is part of a programme to revitalize the Eastern Zone, according to a multisectoral intervention model, which aims to achieve environmental improvement and to attract the establishment of cultural and leisure facilities (Palácio do Freixo and the Leisure-Technology Park). This plan affects the most underprivileged areas of Oporto and aims to take logistic advantage of the new bridge across the Douro and the new access conditions;

- the following investments by central government merit special mention: the expansion of Oporto University, involving the development of new university complexes; the conclusion of the arterial road system; the modernization of the suburban rail service; the construction and extension of major health facilities; the Science and Technology Park project, in the Maia local government area; and two large museums (transport and contemporary art);

- developments worthy of mention in the peripheral local government areas, in addition to the cases already mentioned, are: the South Matosinhos plan, to reconvert the old fish-canning part of the city; the East Maia plan, to create new sports and leisure parks and an industrial zone next to the Science and Technology Park; the V8 plan, in Vila Nova de Gaia, a partnership with the private sector to create a new central artery; or the Vairão agricultural research and development and education complex in Vila do Conde.

In conclusion, it is necessary to state that urban policy at the metropolitan level has been characterized by a serious lack of coordination as a result of the lack of strategic planning, including the formulation of metropolitan policies and the coordination of sectorial actions undertaken by central government.

Whatever the identity of the institution responsible, interventions have helped to accentuate the dualism between municipal centres and the peripheral ring of urban development, where serious problems of lack of infrastructures, urban disorganization and poor environmental quality persist. This polarization is accentuated by the financial and organizational weakness of most peripheral local authorities, which not only have a reduced investment capacity and capacity to submit applications in national and community programmes, but above all are subject to great pressures and deficiencies in terms of urban infrastructures, housing and social facilities.

Strategic areas such as housing, transport and logistics, the environment, social work, culture and economic and employment promotion continue, in most cases, to depend on central government with little coordination at the urban and metropolitan levels.

International (Policies to Internationalize Cities, Including Cross-border Policies)

The European integration process and the general globalization process have exacerbated the design and implementation of policies based on international urban competition.

This process has had a double marginalization effect:

- within cities, change with a major international impact and visibility on specific sites has been given priority, to the detriment of more coordinated measures to improve the existing city. Planning by projects, the creation of special legal frameworks to govern such operations and the presence of private promoters (frequently multinational corporations), are ways to ease and accelerate such operations, by avoiding the rigidity of traditional plans;
- at the level of the urban system, the dichotomy between cities (or metropolises) that possess major advantages in the internationalization process, and those whose influence is limited to nearby territories.

Portugal, as a peripheral country with limited resources and a model of internationalization which is characterized by its dependence on central economies and territories, is confronted with major obstacles to the internationalization of its cities, which affect even the largest cities, i.e., Lisbon and Oporto. In the first place, the growing integration of the Iberian market has meant that Madrid or Barcelona are strong competitors, which is aggravated by the lack of trans-European transport and communication networks.

The EXPO 98 project is a major effort to put Lisbon on the 'international map', by using the very topical theme of the oceans. Lisbon is also favoured by its logistic position on air transport routes, by its links with the Far East

(Macao) and because, at a national level, it agglomerates the main decision-making and international functions. This because it is a capital city and contains almost all the business decision centres, although there is a tendency to lose position in relation to other European capital cities.

The other cities still have very restricted international visibility, even within the Iberian peninsula. Until now, only heritage has provided the basis for a certain international projection (e.g., Evora or Angra in the Azores, both of which are World Heritage cities). At a more local level, the INTERREG Community Initiative has supported some initiatives to functionally strengthen and improve border cities. However, these are small cities with 20,000 inhabitants or fewer, which combine a lack of size with a lack of institutional and economic diversity and the fact that they are located in declining regions.

The Urban Policy Guidelines and Instruments, in the 1997 General Planning Options (GOPs)

The policy for the cities expressed in the document insists on the strategic role of cities as the anchors of regional, economic and social development on a wider territorial scale, as nodal points of transport and communication networks, and as centres of learning and innovation. The policy is urban because it impacts on cities but its objectives are much more ambitious

Cities are assumed to be spaces with problems and opportunities, which means that urban dynamics must be approached from the point of view of the conditions of economic efficiency, social justice, cultural diversity, sustainability and civic participation.

The convergence of sectoral and regional policies with urban impact, and the systematic and prospective vision of the urban framework and its role in the structuring of territory, are indicated as fundamental presuppositions in the formulation of urban policy.

The coordinated management of interventions and the role of inter-sectoral policy rationalization and coordination must be based on negotiation and partnership.

Five city policy objectives are:

1 to organize the territory, attenuate internal territorial imbalances and ensure equity in access to urban services and functions;

2 to promote the competitiveness of the urban system and increase the international projection of the main metropolitan agglomerations;

3   to improve the quality of life, to modernize infrastructures and ensure the economic and social sustainability of cities;

4   to reconcile the increasing process of urban development with environmental interventions and the improvement of rural areas;

5   to improve and promote culture and heritage and promote citizenship and increase social cohesion.

These major objectives involve, above all, intervention priorities in the areas of employment, housing, urban mobility, urban environment, improvement of public spaces and the revitalization of critical urban areas.

The basis of the implementation of urban policy implies the following progressive changes:

1   the improvement and promotion of the potential of the national urban system as a whole, and not only in the major cities and metropolitan areas;

2   a greater coordination of sectoral policies with urban impact, by clarifying the institutional architecture that regulates the various forms of intervention in the city; the reduction of the excessive pulverization of sectoral programmes; the improvement of cooperation between the planning instruments wielded by different ministries, and which overlap each other and are difficult to coordinate at the local level;

3   strengthening of intercity and inter-municipal joint organizations (resources, powers, technostructure) and coordination of urban policy in the configuration of the future administrative regions;

4   financial strengthening of local authorities and the clarification of the legal rules governing mixed capital companies; and measures that render operational urbanism and land use policies viable.

The specific urban policy instruments in the GOPs give particular importance to:

1   a greater coordination of housing policies in the urban development strategy, balancing the reinstatement of existing housing stocks with the construction of new housing stock;

2   increased financial resources for the PROSIURB programme;

3   the launching of the PERIURB programme, to improve the metropolitan peripheries, in terms of urbanism, infrastructures and the creation of conditions for the emergence of peripheral centralities;

4   the coordination of urban rehabilitation programme (national initiative) and URBAN (community initiative), by creating a fund for urban rehabilitation;

5   the coordination of the METROPOLIS programme to make major items of strategic facilities and infrastructure in the metropolitan areas viable, on the basis of state/local authority/private sector contracts;

6   the launching of the 'New Urban Landscapes' initiative in order to support the launching of model operation to improve public spaces, in areas of recent urban growth, which are able to create a structure in the chaotic and infrastructure poor urban fabric which characterizes these areas;

7   the preparation of a 'city image' initiative, based on pilot projects with a strong exemplary effect in areas such as: the promotion of cultural, sporting and leisure events; urban marketing; sign systems; urban furniture and the production of informative and promotional material; the improvement of urban services; the taking advantage of the scenic aspect of urban sites; and operations to improve and promote urban heritage and public spaces.

Assessment of Community Policies

•   The Treaty of the European Union does not deal with the development of a coordinated urban policy, a major contradiction with the strategic role played by cities nowadays as focuses or anchors of development from a local to a European and world scale. It is a matter of common agreement that the major cities and metropolitan agglomerations not only agglomerate resources and population and become true 'innovative environments', but also condense a countless number of problems, which range from environmental degradation to social marginalization and polarization, or the difficulties associated with the modernization of the productive base and the employment market. As has already been stated, the globalization process has also accentuated the gap between those cities which have succeeded in this process and those cities that have been unable to emerge from their problems and from the local nature of their dynamics.

- Accordingly, the effect of community policy on cities is, above all a result of the application of sectoral policies with a major urban impact, above all in the area of infrastructures, which, in most cases, gives rise to the non-coordination of projects which are very difficult to coordinate at the urban level.

- The great utility and adaptation to urban problems of the explicit urban policy initiated by the European Commission (URBAN and Article 10 of FEDER) is well known, but is, however, manifestly insufficient because of its reduced financial resources and because small scale cities are not eligible. The assessment is positive because of the institutional, thematic and operative innovation supported by these instruments (coordination of measures, public-private partnerships, revitalization of private charitable institutions and other local associations, the promotion of citizenship and social cohesion, the fight against exclusion and unemployment, etc.).

- Despite the seriousness of the problems of social exclusion, environmental degradation, unemployment, etc., urban policy objectives should not be confined to the resolution of specific crisis situation. Cities are also spaces of innovation and which drive economic and regional growth, where intervention is necessary to activate or catalyse this potential. Most of Portuguese territory is demographically and economically emptied, cities are the final source of change and initiative and therefore require to have their function as 'anchors' of regional development strengthened. The economy and the environment should in particular be priorities to which special attention is given.

- In the case of Portugal, this lack of coordination at Community level, is reproduced or amplified at the national level, where the same situation of 'institutional drift' of sectoral policies exists. In the case of medium-sized cities, which, in Portugal, are very small cities, coordinated urban policy is confronted with a lack of funds and the absence of specific Community aid. The convergence criteria, which restrict the expansion of public investment, increase this type of problem.

- It should also be stated that most urban problems in Portugal concern the intervention areas of the first generation of urban policies: the provision of basic infrastructures, physical land use controls, housing, transport and environment. The lack of municipal and national resources should therefore be the subject of an aid programme which aims to correct the minimum infrastructure conditions.

- The heart of the question does not reside in whether member states are or are not in favour of the elaboration of a 'common urban policy', and invoke the principle of subsidiarity or the political problems which may be caused by the removal of powers from the state – to the community or regional/local level. In the latter case this would vary according to the territorial scale which is most appropriate to the implementation of urban policy. There can be a common urban policy, which is rendered operational by directives, regulations, programmes, subsidies, funds, etc., provided that a great margin of freedom is given to member states to:
  - adapt these policies to the specific national and regional realities;
  - decide between the structuring initiatives at the macro level (European and national urban framework) and the micro level (at the intra and inter urban level);
  - coordinate and complement community policy with national policy and initiatives;
  - establish priorities in the areas of intervention and the type of objective, measures and initiatives;
  - include city policy within regional development policy;
  - clarify the model of administration in metropolitan areas.
- The existence of this type of 'common urban policy' will require a greater intra and inter-ministerial coordination in respect of city policy, from the institutional architecture of the Portuguese state, namely inside the MEPAT (Ministry of Equipment, Planning and Territorial Administration) and between it and the Ministry of the Environment.

Conclusion

From what has been stated, one can extract some of the main problems to be addressed by an urban policy in Portugal. Some of those problems arise from national specificities:

- a highly unfavourable situation regarding the historic lack of basic urban infrastructures (accessibility, sanitation, public spaces);
- recently instituted urban policy (apart from the conventional tools of physical planning), mainly with regard to the integration of sectoral policies with a strong urban impact and immaterial contents
- absence of administrative regions, as a framework for integration of urban policies with the regional development policy where powers concentrated

in the state at central and local level. The central state has become too scattered by sectors. Local administration is struggling to manage an ever increasing amount of competencies, with clearly insufficient financial, human and organizational resources;

- imbalances in the urban system, specifically with regard to the fragilty of the mid-sized cities network due to their uneven distribution over territory and the reduced dimension of the urban groupings in depressed regions. This situation is further aggravated by the dependence of most of these cities' economy on the central government in terms of investment and employment;
- difficulty on the part of the two major metropolitan areas in asserting themselves internationally, particularly the more vulnerable of the two, centred in Oporto;
- the need to solve problems of urban and environmental dereliction associated to processes of spontaneous urban growth which characterize the metropolitan peripheral areas and the areas of scattered urbanization.

Other issues pertain to problems posed by new urban policies. Regulating the balance between 'private projects' and 'public virtues' becomes more difficult where there is a strong competitiveness between cities and between the strategies of real estate developers, where local governments have only scarce resources that they can manage directly, and where organizational cultures and regulatory tools suitable for that type of solutions are lacking.

The policies drawn up to champion 'sustained', and 'integrated' urban strategies (from physical planning to employment or cultural policy) often turn out to be too ambitious and inoperative due to the excess load of targets to be met, to difficulties in terms of institutional integration and to lack of strategic actions of a more selective nature.

In order to strengthen the internationalization process, of which the EU is a part, the fragility of the Portuguese urban system risks an increase in its own polarities: on the one hand, two metropolitan areas competing on uneven ground at the international level (debating its peripheral position vis-à-vis the Iberian and European space); on the other hand, a group of medium-sized and small cities lacking influence, resources and specialization to sustain their role as anchors in the development of proximity regional areas.

In this context, whatever the scenario of a common urban policy may turn out to be, it is paramount to take these specificities into account. It has been demonstrated in recent years that the strengthening the urban system as a whole does not result from the sum of the urban policies developed by each city. This requires a framework with guidelines for a group strategy and probably an increased selectivity and reinforced support towards the more fragile elements of the urban system. In the absence of such guidelines, the winners will be those who, at the outset, own a larger pool of resources or logistic and economic added value: the losers will turn out to be those with greater difficulty in deploying endogenous resources which complement and regulate outside support.

Note

1   The difficulty in stating a consistent 'urbanization rate' is to a great extent the result of the weight of diffuse forms of urbanization. The statistical authority (National Statistics Institute) tends to underestimate this situation and to treat it as non-urban; other studies, by MEPAT, as an alternative, apply the lower urban threshold to agglomerations with fewer than 10,000 inhabitants. Nevertheless, by applying either criteria, the rate of urbanization is less than 60 per cent. In the section 'The "Archipelago-country": Territorial Dynamics and Urbanization Pattern', we present an alternative hypothesis which in our opinion reflects the realities of the country better.

References

Ascher, François (1995), *Metapolis ou l'avenir des villes*, Paris: Editions Odile Jacob.
Baptista, M. (1993), 'A Rede Urbana Nacional no Contexto Europeu', texto da comunicação colóquio *O Ordenamento Espacial Europeu no Pós-Maastricht*, MPAT/CCRN, Porto (policopiado).
Barreto, A. et al. (1996), *A Situação Social em Portugal, 1960–1995*, Lisboa: Instituto de Ciências Sociais.
CEDRU (1996), *Urbanização e Coesão Social em Portugal; Centro de Estudos de Desenvolvimento Regional e Urbano*, Lisboa (policopiado).
CML (1992), *Plano Estratégico de Lisboa, Direcção de Projecto de Planeamento Estratégico – Câmara Municipal de Lisboa*, Lisboa.
Domingues, A. (1993), *Serviços às Empresas – concentração metropolitana e desconcentração periférica*, 2 vols, (policopiado), Porto: Faculdade de Letras da Universidade do Porto.
EIUA (1992), *Urbanisation and the Functions of Cities in the European Community*, European Institute of Urban Affairs, Liverpool John Moores University/Commission of the European Communities, DG XVI, Bruxelas.
EURICUR (1995), *Effets des Politiques Nationales et Supranationales sur les Grandes Villes (1ère étape)*, (policopiado), Rotterdam: EURICUR/Eurocities.
European Commission (1996), 'Prospects for the Development of the Central and Capital Cities and Regions', *Regional Development Studies*, 22, ECSC-EC, Bruxelas.

Ferrão, J. (1995), 'Que políticas para as Cidades de Média Dimensão' in SEALOT/MPAT, *As Cidades Médias e o Ordenamento do Território*, Coimbra: Comissão de Coordenação da Região Centro.

Ferrão, J. (1997), 'Rede Urbana, Instrumento de Equidade, Coesão e Desenvolvimento?' in colóquio *A Política das Cidades*, Conselho Económico e Social, Lisboa (policopiado).

Gaspar, J. (1993), 'Reordenamento Urbano em Portugal' in *Serviços e Desenvolvimento numa Região em Mudança*, CCRC, Coimbra.

Gaspar, J. and Jensen-Butler (1992), 'Social Economic and Cultural Transformation in the Portuguese Urban System', *International Journal of Urban and Regional Research*, 16, 3.

GEOIDEIA (1993), *Estudo de Avaliação dos Programas Regionais em Portugal (Fase 1)*, GEOIDEIA/Comissão das Comunidades, Lisboa (policopiado).

GEOIDEIA/Ismeri Europa (1995), *Plano Director Municipal de Lisboa*, Vol. I, Lisboa: Câmara Municipal de Lisboa.

Planum et al. (1993), *Estudo Sócio-Económico da Área Metropolitana do Porto*, (documento interno), Porto: Junta Metropolitana.

Portas, N. (1994), 'El Planeamiento Urbano en Portugal' in S.L. Rivas and G. Muzio (eds), *Planeamiento Urbano en la Europa Comunitaria*, Valladolid: Universidad de Valladolid.

Portas, N. (1997), 'Planeamento Urbano e Política de Solos' in colóquio *A Política das Cidades*, Conselho Económico e Social, Lisboa (policopiado).

Quaternaire Portugal (1994), *Cidades Médias em Portugal*, (policopiado), Lisboa: Quaternaire Portugal/DG XVI.

Quaternaire Portugal (1996) *Estudo do Sistema Urbano Nacional*, Vol. I e II, (policopiado), Lisboa: Quaternaire Portugal/DGOTDU.

SEALOT/MPAT (1995), *Ciclo de Colóquios: a Política Urbana e o Ordenamento do Território*, Lisboa: Ministério do Planeamento e da Administração do Território.

14 Spain

ORIOL NEL.LO

Introduction

Spain is a country of old cities and recent urbanization. Many Spanish cities can trace their origins back to Roman times years, and in the middle ages some of them (for example Cordoba, Seville, Valencia and Barcelona) were among the most flourishing urban centres in Europe. However, the difficulties encountered by the processes of industrialization and modernization during the whole of the 19th and most of the 20th century led to a significant delay in the urbanization of Spanish society. As a result, in 1960 – when in many European countries the urban population was already clearly in the majority – over half the inhabitants of Spain still lived in localities of fewer than 20,000 inhabitants.

During the last four decades, however, urban development in Spain has been extraordinary, and Spanish cities have grown faster than at any other time in their history: by 1995, two out of every three Spaniards were living in cities. This process of change has affected the country's urban system as a whole, and the most visible consequence has been the formation of large metropolitan areas, the most important of which are Madrid, Barcelona, Valencia, Seville, Bilbao, Málaga and Zaragoza. The consolidation of these large urban areas – some of which are numbered among the largest metropolitan agglomerations in Europe – opens up new possibilities and presents challenges for the public policies that apply to them. The object of this report is, precisely, to analyse the relationship between the problems and potentialities arising from the transformation of these large Spanish cities and the national public policies that particularly affect them.

The report comprises four sections. The first section outlines the principal characteristics of the Spanish urban system and the place of the major cities in it; the main trends in the internal transformation of the large urban areas are analysed using a series of basic variables (population, employment, travel patterns, etc.). The second section deals with the characteristics of the administrative structure and of the system used to finance large cities in Spain. Sections three and four constitute the core of the report. In the third section

325

the specific problems and potentialities of the large cities are explored, and finally in the fourth section the principal instruments of national intervention in same are described.

It would not have been possible to complete this work without the collaboration of a number of people and institutions. The author would like, in the first place, gratefully to acknowledge the support of the local government bodies of the seven cities listed above. Each of the city councils of these cities – which have grouped together to form the G-7 network in order to debate and formulate a series of joint proposals – was visited expressly in connection with this report, and all of them kindly agreed to receive us and provided us with a great deal of data and information. Moreover, many colleagues were kind enough to collaborate with us, and during our visit to their city were generous with their knowledge and opinions and proved to be expert guides. At the end of this report, the reader will find a list of the discussion partners in each city.[1] We would like to thank them all once again and, at the same time, discharge them of any personal or institutional responsibility for the contents of this report. Finally, it should also be mentioned that the statistical tables and data in this report were compiled and drawn up, under the direction of the author, by the geographer Joan López and the economist Joan Miquel Piqué, both of whom are researchers working in the Institute of Metropolitan Studies in Barcelona.

The Spanish Urban System and the Dynamics of the Transformation of its Largest Cities

The Rapid Transformation of the Urban System: Demographic and Economic Urbanization, the Consolidation of the Axes of Activity, and the Pre-eminence of the Large Metropolitan Cities

The seven largest urban agglomerations in Spain – Barcelona, Bilbao, Madrid, Málaga, Seville, Valencia and Zaragoza – which occupy a surface area equivalent to 1.9 per cent of the Spanish territory, are home to 33.8 per cent of the country's population. This situation is, to a large degree, the result of the transformation of the Spanish urban system that took place between 1960 and 1995, a period during which, as was stated above, Spanish cities experienced the most rapid growth in their history (Guardia et al., 1994; Precedo, 1996; Vinuesa, 1996).

During this period, the population living in towns of over 100,000 inhabitants doubled, rising from 8.5 to 16.8 million people, and increased its relative weight with respect to the country as a whole, going from 27.7 per cent to 41.5 per cent of the total. As can be seen from Table 14.1, two clearly different periods can be distinguished within this evolution: the initial phase (1960–75) was characterized by accelerated and highly polarized growth; and the second stage (1975–95) by slower and more diffuse growth.

Between 1960 and 1975, coinciding with the most acute phase of economic growth and accelerated industrialization, the number of Spanish municipalities with more than 100,000 inhabitants went from 26 to 48, and the population living in this type of settlement increased by 71.4 per cent. During this 15-year period, the large metropolitan areas, where the majority of these municipalities are located, experienced unprecedented growth, over 50 per cent in many cases. The population of Madrid area went from 2.3 to 4.05 million representing a total growth of 76.2 per cent, making it the largest urban agglomeration in the country; Barcelona and Valencia, situated on the Mediterranean coast, shot from 2.5 to 4, and 0.7 to 1.2 million respectively, representing increases of 59.1 per cent and 55.4 per cent; Bilbao, on the Cantabrian coast, and Zaragoza, in the valley of the Ebro, experienced even greater relative growth, 60.5 per cent and 73.9 per cent respectively, going from 0.6 to 0.9, and 0.3 to 0.5 million inhabitants. The increase in the population of the two large metropolitan districts in Andalusia, Seville and Málaga, was slower and occurred later. Their growth during this period (26.3 per cent and 33.6 per cent respectively) was, nevertheless, well above the national average (17.8 per cent).

After 1975 this accelerated rhythm of urban growth decreased considerably. As a result, the relative weight of the sector of the population living in municipalities of over 100,000 inhabitants stabilized with respect to the country as a whole, rising only slightly from 40.4 to 41.5 per cent of the total. Municipalities of over 500,000 inhabitants even experienced a slight drop in relative weight. Today, growth is mainly concentrated in the municipalities with between 20,000 and 100,000 inhabitants, which, between 1975 and 1995, went from housing 19.5 per cent to housing 22.9 per cent of the Spanish population. The largest metropolitan areas have also followed this trend, and have seen their growth rates fall drastically to close to the national average (which was 12.3 per cent for the period 1975–95): Madrid, Zaragoza and Valencia have grown around 15 per cent: Barcelona 8 per cent, and Bilbao even showed a slight decrease of -0.1 per cent. The exceptions are the new metropolitan areas of Seville and Málaga, which grew 30.9 per cent and 43.0 per cent respectively during this 20 year period.

Table 14.1 Evolution of the Spanish population by municipality size (1960–95)

Municipality size	Number of municipalities 1960		1975		1995		Population 1960*		1975		1995		Growth 1960–75		1975–95	
	no.	%	no.	%	no.	%	Population	%	Population	%	Population	%	No.	%	No.	%
≤2,000	6,763	73.5	5,931	72.4	5,923	73.2	4,440,868	14.5	3,346,110	9.3	3,092,179	7.6	-1,094,758	-24.7	-253,931	-7.6
2,001–5,000	1,393	15.1	1,193	14.6	1,026	12.7	4,406,789	14.4	3,655,189	10.1	3,170,048	7.8	-751,600	-17.1	-485,141	-13.3
5,001–20,000	877	9.5	825	10.1	852	10.5	7,781,913	25.4	7,452,905	20.7	8,131,522	20.1	-329,008	-4.2	678,617	9.1
20,001–50,000	108	1.2	153	1.9	178	2.2	3,027,992	9.9	4,289,796	11.9	5,195,443	12.8	1,261,804	41.7	905,647	21.1
50,001–100,000	35	0.4	43	0.5	61	0.8	2,442,326	8.0	2,732,561	7.6	4,093,177	10.1	290,235	11.9	1,360,616	49.8
100,001–500,000	23	0.2	43	0.5	49	0.6	4,160,188	13.6	7,730,613	21.5	9,510,170	23.5	3,570,425	85.8	1,779,557	23.0
>500,000	3	0.0	5	0.1	6	0.1	4,322,860	14.1	6,805,533	18.9	7,267,516	18.0	2,482,673	57.4	461,983	6.8
Total	**9,202**	**100.0**	**8,193**	**100.0**	**8,095**	**100.0**	**30,582,936**	**100.0**	**36,012,707**	**100.0**	**40,460,055**	**100.0**	**5,429,771**	**17.8**	**4,447,348**	**12.3**

*   Actual population.

Table 14.2 Population of the seven major metropolitan areas compared with total Spanish population (1960–95)

		Population			
	Area	1960	1975	1995	Growth 1960–95
Metropolitan areas	9,737.2	7,462,665	11,985,232	13,669,881	83.18%
España	505,992.0	30,777,084	36,012,254	40,460,055	31.46%
% 7 areas with regard to Spain	1.92%	24.25%	33.28%	33.79%	–

Source: INE, *Censos de Población*, several years.

These four decades of evolution of the urban system have had two important consequences: on the one hand, population and activity have tended to concentrate together along certain relatively well defined territorial axes; and on the other, the principal metropolitan areas have established their primacy over the national urban system as a whole (Perpiñà Grau, 1954; Tobío, 1985; Llorens, 1994; Ministerio de Obras Públicas, Transportes y Medio Ambiente (MOPTMA), 1994).

With respect to the configuration of the axes of activity, the first thing that should be noted is the trend towards peripherization of the population. While the mean population density for Spain as a whole is 80 inhabitants per km^2, the 30 coastal provinces and those located along the road network that follows the Ebro valley have a mean density of 127 inhabitants per km^2, five times the mean for the interior of Spain excluding Madrid. This distribution of the population is due to deep-seated historical and geographical reasons, but it was particularly favoured by the spatial dynamics of the economic growth during the period 1960–75. During this period, Spain, like many other Mediterranean countries, experienced large migrations of population from the traditionally rural areas to the provinces where industrial activity and tourism were developing with the greatest force. The road network was later adapted, in part, to these trends, so that the principal axes of activity in Spain today are as follows:

- the Mediterranean coast from Catalonia to Murcia, with a potential prolongation penetrating the coastal provinces of Andalusia;
- the Ebro river valley, from the Basque country and Navarra to Catalonia by way of Aragon;

- the tourist areas of the Balearic and Canary islands;
- the Madrid area in the centre of the Meseta.

The second result of the urbanization process was, as stated above, the reinforcement of the position of the seven largest metropolitan areas at the head of the urban system (Castells, 1990; Precedo, 1996). Home to a third of the Spanish population, these seven agglomeration generate approximately half of the national gross added value, house 43.9 per cent of the industrial work force, and are clearly the principal motors of the Spanish economy. Two of them, Madrid and Barcelona, are metropolises of international importance, while the others are of national and regional significance. Other metropolitan areas are also emerging, such as the tourist areas of Mallorca and Las Palmas de Gran Canarias, Valladolid and the Central Asturian region. The attractiveness of these emerging centres is increasing and they tend to consolidate as metropolitan areas.

Finally, to complete the panorama of questions relating to the urban system as a whole, we must point out its bipolar character. Any conventional measure of the Spanish urban system such as the rank-size method (Díez Nicolás, 1972; Racionero, 1986; Reher, 1994) reveals the almost absolute parity of the metropolitan areas of Madrid and Barcelona. In terms of population they are the fifth and sixth largest metropolitan regions in Europe respectively, coming after London, Paris, the Dutch Randstad and the Ruhr, and ahead of Berlin, Milan, Rome, Athens and Lisbon. The combined population of the two areas is over 9,000,000 (22.3 per cent of Spain as a whole). They contain the principal administrative and financial headquarters of the country, and generate one third of the national gross added value.

The Dynamics of Metropolitan Transformation: Expansion, Decentralization and Increasing Homogeneity

Three processes characterize the current dynamics of transformation of the Spanish metropolitan areas. The first is their tendency to expand their zone of influence and integrate an ever greater area. The second is the progressive decrease in relative weight of the central municipality with respect to the metropolitan area as a whole due to the absolute or relative decentralization of both population and commercial and industrial activity. Both these processes combine, finally, to further the gradual reduction of differences between the centres and peripheral areas of metropolitan agglomerations in terms of amenities, infrastructure and living conditions.

The tendency of large Spanish cities to progressively integrate new territory is clear, and has been closely studied, above all, through the analysis of daily travel patterns. The analyses show that, with the single exception of Zaragoza, the seven principal Spanish cities are clearly supra-municipal in character:

- Madrid, despite the large size of the central municipality (605.8 km^2), not only integrates the labour market of the strict metropolitan area (made up of the 27 municipalities of the abolished Comisión de Planeamiento y Coordinación – 1,942 km^2), but is also showing a tendency to expand its influence to the province as a whole (178 municipalities, 7,995 km^2), and even further, towards Guadalajara and Toledo. The result is that the whole Autonomous Community of Madrid is increasingly becoming a metropolitan reality (Comunidad de Madrid, 1996);

- in Barcelona, where the central municipality is very small (97.6 km^2), the metropolitan dynamic already extends far beyond the 27 municipalities of the old metropolitan administrative area (476 km^2), and increasingly integrates the whole of what is now called the Metropolitan region. This area extends north to the borders of the province of Girona and south to those of Tarragona, and inland to the mountains of Montseny and Montserrat (including a total of 163 municipalities and 3,236 km^2) (Mancomunitat de Municipis de l'Àrea Metropolitana de Barcelona (MMAMB), 1995);

- Bilbao, which has an even smaller core municipality (41.3 km^2) is expanding its metropolitan area to incorporate the entire Bajo Nervión area (25 municipalities and 405 km^2) on both sides of the river (Jauristi, 1985; Gobierno Vasco, 1992);

- in Valencia, the most usual delineations of the metropolitan area include, in addition to the central municipality (134.6 km^2), all the municipalities of the area of l'Horta (44 municipalities and 628.2 km^2) (Rossell et al., 1988; Generalitat Valenciana, 1995);

- in Seville (141.3 km^2), the Junta de Andalucía uses a definition of the metropolitan area that includes 22 municipalities situated in the Vega del Guadalquivir sector, and in the Aljarafe and Guadaira areas (representing a total of 1.502 km^2) (Almoguera, 1989; Junta de Andalucía, 1996a);

- in Málaga (393 km^2), the regional authorities have delimited a metropolitan area comprising ten municipalities, encompassing tourist developments along the Costa del Sol to the east and west of the city and extending inland along the Guadalhorce river valley (representing a total of 962 km^2) (Junta de Andalucía, 1996);

• in the case of Zaragoza, the municipality itself covers a large area (1,063 km^2) so that, in spite of the increasing interrelationship with neighbouring municipalities located along the Ebro, Gállego and Huerva river valleys, it is not strictly speaking a supra-municipal metropolitan phenomenon in the same way as are the other cities (Sancho, 1989; Fernández de Alarcón, 1993).

In recent decades, the dynamics of metropolitan expansion have been accompanied by absolute or relative decentralization of the population and of activity. We described earlier how the rhythm of demographic growth in the metropolitan areas has tended to stagnate in recent years. However, this apparent stagnation conceals very pronounced differences in demographic growth within each metropolitan area. These differences are mostly the result of intra-metropolitan migrations and give rise to the decentralization processes (López Groh, 1988; Castells, 1990; Vinuesa et al., 1994; Arribas and Módenes, 1996).

Table 14.3 shows how the population of the central municipalities in the metropolitan areas of Bilbao, Madrid and Barcelona declined consistently in absolute and relative terms between 1975 and 1995 (-14.0 per cent in Bilbao, 7.8 per cent in Barcelona and -5.4 per cent in Madrid). During the same period, the population of the metropolitan belts of these three metropolitan areas increased by 12.4, 20.5 and 96.5 per cent respectively. The results of the 1996 census, as far as these have been analyzed to date, plainly confirm the continuity of this trend, and as yet provide no evidence of recentralization processes. In the case of Málaga, Seville and Valencia, the central municipalities were still growing during the 1975–95 period (30.3, 22.0 and 7.8 per cent respectively), but at a much more reduced pace than their respective metropolitan belts (which increased 137.4, 53.0 and 25.7 per cent respectively). In Zaragoza, the relative loss in the weight of the old town and other central districts with respect to the municipality as a whole is also noticeable.

It is important, however, to stress that the growth occurring in the metropolitan belts does not tend to be concentrated within the larger urban centres located within these areas. These larger urban centres are even, in many cases, experiencing problems maintaining their own population. The growth tends, rather, to occur in smaller centres and areas characterized by dispersed housing, such as ribbon developments along the La Coruña road in the case of Madrid; the small towns in the Vallès and Maresme districts in the Barcelona metropolitan region; the Aljarafe district in Seville; the right bank of the Nervión and the Mungía hills in Bilbao; the towns of l'Horta along the

Table 14.3 Evolution of population in the seven major Spanish metropolitan cities by territorial area (1960–95)

	Area (sq. km)	1960	1975	1995
Barcelona				
Municipality (NUTS 5)	97.6	1,526,550	1,751,136	1,614,571
Rest of metropolitan area	3,138.0	1,000,697	2,268,577	2,732,593
Total metropolitan area	3,235.6	2,527,247	4,019,713	4,347,164
Rest of province	4,484.1	311,554	370,184	401,072
Total province (NUTS 3)	7,719.7	2,838,801	4,389,897	4,748,236
Bilbao				
Municipality (NUTS 5)	41.3	294,147	431,347	370,997
Rest of metropolitan area	363/5	273.698	479,795	539,144
Total metropolitan area	404.8	567,845	911,142	910,141
Rest of province	1,812.4	183,169	243,723	253,585
Total province (NUTS 3)	2,217.2	751,014	1,154,865	1,163,726
Madrid				
Municipality (NUTS 5)	605.8	2,177,123	3,201,234	3,029,724
Rest of metropolitan area	1,336.1	120,869	847,090	1,664,182
Total metropolitan area	1,941.9	2,297,992	4,048,324	4,693,906
Rest of province	6,053.1	212,225	271,575	487,753
Total province (NUTS 3)	7,995.0	2,510,217	4,319,899	5,181,659
Málaga				
Municipality (NUTS 5)	393.0	296,432	408,458	532,425 *
Rest of metropolitan area	568.7	50,079	54,529	129,475 *
Total metropolitan area	961.7	346,511	462,987	661,900 *
Rest of province	6,344.3	435,179	452,718	563,059 *
Total province (NUTS 3)	7,306.0	781,690	915,705	1,224,959 *

* The municipality of Torremolinos is included in the rest of metropolitan area, because it has been segregated from the municipality of Málaga

	Area (sq. km)	1960	1975	1995
Sevilla				
Municipality (NUTS 5)141.3	441,869	589,721	719,588	
Rest of metropolitan area1,360.6	214,102	238,906	365,481	
Total metropolitan area	1,501.9	655,971	828,627	1,085,069
Rest of province	12,534.2	588,182	549,916	634,377
Total province (NUTS 3)14,036.1	1,244,153	1,378,543	1,719,446	
Valencia				
Municipality (NUTS 5)	124.6	501,777	707,915	763,299
Rest of metropolitan area493.6	261,347	477,820	600,503	
Total metropolitan area628.2	763,124	1,185,735	1,363,802	
Rest of province10,147.8	674,919	749,608	836,517	
Total province (NUTS 3)	10,776.0	1,438,043	1,935,343	2,200,319
Zaragoza				
Municipality (NUTS 5)	1,063.1	303,975	528,704	607,899
Rest of province	16,211.1	337,140	273,327	244,433
Total province (NUTS 3)	17,274.2	641,115	802,031	852,332

Source: INE, *Censos de Población*, several years.

road to Llíria in Valencia; the tourist developments along the coast in the case of Málaga; and the rural districts of the municipality of Zaragoza. Therefore, the shift in demographic growth is not only from the metropolitan centre towards the more peripheral areas (as the data in Tables 14.3 and 14.4 might suggest), but also from all the more densely populated areas and larger towns towards more sparsely populated areas and smaller towns and developments (Salom, 1992; Monclús, 1994; Vinuesa et al., 1994; Nel.lo, 1995; Martín García, 1996; Bilbao Metrópoli-30, 1996).

Many authors have noted the correspondence between the process of territorial diffusion affecting the metropolitan areas and the structural transformation of their economic base, characterized by the fragmentation of the production process and the tertiarization of employment. In the larger Spanish cities, this economic restructuring process has been particularly intense over the last 20 years, and, together with undeniable benefits (Spain's per capita GDP expressed as a percentage of the mean for the countries of the European Union rose from 66 per cent in 1985 to 77 per cent in 1994), it has given rise to high levels of unemployment which, as will be discussed below, constitute one of the main problems of Spanish cities and Spanish society in general. With respect to the sectorial structure, the destruction of industrial jobs was particularly intense in the two oldest large industrial centres (Bilbao and Barcelona), but the relative loss of weight of industrial activities has been general. Tables 14.5 and 14.6 clearly show how the tertiary sector now dominates in all seven metropolitan provinces, both in terms of employment and of Gross Added Value [López Groh, 1988; Méndez and Caravaca, 1993).

The lack of data for the constituent municipalities of each metropolitan area makes impossible to know with exactitude whether the restructuring of employment has been accompanied by a territorial redistribution within these areas. However, the results of studies of certain cities consistently indicate a loss of relative weight of jobs localized in the central areas during both periods of recession (1975–85, 1992–95) and of expansion (1986–91) (Escudero, 1985; Clusa, 1992; Brenes et al., 1993; Celada, 1995; Trullén, 1997).

The third characteristic trait of the metropolitan dynamics in large Spanish cities is the progressive reduction in the differences between the central and peripheral zones of the metropolitan areas. The peripheral areas began, in general, to develop, as we have seen, during the period of accelerated growth in the '60s and late '70s. As a result of these origins, they accumulated serious deficiencies, since the predominance of low quality mass housing was often associated with lack of amenities, deficient infrastructure and bad communications (Capel, 1975; Teran, 1982; Fernández and Gavira, 1986).

Table 14.4   Evolution of the population of the major Spanish metropolitan cities by territorial areas (global data, 1960–95)

G-7	Area (sq. km)	1960	1975	1995
Municipalities (NUTS 5)	2,476.7	5,541,873	7,618,515	7,638,503
Rest of metropolitan areas	7,260.5	1,920,792	4,366,717	6,031,378
Total metropolitan areas	9,737.2	7,462,665	11,985,232	13,669,881
Rest of provinces	57,587.0	2,742,368	2,911,051	3,420,796
Total provinces (NUTS 3)	67,324.2	10,205,033	14,896,283	17,090,677

Source: The author, from INE, *Censos de Población*, several years.

Table 14.5   Employment structure by branch of the seven central municipalities (resident employed population, percentage data 1981 and 1991)

	1981					1991				
	Agriculture	Industry	Construction	Services	Total	Agriculture	Industry	Construction	Services	Total
Barcelona	0.5	35.6	3.6	60.3	100.0	0.7	29.9	5.5	63.9	100.0
Bilbao	0.5	36.1	5.9	57.5	100.0	0.5	26.3	8.2	65.0	100.0
Madrid	0.4	22.9	6.2	70.5	100.0	0.9	20.2	7.0	71.9	100.0
Málaga	2.5	19.2	9.5	68.8	100.0	1.5	16.2	10.4	71.9	100.0
Sevilla	1.8	24.0	6.5	67.7	100.0	1.9	19.2	8.5	70.4	100.0
Valencia	1.7	30.5	5.1	62.7	100.0	1.5	25.8	6.1	66.6	100.0
Zaragoza	2.0	35.8	7.0	55.2	100.0	1.4	31.7	7.6	59.3	100.0
España	16.0	28.2	8.8	47.0	100.0	10.1	24.9	11.0	54.0	100.0

Source: INE: 'Censos de población', several years.

Table 14.6   Gross value-added by branch of activity in the major Spanish metropolitan areas (provincial data 1991)

Province	Gross value-added (million PTA)								
	Agriculture and fishing	%	Industry	%	Construction	%	Services	%	Total	%
Barcelona	56,554	2.1	2,508,651	19.2	601,074	12.3	4,980,045	14.6	8,146,324	14.9
Vizcaya	43,899	1.6	604,946	4.6	128,744	2.6	974,008	2.9	1,751,597	3.2
Madrid	42,173	1.5	1,647,337	12.6	641,450	13.1	6,718,380	19.7	9,049,349	16.5
Málaga	62,658	2.3	134,156	1.0	145,834	3.0	926,366	2.7	1,269,014	2.3
Sevilla	113,357	4.2	291,859	2.2	205,229	4.2	1,144,687	3.4	1,755,132	3.2
Valencia	120.010	4.4	849,376	6.5	252,827	5.2	1,931,486	5.7	3,153,699	5.8
Zaragoza	55,911	2.0	403,865	3.1	100.794	2.1	974,008	2.9	1,534,578	2.8
España	2,729,757	100.0	13,058,571	100.0	4,880,849	100.0	34,113,371	100.0	54,782,548	100.0

Source: Banco Bilbao Vizcaya, 1997, http://www.bbv.es/BBV.servest/madrid/rentapro.htm.

Thus, in general terms, the social profile of the peripheral zones of metropolitan areas tended to be notably lower than their centres.

Today, however, the progressive dispersal of population and activities, aided by the intervention of the central and local authorities, is tending to reduce these differences. In effect, the shift of the population from the central areas to the more peripheral metropolitan zones is closely linked to the evolution of the land and housing market (which are discussed below). Due to this evolution, the housing available in peripheral areas appears to be more attractive and affordable for middle income groups than that available in central areas. Thus, the population moving from the centre is mainly composed of young people with medium income levels and education, whose arrival often contributes to the diversification of the social structure of the peripheral areas (Leal and Cortés, 1995; MMAMB, 1997). These areas have also been favoured – as mentioned above – by the geographical dispersal of industrial and commercial activities and services, and by the efforts of the administration, in particular since the restoration of democratic local government in 1979.

Apart from other problems related to town planning, which will be dealt with below, this migration of middle income groups could, in principle, lead in the central areas towards a situation of greater social polarization, as has occurred in other European cities. As yet, however, there has been no statistical evidence to suggest that processes of this kind have been consolidated. The studies carried out in the capital by the Autonomous University of Madrid for the period 1986–91 show that, while social inequality in terms of income has increased in the city, this is due to a proportionally greater growth of the percentage of income concentrated in the higher strata rather than to a decrease in the income of the least privileged groups (Leal, 1990 and 1994). In the city of Barcelona, according to household surveys, the disparity between the highest and the lowest strata has even diminished: the difference between the aggregate income of the 10 per cent of the population living in the wealthiest households and the 10 per cent who live in the poorest households was 15:1 in 1984 and fell to 1:1 in 1994 (Subirats, 1992; Nel.lo, 1996). These figures, which would indicate the absence of social dualization in the large Spanish cities, are consistent with the data published by the United Nations, which indicate that Spain is one of the countries in the European Union with the least differences in mean income per household (Zaldivar and Castells, 1992; Gaviria, 1996; Programa de Nactiones Unidas para el Desarrollo (PNUD), 1996).

These data do not, however, in any way belie the presence of significant inequalities within the Spanish metropolitan areas. These inequalities occur, in the first place, between districts, in that although the differences between the central and peripheral areas have diminished in general terms, there are still striking contrasts between different municipalities and even between different districts within each metropolis. Secondly, the income distribution among different social groups is far from being equitable and, as will be seen, the living conditions of certain sectors of the population of large Spanish cities are seriously defective.

The Administrative Structure and Financing of Large Spanish Cities

The Administrative Structure: Institutional Fragmentation and Complexity

The administrative structure of large Spanish cities is characterized by the fragmentation of the territory and the complexity of the institutional structure. The promulgation of the Spanish constitution in 1978 brought about a profound reform of the state, the main consequence of which with respect to the organization and government of the territory was the formation of 17 regional communities, each with its own autonomous government. As far as local government was concerned, the constitution retained the two existing basic entities, the province and the municipality, guaranteeing their autonomy and laying the foundation for the democratization and modernization of these administrations. These principles were later further developed by the Ley de Bases de Régimen Local (Local Government Act) approved in 1985. In spite of this notable administrative reform, the essential features of the local government map (which in 1991 had 8,077 municipalities and 52 provinces) have not been modified, and have remained almost unchanged since the promulgation of the constitution.

As we have seen, the urban structure of the large Spanish cities is, in practically all cases, supra-municipal. In response to this situation, the aforementioned Ley de Bases de Régimen Local contemplates the possibility of creating administrative bodies for the metropolitan area as a whole (Martín Mateo, 1988). However, as the regulation of local government falls under the jurisdiction of the autonomous communities, the application of these principles within each autonomous community depends on their respective governments. These bodies have, in general, been remiss in taking steps in this direction, so that (with certain exceptions) large cities in Spain today lack local government bodies on a metropolitan level (Barrero, 1993).

In fact the creation of the autonomous communities led, within a relatively short space of time, to the abolition of the existing bodies charged with the government and coordination of Spain's metropolitan areas. The respective autonomous governments dissolved: in 1980 the Corporación Administrativa del Gran Bilbao (the Administrative Corporation of Greater Bilbao), which had been in existence since 1945; in 1983, the Comisión de Planeamiento y Coordinación del Área Metropolitana de Madrid (the Planning and Coordination Commission for the Madrid Metropolitan area), which had been created in 1963; in 1986, the Corporación Administrativa del Gran Valencia (the Administrative Corporation of Greater Valencia), set up in 1946; and in 1987, the Corporación Metropolitana de Barcelona (Barcelona Metropolitan Corporation), in existence since in 1974. The dissolution of these bodies was no doubt facilitated by the fact that, with the single exception of the Barcelona Metropolitan Corporation, these entities had at the time only very reduced administrative structures, jurisdiction and resources (Ibarra, 1982; Ortega Álvarez, 1983; Castanyer, 1985; Sorribes, 1985). Seville, Málaga and Zaragoza had no formal public administration whatsoever at the metropolitan level.

In the case of the metropolis of Bilbao and Madrid, the functions of the abolished metropolitan bodies were taken over by the respective regional governments, whereas different administrative solutions were adopted to replace them in Valencia and Barcelona. In Valencia, the Consell Metropolità de l'Horta (the Metropolitan Council of l'Horta) was set up in 1986 and intended to have jurisdiction over the supra-municipal coordination and planning of 44 municipalities (Barrero, 1993). However, the inadequate legal definition of these powers, the lack of resources, and on occasion, the refusal of the town councils to cooperate made the Consell Metropolità a barely functional body. In the case of Barcelona, the Corporación Metropolitana was replaced by two specific agencies: the Entitat Metropolitana de Transport (the Metropolitan Transport Authority) with an ambit of 17 municipalities; and the Entitat Metropolitana de Serveis Hidràulics i Tractaments de Residus (the Metropolitan Water and Waste Treatment Authority), whose jurisdiction extends to 33 municipalities. Furthermore, 26 municipalities which disagreed with the abolition of the metropolitan corporation decided to associate and formed the Mancomunitat de Municipis de la Àrea Metropolitana de Barcelona (Association of Municipalities of the Barcelona Metropolitan Area) to cooperate on issues of mutual interest (Mir, 1991; Tornos, 1993). However, despite the efforts made by these new bodies to coordinate their activities, it is generally admitted that the system of metropolitan administration in Barcelona is inefficient and should be subjected to a far reaching reform.

As a result of the fragmentation of the local government map in large Spanish cities, the component municipalities are the key institutions on a local level both with respect to the organization of town planning and to the financing and administration management of services. This fragmentary structure also explains the role played by the central municipalities of each metropolitan area (in spite of the fact that they represent only one sector of these areas) as the promoters of more or less formal mechanisms for cooperation and joint promotion of the image of the area. Two of these city councils, Barcelona and Madrid, also have special charters (established in 1960 and 1963 respectively) which afford them greater powers in terms of administrative action.

Physical and Strategic Planning: the Pre-eminence of Local Plans, the Weakness of Planning on a Metropolitan Level, and the Emergence of Strategic Planning

In Spain, town planning in general falls under the jurisdiction of the autonomous communities. However, the state retains the authority to draw up guidelines concerning land ownership and related matters, which are regulated by the Ley de Reforma del Regimen Urbanistico y Valoraciones del Suelo (Town Planning and Land Valuation Reform Act), which will be modified in the near future. Municipal bodies, including those of large cities, are entitled to propose and draw up plans affecting their own ambit, while the autonomous regional governments generally have jurisdiction over the final approval of such plans (Parejo, 1991; Boquera, 1992; Comisión de Expertos Sobre Urbanismo, 1995; Menéndez, 1996).

   In the large Spanish cities town planning is normally carried out on the municipal level, so that, in principle, an urban plan exists for each constituent municipality within the metropolitan area. As can be seen in Table 14.7, the plans in effect in the majority of the central municipalities of the large metropolitan areas were approved during the '80s. This means that they were

Table 14.7   Urban planning in force in the seven central municipalities of the Spanish major cities

Municipality	Approved	Area	Status
Barcelona	1976	27 municipalities	–
Bilbao	1994	Municipality	–
Madrid	1985	Municipality	Revised (revision approved in 1997)
Málaga	1983	Municipality	Through revising process (waiting for final approval)
Sevilla	1987	Municipality	–
Valencia	1988	Municipality	–
Zaragoza	1986	Municipality	Under revision

Source: The author.

Table 14.8 Metropolitan plans in the major Spanish cities

City	Plan type	Area	Status	Body responsible
Barcelona	Plan Territorial Metropolitano de Barcelona	Metropolitan Region of Barcelona (163 municipalities)	In process	Generalitat de Catalunya
Bilbao	Plan Territorial Parcial del Bajo Nervión	Cuenca del Bajo Nervión (25 municipalities)	In process	Gobierno Vasco
Madrid	Plan Estratégico Regional de Ordenación	Autonomous Community of Madrid (178 municipalities)	In process	Comunidad de Madrid
Málaga	Plan de Orenación del Territorio de la Aglomeración Urbana de Málaga	Urban agglomeration of Málaga (10 municipalities)	In process	Junta de Andalucia
Sevilla	Plan de Ordenación del Territorio de la Aglomeración Urbana de Sevilla	Urban agglomeration of Sevilla (22 municipalities)	In process	Junta de Andalucia
Valencia	Normas de Coordinación Metropolitana	Consell Metropolità de l'Horta (44 muncipalities)	Approved in 1986	Generalitat Valenciana
Zaragoza	Directrices de Ordenación Urbana de Zaragoza	Zaragoza and influence area (21 municipalities)	In process	Diputación General de Aragón

Source: The author.

Table 14.9 Strategic plans in the major Spanish cities

City	Title	Area	Status	Organization in charge
Barcelona	Plan Estrat´gico Barcelona–2000	Muncipality of Barcelona and metropolitan surroundings (undefined)	Approved in 1989 (1st version)	Asociación Plan Stratégico Barcelona–2000
Bilbao	Plan Estrat´gico de Bilbao	Muncipality of Bilbao and metropolitan surroundings (30 muncipalities)	Approved in 1992 and being implemented	Bilbao Metrópolis–30
Madrid	Plan Regional de Estrategia Territorial	Autonomous Community of Madrid (178 municipalities)	Basis Document approved in 1997	Comunidad de Madrid
Málaga	Plan Estratégico de Málaga	Municipality	Approved in 1996 and being implemented	Fundación CIEDES, Centro de Investigaciones Estratégicos y de Desarrollo Económico y Social de Málaga
Sevilla	–	–	–	–
Valencia	Plan Estratégico de Valencia	Municipality	Approved in 1996 and being implemented	Plan Estratégico de Valencia
Zaragoza	Proyecto Zaragoza–2010	Municipality	In process	Ebrópolis, Asociación para el desarrollo de Zaragoza y su área de influencia

Source: The author.

drawn up in the period during which town planning in Spain most flourished, when, with the restoration of democracy, the municipalities were engaged in trying to remedy the disorder and deficiencies caused by the accelerated and untrammelled growth of the '60s and early '70s (Ferrer, 1989; Instituto de Territorio y Urbanismo, 1989; Ezquiaga, 1991; Seguí, 1993). Some of these plans (those relating to Madrid, Málaga and Zaragoza) are currently in an advanced phase of revision. The most notable exception to this general rule is Barcelona, which has a somewhat earlier plan (dating from 1976) that includes not only the central municipality, but also the entire ambit of the former Barcelona Metropolitan Corporation (including a total of 27 municipalities).

This situation, characterized by highly fragmented planning, could be remedied in the immediate future through the approval of a series of plans for each metropolitan region as a whole. In fact, as shown in Table 14.8, metropolitan plans and directives for coordination are being drawn up for every Spanish metropolitan area, with the exception of Valencia where norms of this kind were already approved in 1986. The elaboration and approval of these plans are the result of the regional legislation applicable in each case, and fall under the jurisdiction of the autonomous governments (with the greater or lesser involvement of the municipalities affected). However, the prolonged period of time that has been spent drawing up these plans, and the lack of genuine executive content raise certain doubts concerning their real effectiveness in the long run.

In this context, five of the seven large Spanish cities (Barcelona, Bilbao, Màlaga, Valencia and Zaragoza) have themselves undertaken strategic planning operations (Table 14.9). These plans have in all cases been drawn up at the instigation of the city council of the central municipality, and in general have included the participation of diverse social agents and citizens' organizations. As is usual in such cases, the aim of these plans is to give impulse to local initiative and to foster agreements that pursue common aims and go beyond the institutional fragmentation of local government and town planning. The scope of these plans is municipal in Málaga and Valencia and metropolitan in the other three cases, although the exact territory of application is precisely delimited only in the case of Bilbao. In Madrid, a strategic regional plan is being drawn up by the regional government. One of the most persistent problems relating to the implementation of these plans is the conflict between such metropolitan plans and the local interest of each component municipality. This problem must be seen in the context of the relationship, which is not always an easy one, between the central municipalities and the municipalities of their metropolitan surroundings. The work of drawing up strategic plans has been under way for some years, and started with the initial experience of the first strategic plan for Barcelona, which was approved in 1989.

Financing: Dependence on Own Resources and Budgetary Problems

In Spain, local government financing is regulated by the Ley Reguladora de las Haciendas Locales (the Local Government Finance Act) of 1988 (Albi and García, 1993). Under this law, municipalities obtain income from five main sources: local taxes, municipal charges levied on the use of public facilities, income from assets, inter-administrative transfers and public debt. The first three items, which represent the municipalities own non-financial income, are the principal source, and predominate over the other sources (transfers and debt) in a proportion of 60:40 overall in the municipalities of the country as a whole (Chavero, 1995).

In any analysis of the composition of the income of major Spanish cities, it should be pointed out at the outset that no comprehensive information is available concerning the finances of the municipalities that make up the seven metropolitan areas under discussion. In the absence of this data, Table 14.10 shows the incomes of the central municipalities of each urban agglomeration for the last year for which figures are available (1995). The data reveals that the large cities, with a few variations, conform to the general outlines given above (Centro de Estidios de Planificación (CEP), 1996).

In practice, local taxes (property tax, business tax, vehicle tax and other minor categories) represent on average approximately 33 per cent of total income. Charges and income from assets produce around 14 and 1.5 per cent respectively of the total. Therefore, the municipality's non-financial income from its own sources constitutes on average half (47 per cent) of the total income of the seven cities under discussion. The other half comes from inter-administrative transfers (36 per cent) and public debt. In absolute terms, in 1995 the central municipalities obtained non-financial, budgetary income of 406,114 million pesetas, representing 53,166 pesetas per capita.

In the field of public spending, we must differentiate at the outset between spending related to the obligatory services that municipalities must, by law, provide, and spending related to other demands and needs (Bosch and Espasa, 1994). With respect to mandatory services, significant differences in per capita spending can be observed among the large cities: ranging from 21,675 pesetas per capita annually in Seville, to 38,891 pesetas in Bilbao (1992 data). Possibly, these variations can be attributed, among other factors, to each municipality's position with respect to its metropolitan surroundings. Central municipalities

Table 14.10 Budget review structure of the seven central municipalities, 1995 (million PTA)

	Barcelona		Bilbao		Madrid		Málaga		Sevilla		Valencia		Zaragoza	
	Total	%	Total	%	Total	%	Total	%	Total	%	Total	%	Total	%
Non-financial own revenue	132,494	50.21	21,613	46.96	138,373	51.77	19,059	44.17	26,369	30.61	36,119	51.64	32,088	51.05
Chapter 1 Direct taxes	86,226	32.68	9,792	21.28	92,071	34.44	13,487	31.26	17,670	20.51	23,396	33.45	17,496	27.84
Property tax	42,860	16.24	4,253	9.24	38,637	14.45	6,730	15.60	8,643	10.03	12,606	18.02	7,853	12.49
Vehicle tax	11,301	4.28	1,555	3.38	14,747	5.52	2,029	4.70	2,890	3.35	3,368	4.81	2,636	4.19
Business tax	24,689	9.36	3,178	6.90	27,128	10.15	3,524	8.17	4,917	5.71	5,392	7.71	5,228	8.32
Chapter 2 Indirect taxes	2,360	0.89	1,307	2.84	9,709	3.63	506	1.17	1,072	1.24	2,429	3.47	2,638	4.20
Chapter 3 Other income	37,122	14.07	10,012	21.75	31,270	11.70	3,575	8.29	7,367	8.55	9,859	14.09	11,7769	18.73
Chapter 5 Patrimonial income	6,786	2.57	502	1.09	5,323	1.99	1,491	3.46	259	0.30	435	0.62	184	0.29
Transfers	86,332	32.72	18,075	39.27	92,726	34.69	19,179	44.45	25,153	29.20	27,658	39.54	19,813	31.52
Chapter 4 Current transfers	82,619	31.31	17,085	37.12	91,458	34.22	18,773	43.51	25,153	29.20	27,011	38.62	18,105	28.81
Chapter 7 Capital transfers	3,712	1.41	990	2.15	1,268	0.47	407	0.94	–	–	647	0.93	1,708	2.72
Real investments alienation (Chap. 6)	1,234	0.47	284	0.62	–	–	0	0.00	25	0.03	373	0.53	200	0.32
Financial revenue	43,820	16.61	6,054	13.15	36,200	13.54	4,907	11.37	34,604	40.17	5,798	8.29	10,751	17.11
Chapter 8 Financial assets	0	0.00	1,754	3.81	200	0.07	228	0.53	128	0.15	38	0.05	469	0.75
Chapter 9 Financial liabilities	43,820	16.61	4,300	9.34	36,000	13.47	4,679	10.84	34,476	40.02	5,760	8.23	10,282	16.36
Total revenue	263,880	100.00	46,026	100.00	267,299	100.00	43,145	100.00	86,151	100.00	69,949	100.00	62,853	100.00

Source: Centro de Estudios de Planificación (1996), *Evolución de las grandes magnitudes presupuestarias y contables de las grandes cuidades españolas en el periodo 1991–1995*, Ayuntamiento de Barcelona.

Table 14.11 Evolution of the share of local, autonomous and central governments with regard to total public expenditure in Spain (percentage data, 1981–95)

Year	Total consolidated expenditure				Non-financial consolidated expenditure			
	Central gov't	Autonomous gov't	Local gov't	Total expenditure	Central gov't	Autonomous gov't	Local gov't	Total expenditure
1981	86.95	2.88	10.17	100.00	87.33	2.95	9.72	100.00
1982	84.29	5.91	9.80	100.00	84.57	6.08	9.35	100.00
1983	80.09	7.62	12.29	100.00	80.22	7.92	11.86	100.00
1984	75.96	11.54	12.50	100.00	75.65	12.20	12.15	100.00
1985	74.11	13.12	12.76	100.00	73.15	14.12	12.73	100.00
1986	73.84	13.39	12.77	100.00	72.62	14.60	12.78	100.00
1987	72.30	14.93	12.77	100.00	71.28	16.13	12.59	100.00
1988	68.49	17.85	13.66	100.00	67.29	19.34	13.37	100.00
1989	67.59	18.33	14.08	100.00	66.44	19.75	13.81	100.00
1990	68.02	18.25	13.73	100.00	65.78	20.21	14.01	100.00
1991	66.89	19.46	13.65	100.00	64.78	21.51	13.71	100.00
1992	66.87	19.94	13.19	100.00	64.27	22.35	13.38	100.00
1993	66.95	20.28	12.77	100.00	64.18	22.76	13.05	100.00
1994	67.76	20.46	11.78	100.00	64.98	22.85	12.17	100.00
1995	67.58	21.22	11.20	100.00	65.46	23.27	11.27	100.00

Notes

1 Consolidated expenditure excludes transfers to other government levels.
2 Financial expenditure refers to Chapters 3 and 9 (Financial expenditure and Financial liabilities).

Source: Ministerio para las Administraciones Públicas (1995), *Informe Económico-Financiero de las Administraciones Territoriales en 1994.*

with smaller municipal areas, which therefore only encompass the very central areas of their respective agglomerations (which is the case of Bilbao, Valencia and Barcelona), incur higher costs per capita because they have to support a proportionally greater weight of the expenditure associated with central functions. What happens with spending on obligatory services is, therefore, the expression of a more generalized situation: the fact that large Spanish cities must support costs arising not just from the needs of their inhabitants, but also from the provision of services and infrastructure used by a large sector of the Spanish population as a whole, as well as by business and institutions.

It is this consideration that has led the mayors of the G-7 Group (the association formed by the seven largest municipalities in the country) to affirm that 'the organisation of the local fiscal system in general, and consequently the Ley de Financimiento de las Haciendas Locales (Local Government Finance Act) in particular, is proving increasingly inadequate as a means of providing municipalities with the resources they need' (Comunicado de Prensa, 1993, p. 2). In this context, they went on to say that, 'the problems of insufficient financing experienced by large cities are greater than those experienced by other municipalities' (Criterios para la Ley de Grandes Cuidades, 1996, p. 26). In fact, the complex financial situation of large cities forms part of the problem of Spanish local government financing and tax management, which is, to a large degree, a result of its highly subsidiary position with respect to the fiscal system as a whole (Ministerio para las Administraciones Públicas, 1995). Table 14.11 shows that, in 1995, the consolidated non-financial spending of local government in Spain represented only 11.3 per cent of total public expense, as compared to the expense of central government (65.5 per cent) and the autonomous communities (23.3 per cent). The data relating to the evolution of these figures even reflect a certain trend towards the reduction of the relative weight of local expense, both in proportion to other administrations, and, which is even more significant, in proportion to the GDP.

In light of this situation, the Federación Española de Municipios y Provincias (Spanish Federation of Municipalities and Provinces), and the mayors of the largest cities, have proposed a 'local pact' which would involve a redistribution of public spending among the administrative subsectors (Federación Española de Municipios y Provincias (FEMP), 1996; Criterios para la Ley de Grandes Cuidades, 1996). Under the terms of this proposed agreement, 50 per cent of total spending would correspond to the central government, and the rest would be divided equally between local government and the autonomous communities (Criterios para la Ley de Grandes Cuidades, 1996). It should be noted that, as a result of the extremely rapid growth of the last 15 years, the spending of the autonomous communities already represents close to 25 per cent.

Within the context of general containment of public spending and deficit, a plan for redistribution such as the one proposed should provably be based on an increase in the transfers from the other administrations to local government bodies. In fact, as we have seen, Spanish municipalities including those of the large cities depend twice as much on income from their own sources as they do on transfers from other administrations. This undoubtedly allows them a certain degree of financial autonomy, but in a situation characterized by increasing demands, it also gives rise to budgetary problems. It is, however, commonly agreed that, in general terms, the weight of local taxes as a proportion of total income cannot be further increased. Furthermore, as mentioned above, the debt level is already high. Nevertheless, the proposal to increase the weight of transfers is also fraught with complications (Castells and Bosch, 1993).

Transfers received by municipalities in the majority of cases correspond to their share of the general revenue of the state. The transfers received from the state are generic and therefore not tied to any particular use. The monies are distributed among local governments in order to guarantee a minimum income for each municipality, and according to population, relative fiscal contribution, and other minor considerations. The municipalities located in the Madrid and Barcelona metropolitan areas receive special consideration to compensate for expenses arising from the characteristics of these areas. For the municipalities of Spain taken overall, the total amount of share in the state income represents 3.65 per cent of the total, so that for the period 1994–98 funds distributed amounted to some 700,000 million pesetas annually (Chavero, 1995).

In addition, lesser contributions are also received from the European Union, the autonomous communities, and the provincial councils. In the large Spanish cities (with the exception of Bilbao owing to the particular characteristics of the Basque tax system) these contributions generally do not exceed 25 per cent of the total income received from transfers. As far as EU transfers are concerned, a fund providing 50,000 million pesetas annually has been established by the state for the period 1994–98, using monies coming from FEDER programmes and the European Cohesion Fund. A total of 30,000 million of this fund is being used to finance infrastructure operations in municipalities of over 50,000 inhabitants (Landaburu, 1993; Chavero, 1995).

The autonomous communities have also established and begun to provide for local cooperation funds. For the large Spanish cities overall, the total amount of inter-administrative transfers received in 1995 amounted to some 288,937 million pesetas (280,204 of which came from current transfers and 8,737 from capital transfers). This represents 37,826 pesetas per capita.

The solution proposed by the city councils of the G-7 Group calls for the creation of a specific fund for transfers to large cities that would form part of the general state budget. The amount to be allocated to this fund would be calculated on the basis of the real cost of the services provided by the city governments. At the same time, the cities also propose that the autonomous communities should allocate part (5 per cent) of the percentage of personal income tax collected by them to contribute to the Fondos Autonómicos de Transferencia de Cooperación Local (Regional Funds for Local Cooperation Transfers), which as we have seen currently account for only a insignificant part of the transfers received by the municipalities (Criterios para la Ley de Grandes Cuidades, 1996).

The Specific Problems of Large Cities: Challenges and Opportunities

As we have seen, the large Spanish cities are currently going through a pronounced process of change affecting their economic base as well as their physical structure. The modernization and opening up of the Spanish economy, a process which accelerated after the country became fully integrated into the European Community in 1986, has brought about large scale structural adjustments. These changes have played a particularly significant role in the economies of the principal cities, which moreover constitute the principal motor of the ongoing transformation. The economic structure of the large Spanish cities is, therefore, in the throes of an acute process of modernization, flexibilization and tertiarization, as has been noted in the first section.

These economic transformations have been accompanied – and this is no mere coincidence – by an intensification of the dynamics of metropolitan expansion and integration. These dynamics have led to the expansion of large cities into new areas, which in most cases are characterized by low density urban development. As a result, the traditional and characteristic Spanish urban model, a very dense and compact one, is gradually being replaced by more diffuse and less dense development. Furthermore, these new urban areas are clearly supra-municipal in character and consequently their administration, planning and financing poses specific problems.

Undoubtedly, the processes of change described in the previous sections give Spanish cities new potential and increased capacity. Firstly, the diversification and opening up of their economies together with the change of scale brought about by their expansion tend to make them more competitive in the international arena. Secondly, the tendency of population, facilities, and activity in general to be relocated in a more diffuse manner throughout the whole metropolitan area is creating a more integrated and relatively more homogeneous whole. However, the current dynamics of change also involve a considerable number of problems and unknowns, the most important of which are described below, grouped into six broad categories: accessibility, travel patterns, the environment, housing, social problems and governance.

Accessibility: Growth in Demand and Infrastructural Deficiencies

The internationalization of the Spanish urban economies has resulted in an extraordinary increase in their external connections. The consequent increase in demand has not, despite the efforts made, met with an adequate response in the provision of infrastructure. The deficiencies in the road system and the transport infrastructure in general are, therefore, one of the principal bottlenecks holding back the development of large Spanish cities.

In 1995, airport traffic in the seven large cities (with the exception of Zaragoza where the air traffic is low) accounted for the movement of 41.8 million passengers, representing 76.6 per cent of the total traffic for peninsular Spain. Passenger travel increased between 1991 and 1995 by 21.4 per cent despite the economic recession during part of this period. Of particular interest are the figures relating to the absolute increases experienced over the last five years by Madrid (which gained five million passengers and reached a total of 19.6 million), Barcelona (showing a gain of 2.3 million and surpassing 11.3 million in total number of passengers), and Málaga (which gained 1.4 million to reach a total of over 6.3 million). However, recent studies on air traffic have shown that Spanish cities have a relative accessibility by air very much below that of other European cities. If we consider London as having an index of 100 and Paris one of 99, the largest peninsular Spanish airports, Madrid and Barcelona, would be situated at 73 and 67 respectively (Bruinsma and Rietveld, 1993; Gutiérrez Puebla et al., 1996). This situation, together with the increase in demand, has resulted in problems of congestion, which threaten to saturate the system, particularly in the Madrid-Barajas and Barcelona-El Prat airports. The *Plan Director de Infraestructuras 1993–2007* (National Plan for Infrastructure), estimates that, to overcome these problems, investment in airport expansion and the improvement of the aerial navigation control system for all the state airports will amount to 800,000 million and 200,000 million pesetas respectively (in 1992 pesetas). Specific and more recent calculations for the Madrid and Barcelona airports reveal the need for an investment of 203,000 and 154,000 million pesetas respectively for these two facilities (excluding improvement of access roads) (MECSA, 1995; Barcelona Regional, 1996).

The tonnage of goods transported by sea has also increased considerably. The ports of Barcelona, Bilbao, Málaga, Seville and Valencia together handle some 80 million MT of cargo, a figure that has increased 9.3 per cent between 1992 and 1995. The increase in the volume of general cargo handled, 42.5 per cent in four years, has been particularly notable. The ports with the largest absolute increases are Valencia and Barcelona (in bulk and general cargo), and Bilbao (which despite a decrease in bulk cargo showed a notable increase in general cargo). These three ports, together with Algeciras (which is also closely related to the Seville area), form the basic structure of the port system of peninsular Spain. Valencia and Barcelona primarily handle traffic from the Pacific and Indian Oceans (via the Suez canal), and Bilbao and Algeciras deal primarily with traffic from the Atlantic. Once again, however, the infrastructure suffers from significant limitations affecting the docking facilities as well as the support facilities on land, and road and rail access. The projected expansion of the ports of Bilbao and Barcelona, and the improvement of access to same are particularly important projects owing to their large scale, and because they involve the creation of logistic centres. The investment needed to implement the *Plan Director de Infraestructuras* in this area have been evaluated at 800,000 million pesetas for the Spanish port system as a whole (Huertas and Barreiro, 1993; MOPTMA, 1994).

The increase in land transport has also been notable: traffic on the state road system doubled between 1985 and 1996 with respect to both light and heavy vehicles. Road infrastructure has increased greatly in the past 15 years, with the total route length of high capacity roads (motorways and trunk roads) rising from 1,933 km in 1980 to 8,133 in 1995. Despite this, the density of the system both in km/km^2 and in km/1,000 inhabitants is still considerably below the European average. Furthermore, the railway system, most of which has a different gauge from the rest of Europe, is not growing, and the number of kilometres of track in the system actually decreased between 1980 and 1995 (from 15,724 km to 14,291 km) (Ministerio de Fomento, 1996a). Passenger and freight traffic have also stagnated. The first high speed line did not come into service until 1992, and Madrid and Seville are the only large Spanish cities connected by the TGV (RENFE, 1993; Inglada, 1994). Plans for expansion include the connection of Madrid with the French border via Zaragoza and Barcelona, as well as links between Madrid and the Basque Country (MOPTMA, 1994). These two operations have been classified in this order as high priority projects, and they have been selected as one of the 14 higher priority projects in the EU within the framework of the Trans-European Networks Scheme (Vázquez and Álvarez, 1995; European Union, 1996). There are also plans for TGV links between Madrid and Valencia, and Málaga and Córdoba. Upon completion of these connections, the seven largest Spanish cities will be integrated into the European highspeed rail system. For the period 1993–2007, the *Plan Director de Infraestructuras* estimates the investment needs for the general road system at 2,920,000 million pesetas for connecting roads and high capacity roads, and at 1,718,000 million for the development of the highspeed rail system (MOPTMA, 1994).

A final element in the description of communication infrastructure is the field of telecommunications. In this area, Spain has also recently emerged from a poor situation. However, in the last few years, development in this area has been very rapid. Between 1988 and 1995, the installed base of telephone lines went from 12 to 16.3 million (Ministerio de Fomento, 1996a). During the same period, the number of lines in service per 100 inhabitants rose from 28.1 to 38.5. In order to plan and promote development in this field, the state passed the Plan Nacional de Telecomunicaciones 1991–2002 (National Telecommunications Plan), with important financial provisions that are detailed below (MOPTMA, 1995a). With respect to telecommunications and high technology research and production, there are nine technology parks in Spain, six of which are in the major Spanish cities (Asociación de Parques Tecnológicos de España, 1996).

Daily Travel Patterns: Increasing Demand and the Predominance of the Private Vehicle

As indicated above, the expansion of the metropolitan areas is bringing with it the dispersion of population, jobs and services across increasingly wider urban areas. Logically, these processes are complemented by new forms of functional specialization and urban hierarchization, which in turn lead to an increase in the travel needs of the citizens. Consequently, the number and length of mechanized trips per inhabitant is increasing consistently in all of the large Spanish cities for which data is available (Torres et al., 1990; Ministerio de Fomento, 1996b).

The private vehicle accounts for an ever increasing proportion of travel, so that now public transport (underground, bus and commuter trains) only predominates with respect to internal trips within the municipalities of Madrid and Barcelona, and to the connections between these cities and their metropolitan belts. The seven large cities and their respective provinces account for 44.1 per cent of all vehicles in the country, and the vehicle ownership rate is 486 vehicles/1,000 inhabitants. In the seven municipal capitals, the average rate is 516 vehicles/1,000 inhabitants compared to a Spanish average of 466. Moreover, 60.6 per cent of all accidents involving injuries that occur within urban zones in Spain now happen within these seven provinces where, particularly in the case of Madrid and Barcelona, this type of accident represents an ever-growing proportion of total accidents.

The increasing use of private vehicles has logically resulted in an unprecedented increase in the congestion of the accesses to the cities, and a concurrent decrease in the commercial speed of surface public transport, while also affecting energy consumption and atmospheric pollution. The entry into service of new ring roads (such as the M40 in Madrid, the 'Rondas' in Barcelona, and the Seville, Málaga and Valencia ring roads), despite the fact that they have provided a temporary respite, cannot in any way be considered to represent a definitive solution to this problem.

To deal with this situation, the Spanish government has instigated the elaboration of a series of intermodal transport plans for the main urban areas with the object of integrating the activities of the different public administrations in this field, coordinating traffic management, and making a determined effort to promote public transport (García Alcolea and Marinas, 1993). The intermodal transport plans for the seven large metropolitan areas are currently being drafted. The investment required to finance these plans has been estimated at 2,215,000 million pesetas (this includes the plans for the seven largest urban agglomerations together with those for the central area of Asturias and the Bay of Cádiz) (MOPTMA, 1994).

Housing: High Prices and Difficulty of Access

The demand for housing in large Spanish cities has been affected in recent years by the coming of age of the generations born during the 'baby boom' of the '60s and early '70s. This demographic factor has been accentuated by a decrease in the average household size, a generalized phenomenon in many European countries which in Spain has meant a decrease from 3.9 persons per dwelling in 1970 to 3.3 in 1991. The resulting growth of demand has coincided with a significant increase in house prices and rents, so that a considerable segment of the population living in large cities currently experiences considerable difficulty in acquiring or renting a home (Cortés, 1995).

In effect, the housing needs in urban and metropolitan Spain for the period 1991–2011 have been estimated to be 1,443,087 units on newly developed land, 83 per cent of which is situated in municipalities of over 50,000 inhabitants. To satisfy this demand would require the development of 36,000 hectares of previously unserviced land, an area equivalent to over three-quarters of the total area of land currently urbanized in the Barcelona metropolitan region.

Average house production during the period 1981–91 was 248,023 units per year, representing a total increase in the housing stock of 16.8 per cent for the decade. However, it should be noted that in Spain the proportion of unoccupied dwellings and secondary residences is very high: of the 17.2 million existing dwellings, only 11.7 million are principal residences, while secondary residences and unoccupied dwellings account for 3 and 2.5 million respectively. Furthermore, the number of properties in need of replacement or rehabilitation is high since, in the cities of over 500,000 inhabitants, for example, more than 20 per cent of residential buildings have more or less serious defects. Finally, it should be noted that the availability of houses and flats for rent is among the lowest in Europe in relative terms; in urban areas 76.2 per cent of homes are owned by their inhabitants (Ministerio de Fomento, 1996b).

The price of housing rose very rapidly during the period of expansion 1986–91, when prices in urban areas doubled in general terms. Since 1991, prices have stabilized, and even slightly decreased (Leal and Cortés, 1995; Clusa, 1995; Naredo, 1996). However, the price of a new home in the municipalities of Barcelona, Madrid and Bilbao is still over 200,000 pesetas/m^2 of floor space, and in Málaga, Seville, Valencia and Zaragoza ranges from 110,000 to 145,000 pesetas/m^2. This represents an average price for a 100 m^2 dwelling of over 20,000,000 in the largest municipalities, and in any case more than ten million in the rest. The differences in price between the central municipalities and their metropolitan surroundings are considerable (prices in Madrid and Barcelona are 1.65 and 1.56 times higher respectively than in their metropolitan belts). The relationship of these prices to the average annual income per Spanish household was estimated for 1994 at over seven times the average income for the Madrid metropolitan area, and more than six times the average income for the Barcelona metropolitan area. For Spain as a whole the economic effort required to purchase a home amounts to 4.6 times the average annual household income (Ministerio de Fomento, 1996b).

Taken together, these factors reveal that, in general terms, the problem of housing is more one of affordability than availability. In an attempt to improve this situation, the state, in collaboration with the autonomous communities, has implemented the Plan Nacional de Vivienda (National Housing Plan), the objective of which is to facilitate access to housing to those for whom this is impossible under current market conditions. Accordingly, in addition to the tax deductions currently allowed for the purchase of a home, a system of direct subsidies was set up to help families with low purchasing power to acquire certain types of dwellings (MOPTMA, 1995b). However, as will be shown below, the impact of the plan – which has been extended for the period 1996–99 – in the large cities has been greatly diminished by the high price of land. In fact, the repercussion of the price of land in the final price of the dwelling is such that the majority of new homes reach the market at prices that make them ineligible for subsidies because they exceed the maximum price limits established by the plan.

The Environment: High Land Occupation and Limited Control of Waste Water, Solid Waste and Contamination

The expansion of the city – of which one of the principal causes is precisely the differences in the price of land and housing in different areas – is also having great impact on the environment. The most important consequence is obviously the high consumption of land. In fact, it has been asserted that the large Spanish cities have occupied as much land over the last 30 years as in their entire previous history (Ministerio de Fomento, 1996c). In the Barcelona metropolitan region, for example, it has been estimated that the amount of urban land went from 21,482 hectares in 1972 to 45,036 in 1992 (Serratosa, 1994). In Madrid, for the period 1957–80, José M. Naredo has calculated that the occupied area per inhabitant doubled, which is even more significant in view of the demographic growth during the same period (Naredo, 1994). The areas affected by this phenomenon are mostly flat areas, coastal sections, fertile lands, plains and deltas (and this occasionally causes conflicts with agricultural activities, for example in l'Horta de Valencia and the Llobregat delta in Barcelona). Furthermore, besides mortgaging future use, the increase in urban land area tends to isolate open spaces in metropolitan surroundings and make them increasingly marginal.

Another crucial environmental problem is caused by the inadequate control of the water cycle. Water use is very high in Spain as a whole (Dirección General de Planificación Territorial, 1995; Segura, 1995). The country ranks amongst those of the world with higher water consumption per inhabitant (some 300 litres daily per inhabitant). Experts agree that these figures are disproportionate for a country that receives less than 600 litres/m^2 of rainfall annually over most of its territory, and where precipitation is characterized by its lack of regularity. Despite the fact that the high consumption has its origin primarily in agrarian irrigation, this lack of water is an important conditioning factor in the development of large Spanish cities. In addition, water treatment is only available to 40.6 per cent of the equivalent population served (calculated according to Community Directive 91/271). Infrastructure is now under construction which will shortly make possible treatment of water for 12 per cent more of the equivalent population (Martínez Císcar, 1995; MOPTMA, 1995). Thus, despite the great efforts made in recent years in this field, the levels are still far from those required by European regulations.

Pollution of the atmosphere with sulphur dioxide (SO_2) and smoke are at acceptable average levels in the large Spanish cities. However, seasonal fluctuations mean that the limit values are sometimes above permitted levels (particularly in Madrid during the winter months) (Monzón et al., 1995). Nonetheless, the data reveal that in the three largest cities (Barcelona, Madrid and Valencia) the average levels of SO_2 and smoke are currently reducing sharply.

Soil contamination also continues to affect large areas, and some sites of great seriousness exist within metropolitan areas. According to 1994 data, there are 18,142 industrial facilities which, because of their characteristics, were potential sources of edaphic contamination, and 4,532 potentially polluting sites. Some 75.5 per cent of the former and 57 per cent of the latter were located in the six autonomous communities where the largest metropolitan areas are situated (Andalusia, Aragon, the Basque Country, Catalonia, Madrid, and Valencia) (MOPTMA, 1995d).

Finally, solid urban and industrial waste produced in Spain amounts to 14 million tons annually, a third of which is handled without appropriate control. The production of dangerous waste has been estimated (for 1994) at 3.4 million tons. Some 54.6 per cent of this is generated in the six autonomous communities listed above (MOPTMA, 1995e; Ministerio de Fomento, 1996c).

The Spanish government, the autonomous communities and local governments have taken different steps to improve this situation. With respect to land use, it was noted in the *Agenda Habitat* document (Spain) that 'over the last fifteen years the area of protected natural spaces in the country has multiplied by a factor of thirteen and, with an area of 3 million hectares, today represents over 40 per cent of the European total' (Ministerio de Fomento, 1996c, p. 12). In addition, in 1995, national plans for the treatment of waste water, dangerous waste and for the recuperation of contaminated land were approved which call for a total investment of over two billion pesetas. The content of these plans is detailed in the next section.

The Social Problems: High Unemployment, an Ageing Population, and Poverty

From the point of view of social questions, unemployment is undoubtedly the main problem affecting large Spanish cities. Despite the continued growth of the GDP (2.59 per cent annual accumulative in the last 15 years), and the internationalization of the Spanish economy, the economy does not generate enough employment for the country's population (Fernández et al., 1991). Consequently, the rate of economically active population remains one of the lowest in Europe: 50.9 per cent for Spain as a whole and 51.6 per cent for the seven largest metropolitan areas. The delay in the incorporation of women into the labour force has been one of the main causes of this low rate.

The low rate of economically active population coincides with an extremely high rate of unemployment. In 1995, a total of 2.5 million people was registered as unemployed in the country as a whole, and the mean unemployment rate in Spain was 16.3 per cent. The seven large metropolitan areas had, overall, a slightly higher rate of unemployment than the country as a whole, and were home to some 900,000 unemployed persons. There are, however, important differences between cities. The areas of Barcelona, Zaragoza and Madrid have an unemployment rate lower therefore than the average for the country. Bilbao and Valencia have slightly higher unemployment than the national average. And Seville and Málaga, with registered unemployment figures close to 25 per cent, are among the urban areas in Europe with the worst employment conditions.

It should also be stressed that substantial differences also occur within each area. The central municipalities have in all cases unemployment rates lower than their respective metropolitan belts, to the point that the rates in the municipalities of Barcelona and Madrid are close to the European average. The unemployment rate for the population resident in the metropolitan belts is also higher in all cases than that of the rest of the respective provinces.

A second source of concern from the point of view of social questions, is the progressive ageing of the population of the large Spanish cities (Pérez, 1996; Vinuesa, 1996). This phenomenon is the result of the combination of an increase in life expectancy and low birth rates. In the urban centres, the trend is accentuated by the exodus of the young population of childbearing age. Thus, while the ageing rate for Spain as a whole is 0.61, in the seven metropolitan areas it can be as high as 0.63. Once again, however, there are important variations between the different areas. Barcelona, Zaragoza and Bilbao have ageing rates higher than the Spanish mean, while in the rest of the metropolitan areas the rate is lower than the mean. The areas of Seville and Málaga stand out in this respect owing to the youthfulness of their demographic structure. The difference between the ageing urban centres, and the younger metropolitan belts is particularly notable in the case of Barcelona (where 18.5 per cent of the population of the central municipality is over 65 years of age), and also in Madrid.

High unemployment rates, the ageing of the population and other factors (such as the precarious employment conditions and differences in levels of training and education) mean that some segments of the population of the large Spanish metropolitan areas endure grave living conditions (Córdoba and García, 1991; FOESSA, 1995). The proportion of Spanish households with an income of less than 50 per cent of the national average (which has conventionally been defined as the poverty line) is 19.4 per cent. The situation is worse in four metropolitan provinces Zaragoza, Valencia, Seville and Málaga where the percentage of households living below what is considered to be the poverty line is over 20 per cent. The provinces of Madrid, Bilbao and Barcelona, on the other hand, have a much lower incidence of poverty. Households whose members are old people, and those where the head of the family is a woman are particularly prone to be affected by poverty.

The schemes implemented by the public authorities to deal with these problems are not, in the main, specific to urban areas, but they have had a profound affect on such areas. In the field of social policies, it should be indicated that over the last 15 years the scope of unemployment has been increased to the point where benefit is received by 50.7 per cent of unemployed persons. There has also been an extension in the payment of public pensions to people who, for various reasons, did not contribute to pension schemes before retirement. Finally, the state has made access to the Social Security health system universally available, and now guarantees public and obligatory education up to the age of 16. These policies (together with other factors, such as the solidity of family networks) have undoubtedly slowed down the process of social dualization, which social problems like those described above might have given rise to in the large Spanish cities (Zaldívar and Castells, 1992; Gavira, 1996).

The Administrative Question: the Cost of Institutional Fragmentation

To close this section on the challenges faced by the large Spanish cities, the problems that arise from their administrative organization should be mentioned. It has been explained above how one of the principal characteristics of the Spanish metropolitan areas is the institutional fragmentation and administrative complexity of the local government structure (Barrero, 1993). In certain cases, this reaches extremes (for example in the metropolitan region of Barcelona, where in a area of 3236 km^2 there are 202 governing bodies belonging to six different tiers of local government), making the administrative structure of large Spanish cities confusing and potentially conflictive.

There are numerous disadvantages associated with this situation. In the first place, loss of efficiency, owing to the difficulties of coordination and the prevalence of sectorial and local viewpoints in the actions of institutions and public companies. The administrative costs are also high owing to bureaucratic hypertrophy and, very commonly, institutional redundancy. This situation also produces difficulties with respect to legitimacy and accountability, owing to the complexity of the administrative apparatus and the fact that the constituencies where the representatives are elected fail to correspond to the reality of the citizens' urban experience. And finally, there are institutional costs, such as the loss of capacity for negotiation and representation when dealing with third parties (companies, administrations, European institutions, etc.) (Nel.lo, 1995).

The reform needed to adapt the administration and planning procedures to the new metropolitan situation is, as has been explained, a task that falls under the jurisdiction, in the first place, to the state and to the autonomous communities, and it is still in an preliminary stage. The advances achieved to date on the local level in the creation of mechanisms of coordination and concentration continue to be modest. In the following section we will analyze some of the work being done in this sphere, and the national policies that apply in the large cities.

The National Policies Affecting Cities

Spanish cities today are at a crossroads. Previous sections of this document detail the ways in which large urban areas have consolidated their pre-eminence over the Spanish urban system as a whole, and are continually expanding to integrate an ever larger area. At the same time, as their economies have opened up to international markets, these cities have experienced a rapid increase in connections and relations with the exterior. In this context, they have had to modernize their economies by way of complex structural adjustments, and in general they have managed to accomplish this without destroying their social cohesion. Many more facilities and much more extensive urban infrastructure exist now than just 15 years ago, and during this period a democratic system of local government has been established. The large Spanish cities have, therefore, experienced rapid improvement, have seen the quality of life of their inhabitants improve, and are now more competitive and attractive in the context of the international scene.

However, it is also true that the cost of this process has been significant, and that significant deficiencies persist in infrastructure, the environment and the social arena. An adverse consequence of the economic transformation has been the creation of a high rate of structural unemployment. This is particularly bad in some urban areas, and can drive sections of the population into situations of poverty and social marginalization. It has also been noted that if finding work is a problem for broad sections of the urban population, access to housing, a basic requirement for enjoying urban living, is no less a problem. Furthermore, serious questions have been raised about the functionality, social equitableness and ecological viability of the urban growth model that has emerged, which involves increasingly extensive urbanization. Finally, large Spanish cities still suffer from notable infrastructural deficiencies, which limit their proper internal functioning and hinder access from the outside.

The current situation is, therefore, characterized by significant potential on the one hand, and important challenges on the other. The policies and projects drawn up and implemented by the different levels of public administration play a key role in the effort being made to take advantage of this potential and meet these challenges. With respect to national policies relating to cities, that is those implemented by the national government, it should be noted that at present no single integrated policy exists (Arias, 1996; Ministerio de Fomento, 1996a). This is in part owing to the decentralization of the Spanish administrative structure, which grants important powers in this area to the autonomous communities. However, as stated in the working document presented by the Spanish government at the *Habitat 2* conference in June 1996, it is also true that 'neither is there any national policy for cities that develops inter-administrative co-operation' (Ministerio de Fomento, 1996c, p. 12).

In this context, the principal national initiatives relating to cities are: the *Plan Director de Infraestructuras*, the *Plan de Vivienda* (the Housing Plan), the sectorial plans for the environment, and the *Plan Nacional de Telecomunicaciones*. It should be noted that these measures were mainly adopted in recent years by governments of socialist orientation. Their continued implementation may be influenced in the future by the change of government which occurred in Spring 1996. A brief account is given below of the content of these plans. Also described because of its relevance to this field is the *Draft Bill on Urgent Measures* for large Spanish cities, which has been drafted by the mayors of the seven largest cities.

The Plan Director de Infraestructuras and the Competitiveness of the Cities

The *Plan Director de Infraestructuras 1993–2007*, approved by the cabinet on 4 March 1994, was conceived as 'the fundamental instrument of State regional policy' (MOPTMA, 1994). The plan's central aim is to provide a framework for strategic global planning with respect to the basic infrastructure for transportation, waterworks and the environment that would deal with the accumulated deficiencies in this field (Gutiérrez and Monzón, 1993; Vigil, 1993; Vázquez and Álvarez, 1993; Ministerio de Fomento, 1996a).

In order to fulfil this objective, the PDI proposes going beyond sectorial policies and defines an integrated policy for infrastructure based on five criteria: increasing the competitiveness and productivity of the territory as a whole; promoting balanced development among different areas; improving the quality of life and standard of living of the population; fostering responsible resource management while internalizing environmental costs; and guaranteeing the conservation of the historical and cultural heritage of the country. In short, the plan proposes the design of a policy on infrastructure that would serve as an instrument of regional policies.

The plan involves action in four broad areas: inter-urban transport, urban transport, waterworks, and environmental infrastructure. The proposed lines of action are shown in Table 14.12, and entail a total investment of some 18.7 billion pesetas for the period 1993–2007. In principle, 70 per cent of this financing will come from the general state budget; the rest will come from non-budgetary sources, involving private financing and user payment. Expenditure on interurban transit, amounting to some 10.7 billion pesetas, accounts for the largest portion of this investment (details of the most important items in this field have been described in the previous section). Other large items are investments in urban transport (3.4 billion), waterworks (2.2 billion), environmental infrastructure (1.8 billion), and coastal projects (0.4 billion).

Because of their impact on large cities, a more detailed description of the

Table 14.12 Summary of the valuation of the National Plan to Infrastructure actions (thousand million PTA)

Action programme	Total plan		General state budget		Extra-budget financing	
	Total	Annual average	Total	Annual average	Total	Annual average
Interurban transport	10,739	715.9	7,383	492.2	3,356	223.7
Roads	5,468	364.5	5,223	348.2	245	16.3
Railways	3,222	214.8	1,981	132.1	1,241	82.7
Harbours	800	53.3			800	53.3
Airports	1,000	66.7			1,000	66.7
Combined transport	121	8.1	101	6.7	20	1.3
Environmental actions	128	8.5	78	5.2	50	3.3
Urban transport	3,440	229.3	2,752	183.5	688	45.9
Transport intermodal plans in metropolitan areas	2,215	147.7	1,658	110.5	557	37.1
Urban sectoral actions	1,105	73.7	1,025	68.3	80	5.3
Improvement of urban environment actions	75	5.0	60	4.0	15	1.0
Concerted transport and urban actions	45	3.0	9	0.6	36	2.4
Hyrdaulic actions	2,225	148.3	2,225	148.3		
Growth of hyrdaulic resources	890	59.3	890	59.3		
Flooding protection and improvement and environment protection	550	36.7	55	36.7		
General interest irrigations	375	25.0	375	25.0		
Replacement, conservation and other actions	410	27.3	410	27.3		
Environmental infrastructures	1,854	123.6	573	38.2	1,281	85.4
Adjusting of water quality	1,500	100.0	325	21.7	1,175	78.3
Urban solid residues actions			160	10.7	160	10.7
Industrial residues actions	169	11.3	63	4.2	106	7.1
Equipamientos de vigilancia y control	25	1.7	25	1.7		
Coast actions	450	30.0	225	15.0	225	15.0
Improvement, enlargement and regeneration of beaches and other litoral sites	272	18.1	136	9.1	136	9.1
Rehabilitation of the seaside and coast defences	158	10.5	79	5.3	79	5.3
Accessibility to beaches and seaside	20	1.3	10	0.7	10	0.7
Research and development	45	3.0	15	1.0	30	2.0
Total actions	18,753	1,250.2	13,173	878.2	5,580	372.0

Source: MOPTMA (1994), *Plan Director de Infraestructuras 1993–2007*, 2nd edn.

planned urban transport projects is necessary. In line with its overall approach, the PDI proposes to carry out urban transport projects within the framework of a strategy for integrated action in the cities (García Alcolea and Marinos, 1993; Fernández Lafuente, 1994; Ministerio de Fomento, 1996a). This integrated strategy will be implemented by the government in accordance with the guidelines laid down in the plan, and its application in each city will be by agreement with the respective authorities (autonomous communities and local governments). The lines of action contemplated include the following programmes (for budgetary details see Table 14.12) (MOPTMA, 1994):

- intermodal transport plans. The object is to provide every large city with a plan for the configuration of an integrated transport system. It also aims to define and promote the role played by mass transport in these systems. As noted above, it is foreseen that the seven large Spanish metropolitan areas will each have an intermodal plan in the near future;
- sectorial actions in the urban context. These plans cover efforts undertaken in two fields: firstly road systems, to ensure the continuity of and access to the state system within urban agglomerations; and secondly the reorganization of railway systems passing through the cities;
- improvement of the urban environment. This programme covers a set of operations designed to facilitate the urban integration of transport infrastructure, and the reuse of land left vacant as a result of these changes;
- exceptional projects related to transport and urban planning. This heading covers a group of operations that are considered to be national projects because of their scale, complexity, repercussions on the city, national importance and international relevance. In these cases, the Spanish government promotes the creation of joint bodies and agreements between administrations which make it possible to work towards solutions that meet the needs of all the numerous agents involved. These operations normally include the improvement of the transport infrastructure (railways, roads, airports, etc.), their integration into the city, control of their environmental impact and the reuse of spaces left vacant as a result of modernization. The most characteristic projects are those dealing with the Ría de Bilbao and the Llobregat delta in Barcelona. Concerted projects of this type are also under way in Madrid (the Barajas and Campamento projects), Valencia (the Valencia intermodal scheme) and – outside of the seven largest cities – in Oviedo (the Oviedo green belt project).

The Plan Nacional de la Vivienda and the Right to the City

In Spain housing policy falls, in principle, under the jurisdiction of the autonomous communities. The central government is, however, responsible for monitoring the situation to ensure that the general conditions calculated to make housing available and accessible to all citizens are achieved and maintained. The citizen's right to housing is recognized by the Spanish constitution. As has been mentioned above, the evolution of the real estate market has been subjected in the last ten years to strong tensions, and prices have risen to levels outside the reach of a large section of the population. In order to deal with this situation, the state drew up and implemented the *Plan Nacional de la Vivienda 1992–1995* (National Housing Plan), mentioned above. This plan contemplated a series of measures including the provision of subsidies to aid prospective home buyers, fomenting the development of land suitable for construction, encouraging the renovation of real estate, etc. This plan, which was implemented by the autonomous communities by way of annual schemes, made it possible to finance, over the four-year period, more than 400,000 housing interventions, and to develop land for a further 100,000 dwellings (Carreras, 1994; Ministerio de Fomento, 1996a).

For the period 1996–99, the Spanish government, with the agreement of the autonomous communities, approved by way of the Royal Decree of 28 December 1995 the prolongation of the legislation in force with certain modifications. It is hoped that by using these measures, it will be possible to finance a total of 500,000 housing interventions during the four-year extension (MOPTMA, 1995). The total number of housing interventions foreseen in these agreements is 286,607, together with serviced land for 70,895 more, involving a total cost of 233,550 and 11,471 million pesetas respectively.

However, the application of these measures comes up against substantial problems in the large cities, as has been noted above. These problems are in the main caused by high land prices and construction costs, as a result of which practically all new housing in the major cities is ineligible for subsidies because the final price exceeds the maximum limit set for this purpose. Some of the modifications incorporated into the legislation, such as the reinforcement of the policies relating to urban renewal, and the creation of publicly owned and serviced land to be used for the construction of subsidized housing, could serve to remedy this situation to some degree.

The Environmental Plans and the Sustainability of Development

In the area of the environment, national policies relating to cities are covered by three plans: the *Plan Nacional de Saneamiento y Depuración de Aguas Residuales 1995–2005* (the National Plan for Treatment of Waste Water); the *Plan Nacional de Recuperación de Suelos Contaminados 1995–2005* (the National Plan for the Recovery of Contaminated Land); and the *Plan Nacional de Residuos Tóxicos y Peligrosos 1995–2000* (the National Plan for Dangerous Toxic Wastes). These three plans were approved by the cabinet on 17 February 1995.

The aim of the Plan Nacional de Saneamiento is 'to assure the quality of the treatment and dumping of urban waste waters in accordance with European Union standards by ensuring the integration and coherence of the actions taken by the three levels of administration', and to facilitate the development of adequate regulations (MOPTMA, 1995c, p. 13808). Total financing needs in this field in which the situation, as noted above, are still far from optimal have been estimated at 1.8 billion pesetas. 59 per cent of the needs are accounted for by the autonomous communities that contain the seven largest metropolitan areas. The central government and the European Cohesion Fund will finance 25 per cent of the investment up to the year 2005, and the balance will be paid by the regional governments. The majority of these governments have already established surcharges levied on consumption to cover the cost of the water treatment operations.

The objective of the *Plan Nacional de Recuperación de Suelos Contaminados* is to add to the inventory of contaminated areas already compiled and to undertake the recovery of 275 of these areas (MOPTMA, 1995d). These are the sites which, because of the danger they present, and in many cases because of their proximity to urban centres, require more urgent action. Total expenditure forecast for the period 1995–2005 is 132,000 million pesetas. 50 per cent of this amount will be provided by the central government, and the rest will be financed by the autonomous communities. The administrations will eventually be able to recover their expenditure through income generated by legal actions brought against the entities responsible for the contamination, and through the increase in value of the land that has been rehabilitated. 79.4 per cent of the investment needs forecast corresponds to the six autonomous communities having the largest metropolitan areas.

Finally, the *Plan Nacional de Residuos Peligrosos* has three primary objectives: the progressive reduction at source of general dangerous waste, the promotion of recycling and reuse, and the correct environmental treatment of waste (MOPTMA, 1995e). The total investment required to implement this plan has been estimated at 180,000 million pesetas for the period 1995–2000, of which 45.2 per cent is allocated to the reduction at source of dangerous waste, and 41.7 per cent for waste management. Some 25 per cent of the necessary funds will be provided by the central government, and the rest will come from the autonomous communities.

The Plan Nacional de Telecomunicaciones and the Informational City

The general framework for the regulation of telecommunications in Spain is provided by the Ley de Ordenación de las Telecomunicaciones (Telecommunications Act), passed in 1987. There is also a *Plan Nacional de Telecomunicaciones 1991–2002*, which was conceived as 'the basic instrument that directs the development and evolution of public, official and state-reserved civil telecommunications services, and of all the telecommunication infrastructure associated with such services' (MOPTMA, 1995a, p. 49). The plan called for a total investment of seven billion pesetas (in 1991 pesetas), of which 5.8 billion were allocated to the upgrading of public and para-public telecommunications infrastructures .

The accelerated development of this sector, and its progressive deregulation have led to the adoption of new regulatory measures, prominent among which are the Ley Reguladora de Telecomunicación por Satélite (which regulates satellite telecommunications) and the Ley Reguladora de Telecomunicación por Cable (which regulates telecommunications by cable), passed on 12 and 21 December 1995 respectively. The latter has specific repercussions on large cities. The Act establishes that territories will be defined in order to organize telecommunications services by cable. Each territory will be served by Telefónica de España SA and a second operator. Such operators will bid to obtain a concession from the government to provide the service in question, and will be obliged to provide the service throughout the entire territory. The territories may range from being part of a municipality to including a group of municipalities. They will have no fewer than 50,000 and no more than 2,000,000 inhabitants so that they could, in principle, exclude sparsely populated areas which would, therefore, be left out of the large groupings. To avoid this, the local administration has signed agreements in various autonomous communities that have made it possible to divide up the central metropolitan areas and group them with less populated areas. In this way groups of municipalities have been defined that cover the entire regional territory. The municipalities have also requested control over the licences for the occupation of land, subsoil and air by cable installations and other transmission elements; likewise the large cities have demanded the possibility of establishing and maintaining local telecommunications and telematic networks, including radio and television broadcast facilities.

The Draft Bill on Large Cities and the Governance of Urban Areas

The success of the policies affecting large urban areas largely depends on their governance. In fact, it is commonly accepted that the potential beneficial impact of national policies is diminished in urban areas lacking a balanced system of institutional relations. This is owing as much to the administrative difficulties of applying these national policies as to the possibility that parts of the urban area may make use of their administrative situation to appropriate benefits that would otherwise enrich the entire urban community.

Various proposals have been made in Spain regarding this question, some by the administration itself. In the first place, the *National Report* presented by the Spanish government at the *Second UN Conference on Human Settlement* held in June 1996. This report argues for the necessity of implementing urban policies through integrated schemes rather that solely sectorial schemes. In order to achieve this, the document proposes, on the one hand, the fostering of cooperation between administrations, and on the other, the strengthening of local autonomy and citizen participation (Ministerio de Fomento, 1996a).

In line with this proposal, the mayors of the seven largest Spanish cities (the G-7 group) have agreed to demand the elaboration of a Ley de Grandes Ciudades (Large Cities Act). The object of this Act, according to the criteria approved by the mayors in July 1996, will be precisely to introduce amendments into various sectorial national laws affecting their specific application to large cities. The proposed scope of the act would be 'cities whose government and administration poses singular problems owing to their large populations'. It is therefore considered that the Act should apply to the municipalities of Madrid, Barcelona, Valencia, Seville, Zaragoza, Málaga and Bilbao, 'and to the local government associations created around these municipalities to manage the utilities and services that would be regulated by the Ley de Grandes Ciudades' (Criterios para la Ley de Grandes Cuidades, 1996, p. 6-7).

The Act would cover a wide range of topics, and the regulation of these areas will tend to increase the capacity of local governments to intervene in these matters. Accordingly, the G-7 propose that specific measures be passed in relation to large cities, covering town planning, housing, the environment, infrastructure, public transport, taxation, finance, social policies, municipal justice, public safety and traffic management.

The governance of large Spanish cities depends to a large degree on the evolution of the debate on these proposals. And the success of national and European policies that are applied in these cities depends on their governance.

Summary and Conclusions

The Spanish Urban System and the Dynamics of the Transformation of its Largest Cities

Over the last four decades, urban areas in Spain have evolved more rapidly than at any other time in their history. Today, two out of three Spaniards live in urban areas, and the resident population of municipalities of over 100,000 inhabitants, some 16.8 million people, represents 41.5 per cent of the country's total population.

Seven large metropolitan areas – Barcelona, Bilbao, Madrid, Málaga, Seville, Valencia and Zaragoza – are at the head of the Spanish urban system, and are the principal motors of the Spanish economy. Together these areas are home to 33.8 per cent of the country's population, account for two-fifths of the industrial work force, and produce nearly half of the national gross added value.

The demographic growth of these large urban areas is now slowing down. In spite of this, the major Spanish agglomerations are expanding to include an ever larger area, and are becoming clearly supra-municipal metropolitan phenomena.

This rapid increase in the size of the major Spanish cities has been accompanied by structural adjustments of their economies, including a shift to the services sector as well as the flexibilization and internationalization of their economic base. As a result, despite the industrial tradition of some of the large Spanish cities, the relative weight of services is increasing, and this sector accounts now for over 60 per cent of the jobs in these areas.

The territorial expansion and economic transformation of the cities is also leading to the decentralization of both population and activities. As a result of these trends, large Spanish metropolitan areas are becoming more homogeneous spaces, in which the differences between the once totally dominant metropolitan centres and their surrounding areas (in terms of population density, employment, amenities, infrastructure and services) are being reduced. The growth in population, for example, is now in all cases greater in the metropolitan belts than in the central municipalities.

The Administrative Structure and Financing of Large Spanish Cities

The administrative structure of the major Spanish cities is characterized by territorial fragmentation and institutional complexity. In general, large Spanish cities lack administrative bodies responsible for metropolitan coordination.

Likewise, considerable fragmentation also exists in the area of town planning. With certain exceptions, in each metropolitan area there are in principle as many town plans as component municipalities. However, metropolitan planning guidelines are currently being drawn up for most of the seven major cities.

During the '90s, almost every major Spanish city has drawn up and implemented a strategic plan. In general, the central municipalities have taken the initiative in these projects with a view to mobilising local energies and promoting agreements that will further common aims, transcending administrative barriers and the fragmentation of physical planning.

Local government financing in the major Spanish cities depends more on the cities' own income than on transfers from other administrations. In the seven central municipalities, local taxes, municipal charges, and income from assets constitute on the average 47 per cent of the total, while debt accounts for 17 per cent, and transfers for 36 per cent. Transfers come in the main from the central government, with only a small percentage (generally less than 25 per cent) coming from the autonomous communities and the European Union.

This income structure gives the governments of major cities a certain degree of financial autonomy, but also gives rise to budgetary problems. Despite the considerable increase in the services provided by local government in recent years, their total expenditure as a percentage of the gross domestic product (4.8 per cent) and of public spending as a whole (11.3 per cent) has declined. The present situation is, therefore, still far from the ideal distribution proposed by the associations of local governments, according to which, the state would manage 50 per cent of total expenses, the autonomous communities 25 per cent and local governments the remaining 25 per cent.

The Specific Problems of Large Cities: Challenges and Opportunities

The internationalization of their economies has opened up new opportunities for the major Spanish cities, but has also given rise to significant challenges with respect to the infrastructure of external access, an area still affected by significant deficiencies. Between 1991 and 1995, air and sea traffic have increased sharply, making the expansion of Madrid and Barcelona airports and the improvement of Bilbao, Barcelona and Valencia ports urgent priorities. Traffic on the national road system has doubled between 1985 and 1995, while rail traffic has remained the same. In both cases, the density of Spanish systems is below the EU average, and major expansion projects are currently under way (the motorway system, the TGV, etc.). Finally, with respect to telecommunications, despite the rapid development seen in recent years, Spanish networks are still below the European level.

The expansion of the metropolitan cities, and the consequent jump in physical scale, while it has made them more integrated and competitive, has, at the same time, increased the need for internal travel, and exacerbated congestion and traffic problems. Despite the considerable effort invested in this field, the cities' public transport systems are still weak, so that the private vehicle remains the primary means of transport. The rate of vehicle ownership in the central municipalities of the seven metropolitan areas is 516 vehicles/ 1,000 inhabitants (while the Spanish average is 466).

Since 1986, the Spanish housing stock has undergone an extraordinary increase in value. This increase has coincided with the coming of age of the 'baby boom' generations of the '60s and early '70s. The combination of these two circumstances and other contributing factors has given rise to tensions between supply and demand, putting the possibility of buying a home beyond the reach of large sections of the population. The need for housing constructed on newly developed land in municipalities with over 50,000 inhabitants has been estimated at some 1.2 million units for the period 1991–2011. The relationship between the average price of a dwelling and the average income of Spanish households is 7:1 in the Madrid metropolitan area, and 6:1 in the Barcelona metropolitan area (while the overall Spanish average is 4.6:1).

The increase in the size and activity of the cities has also left its mark on the landscape, and has created significant environmental problems. During the last 30 years, the major Spanish cities have occupied as much new land as during their entire previous history. The level of water treatment in the country as a whole, which has been improved considerably, has still only reached 40.6 per cent of the equivalent population served. Urban areas are also experiencing problems owing to air pollution, soil contamination, and the production of solid and industrial waste.

Finally, the economic transformations – which have made it possible for Spain to progress from 66 to 77 per cent of the European average gross domestic product per capita between 1985 and 1994 – have also had serious consequences in terms of social problems in the large cities, among which unemployment, ageing of the population and poverty are the most prominent. In 1995, some 900,000 of the 2.5 million people unemployed in Spain live in the major urban areas. These areas had rates of registered unemployment ranging from 13 or 14 per cent in Barcelona and Madrid, to 26 or 27 per cent in Seville and Málaga. In addition to unemployment there is also concern about the progressive ageing of the population. Furthermore, situations of relative poverty (which affect 19.4 per cent of Spanish households) are found in all the major cities although distributed unevenly: ranging from 9 to 13 per cent of households in Bilbao, Barcelona and Madrid, to over 20 per cent in Màlaga, Seville, Valencia and Zaragoza.

The National Policies Affecting Cities

There is no single, integrated, national policy for cities in Spain. This is due in large part to the decentralization of the Spanish administrative structure, which grants considerable powers in this area to the autonomous communities. There are, however, several sectorial plans and projects that have a significant impact on the large cities. These are the National Infrastructure Plan, the National Housing Plan, three national plans relating to different aspects of the environment, the National Telecommunications Plan and the Draft Bill on Large Cities.

The National Infrastructure Plan 1993–2007 develops lines of action in four different areas: interurban transport, urban transport, waterworks, and environmental infrastructure. Of particular relevance to urban areas are the projects relating to accessibility (ports, airports, roads, and railways), for which finance needs are estimated at 10.7 billion pesetas (in 1992 pesetas). Also of great importance are projects relating to transport within urban areas, which include certain large scale projects and intermodal transport plans for each major city, representing the investment of a further 3.4 billion pesetas. It is estimated that a total of 18.7 billion pesetas will be required to implement the *Plan Director* during the period 1993–2007.

The objective of the National Housing Plan 1996–99 is to facilitate access to housing to citizens who cannot afford to purchase or rent a home under present market conditions. The plan, drawn up by the state in collaboration with the autonomous communities, calls for the financing of 500,000 housing interventions during this period.

The objectives of the National Plan for the Treatment of Waste Water

1995–2005, the National Plan for the Recovery of Contaminated Land 1995–2005, and the National Plan for Dangerous Toxic Wastes 1995–2000 are to improve the situation in their respective spheres of action in accordance with the standards established by European and Spanish regulations. It is estimated that over two billion pesetas will be required during the 1995–2005 period to implement these plans. This financing will be provided by the state (from its own resources or from the European Cohesion Fund), and by the autonomous communities.

The National Telecommunication Plan 1991–2002 was conceived as the basic instrument for directing the participation of the state in the development and evolution of civil infrastructure and services in this sector. When it was drawn up, the plan foresaw investment needs amounting to some seven billion pesetas. Regulations in this area have recently been updated, and the new legislation involves measures of particular relevance to the cities, especially in the field of cable telecommunications.

Finally, in an attempt to deal with the specific problems affecting large agglomerations, the mayors of the seven major Spanish cities have recently proposed the promulgation of a Large Cities Act. The proposed Act would change the way in which sectorial legislation is applied to the major Spanish cities whose government and administration pose particular problems owing to the size of their population. Under this Act, the local governments of these areas would be granted greater capacity and power to intervene in fields, such as urban development, housing, the environment, infrastructure, public transport, fiscal measures, financing, social policy, municipal justice, public safety and traffic management.

Note

1   Madrid: Mr Luis Felipe Alonso Teixió, architect, Professor, Escuela de Arquitectura de Madrid; Mr Félix Árias, architect, Technical Director, Dirección General de Actuaciones Concertadas con las Ciudades, Ministerio de Fomento; Mr Jesús Leal, sociologist, Professor, Universidad Autónoma de Madrid; Mr Ignacio del Ro, Segundo Teniente de Alcalde, Concejal de Urbanismo, Ayuntamiento de Madrid.
Barcelona: Mr Lluís Ballbé, lawyer, Secretary, Federación de Municipios de Cataluña; Mrs Núria Bosch, economist, Professor, Departamento de Hacienda Pública, Universitat de Barcelona; Mr Ernest Maragall, economist, Regidor Ponente de Función Pública y Calidad, Ayuntamiento de Barcelona; Mr Guillem Sánchez, economist, Director adjunto a la Gerencia y delegado de Hacienda, Ayuntamiento de Barcelona.
Zaragoza: Mr Francisco Javier Monclús, architect, Professor, Escuela de Arquitectura de Barcelona; Mr José Enrique Ocejo, civil engineer, Director Centro Municipal de Ordenación

del Territorio, Ayuntamiento de Zaragoza; Mr Manuel Ramos, architect, Jefe de la Oficina Municipal del Plan de Ordenación, Ayuntamiento de Zaragoza.

Bilbao: Mr Ibon Areso, architect, Teniente de Alcalde de Obras y Servicios, Ayuntamiento de Bilbao; Mr Jaime del Castillo, economist, Director, Información y Desarrollo SL; Mrs María Angeles Diez, economist, Información y Desarrollo SL; Mr Alfonso Martínez Cearra, engineer, Director general, Metrópolis 30.

Málaga: Mr Francisco Carmona, civil engineer, Gerente de Urbanismo, Ayuntamiento de Málaga; Mr José Estrada, Treasurer, Fundación CIEDES

Mr Pedro Marín, Jefe de programas europeos, Ayuntamiento de Málaga; Mr José Seguí, architect; Mr Luis Guillermo Tapia, economist, Secretario, Fundación CIEDES; Mr Francisco de la Torre Prado, agricultural engineer, Primer Teniente de Alcalde, delegado de la Agencia Municipal de Urbanismo, Vivienda y Transporte.

Sevilla: Mr Manuel Benavent, geographer, Arenal grupo consultor SL; Mr José García Tapial, architect, Jefe del Servicio de Planeamiento Urbano, Gerencia de Urbanismo, Ayuntamiento de Sevilla; Mr Antonio Martín, geographer and lawyer, Gerencia de Urbanismo, Ayuntamiento de Sevilla; Mr Miguel Angel Pérez, geographer, Director, Gruptec.

Valencia: Mr Luis Alonso de Armiño, architect, Professor, Escuela de Arquitectura de Valencia; Mr Álvaro Aleixandre, lawyer, Asesor de la Concejala del Área de Urbanismo, Ayuntamiento de Valencia; Mrs Júlia Salom, geographer, Professor, Departamento de Geografa, Universidad de Valencia; Mrs Elizabeth Delios, geographer, Departamento de Geografa, Universidad de Valencia.

References

Albi, Emilio and García, José Luis (1993), *Sistema fiscal español*, Barcelona: Ariel.

Almoguera, Pilar (1989), *El área de Sevilla como sistema metropolitano*, Sevilla: Instituto de Desarrollo Regional, Universidad de Sevilla.

Arias, Félix (1996), 'La política de ciudades de los gobiernos nacionales', *Cuadernos Economicos de Granada*, XI.

Arribas, Ramon and Módenes, Juan Antonio (1996), 'La població en la nova estructuraci territorial de la regió metropolitana de Barcelona, 1981–1991', *Nota d'economia*, 54, pp. 71–84.

Asociación de Parques Tecnológicos de España (1996), *Directorio*, Ourense: APTE.

Barcelona Regional (1996), 'Les infrastructures metropolitanes de Barcelona: una aproximació als projectes en curs', *Memòria econòmica de Catalunya*, Barcelona: Cambra Oficial de Comerç, Indústria i Navegació de Catalunya, pp. 248–68.

Barrero, Maria Concepción (1993), *Las áreas metropolitanas*, Sevilla: Instituto García Criado, Universidad de Sevilla-Civitas.

Bilbao Metrópoli-30 (1996), *Informe Anual de progreso 1995*, Bilbao: Bilbao Metrópoli-30 Asociación para la revitalización del Bilbao Metropolitano.

Boquera, José M. (ed.) (1992), *Derecho urbanístico local*, Madrid: Civitas.

Bosch, Núria and Espasa, Marta (1994), *Coste de los servicios obligatorios en las grandes ciudades españolas*, (mimeo), Barcelona: Centro de Estudios de Planificación.

Brenes, R. et al. (1993), 'Reestructuración productiva y comportamiento de la industria en la aglomeración urbana de Sevilla', *Ciudad y Territorio. Estudios Territoriales*, I, 98, pp. 553–77.

Bruinsma, Frank and Rietveld, Piet (1993), 'Urban Agglomerations in European Infrastructure Networks', *Urban Studies*, XXX, 6, pp. 919–34.

Capel, Horacio (1975), *Capitalismo y morfología urbana en España*, Barcelona: Libros de la Frontera.

Carreras, Borja (1994), 'Líneas básicas de la actual política estatal de vivienda', *Ciudad y Territorio. Estudios territoriales*, II, 99, pp. 9–17.

Castanyer, Jorge (1985), 'Evolución del marco institucional en las áreas metropolitanas españolas', *Estudios territoriales*, 19, pp. 191–203.

Castells, Antoni and Bosch, Núria (1993), *Informe sobre el finançament municipal a Catalunya. Problemàtica i línies de reforma*, Barcelona: Federació de Municipis de Catalunya.

Castells, Manuel (1990), 'Estrategias de desarrollo metropolitano en las grandes ciudades españolas: la articulación entre crecimiento económico y calidad de vida' in Jordi Borja et al. (eds), *Las grandes ciudades en la década de los noventa*, Madrid: Sistema, pp. 17–64.

Celada, Francisco (coord.) (1995), *La economía en Madrid. Análisis espacial de la estructura económica de la región desde 1980*, Madrid: Consejería de Política Territorial de la Comunidad de Madrid.

Centro de Estudios de Planificación (1996), *Evolución de las grandes magnitudes presupuestarias y contables de las grandes ciudades españolas en el período 1991–1995*, (mimeo) Barcelona: Ayuntamiento de Barcelona.

Chavero, Joan (1995), 'Els ingressos econòmics municipals' in Josep Mir (ed.), *Manual de govern local*, Barcelona: Federació de Municipis de Catalunya, pp. 111–31.

Clusa, Joaquim (1992), 'La distribució territorial de la indústria i els serveis a la regió metropolitana de Barcelona als sis anys de la recuperació econòmica', *Papers, Regió Metropolitana de Barcelona*, 12, pp. 9–39.

Clusa, Joaquim (1995), 'Argumentos alternativos sobre el dimensionamiento del suelo urbanizable y el contenido económico de la propiedad del suelo', *Ciudad y Territorio, Estudios Territoriales*, III, 103, pp. 133–53.

Comisión de Expertos sobre Urbanismo (1995), 'Recomendaciones finales de avance normativo y política de suelo del Informe sobre suelo y urbanismo', *Ciudad y Territorio. Estudios territoriales*, III, 103, pp. 165–89.

Comunicado de prensa, (mimeo), Madrid, II Reunión de Alcaldes de las Grandes Ciudades, 26 October 1993.

Comunidad de Madrid (1996), *Plan Regional de Estrategia Territorial. Bases*, Madrid: Consejería de Obras Públicas, Urbanismo y Transportes de la Comunidad Autónoma de Madrid.

Córdoba, Juan and García Alvarado, José M. (1991), *Geografía de la pobreza y la desigualdad*, Madrid: Síntesis.

Cortés, Luis (1995), *La cuestión residencial. Bases para una sociologa del habitar*, Madrid: Fundamentos.

Criterios para la Ley de Grandes Ciudades, (mimeo) Málaga, VI Reunión de Alcaldes de las Grandes Ciudades, 1 July 1996.

Díez Nicolas, Juan (1972), *Especialización funcional y dominación en la España urbana*, Madrid: Guadarrama-Fundación Juan March.

Dirección General de Planificación Territorial del Ministerio de Obras Públicas, Transportes y Medio Ambiente (1995), 'Recursos hídricos y marco territorial', *Ciudad y Territorio. Estudios territoriales*, III, 105, pp. 517–40.

Escudero, Manuel (1985), 'Esplendor y caída del Gran Bilbao', *Estudios Territoriales*, 19, pp. 113–31.

Ezquiaga, José Maria (1991), 'De la recuperación de la ciudad a la articulación del espacio metropolitano' in Javier Echenagisia (ed.), *Madrid, punto y seguido. Una propuesta de lectura (1985–1990)*, Madrid, pp. 216–36.

European Union (1996), *Trans-European networks (TENs)*, Brussels: EU.

Federación Española de Municipios y Provincias (1996), *Bases para el pacto local*, (mimeo), Madrid: FEMP, September.

Fernández, Antonio and Gavira, Carmen (1986), *Crónicas del espacio perdido. La destrucción de la ciudad en España, 1960–1980*, Madrid: Ministerio de Obras Públicas y Urbanismo.

Fernández, Fernando et al. (1991), 'Empleo y paro en España, 1976–1990' in Fausto Miguélez and Carlos Prieto (dir.), *Las relaciones laborales en España*, Madrid: Siglo XXI, pp. 42–96.

Fernández de Alarcón, Rafael (1993), 'Gestión territorial en los ejes de desarrollo de la ciudad de Zaragoza' in Manuel Ferrer (ed.), *Planeamiento y gestión metropolitana, comarcal y municipal*, pp. 131–47.

Fernández, Lafuente, Francisco (1994), 'Una política para las ciudades. Desarrollo del Plan Director de Infraestructuras en Medio Ambiente Urbano' in *Ciudad y Territorio. Estudios territoriales*, II, 99, pp. 19–30.

Ferrer, Amador (1989), 'El planejament urbanístic' in Oriol Nel.lo (dir.), *Deu anys d'ajuntaments democràtics (1979–1989). Elements per a un balanç*, Barcelona: Federació de Municipis de Catalunya, pp. 131–79.

Fundación FOESSA (1995), *V Informe sociológico sobre la situación social en España*, Madrid: FOESSA.

García Alcolea, Rafael and Marinas, Ignacio (1993), 'Estrategia para concertar la intervención de la Administración central en la ciudad', *Ciudad y Territorio. Estudios territoriales*, I, 97, pp. 411–21.

Gaviria, Mario (1996), *La séptima potencia. España en el mundo*, Barcelona: Ediciones B.

Generalitat Valenciana (1995), *Estrategias de vertebración territorial. Documento II del Avance del Plan de Desarrollo Urbanístico de la Comunidad Valenciana*, Valencia: Conselleria d'Obres Públiques, Urbanisme i Transports de la Comunitat Valenciana.

Gobierno Vasco (1992), *Directrices de ordenación del territorio de la Comunidad Autónoma del País Vasco, Avance*, Vitoria: Departamento de Urbanismo y Vivienda del Gobierno Vasco.

Guardia, Manuel et al. (1994), *Atlas Histórico de las ciudades europeas, Vol. I, La Península Ibérica*, Barcelona: Centre de Cultura Contemporània de Barcelona-Salvat editores.

Gutiérrez, Javier et al. (1996), 'Accesibilidad en la Unión Europea: un análisis comparado según modos de transporte', *Estudios de Transportes y Comunicaciones*, 70, pp. 7–19.

Huertas, Juan Carlos and Barreiro, Javier (1993), 'Zonas de actividad logística. Perspectivas de futuro', *Ciudad y Territorio. Estudios territoriales*, I, 9, pp. 423–42.

Ibarra, Juan Luis (1982), *Las áreas metropolitanas en el modelo autonómico*, Vitoria: Publicaciones del Gobierno Vasco.

Inglada, Vicente (1994), 'Análisis empírico del impacto del AVE sobre la demanda de transporte en el corredor Madrid-Sevilla', *Estudios de Transporte y Comunicaciones*, 62, pp. 35–51.

Instituto del Territorio y Urbanismo (1989), *Diez años de planeamiento urbanístico en España, 1979–1989*, Madrid: Ministerio de Obras Públicas y Urbanismo.

Jauristi, Joseba (1985), *La estructura urbana de Vizcaya*, Bilbao: Universidad del País Vasco.

Junta de Andalucía (1996a), *Plan de Ordenación del Territorio de la Aglomeración Urbana de Sevilla. Documento de Diagónstico*, 2 vols, Sevilla: Consejería de Obras Públicas y Transportes de la Junta de Andalucía.

Junta de Andalucía (1996b), *Aglomeración urbana de Málaga. Plan de Ordenación del Territorio*, 2 vols, Sevilla: Consejería de Obras Públicas y Transportes de la Junta de Andalucía.

Landaburu, Eneko (1993), 'El papel de las infraestructuras en el desarrollo regiona y en la política regional de la Comunidad', *Ciudad y Territorio. Estudios territoriales*, I, 97, pp. 341–7).

Leal, Jesús (1990), 'Crecimiento económico y desigualdad social en la Comunidad de Madrid', *Economía y Sociedad*, 4, pp. 55–66.

Leal, Jesús (1994), 'Cambio social y desigualdad espacial en el área metropolitana de Madrid', *Economía y Sociedad*, 10, pp. 61–81.

Leal, Jesús and Cortés, Luis (1995), *La vivienda en Madrid. Análisis espacial de la dinámica residencial de la región*, Madrid: Consejera de Política Territorial de la Comunidad de Madrid.

Ley (37/1995) de 12 de diciembre, reguladora de las telecomunicaciones por satélite, *Boletín Oficial del Estado*, 13 de diciembre 1995.

Ley (42/1995) de 22 de diciembre, reguladora de telecomunicaciones por cable, *Boletín Oficial del Estado*, 23 de diciembre 1995.

López Groh, Francisco (1988), *Áreas metropolitanas en la crisis*, Madrid: Ministerio de Obras Públicas y Urbanismo.

Llorens, Vicente (1994), *Arco mediterráneo español. Eje europeo de desarrollo*, Valencia: Conselleria d'Obres Públiques, Urbanisme i Transports de la Generalitat Valenciana.

Mancomunitat de Municipis de l'Àrea Metropolitana de Barcelona (1995), *Dinàmiques metropolitanes a l'àrea i regió de Barcelona*, Barcelona: Mancomunitat de Municipis de l'Àrea Metropolitana de Barcelona.

Mancomunitat de Municipis de l'Àrea Metropolitana de Barcelona (1997), *Migracions metropolitanes 1991–1996*, (mimeo), Barcelona.

Martín García, Antonio (1996), *Sevilla (1872–1994), Ciudad y territorio. De lo local a lo metropolitano*, Sevilla: Fundación Cultural del Colegio Oficial de Aparejadores y Arquitectos Técnicos de Sevilla.

Martín Mateo, Ramon (1988), 'Las áreas metropolitanas' in Santiago Muñoz Machado (dir.), *Tratado de derecho municipal*, Vol. I, Madrid: Civitas, pp. 855–63.

Martínez Císcar, José S. (1995), 'El Plan Nacional de Saneamiento y Depuración. Indispensable para el desarrollo sostenible', *Ciudad y Territorio. Estudios territoriales*, 105, III, pp. 497–502.

MECSA (1995), *Aeropuerto y región. Experiencias internacionales*, Madrid: Consejería de Política Territorial de la Comunidad de Madrid.

Méndez, Ricardo and Caravaca, Inmaculada (1993), *Procesos de reestructuración industrial en las aglomeraciones metropolitanas españolas*, Madrid: Ministerio de Obras Públicas y Transportes (MOPT).

Menéndez, Ángel (1996), 'Constitución y democracia 1976–1996: la segunda reforma de la ley del suelo', *Ciudad y Territorio. Estudios territoriales*, XXVIII, 107–108, pp. 127–48.

Ministerio para las Administraciones Públicas (1995), *Informe Económico-financiero de las Administraciones Territoriales en 1994*, Madrid: MAP.

Ministerio de Fomento (1996a), *Los transportes y las comunicaciones. Informe anual 1995*, Madrid: Ministerio de Fomento.

Ministerio de Fomento (1996b), *Informe Nacional de España, II Conferencia de Naciones Unidas sobre Asentamientos Urbanos, Habitat II*, Madrid: Ministerio de Fomento.

Ministerio de Fomento (1996c), *Agenda Habitat España. Documento de trabajo*, Madrid: Ministerio de Fomento.

Ministerio de Obras Públicas, Transportes y Medio Ambiente (1994), *Plan Director de Infraestructuras, 1993–2007*, Madrid: Ministerio de Obras Públicas, Transportes y Medio Ambiente.

Ministerio de Obras Públicas, Transportes y Medio Ambiente (1995a), *Plan Nacional de Telecomunicaciones (1991–2002)*, Madrid: Ministerio de Obras Públicas, Transportes y Medio Ambiente.

Ministerio de Obras Públicas, Transportes y Medio Ambiente (1995b), 'Real Decreto 2190/ 1995 de 28 de diciembre. Vivienda y suelo. Medidas de financiación de actuaciones protegibles para el perodo 1996–1999', *Boletín Oficial del Estado*, 312, 30 de diciembre.

Ministerio de Obras Públicas, Transportes y Medio Ambiente (1995c), 'Plan Nacional de Saneamiento y Depuración de Aguas Residuales (1995–2005), *Boletín Oficial del Estado*, 113, 12/V/1995, Madrid.

Ministerio de Obras Públicas, Transportes y Medio Ambiente (1995d), 'Plan Nacional de Recuperación de Suelos Contaminados (1995–2005)', *Boletín Oficial del Estado*, 114, 13/ V/1995, Madrid.

Ministerio de Obras Públicas, Transportes y Medio Ambiente (1995e), 'Plan Nacional de Residuos Peligrosos (1995–2000)', *Boletín Oficial del Estado*, 114, 13/V/1995, Madrid.

Mir, Josep (1991), *La reforma del règim local a Catalunya*, Barcelona: Escola d'Administració Pública de Catalunya .

Monclús, Francisco Javier (1994), 'Zaragoza' in Manuel Guardia et al. (eds), *Atlas Histórico de las ciudades europeas, Vol. I, La península ibérica*, Barcelona: Centre de Cultura Contemporània-Salvat editores, pp. 239–65.

Monzón, Andrés et al. (1995), 'La contaminación atmosférica y el transporte urbano en Madrid. Problemática actual y campos de actuación', *Estudios de transportes y comunicaciones*, 68, pp. 57–74.

Naredo, José Manuel (1994), 'El funcionamiento de las ciudades y su incidencia sobre el territorio', *Ciudad y territorio. Estudios territoriales*, II, 100–101, pp. 233–49.

Naredo, José Manuel (1996), *La burbuja inmobiliario-financiera en la coyuntura económica reciente (1985–1995)*, Madrid: Siglo XXI.

Nel.lo, Oriol (1995), 'Dinàmiques territorials i mobilitat urbana a la regió metropolitana de Barcelona', *Papers. Regió Metropolitana de Barcelona*, 24, pp. 9–37.

Nel.lo, Oriol (1995), 'Políticas urbanas y gobierno metropolitano en el proceso de integración europea', *Ciudad y territorio. Estudios territoriales*, III, 106, pp. 783–92.

Nel.lo, Oriol (dir.) (1996), 'Enquesta de la regió metropolitana 1995. Primers resultats referents a la mobilitat, els canvis de residència, el mercat de treball i la distribució dels ingressos familiars', *Barcelona economia*, 28, pp. 87–98.

Ortega Álvarez, Luis Ignacio (1983), 'La Comunidad Autónoma de Madrid como área metropolitana' in Eduardo García Enterra (ed.), *Madrid, Comunidad autónoma metropolitana*, Madrid: Instituto de Estudios Económicos, pp. 127–69.

Parejo, Luciano (1991), *Suelo y urbanismo: el nuevo sistema legal*, Madrid: Tecnos.

Pérez, Julio (1996), *La situación social de la vejez en España a partir de una perspectiva demográfica*, Madrid: Fundación Caja de Madrid.

Perpiñà Grau, Romà (1954), *Corología. Teoría estructural y estructurante de la población de España*, Madrid: Consejo Superior de Investigaciones Científicas.

Precedo, Andrés (1996), *Ciudad y desarrollo urbano*, Madrid: Síntesis.

Programa de las Naciones Unidas para el Desarrollo (1996), *Informe sobre desarrollo humano*, Madrid: Ediciones Mundi Prensa.

Racionera, Luis (1986), *Sistemas de ciudades y ordenación del territorio*, Madrid: Alianza.

Reher, David-Suer (1994), 'Ciudades, procesos de urbanización y sistemas urbanos en la península ibérica, 1550–1991' in Manuel Guardia et al., *Atlas Histórico de las ciudades europeas, Vol. I, La península ibérica*, Barcelona: Centre de Cultura Contemporània de Barcelona-Salvat editores, pp. 1–29.

RENFE (1993), *Un año de AVE*, Madrid: RENFE-MOPT.

Rosselló, Vicent M et al. (1988), *La comarca de l'Horta. Àrea metropolitana de València*, Valencia: Conselleria d'Administració Pública de la Generalitat Valenciana.

Salom, Julia (1992), *Sistema urbano y desarrollo regional en la Comunidad Valenciana*, Valencia: Edicions Alfons el Magnànim.

Sancho, José (1989), *El espacio periurbano de Zaragoza, Vols I and II*, Zaragoza: Ayuntamiento de Zaragoza.

Seguí, José (1993), 'El planeamiento en Andaluca: breve análisis de una década (1982–1992)', *Geometria*, 15, pp. 2–11.

Segura, Ricardo (1995), 'Referencias básicas del Plan Hidrológico Nacional', *Ciudad y Territorio. Estudios territoriales*, III, 105, pp. 559–65.

Serratosa, Albert (1994), 'Els espais oberts en el planejament metropolità: realitats y propostes', *Papers. Regió Metropolitana de Barcelona*, 20, pp. 37–47.

Sorribes, Josep (1985), *Desarrollo capitalista y proceso de urbanización en el Pas Valenciano (1960–1975)*, Valencia: Edicions Alfons el Magnànim.

Subirats, Marina (dir.) (1992), *Enquesta de la regió metropolitana de Barcelona 1990. Condicions de vida i hàbits de la població, Vol. II, Treball, Condicions econòmiques i formes de consum*, Barcelona: Institut d'Estudis Metropolitans de Barcelona.

Terán, Fernando de (1982), *Planeamiento urbano en la España contemporánea (1900–1980)*, Madrid: Alianza.

Tobío, Constanza (1985), 'Freno y redistribución del crecimiento demográfico en España, 1971–1975 y 1975–1981', *Estudios territoriales*, 19, pp. 57–67.

Tornos, Joaquim (1993), 'Las ciudades metropolitanas. El caso de Barcelona (nacimiento, desarrollo, muerte y resurrección del área metropolitana de Barcelona)', *Revista aragonesa de administración pública*, 3.

Torres, Joan et al. (1990), 'Políticas de transporte, tráfico y circulación: como articular los diversos modos de transporte' in Jordi Borja et al., *Las grandes ciudades en la década de los noventa*, Madrid: Sistema, pp. 409–25.

Trullén, Joan (1997), *La regió metropolitana de Barcelona: competitivitat en una economia global*, (mimeo), Barcelona: Pla Estratègic Barcelona-2000.

Vázquez, Pablo and Álvarez, Óscar (1995), 'Las redes transeuropeas y las líneas presupuestarias comunitarias. Su relación con el PDI', *Ciudad y Territorio. Estudios territoriales*, I, 97, III/1997, pp. 443–53.

Vigil, Carmen (1993), 'Financiación de infraestructuras', *Ciudad y Territorio. Estudios territoriales*, I, 97, pp. 433–42.

Vinuesa, Julio (1996), 'Dinámica de la población urbana en España (1857–1991)', *Ciudad y Territorio. Estudios territoriales*, XXVIII, 107–108, pp. 185–216.

Vinuesa, Julio et al. (1994), *La población de Madrid. Análisis de la dinámica demogárfica de la región, 1981–1991*, Madrid: Consejería de Política Territorial de la Comunidad de Madrid.

Zaldivar, Carlos Alonso and Castells, Manuel (1992), *España, fin de siglo*, Madrid: Alianza.

15 Sweden

JAN-EVERT NILSSON

Sweden is a country large in area and small in population, located on the northern fringe of Europe. It is characterized by sparseness of population between urban areas, which are themselves small in terms of population, and great distances to the large markets.

National Spatial Development Pattern

In area, Sweden is the third largest country in the European Union (EU) – nearly 11 times the size of the Netherlands, for example. In terms of population, however, Sweden has just under 60 per cent of that of the Netherlands, which means that Sweden is one of the smaller countries in the EU. A population density of 21 inhabitants per km^2 corresponds to about one-tenth of the EU's. About 83 per cent of the inhabitants lives in urban areas – i.e., population centres of at least 200 people. Of these, only 40 per cent, which corresponds to one-third of the total population, live in urban areas with populations over 50,000. Half of the Swedish population lives in urban areas with fewer than 10,000 inhabitants, or in rural areas.

Thus the statistics reveal that Sweden is similarly urbanized to other industrial countries in Europe. However, Sweden is distinguished by the lateness of its urbanization, similar to that in Finland and Norway. Not until the 1940s did the population of the urban areas exceed that of the rural areas. This late urbanization helps to explain why Sweden, despite its high level of urbanization, is perceived as lacking urban cultural traditions (Wiklund, 1995). Swedish urbanization coincides with the creation of the Nordic welfare state. The rapid, well-planned expansion of Swedish cities during the past half century is closely comparable to suburbanization.

Urbanization in Sweden emerged in the mid-19th century. That was when the degree of urbanization began to continually grow, as a result of the expansion of the manufacturing sector combined with a continuing increase in the birthrate of city dwellers. At that time, urbanization expressed itself partly in the growth of existing cities and partly in the emergence of new cities that blossomed in the fertile ground provided by expansive industries. Primarily, industrialization implied the rapid growth of coastal cities with good harbours. This was the period during which the Swedish city system was formed, and the population of these areas has continued to increase even though the rate of growth has subsided.

The Swedish City System

The Swedish urban system can be described as follows. There are three metropolitan areas – the Stockholm, Göteborg and Malmö regions – which together comprise 35 per cent of the country's population. The service sector is dominant in all three metropolitan regions – accounting for 71–81 per cent of the work force in these regions. Business-related services and communications are particularly over-represented, along with personal services and public administration. On the other hand, the industrial sector is gravely under-represented in the Stockholm region. The share of people employed in industry amounts to only about 60 per cent of the average for the country. In this respect, the picture is different in the other two metropolitan regions. In Göteborg there is a large concentration of engineering industries in the centre of the region, while the Malmö region is heavily specialized in the consumer goods field. The share of people employed in these industrial areas is nearly double that for the country as a whole.

Uppsala, the fourth largest city, with 185,000 inhabitants, lies 60 kilometres north of Stockholm and has a labour market with strong ties to the Stockholm region. Outside of the metropolitan regions there are 23 medium-sized cities of between 55,000 and 135,000. Of Sweden's 23 counties, only two lack a city of this size. With four exceptions, these medium-sized cities are regional centres, i.e., cities containing regional hospitals, county councils and institutions of higher education. In general in these cities, the industrial sector accounts for 15–25 per cent of employment, while 40–50 per cent is in the public sector. These cities constitute centres in local labour markets with 55,000–300,000 inhabitants.

The pace of urbanization dropped significantly during the 1970s, when the population of built-up areas grew by only 4.4 per cent, a figure that can be compared with an increase of 15.4 per cent during the 1960s. At this time, the form of urban development also changed; the growth of metropolises was replaced by an increase in suburban areas around these cities. One prerequisite for this development was to improve the possibilities of commuting by expanding public transportation and an increase in the use of private cars. The latter, in particular, played an important role in extending the range of people's activities. The new pattern of urbanization meant that the population increase in the cores of cities was replaced by a trend towards regional diffusion: the growth of cities took the form of geographical expansion. The daily urban regions of human beings grew. The result has been that the proportion of the country's population that has access to the city's varied offerings of employment opportunities and services has grown faster than the increase of residents in the cities.

Access to the cities' varied job opportunities led to increased commuting. There has also been a very rapid increase in commuting to work across municipal boundaries in Sweden, from about 0.5 million 15 years ago to about 1.2 million today. One factor contributing to this is, no doubt, the increasing numbers of women employed outside the home. If the demand for jobs for both husband and wife in a family is to be realized, access to a differentiated labour market is necessary. This can be achieved either by the family's settling down in larger cities or by one or another family member's accepting a sizeable commute to work. In this way, the geographical extension of metropolitan regions becomes an alternative to urbanization. Developments since the 1970s suggest that many people feel that they achieve an enhanced quality of life by enlarging their geographical scope.

Table 15.1 shows that among the metropolitan regions, only Stockholm has demonstrated strong economic growth. The reason for this is that the expansion of the service sector since the 1960s has been greater than the decrease in employment in the industrial sector. During the 1960s, industrial employment in the region dropped by 37 per cent. Despite this, total employment in the region grew by 17 per cent as the result of a strong increase in the area of business-related services.

Among the other 20 city regions, four reveal strong development. Three of them – Uppsala, Linköping and Umeå – are university cities with a large public sector and a relatively small but dynamic industrial sector. During recent years, a significant number of rapidly growing companies in the fields of IT and biotechnology have sprung up in association with the universities. Most of the ten city regions that show weak development involve cities that emerged as important industrial areas when Sweden was industrialized during the late 19th century – Norrköping, Borås, Gävle, Eskilstuna, Sundsvall, Skellefteå and Örnsköldsvik – and that have been hard hit by the structural transformations that have occurred in Swedish industry since the 1960s (Nilsson, 1995).

Table 15.1 Characteristics of urban regions in Sweden 1996

Rank	Name	Inhabitants City	Inhabitants Region	Economic performance	Tertiary/ secondary*
1	Stockholm	761,511	1,761,511	strong	81/19
2	Göteborg	454,046	788,984	poor	71/27
3	Malmö	247,382	618,382	poor	72/24
4	Helsingborg	114,849	292,095	average	
5	Uppsala	184,544	276,915	strong	
6	Linköping	131,907	242,635	strong	
7	Örebro	120,783	178,782	average	
8	Västerås	124,087	172,900	average	
9	Norrköping	123,560	168,842	poor	
10	Falun	55,033	152,278	average	
11	Borås	96,240	151,654	poor	
12	Luleå	71,239	151,253	average	
13	Jönköping	115,654	144,964	average	
14	Gävle	90,691	144,853	poor	
15	Umeå	102,512	136,094	strong	
16	Karlstad	79,475	127,899	average	
17	Växjö	73,107	125,760	average	
18	Kristianstad	73,722	117,518	average	
19	Eskilstuna	88,693	117,457	poor	
20	Sundsvall	94,464	113,048	poor	
21	Kalmar	58,778	112,512	poor	
22	Östersund	58,492	107,508	poor	
23	Halmstad	83,533	106,555	strong	

*   These data are for 1994.

Metropolitan Regions

The population of Sweden's three metropolitan regions grew by 62 per cent during the period 1950–96. During this time, the metropolitan regions' share of the Swedish population increased from 27 to 35 per cent. This expansion has entailed a change of character in the three metropolitan regions.

In 1950, neither Stockholm, Göteborg nor Malmö were regarded as metropolitan regions, but rather as Sweden's three largest cities that dominated the surrounding countryside in terms of population. At that time, 83 per cent of the population resided in the six municipalities that constitute the core of the Stockholm region. These cities' share of the region's employment was even greater (85 per cent), but there was still little commuting to work in the centre of Stockholm. The situation was similar in Göteborg. 80 per cent of the population and 88 per cent of the jobs were located in the three municipalities that make up the core of the region. In this respect, the situation was different in Malmö, where only 55 per cent of the population and 53 per cent of the jobs were located in the city. This reflects the fact that the Malmö region should actually be regarded as a multicore region, with the university city of Lund, 13 kilometres north of Malmö, as the region's second significant core. In 1950, with its 204,000 inhabitants, Malmö was more than four times the size of Lund. Hence, at that time, 68 per cent of the population of the Malmö region was located in Malmö and Lund. The latter city's rapid growth during recent decades has gradually increased its relative significance in the region. In 1996, as the population of Lund has grown to 97,000, Malmö is only 2.5 times larger.

During the period 1950–70, the population of the metropolitan regions grew by almost 40 per cent, an increase primarily achieved through a large surplus in-migration. The great streams of population flowed from regions in northern Sweden, where many people worked in forestry and agriculture, to the country's three metropolitan regions. Urbanization presupposed comprehensive investments in housing in these regions. Urban policy in Sweden at the time was aimed at the expansion of new residential areas in combination with investments in public transportation. Improved communications provided new opportunities for expansion outside the cities.

An increasing part of the expansion in the Stockholm region therefore took place in suburbs and 'satellite towns'. The latter were distinguished by being geographically detached from the actual city, which gave them the character of being neighbourly villages. Good communications provided the inhabitants access to the cultural, educational and recreational offerings of the big city. The requirement that these 'satellite towns' be geographically detached meant that they were situated in municipalities adjacent to Stockholm (Wiklund, 1992).

In the municipality of Stockholm, a good deal of the expansion occurred in the form of new city districts that made up clearly defined local labour markets in the vicinity of the newly expanded subway. A centre was erected around the subway station with a concentration of apartment houses complemented by commercial and social services and work places. An interesting centre was expected to attract businesses, and thus contribute to the creation of a versatile local labour market. These suburban centres were surrounded by park-like landscapes containing schools, day nurseries, playgrounds and sports facilities. Beyond the parks, areas of row houses with small local centres were located, with detached houses still further from the subway station. Vällingby, the first suburb built on the basis of these new ideas, became a success and attracted international attention (cf. Hall, 1988).

The reshuffling of the population from the thinly populated parts of the country to metropolitan regions led to a political reaction, from which emerged an active localization policy with the task of developing the industrial base in the areas of out-migration. In this way, the governmental authorities hoped also to be able to limit the growth of population in the metropolitan regions. Since the 1960s, investments in regional policy have gradually increased in scope, while political interest in urban policy has dwindled. Influential political circles are clearly inclined to place these two policy areas in an adversarial relationship. Investments in urban policy have been considered as counteracting the goal of achieving regional balance, a goal that had been a lodestar for regional policy.

In 1970, the metropolitan regions' share of the country's population had grown to 33 per cent. During the '70s there was a drastic reduction in the rate of urbanization. The population of the metropolitan regions grew by only four per cent. A new situation arose, revealing a surplus of apartments in certain areas. This was exactly when the 'million programme' terminated. Within the space of a few years, the construction of apartments in multiple-family dwellings declined from 110,000 per year to 50,000. The construction of one-unit housing maintained its previous level – 25,000 units annually. The change in the composition of new construction contributed to the generation of a new wave of migration from the big 'million region' modern apartments to newly-built, one-family-domicile areas. It was not difficult to discern a development of segregation.

The stagnation in the population growth of the metropolitan regions was primarily a result of the fact that there was a reduction in the populations of the three metropolises. Hence, from 1970 to 1985 the population of Stockholm went down by 80,000 people, which corresponds to eight per cent, at the same time as the periphery of the Stockholm region grew by 181,000 people, which is the equivalent of 36 per cent. The proportion of the centre's share of the region's population went down to 56 per cent. Despite the population decrease in the centre of the Stockholm region, employment rose by 14 per cent. This indicates that the decrease in population in the central parts of the Stockholm region was primarily a result of the changes in the preferences of people who would live there. An increasing number of Swedes preferred to live in one-family dwellings in more thinly-populated areas of the region, rather than living in apartments in the asphalt jungle.

One consequence of this prioritizing was a great increase in the amount of commuting in the region. However, the large increase in population on the periphery of the metropolitan region was not only the result of increased commuting. There was a simultaneous surge in employment in this part of the Stockholm region – an increase of 79 per cent during this period. This implies that the increase in employment in the suburban municipalities, in absolute numbers, exceeded the increase in the city centre. During this period, Stockholm was transformed from a metropolis into a metropolitan region.

There was a similar development in the other two metropolitan regions, where the populations declined in the central parts and rose in the peripheries. During the period from 1970 to 1985, the population in the central parts of the Göteborg region dropped by five per cent; in Malmö the figure was 11 per cent. In the Malmö region, this decrease was partially counterbalanced by rapid growth in Lund, whose population went up by 21 per cent.

Thus developments since the 1950s have been characterized by a high rate of population growth on the peripheries of the metropolitan regions. The share of the population living in the centres of these regions has gradually decreased, amounting in 1996 to 55 per cent in the Stockholm region, 69 per cent in the Göteborg region and 43 per cent in the Malmö region. If Lund is included, the share for the Malmö region rises to 61 per cent. These figures indicate that, relatively speaking, the expansion of the periphery has been weakest in the Malmö region.

Administrative and Financial Framework

In the 1970s and 1980s the Ministry of Environment was responsible for national urban policy. In 1994 the government reintroduced the Ministry of Domestic affairs and moved urban policy to that ministry, which is also in charge of other issues dealing with the municipalities. However, because urban policies in Sweden are primarily directed towards the three metropolitan areas in Sweden, other ministries are involved, too. The Ministries of Transportation and Communication, Environment and Social Affairs are examples of ministries directly involved in national urban issues.

Local autonomy is one of the cornerstones of Swedish polity. Municipal autonomy is exercised locally, in municipalities, and regionally, in county council districts, which rest on a long historical tradition. These basic principles have been written into the Swedish constitution, which decrees that municipalities and county council districts have taxation authority and that the right to make decisions lies with elected representatives. There is legislation covering the fundamental regulations concerning division into municipalities and their organization and how their activities are to be conducted, as well as their powers and responsibilities.

In addition, in every county there is a county administration which is a state authority led by a county governor appointed by the national government.

When the county council districts were introduced in the 1862 municipal ordinances, a peculiarly Swedish regional administrative pattern was created. In every county there is both a state county administration and a county council elected directly by the inhabitants of the county. The picture is complicated by the fact that for a long time there were three municipalities without county councils, two of them being Göteborg and Malmö, where the municipality is also responsible for health care.

The geographical areas of the county administrations and the county councils are the same, but their areas of responsibility are different. The county administrations have primary responsibility for a number of state assignments in the county – regional social planning (regional policy, physical planning and state sector planning) – as well as coordination of state, county council district and municipal government services. The county council municipalities have primary responsibility for health care services, which is their dominant activity, but they also contribute to public transportation, business sector development, culture and the field of social activities. In 1996, the Swedish parliament voted for an experiment in certain counties, entailing the transfer of tasks from county administrations to county councils.

The geographical area of the county of Stockholm's county council corresponds fairly well with the expansion of the Stockholm region, so the county council in this case functions as a metropolitan authority with responsibility for the region's health care, public transportation and regional planning. The regional plan adopted by the county council allocates areas for residential housing, work places, traffic connections, recreation, etc. for the coming 10–15 years. In this way, the regional plan will guide the development of the region's physical structure.[1]

The situation is different in the other two metropolises. The Göteborg region crosses the boundaries of three counties and county councils. The picture is further complicated by the fact that the municipality of Göteborg is not included in any county council. Hence, in the Göteborg region, there is no given organizational platform for managing the region's development. The number of county councils and county administrations has complicated the effective coordination of public transportation and investments in the infrastructure. Instead, planning is done in an Association of Local Authorities, which is a voluntary affiliation of municipalities included in the region. The association, however, has no statutory right to make decisions about the Göteborg region. In 1997 the Swedish parliament approved a bill that combines three counties in western Sweden into one large county. At the same time, the three county councils will be merged, and the municipality of Göteborg will enter the new county council. When this decision is carried through, the planning situation in the Göteborg region will be simplified.

An association of local authorities is also the forum in which the development of the Malmö region is being discussed. Malmö, which up to now has been, like Göteborg, a municipality not included in the county council, also lacks a functioning regional authority. The location of the Malmö region in southwest Skåne means that the metropolitan region is included in one county and one county council, and this has simplified the development of regional public transportation. The institutional framework for the Malmö region is presently undergoing change. On 1 January 1997, the counties of Kristianstad and Malmöhus were merged into one county – Skåne County. Simultaneously, the two old counties' county councils were combined into a single county council and Malmö was included in the new county council.

A decision has also been reached to transfer responsibility for regional development work from the county administration to the region's politicians in stages, as an experiment. Responsibility was switched to a regional association on 1 July 1997, and assumed by the Skåne County county council in 1999. The argument given for this experiment is that it will strengthen and develop Skåne, and facilitate the use of common resources more effectively from an overall point of view. The experiment will run from 1999 to 2002 and then be evaluated. Thereafter, the Swedish parliament will decide on the design of the county organization in the future.

The organizational framework in the Malmö region is further complicated by the ambitions of representatives of the region to utilize the Öresund bridge to develop a functional transnational metropolitan region, the Copenhagen-Malmö region, united by an integrated system of public transportation. An Öresund Committee has been formed for this purpose. The committee is charged with bringing about greater cooperation, e.g., in communications and infrastructure, traffic, business, research, education and culture. The committee is made up of leading politicians from counties, county councils and municipalities on both sides of Öresund, as well as representatives of the Danish and Swedish governments. There is a subcommittee of leading officials from the member organizations. Day-to-day operations are conducted by a secretariat, whose main office is in Copenhagen. Among the initiatives of the

Öresund Committee is an environmental programme for the Öresund region; it has also worked out a plan for public transportation in the united Öresund region. The Öresund Committee was also responsible for drawing up an INTERREG-II programme for the Öresund region.

During the postwar period the number of municipalities in Sweden has steadily decreased. In 1950 there were 2,500; at present there are 286. Among other things, this reduction in the number of municipalities can be attributed to the desire to strengthen the municipalities' economic and administrative resources, and consequently their ability to offer public services to their inhabitants. Simultaneously with the reduction in the number of municipalities, the scope of municipal activities has increased dramatically.

To a considerable extent, the Swedish 'welfare state' is local; it is rather a question of 'welfare municipalities' than of a welfare state. Kindergartens, schools, health care, geriatric care, housing construction and public transportation are mainly municipal responsibilities, and until recent years the municipalities have had a monopoly on conducting some of these activities. The municipalities have responsibility for most of the tasks in the public sector that directly affect Swedish citizens.

Table 15.2 reveals that education, geriatric care and child care are the three major items in municipal expenditures. Altogether, these three areas account for 64 per cent of total outlays. The table also shows that the expenditures of metropolitan municipalities per inhabitant exceed the national average by 10 per cent, whereas the expenditures per inhabitant for suburban municipalities are on average 12 per cent below the national average.

The high costs for the metropolitan municipalities are primarily explained by the fact that investments in social services and culture are significantly higher in these areas than in the country at large. The three metropolitan municipalities are distinguished by the number of residents entitled to social assistance, which exceeds the national average. The high costs of geriatric care in the metropolises are explained by the relatively greater number of elderly people in the population. The expenditures of suburban municipalities are lower than the national average for most areas of activity. Only those for child care and education exceed the national average. The comparatively high expenditures in these areas can be partially explained by the age distribution in the population.

Between 1950 and 1995, municipal (including county council district) consumption rose by 474 per cent, and municipal investments by 390 per cent. During the same period, Sweden's GNP went up by 245 per cent. This implies that the municipal and county council district share of GNP rose during

Table 15.2   Municipal expenses by activity 1995 (SEK/resident[a])

Activity	Sweden	Metropolitan municipalities[b]	Suburban municipalities[c]
Political activities[d]	558	554	646
Infrastructure	2,468	2,596	1,948
Recreation	1,028	1,173	911
Culture	812	1,139	547
Child care	4,493	4,515	5,311
Education	8,197	6,963	8,264
Geriatric care	7,656	8,693	5,094
Individual + family care	2,280	4,007	1,970
Dedicated contributions[e]	1,214	1,527	757
Business activities[f]	2,904	3,606	1,910
Total	31,610	34,773	27,718

Notes

a   1 SEK = 8.70 ECU.
b   The municipalities of Stockholm, Göteborg and Malmö.
c   Suburban municipalities with large work commuting to a metropolis.
d   Costs for municipal political organizations and support for political parties.
e   Costs for refugees received and job-creating measures.
f   Covers business activities conducted under the auspices of municipalities.

Source: Svenska Kommunförbundet, 1996.

this period from 11 to 19 per cent. The increase in municipal consumption has been financed by tax hikes and transfer payments from the national government. The average municipal tax (which is proportional and levied on the incomes of municipal residents) has grown from SEK10 in 1950 to SEK31.5 in 1995. Since the start of the 1990s, the government has limited the possibilities of the municipalities to raise taxes. In 1995 the average tax rise was only SEK0.35. The government redistributes some of the municipal tax revenues among the municipalities. It withdraws resources from municipalities with strong tax bases and transfers them to those with weak tax bases.

On average, nearly 60 per cent of municipal revenues come from municipal taxes, 25 per cent from fees and just under 20 per cent in the form of government subsidies. These state contributions were formerly earmarked for specific areas. In 1993 a general state subsidy system was introduced, which meant that about 80 per cent of the contributions formerly earmarked were transformed into general revenues. Thus the specially-designated state subsidy share of municipal revenues has decreased significantly. This reorganization was preceded by a heated political debate over 'winners' and 'losers' from the new distribution system. One result of the reorganization was an increase in transfers to metropolitan municipalities.

The general state subsidy system consists of three parts. The so-called base amount accounts for the largest part of the total subsidy. This base amount is used for equalizing municipal taxable incomes up to a general guaranteed level. In Stockholm county there is also a regional equalization subsidy financed by the municipal taxes in the county's municipalities. The equalization subsidy redistributes tax revenues from municipalities with strong tax bases in the country's heavily populated areas to small municipalities in thinly populated areas. Of the total tax revenues commanded by municipalities, the equalization subsidy accounts for 43 per cent in rural areas. The corresponding share in suburban municipalities is only nine per cent. The equalization subsidy is a means of ensuring that comparable services can be offered in different municipalities.

The three metropolitan municipalities differ in one obvious respect from the average. Approximately equally large parts of their resources, around 40 per cent, come from fees and municipal taxes. The picture is different for the suburban municipalities that surround the metropolises, where municipal taxes account for more than 60 per cent of revenues and fees for only 25 per cent. The high share of financing from fees in the metropolises is explained by the fact that these municipalities carry on extensive activities in municipally owned public utilities corporations – real estate companies, harbour facilities, power authorities, grounds and industrial location works, etc. – which are mainly financed by fees and rentals. Such businesses account for nearly 25 per cent of the activities of the metropolitan municipalities.

Urban Issues and Challenges from the National Perspective

Three questions have occupied a central position in discussions of urban issues in recent years. Great attention has been devoted to the economic situation of municipalities, to environmental and traffic matters, and to the social segregation that exists in the metropolitan regions.

Several factors contributed to the strained economic situation of municipalities during the 1990s. Sweden was afflicted by a severe recession that resulted in a 4.7 per cent decrease in GDP between 1991 and 1993. This was the first time in the 20th century that GDP declined three years in a row. Unemployment, including people covered by labour market policy programmes, rose from 4.5 to 12.2 per cent, and the number of people employed in the country fell by 10 per cent. Falling employment and rising unemployment had a negative effect on the tax revenues of the municipalities, while simultaneously resulting in greater expenditures for individual and family care. Municipal revenues were further weakened by a 22 per cent reduction in state transfer payments to municipalities in the space of a few years.

The effect was to halve municipal surpluses, which had been used to finance investments or improve liquidity, between 1992 and 1993. In the metropolises, a surplus was transformed into a deficit, while the suburban municipalities came out better. The picture for the metropolises is complex, however, as they also carry on extensive activities in corporations wholly owned by the municipality. If the activities of municipally owned corporations are included in the analysis, the surplus of the metropolitan municipalities per resident is nearly twice that of the national average.

The municipalities cope with their reduced revenues by economizing. Municipal investments were cut back by 12 per cent between 1991 and 1993, while municipal consumption declined by 3 per cent. At the same time, employment in municipalities fell by 8 per cent. The reduction in employment in the municipal sector has continued, falling by 12 per cent between 1991 and 1995.

In most municipalities, the politicians have had trouble establishing priorities. The result has been that cutbacks have hit all types of activities. Since child care, education and geriatric care account for most municipal outlays, palpable reductions have been made in these areas. The cutbacks, whose consequences have been constantly presented in the mass media, have created strong political reactions. Parents complain about hikes in the fees for child care and the reduction in personnel in nursery schools. Parents of schoolchildren are displeased with economies in the school which result in the reduction or elimination of peripheral resources as remedial instruction, substitute teachers, school nurses, libraries, etc. Many people protest the effects of the cutbacks in geriatric services. Reports about how elderly people in institutions are forced to go to bed in the early afternoon because of the shortage of personnel upset the feelings of many citizens. Their dissatisfaction with the political parties and their representatives has increased. The cutbacks in the municipal sector have contributed to a decline in the legitimacy of the political system. There has been rising distrust of politicians and their promises.

The relatively high inflation that marked the Swedish economy up to the beginning of the 1990s (the annual average increase in the consumer price index during the 1980s was 7.6 per cent) has reinforced the trend towards segregation. Inflation boosted the costs of new housing construction, which in turn entailed a rise in the price of existing houses. The pace of the price increase was determined by the balance between the availability of and demand for houses in the various regions. The price increases were greatest in the overheated housing market in the Stockholm region. Large numbers of people experienced difficulty in financing the purchase of houses in the central parts of the metropolitan regions.

The three metropolitan regions are among the most environmentally defiled areas in Sweden. This environmental depredation in part reflects the encumbrances on the environment, and partly the effect of the environmental situation on many people who live in these regions. Both Göteborg and Malmö are situated in coastal areas that are particularly exposed to air and sea pollution emanating from other parts of Europe. Both regions are also home to industries that have a burdensome impact on the environment. A large part of the acreage in the Malmö region and its surroundings is used for intensive agricultural production. Household wastes and traffic also encumber the environment.

In the Göteborg region, many areas of both land and water are heavily acidified. The seas nearest the coast suffer from eutrophication, which has negative consequences for the ecological system. Vehicular traffic, heating operations and industrial processes all contribute to air pollution. The more northern sections of the city of Göteborg constitute one of Sweden's most vulnerable areas in terms of air pollution.

The environmental situation of the Malmö region is affected by its geographical situation. Southwest winds carry pollutants from large Continental industrial districts in over Skåne. Over 80 per cent of the sulphur and a somewhat smaller percentage of the nitric oxides in the area are estimated to be wind borne. This fallout is up to ten times larger than the capacity of the land to receive it. Water pollution in Öresund also has an international background. In addition to the emissions from its own region, the water quality, living conditions and production in Öresund are affected by pollutants from Denmark and the countries bordering the Baltic and the Kattegat. This is why efforts to improve the environment of the Malmö region will require a major international input.

With respect to natural conditions, the prospects are different in the Stockholm region. Furthermore, industrial activities and agricultural production play a less prominent role there. Traffic accounts for most of the emissions in the air. Considering that air pollutants – emissions of carbon monoxide, nitric oxide and ozone, along with noise – are the greatest environmental problem for the Stockholm region, great attention has been devoted to the possibilities of improving the traffic situation in the central parts of the region (SOU, 1990:39).

National Policy Response to Urban Issues, Challenges and Development

In Sweden, national urban policy is primarily directed at the three metropolitan regions, and this is a policy area to which little attention has been devoted during the past 25 years. Political interest has been much more directed to the regional policies involving the country's peripheral areas. Periodically, there have also been heated confrontations between the champions of metropolitan regions and those who represent less populated regions in Sweden. The ambitions of regional policy have often been expressed in terms of transferring resources from the metropolitan regions to other parts of Sweden. Following this line of thought, urban policy has primarily become an urgent matter for local and regional politicians in the three metropolitan regions, who had experienced difficulties in winning political support for their concerns in parliament.

The structure of the Swedish city system has contributed to great political attention being paid to the medium-sized cities. Among Swedish planners, 'the suitable city' represents an ideal, one which is emphasized in the vision of 'Sweden 2009' that has been prepared as a national document in the EU project, European Spatial Development Perspective. The vision maintains that these cities are distinguished by being relatively well able to unite the big city's offerings of housing, employment, service, recreational facilities, etc. with the small town's access to the benefits of the big city and to the surrounding natural environs. The suitable city is thought to offer better contacts between people and proximity to commerce, service, employment and education. The geographical closeness of these various components means that the inhabitants can get around on foot or by bicycle. These medium-sized cities are reckoned to offer much of what Swedish planners associate with a good urban life (*Sverige 2009 – förslag till en vision*, 1994, p. 72).

The focus of urban policy has changed over time. During the 1960s, housing policy was at the very centre of political interest. The housing shortage was viewed as a major problem. Parliament passed an ambitious housing programme. This so-called 'million programme' was launched in 1964; its goal was to create one million new apartments over a period of ten years. Annual housing construction was raised from 65,000 to 100,000 apartments. This housing production was financed by state pension funds, and the state played an active role in the allocation of borrowing resources. Priority was given to the production of multiple dwelling units; only one-third of the effort went into one-family houses. Housing contractors who invested in large projects, i.e., projects involving more than 1,000 apartments, were given certain advantages. Municipally owned housing companies were given priority over private landlords, social housing was given high priority. The ambitious quantitative goals for housing production implied that planning was speeded up. The number of apartments was prioritized at the expense of the living environment

The 'million programme' was terminated as planned in the 1970s and the focus of interest moved to the relocation of state agencies from Stockholm to other parts of Sweden. The relocation of state agencies from Stockholm to designated primary centres – 23 urban regions with 45 000–136 000 inhabitants – became one important element in the new city system policy formulated in the beginning of the 1970s. In 1971, parliament passed a bill on relocation of state agencies from Stockholm and the wave of relocation had started. 32 state agencies, with a total of 5,890 employees, were moved to 13 primary centres. A few years later, another ten agencies, with 2,810 employees, were relocated to eight primary centres, of which seven also received state agencies in the first round. After that, the relocation process was discontinued. One reason for this was the fact that the growth of the metropolitan areas stopped and the regional imbalances were thereby reduced. However, at the end of the 1980s a third wave of relocation from Stockholm was initiated. In 1988/89 another four state agencies with 600 employees in total were relocated. In total, 9,300 jobs were relocated from Stockholm in the three waves of relocations described above. Another 1,020 jobs, relocated on special terms during this period, might be added. Thus, in total 10,320 jobs were moved from Stockholm to other cities. However, the number of employees who agreed to leave Stockholm was considerably lower, at about 2,500 (Nilsson, 1992, p. 114). In 1997 the government suggested the relocation of another 300–600 state agency jobs from Stockholm to two smaller cities which had been hit by reductions in the defence budget.

In the 1990s, organizational changes have been the most important urban issue. Changed economic conditions for municipalities have forced them to initiate thoroughgoing organizational changes in the 1990s. One cardinal idea that began to be adopted in many municipalities was to utilize the experiences of the private business sector. Municipal activities were divided up into purchaser and supplier organizations. The purchaser organizations were expected to formulate the goals for and demands on the production for which the municipalities are responsible. These 'orders' could then be filled either by municipal entities or by private organizations. The main point was that politics should concentrate on the purchaser organizations. Local politicians should act as though they were members of the board of a private company.

Their attention should be focused on formulating the frameworks for the activities financed by the municipalities. Responsibility for 'delivery' should then be allocated to independent municipal or private actors under professional management. In this way, many municipalities gave up their monopoly on operating institutions that delivered municipally-financed services to municipal residents.

Many municipalities, especially suburban municipalities in metropolitan regions governed by centre-right administrations, concentrated on stimulating the growth of private alternatives. They encouraged the establishment of nursery schools, schools and geriatric facilities run under private auspices. Simultaneously, municipal residents were given greater freedom to choose nurseries or schools for their children, a choice that was not limited to institutions in their own municipalities. Extensive establishment of new nurseries and schools took place in the metropolitan regions.

One dilemma for this organizational model was that politics was cut off from many concrete decisions about how activities should be run. Specific changes in nurseries, schools, geriatric institutions, etc. were placed beyond the reach of politicians. This meant that local politicians could do nothing when there was local dissatisfaction with the activities of an individual institution. They could only refer complaints to those who were responsible for operating the institution.

The growth of private alternatives in nurseries and schools has been followed by growing discussion of the distributional effects of the policy. The debate encompasses two issues. In the first place, there is a risk of growing regional differences. The offerings of alternatives are concentrated in the metropolitan regions whose large populations prepare the ground for a 'market' of nurseries and schools with special orientations. In smaller municipalities, there is often no alternative to the municipal institutions. In the second place, there is a risk that freedom of choice will lead to greater social segregation. Many people maintain that the alternatives are primarily available to the well-educated middle class. The parents' conscious choice of nurseries and schools represents a risk that there will be a concentration of the children of the middle classes in selected nurseries and schools. If that occurs, the new freedom of choice will result in the creation of a dual system, both parts of which are financed by the public sector.

The counter argument is that the municipal system is already segregated, since the possibility of choosing nurseries and schools is primarily determined by where you live. In this context, segregation means that different population categories live in different areas. Residential segregation makes itself felt in nurseries and schools. Living conditions are different in different municipalities in the metropolitan regions. Groups with solid resources are heavily over-represented in certain municipalities, while those with scanty resources are over-represented in others.

In the Götenborg and Malmö regions, those with scanty resources are over-represented in the regions' two largest municipalities. In the Stockholm region, on the other hand, there are other municipalities that have a high share of households with meagre resources. One metropolitan study commissioned by the government identified the residential areas that in 1980 had more than twice the number of recipients of social assistance as the region on average. 51 residential areas in the three metropolitan regions fulfilled the requirement. In the Göteborg and Malmö regions, these areas were heavily concentrated in the municipalities of Göteborg and Malmö. In the Stockholm region, however, nearly three-quarters of these residential areas were in suburban municipalities (SOU, 1989:67). These areas were also characterized by a high proportion of immigrants, people with low incomes and people with health problems.

The differences mainly reflect the way in which the 'million programme' was implemented in the three regions. In the Göteborg and Malmö regions, the million-programme housing units were for the most part built within the boundaries of the municipalities of Göteborg and Malmö, whereas in the Stockholm region a large number of the million-programme residences were constructed in Stockholm's neighbouring communities – especially in the southern part of the region.

The municipality of Malmö, with financial assistance from the EU, has launched a project – Urban Malmö – to improve conditions in five residential areas that had become slums. These areas contain somewhat more than 14,000 residences and some large industries. The goal of the project is to lay the ground for new companies, increase employment and improve the outdoor environment. 11.5 million ECU will be invested during the period 1997–99; the EU contribution is somewhat under five million.

Developments in the housing area since the 1980s have implied the cementing of segregation. Renovation of apartment units in the central areas of the metropolitan regions has entailed a rise in housing costs, which has made it difficult for the economically weak households that had previously lived in them to move back in. These people are now concentrated in less attractive residential areas. The transformation of rental apartments into cooperative apartments has had a corresponding effect. The number of cooperative apartments in the inner city area of Stockholm grew very rapidly during the 1980s. A similar development has transpired in Göteborg and

Malmö. The increasing stock of cooperatives means that increasing economic
investment is required to enter the housing market in the regions' central city
areas. The change in the housing market has led to an increasing over-
representation of high-level white collar workers in the inner city.

During the second half of the 1980s, population growth once again
increased in the three metropolitan regions, by 10 per cent during the period
1980–96. The greatest growth (14 per cent) occurred in the Stockholm region,
and the smallest (9 per cent) in the Malmö region. For the first time since the
1950s (Stockholm) and 1960s (Göteborg and Malmö), there was also an
increase in the populations of the centres of the metropolitan regions, even
though the greatest rate of increase still occurred in the peripheral areas. The
expansion in the centres of the metropolitan regions contributed to the
stimulation of interest in development projects in the city centres. In all three
regions, development of new housing areas in the old harbour districts is
either going on or being planned.

The municipal council in Stockholm decided to convert the harbour and
industrial sites just south of inner city Stockholm into a residential area. In
Göteborg, similarly, there are plans for creating a new, integrated city
environment on northern Älvstrand, where formerly heavy shipbuilding
industries and harbour activities had been operating for decades. This area
will now be home to a mixture of homes, offices, industries and social services.
This building project is estimated to continue for 30 years. When completed,
the area will contain 20,000 residents and about as many work places. In
Malmö, the plan is to expand the old shipbuilding area in the harbour; among
other things, it will be the home of a new university.

Political attention to the situation of the metropolitan regions increased
during the late 1980s. One reason for this was the downturn in the political
activity of Swedish citizens – e.g., in terms of participation in elections – that
could be observed in these regions. The current Social Democratic government
therefore commissioned an investigation to suggest measures and to increase
the political participation in the metropolises. This investigation published a
total of 13 expert reports and a final report (SOU, 1990, p. 39).

The final report noted that the prospects for rapid economic growth in the
Göteborg and Malmö regions were not particularly good. On the other hand,
it found much to indicate that the Stockholm region would continue to enjoy
a positive economic development in the coming years. Therefore, the
investigation concluded that there were strong reasons to stimulate
development in the Göteborg and Malmö regions. One reason was national in
character. The investigation thought that it would be advantageous for the

development of the entire country if the economic potential of these two metropolitan regions could be better utilized. Another argument was municipal in character. Greater economic growth in these two regions was regarded as a means to achieve a long term solution to the municipal economic problems that exist in the cities of Göteborg and Malmö.

The metropolitan study also observed that from the national perspective there was no reason actively to stimulate economic growth in the Stockholm region. At the same time, however, it warned the government against adopting measures designed to slow the economic growth of that region, because in the worst case such measures could create obstacles to the importation of new knowledge and technology and to Sweden's possibilities of keeping pace with international economic development. The metropolitan areas, primarily the capital region, were considered as national import ports for new technology.

The final report emphasizes that the investigation has indicated many paradoxical features in the development of the metropolises. Economic developments have been relatively favourable and the employment situation comparatively advantageous. At the same time, they have evinced such deficiencies in wellbeing as exclusion of people from the labour market, greater dependency on social assistance and increasing residential segregation, which were intensified during the long economic boom of the 1980s. The investigation's final report submitted 40 proposals relating to expansion of the infrastructure, measures for improving the wellbeing of vulnerable groups, regeneration of the public sector, stimulation of citizen participation and ways to enhance the ability of politicians to take action.

Many of the proposals submitted by the metropolitan study have been realized. Accordingly, the study suggested that the government take the initiative for a programme for expanding the traffic network in the three metropolitan regions. Before the investigation's final report had been published, the government had appointed three negotiators who, at the government's instigation, would consult with the affected municipalities to draw up proposals for investments in traffic in these three regions. These negotiations resulted in three agreements in principle for expansions of the traffic systems (SOU, 1991, p. 19).

The main thrust of the agreement in the Stockholm region was on investments in the highway network. A complete six lane beltway around the centre of Stockholm and one thoroughfare to the west of the city for through traffic would be constructed. The argument for the beltway was that a growing Stockholm, where a large amount of automobile traffic passes through the city, has created a poorer environment and low accessibility for traffic. The beltway would make it possible to lead traffic around the core of the city. These thoroughfares would be financed by tolls. In addition, a rapid streetcar system would be laid out, the capacity of the railways would be expanded and the subway system would be improved. The national government and the county council together would finance the investments in public transport.

The agreement between the government and Stockholm has been subjected to much criticism both from concerned citizens and in political circles. There have been opponents in all parties. The entire plan, specific parts of the plan and the proposed financing have all been opposed. With the passing of time, the estimated costs for the expansion have gradually been adjusted upwards. In February 1997 the Minister of Transport and Communications stepped in, stating that the government no longer backed the plan. The government proposed that the eastern part of the beltway not be built and that the thoroughfare west of the city for through traffic be postponed. At the same time, the proposal to finance the investments by means of tolls was withdrawn. The government promised to come back with a new proposal for how the region will pay its share of the costs. For his part, the minister recommended a regional payroll tax.

The agreement in Göteborg comprised the improvement of public transportation to and within the region's centre, construction of a beltway to the east of the city and stipulation that road construction inside the beltway be carried out only if it were required to improve the conditions for public transport. Some of the expansion in the Göteborg region was also to be financed by tolls.

The negotiating situation in Malmö was unique. At the time set for the negotiations, planning was under way for a bridge over Öresund, but the decision to build one had not yet been made, leading to a good deal of uncertainty about connections to the bridge. To a large extent, the investments included in the agreement focus on public transportation. A programme for improving public transport will be carried out, and rail traffic will be expanded where the appropriate conditions exist. The orientation of the agreement is determined by the fact that the Malmö region is a multicore metropolitan region where improvements in transport among the cores are more important than traffic within the cores.

Arguably the most important infrastructure investment for the region, the City Tunnel, which is a rail connection between the centre of Malmö and the Öresund bridge, was not included in the agreement. The City Tunnel is calculated to play a major role in terms of improving the environment, increasing accessibility and stimulating economic development in the region.

It is expected to provide the Öresund bridge with better links to the regional rail network, which can facilitate the dissemination of the bridge's economic effects to other parts of the region. An agreement on financing the City Tunnel was reached in 1996 between the government and the municipality of Malmö.

When Sweden joined the EU in 1995, the EU Commission decided to designate Malmöhus county as an entitlement area for cooperation with Denmark in the Öresund region within INTERREG-II. The programme, which will be carried out during 1995–99, has an appropriation of 28 million ECU. The background was that in 1994, the EU Commission designated the Copenhagen region as an entitlement area within the framework for the 1994–99 INTERREG-II programme.

The purpose of the programme is to foster the integration of Skåne and the Copenhagen region by supporting existing – and promoting the growth of new – cooperative relations in the region. The programme encompasses six areas of effort, the largest being the development of the business sector in the region. This large investment in the business sector is explained by the fact that unemployment is one of the greatest problems in the Öresund region. The aim is to remove or diminish the barriers that complicate cooperation between the business sectors in Skåne and the Copenhagen region, and by so doing contribute to promoting cooperation and strengthening competitiveness in the business sectors of the two regions.

Another high priority area is the development of regional competence and integration. Three types of effort are included here. One focuses on analytical activities and drawing up plans for development. Among other things, this gives high priority to analyzing the consequences of the Öresund bridge, analyses of barriers affecting the business sector, development plans for peripheral parts of the Öresund region, and developing methods for border region statistics. The second effort concerns cooperation in the field of health care services and in the area of social services. Among high priority themes are the principles governing the citizen's choice of hospitals in the Öresund region, analyses of development trends for the health care sector in the integrated region, and programmes for mutual research efforts at different hospitals in the Öresund region. The third effort is research, development and higher education. Here the effort will be to support greater cooperation among colleges and universities in the region, to intensify cooperation among research centres, to adopt measures to facilitate educational opportunities in the region, to support preparations for cooperative initiatives aimed at EU educational and research programmes, and cooperatively to develop strategic research areas of importance to the Öresund region (INTERREG-II, 1995).

The measures proposed by the metropolitan study for improving the welfare of vulnerable groups in the metropolitan regions basically had to do with labour market policy, renovation of residential areas and efforts to improve law and order. The conditions for realizing these proposals changed dramatically with the recession at the beginning of the 1990s. As indicated earlier, this involved a rapid rise in unemployment and a dramatic deterioration in government finances. A period of cutbacks in public expenditures began. The economic possibilities of improving the welfare of vulnerable groups in the metropolitan regions were consequently diminished.

The metropolitan study further proposed that regional planning also be transferred to directly elected county councils in the Göteborg and Malmö regions. This presumed a change of the mapping out of counties in the Göteborg region, and that Malmö join its county council with regard to regional planning. The decision has been made that the new county council in Skåne will assume responsibility for regional planning in 1999. The confirmed merger of three counties in western Sweden is the first step on the way to a similar development in the Göteborg region.

In 1994 the Swedish government commissioned a second investigation to work on living conditions in metropolitan areas. This time it was a parliamentary commission assigned to initiate and implement projects to ameliorate the situation in about 20 exposed housing areas in the three metropolitan regions.

Note

1   The latest regional plan encompasses the period 1990–2020 (*Regionplan*, 1992).

References

Hall, Peter (1988), *Cities of Tomorrow*, Oxford.
INTERREG-II (1995), *Öresundsregionen* [The Öresund Region].
Nilsson, Jan-Evert (1992), 'Relocation of State Agencies as a Strategy for Urban Development: The Swedish Case', *Scandinavian Housing and Planning Research*, 9, p. 113–8.
Nilsson, Jan-Evert (1995), *Sverige i förändringens Europa* [Sweden in a Changing Europe], Malmö.
Regionplan 1991 [*Regional Plan 1991*] (1992), Stockholm.
SOU (1989), *Levnadsvillkor i storstadsregioner* [*Living Conditions in Metropolitan Regions*].
SOU (1990), *Storstadsliv. Rika möjligheter – hårda krav* [*Big City Life: Rich Opportunities, Exacting Demands*].

SOU (1991:19), *Storstadens trafiksystem – Överenskommelser och miljö i stockholms-göteborgs-och malmöregionerna.*

Svenska kommunförbundet [Swedish Association of Local Authorities and Statistics] (1996), *Vad kostar verksamheten i Din kommun? Bokslut 1995 [What Do the Stockholm Activities in Your Municipality Cost? Balance Sheet 1995]*, Stockholm.

Sverige 2009 – förslag till en vision [Sweden 2009 – Proposal for a Vision] (1994), Karlskrona.

Wiklund, Tage (1992) *Storstaden i all ära. Stockholm och den moderna storstadsförorten [With All Due Respect for Metropolis – Stockholm and the Modern Metropolitan Suburb]*, Stockholm.

Wiklund, Tage (1995), *Det tillgjorda landskapet [The Artificial Landscape: An investigation into the conditions for urban culture in the Nordic countries]*, Göteborg.

16 The United Kingdom

MICHAEL PARKINSON

Introduction

This report on the structure, development and impact of urban policy in Britain during recent years is divided into six sections. The first identifies the key economic, social and institutional changes that have occurred in Britain during the past two decades and the challenges and opportunities they present to urban policy. A second section examines the national spatial pattern, identifying in particular the key trends affecting large cities. The third section identifies the financial and administrative framework in which urban policy is made and discusses key changes in the structure, role and operation of local government. A fourth section discusses the national government's perspective upon urban issues and challenges and how that perspective has changed over time. The fifth section provides a detailed assessment of the impact of national policy during the past two decades with particular focus upon developments in policy during the past five years. The sixth section identifies a number of crucial current policy concerns as well as the debate about future policy that is taking place in Britain. The final section identifies the key findings of the report.

The Context of Urban Policy

Britain is an important case study for this European Commission survey of national urban policies in Europe. It was one of the first European nations to industrialize and urbanize during the 19th century and one of the first to deindustrialize and deurbanize at the end of the 20th century. As a result, it was also the first European country to introduce an explicit urban policy in 1968. Britain now has more experience of devising policies to help cities restructure than any other European country. Its achievements in the past 30 years should prove an important guide to what is desirable and possible in urban policy terms for the European Commission.

The economic, social and environmental difficulties facing British cities have been an issue for public debate for the past 30 years. But they have become more intense in recent years in the face of a rapidly changing economic environment. The internationalization and restructuring of the economy has increased the problems that many cities face. But it has reduced the control that either their public or private sectors have over the economic decisions that affect their communities' wellbeing. The decline of manufacturing and the rise of the service sector economy with its bifurcated labour force, has brought the decline of well paid manufacturing jobs, chronic structural unemployment, the fragmentation of the labour force, an increase in part time employment and a shift in the balance of male and female employment. Social trends – changes in the nuclear family, demographic change and an ageing population, the decentralization and suburbanization of jobs and people especially the skilled and young, the fracturing of community and the loss of social cohesion – have reinforced the consequences of economic change. Together they have created in many urban areas an uneven distribution of prosperity and the marginalization of particular economic and social groups, especially, if not exclusively, ethnic minorities, which is reflected in different patterns of employment and unemployment, access to housing, education, health care and vulnerability to crime and racism.

During the past 15 years, there have also been important changes in the institutional landscape in which urban policy has been implemented which have matched the pace of economic and social change. In local government, for example, the Conservative government's attempts since 1979 to reduce the role of the public sector has dramatically affected the responsibilities, powers and resources of local authorities. During the past decade, many former local authority services in the field of housing, education, social services, transport and environmental maintenance have been privatized or opened up to competitive tendering. Local control over revenue and capital expenditure has been constrained and reduced and local authorities have had to look beyond public funds to private sources to deliver both large and small local projects. New players have been brought in to the provision of services. And new models of mixed provision have been created. At the same time, the traditional model of the centralized, paternalist state has been eroded by the increase in special interest group politics, growing professionalism of local voluntary and community organizations and the rising expectations of the recipients of local authority services. There has also been an increasing number of actors in urban regeneration and a continuing central government emphasis on the role of the private sector.

As a consequence of such changes, urban policy in Britain is being implemented in the context of:

- constrained public resources;
- a high degree of fragmentation between local service providers;
- a reduced executive role for local government;
- a national urban policy agenda which goes beyond physical change but is only indirectly linked to the mainstream programmes that impact most heavily on cities financially;
- a new quasi-prefectoral role for regional government departments;
- central government policies which increasingly allocate resources through competitive bidding and reward areas that display a high degree of public entrepreneurialism and partnership;
- a growing role for the European Commission.

This essay concentrates on the experience of the past decade and current policy issues (cf. Parkinson, 1989, 1996a, 1996b; Atkinson and Moon, 1994; Deakin and Edwards, 1993, Lawless; 1996, Wills-Heeg, 1996). But it starts by identifying some key trends and problems in British cities which government policy is trying to address.

National Spatial Development Pattern

In Britain, as in the rest of the Union, defining a large city is not straightforward. Since it was one of the first industrialized countries in Europe, Britain has also long been one of its most urbanized. The majority of its population already lived in urban areas as early as 1850 and in the 1990s over 80 per cent of its population did so. However, the term urban includes many areas which are not large cities. Also, the definition of a city – let alone a large city – is itself a matter of interpretation and varies between European countries. In particular, the way in which administrative boundaries are drawn – distinguishing the core city from its wider metropolitan area – affects the population size of cities. Obviously, the metropolitan area, which is often the more appropriate economic unit is larger than the central administrative city – but population figures are typically provided for the latter. Hence clear definitions, discussions and comparisons of 'large cities' within the Union is not simple.

It is also important to recognize that urban problems are not confined to the large cities. In Britain, government policy has identified 57 cities and towns as Urban Priority Areas, which, on objective indicators of economic and social need, deserve financial support. This list contains cities with populations as low as 50,000. Such places benefit from urban policy – even if the scale of need and the financial resources they have received from government have been smaller than those in larger cities. Hence, although this essay primarily focuses upon the profile, problems and prospects of large cities, it is important to remember that urban policy in Britain recognizes there is a hierarchy of urban areas in terms of population, needs and the distribution of public resources rather than a simple distinction between 'the large cities' and 'the rest'.

In attempting to discuss the larger cities, the most sensible classification to use is that developed by the Office of Population Censuses and Surveys for England and Wales. Its most useful classification for our purposes is the following four types of urban areas: i) London (which is divided into 33 local authority areas); ii) six principal metropolitan cities – Birmingham, Leeds, Liverpool, Manchester, Newcastle-upon-Tyne and Sheffield; iii) 30 other metropolitan districts; and iv) nine large non-metropolitan cities. Historically, the seven cities in categories i) and ii) have been the largest and the most important in economic terms. However, economic restructuring and population change mean that some of the other cities outside that list of seven are now actually larger and as important economically as those outside it. Table 16.1 indicates the top 20 cities in terms of population in Britain, including Scotland and Wales, during the past 30 years. In 1991 there were 19 cities with populations over 200,000 and nine with populations over 400,000. Those nine include all but one – Newcastle – of England's seven traditional industrialized cities which have typically been the central focus of urban policy. They can be regarded as England's large cities in this essay.

What are the most important trends affecting cities during the past decade? The most authoritative recent answer is provided in a government sponsored study (Atkins et al., 1996). This review discussed all urban areas in England but concentrated upon the 12 large cities – the traditional large seven plus Bristol, Nottingham, Plymouth, Preston and Coventry. It identified four major trends affecting cities – economic restructuring, counter-urbanization, social polarization and the dominance of London. The broad message that emerged from the study was that, although there was a variation between places, the division between urban and rural areas widened during the 1980s.

Economic Restructuring

The key feature affecting Britain's larger cities in recent years has been the process of economic restructuring and changes in the nature and distribution of employment. Simply put, the large cities, and particularly their inner areas,

Table 16.1 Top twenty cities in Britain in terms of population (including Scotland and Wales) during the past 30 years

Population 000

	1961		1971		1981		1991	
1	London	7,992	London	7,454	London	6,696	London	6,890
2	Birmingham	1,107	Birmingham	1,015	Birmingham	1,007	Birmingham	938
3	Glasgow	1,055	Glasgow	897	Glasgow	766	Leeds	677
4	Liverpool	746	Liverpool	610	Leeds	705	Glasgow	654
5	Manchester	662	Manchester	544	Sheffield	538	Sheffield	503
6	Leeds	511	Sheffield	520	Liverpool	510	Bradford	451
7	Sheffield	494	Leeds	496	Bradford	457	Liverpool	450
8	Edinburgh	468	Edinburgh	454	Manchester	449	Edinburgh	422
9	Bristol	437	Bristol	427	Edinburgh	437	Manchester	400
10	Belfast	416	Belfast	362	Bristol	391	Bristol	372
11	Nottingham	312	Coventry	335	Belfast	314	Coventry	295
12	Coventry	306	Nottingham	301	Coventry	314	Belfast	279
13	Kingston-upon-Hull	303	Bradford	294	Leicester	280	Cardiff	277
14	Bradford	296	Kingston-upon-Hull	286	Cardiff	274	Leicester	272
15	Leicester	273	Leicester	284	Nottingham	272	Nottingham	262
16	Stoke-on-Trent	265	Cardiff	270	Kingston-upon-Hull	270	Kingston-upon-Hull	253
17	Cardiff	257	Wolverhampton	269	Wolverhampton	255	Stoke-on-Trent	244
18	Aberdeen	185	Stoke-on-Trent	265	Stoke-on-Trent	253	Wolverhampton	241
19	Dundee	183	Aberdeen	182	Aberdeen	204	Aberdeen	210
20	Wolverhampton	151	Dundee	182	Dundee	180	Dundee	166

Source: Pocket Britain in Figures, The Economist, 1997.

have been losing jobs at steady rates for the past 30 years. These trends have continued during the 1980s as there was a widespread reduction in employment in urban England in contrast to general increases in the rest of the country. The inner areas of the largest cities fared worst. In 1991, of the study's 12 large cities, there was at least 9 per cent less employment in London, Liverpool, Newcastle and Plymouth than there had been in 1984. There were significant increases in work in only two – Bristol and Leeds. Unemployment rates rose more quickly than the national rates over the 1980s in the inner and outer areas of cities, especially in London, the largest non-metropolitan cities and the principal metropolitan cities. In terms of households, by 1991 in the seven principal metropolitan cities, one in every three households had no-one in the labour force. Inner city residents face increasing competition for jobs in the inner city at a time when the jobs there are are declining in number and shifting away from the manual jobs on which they largely depended. The number of households with no member in the labour market increased steeply in metropolitan areas whereas in the more rural districts the number of households with at least two earners grew more rapidly.

There were important changes in the gender distribution of labour. During the 1980s, national employment rates for men fell by three per cent, whereas it rose for women by seven per cent, but the trends were even greater in the large cities. The report concluded that the 1991 census painted 'a depressing picture' of the labour market opportunities for people in urban England, especially those in the inner areas of the large cities. During the 1980s, self-employment grew more slowly than average in all 12 inner areas and all six metropolitan and city type districts except outer London. Unemployment rates for both men and women in 1991 were higher than average in all the urban England district types except outer London.

Counter-urbanization

The second key trend affecting large cities is the loss of population as people move away from the large urban towards more rural areas. The trend has slowed since the 1970s, but still continues in 1990s Britain. Apart from London, which we shall discuss later, there is a close inverse relationship between rate of overall population growth and the level in England's urban hierarchy, together with a very widespread shift in population distribution from the inner to outer areas of large cities. Internal migration within Britain is the primary cause of the population decline of larger cities. Between 1961–91, rural areas grew most strongly and the principal metropolitan cities and other metropolitan districts had the largest losses. This trend can be seen in Table 16.2, which indicates the population changes in the top seven cities and their surrounding conurbations during the past 30 years.

Table 16.2 Population changes in the top seven cities and their surrounding conurbations during the past 30 years

Area	Population (000s)			
	1961	1971	1981	1991
England and Wales	46,196	49,152	49,634	51,099
England	43,561	46,412	46,821	48,208
Wales	2,635	2,740	2,813	2,891
Greater London	7,977	7,529	6,806	6,890
Inner London	3,481	3,060	2,550	2,627
Outer London	4,496	4,470	4,255	4,263
Greater Manchester	2,710	2,750	2,619	2,570
Manchester	657	554	463	439
Merseyside	1,711	1,662	1,522	1,450
Liverpool	741	610	517	481
South Yorkshire	1,298	1,331	1,317	1,302
Sheffield	581	579	548	529
Tyne and Wear	1,241	1,218	1,155	1,130
Newcastle-upon-Tyne	336	312	284	278
West Midlands	2,724	2,811	2,673	2,629
Birmingham	1,178	1,107	1,021	1,007
West Yorkshire	2,002	2,090	2,067	2,085
Leeds	710	749	718	717

Source: *1995 Annual Abstract of Statistics*, Office of Population of Censuses and Surveys.

Although counter-urbanization is an important trend, it slowed significantly from its peak in the mid-1970s. Population losses were much smaller in the 1980s than in the 1970s. Migration rates reveal the picture. Between 1990 and 1992, England's metropolitan areas showed a net loss of 80,000 a year from migration with other parts of Britain. This was down by 35 per cent on the average for 1984–87 and 40 per cent below the rates in the mid-1970s. Within cities, the key trend was the continuing shift in population from their inner to their outer areas. Ten of the 12 large cities in the DOE study showed such shifts. The only exceptions were Nottingham and London, which had population growth in the inner areas and stabilization in the outer areas. In terms of net migration exchanges with the rest of Britain, the inner areas of all 12 cities lost at least 0.6 per cent of population – with highest losses in

Newcastle, Manchester and London. The study's conclusion was that counter-urbanization was likely to continue, despite the slowing down in recent years for most cities. If economic restructuring continued along the same lines with jobs moving to smaller urban and rural areas, population was likely to move along the same lines.

As the government report indicated, social polarization is an increasingly important policy issue in Britain. Its significance has been increased by economic restructuring, counter-urbanization and the dominance of London, which have had an impact upon levels of both social and spatial polarization. Social polarization in essence means a widening of the gaps that exist between groups of people in terms of their economic and social opportunities and circumstances. Although census data is not the most valuable for demonstrating this issue, the report did demonstrate the growing gap between urban and rural, between earners and non-earners and between inner and outer urban areas. The census data were unable to demonstrate that social polarization had actually increased during the 1980s, but confirmed that levels were higher in cities than outside. Examining households with children and no earners, those with no earners and no children, and those with earners, it found the following pattern:

- wards with the proportion of households with at least one earner above the national average were concentrated in the southeast of England around London and in belts of affluence around major cities;
- wards with above the national average proportion of households with no earners were particularly prevalent in Inner London and in the inner areas of other metropolitan centres;
- the inner areas of all cities except London had above average proportions of both households with children and no earners and households with no children and earners. They had below average proportions of households with earners;
- 22 per cent of children live in households with no earner as well as having at least two of the three problems of lacking amenity, being overcrowded and not having a car. The percentage was highest in the inner urban areas, declined to outer metropolitan areas and were lowest in rural areas.

This concentration of types of households is likely to continue. Households leaving inner urban areas are more likely to be owner-occupiers and less reliant upon local authority or housing association housing. Those living in the inner cities are more likely to be ethnic minorities and hence discriminated against in access to employment and services. By contrast, in rural areas there has been a growth in new service sector industries in the past decade. Those areas also have higher proportions of families with one person in work and of home owners.

The Dominance of London

In terms of the large cities, one fact stands out, as Table 15.1 demonstrated. London dominates the British urban hierarchy – economically, institutionally and culturally. Even though its economy has outperformed other large cities, London's sheer size also means that it has a very high proportion of the country's urban problems. As the DOE report indicated, in many respects, London is a global city like Paris, New York, Tokyo and Los Angeles, and exhibits many of the trends found in such cities during the 1980s. For example, like those cities – in contrast to the national pattern – its population ceased to decline, and in the inner areas actually grew in the 1980s. It attracted higher rates of international migration than other British cities. It has higher percentages of black and other ethnic minorities than other British cities. It also has higher levels of polarization than any other cities, with more of its 33 local authority areas having the highest concentration of people from the highest social classes, as well as areas with the highest concentrations of economic and social problems.

The Administrative and Financial Framework

The Local Government System

To understand urban policy in Britain in the 1990s, it is important to appreciate the position of local authorities. In the past 15 years, national government has made a large umber of reforms to their structure, roles, finance and operation which have dramatically affected relations between national and local governments and urban policy. Stoker and Stewart (1995, p. 78) argue that '[t]he emphasis of many of these measures and the central thrust of the Government concern was with increasing the control of central government over local authorities and in particular on restraining local authority expenditure'. They identify the key themes of the government's policy in relation to local authorities since 1979 as:

- financial constraint, with real cutbacks or increases failing to keep pace with inflation as well as concern with value for money and more outputs for fewer resources;
- the fragmentation of local government as elected local authorities increasingly share their service delivery, regulatory and strategic responsibilities with a range of other agencies and institutions;
- a commitment to competition with local services open to provision by the private sector;
- the separation of responsibility for a service from the act of providing it, with local authorities retaining responsibility but passing on the doing of it to others;
- the development of an enabling role for local authorities rather than an all-providing role;
- a closer relationship between paying for and receiving local services;
- a greater emphasis on customer choice;
- a greater scope for individual and private sector provision of local services;
- a commitment to developing more businesslike management.

It is worth underlining a number of key issues which particularly impact upon cities and which flow from those general trends in national policy towards local government.

Metropolitan government There have been major changes in the structure of metropolitan government. Local government reform in 1974 created elected metropolitan government in the largest seven cities. These levied charges upon their constituent local authorities and in return provided a range of services – strategic planning, transport, police and fire services and economic development across the metropolitan areas. However, these Metropolitan County Councils were abolished by national government in 1986. As a consequence, there are no levels of government which are responsible for wider policy matters across the largest conurbations. Instead, a number of local authorities – 33 in London, 12 in greater Manchester, for example – have to engage in a variety of voluntary and semiformal arrangements to provide strategic services across the metropolitan areas.

Although the government would not accept the point, many commentators argue that the absence of such directly elected organizations with powers to provide strategic services restricts the ability to respond coherently to economic and social changes across the wider metropolitan areas. They also suggest that it has encouraged conflicts of interests between the more and less affluent parts of large urban areas. The argument is most typically made about London, which it is argued suffers in comparison with other major European cities. There is a considerable debate within the city about the merits of recreating some form of London-wide government.

Local government functions Local authorities have traditionally had responsibility for providing directly a wide range of services to their citizens – including education, housing, social services, transportation, environmental services, highways and planning. Services were paid for from a variety of sources – grants from national government, income raised from local taxation and charges for services from users. However, during the past 15 years, government policy has been to privatize the provision or open up to competition many services which were provided directly by local authorities. As a consequence, the provision of local services is now much more complex and local authorities are no longer the single monopoly provider of services. Some local authorities have competed against the private sector on price and quality and have retained contracts to provide traditional services. In other cases, the private sector has won contracts. As a result there is a wide variety of public and private suppliers of services operating in cities.

Local government finance Local government finance has been a source of constant public debate and controversy for over 20 years, since the Labour government in 1976, and more particularly the Conservative government, tried to reduce public expenditure and particularly that of local government. Central controls over local revenue and capital expenditure have become increasingly tight during this period and the argument has become more complex and heated over the years. There have been many changes in an extraordinarily complex system. But the essential features are now clear. As one eminent commentator has observed, the system of local government finance was massively reformed in the years 1989–97. A new local tax was introduced, then abolished. 'Capping' of all local authority expenditure was extended so that all local authorities in effect have their expenditure limited by national government. The proportion of income raised from local taxation was reduced from about 60 per cent to under 20 per cent. Local government is now heavily dependent on central government support. Small changes in the level of Revenue Support Grant have a far greater effect on local taxation and expenditure than decisions made by locally elected councillors.

    There is continuing dispute about where the formulae used to distribute resources to local authorities are either large enough to meet their social needs or distinguish fairly between different types of local authority. Local taxation in 1993–94 accounts for about 20 per cent of all local authority income. A further 28 per cent comes from national non-domestic or business rates, 10 per cent from specific central government grants, 1 per cent from the community care grant and 41 per cent from the general Revenue Support Grant from central government. The heavy reliance on non-local revenue creates a substantial opportunity for central government to dictate the level of local spending in aggregate terms. But also, central government can influence the spending decisions of individual authorities through defining what needs to be spent by way of the Annual Standard Spending Assessment and by holding capping powers over local budgets to ensure that they do not rise above government approved levels. The degree of central control over local authority capital activity is very considerable.

Regional administration Just as there is no metropolitan-wide government, there is no form of elected regional government in Britain, and no formal intermediary between the nation state and local authorities. However, partly in response to the European position, there is growing voluntary cooperation between local authorities at regional level. All of the major English regions now have regional associations which combine elected local authorities with representatives from the private and community sectors. There is considerable debate about the potential advantages and disadvantages regional government might bring to regions and to the large cities which are at their heart. The Conservative government was opposed to any devolution of taxing or spending powers to any unit of government in Scotland, Wales or the English regions. But the Labour government after its election in 1997 introduced major policy changes. Scotland will be given a separate parliament, Wales an elected Assembly and the English regions will be given Regional Development Agencies (RDAs). These new agencies will take control of many programmes and budgets of a range of public agencies and will be responsible for creating economic development strategies for their regions and improving their economic competitiveness. The agencies will not be elected but appointed by government. But they will be accountable indirectly to voluntary Regional Chambers consisting of public and private agencies in each region. Although their powers and resources are constrained, the RDAs mark an important innovation in policy making and may create a foundation for regional government and increased regional democracy in the future. At present, the links between national government, regional organizations and local authorities remain uncertain. In many commentators' eyes, this also affects the capacity of larger cities to respond on a strategic level to economic, social, cultural and technological changes which cross narrowly defined local authority administrative boundaries. However, as we shall discuss later in this paper, there have been important administrative developments at regional level with the creation of Government Offices for the Regions. These have integrated the activities of the four government departments whose activities impinge most directly upon cities and one of their primary responsibilities is to administer the government regeneration programme at regional level.

More complex urban governance In addition to opening service provision to competition, government policy has also created a number of non-elected agencies such as Urban Development Corporations, Training and Enterprise Councils, Housing Action Trusts, which provide services for cities in housing, training, education, physical renewal that were once provided by local authorities. These initiatives were introduced at different times, with different responsibilities, agendas, budgets and timetables. But it means that the institutional framework of governance at local level is now increasingly complicated. Regeneration has to be achieved through the interactions of many players. In a single urban area this can include: national government departments and their regional offices; several local authorities and their different departments; task forces; City Action Teams; Urban Development Corporations; Training and Enterprise Councils; Enterprise Zones; City Challenges; Single Regeneration Partnerships; private firms; private or voluntary sector advice and training organizations; institutions of further and higher education; and tenants' and residents' associations. Again, although the government would not accept this point, critics often argue that this fragmentation of government constrains cities' capacity to achieve regeneration – the goal of government policy.

   In understanding the complexity of patterns of the governance of British cities, it is particularly important to appreciate the contribution that different government departments make to urban affairs. The most significant is the Department of the Environment, which has had formal responsibility for urban policy since 1970. The department manages the programmes and policy sectors which probably have greatest impact upon urban areas. Its most important urban responsibilities include local government and its finances, regeneration programmes, housing, the environment and land use planning. But other departments are responsible for a wide range of programmes which have an important impact upon large cities. For example, the Department of Trade and Industry looks after regional policy, European programmes and structural funds and is responsible for encouraging economic competitiveness. The Department of Transport is responsible for much of the urban transport infrastructure. The Department for Employment and Education is responsible for a wide variety of programmes in education, training and support for business which impact upon cities. The Home Office has responsibility for policing and programmes to reduce crime in cities as well as a range of initiatives to improve the social and economic standing of ethnic minorities. The Department of Social Security is responsible for many welfare state programmes which particularly impact upon low income people in British cities. Overall responsibility for public expenditure is exercised by the Treasury. All play an important part in the development of cities and urban policy. In recent years there have been continuing efforts to integrate their budgets, programmes and policies.

Urban Issues and Challenges from a National Perspective

Britain has had an explicit urban policy since the introduction of the Urban Programme in 1968. However, its shape and resources have changed many times since that date. In devising urban policies to respond to economic and social changes in the past 30 years, successive governments have had to face a common set of questions. They include:

- What is the target of the policy – 'inner city problems' or urban challenges?
- Is the problem economic, social or environmental – or some combination of all three?
- What is the right balance of power and responsibility between national and local government?
- What is the best mix of public, private and community intervention?
- should social need or economic opportunity determine policy priorities and the flow of public resources to cities?
- How can government best achieve an integrated approach to a multifaceted set of problems?
- How can government get the best out of other partners?
- Are competition and partnership mutually reinforcing – or mutually exclusive – ways of delivering urban policy?

Different governments have given different answers to these questions. On occasions the target of policy has been narrowly defined; for example, particular social groups or limited areas within the 'inner cities'. But there has occasionally been a recognition that the challenge is more pervasive and touches many groups who are not confined to particular areas of our cities. At times, a pathological view of the 'inner city problem' has emphasized the individual inadequacies of urban residents; at others, policy has more clearly recognized the structural causes of their exclusion. Sometimes the existence of need has been regarded as enough to require a policy response; at others economic potential has been required as a justification for public expenditure. At times it has been assumed that a single actor – local authorities, national government, the public sector, the private sector – could resolve the problem. At others the need for partnership has been more clearly recognized. Sometimes is has been assumed that the cities are the concern of a single government department; at others the importance of other departments has been recognized. At key points 'the community' has been given a prominent role – at others it has had to take a back seat.

Despite such differences, we can detect a broad pattern in the evolution of urban policy. Throughout the 1970s, after a Labour government's introduction of the first Union Programme in 1968 and despite shifts in government, urban policy rested on two shared assumptions. First, it was as much designed to provide social and welfare support services to those experiencing economic change in the inner cities as it was to create wealth in those areas. Second, since disinvestment by the private sector was seen as the cause of many inner city problems, the public sector, including local authorities, was regarded as the natural mechanism to promote urban reconstruction.

During the 1980s, however, the Conservative government challenged both those assumptions. In particular the market not the state was regarded as the primary response to urban decline. The values of urban entrepreneurialism replaced those of public intervention. Investment in physical capital – property – rather than investment in social capital – people – became a policy priority. Wealth creation became as important a goal of policy as the delivery of welfare. National government control was increased at the expense of local authorities. But in the 1990s urban policy is changing once again and there is evidence of earlier approaches and values re-emerging. In particular, City Challenges and the Single Regeneration Budget attempt to provide different answers to our key questions, as many of the answers from the 1980s have been increasingly challenged.

The development of urban policy in Britain has been politically controversial. It is, therefore, difficult to provide an analysis that every partner would agree upon. Possibly the most neutral description of its development can be found in the study of the Action for Cities programme, *Assessing the Impact of Urban Policy* (Robson, Parkinson et al., 1994), which the Department of the Environment commissioned. Reviewing 25 years of urban policy, it identified the five main periods of policy in the following terms:

i) with the introduction in 1968 of the Urban Programme policy focused upon community-based projects and addressing the needs of social deprivation;

ii) after the enhancement of the Urban programme in 1978, the focus of policy was increased to include economic and infrastructure needs. The delivery of policy was through the creation of partnership between central and local government with the identification of seven partnership areas in the largest cities and programme areas in smaller cities;

iii) from the 1980s, the emphasis upon economic and infrastructure was reinforced with a switch of spending from revenue to capital expenditure. The stress on creating partnerships which had originally been seen in terms of central and local government, was transformed to partnerships which involved the creation of new agencies such as Urban Development Corporations, one of the key developments of the 1980s. Also in this period there were many new policy instruments whose objective was to lever private sector investment into urban areas through enterprise zones and successive grant systems such as Urban Development Grants, Urban Regeneration Grants and City Grants;

iv) in the later 1980s, issues of coordination became a more important feature of urban policy. New administrative arrangements like City Action teams and task forces were added to locally based agencies. Particularly importantly, in 1988 the government rolled together a whole range of urban related policies into its programme Action for Cities;

v) in the 1990s, attention was focused most specifically upon area-based interventions, targeting, the allocation of resources according to competition and the integration of the regeneration programmes of different government departments.

National Policy Responses to Urban Issues, Challenges and Development 1979–97

Urban Policy 1979–91: Encouraging Urban Entrepreneurialism

Despite shifts in emphasis between 1968 and 1979, there were several continuities in policy during this period. The delivery of welfare remained a central goal. Public expenditure was seen as crucial. Local government was regarded as an important actor in urban regeneration. After the election of the Conservative government in 1979, however, those three key assumptions of policy were fundamentally challenged. During the next decade the institutional and policy framework which they underpinned was gradually changed as the government attempted to encourage its new strategic response to urban decline – private sector-led urban entrepreneurialism. During the 1980s, the government devoted considerable attention to local government. Metropolitan councils were abandoned. Local services and finances were restructured. A host of central government initiatives – task forces, City Action Teams, Enterprise Zones, Development Corporations, Housing Action Trusts, English Partnerships – were introduced. The government's original stated strategy for the regeneration of cities involved a major redistribution in political power, including the decentralization of power and shift in control of policy from central to local level and the use of private markets to break the control of monopoly public suppliers at local level. However, during this period the government also decided it had to reduce public sector expenditure, especially that of local authorities. As a consequence, many have argued that in contrast to its stated intentions, the government minimized local government's role in urban regeneration while increasing that of the private sector and central government itself.

Although government policy for the cities has never been made entirely explicit, the Action for Cities programme gave its most comprehensive account. Policy was designed:

- to encourage enterprise and new business and help existing businesses to grow stronger;
- to improve people's job prospects, their motivation and skills;
- to make areas more attractive to residents and to business by tackling dereliction, bringing buildings into use, preparing sites and encouraging development, and improving the quality of housing;

- to make inner city areas safe and attractive places in which to live and work.

What Was the Policy Impact in the 1980s and 1990s?

What was the impact of this policy approach in the 1980s? Which groups benefited and which lost? What implications were there for urban policy? *Assessing the Impact of Urban Policy* threw considerable light on these issues. Funded by the government, this report is regarded as the definitive account of the impact of urban policy during the past 15 years. It examined the impact of policies and resources spent through the Action for Cities programmes over 120 British cities during the 1980s and early 1990s and compared the position of the 57 Urban Programme authorities with other less deprived areas. It concentrated in detail on the experience of three major conurbations – Manchester, Liverpool and Newcastle. Essentially, it made five points about the impact of urban policy during the 1980s and early 1990s.

Limited resources Total government expenditure on cities was relatively limited. The report estimated that the money spent by government in all its programmes which impacted upon cities at that time was £4 billion, a modest proportion of the total spend of £200 billion by government. Urban expenditure, the government's explicit urban policy, in 1993–94 was rather less, at £1.01 billion. Equally importantly, that figure had gradually risen throughout the 1980s but was planned to decline by 1993–94. Whatever positive impact government policy had had in the past, expenditure cuts suggested it would be reduced in future.

Smaller not larger cities benefit The study measured change in the conditions of different cities in terms of employment prospects, the attractiveness in terms of the numbers of younger age groups living there, as well as the demand for private housing. Here the evidence was mixed. At one level government policy had an impact and improved the position of the 57 cities in greatest need. Government resources spent on those areas reduced unemployment, attracted younger residents, and raised demand for private housing in comparison with other areas which had not received that expenditure. In addition, the gap between the Urban Programme areas in greatest need and the remainder closed as the overall position of the 57 most deprived areas relatively improved.

However, the problem was that larger cities did not share in that relative progress. The seven largest cities experienced both absolute and relative decline, with the problems traditionally associated with inner cities spreading more generally across the wider urban area. Urban policy had improved conditions in some of the medium- and smaller-sized cities or outlying parts of the larger cities. But there had been an intensification of economic distress at the hearts of the biggest cities which had continued to deteriorate, regardless of financial expenditure.

Declining resources A stable or growing proportion of explicit urban funds was targeted at the 57 cities in greatest need. However, the major sources of funding for cities were still the Rate Support Grant and the Housing Investment Programmes. And these were substantially reduced during the decade. At the beginning of the 1980s they had accounted for up to 90 per cent of expenditure in larger cities. But cuts in government support for those main programmes meant that in some cases they had fallen to 70 per cent of local authority expenditure. Although cities continued to receive special Urban Programme funding throughout the 1980s, their larger sources of government income were reduced.

Insufficient coordination The research identified a number of administrative weaknesses. There was insufficient coordination of the policies and efforts of the different government departments whose work impacted upon cities. Some government departments operated with different spatial priorities – for example, the wider region as opposed to the city. Others had no spatial priorities and no overt commitment to cities at all. Not enough attention had been paid to creating linkages between different policy sectors such as training, education and job creation or to strengthening the capacity of local communities.

Building partnerships The report identified substantial limitations of government strategy to create partnerships to deliver urban regeneration during the 1980s. The emphasis had been on private sector leadership. But the contribution and commitment of the private sector to the partnership process had been exaggerated by government. The sustained commitment of public resources and an agreed policy environment which would attract the private sector into longer term partnerships had not been provided. Local authorities had been excluded from the process. The report argued that they had an important part to play in creating coalitions to achieve long term regeneration. But limits upon their powers and resources had limited their ability to play a constructive role. The study also found the local communities had not been given a sufficiently large role. It argued that the process ought to be opened up to engage both the local authorities and the community sector more in future.

Lessons for Policy

The research identified five main lessons for a future policy. Public-private partnerships and coalitions of local players were a desirable method of attempting urban regeneration. Local authorities should be given greater opportunities, powers and resources to play a significant part. Local communities should also be given greater opportunities. Specific resources should be provided to encourage community capacity building within deprived areas. Greater coherence was needed between the programmes of the different government departments which impacted upon the inner cities, as had been achieved in some area-based programmes. There should be greater flexibility of expenditure between different departments and between different years. There should be less ambiguity in the targeting of resources to cities with a single urban budget, uniting all the resources of the departments, which should be administered at regional rather than national level.

Urban Policy 1992–97: Between Partnership and Competition; City Challenge and the Single Regeneration Budget

In the early 1990s such criticism, amongst other pressures, encouraged the government to change policy focus. It made substantial changes to the organization, financing and priorities of urban policy with the introduction in 1992 of the City Challenge initiative and even more important in 1994, the Single Regeneration Budget (SRB). The SRB brought together all government regeneration programmes under a single heading. Critics have two major reservations about these initiatives. They have argued that a competition between local authorities and partners is not the best way of allocating resources to urban areas. They have also observed that the money was new but found from existing programmes. Despite those two important reservations, City Challenge and the SRB are a important attempt to address some of the key problems of urban policy and have a number of features which differentiate it from the policies of the 1980s.

City Challenge City Challenge was introduced in 1992 as a five year programme for which the 57 Urban Programme authorities were eligible to compete. In two rounds of competition, 31 local partnerships of local authorities, TECs, the private sector and community made successful bids to government to achieve Challenge status and were each allocated £37.5 million over a five year period. City Challenge has wider goals than economic and physical regeneration. These are retained, but social and human capital are given higher priority. Local partners are required to define a wider vision for their area and to link programmes, projects, resources and mechanisms to that vision in a strategic way. Challenge focuses upon the quality of the programmes as well as a need. It uses the principle of competition to encourage the focus on quality. Local authorities and local communities are given a more substantial role. It involves a range of government departments – not simply the DOE. It is meant to bend mainstream resources in the process attracting increased private resources to the area. It is a five year initiative designed to give greater certainty and continuity for local players.

How well is City Challenge performing? An independent review of the City Challenge initiative prepared for the Department of the Environment found substantial support for the policy (Russell, Parkinson et al., 1996; Parkinson, 1993). Its key findings were:

i) City Challenge was the most promising regeneration scheme so far attempted. There was widespread support from a range of partners for most aspects of its design. They saw it as an advance upon previous initiatives, particularly because of its partnership basis, its community and private sector involvement, its strategic and targeted approach and its implementation by dedicated multi-disciplinary teams;

ii) it was more than meeting its leverage and output targets. In its first three years the 31 Challenges had:

- levered in nearly £1.3 billion private sector funds;
- completed/improved nearly 39,200 dwellings;
- created/preserved over 53,000 jobs;
- reclaimed/improved nearly 1,900 ha derelict land;
- created/improved over 1,257 m^2 of floor space;
- promoted nearly 3,150 business start-ups;

iii) competition had advantages as a management tool. It galvanized cross-sectoral involvement, required commitment to future delivery and produced more positive and imaginative proposals for change. However, for some people, competition was problematic as a basis for allocating urban resources in being potentially divisive and penalizing areas without conspicuous development opportunities to deliver;

iv) the scale of City Challenge resource and its area targeting made possible a more strategic integrated approach to regeneration. Challenge allowed developments to occur which required substantial pump priming to take place. It speeded up development which otherwise would have been more piecemeal. It triggered further investment and related activity. It added value by linking separate programmes, agencies and types of expertise;

v) Challenge also influenced the way in which partner organizations worked together. It encouraged cross-sectoral understanding. It stimulated more corporate working within local authorities. It led to tighter project management. Partnership at programme and project level was bringing new alliances in other areas.

Extending the Challenge Model – the Single Regeneration Budget

In 1994, there were further substantial organizational and policy changes as the government extended the principles of City Challenge with the creation of the Government Offices in the Regions and the Single Regeneration Budget (Department of the Environment, 1996). Government Offices in ten regions bring together the four departments whose activities most clearly impact upon cities – Environment, Employment, Training and Industry and Transport – led by a regional director. They are responsible for, amongst many other things, allocating the Single Regeneration Budget (SRB). The SRB integrated 20 different grants from five government departments affecting regeneration into a single budget worth £1.4 billion. An increasing proportion of that total will be made available annually on a competitive basis to partners in the regions – local authorities, Training and Enterprise Councils, Urban Development Corporations, the private and voluntary sectors. At national level, policy on the SRB is coordinated by a ministerial Committee on Competitiveness. A network of sponsor ministers supports regeneration initiatives in their area, with ministers acting as channels of communication between local areas and Whitehall.

The Single Regeneration Budget, now the explicit urban policy of the government, is intended to support existing continuing programmes including

City Challenge, Urban Development Corporations and Estate Action. Through the SRB Challenge Fund and English Partnerships, it provides funding for new regeneration activities. The SRB is intended to complement main programme spending. The Challenge Fund of the SRB initiative makes resources available annually on a competitive basis for local partnerships to support regeneration schemes lasting between 1–7 years. It builds upon past strengths of regeneration policy but introduces a new local focus to the delivery of government services. Its objectives are to:

- build on initiatives proposed by local partners;
- ensure flexibility and effective use of public money;
- link into other regeneration strategies;
- be responsive to local needs and priorities;
- attract private and other public sector investment;
- harness the talents and resources of community groups and the voluntary sector.

The aim of the policy is to achieve sustainable regeneration through the formation of strong local partnerships which involve local communities to ensure the long term success of regeneration activities. The priorities for SRB are to:

- enhance the employment prospects, education and skills of local people, particularly the young and those at a disadvantage and promote equality of opportunity;
- encourage sustainable growth and wealth creation by improving the competitiveness of the local economy, including support for existing and new businesses;
- protect and improve the environment and infrastructure and promote good design;
- improve housing and housing conditions for local people through physical improvement, better maintenance, improved management and greater choice and diversity;
- promote initiatives to benefit ethnic minorities;
- tackle crime and improve community safety;
- enhance the quality of life of local people, including their health, cultural and sports opportunities.

The Delivery Mechanism

Financial support for new regeneration initiatives from the Challenge Fund is allocated through a national competitive bidding process. The first bidding round took place in 1994 for schemes beginning in 1995. Bids from local partnerships were appraised by the government offices in accordance with criteria set out in bidding guidance prepared by Whitehall. Final decisions were taken by ministers. Over 200 bids were successful, involving support for employment, training and education, enterprise, housing projects, crime prevention schemes and initiatives directed specifically to ethnic minorities. 172 were approved for the year beginning 1996. The bids came from a range of partnerships typically involving local authorities, Training and Enterprise Councils, the private, community and voluntary sector. Third and fourth rounds of the Challenge have been committed by the government.

Total expenditure is planned to increase from £125 million during 1995–96 to £600 million by 1998–99. In total over £1.3 billion will be available for all four bidding rounds for new regeneration projects over the three years to 1998–99. Government estimates that rounds 1 and 2 will attract more than £10 billion total expenditure over their lifetime, including private sector investment of £5 billion. Table 16.3 indicates the budgets that make up the SRB.

In addition to new projects and expenditure met by the Challenge Fund, there is a series of continuing commitments which are part of the Single Regeneration Budget. The most important include Estate Action, which is designed to help local authorities transform unpopular housing estates into places where people wish to live. It provides funds for local authorities to tackle the physical condition of their estates, improve housing management, secure greater tenant involvement, provide variety and choice in housing and create opportunities for training and enterprise. The Urban Programme, which was established in 1969, primarily supports local authority and voluntary sector projects. It will be ended in 1996–97. There are three important non-departmental public bodies – Urban Development Corporations, Housing Action Trusts and English Partnerships. The Urban Development Corporations were created in 11 cities throughout the 1980s. They will expire by 1998. The Corporations were designated, financed and appointed by central government. Their goals were to:

- bring land and buildings into effective use;
- encourage the development of existing and new industry and commerce;

Table 16.3 Regeneration expenditure

£ million

	1990–91 outturn	1991–92 outturn	1992–93 outturn	1993–94 outturn	1994–95 outturn	1995–96 estimated outturn	1996–97 plans	1997–98 plans	1998–99 plans
Single Budget Regeneration									
UDCs	553.2	508.6	430.6	343.1	258.0	217.8	190.0	168.0	69.3
Docklands Light Railway	54.0	93.2	84.4	28.1	29.1	37.1	18.1	18.9	20.0
English Partnerships (URA)	118.9.	99.1	153.3	164.9	191.7	210.3	209.6	209.6	209.6
Housing Action Trusts	–	1.1	26.5	78.1	92.0	90.0	89.0	88.9	89.0
Challenge Fund	–	–	–	–	–	125.0	265.1	483.1	600.3
Estate Action	180.0	267.5	348.0	357.4	372.6	313.8	256.1	117.8	114.8
City Challenge	–	–	72.6	240.0	233.6	241.6	224.4	143.0	7.0
Other SRB									
Urban Programme	225.8	237.5	236.2	166.5	67.8				
Task Forces	20.9	20.5	23.6	18.0	15.7				
Business Start-up Scheme	113.1	90.1	62.1	81.9	63.8				
Local Initiative Fund	19.9	48.2	49.7	45.9	34.5				
Compacts	5.8	5.5	5.4	5.7	5.2				
Teacher placement	–	3.7	3.4	3.3	3.3				
Education Business Partnership	0.7	3.2	2.0	1.7	2.5				
TEC Challenge	–	–	–	9.1	3.5		65.8	38.6	23.4]
Programme Development Fund	2.1	1.9	3.5	2.9	3.1	[123.2			
Regional Enterprise Grants	8.4	7.3	5.8	8.2	11.8				
Section 11 (part)	74.1	61.8	70.9	74.8	65.3				
Ethnic Minorities Grant	–	–	4.0	5.4	5.7				
Safer Cities	–	–	–	–	1.9				
Ethnic Minority Business Initiative	0.4	0.4	0.3	0.6	0.6				
GEST 19	–	–	3.3	6.1	4.2				
City Action Teams	7.7	8.4	4.6	3.4	0.2				
CFERS	-4.4	-7.2	-5.4	-7.6	-7.8				
Total SRB	1,370.5	1,459.8	1,584.7	1,627.7	1,468.3	1,358.9	1,318.1	1,327.9	1,334.1

Source: Department of the Environment, *1996 Annual Report and Expenditure Plans 1996/7 to 1998/9.*

- create an attractive environment;
- ensure that the housing and social facilities were available to improve the quality of life for people who live and work in the area.

English Partnerships' objectives are to promote job creation, inward investment and environmental improvements through the reclamation and development of vacant, derelict or contaminated land. They operate through six regional offices in England. Using their mix of instruments of grants, loans, guarantees and joint ventures, they operate as a strategic partner and investor in regeneration. EP is funded through the SRB and attempts to attract complementary funding from the European Regional Development Fund and maximize the leverage of private sector investment.

Future Policy Issues and Concerns

Where does urban regeneration policy stand in the mid-1990s? The focus is upon partnership, spatial targeting, integration and competition with a commitment to economic, social and environmental regeneration. In terms of policy design, there is some consensus that progress has been made under the SRB and City Challenge. Local authorities, the private sector and the community sector have welcomed the fact that policy:

- encourages the integration of departments and funding, partnership and a regional approach;
- adopts an expansive definition of the urban problem, recognizing the importance of, and the links between, the economic, social and environmental dimension;
- recognizes that the problems are not narrowly geographically confined;
- recognizes the importance of assessing how policy is performing and how resources are being spent, as well as simply identifying the need that the policy is meant to meet;
- recognizes the importance of partnership and accepts that this means that the local authority and the local community, as well as the national government and the private sector, need to be at the table;
- recognizes that many departments affect cities and they need to be at the same table. SRB in particular has made many departments put their money on the table.

But if those are the virtues of current policy, a number of criticisms have been made. Some are specific to the SRB. But the majority have been faced many times during the past 25 years. In terms of the SRB there is a concern that:

- there is not a sufficiently clear regional strategy to make the selection process transparent or relevant to regional needs;
- SRB, in contrast to City Challenge, spreads resources too thinly across too many projects within regions, as well as across too many regions, some of which have traditionally not received urban programme funding. Some critics have argued that there is a risk that the strategic dimension of the initiative may be lost as the SRB becomes a collection of discrete projects rather than an integrated and strategic approach to a clearly specified area.

Other concerns are more general. They include concerns about declining resources, the equality of partners, inter-departmentalism and the use of competition as opposed to need to determine priorities and allocate resources.

Resources

There are two resource issues – one longer term, the other short. Like many programmes before them, City Challenge and the SRB – despite the breadth of the latter's constituent programmes – are essentially special initiatives. They constitute government's explicit urban policy. But the resources which flow to cities through such initiatives are far smaller than resources that flow in – or out – of them through mainstream programmes. Housing, education, transport, health, social services, policy and infrastructure policies constitute the implicit urban programme which has a far greater impact upon the fortunes of cities and the people who live and work in them. As the Action for Cities evaluation indicated, in recent years, cuts in mainstream programmes have not been compensated for by special monies, however valuable they may be to financially hard-pressed areas. Many argue that special initiatives should be regarded as an addition to – not a substitute for – wider government policies for cities.

In addition, the resources invested in the current special initiatives are vulnerable. For example, the resources invested in the constituent programmes of the SRB rose from £1,204 million in 1989–90 to a peak of £1,603 million in 1993–94. But after the creation of the SRB, they are estimated to decline to £1,324 million in 1997–98. Equally importantly, it is uncertain what will happen to the resources that are currently going into those constituent SRB programmes such as the UDCs – planned at £209 million for 1997–98 – and City Challenge – planned at £150 million – which will be ending in 1997 and 1998.

Integrating Government Departments

Urban issues do not respect departmental boundaries. Over 25 years, successive administrations have been faced with the attempt of breaking down departmental barriers both in Whitehall and in the regions to achieve a more integrated response to urban decline or regeneration. How well is current policy doing in building bridges? The answer must be that at least much more effort is being invested under current policy. The Urban Programme of the 1960s did not recognize the need. The Inner City Partnerships recognized it in the 1970s, but did not provide enough inducement for departments sufficiently to change their behaviour. In the 1980s, the Merseyside Task Force and the City Action Teams represented an effort to achieve greater integration, but their resources and powers were too modest to have major impact. Despite the repackaging of many existing programmes in the Action for Cities initiative, increased coordination was not a major policy thrust, as its evaluation confirmed. The Audit Commission designation of government initiatives and programmes for urban regeneration as a 'patchwork quilt' remains the most vivid sobriquet for that period.

In the 1990s City Challenge more clearly recognized the need and has got government departments around the table. However, it did not force them to put their own money on that table. Nor did it provide them with enormous sanctions to change their behaviour. Despite this, there is evidence of increased inter-departmentalism. The Government Offices in the Regions and the SRB have encouraged the integration of government departments. It is unwise to underestimate the problems in reconciling different departmental cultures as well as administrative styles. There has been a great deal to do in simply sorting out internal administrative issues. Equally, not all government departments whose actions affect cities have been integrated into the office. Nor is it clear that all departments are equally committed to the integration of policy. Nevertheless, the evidence is that the Government Offices provide increased policy flexibility which both government and their partners welcome. The SRB has required departments to put their money on the table and risk the chance of losing some of it. The first rounds of bidding in the SRB has already provided evidence of internal redistribution of resources.

Partnership

City Challenge and SRB place partnership at the top of the political agenda. There is clear evidence that partnership is developing. But there are also concerns that not all partners are equally positioned in the policy. In particular, there is a concern that the local authorities have lost so many powers and resources that they cannot be equal partners in the regeneration game. There is also concern that the community is not equally powerful. City Challenge did empower many communities. But there is a feeling that in the SRB community groups have lost some ground in the decision-making process.

Competition

A key concern is about the principle of competition which underpins much current regeneration policy. Competition has been used at least partly to address criticisms of more traditional approaches like the Urban Programme. It was indeed often difficult to see how social need was related to the quality of the programmes and the achievements that were gained from the use of public money. There was a consensus that the traditional Urban Programme needed reinvigorating. In a narrow sense there is evidence that competition has encouraged innovation, collaboration and partnership within particular areas around specific programmes. But as a wider principle of determining priorities and allocating resources, a number of issues remain to be faced:

- competition may have had a beneficial impact upon the winners, but what long term impact does it have upon losing local authorities, communities and projects?;
- competition may create excitement and innovation initially, but will diminishing returns set in over the years as local authorities find themselves competing in more competitions in more policy areas for declining rewards?;
- how compatible is the competition for nationally allocated funds with the strategic choice of local and regional priorities?;
- will competition reinforce or undermine the government effort to promote local partnerships?;
- where should the balance between need and opportunity lie as a source of priorities and the allocation of resources? What should be the relationship between the search to increase economic competitiveness and to reduce social exclusion? What are the limits to the withdrawal of resources from

needy areas, communities and projects because they fail to win competitions? In principle, at what point would it stop?

The Role of European Policy

Until the change of government in 1997, there were probably two schools of thought about European involvement in urban policy – that of local authorities and that of central government. On balance, local authorities welcomed the Commission's increased concern with urban issues, for two kinds of reasons. The first is that European funds, however modest, are valuable at a time when local resources are very constrained. Also, European grants often have a degree of status which local authorities can use to encourage other investment into projects from the public and private sector. The second reason is more to do with high politics. As national government has increased its control over local authorities, many of them in turn have seen Brussels and the Commission as a way of short-circuiting Westminster and Whitehall as alternative power base, source of ideas, funding and influence. Local authorities would probably wish to see more Commission involvement in cities.

The Conservative government was sceptical of an increased Commission competence in urban policy, precisely for the reverse reasons to those advanced by local authorities. It did not wish to see an increased urban competence for two kinds of reasons. The first was because of the government's reservation about increasing the role of the Commission in British economic and social life in general. More specifically, the government probably believes that British cities would not benefit substantially from an increased urban stance by the Commission, since its cities would qualify for fewer resources than those in other parts of the Union if they were allocated on the basis of economic and social need. In other words, Britain would probably lose rather than gain resources. The Labour government is less opposed to the principle of European involvement in urban policy. How this will be translated into practice remains to be seen.

In terms of existing EU programmes, national government, like individual cities, is obviously anxious to maximize the resources that can be attracted to Britain, and hence does not reject any programmes. URBAN is regarded as a reasonably efficient administrative device. However, it is seen as reflecting what has been current policy in Britain for some time through City Challenge and SRB. Policy makers do not therefore regard it as innovative in a British context, even though it might be in other countries which have less experience of, or less well-developed, urban strategies. Also, the level of resources in the programmes are not regarded as commensurate with the effort required to win them. Structural Funds are seen as rather dated in their approach. They are seen as too project-oriented rather than strategic in approach. The division between ERDF and ESF programmes is regarded as unhelpful in Britain, which has been attempting to pursue an integrated holistic approach to urban issues. ERDF is still regarded by some policy makers as focusing too much upon physical infrastructure.

Conclusion

This report has discussed the key issues affecting the development of urban policy in Britain during recent decades but has focused upon developments during the past five years. It identified the changing institutional framework in which urban policy is made, in particular: constrained public resources; a high degree of fragmentation between local service providers; a reduced executive role for local government; the rise of regional administration; the increased use of competition to allocate resources to urban areas; and a growing role for the European Commission. The report indicated there was a hierarchy of urban areas in terms of size, resources and need rather than a simple division between the large cities and the rest. But it did identify four major trends which particularly affected large cities: continued economic restructuring; counter-urbanization; increasing social polarization; and the continuing economic social dominance of London in the urban hierarchy. In a review of administrative arrangements the report noted the growing complexity of urban governance caused by the increase in public and private partners in urban regeneration, the disappearance of metropolitan government, the absence of regional government, the loss of local government powers and finance and the growth in regional administration. The discussion of national perspectives observed the changes in views over time about the respective roles of the public, private and community sectors as well as those of national and local levels of government.

The main section of the report which assessed the effectiveness and impact of recent urban policy, drew upon a series of independent evaluations commissioned by government and parliament during the past four years. These indicated a range of limitations to policy during the 1980s. They also identified a number of continuing concerns, in particular the reduction of public resources for urban policy and the need to integrate the efforts of central government departments more effectively. Nevertheless, all indicated growing support amongst the public, private and community sectors for the approach to urban policy during the 1990s. Although there were some concerns about the limits of competition as a method of allocating resources, the current principles enshrined in City Challenge and the Single Regeneration Budget – the focus upon partnership, the involvement of the local authority and community organizations, the richer mix of policy goals, the spatial concentration of resources, the longer time frame of policy initiatives, the concern to assess effectiveness of programmes and the integration of the programmes of a range of government departments – are regarded as crucial to the success of urban policy. After its election, the Labour government set in motion a review of local democracy and urban policy, focusing upon many of the issues raised in this chapter. It also endorsed greater European involvement. Combined with the new regional agenda, it is clear that urban policy in Britain is set to depart on a new phase of its journey. It will be the next millennium before we will know where the odyssey will end and how successful it will be.

References

Atkins, David et al. (1996), *Urban Trends in England: Latest Evidence from the 1991 Census*, London: HMSO.

Atkinson, R. and Moon, G. (1994), *Urban Policy in Britain: the City, the State and the Market*, London: Macmillan.

Deakin, N. and Edwards, J. (1993), *The Enterprise Culture and the Inner City*, London: Routledge.

Department of the Environment (1996), *Annual Report and Expenditure Plans 1996/7–98/9*, London: SO.

Lawless, Paul (1996), 'The Inner Cities', *Town Planning Review*, Vol. 67, No. 1.

Parkinson, Michael (1989), 'The Thatcher Government's Urban Policy 1979–89: a Review', *Town and Country Planning Review*, Vol. 60, No. 4.

Parkinson, Michael (1993), 'City Challenge – a new strategy for Britain's cities?', *Policy Studies*, No. 3.

Parkinson, Michael (1996a), 'Twenty Five Years of Urban Policy in Britain – Partnership, Entrepreneurialism or Competition?', *Public Money and Management*, July.

Parkinson, Michael (1996b), *Strategic Approaches to Area Regeneration*, York: Joseph Rowntree Foundation.

Robson, Brian, Parkinson, Michael et al. (1994), *Assessing the Impact of Urban Policy*, London: HMSO.

Russell, Hilary, Parkinson, Michael et al. (1996), *City Challenge: Interim National Evaluation*, London: SO.

Stewart, John and Stoker, Gerry (eds) (1995), *Local Government in the 1990s*, London: Macmillan.

Wills-Heeg, Stuart (1996), 'Urban Experiments Limited Revisited: Urban Policy Comes Full Circle', *Urban Studies*, Vol. 33, No. 8.

17 Synthesis

LEO VAN DEN BERG, ERIK BRAUN AND JAN VAN DER MEER

Introduction

This final chapter synthesizes the main features of the comparative investigation into national urban policy in the European Union. The main objective of this study is to present the 'state of the art' concerning the explicit national urban policies in the member states of the European Union, but the investigation has also taken other national policies into consideration as far as they make a substantial impact on the development of the cities. The specific circumstances in the member states account for the differences and similarities in national urban policy in the European Union. In this investigation the national urban policies have been discussed in the context of the national spatial development pattern, the administrative and financial framework and the urban issues and challenges perceived at the national level. A high degree of urbanization in the national spatial development can be an inducement to city- or town-related policies from the national government. The administrative and financial framework explains the ability of the local, regional and national government to respond to urban problems. Another factor that plays a role is the national government's perception of urban issues and challenges. To some degree, these factors influence the national urban policy as conducted in the member states. Next, this synthesis is concerned with the national spatial development pattern in the member states, to follow it up by a comparison of the administrative and financial circumstances. After that the attention shifts to similarities in what the national governments consider to be urban issues and challenges, followed by a discussion of the main features of national urban policy in the European Union. Finally, the last section puts the national urban policies in perspective.

National Spatial Development Pattern

Introduction

A complexity of social, cultural, economic, technological and political changes underlies the processes of growth and decline of the European cities. When we compare the urban dynamics and spatial patterns internationally, we find wide differences as well as striking similarities both between the regions of one country and between the regions of different countries. From the national reports, we will endeavour to draw an overall picture of the main differences and similarities among the countries. The first conclusion, supported by international literature on the subject, is that the evolving urban systems and patterns are largely nationally determined and that national frontiers still form the dividing line between sometimes far divergent spatial patterns. Some significant differences between the member states have to do with their degree of urbanization, the balance in their urban system and the phase of urbanization in which their cities find themselves, and of course the socioeconomic position and performance of the various towns and the way that position has found spatial expression. The phase of urbanization, the socioeconomic performance and the intra-regional spatial patterns also appear to vary widely within countries. We shall now briefly discuss differences as well as similarities in spatial structures, with special attention to the situation of, and within, towns.

Degree of Urbanization

To make a straightforward comparison of the degree of urbanization in which countries find themselves seems hardly possible, for almost all countries define 'urbanized' in their own special way. The definitions vary from more than 200 inhabitants in Sweden to over 10,000 in such countries as German, Greece and the Netherlands. If the degree of urbanization is judged by the proportion of population living in (large) towns, the – hardly surprising – conclusion is that Europe counts strongly urbanized countries (such as Germany, the United Kingdom, Belgium, the Netherlands, Denmark) and slightly urbanized ones (Sweden, Finland, Austria, Portugal and Ireland), as well as a number of countries occupying a position between the two extremes (Italy, France, Spain, Greece and Luxembourg). In spite of wide differences, a common trend can be observed, namely, a continuous concentration of people (and economic activities) in the major urban regions, which therefore go on expanding their sphere of influence. Especially in the last decade, even the least urbanized countries have registered a strong expansion of both the largest cities and the regional centres. Ever more Europeans have come to live in an urban environment and the process seems to be intensifying. In some still hardly urbanized countries (Spain, Portugal, Austria, Greece, etc.) the ongoing concentration is confining some rural areas to the periphery.

National Urban Systems

Urban systems in Europe show very different forms as well. Most countries have not reached a balanced urban system in which the various levels of the urban hierarchy are adequately filled. In most of the countries a primary city (always the capital) dominates the urban system. London, Paris, Dublin, Lisbon, Copenhagen, Vienna, Stockholm, Helsinki, Athens and Luxembourg are such distinctly primary cities. In Spain, the towns of Madrid and Barcelona are almost on a level, while Germany (after Berlin), Belgium (after Brussels), Italy (after Rome), and the Netherlands have some roughly equivalent cities and/or a well-balanced urban system. In several countries, the level between the primary city and the rest of the towns is not, or incompletely, comparable. That is notably true of France, Austria, Denmark, Ireland and Finland. Sometimes the intermediate level counts only one or a few towns (such as Oporto in Portugal, Gothenburg and Malmö in Sweden, and Saloniki in Greece). Belgium, Italy, Spain and United Kingdom do enjoy a relatively balanced hierarchy in which the various urban size classes are reasonably to well represented. From the national c hapters, in many countries a relatively large proportion of the national populations is spatially concentrated in only a few urban regions. That can be said of Spain (34 per cent in seven urban regions), Belgium (55 per cent in five), Sweden (35 per cent in three), Finland (22 per cent in one), Denmark (34 per cent in one), Portugal (39 per cent in two), Luxembourg (55 per cent in one), England (36 per cent in seven), The Netherlands (40 per cent in the Randstad), Greece (37 per cent in two), and France (16 per cent in one). The urban concentration seems to proceed fastest in those countries that have come relatively late to urbanization, mostly countries that are peripheral to the European core area, such as Finland, Sweden, Ireland, Portugal, Spain, Italy (the south), Greece and Austria. Dominance in size coincides often, but not always, with economic dominance. In most countries the primary city is also economically dominant. Italy is an exception: cities like Bologna, Milan and Turin vie with Rome for economic supremacy. In the countries that lack a distinct primary city (Germany, the Netherlands) there are several cities of equal worth.

Stages of Urbanization

In the introductory chapter we argued that the phase of urbanization in which a country, or more accurately, the towns in a country, find themselves, determines what kind of problems confront these towns, and also what is the best policy to cope with them. The problems of old industrial towns at a stage of decline are hardly comparable with those of fast-growing cities in countries that until recently were largely agrarian. Europe encompasses the full range of urban development phases. The Finnish towns are at the stage of urbanization; Helsinki is the fastest growing major city in the EU. Urbanization also marks many (but not the largest) cities in southern Europe. Suburbanization – the stage at which the urban region is still growing, but mostly thanks to the surrounding towns – is at the moment the commonest trend, though not everywhere equally advanced. Some countries have been suburbanizing for a long time (especially such old industrial countries as the United Kingdom, Belgium, Germany, the Netherlands, and Luxembourg), and some have only recently joined in. Suburbanization is a relatively new phenomenon (since the 1970s) in the towns in Italy (the north), France, Austria, Spain, and even newer (since the 1980s) in Portugal, Ireland, Italy (the south), Greece (Athens) and Sweden. From that enumeration, clearly the part of Europe that was in the vanguard of industrialization and the first to attain prosperity is at a more advanced phase of suburbanization than the part that industrialized later. A number of European cities suffer from disurbanization, that is, decline of the entire urban region, a development often attended by problems of economic structure. The affected cities are mostly old industrial and harbour cities based on one or only a few sectors of economic activity; examples can be found in the United Kingdom (most large urban regions), the Walloon region, the Ruhr Area, the new German states, Italy (the north), Spain (the region of Bilbao, among others), and France (Marseilles). With the exception of the new German states, these cities had often achieved considerable industrial growth in the past, but found it hard to compensate for the decline in the basic industrial sectors or other dominating (port) activities by attracting new economic activity. Various large European towns suffer from the phenomenon of disurbanization and the related socioeconomic problems (notably unemployment and its social aftermath). Finally, some places have entered the stage of reurbanization, in which large towns begin to pick up (after a period of decline) thanks to new economic growth or urban renewal policy. Reurbanization has been recorded among other places in Vienna (town renewal), Stockholm (economic growth), Milan, the major Dutch cities (urban renewal), and several German towns. A phenomenon specific to the most urbanized regions of the EU is the emergence of polycentric regions or conurbations, with the urban regions formed around some central cities amalgamating into vast urbanized areas. Examples of such polycentric regions are the Rhein-Ruhr area, the Rhein-Main area, the regions of Berlin and

Stuttgart, the Randstad, and the London and Paris regions. In Denmark and Sweden, the formation of the Copenhagen-Malmö-Lund region is envisaged.

Intra-urban Patterns; Core versus Ring

Growth and decline are, as previously noted, the result of a complexity of mutually reinforcing or opposing forces. From theories on the subject, which seem to be largely confirmed by the national reports, economic growth and the resulting prosperity are inseparable from urban development. However, that hypothesis does not seem to apply to some areas, such as the south of Italy and some old industrial zones in the European core land and in the new German states. In those areas, the cities cannot, or only with supreme effort, develop under their own steam and the private sector is very cautious with investment. Another observation is that a period of urban prosperity is often followed by a period in which negative aspects disturb or jeopardize urban development and economic growth. The negative aspects can take various forms, dependent among other things on the phase of urbanization, for instance an excess supply of workers, a qualitatively trailing supply of labour, disintegration of the economic basis, congestion, unpleasant living environment, etc. The situations can widen social discrepancies among the demographic categories in an urban region. Such discrepancies often find expression in the spatial pattern. A feature of most urban regions is that the problem categories are left in the least attractive parts of the town (or settle there for lack of alternatives), while the intermediate groups move to the suburban municipalities. That situation is typical of, among other countries, the Netherlands, the United Kingdom, Germany, Belgium, Denmark, and, to a lesser extent Austria and Sweden (Stockholm excepted). In other urban regions, the socially weak are, on the contrary, found mostly in the suburbs (France, Finland, Stockholm). Finally, there are countries where social discrepancies manifest themselves in the core cities as well as in the suburbs (Spain, Italy, Portugal, Ireland and Greece). In most national chapters it is stated that social segregation puts the economic function of the towns in jeopardy. The tenor is that urban regions in particular are increasingly beset with serious social problems, mostly through extensive unemployment. That tendency was recently (early 1990s) observed even in such 'young' urbanized countries as Ireland, Finland, Sweden and Austria.

Some National Details

A few details are offered in conclusion. In Finland urban development is mostly coupled to the university function. In Finland, Sweden, Ireland and (already since the 1960s) and France attempts are made to render the urban system more balanced. In the Scandinavian countries that is an element of regional policy. Mostly in the southern, but also in other countries, the lack of spatial planning to respond to the recent boom in car-ownership has caused tremendous problems of congestion and accessibility. In Belgium and the Netherlands 'corridors' are being formed along the main traffic axes; in those countries, non-urban areas that are easily accessible by motorcar seem to enjoy considerable economic growth. In Spanish urban regions, social and spatial cleavages is diminishing rather than worsening; the differences between the lowest and highest incomes seem to be contracting. Especially in the United Kingdom, social segregation appears to be a problem that is not limited to the large towns; small (industrial) towns also suffer from such problems.

Administrative and Financial Framework

Introduction

The member states differ widely in administrative structure. Two main types can be distinguished: unitary states (12) and federal states (three), but these main types show great diversity, for instance in the number of administrative levels. Moreover, the roles, functions, competencies, services, budgets, income sources, expenditures, etc. tend to be differently divided between the administrative levels of a country and the divisions also vary from one country to another. To go into detailed administrative and financial aspects would stretch beyond the framework of this inventory of national urban policy. Instead, we will confine ourselves to a bird's eye view of aspects that may help us compare and interpret national urban policy. To that end, we propose to look successively at the administrative structures, the ministries involved in national urban policy, the degree of (de)centralization of public responsibilities, urban finance, and the emergence of metropolitan authorities.

Administrative Structures

Of the 12 unitary states, France, Italy and Spain have four levels of administration. Quite recently (in the 1970s), these countries considerably strengthened the regional level, primarily because they wanted to decentralize certain competencies. In 1978, Spain reinforced the intermediate level (17 autonomous communities) to such an extent that a 'quasi-federal constitutional setting' can be said to have ensued (Pola, 1996). Three-tier structures are found in the three northern countries, the Netherlands, and very recently in Ireland and Greece. In most of these countries the intermediate level counts for less than the local level in task load, budget, and influence. That is specifically true of the three northern countries, where local autonomy is strong. Ireland introduced an intermediate level in 1994, likewise inspired by the need for more decentralization. As a matter of fact, until 1996 Greece had had only one level, the central one. Local authorities acted primarily as executors of state policy. But decentralization is waxing here, too; formal responsibilities having been bestowed on 54 provinces, and equal competencies given to some municipalities. Finally, there are the unitary, two-tier states: the United Kingdom, Portugal and Luxembourg. The United Kingdom is not fully two-tier, however. Above the diversity of local administrative units (London boroughs, metropolitan districts, unitary councils and districts), there is in parts of England an intermediate level (counties). Remarkably enough, about ten years ago, the intermediate level was present throughout the United Kingdom (in the shape of metropolitan counties and regional councils). The United Kingdom is the only member state where the central authority has retrieved responsibilities from the local administrative levels. In Portugal, the creation of regions has been in discussion since the 1970s, but so far without concrete results. In the three federal states, Germany, Austria and Belgium, the intermediate level (Länder in the German-speaking countries) has in fact responsibilities that compare to those of the national governments in the unitary states. Austria has three administrative levels. Germany counts two levels in the Länder of Hamburg and Bremen, three levels in the larger cities, and a second local level in the non-urban areas to coordinate the municipalities. The Belgian administrative structure is beyond doubt the most complicated within Europe, with not only three regional units (Flanders, Wallonia and the Brussels region) but also three cultural units (communities based on linguistic differences), which do not fully coincide. Belgium has four administrative levels, of which the provinces carry the least weight.

Ministries Involved

Although the relevant information is not complete,[1] our presumption is that nowhere in the EU is there a ministry exclusively occupied with the (major) cities and their development. There is, however, in some countries an explicitly city oriented section or state secretary's office whose concern is not exclusively with financial or constitutionally embedded relations (with, respectively, the ministries of Finance and of the Interior). Examples of (very recently created) sections specifically oriented to urban development occur in Italy (Delegation for Urban Areas, section of the Ministry of Public Works), and the Netherlands (State Secretary for Major-City Policy, section of the Ministry of the Interior). The Ministry of the Interior in Finland also plays a role in regional development. Germany has a Federal Ministry for Regional Planning, Building and Urban Development, but for urban policy the Länder are primarily responsible. Each Land has organized itself in its own specific way. Thus, Rhineland Westphalia has a Ministry for City Development, Culture and Sport. In Germany, there are on the national level two standing conferences of Länder ministers (involved in spatial planning and housing) relevant to national urban planning. In Austria there is a comparable standing conference with respect to spatial planning; however, on the federal level there is no ministry for spatial planning. The spatial development is entrusted to the local level, which can give rise to problems of adjustment. In France there are two inter-ministerial delegations, one specifically concerned with spatial-economic matters (DATAR), the other with sociocultural aspects (DIV). Greece also possesses an inter-ministerial organism specifically charged with spatial planning and the environment. In Portugal, the Ministry of Equipment, Planning and Territorial Administration (MEPAT) is directly involved in urban policy. In the United Kingdom – as in Denmark and Ireland – the Ministry of the Environment is the directing and coordinating ministry for urban policy, with some other sectorial ministries functioning as 'sponsors'. In Spain too, the Ministry of the Environment is involved in urban affairs together with the Ministry of Public Works. Naturally, in most countries the ministries of Housing, Spatial Planning, Transport, Social Affairs, Employment, Economic Affairs, etc. have an influence on cities and their development, mostly through sectorial policy. The distribution of sectorial tasks among ministries is organized by each countries in its own specific way. Moreover, in every country the tasks are regularly recombined or uncoupled, depending on the government in office. Policy with influence on urban development is mostly spread among many ministries. It is often sectorial and not explicitly oriented to cities. In the Netherlands, 11 of the 14 ministries are involved in the Major-Cities Policy, a separate state secretary being in charge of the coordination.

Centralization versus Decentralization: Urban Autonomy

In the preceding sections, the increasing decentralization of responsibilities has already been referred to. The decentralization works out differently, however, on the position of the towns. The financial resources or competencies for local authorities to develop an autonomous policy are still relatively limited in France and Italy (although increasing in both countries), and very constrained in the United Kingdom, Ireland, Portugal and Greece. The other extreme is represented by the northern countries and Luxembourg, where the local autonomy is in fact the basis of the administrative system, although in Denmark the national government is increasingly assuming control. Relatively much autonomy for the local authorities is also a characteristic of the three federal states and Spain. In cases where municipalities enjoy a high degree of autonomy, the adjustment among municipalities in the same urban region tends to be more difficult, especially in matters of spatial economics or transport. Fragmentation of policy (reported for Spain, for instance), and intra-regional competition (in Austria, for one) are counterproductive to the development of functional urban regions. In the United Kingdom, local autonomy has been seriously curtailed, and in Portugal and Greece the local level has hardly any competency at all. In the Netherlands, finally, the policy freedom of municipalities has also increased, but that finds no direct expression in the financial relations between state and local government, although some national grants have been combined into generic payments, which gives municipalities more freedom to decide how to spend the money.

Urban Finance

The degree of local autonomy is largely tied up with the financial relations. This topic appears to be extremely complex, and to deal with it in detail would be beyond the scope of this exercise. Moreover, the information in the national chapters does not permit an adequate comparative analysis, nor would that be the purpose of the present report. Therefore, we will content ourselves with presenting some indicative results, based among other sources on the summary (by Pola, 1996) of a recently published comparative analysis of local public finance in the EU member states. There seems to be an infinite variety of ways to acquire local revenue. Taxation is an important source, but not always the most important, as is evident from the situation in six member states. In Swedish and Spanish cities, tax returns account for over six-tenths of the municipal budget. Austria, Denmark, Finland and France follow close (about five-tenths). Income from taxation is relatively low (about one-tenth) in the Netherlands, Greece, Ireland, Italy and the United Kingdom (Committee of the Regions, 1996). However, high tax returns do not always mean much autonomy, for often the levy of taxes is purely the execution of an imposed task. Other important sources of income are the grants and subsidies allotted by higher administrative levels. Their share in municipal income varies from very low in Sweden, Austria, Spain and Germany (about one-fifth) to very high in the United Kingdom, Ireland, Italy, Greece, and the Netherlands (between three- and four-fifths). In many countries, block grants have replaced specific grants. In Germany, the United Kingdom and the Netherlands a considerable portion of the grants is still paid in the shape of specific grants. The third, 'non-tax non-grant', source of income consists of charges for services and commercial transactions. Especially in Luxembourg, Germany and Austria, that category contributes quite a lot to municipal income (over three-tenths). In several countries (the Netherlands among them) such revenues are needed to compensate for the loss of income from the state which attends the decentralization of tasks. Furthermore, the private sector is increasingly involved in the implementation of policy, for instance through public-private partnerships (in many countries) and the privatization of public services (in particular in the United Kingdom). Finally, borrowing is an accepted way of finding funds for investment in most (but not all) member states.

Among the purely local taxes, property tax is the most common, albeit in very divergent forms. Income taxes exclusively for local use occur in the Scandinavian countries and Belgium. Business tax is usual in the French, German, Italian, Portuguese, Spanish and – until recently – Austrian cities, and its application is very diverse (for instance on value added, jobs, 'fiscal potential', profits, etc.). Finally, local authorities levy taxes on specific items of consumption as well as on specific transactions. 'The Netherlands deserve to be singled out for its environmental taxes' (Pola, 1996, p. 4), a kind of tax hardly yet considered in the rest of Europe. From various national chapters, the existing financial framework can lead to biased relations, because insufficient account is taken of the measure in which the spending of 'impoverished' local units is covered by revenue. The large central cities especially in Germany, Italy, the United Kingdom, Spain, Belgium and the Netherlands, appear to encounter difficulties of that kind, which can frustrate their policy actions. In the Netherlands (recently), France, Austria, Finland, Belgium (recently), Sweden and Luxembourg methods of equalization or compensation have been developed to relieve or solve such problems.

EU-funding

Although not all national chapters explicitly refer to the role of the EU, some cities appear to profit from EU-contributions, especially from the URBAN programme. This programme is considered useful for its integral approach, but makes little spatial or financial impact to contribute significantly to the solution of urban problems. A greater impact is evidently due to the funds set aside for the Objective 1 and 2 regions. That impact is highly appreciated, notably in the Objective 1 areas (in Portugal, Ireland and Spain, for example). Some reports do point out that EU funds are project-oriented rather than strategic (the United Kingdom and Portugal), and focus too much on situations of crisis and too little on cities needing support for their innovative potential (Portugal). In Italy (the south), it appeared that only between 16 and 20 per cent of the structural funds end up in cities; the deficient sectorial weigh-off on the national level results in lack of support on the local level. The financial influence of the EU on the towns is judged to be 'modest' in other than Objective 1 countries. The status evidently attached to the designation as an European project does seem highly appreciated in some instances (United Kingdom). The three recently (1995) joined member states have not yet formed an opinion about the financial impact of the EU on their towns. Only Sweden mentions the INTERREG-II programme, which gives financial support to the Öresund project.

The Emergence of Metropolitan Authorities

In various national chapters (notably those of Spain, Austria and the Netherlands) the observation is made that the existing administrative framework could complicate the adjustment of supra-local tasks on the metropolitan level. The counterproductive effects of intra-regional competition (for companies and people, or by means of tax facilities) are also pointed out. Research has disclosed the eminent importance of the efficient and effective integration of organizing capacity in metropolitan administration (van den Berg, Braun, and van der Meer, 1997). Some form of administration and management on the level of the functional urban region seems an attractive proposition in that context. While such a model is applauded by many, the European practice displays very few successful examples of it. Admittedly, in some countries efforts have recently been made to stimulate the creation of metropolitan administrative bodies. The legal foundations for it have already been provided in Italy (for the ten largest metropolises) and Portugal (for

Lisbon and Oporto). In Italy the discussions are for the moment confined to three cities, nor has much concrete progress been made in Portugal. In the Netherlands plans are in the making to form 'city provinces' (with regional as well as local tasks) for the largest urban regions, but the process has been delayed by the lack of societal support. In some Spanish cities (Barcelona and Valencia) metropolitan agencies do exist and in Germany (Ruhr area, Frankfurt, Hanover, Mittlerer Neckar and Berlin/Brandenburg) voluntary public-public partnerships have been concluded, but in both cases with rather narrow task loads and responsibilities. In some cities the functional metropolitan region coincides more or less with a regional administrative unit, which presumably should favour internal adjustment (in Madrid, Stockholm, Vienna, Brussels, Hamburg and Bremen, among other cities). For the Brussels region that is no more than theory since the competency for cultural policies is lacking and the functional urban region is stretching beyond the borders of the Capital Region. With the exception of France and Finland, nowhere in Europe are there (as yet) metropolitan authorities. Nevertheless the Netherlands, Denmark, Spain and the United Kingdom have experimented with such forms of administration in the past. These metropolitan authorities were all abolished, however, in the 1980s for various reasons (political arguments, lack of success). France is an exception with its 10 'Urban Communities'. These regional administrative bodies exist in fact alongside the municipalities and have assumed a significant portion of the metropolitan tasks without en-croaching upon the formal autonomy of the local units. Founded in the 1960s – and not abolished as elsewhere – that formula now seems to be successful (in Lille and Lyon, for instance). In Finland the Helsinki Metropolitan Area Council (a legal organ) is in operation, with in fact a rather narrow task load. In most other countries the gap in supra-municipal administration is filled by (obligatory or voluntary) cooperation, for instance for the purpose of joint exploitation of public services, or under the stimulation of the policy of the European Union, which is primarily addressed to the regions.

Urban Issues and Challenges in the National Perspective

Introduction

The general conclusion of the present investigation may be that in more and more member states attention is given to the position and the role of the towns in regional and national development. Of course, the measure of attention is bound up with the degree of urbanization and the administrative structure. In federal Germany and in Belgium many competencies with respect to urban development are vested in the Länder (Germany) or the regions (Belgium), so that the national government looks at the towns from a distance. In the other countries of advancing and advanced urbanization, the importance of a growing number of urban concerns and challenges has been recognized for some time on the national level. And in some of the less urbanized countries the debate about the position of towns in the national development has recently got under way. At first, the attention tends to focus on the growing socioeconomic problems, but increasingly some member states also stress the potential of towns for stimulating the economy.

Cumulation of Widespread Social Problems in the Medium-sized and Larger Cities

Nevertheless, the socioeconomic problems of the towns are still an important national concern. The investigation has confirmed that a growing number of cities are confronted with such fundamental social problems as unemployment, poverty, (youth) crime, arrears in education, drugs consumption, and the integration of minorities and persons claiming asylum. The fight against unemployment in particular has a high priority in almost all countries, and persistent unemployment is one of the very problems that are increasingly concentrated in urban areas. In the early industrialized north European countries and in the metropolitan regions in Italy and Spain, urban concentration of unemployment is a well known phenomenon, but in the other member states, too, it is increasingly an urban concern. In Greece, for instance, unemployment and poverty used to occur mainly in rural parts, but progressive urbanization has clearly caused a shift to the urban regions. In Finland and Ireland as well, the unemployment problem is shifting from the periphery to the towns. In short, whatever the degree of urbanization which the member states of the European Union have reached, unemployment notably scourges the cities in the whole of Europe.

Besides unemployment, the integration of minorities and asylum seekers in the urban society claims much attention from national and local governors. These groups in society appear to live mostly in the cities, and their massive throng to the towns and spatial concentration within the towns obstructs the integration. The traditional inflow from other parts of the world has, in many member states, greatly swollen under the influence of the war in former

Yugoslavia, especially in the towns of south Germany, north Italy and Austria, which already used to exert great attraction on former Eastern bloc countries.

In a growing number of member states, urban safety is increasingly important, and so are, in its wake, the problems of drugs consumption and (youth) crime. Evidently, citizens in the larger towns are increasingly (feeling) insecure. The nature and intensity of other social problems besetting the towns, such as the concentration of educational arrears, is consistent with the degree of urbanization.

That all these social worries are to be found notably in the towns is an interesting finding, but what causes the typically metropolitan problems, explicitly recognized by most national governments of the member states, is their mutual reinforcement and their cumulation in certain quarters or neighbourhoods of the central cities or suburbs. The danger of socioeconomic and spatial segregation, a situation in which exclusion from the labour market, educational level, ethnic descent and social origin raise barriers to a certain group within the urban community, is recognized in all to some degree urbanized, member states.

Balance in the National Urban System

The interest of the national governments in the typically metropolitan problems and in a balanced social development of the towns, has greatly increased in the past few years. In some countries the national authorities attach much worth also to a balanced development of the national urban system. Their interest springs on the one hand from the desire to limit regional discrepancies in economic and social development, and on the other from the growing recognition of urban centres as potential motors of (peripheral) backward areas. France also looks upon the biased relation between Paris and the other major cities as an obstacle to the latter's development and as a threat to the national competitive position. The Finns regard the balanced spread of urbanization as a comparative advantage. Germany, the Netherlands, the United Kingdom and recently also Belgium are all to some extent striving for a balanced national urban development.

Infrastructure and Housing

In such countries as Spain, Portugal and Greece, urbanization has only gained momentum in the last few decades. Their governments have had little grip on the urbanization process, and there has been no question of coordinated spatial development. Through the lack of coordination and the speed of the urbanization process, the pressure on the existing urban infrastructure (road network, public transport) has risen to unprecedented heights, despite significant investments in the past ten years. With the access to urban centres and hence their economic potential in danger, and even more because most of the population moves by motorcar, the national governments in those countries naturally very much want to raise the level of the infrastructural provisions. In Spain, the fast urbanization has been coupled, especially in the last 10 years, with a tight housing market, the metropolitan areas having a great shortage of adequate and reasonably priced housing. In Portugal, too, housing is high on the government's list of priorities. However, other countries stress the developments in the housing market as well. For instance, the federal government of Germany also mentions the availability of affordable housing as a priority.

Urbanization, Accessibility and the Environment: Attention to Sustainable Development

The advanced urbanization in the Union makes sustainable development very important, especially in the urban regions. In such regions, accessibility, quality of the environment and economic development are closely interwoven. In all member states these aspect are perceived as important urban issues and at the same time give direction to some of the policy responses. In countries like Spain, Portugal and Greece the accent is mainly on infrastructure and accessibility, which does not detract from the growing importance of the environment. In the more urbanized countries like Denmark, the Netherlands and Germany, and also in Luxembourg, Finland and Sweden, the value attached to the environment rises all the time, which does not make accessibility less important, however. It does mean that high standards are set for new infrastructure and that much attention is also given to excellent access by public transport, especially in urban centres.

Cultural Heritage

In many of the member states, towns are increasingly regarded as elements of the national cultural heritage. Some cities represent a unique and increasingly valued combination of history, tradition and characteristic buildings. To conserve historical and cultural values is an important concern. But the conservation and maintenance of such carriers of cultural heritage can also contribute to the attractiveness of towns and the appeal of the residential and living environment. In short, cultural heritage has acquired economic value as well, as a locational condition and in the shape of urban tourism.

How to Cope with Metropolitan Problems?

Even in countries that already have gained experience with the typically metropolitan problems, such as the United Kingdom, the Netherlands and France, the question how to cope with them remains on the agenda. On the one hand, there is a continuing search for new policy instruments which enable the various tiers of government to deal better with the problems. On the other hand, some countries try to come nearer to a solution by reforming the administrative structure. Some other member states (Italy, Portugal, Finland, Belgium), have recently shown an increasing interest in ways and means of dealing with metropolitan problems, or are drawing up inventories of the possibilities. What is the role of the national government? How can a coherent integral policy be conducted on the local and national levels?

National Policy Responses to Urban Issues and Challenges

Introduction

In the first chapter we explained the need to make a distinction between explicitly town oriented policy and policy measures that, while having a great impact on towns, are not explicitly tailored to them. These policies are themes of sectorial policy or groups in society. Which countries *do* pursue an explicit urban policy? What is the vision underlying that policy and what instruments are put in for its implementation? Is the national urban policy of an integral nature or is it not? In what follows we shall try to answer these questions. Attention will also be paid to national policy that is not explicitly town oriented but does have great influence on towns.

Examples of Explicit National Urban Policy

For the present, the countries whose national governments have advanced furthest in substantiating the (heightened) interest for cities into explicitly city oriented policy, are the United Kingdom, France and the Netherlands. In the United Kingdom such a policy has been conducted since the late 1960s, but the approach, the priorities and the financing have altered in the course of the years. The policy now in force is the City Challenge, initiated in 1992, and since combined with the Single Regeneration Budget (1994). These explicit urban policy initiatives emphasize the economic revitalization of the urban regions. As in the United Kingdom, in France the foundation for explicit national urban policy was laid in the 1960s with the policy of *Métropoles d'équilibre*, continued since 1990 in the form of the *Chartes d'objectifs* (large-cities charters), which come under the Ministry of Public Works and the national planning office (DATAR). The latter body is also responsible for the policy of *réseaux de villes* (urban networks). Besides, the socially oriented measures of national urban policy have been combined in the *Contrats de Villes* (Urban Contracts policy), often jointly with the 'Programmes de Aménagement Concerté du Territoire'. In the Netherlands, policy makers have shown explicit interest in urban development, in particular in the context of spatial planning. Since the late 1980s the explicit attention to urban affairs has been broadened to other policy areas as well, because of the socioeconomic problems of the cities. The increased attention resulted, in 1994, following a strong plea from the four major cities, in the Major-Cities Policy. That policy is coordinated by a project state secretary for the major cities, coming under the Ministry of the Interior, and can be considered the first integral explicit national urban policy in the Netherlands.

Visions and Objectives Underlying the Explicit National Urban Policy

In the United Kingdom, in the 1980s the focus of national urban policy was on the economic performance of the cities, economic and physical regeneration being key concepts of policy. The adjustment to the City Challenge policy has not shaken the foundations of that vision, but served to give investment in, and preservation of, social and human capital its proper place. The Dutch government has issued an explicit statement about the role of the cities in national development. The Major-City Policy is concerned not only with the problems of the major cities but also with their economic potential. The Dutch government regards cities as the motors of the national economic, cultural and social development, and has woken up to the fact this motor function is impeded by certain social problems. The Major-City Policy is supposed to change that situation. In France, most efforts and resources are directed to the fight against social discrepancies among and within towns. The *Contrats de Villes* focuses on fighting the concentration of arrears and spatial and social segregation, whereas the policy pursued to reinforce the position of the major (provincial) towns (Large City Charter), is of an economic nature; its main objective is to restore balance to the national urban system.

National Urban Policy: Top-down and Bottom-up?

The relation between the national government and the local authorities determines to a high degree the principles and implementation of policy. The choice of a policy directly addressing the cities is inspired (among other considerations) by the idea that an area-oriented policy can better than others deal with the specific problems of towns, and thus increase its effectiveness. The Dutch national government hopes that the Major-City Policy will create the conditions enabling local authorities to get themselves a grip on the problems. The national government has reserved to itself a coordinating, and in some areas a controlling part, but the cities have to give substance to the Major-City Policy. On the whole, the position of the national government in the United Kingdom towards the towns was reinforced in the 1980s, giving it more control over local policy. Nevertheless the government's explicit intention is to have its explicit national urban policy given substance on the local or regional level, the initiative being by definition not with the local government but with local partners, often a coalition of public, semi-public, public-private and private parties. These urban development authorities are required to define a wider vision for their area and to link programmes, projects, resources and mechanisms to that vision in a strategic way. On that basis, the cities have to vie with others for payments from the available funds. In France, in the 1980s the local authorities were given more elbow room. However, the influence of the national government is still very large which can be explained among other things from the traditional centralist structure of French public administration. Representatives of the national government exert substantial influence on local development, among others through the allocation of resources, specifically in the *Chartres d'objectifs* but also in the *Contrats de Villes*.

The Integrality of Explicit National Urban Policy

One spearhead of the Dutch Major-City Policy is to make policy more comprehensive, not only on the national level in terms of input from the 11 ministries involved, but also on the local level, where bottlenecks in the approach to metropolitan problems are just as likely to develop when sectorial initiatives are not properly adjusted. An integral approach implies on the national as well as on the local level a restyling of administrative culture. That is a necessary condition for a successful Major-City Policy. In the United Kingdom the principle is that integrality has to be encouraged on the national and local levels. The four ministries (Environment, Employment, Training and Industry) most involved in the national urban policy are working together in the newly created 'Government Offices in the Regions'. To stimulate cooperation on the local level, only qualitatively good and integral plans are accepted for financing. The philosophy underlying that strategy is that competition of local plans will push up their quality. In France, integrality is an aspect of the *Contrats de Villes*, which are put up for discussion among the parties involved, who will then try to reach agreement on a joint approach. However, the integration refers only to social questions, for integration with economic policy is not guaranteed. The *Chartes d'objectifs* do not aim at integral policy on the local level, but great store is set by an integral development of the national urban system. The medium-sized towns involved may be encouraged to choose a functional economic specialisation for the sake of proper national spread.

Explicit National Urban Policy and the Channelling of Financial Flows

The explicit policy in the United Kingdom and in the Netherlands is supported in the two countries by different methods of financing. In the United Kingdom, the City Challenge programme has been completed with the Single Regeneration Budget, in which all urban-regeneration funds of the above mentioned ministries have been combined. Moreover, the funding of local initiatives is not a matter of course. Several local plans compete for the available resources (31 out of 57 proposals have been accepted). In the Netherlands too, the idea of a fund coupled to the Major-City Policy was considered, but in the end the decision was to channel the financial flows within each department concerned and give the municipalities more freedom of expenditure, thus widening their scope for independent policy making. Actually, in the Netherlands as well the quality of the local plans is tested by the national government. In France, local authorities are less free to dispose of their means. The state furnishes the money needed and also keeps an eye on its spending.

Area-oriented Approach: Neighbourhood Level, Town, or Urban Region?

The present spatial scale of the Dutch Major-City Policy is in certain respects an impediment. The policy focuses on towns rather than metropolitan regions, which is due, for one thing, to the delayed creation of town provinces. Within the town borders there is room for some spatial flexibility. In the United Kingdom, the explicit national urban policy is not tied to administrative borders; the national government concludes deals with 'urban areas'. In France, too, the spatial scope is wider, because the state bargains with the regional bodies and allocates its resources through the regions. That spatial flexibility is indeed necessary, since certain problems cannot always be solved within the borders of an administrative spatial unit, but the solution may be found in a neighbouring commune.

A clear example of the focus on area oriented policy measures can be found in the so-called 'entrepreneurial zones'. Last year, the French government pointed out 44 *zones franches* to promote economic development in urban areas that suffer from high unemployment and other social problems, by means of fiscal exemptions. The Dutch government has also launched the notion of entrepreneurial zones in the Major-Cities Policy, aiming to promote economic regeneration in deprived urban areas. In the United Kingdom similar policy measures have already been introduced in the 1980s.

Ireland: the Explicit Urban Renewal Act

The policy of the national government in Ireland is not comparable to the explicit policies conducted in the United Kingdom, the Netherlands and France. Most of Irish national policy affecting cities is sectorial policy, but Ireland also pursues explicit urban policy of a kind in the shape of the Urban Renewal programme ensuing from the Urban Renewal Acts of 1986 and 1987. These Acts focused first and foremost on the redevelopment of urban areas, in particular the Irish inner cities. The first emphasis is on physical regeneration, but schooling opportunities and the quality of the living environment also figure in the programme, although the financial structure of the policy has stimulated mostly commercial development (offices). At first, the policy addressed only a few zones in five cities, but by now 100 programmes are operative in 35 urban centres. In contrast to, for instance, Dutch town renewal, which addressed not only the cities but all local units, Irish renovation is mainly directed to the inner city areas. At present, the policy is co-funded from the European Union. Moreover, in Dublin a separate independent organization has been formed to attend to the process of urban renewal.

Spatial Planning and Sectoral Policies

Next to the explicit urban policy responses, the United Kingdom, France and the Netherlands pursue a broad range of other national policies that have a major impact on cities. These policy responses still take up a great part of the policies that influence urban development. For instance, since the 1980s, urban centres have been made the core of Dutch spatial planning policy. In the other member states (with the exemption of Ireland, mentioned above) the national responses to urban issues and challenges have not been shaped into explicit national urban policy. In these counties the national policy responses are to be found in the spatial planning policy and other sectorial policy measures.

City Development in Discussion: Portugal and Italy

In Italy, there had hardly been any interest for the problems of towns until the 1990s. Since 1990 a different course has been taken; a law has been passed to open the way for administration on the level of the metropolitan region, though no final decision has yet been made in any of the selected urban areas. In addition, the Minister for Public Works has had 'urban areas' added to his portfolio. The remaining sectorial policy now also takes the cities into account. The government aims at more integration in land management, urban planning and environmental policies, to achieve the sustainable development of urban areas.

Until shortly, urban changes in Portugal were mostly due to sectorial investment. Explicit national urban policy has only recently become a Portuguese concern, and the first cautious steps forward have just been taken. The possibilities of a more explicit national urban policy are being considered, in particular the coordination of such a policy on the national level. At present, many urban affairs come under the responsibility of the Ministry of MEPAT. An object of debate is improved coordination with other ministries involved in urban development, namely, those of Culture, Economy, and Social Solidarity and Employment. The Ministry MEPAT coordinates the PROSIURB programme initiated in 1994, a programme explicitly oriented to the development of urban centres outside the metropolitan regions of Lisbon and Porto. PROSIURB has a very small budget and is mainly regarded as an additional financing programme along with the resources from the European Commission.

In a sense, the EXPO '98 project is also an exponent of national urban policy, because it is an initiative of the national government, which is also the leading partner in the firm EXPO '98 that carries out the project. The present government considers national urban policy a matter of importance, because it perceives a distinct role for the larger towns in the internationalization of the Portuguese economy. Such a policy can be implemented only if, in the eyes of the government, certain conditions are fulfilled.

The Special Position of the Federal Member States and Spain

The administrative organization in the federal states of Germany, Belgium and Austria, as well the administrative organization in Spain mean that the national governments in these member states are not in the position to pursue explicit urban policy to the same extent as the United Kingdom, France or the Netherlands. The intermediary level of government comprises most of the competences for urban policy. In fact, some of these 'regional' authorities are urban regions: Hamburg and Bremen are *Bundes Laender*, Brussels is one of the three Belgian regions (*gewest*), Madrid is an autonomous community in Spain and the urban region of Vienna is one of the Austrian states.

In federal Germany, most competencies are on the level of the 16 states and on the local level. On the national level, the Ministry for Regional Planning, Building and Urban Development and the Ministry of Transport and the Environment have influence on urban development. The Regional Planning ministry formulates the guidelines and principles for spatial development in Germany, and recently refined them in the *Raumordnungspolitische Orientierungsrahmen* in view of the German reunion and the spatial integration of the new federal states. The most important task of the federal government is to create the marginal conditions for the lower authorities, and notably to put certain matters of urban interest on the agenda, such as the importance of sustainable urban development. The German government tries to give more and more substance to that task in view of the intensifying international competition among cities and the necessary spatial integration of the 'new German towns'.

Belgium, like Germany, is a federal state, where many of the responsibilities concerned with urban development are vested in the regional authorities. Under the infrastructural policy of the Belgian state, relatively much is invested in the infrastructure needed for towns (among other things, the connection to the high speed rail network). Before Belgium became a federal state, there was not really a national vision of urban development, nor has federalization changed that, which is logical. This is changing on the regional level, especially in Brussels and Flanders, concern for the situation

of towns has increased, and a vision of urban development is being developed
as a first step to a more integral approach. The measures carried through in
the past few years have been mostly sectorial, and very few efforts have been
made to harmonize policy initiatives. In the fight against urban poverty the
Flemish government has recently integrated a number of individual measures
in the Social Impulse Fund (SIF). The government allocates funding to the
cities with the largest problems on the basis of locally formulated integral
plans.

In Austria, urban development has only recently become a concern, now
that suburbanization encroaches more and more upon the scarce space, and
increases the need for infrastructure. The national government draws up the
framework for spatial development, and gathers and distributes information,
but the cities are highly autonomous in their policy making. Given the
progressive urbanization and the fact that houses tend to be built on generous
plots of land, the expectation is that the national government will move
coordinated spatial development higher on the political agenda.

In Spain, where the responsibilities are highly decentralized to the
autonomous communities, there is no explicit national urban policy either.
But sectorial policy in Spain – more than in Germany, for example – is relevant
to urban development. In the National Infrastructure Plan, the connections
among towns and also internal urban transport are important aspects, on the
consideration that external and internal accessibility is a necessary condition
for economic development. Besides, national housing policy, intended to
relieve the tension on the housing market, expressly addresses the cities. The
national environmental policy, too, is clearly concerned with the position of
the larger cities. All policy measures spring from sectorial policy, and as in
other countries, the (seven) major cities have pointed out the drawbacks for
the quality of urban development. They plead an approach in which the major
cities themselves can take decisions and thus stimulate a more integral urban
development.

*Explicit Regional Policies with Increasing Attention to the Functioning of
Cities in the Nordic Countries*

In Denmark, Sweden and Finland, urban development in the past few decades
has given less rise to an explicit urban policy. In these countries the main
focus is on explicit regional policies. Increasingly, the functioning of cities
becomes an important part in these policies. Cities are seen more and more as
a stimulator of regional development.

In Sweden, a high degree of local autonomy is laid down in the constitution, and moreover, as Sweden is not yet very urbanized, the national government feels no urge to conduct an explicit urban policy. Nevertheless, in the context of regional policy, a study has been made of the problems of the metropolitan regions of Sweden, the conclusion of which is that 'a favourable development of the towns can also benefit the development of the national economy'. That study has induced the Swedish government to enter into agreements with the three regions with the highest investment in road infrastructure and public transport.

In Finland the role of cities is placed in the context of regional policy as well. However, some informal research has already been carried out into the aspects of a more explicit urban policy. One point made in that investigation is that the cities are in potential the engines of the future economic growth of Finland. The government has appointed a work group, consisting of representatives of the ministries and the towns, which will continue the study of urban questions. One important task of the work group is to exchange experiences and best practices, and another is to draw up a document in preparation of a more explicit urban policy. Recently, the Ministry of the Interior increased its attention to the development of cities through the Centres of Expertise policy that promotes the development of knowledge-intensive activities.

In Denmark, Copenhagen is by far the largest city: with one-third of the population living in the Greater Copenhagen area, a policy explicitly addressing cities is a delicate matter. In Denmark, internationalization and increasing awareness of the environment are important aspects of spatial planning policy and regional policy. Against that background, the Danish government encourages the creation of strategic networks among cities (exchange of knowledge, check on unhealthy competition) and the planning of urban and regional development from a national point of view.

The Impulse of the European Programmes: the Example of Greece

In Greece, an explicit national urban policy does not yet figure on the national agenda. The recent reorganization of the administrative system implies for Greece that they are now able to make the first steps towards the development of explicit national urban policies. In the past, the policy of the national government has not been explicitly targeted to cities, although Athens has benefited from some national decisions. In recent years, the Greek cities have been given more attention within sectorial policies. In transport policy, for instance, improvement of the deficient infrastructure in urban areas is now a spearhead. Moreover, the extensive support from the European Union has put the national urban development higher on the national political agenda, and policy measures with a clear urban dimension have been initiated in the framework of one of the European programmes.

Bilateral Consultation in Luxembourg

It is comprehensible that Luxembourg does not pursue explicit national urban policy. Policies with regard to the city of Luxembourg are mainly formulated at the local level. The national sectorial policies, in particular housing and spatial planning, are coordinated through bilateral consultation between the national and local level.

Increasing Attention to Intercity Links: Urban Networks

In a growing number of member states the physical and 'material' connections among the cities in the national urban system receive high priority. A number of examples suggest themselves. A large part of the national infrastructure investments in Spain go to the external and internal accessibility of cities. In Germany, the links among cities play an important role in the integration process of the cities in the former 'German Democratic Republic'. Moreover, in most of these countries the focus is not only on national links among cities but increasingly on the links to other cities in Europe as well. The European policies that promote the Trans-European Networks have been integrated in the national policy framework of many countries. In France, the national government pays special attention to the cities that are situated on European corridors and to other cities with an important logistic function as well. The Dutch spatial planning policy and national transport and infrastructure policy attribute a lot of weight to the accessibility and the national and international connections of the major Dutch cities. The Portuguese government recognizes the importance of good (inter)national connections for their major cities as well. The Danish government and the German government also promote the starting-up of strategic networks between cities. In Denmark, the new bridge to Sweden is another example of a new physical link. Also in Italy, the government has started to promote strategic network among cities.

National Urban Policy in Perspective

In spite of wide differences in the degree of urbanization, the structure of the national urban systems and the development phase at which the various urban regions find themselves, there are some similarities among the member states (see also Table 17.1). For one thing, urbanization is advancing most rapidly in those countries that were until recently hardly urbanized. Urban growth manifests itself more in the ring zones around the major cities rather than in those cities themselves. Everywhere the ring zones of the largest cities are the fastest growers. The result is progressive concentration of activity in the largest urban regions. That process is especially striking in the countries of relatively late urbanization. More and more Europeans belong to the urbanized population. In quite a lot of countries social and spatial segregation in the urban regions is a severe problem. The highest concentrations of unemployment and problems as low residential and living quality, crime, vandalism and health concern are found in the urban regions, often in the central cores, sometimes in the suburbs, and sometimes in both. There are sizable differences in the degree in which major cities are threatened by social, living climate and safety problems. These differences appear to depend, among other things, on the phase of development to which a region has progressed. The typically urban problems seem to develop fast in the countries that until recently had remained unaffected.

Differences in administrative and financial structure within Europe appear exceptionally wide. These differences appear to have an effect on the urban development and the nature and form of the national policy with respect to the towns. On the other hand, the administrative and financial structures are highly dynamic. The last two decades have shown drastic administrative reforms in at least seven of the 15 member states. With the exception of the federalization of Belgium, almost all changes have given shape to the wish for more decentralization of competencies in those countries which in the past had a strictly centralist government system. A second exception is the United Kingdom, where the central authority has rather assumed more power at the expense of the competencies of local authorities. However, the recent change of government might change this situation.

The spectrum of organizational structures shows that on the ministerial level there is hardly any explicit urban approach. Only in a limited number of countries are the (major) towns emphatically highlighted. Most countries display very little integration or coordination among the various sectorial ministries in favour of a specific approach to urban prospects and threats.

Table 17.1 Spatial pattern and urbanization

	Degree of urbanization	Balanced urban system	Primary city	Stage of urbanization	Urban problem areas	Cities >100,000	Metropolises >1 million	National population
Austria	low	no	yes	suburbanization	inner cores	6	1	7.8
Belgium	high	yes	no	sub/deurbanization	inner cores	8	2	10.0
Denmark	high	no	yes	suburbanization	inner cores	4	1	5.2
Finland	low	no	yes	urbanization	inner cores	6	1	5.0
France	average	no	yes	suburbanization	suburbs	46	3	58.0
Germany (west)	high	yes	no	sub/reurbanization	inner cores	83	8	81.3
Germany (east)				sub/deurbanization				
Greece	average	no	yes	urb/suburbanization	mixed	6	1	10.3
Ireland	low	no	yes	urb/suburbanization	mixed	3	1	3.6
Italy (north)	average	yes	no	sub/deurbanization	mixed	46	4	57.9
Italy (south)				urb/suburbanization				
Luxembourg	high	–	yes	suburbanization	suburbs	0	–	0.4
Netherlands	high	yes	no	sub/reurbanization	inner cores	23	2	15.5
Portugal	low	no	yes	urb/suburbanization	mixed	5	1	9.3
Spain	average	yes	no	suburbanization	mixed	48	3	39.3
Sweden	low	no	yes	urb/suburbanization	mixed	11	1	8.9
United Kingdom	high	yes	yes	sub/deurbanization	inner cores	57 *	7	58.1
EU total						352	36	370.6

* Eurocities documentation, Barcelona, 1989.

There are wide discrepancies in the degree of autonomy among the cities of Europe. Autonomy ranges from all-but-none in Greece to all-but-complete in Sweden. Although the tendency towards decentralization is manifest, that does not invariably mean that the formal responsibilities and opportunities to conduct an autonomous and integral policy on the municipal or metropolitan level have been much extended. Concerning municipal finance, no clear trends are perceivable, although the observation is warranted that as decentralization proceeds, the grants allocated by the state are reduced. On the other hand, specific grants have gradually supplanted by generic grants. The towns have been forced to compensate the reduction by raising charges or introducing new ones, by levying local taxes or by involving the private sector (public-private partnership and the privatization of public services). Although in some countries the national government tries by financial equalization to adjust the means given to towns in proportion to their real needs, in many countries the largest central cities find themselves in the worst financial straits, and thus seriously hampered in the pursuit of their policy.

Metropolitan authorities are few and far between in the EU. We have counted 25 of them, of which ten are in France (Urban Communities). Of the others, some coincide with a higher administrative level, and the remainder have been created on a voluntary basis and have hardly any authority at all. In Italy and Portugal the law provides for the formation of metropolitan administrations, but no great progress has been made with the implementation. In the Netherlands, plans for three 'city provinces' have been delayed. In the other countries, 'urban management on the proper level' does not seem to have political priority as yet, notwithstanding pleas to that effect in the chapters on Spain and Austria, among others.

It is difficult to separate the national perception of and priority to urban issues and challenges from the similarities and differences in the national spatial-development pattern and the administrative and financial framework. In countries where much authority is vested in the local government, the national government will intervene the less explicitly in the debate and give less attention to details. But in all countries where urbanization started early, the typical metropolitan problems (concentration of long term unemployment, social and spatial segregation, safety) have been high on the agenda for quite some time. Increasingly, the same problems confront countries that were late urbanizers. In the strongly urbanized Netherlands, for instance, the predicaments of cities are getting full attention, but also in countries where the urbanization degree is still below the European average (such as Portugal and Finland) the way things are developing is seen as a threat. Sustainable urban development has become a primary concern wherever a balance has to be struck between the economy, transport and the environment. The accents vary among the member states: while Portugal and Greece and to a lesser degree Spain and Italy give priority to the adjustment and expansion of urban infrastructure in response to their poorly coordinated urbanization, Germany, Denmark, the Netherlands and the other Scandinavian countries are more inclined to relate accessibility to the environment. Dependent on the spatial development but also, and especially so, on the administrative and financial organization, the approach to urban problems is increasingly a matter of government concern.

In the United Kingdom, the Netherlands and France, urbanization and the related social problems have given rise to an area oriented, more or less integral policy, targeted explicitly to the towns and cities. In Ireland as well, an explicit national urban renewal policy has been adopted. In some countries where the urbanization pattern might also have given rise to such an explicit national urban policy, the lack can be explained by the specific administrative situation (Germany, Belgium, Austria and less so, Spain) or the spatial conditions (the relation between Copenhagen and the rest of Denmark, and the place of the town of Luxembourg within the Grand Duchy). In some less-urbanized, non-federal states (Portugal, Italy, Sweden, Greece and Finland), policy attention for urban development is on the increase. Finland has appointed a work group to study the outlines of a national urban policy, and from the Portuguese chapter, that country is moving towards such an explicit policy. The observation is in order, however, that in all member states, even those practising an explicit national urban policy, most of the national policy that affects the towns, is spatial planning policy and sectorial policy. Within those policies, the relevance of the towns and cities is increasingly acknowledged. But the adjustment of the policy efforts deserves more attention in the future, for urbanization is progressing in the countries of the European Union. The logical consequence is that more and more states include the results of urbanization in their policy. Indeed, national urban development appears more and more on the political agendas of the national governments of member states. An additional stimulus is that national governments are more and more aware of the cities' function as motors of the national economy, as well as the fact that the serious social problems are most manifest and concentrated in those very towns. Nevertheless, from the country cases presented, the majority of EU countries have not yet proceeded to a genuine, explicit, national urban policy. Still, the national chapters presented warrant the expectation that more and more countries will in the future develop an explicit, integral, city oriented policy.

To the future prosperity of the member states, the development of an explicit national urban policy is highly relevant. That is pleaded not only by the arguments offered above, but also by the fact that cities are more and more functionally related. To achieve a balanced development of the national urban system, the national government needs a clear vision of the preferable evolution of the towns within the national system. Naturally, that vision should do justice to the development potentialities of the several towns and their important role for stimulating wider regional development. To that end, the towns themselves must draw a clear picture of their development potential.

Indeed, the voice of the towns should be heard in the development of a national urban policy. European cities need a clear vision and strategy as a basis for their own policy, to increase their own competitive power, and to deal adequately with their socioeconomic problems. An indispensable element of such a strategy is good cooperation with the higher authorities, based on a jointly evolved vision of urban development that is advisable on the local, regional and national levels. Such an atmosphere of cooperativeness is conducive to the most efficient use of all resources available for urban development. A fact to keep in mind in that context is that the strategic cooperation between towns and the higher authorities cannot remain confined to one country, since united Europe is diligently striving to strengthen its own competitive power. From the European point of view as well, and with the cities' function as economic motor in mind, to make the most of their economic potential is of the essence. Moreover, the tendency of cities to combine into urban systems appears increasingly to ignore national frontiers. On the European level as well, cities on both sides of a national border tend to join the same functional urban network. All in all there is every reason for the EU to try for a European vision of preferable paths of urban evolution. Again, such a vision should be reached in close cooperation with the European cities themselves.

There is no need to argue that the above expectations refer to a remote future. Nevertheless, now is the time to design, on the basis of a clear vision, a policy for cities that does justice to their potential as well as to the need to support the European cities fast and efficiently in their efforts to prevent and solve the grave social problems which are, or will be, confronting them.

From the above presentation of the 'state of the art' of national urban policy in the 15 member states of the European Union, most of them so far have taken only a very modest step towards the model we have sketched, by which the various authorities in Europe display an interactive and integrated approach to an efficient and effective explicit urban policy. The full realization of such a model requires a great deal of organizing capacity on all levels, especially so as private enterprise, too, should be actively involved in the design and implementation of the policy. For the sake of the future of EU cities, and hence of the future of the entire Union, cities, member states and EU alike should invest generously and willingly in the quality of their own organizing capacity.

Note

1   In four of the national chapters, ministries are not referred to.

References

Berg, van den, L., Braun, E. and Meer, J. van der (1997,), *Metropolitan Organising Capacity*, Aldershot, UK: Ashgate
Pola, G. (1996), *Summary of comparative study, in: Local public finance in Europe (Seminar proceedings)*, Siena, Italy: European Commission DG XXI and Ministerio delle Finanze.